Bc

# RACE

# RACE

John R. Baker

1974
*Oxford University Press*
NEW YORK AND LONDON

© JOHN R. BAKER 1974
*Library of Congress Catalogue Card Number: 73-87989*
*Printed in the United States of America*

TO

C. P. BLACKER

M.C., G.M., M.A., M.D., F.R.C.P.

*lifelong friend*

De-là est venu ce bel adage de morale, si rebatu par la tourbe Philosophesque, que les hommes sont par tout les mêmes, qu'ayant par tout les mêmes passions & les mêmes vices, il est assés inutile de chercher à caractériser les différens Peuples; ce qui est à peu près aussi bien raisonné que si l'on disoit qu'on ne sauroit distinguer Pierre d'avec Jaques, parce qu'ils ont tous deux un nés, une bouche & des yeux.

Ne verra-t-on jamais renaître ces tems heureux où les Peuples ne se mêloient point de Philosopher, mais où les Platons, les Thalés & les Pythagores épris d'un ardent desir de savoir, entreprenoient les plus grands voyages uniquement pour s'instruire, & alloient au loin secouer le joug des préjugés Nationaux, apprendre à connoître les hommes par leurs conformitès & per leurs différences...?*

JEAN JAQUES ROUSSEAU

*See page 16.

# Preface

THIS BOOK is intended for everyone interested in the problems of race, whether a specialist in some branch of knowledge directly connected with the subject or not. An author who addresses both specialists and non-specialists may feel himself in a quandary. How shall he remain comprehensible to all his readers, yet not bore or irritate the specialists? Perhaps he cannot altogether achieve his aim. Nevertheless, in this respect the subject of race plays into the author's hand; for specialists in branches of knowledge bearing on racial problems have not, as a general rule, settled down to the formidable task of acquainting themselves with all aspects of it. For instance, there are probably many authorities on human genetics who have not studied the assessment of cognitive ability, and by no means every social anthropologist would lay claim to a detailed knowledge of anatomy or taxonomy. They could all have grasped every aspect of the subject, had they wished; but the majority have not in fact done so, and as a result they are in certain respects non-specialists. I therefore offer this book to the public in the hope that some of it may be useful to all its readers, and all of it to some. Those parts that are more technical or more detailed than the rest (though not necessarily less interesting) are distinguished by smaller type. Readers who decide to skip these passages will find that they have not lost the thread.

Most of the passages taken from writings in foreign languages are rendered in this book in English. The translations, except from Russian and Dutch, are my own. My aim has been to err, if at all, on the side of being too literal rather than the reverse, but I have avoided the use of grammatical constructions that are foreign to our tongue. I have not interrupted the text by statements that the original language was foreign. In many cases this will be obvious. If in doubt, the reader has only to look up the reference in the list at the end of the book, and note the language in which the title of the original publication was written.

In passages quoted directly, without translation, I have followed the original spelling exactly, with the exception that in Latin words I have substituted $u$ for $v$ wherever $u$ was obviously intended.

Most of the measurements recorded in this book are expressed in metric terms, in accordance with the Système International d'Unités. It will be remembered that in this system, what used to be called the micron ($\mu$) is now the micrometre ($\mu$m), and what was the millimicron is the nanometre (nm).

After a lot of hesitation I have decided not to make acknowledgements for help in writing this book, except to those whose assistance has been such that no one could regard it as indicating agreement with what I have written. The fact that a person's photograph appears in the book, to illustrate points in physical anthropology, must not be taken to imply acceptance of my opinions. Naturally I am indebted to others, as every author is; but parts of the book deal with controversial matters, and if I were to offer thanks, it might be supposed by some readers that those who had helped me necessarily shared my views. The fact is that many of them do not know what my views are, and I do not know theirs. No one, except typists and persons concerned with publication, has seen the manuscript. If anyone wishes his or her help to be acknowledged, it shall be done most willingly if a reprint or second edition should ever be published. Two exceptions, though, must be made to the general rule against naming those who have given me information, advice, or encouragement. The dedication of the book reveals the identity of one; and there is another of whom I can say with confidence that she will approve of what she has not seen, and whom I can therefore thank for her encouragement and the assurance of her support—my wife, Liena.

JOHN R. BAKER

P.S. A new taxonomic term, *stirps*, is suggested in a footnote to p. 5. It is hoped that this term will be found useful in anthropology. The footnote was added after the rest of the book was complete.

# Contents

## Part 4   Criteria of superiority and inferiority   419

# List of Appendices

# List of illustrations

*For acknowledgements see pp. xvii–xviii*

# Acknowledgements

I TAKE this opportunity to express my deep gratitude to the past and present staffs of the Bodleian Library and its dependent and associated libraries in Oxford, especially the Radcliffe Science Library, for their invariable helpfulness over a period of half a century.

I am greatly indebted to Mrs. J. A. Spokes for her secretarial help in the early stages of the preparation of this book. Mrs. R. Keeys and Mrs. S. Freeborn, of Hunts Typewriting Bureau, Oxford, copied most of the manuscript. I thank them for their very accurate work.

Those who have given permission for the reproduction of illustrations are listed below. I have taken a lot of trouble in seeking to obtain permission in the case of all those illustrations that were published during the last eighty years, but I have not in every case been successful in locating the person who could give it. If I have made omissions that can be corrected, I hope to be informed and thus to have the opportunity to make amends in a reprint or later edition of the book. In those cases in which I have based new illustrations, drawn by myself, on information published by others, I have thought it unnecessary to do more than give references to the sources of the information. This applies to Figs. 6, 7, 10, 12, 14, 16, 35, 38, 73, and 76–80.

| Figure | |
|---|---|
| 1 | Masson & Cie, Paris |
| 2 | The Royal Society of London |
| 3 | The Bodleian Library, Oxford |
| 4 | Bibliothèque nationale et universitaire, Strasbourg |
| 9 | University Museum, Oxford (Dr. T. S. Kemp, Curator of the Zoological Collections) |
| 11 | Longman Group Ltd., London |
| 15 | The Royal Society and Professor H. G. Callan, F.R.S. |
| 17C. D | *Biological Journal of Okayama University* and Professor Siro Kawaguti |
| 22A | VEB Gustav Fischer Verlag, Jena |
| 23A–D | E. Schweizerbart'sche Verlagsbuchhandlung, Stuttgart |
| 25 | Berliner Gesellschaft für Anthropologie, Ethnologie und Urgeschichte (Professor Dr. Hermann Pohle, Vorsitzender) |
| 28A–D | University Museum, Oxford (Dr. T. S. Kemp) |
| 29A | Press Association, London |
| 29B | Associated Press, London, & Wide World Photos, New York |
| 29C | Bassano & Vandyk Studios, London |
| 29D | Musées royaux d'Art et d'Histoire, Brussels (M. Jean Ch. Balty) |
| 30A. B | Hutchinson Publishing Group, London |
| 30C. D | Associated Press, London, & Wide World Photos, New York |
| 31B | *Daily Telegraph*, London (photograph by Mr. Murray Irving) |

| 32A | Link Information Services, London |
| 32B | The Trustees of the British Museum (Natural History) |
| 33A | United Press International (U.K.), London |
| 33B | Muséum d'Histoire naturelle, Lyon (M. L. David) |
| 33C | Musée du Louvre, Paris (M. André Parrot and M. Pierre Amiet) |
| 40 | The Visitors and Keeper of the Ashmolean Museum, Oxford |
| 42 | The Trustees of the British Museum |
| 43 | The Trustees of the British Museum |
| 44A. B | Hutchinson Publishing Group, London |
| 45A–C | The Trustees of the British Museum (Natural History) |
| 46A. B. D | University Museum, Oxford (Dr. T. S. Kemp) |
| 46C | Anthropology Laboratory, Department of Human Anatomy, Oxford University (Dr. G. A. Harrison) |
| 48A–E | University Museum, Oxford (Dr. T. S. Kemp) |
| 49A | *Anatomischer Anzeiger* (Professor Dr. Max Watzka) |
| 49B | Cambridge University Press |
| 52 | VEB Gustav Fischer Verlag, Jena |
| 55A. B | Berliner Gesellschaft für Anthropologie, Ethnologie und Urgeschichte (Professor Dr. Hermann Pohle) |
| 55C | The late Mrs. E. Goodall, Queen Victoria Museum, Salisbury, Rhodesia, and Mr. Roger Summers, F.S.A., Kommetjie, South Africa |
| 56B | VEB Gustav Fischer Verlag, Jena |
| 57B | The Trustees of the British Museum |
| 57C | The Bodleian Library, Oxford |
| 60A. B | Buch- und Kunstverlag Anton Schroll, Vienna |
| 60C | Hutchinson Publishing Group, London |
| 63A. B | Mr. J. P. Maule, M.A., Edinburgh |
| 71A. B | The Trustees of the British Museum |
| 72A | Mr. Gerry Cranham, Coulsdon |
| 72B | Associated Press, London, & Wide World Photos, New York |
| 74 | Professor J. LeR. Conel, Boston (Mass.) |
| 75 | *Journal of Comparative Neurology* and Professor Murray L. Barr |
| 81 | The Visitors and Keeper of the Ashmolean Museum, Oxford |
| 82 | The late Mrs. E. Goodall, Queen Victoria Museum, Salisbury, Rhodesia |

# INTRODUCTION

# Introduction

THE SUBJECT of race is so vast and so diverse that an author might feel at a loss when he sets out to introduce what he has written about it. Briefly, the intention has been to establish facts and to record ideas about race, with special reference to man. There is nothing in the book about any practical applications of the conclusions reached; but with this exception, the attempt has been made to look at the subject in all its aspects.

Throughout the book, what may be called the historical method has been adopted as a matter of deliberate policy. It is hoped that readers may approve of this approach; for what seem to be new ideas strike suddenly on the mind as novelties when they reappear out of the distant past in the writings of authors now long in their graves. The stimulating effect is due to the fact that the writers had not been influenced by the conventional ideas of modern times. One is surprised and forced to think—and sometimes to think new thoughts. In those branches of science in which deduction plays a large part, modern ideas may readily be introduced without need to recite the opinions of our forefathers; but where knowledge accrues gradually by long-sustained thought and argument about a vast body of information, one cannot fully understand or assess the ideas of the present without going back to look at origins.

It is the human aspect of race that chiefly interests most people, and in the writing of the book this fact has been kept constantly in mind. Nevertheless it is written by a biologist who believes that racial problems cannot be understood by anyone whose interests and field of knowledge stop short at the limit of purely human affairs. 'One must not remain fastened to man and act as though he were the only organism in nature.' So wrote that great anthropologist and humanitarian of the eighteenth century, Johann Friedrich Blumenbach, when considering the equality or inequality of human races.[109]* T. H. Huxley stressed the same point, in his *Essay on the methods and results of ethnology*. 'Anthropology is a section of ZOOLOGY,' he wrote; '... the problems of ethnology are simply those which are presented to the zoologist by every widely distributed animal he studies.'[536] The present work is written in the spirit that inspired these sentences. If the relevance of some of the zoological parts of the book is not obvious to the reader at first sight, it will become so when he has passed on to the chapters devoted to selected human groups.

The book deals with the question whether there is reality behind the idea of

---

* Throughout this book, the numerals in square brackets refer to the bibliography on pages 560–605.

race. The subject can only be rationally discussed if certain words that will be used over and over again are clearly explained at the outset. Anyone who happens not to be familiar with the technical terms used in systematic zoology will find the book much more readable if he will take the trouble to note carefully what meanings will be attached to a few terms that are indispensable in a study of this kind.

The reader will be aware that organisms are grouped together if they show resemblances that are considered to be due to descent from common ancestors. A group of this kind is called a *taxon*, and the branch of knowledge concerned with the principles and practice of the classification of organisms is called *taxonomy*. The group that includes all the hairy animals whose young are suckled by their mothers is a taxon known as the Mammalia, which includes animals so diverse as the shrew, hippopotamus, fruit-bat, and man. A taxon that includes such very different animals as these is called a *class*. Each class is divided into subsidiary taxa called *orders*, and these successively into *families*, *genera*, and *species*. Each of these groups is itself a taxon, and it thus follows that there is a hierarchy of taxa.

A family (the Pongidae or anthropoid apes, for instance) is a very minor taxon in relation to the Mammalia as a whole, but major in relation to each of the species which compose it. It is convenient to use the words 'major' and 'minor' in this relative sense, to indicate the place of a taxon in the hierarchy of taxa. It must be understood that these words will never be used in an appreciative or disparaging sense: they are entirely objective.

The meaning of the word species will be considered in some detail in Chapters 5 and 6. For the present it must suffice to say that it must be regarded provisionally as a group of animals that interbreed with one another. When a species has a wide distribution, it often shows differences of structure in different places, though intermediates occur. Each recognizable group constitutes a taxon called a *subspecies* or *race*. Thus the race is a minor taxon in relation to the species. Many authorities subdivide the races of man into taxa called *subraces*; for instance, two of the subraces into which the Europid (so-called 'Caucasian') race is divided are the Nordids and Alpinids. Some go so far as to recognize subdivisions of subraces, the taxa called *local forms*. In discussions of the problems with which this book is concerned, one repeatedly finds the need for a comprehensive term that can be used without distinction for any of the taxa that are minor to the species; that is to say, races, subraces, and local forms. No one has previously suggested a term having this meaning, and it is therefore necessary to propose one. Throughout the book *ethnic taxon* will be used for the purpose. It is open to the objection that English words derived from the Greek ἔθνος (ethnic, ethnology, ethnography, and others) are used by some authors in reference to groups of mankind distinguished by cultural or national features, rather than descent from common ancestors. This usage, however, is not universal; and it seems impossible to think of an acceptable substitute for *ethnic*. Most of the Greek and Latin words that might have been chosen are either so unfamiliar that they would convey no idea to most readers, or else have already been taken into our language with senses that make them inapplicable here (γένος, for instance, in its Latin form *genus* is already used).* It is particularly important that the meaning of the term 'ethnic taxon' should be clearly understood. It does not supplant the words race, subrace, and local form, but comprehends these three, and can be used in place of any of them.

Some authorities think that in certain cases the race is more significant than the species. They may study an interbreeding group of animals over a vast area of the surface of the globe, and concentrate their attention on the particular 'forms' or races that represent it in various localities. To these investigators these 'forms' are the realities. They consider that species have been founded too readily on the evidence of structural resemblances studied in the museum or laboratory, without sufficient attention having been paid to the question whether proof has been obtained by field studies that interbreeding between one form and another does in fact occur in nature. Wherever there are forms that replace one another geographically, and especially if they appear to merge into one another in the intermediate territory, they refer to the whole series of forms or races as a *Formenkreis*, and discard the word species altogether. The *Formenkreis*, then, is a set or series of races. This is a matter of considerable importance, for mankind should perhaps be regarded as constituting a *Formenkreis* rather than a species. The subject is carefully discussed in Chapter 5. Here it is only necessary to mention that the *Formenkreis* is a taxon and that it is divisible, like the species, into races, subraces, and local forms.

If 'ethnic taxon' had been a generally recognized term, this book might have been called '*Ethnic taxa*', for it is concerned with subraces as well as races, and indeed occasional mention is made of local forms; but the title of a serious work must necessarily be comprehensible, and precision must defer to necessity.

It is thought by some students of the subject that all attempts to classify mankind into ethnic taxa are vain. Those who hold this view lay stress on the prevalence of intermediates, and on the difficulty of laying down strict criteria for the recognition of races and subraces. They consider that those who describe these taxa are really only listing the characters of ideal types, non-existent except in the minds of men. For them, the only reality is the whole *population* of a particular place at a particular time. The ethnic constitution of the population is regarded as of little consequence in comparison with the environmental circumstances that mould the minds and activities of the men and women who compose it. Full weight should be given to this point of view, and in particular to the fact that large-scale hybridization between races and subraces has in fact occurred. Nevertheless it will be argued in this book that race and subrace do represent a truth about the natural world, which cannot be adequately described without consideration of them. For this reason a classification of mankind into ethnic taxa is set out in the table placed at the end of the book for easy reference. Nearly all the taxa mentioned in the book are listed in it. All classifications of this sort are provisional in the sense that no

---

* The Latin word *stirps* (plural *stirpes*) may be suggested as a synonym for ethnic taxon. Indeed, it might well replace the latter term. Not only does it avoid the objection to *ethnic*, mentioned above; it has the added advantage that an adjective can be derived from it. Thus, for instance, one may say that there is a 'stirpal difference' between two peoples.

two authorities are likely to be in complete agreement about them, and the growth of knowledge will no doubt necessitate changes. Nevertheless such tables do contain an important element of truth, which is hidden if no such classification is attempted. This is proved by the fact that random alterations in them produce nonsense, which certainly cannot be said of a carefully constructed table. For instance, no one with any knowledge of physical anthropology will deny that it would be absurd to make the Nordids into a race that included the Sinids and Khoisanids as subraces, or to place the Mongolids as a subrace of the Australasids.

The subject of ethnic taxa is of great interest from the purely biological point of view, without consideration of man, and a very large literature has grown up around it. Public interest, however, is centred on human aspects of the matter, and primarily on the question whether all the ethnic taxa of man are to be regarded as 'equal' or as in some sense 'unequal', and if 'unequal', whether some may be regarded as 'superior' to others. For instance, it has been claimed (by certain Europids) that the Europid race is superior to other races, and (by certain Nordids) that among the Europids, the Nordid subrace is superior to other subraces. One needs a technical term that will cover this whole subject of equality or inequality among the ethnic taxa of man. The term used throughout this book with this particular meaning is 'the ethnic problem'. It will be understood that there are many biological problems concerned with ethnic taxa; but one needs a short phrase in a book such as this, and the explanation that has been given here will ensure that the words will not be misunderstood.

Every ethnic taxon of man includes many persons capable of living responsible and useful lives in the communities to which they belong, while even in those taxa that are best known for their contributions to the world's store of intellectual wealth, there are many so mentally deficient that they would be inadequate members of any society. It follows that no one can claim superiority simply because he or she belongs to a particular ethnic taxon. It does not inevitably follow, however, that all taxa can properly be said to be 'equal'. It is necessary to consider carefully whether any meaning can be attached to the statement that one ethnic taxon is 'superior' to another. If the statement is not meaningless, one wants to know with some precision what it means, and if this could be defined, it would still be questionable whether any one taxon were in fact superior to another. These problems are considered in this book.

The subject is necessarily controversial. It is hoped that those readers who disagree with some of the opinions expressed will nevertheless find something of value to them in particular parts of the book. It will have served its purpose if it has cleared away those misapprehensions that cannot be helpful, in the long run, to either side in the controversy.

PART ONE

# The Historical
# Background

# 1 From Neanderthal man to the philosophers of the eighteenth century

THE FOUR historical chapters that constitute Part 1 of this book are concerned with the thoughts of man. They do not deal with actions taken in the political field to apply in practice the ideas present in the mind. For example, no mention is made of the work of the great humanitarians, such as William Wilberforce and Thomas Clarkson, in the suppression of Negro slavery; and indeed this would be unnecessary, because the facts are readily available to everyone interested in history or biography.[211, 229, 438] The subject dealt with here is less familiar, because the information is scattered among many very diverse and in some cases unexpected, little known, and even rather inaccessible sources of information. Hitler is the only author mentioned in the four chapters who is chiefly known as a man of action. It has seemed necessary to record something about his views on the ethnic problem as expressed in *Mein Kampf*,[494] because his subsequent actions had such a profound effect on human thought.

The subject considered in these chapters is not only intrinsically interesting: it has a message also for the present day. Although many of the early thinkers were mistaken in their beliefs, some of them afford examples that might well be followed today. In particular one thinks of that quartet of distinguished biologists, Blumenbach, Sömmerring, Camper, and Tiedemann, whom we shall meet in Chapter 2. Here were men who addressed themselves fearlessly to the ethnic problem. They did not by any means agree exactly with one another, but they indulged in no personal attacks. To the best of their ability they brought to bear on a difficult subject such information as was available in their time. They were men of wide knowledge and level judgement, open-minded searchers after truth.

Chapters 3 and 4 bring the history up to the end of the third decade of the twentieth century. They deal with only one side of the problem, in considerable detail. The reason for ending the purely historical part of the book at this point is explained on p. 61.

This first chapter, dealing as it does with the earliest part of the history, is inevitably somewhat desultory, because the lack of relation between most of the available sources of information makes it almost impossible to weave them together into a continuous whole.

In a study of the subject with which this book is largely concerned, it might seem a waste of time to search for evidence regarding man's remote ancestors in the mid-Pleistocene, perhaps fifty thousand or more years ago, during the last great glacial phase. How did the various ethnic taxa of man react to one another in the remote past? It is true that at present we have not enough evidence to enable us to reach a firm conclusion, but in fact we can at least see how a certain amount of knowledge might one day be obtained.

In the early part of the last glacial phase, humanity was represented in Europe by Neanderthal man.[129, 130, 131] He was short, in comparison with most modern men, but massively built. Huge eyebrow ridges joined one another above the nose (Fig. 1); the forehead was very low and sloping; the

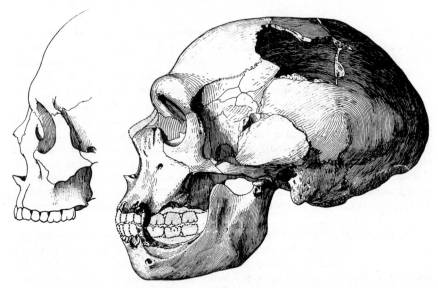

1   *A skull of Neanderthal man, with part of a skull of a modern Europid (a Frenchman) for comparison*

The Neanderthal skull represented here, from La Chapelle-aux-Saints, Corrèze, France, is the most complete in existence, but it lacks the nasal bones and most of the teeth. The missing parts are present in other specimens of the same ethnic taxon, and it has therefore been possible to add them in the drawing.
*From Boule.* [130]

skull was rather long in proportion to its breadth, flattish on top, and curiously flattened from above and below in the occipital region, so that it almost resembled in form the *chignon* of a woman's hair.[129] The massive maxillary bone of each side extended forward in a large process (apophysis) that pushed the nasal bone before it so as to make the nose project prodigiously; the foramen magnum was situated rather far back. The cavity of the skull was large, but casts of the brain-case indicate that the frontal lobes were small and the convolutions of the brain-surface somewhat primitive in arrangement. The lower jaw sloped away below so that one can scarcely speak of a chin. The legs were short in relation to total stature. There has been some tendency in recent years to minimize the characters that distinguish Neanderthal anatomy from that of modern man. It is legitimate to doubt whether this tendency can be fully justified by the facts. Apart from the grosser features that have been mentioned, there are marked differences in the teeth, especially the lower molars.[433] Many authorities place him in a separate 'palaeospecies', *Homo neanderthalensis*, and its European race has been named *proto-europaeus*.[302]

Neanderthal man was replaced in Europe during the last glacial phase by *Homo sapiens*, exemplified by Cromagnon man, named after a place in the Dordogne (south-central France) where the remains of five human bodies were found. Whether any Cromagnids coexisted in Europe with Neanderthal man is uncertain, but it is usually supposed that the latter died out before the others arrived. Since, however, there are 'Neanderthaloid' characters in certain early forms of *H. sapiens*, some authorities consider that there was overlapping in time and some hybridization.[227] If so, Neanderthal man can scarcely be regarded as a separate species.

Very strange facts are revealed when we turn to the Neanderthaloid remains of the mid-Pleistocene found on Mount Carmel, south of Haifa in Israel, and in other parts of Palestine. A considerable number of rather well preserved specimens have been studied in great detail by McCown and Keith.[720] The people who lived in this area at the time were remarkably varied in structure, some of them verging towards the Neanderthal, others towards the early *sapiens* type, others again intermediate. It was suggested by the American anthropologist C. S. Coon that hybridization between Neanderthal man and *sapiens* might be the explanation.[226] This view was strongly supported by Dobzhansky,[277] an authority on the origin of species and races. Since Neanderthal man differs more markedly from any of the races of man living today than any of these races differ from one another, it follows that if hybridization occurred, primitive men and women had not at that time and place a strong repugnance against extreme difference in sexual partners.

McCown and Keith[720] had themselves seriously considered the possibility of hybridity and rejected it. If it had occurred, one must suppose that there was already present in Palestine at that time (the Levalloiso-Mousterian culture period of archaeologists) a fully developed form of Neanderthal man and also a fully developed form of *sapiens*; and no evidence of this exists. In their book *Fossil men*, the French palaeontologist Marcellin Boule and the anthropologist H. V. Vallois agree with McCown and Keith in rejecting the possibility that Palestine man was a hybrid.[131] The matter cannot be regarded as settled, but when further evidence becomes available, we shall be better able to form an estimate of the interethnic relations of early man. It is possible that new ethnic taxa were evolving rapidly in Palestine in the period under consideration—that there was a branching of the evolutionary tree, rather than a grafting together of previously separate twigs.

A moment's reflection will show that the great majority of man's remote ancestors can have had only a faint idea, or none at all, of the physical differences between the ethnic taxa of man. Even today, with the enormous increase in population and ease of travel, it seems certain that only a small minority of the inhabitants of Great Britain has ever seen a Bushman (Sanid) or Hottentot (Khoid), and there must be many in Australia who have never seen a Negrid. Population gradually increased in Neolithic times as knowledge of agriculture began to spread over the world, and subraces must then have tended to meet more often than races; but there were certain wide areas where races did meet and hybridize to some extent with one another. In such cases the resulting hybrid peoples were commonly not exactly intermediate, because the majority of the ancestors of the partially hybrid group belonged to one of the two races. An example is provided by the Turanids of the country north of Iran, Afghanistan, and Pakistan. These people are hybrids between Europids and Mongolids, but the former stock evidently predominated, presumably because the original hybrids tended to intermarry with Europids more often than with Mongolids. The Turanids are regarded as a subrace of Europids, characterized by the possession of certain Mongolid traits in their physique.

Similarly, the Aethiopids of Ethiopia and elsewhere (Galla and other tribes) are almost certainly hybrids between Europids with some Negrid admixture, but certain authorities[303, 836] regard them as Negrids with Europid admixture.

A remote possibility exists, however, that the Aethiopids are the descendants of a group from which both Europids and Negrids are derived. [1085]

There are several tribes commonly grouped together as 'Nilo-Hamites', because they are supposed to have Nilotid Negrids and Aethiopid Europids as ancestors; but different tribes were probably derived from different Negrid subraces and/or different Europid subraces, and if so, the grouping under a single name is misleading because it does not reflect a common ancestry.

Sufficient examples have been quoted to show that subraces and even races sometimes hybridize where they meet, but this really almost goes without saying; for if sexual revulsion against intersubracial and interracial marriages were complete, one set of genes would have no chance of intermingling with another, and the ethnic taxa would be *species* by the commonly accepted definition (see p. 74). It cannot be too strongly stressed that intersubracial and interracial hybridization is so far from indicating the unreality of subraces and races, that it is actually a *sine qua non* of the reality of these ethnic taxa.

Strong feelings against intersubracial and interracial hybridization do, however, sometimes manifest themselves. When Nordindids ('Indo-Afghans') began to penetrate into India from the north-west from about 1500 B.C. onwards, and came into contact with various peoples differing from themselves in physical features as well as in culture, social barriers against free hybridization were set up and the 'caste' system gradually evolved. This was perhaps the most elaborate and effective barrier against the mixing of contiguous ethnic taxa that the world has ever known.

Palestine is a region from which we have historical evidence of hybridization and of steps taken to prevent it. Unfortunately we have no reliable evidence of the physique of the peoples concerned, though we have names that are intended to identify them. In the Bible three ethnic taxa are fancifully supposed to have sprung from the three sons of Noah (*Genesis*, x). It is generally taken for granted that the supposed descendants of Shem were the 'Shemites' or 'Semites',[19, 674, 39] but unfortunately this does not carry us much further, because we do not know who the Semites might be. Possibly the Orientalids

('Arabs') are meant; possibly the Armenids, who are physically very different; possibly both of these and their hybrids.[674] It has been argued, however, that there was a Nordid element in the 'Shemites', and therefore in the Hebrew patriarchs.[395]

The descendants of Ham were the Hamites, but here again we are in difficulty, because it is uncertain who the Hamites were. Since Canaan was one of the sons of Ham, it seems reasonable to suppose that the Canaanites were Hamites. Usually, however, the Hamites of the Bible are assumed to have been the early Egyptians, [674] who are thought to have been Protomediterranids hybridized with Orientalids; [302] but Chapter x of *Genesis* makes it clear that the Sumerians and Assyrians, among others, were also descendants of Ham. Certain authorities [39] have supposed that the Hamites were Negrids. It has, indeed, been claimed [211] that the latter were descendants of Phut, one of Ham's sons; but it is doubtful whether much was known of Negrids by the writers of *Genesis*, x, and Phut's descendants do not appear to have made any clear mark on the available historical records.

The Japhetic peoples are usually supposed to have been of 'Indo-European' [19, 674] or 'Indo-Germanic' [39] stock; but these expressions, based on linguistic studies, are not translatable into ethnic terms. Evidence has been brought forward for the view that the Japhetic peoples were in fact Armenids and Alpinids. [395]

It is impossible to draw any definite conclusions from the account in *Genesis* of the origin of the various peoples to whom reference is made, beyond the fact that they were all supposed to have sprung from a common ancestor; but it seems very probable that they were all Europids. Whatever the correct interpretation may be, there is no doubt that hybridization among subraces occurred in Palestine and Mesopotamia in biblical times, and that the Hebrews were strongly urged by some of their spiritual leaders to avoid it. Although the ethnic taxa in question were only subraces of the same (Europid) race as themselves, there was no question of 'equality' in the minds of the leaders. It was legitimate to despise people of another taxon that was regarded as more primitive. Noah, it will be remembered, had condemned Canaan (i.e. one of Ham's sons and his descendants) to be 'a servant of servants . . . unto his brethren', that is to say, a servant to the Shemites and Japhetites (*Genesis*, ix, 25–7). Strongly expressed opinions on the ethnic problem such as these no doubt had an influence on Jewish, and later to some extent on Christian, thinking. A striking example appears, for instance, in the book of *Job*. It seems that this unfortunate man was mocked by youthful members of a primitive, cave-dwelling, pre-agricultural (food-gathering) tribe (*Job*, xxx, 1–10). This is the interpretation placed on the words by several commentators, and indeed no other seems possible. As a young man, Job had known the fathers of his persecutors, and he remarks of them, 'I would have disdained to set [them] with the dogs of my flock. . . . they were viler than the earth.'

A group of Canaanites called the Hivites were regarded by the Hebrews with marked disrespect. It will be remembered how Joshua imposed his will upon them, by assigning to them the tasks of hewing wood and drawing water for their Hebrew masters. They still retained this lowly status when the chapter of the Bible describing these events (*Joshua*, ix) was written down, probably some centuries later.

Christian ethics brought about a less severe attitude in people towards persons of ethnic taxa other than their own, but it must be remembered that the early Christians had little or no acquaintance with people so different from themselves in physique as to belong to another race. St. Paul played a prominent part in encouraging a more tolerant attitude. The words he used in speaking to the Athenians at Mars' Hill are given in the Revised Version of the Bible thus: 'God . . . hath made of one blood all nations of men,' but it is not always remembered that he added, 'and hath determined . . . the bounds of their habitation' (Revised Version, *Acts*, xvii, 24–6). The translation of this passage in the New English Bible is as follows: 'He [God] created every race of men of one stock. . . . He fixed . . . the limits of their territory.' (New English Bible, 1961). It is questionable whether Paul actually used a word meaning 'blood'. This word is stated not to occur here in the early Greek texts, and it was rejected by the Catholic Church from the time of St. Jerome.[808] The New Testament in Greek carefully compiled by the British and Foreign Bible Society[791] says simply that God made every race of man 'ἐξ ἑνὸς'. Canon G. W. Wade's version of this passage is 'from a single ancestor'.[1112] The common use of the word 'blood' to indicate relationship can be traced back to Erasmus's Bible of 1516.[311] He may have been deliberately using a current European idea when he wrote 'ἐξ ἑνὸς αἵματος' in his Greek version and '*ex uno sanguine*' in the Latin. Luther may well have been influenced by this when he wrote '*von eynem blut*' in his translation.[688] It would not appear that the early Jews associated blood with race. The use of the word 'blood' to indicate relationship has nothing to commend it and might well be abandoned with other mediaeval superstitions. Lest anyone should imagine that Erasmus had prescience of the blood-groups, it should perhaps be mentioned that members of a single ethnic taxon, indeed often of a single family, may belong to different groups.

It is clear that the early Christians did not altogether disregard the ethnic cohesion of the Jews. *The Epistle of St. James* appears to be directed to those who were ethnically Jews, but who lived outside Palestine and had been converted to Christianity.[1112] It is not clear to whom precisely *The First Epistle General of St. Peter* was addressed. The Revised Version of the Bible translates I *Peter*, ii, 9, 'But ye are a chosen generation, a royal priesthood, an holy nation, a peculiar people,' but Wade writes instead, 'But you are a Chosen race. . . .' The rendering in the New English Bible is this: 'But you are a chosen race, a royal priesthood, a dedicated nation, and a people claimed by God for his own.' It seems to be uncertain whether the 'strangers' (Revised Version), 'Sojourners',[1112] or 'scattered people' (New English Bible) in Pontus, Galatia, and certain other places, to whom St. Peter addressed his Epistle, were specifically the Christian strangers of *Jewish* origin.

That persons of different ethnic groups are not necessarily immediately unattractive to one another is attested by the familiar tradition, passed down from the sixth century, of Gregory (afterwards Pope Gregory I) at his first sight of persons of the Nordid subrace. The Venerable Bede tells us that Gregory saw some Anglo-Saxon boys exposed for sale in the market-place of Rome.[67, 68]

He described their countenances as 'bright' and 'charming' (the adjectives were *lucidus* and *venustus*). On being told that they were called Angles, he replied 'Rightly, for they have an angelic appearance, and it is proper for such persons to be the associates of the angels in heaven.' (Not everyone is aware of the further puns perpetrated by His Holiness on this memorable occasion and duly recorded by his venerable historian.) It must be remembered, however, that the Nordid boys differed only in rather unimportant points of physique from the familiar Mediterranids of Rome, apart from the minor character of colour. These two subraces are closely allied.

A leap to the sixteenth century brings us to Montaigne's essay entitled '*Des Cannibales*'.[756] The ostensible purpose of this short paper is to exhibit a primitive people in a favourable light in relation to the members of civilized societies. At this distance of time it is difficult or perhaps impossible to be quite certain whether in this particular essay Montaigne was writing with his tongue in his cheek, deliberately hiding from the unsuspecting reader what he intended to spring on him towards the end. He appears to be describing the Caribs of the West Indies, though he does not make this perfectly clear. For his information he relies mainly on one of his servants, who has been in that part of the world and whom he describes as being '... simple and uncouth, which is a suitable state for rendering true evidence. . . . One needs either a very reliable man, or one so simple that he has not the wherewithal to create and give verisimilitude to his false inventions.' This man's story is confirmed by several sailors and merchants who had voyaged with him. Montaigne draws a remarkable picture of the superiority of the '*Cannibales*' over civilized people. One example among many is that they eat wild fruits; civilized men should be termed savage, because instead of using what nature provides, they artificially deform its vegetable products. 'I find', he tells us, 'that there is nothing barbaric or savage in this nation in what has been reported to me, unless it can be that each person calls Barbarity what is not customary with him, or that we have no other measure of truth and reason than the example and idea of the opinions and customs of the country in which we live.' He goes smoothly on to tell us that these people take prisoners in war and keep them alive for two or three months, during which period they use every possible method they can think of to induce them to say something that would indicate fear. For this purpose they tell them exactly what is going to happen to them: the tortures they are going to suffer, the preparations that are being made for this purpose, and the intention to slice up their limbs for the banquet that will be made of their flesh—all of which is in due course carried out.

Those in modern times who overstress the significance of 'colour' would receive a wholesome corrective on reading the excellent essay on physical anthropology written by an anonymous traveller and published in the *Journal des Sçavans* in 1684.[24] In this very remarkable work on the geographical distribution of human '*Espéces ou Races*', the author clearly recognizes that the people of North Africa, Arabia, and India belong to the same race as those of Europe. He writes on the subject of colour as follows.

For although the Egyptians, for instance, and the Indians are very black, or rather tawny [*baganés*], this colour is nevertheless only accidental to them, and comes only because they expose themselves to the sun; for those who take care of themselves and are not obliged to expose themselves to it as often as the [common] people are, are not blacker than many Spaniards. It is true that most Indians have something rather different from us in the expression of the face and in the colour, which often tends towards yellow; but that does not seem sufficient to make a particular species; for otherwise it would be necessary to make one also for the Spaniards, another for the Germans, and similarly for several other peoples of Europe.

The author sharply distinguishes certain other 'coloured' races from the Indians, by morphological criteria. He considered the women of Lahore the most beautiful of India. These would have been Nordindids (Indo-Afghans).

Some of the important facts first clearly established by the anonymous traveller were well exhibited in the atlas published by de Vaugondy nearly a century later.[1087] The area of '*Les Européens*', identified by the appearance of the face (*visage*), includes not only Europe itself (apart from the extreme north of Scandinavia and the region north of the Black Sea), but also Africa north of the Sahara, Arabia, Iran, Afghanistan, Pakistan, and India as far south as the River Ganges.

It was already recognized in the seventeenth century that the skin-colour of certain races of man was not solely due to the action of the sun's rays during the life of the individual. One Leutholf or Ludolfus, writing in 1691, put the matter very clearly in a commentary[679] published separately from his book on Africa. 'But still', he says, 'within the range of the [tropical] sun there are nations if not actually white, at any rate not actually black; many are far distant from the equator, beyond one tropic or the other, such as the inhabitants of Persia or Syria, or the Cape of Good Hope, for example, and nevertheless they are very black.' Ludolfus refers to the blackness of the native inhabitants of Ceylon and other countries and remarks, 'If you attribute the natural cause [of their skin-colour] to the heavens and the sun, why do not white men who grow old in these regions become black?' There is here clear recognition of the reality of genetic differences between ethnic taxa.

From this lack of knowledge there has arisen that fine dictum of morality so much bandied about by the philosophical crowd, that men are everywhere the same, and that having everywhere the same passions and the same vices, it is rather useless to attempt to characterize the different races; which is just about as reasonable as if one were to say that one could not distinguish Peter from James, because each of them has a nose, a mouth, and eyes.

Will one never see the return of those happy times when people did not concern themselves with philosophy, but when such men as Plato, Thales, or Pythagoras, smitten with an eager desire for knowledge, undertook the longest journeys solely to obtain information, and went far away to shake off the yoke of national prejudices, to learn to know men by their conformities and by their differences . . .?

Those who are unfamiliar with this passage would be unlikely to ascribe it correctly to its author; but readers of these historical chapters will find that during the eighteenth and nineteenth centuries thinkers who were irreligious and radical or 'progressive' in their political views often tended to believe in the inequality of the races of man. The passage was in fact written by Jean-Jacques Rousseau. It is printed in its original French as an epigraph to this book.

The circumstances in which Rousseau came to write his famous *Discours sur l'origine et les fondemens de l'inegalité [sic] parmi les hommes*|918-920| may be remembered. The Academy of Dijon had offered a prize for a discourse on this subject: 'What is the origin of inequality among men, and is it authorized by natural law?' In his attempt to answer this question, Rousseau was not primarily concerned with the ethnic problem; but, as the extract given above shows, he allowed that the various ethnic taxa differed mentally as well as physically. He stressed the importance of the environment in causing the diversity of human beings in different parts of the world, especially when the environment acted over a long series of generations. His main concern, however, was with the degree of happiness of persons in solitary and social life. He believed that man's unhappiness was largely due to inequality among people living in the same society. He distinguished two varieties of inequality: *naturelle ou physique* and *morale ou politique*. The former was the sort caused by differences of age, health, or intellect; the latter by those due to convention or the consent of fellow-men. It was Rousseau's belief that primitive man, '*l'homme dans l'état de nature*', was solitary: there was not even such an association of the sexes as occurs in many non-social animals. 'The males and females united at random, by chance meeting, opportunity, and desire. . . . they left one another with the same readiness. . . . the two sexes did not recognize one another again, and even the child was nothing more to the mother, as soon as he could manage without her.' In this state of society man was *happy*, because inequality did not have an opportunity to express itself. As social institutions developed, inequality became apparent and caused misery.

Rousseau does not argue that the primeval savage was morally superior. On the contrary, he says distinctly that men in a state of nature 'could not be either good or bad, and had neither vices nor virtues. . . . they had no dealings of any kind with one another, and as a result knew neither vanity nor consideration nor esteem nor scorn; they had not the least notion of thine or mine, and had no idea of justice.' He regarded the Caribs (Indianid race, Brasilid subrace) as approaching more closely to the state of nature than any other people known at the time; but he only mentions them very briefly, and there is no indication that he had any detailed knowledge of their mode of life. As a matter of fact the Caribs were not particularly unsocial in early times: they had their *carbets*, or communal houses, and so far was the husband from deserting his wife that he underwent the strange custom of the *couvade* when his child was born.|268| Rousseau's belief in the solitary state of primitive man was almost entirely hypothetical, as he himself freely admitted. His ideas on this subject would not be likely to find acceptance among modern students of primitive culture.

The prize was awarded to Rousseau in 1750, but the *Discours* was not published till five years later.|918| The French physiologist C. N. Le Cat, who was one of the judges, strongly opposed the award and published a '*Refutation*' in the form of a book printed in columns, with extracts from the *Discours* on the left and his own criticisms of them on the right.|193| Most of the latter are given in very matter-of-fact style, without any attempt at satire, or rhetoric of any kind. He stresses, however, some of the horrors of savage life. 'Tell me, I beg you, illustrious orator,' he writes, 'is it among the realms in which universities and academies flourish, that one finds the gallant nation of cannibals?' It should be mentioned that Le Cat was by no means contemptuous of persons belonging to races other than his own. In another book he writes favourably of Negroes, and in particular opposes the idea that darkness of skin indicates inferiority. 'Does one believe', he writes, 'that Negroes have a lower estimate of themselves, and are indeed less estimable, because ordinary white people regard their appearance with horror? They are very good-natured and much more sensible than we, if they do not give us tit-for-tat.'[194]

Rousseau was by no means the only celebrated author of the eighteenth century who contributed to the discussion of the ethnic problem. Some of the greatest philosophical and political thinkers of the period—Montesquieu, Hume, Kant, and Voltaire among them—made comments, though mostly short ones. Some of these were merely satirical, and therefore not helpful in the search for truth. Thus Montesquieu wrote of the Negro in *De l'esprit des lois*: 'Those concerned are black from the feet to the head; and they have the nose squashed so flat that it is almost impossible to pity them. One cannot take it into one's mind that God, who is a wise being, has placed a soul, especially a good soul, in a wholly black body.'[759] The irony is so heavy-handed in the passage from which this extract is taken, that it cannot be regarded as effective even by the standards according to which this kind of rhetoric is commonly judged.

The Scottish philosopher and historian David Hume was one of those opponents of conventional religious thought who did not hesitate to express their belief in the inferiority of certain ethnic taxa. In his *Essays, moral and political* he writes, 'And indeed, there is some Reason to think, that all the Nations, which live beyond the polar Circles or betwixt the Tropics, are inferior to the rest of the Species, and are utterly incapable of all the higher Attainments of the human Mind.'[523] He remarked, however, that there was no relation between intelligence and latitude within the limits of the temperate zone. Hume was particularly impressed by the ease with which Negroes could be bribed by the gift of alcoholic drinks. He noted that the character of the Chinese was remarkably uniform over a huge area, in which the climatic conditions varied widely from place to place, and he concluded that the differences in 'Temper' of the various nations could not be due solely to the physical environment. He thought, however, that fortuitous circumstances might have produced some of the differences. In developing nations, a few persons gain control and eventually influence the mass of the people. Since the governing body is small, there must be a large element of chance in its composition.

The philosophers of the eighteenth century did not always draw a sharp distinction between nations and ethnic taxa. In his *Beobachtungen über das Gefühl des Schönen und Erhabenen*[569] Immanuel Kant gives rather elaborate accounts of the mental characters of the Germans, English, Dutch, French, Italians, Spaniards, Arabs, Persians, Indians, Japanese, and Chinese, but he makes no genuine attempt to say anything about the general character of the

Europid race in contrast to that of the Mongolid, or to differentiate between the various subraces among the Europids, though sufficient anthropological knowledge was available at the time (1764) to make a start in this direction. He does, however, distinguish the Negrid race from others, makes general remarks on the mental powers of persons belonging to it, and quotes Hume in support of his opinions.

The Negroes of Africa have received from nature no intelligence that rises above the foolish. Hume invites anyone to quote a single example of a Negro who has exhibited talents. He asserts that among the hundred thousands of blacks who have been seduced away from their own countries, although very many of them have been set free, yet not a single one has ever been found that has performed anything great whether in art or science or in any other laudable subject; but among the whites, people constantly rise up from the lowest rabble and acquire esteem through their superior gifts. The difference between these two races of man is thus a substantial one: it appears to be just as great in respect of the faculties of the mind as in colour.|569|

The use of fetishes by certain Negrid tribes had a strong influence on Kant's judgement. 'The religion of fetishes,' he writes, 'which is widely spread among them, is perhaps a sort of idolatry that sinks as deep in foolishness as seems to be possible for human nature. A bird's feather, the horn of a cow, a mussel, or any other common article becomes an object of veneration and invocation in oaths as soon as it has been consecrated by a few words.'|569|

Kant considered that no other uncivilized people showed such a high degree of intelligence as those of North America.

Kant's *Anthropologie in pragmatischer Hinsicht*|568| is really a work on psychology rather than anthropology in the modern sense. In this book he once more summarizes his opinions about the mental characters of various nations, but more shortly than in the earlier work. He particularly emphasizes the virtues of the Armenians, whom he describes as a unique people, sensible (*verünstig*), peaceful, and of superior character. It may be remarked that Hume also regarded the Armenians highly. He says that they 'have a peculiar Character' and are 'much noted . . . for Probity'.|523|

Voltaire, like Rousseau, was a radical in politics who did not believe in racial equality; but he expressed himself on this subject much more forcibly than his fellow-countryman. He was more impressed by the physical differences between the races than most of the philosophical and political thinkers who addressed themselves to the ethnic problem. He was particularly struck by the '*tablier*' (apron) of Hottentot (Khoid) women, exaggerated accounts of which were current in the eighteenth century. The subject is treated in some detail from the anatomical point of view in Chapter 17 (pp. 313–17) of the present book.

It was in his book *La philosophie de l'histoire*, published in 1765 over the pseudonym of l'Abbé Bazin, that Voltaire first broached the subject in print.|1108| It is to be remarked that he uses the words *espèces* and *races* interchangeably, and that he wrongly attributes the *tablier* to the '*Caffres*'.

Voltaire writes of the Negroes that 'Their round eyes, their flat nose, their lips that are always thick, their differently shaped ears, the wool of their head, even the measure of their intelligence, place prodigious differences between them and other *espèces* of men.' He denies that the differences are the effect of climate, because Negroes transported to cooler countries produce offspring of their own kind. 'The apron that nature has given to the Kaffirs, the loose, soft skin of which hangs from the navel to half-way down the thighs, the black teats of the Samoyed women, the beard of the men of our continent, and the always beardless chin of the Americans, are such marked differences that it is scarcely possible to imagine that these people are not of different *races*.'[1108]

Voltaire reverted to the *tablier* in *Les lettres d'Amabed*.[1110] This work of fiction consists mainly of letters written by one Amabed, an Indian of Benares, to Shastasid, the '*Grand Brame de Maduré*', and of the latter's replies. During his visit to South Africa, Amabed was much struck by the peculiar anatomy of the Hottentot women. He writes to Shastasid from the Cape of Good Hope:

> These people do not appear to be descendants of the children of Brama. Nature has given to the women an apron formed from their skin; this apron covers their *joyau*, of which the Hottentots are idolatrous ... The more I reflected on the colour of these people, on the clucking they use instead of an articulate language to make themselves understood, on their face, and on the apron of their women, the more I am convinced that these people cannot have the same origin as ourselves. Our chaplain claims that the Hottentots, Negroes, and Portuguese are descended from the same father. The idea is certainly ridiculous.

Once more Voltaire insisted on the diversity of man in his *Questions sur l'encyclopédie*.[1109] 'The inclinations, the characters of men differ as much as their climates and their governments. It has never been possible to form a regiment of Lapps or Samoyeds, while their neighbours, the Siberians, are intrepid soldiers. ... Only a blind person, and indeed an obstinate blind person, could deny the existence of all these different *espèces*.' He was under no misapprehension, however, about the intellectual level of the common run of mankind as a whole. 'In general,' he writes, 'the human species is not more civilized by two or three degrees than the people of Kamchatka. The multitude of brutal animals called *men*, compared with the small numbers of those who think, is at least in the proportion of 100 to one in many nations.'[1109] It may be remarked incidentally that in his *Questions* Voltaire pours scorn on 'certain bad jokers' who have claimed that man was originally solitary. This is obviously a reference to Rousseau. Voltaire had already denied that ancestral man was solitary in *La philosophie de l'histoire*.[1108]

The diversity of man was emphasized even more strongly by Henry Home, Lord Kames (1696–1782), than by Voltaire.

Kames, a Scottish lawyer and philosopher, was a man of very wide interest. Towards the end of his life he published anonymously a book in two volumes entitled *Sketches of the history of man*[563]—'not intended', as he modestly but with some justice admits, 'for the learned; they are above it'. It is a strange work. He dismisses Linnaeus's classification of animals contemptuously.

> It resembles the classing books in a library by size, or by binding, without regard to the contents. It may serve as a sort of dictionary; but to no other purpose so far as I can discover. ... What will a plain man think of a method of classing that denies a whale to be a fish?

Kames's purpose is to contradict the idea that the differences between the kinds of human beings can be due to environmental effects. He devotes many pages to the mental differences between peoples and to the improbability of their being caused by the environment. He dubs Montesquieu 'a great champion for the climate' as a cause of these differences. He says that the argument on which he himself chiefly relies is this, 'That were all men of one species, there never could have existed, without a miracle, different kinds, such as exist at present'. He thinks that the obvious conclusion would be that God created not one pair of human beings, but many pairs with different characters, all suited to the environments in which he placed them. This, however, he regards as unacceptable, because it is contrary to the biblical account; and he therefore concludes that when the people were scattered from Babel, God divided them into different kinds, already fitted for different climates.

Kames's book is worth mentioning not so much for any merit it may possess as from the stimulus to controversy it aroused in the years following its publication. Blumenbach refers to him several times (generally under the name of Henry Home), and in each case he disagrees. The Revd. Samuel Stanhope Smith, Professor of Moral Philosophy in the College of New Jersey, wrote a special article entitled 'Strictures on Lord Kames's discourse on the original diversity of mankind', which he appended to his book entitled *An essay on the causes of the variety of complexion and figure in the human species.*|984| Smith's 'Strictures' are quite effective, but the task was not a difficult one. He points out a number of demonstrable errors committed by 'this celebrated philosopher. . . . In all the writings of this author, there is not another example of so much weak and inconclusive reasoning.' The main part of Smith's book, which was based on a lecture delivered in Philadelphia in 1787, consists of support for the belief that all human beings have a common ancestry. He uses some ingenuity in explaining away certain facts that appear at first sight to contradict this theory. He believes that differences in climate are the chief cause of the diversity of races, but he regards 'the state of society' as another important factor; and he supposes that migrations account for some of the facts that are not otherwise easily explained. There are also 'secret causes of difference, as there are varieties of the same family'. He makes it perfectly clear that in his opinion the changes produced by the environment are inherited, and cumulative in effect.

The effect proceeds increasing from one generation to another. . . . resemblances of parents are communicated to children. . . . We see that figure, stature, complexion, features, diseases, and even powers of the mind become hereditary. . . . when any change becomes incorporated, so to speak, it is, along with other constitutional properties, transmitted to offspring.

It is to be noted that Smith and the other philosophers and scientists of pre-Darwinian days who believed in the ancestry of all mankind from a single stock—the 'monogenists', as they came later to be called—were in a limited sense evolutionists, though their views on the causes of the evolutionary process were incorrect.

His belief that all mankind shared a single ancestry was far from making Smith an egalitarian. 'And the Hottentots, the Laplanders, and the people of New-Holland', he writes, 'are the most stupid of mankind. . . . they approach . . . the nearest to brute creation.' He is particularly severe on the Hottentots, describing them as 'In their manners the most beastly, and the faculties of their minds approaching the nearest to brutes of any of the human species'.

Smith's opinions on the origin of mankind were to some extent shared by Johann Gottfried Herder (1744–1803), though the latter looked more favourably on the less advanced peoples of the world. This German philosopher, theologian, and authority on linguistics had a fellow-feeling towards the *Völker* of the world, and he was a student and admirer of the folk-songs of various nations. His *Ideen zur Philosophie der Geschichte der Menschheit* [487] is regarded as his masterpiece. The first edition appeared in separate parts from 1784 to 1791. In what he writes in this book on the subject under discussion here, it is difficult to visualize him as the associate (and in later years the adverse critic) of Kant, or as the close friend and inspirer of Goethe; for his arguments appear rather feeble and in places actually foolish. For instance, he says that all men are the same in internal anatomy, and even—almost unbelievably—that a few hundred years ago the inhabitants of Germany were Patagonians. He mentions Blumenbach (p. 25), but will not agree to the division of mankind into races. '*Race* [he uses this actual word] implies a difference of origin,' he claims; and this difference he denies. '*Denn jedes Volk ist Volk*,' he insists; for him, the reality is not the race but the nation with its national speech. His emphasis on the *Volk* foreshadows Spengler's (pp. 53–5), though the latter was not much interested in language as a binding force.

Herder shows better sense than some of the philosophers of his time in rejecting the idea that anthropoid apes could be regarded as human. He tells us that Nature has divided the apes and monkeys into many genera and species, but man is unitary. 'Neither the Pongo nor the *Longimanus* is your brother; but truly the American and the Negro are.'*

The tendency of certain philosophers of the eighteenth century to attribute more intelligence to the anthropoid apes than could reasonably be ascribed to them from the available evidence, is of special interest to the student of the ethnic problem. It may surprise some readers to learn that Rousseau regarded the chimpanzee as human.[918, 919] Having recorded certain observations made on these animals in the Congo, he continues thus:

> One does not see in these passages the reasons on which the authors base themselves in refusing to the animals in question the name of savage men; but it is easy to conjecture that it is because of their [the chimpanzees'] stupidity, and also because they do not speak: these are feeble reasons to those who know that although the organ of speech is natural [innate] to man, speech itself is nevertheless not natural, and who understand to what point his capacity for improvement may have raised civilized man above his original state.

Rousseau accepted whatever in the records of travellers supported the intelligence and humanity of the chimpanzee, and rejected contrary evidence. He regarded the capacity for self-improvement as 'the specific character of the human species', and he considered that this criterion had not been applied to

---

* The 'Pongo' referred to here was probably the chimpanzee, since the gorilla was scarcely known at the time; the name was subsequently applied to the latter animal (see p. 32). The '*Longimanus*' was the gibbon (and the 'American' of course the Indianid).

the chimpanzee with enough care to support the conclusion that it was not human.

The learned but eccentric Lord Monboddo, Scottish lawyer and philologist, shared Rousseau's outlook on the anthropoid apes. In his anonymous work *On the origin and progress of language*[752] he mentions the 'Ouran Outangs' of Angola and several parts of Asia. (The confusion of the orang-utan with the chimpanzee is evident here, as in so many writings of the eighteenth century.)

> They are exactly of the human form, walking erect, not upon all-four. . . . they use sticks for weapons; they live in society; they make huts of branches of trees, and they carry off negro girls, whom they make slaves of, and use both for work and pleasure. . . . But though from the particulars mentioned it appears certain that they are of our species, and though they have made some progress in the arts of life, they have not come the length of language.

What surprised Monboddo was not that they could not speak, but that they could not learn to speak. He agreed with Rousseau in rejecting the opinion that speech is 'natural' to man. 'Now if we can get over that prejudice,' he says, 'and do not insist, that other arts of life, which the Ouran Outangs want, are likewise natural to man, it is impossible we can refuse them the appellation of *men*.'

Edward Long, the historian of Jamaica, agreed with Rousseau and Monboddo in attributing intellectual powers to the anthropoid apes, but gave a twist to his opinion to which these authors would scarcely have assented; for he remarks of the orang-utan, '. . . nor, for what hitherto appears, do they seem at all inferior in the intellectual faculties to many of the Negroe race'. He supposed that the orang-utan (or the chimpanzee—it is impossible to be sure which he meant) was 'in a close affinity to man'. [678]

Maupertuis would seem to have gone to even further lengths than Rousseau, Monboddo, and Long in overestimating the intellectual potentialities of the anthropoid apes. The French zoologist Étienne Geoffroy Saint-Hilaire has related a curious anecdote about the illustrious mathematician. It evidently made a profound impression on him, for he published it in 1798[398] and repeated it in an entirely separate work thirty-one years later.[399] If the story is true, Maupertuis made the announcement that he would take greater pleasure and would learn more in the society of apes than in that of the most learned men of his time. Saint-Hilaire mentions this as one of the '*écarts*' of a philosophy that was fashionable at the end of the eighteenth century. (Maupertuis died in 1759. I have not found anything in his own writings to substantiate Saint-Hilaire's story.)

# 2 Blumenbach and his scientific contemporaries

IN THE eighteenth century the philosophers, political writers, and historians were by no means the only people who interested themselves in the ethnic problem. Certain distinguished biologists wrote at much greater length—and, let it be said at once, with much more restraint and better sense—on the same subject. The works of such men as Blumenbach retain their interest and a good deal of their value today. In order, however, to appreciate what they were trying to do, it is necessary to feel one's way into the biological thought of the eighteenth century. Blumenbach and his associates were not concerned to prove that all races of mankind were necessarily 'equal', but they did want to show that all races were human, and to convince others that the differences had been exaggerated. It must be remembered, too, that the idea of human evolution from an anthropoid stock was scarcely present in most men's minds; indeed, evolutionary thought was in its infancy even in scientific circles.

Linnaeus was so far from accepting the idea of equality among men that he listed the mental qualities of each race as distinguishing characters, comparable with the physical ones. The people whom he grouped under the name of *Europaeus* clearly belonged to the Nordid (and perhaps also Osteuropid) subraces of modern terminology; this follows from his description of their physical characters. With his customary terseness he says that this section of mankind is 'active, very acute, a discoverer'.[669] It is worth mentioning, as a curiosity of the history of science, that in the twelfth edition of the *Systema naturae*[670] Linnaeus changed *acutissimus* in his characterization of *Europaeus* to *argutus* (quick-witted).[670] One cannot guess what might have been the cause for this slight change, which was accepted by Gmelin in the edition (thirteenth) for which he was responsible.[671] In striking contrast to what he says about *Europaeus*, Linnaeus stigmatizes the section *Afer*, which is shown by his physical description to comprise the Negrid and Khoisanid races, as 'crafty, lazy, careless'. Linnaeus's opinions on the status of the anthropoid apes are deferred to a later page (p. 31).

In 1775, the year before Blumenbach's first edition appeared, a physician named John Hunter published the *Inaugural dissertation* that he had delivered on the award of the degree of Doctor of Medicine in the University of Edinburgh.[524] It dealt with the differences between the various kinds of human beings, and claimed to expound their causes. It was written in Latin, but a translation was eventually published as an Appendix to the English edition of Blumenbach's book.[525] Several writers have supposed that the author was the great surgeon and anatomist of the same name, but this was not so. It should have been realized that the latter was not likely to have taken the degree of Doctor of Medicine at the age of forty-seven, and indeed it does not appear that he was ever an M.D.

Although the *Dissertation* is not a work of much importance, it has some interest as an immediate forerunner of Blumenbach's book; but unlike the latter, it contains no attempt at a classification of mankind into 'varieties' (races). Hunter attributes the physical and mental differences between various groups of mankind to the direct effect of the environment and their transmission from generation to generation, with cumulative consequences. He says that '. . . many properties which have been acquired by the parent are transferred to the offspring. . . . The black colour of the parent may become blacker in the son.' It is his object to show that all human beings are of the same species, and that the differences between them are due to 'natural causes', not to separate creation. Hunter's message is very similar to Stanhope Smith's, published thirteen years later (see pp. 21–2).

2   *Johann Friedrich Blumenbach*

Blumenbach was the author of *De generis humani varietate nativa liber.* |106|
*From an engraving in possession of the Royal Society*

Johann Friedrich Blumenbach (Fig. 2) was born at Gotha, eastern Germany, in 1752, and started teaching at Göttingen University almost immediately after taking his degree there in 1775. He became Professor of Medicine, but his chief publications were in the fields of anthropology, physiology, and comparative anatomy. He died at Göttingen in 1840, having stayed there most of his life and travelled very little.|345, 346, 709| His contributions to the study of the ethnic problem are contained in his famous work *De generis humani varietate nativa liber*, which went through three editions,|106, 107, 108| of which the first and third were translated into English,|110| and in his *Beyträge zur Naturgeschichte*.|109, 110|

Blumenbach had no conception of the evolution of man from apelike ancestors, nor, indeed, any idea of evolution at all, in the modern sense; but he recognized that plants and animals were capable of becoming modified in form as a result of domestication or change of climate, and he supposed that new characters artificially imposed during the lifetime of the individual were inherited. All changes in a species resulting from these causes were examples of what he called the *Degeneratio*|108| or *Degeneration*|109| of the *Varietas primigenia*|107| or *Stammrace*.|109| New species could arise only by special creation.|109| It was his contention that there was only a single species of man. The *Varietas primigenia* was what he called *Caucasiana*, which corresponds roughly to the Europid race in the terminology used in the present book. From this *Varietas* the others had arisen by the process of degeneration, which resulted from the fact that man is exposed to climatic extremes, is by far the most domesticated of all organisms,|108| and sometimes interferes artificially with the structure of his body.

From his use of the word *Degeneratio* one might well suppose that it was Blumenbach's purpose to assert the superiority of the Europid over other races; but this would not be quite correct, for his whole intention was to stress the unity of man, and to correct the common belief in the marked inferiority of certain races. He allowed the existence of certain obvious structural differences. Referring to the facial characters of Negrids he remarks, for instance, 'Although, therefore, almost all human embryos are flat-nosed, nevertheless the Ethiopians of whom we speak have such very wide noses and *intersinia* (if I may use Isidore's expression [for the nostrils]), that everyone recognizes that race by these characters alone, even if the swollen lips are disregarded.'|106| He also remarks that even a blind man, if he had any idea of the great difference between the faces of Mongolians and 'Ethiopians', could at once distinguish the skull of a Kalmuk from that of a Negro merely by touch. He was anxious, however, to minimize those characters that might be thought sufficiently important to warrant the separation of any group of human beings as another species; and he underestimated the peculiarity of the *tablier* or *ventrale* as much as Voltaire exaggerated it. 'The most recent testimony of travellers', he writes, 'commands us to put the cutaneous *ventrale* of female Hottentots (the existence of which was asserted by the early travellers) in the same category as the human tail, and in like manner to relegate it to the fables.'|106| Blumenbach is right, however, when he denies that colour can establish a difference of species.|106|

There is no perfectly clear statement in Blumenbach's writings to the effect that degeneration implies inferiority, and with the single exception that people of the *Varietas prima*\* (Europids) are said to be 'of the most beautiful form' (*pulcerrimae formae*) in comparison with those of all other races.|107|

---

\* Elsewhere Blumenbach uses the term *Varietas primigenia* with the same meaning.

Blumenbach made a special plea for a more favourable attitude towards Negroes. 'No so-called *savage* people is known to us', he writes, 'that has so distinguished itself by such examples of perfectibility and even of capacity for learning and culture, and has thereby fastened itself so closely to the most cultivated people on earth, *as the Negro*.'[109] He gives many remarkable examples of the intellectual powers of particular Negroes.

Brief mention must be made of a colleague of Blumenbach's who had been appointed a lecturer in philosophy at Göttingen University [730] two or three years before Blumenbach had become a member of the teaching staff there. Two men more radically different in outlook on the ethnic problem it is scarcely possible to imagine. Christopher Meiners sought to influence opinion on this subject by writing in scathing terms about Negroes and other non-European peoples. In one of his papers he asks jurists and other authorities on mankind whether they consider that freedom and other rights are owed to people 'so devoid of feeling, so excitable and indolent, so stupid and ill-natured (*übelartigen*) as Negroes are', and gives it as his opinion that 'the black, brown, and red peoples' not only did not invent arts and sciences, but were incapable of accepting them when offered by Europeans. [728] In another paper he refers to the 'ugly, stupid, and ill-natured Negro'.[729]

Samuel Thomas Sömmerring (1755–1830) was a close friend of Blumenbach's when they were undergraduates at the University of Jena,[345] and afterwards a pupil of the latter's at Göttingen; he also studied under Camper (pp. 28–30) in Holland. He passed through a period during which he was interested in magic and became a Rosicrucian, but subsequently he devoted himself wholeheartedly to scientific studies. He became a distinguished human anatomist, holding professorships in several German universities.[807] He is known today chiefly for his pioneer work on the sympathetic nervous system. He was a friend of Goethe, who warned him against his tendency to speculate too freely. He remained a friend, too, of his former teachers, Blumenbach and Camper, and it is evident that he was familiar with the latter's *Dissertation* [186] long before it was published.

In 1784 Sömmerring published a small book on the anatomy of the Negro compared with that of the European.[987] The following year he published a much enlarged second edition.[988] It is worth remark that in the title of the first edition he referred to *Mohren*, but both editions are concerned with Negroes, not Moors. He announced clearly at the outset that his main purpose was to discover 'whether the Negroes or the Europeans approximate more closely to the apes'. These little volumes contain a remarkably objective and in most (though not all) respects accurate account of the physical differences between Negrids and Europids. So far as the former were concerned, he based his account chiefly on three skulls in his possession, and on his dissections of four corpses. He goes systematically through the body, noting the differences. Apart from the obvious ones he mentions the following, among others. The eyeball and eye-socket of the Negro are slightly larger; the homologue of the third eyelid is better developed; in the skull the anterior nostrils (*nares*) are not separated from the nasal cavity by a sharp ridge, and the posterior openings of the nasal cavity are much larger than those of the European, since the pterygoid processes are further apart; the upper and lower incisor teeth project forward so as to meet at an angle; the lower jaw is much more robust, and the part to which the masseter muscle is attached is very broad; the fingers and toes are longer, and the hips more slender.

When his studies were complete, Sömmerring could justly claim that he had carried out his work without prejudice.

> One will see from my whole treatise that in this study my intention was simply to discover whether Negroes or Europeans approximated more closely to the apes. At the end it was as much a matter of indifference to me to assert this for white men as for black, only I must find grounds for my assertion: but the more I pursued this study cold-bloodedly, the more I became well aware that it obviously held true for the Negro. . . . But they remain nevertheless men, and very much raised above that class [the apes] of true four-footed animals; they are indeed very strikingly distinguished and separated from them. . . . I am in that matter fully of his [Camper's] opinion, as I have already said in the Preface, that the Negro is not simply man, but of the same species with us; that he shades off as well through imperceptible nuances in structure, colour, etc., into the Abyssinian and Hottentot, as other varieties of man shade off into one another through equally imperceptible transitions.

He remarks, however, 'I think that the distinguishing organs of the understanding, that prove our difference from the animals, probably leave the Negro somewhat behind us on the average,' but 'among the blacks there are a few who approach near their white brothers, and surpass many of them in intelligence'. It will be allowed by any unprejudiced person who studies Sömmerring's book that, whatever mistakes he may have made in points of detail through lack of adequate anatomical material, he was guided solely by desire to establish the truth.

The celebrated Dutch comparative anatomist Petrus Camper (1722–1789) is of interest to students of the ethnic problem mainly because he introduced a quantitative method for the objective comparison of the races of man with one another and with certain animals. His 'facial line' might almost be considered as the starting-point from which modern craniology has developed, though the artist Albrecht Dürer had studied the living face in a comparable way nearly 250 years before.[295] Camper wrote the first sketch of his *Dissertation* on this subject in 1768 and added to it from time to time till it was more or less in its final form in 1786. He was, however, a busy and versatile man: not only an anatomist, but a distinguished surgeon and obstetrician, an authority on medical jurisprudence, and an artist and sculptor of considerable skill. He was just about to arrange publication of his book when he died unexpectedly in 1789. It was published two years later by his son, in the form of a translation into French.[187]

Camper proceeded as follows. He set up the skull in a position arbitrarily chosen as horizontal. This was achieved when the orifices of the ears (bony external auditory meatus) and lowest part of the nasal aperture were in the same horizontal plane. He does not say exactly where these points were, but it seems probable from his drawings that he usually (but not always) used what are nowadays called the *porion* and *nariale* as the exact points on the bony orifices of the ear and nose respectively that were to be held in the same horizontal plane. He then made an accurate drawing of the left side of the skull from '*un point de vue ambulant*', so that every point in the object would be represented in the drawing by a point immediately opposite it, without distortion by perspective. He then drew a line (ND in Fig. 3A, B, C), through or close by the *nariale* and *porion*, and a second line, GM in the figures, grazing the front surface of the first incisor tooth and the forehead (neglecting the fact that this line might intersect the nasal bones at their junction). This second line is the celebrated 'facial line' of Camper. Arrows have been inserted in Fig. 3 to call attention to this line. The angle formed by the facial line with the horizontal plane is commonly called the 'facial angle'. Camper himself does not appear to have used this expression, though he always measured and recorded the angle.

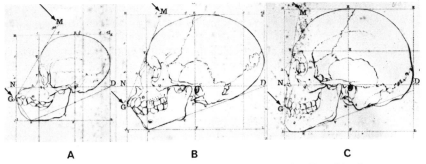

**A**                    **B**                    **C**

3   *Camper's drawings of skulls, to illustrate his 'facial line'*

The skulls are of a young orang-utan (A), a young Negro (B), and of a typical European (C). The lines marked ND indicate Camper's horizontal plane. The facial line is that which connects the letters M and G in each drawing. Arrows have been added to call attention to these letters. The original plates from which these illustrations were copied photographically were discoloured by age.            *From Camper* [187]

If the upper part of the face, below the forehead, and also the upper jaw project forward, the facial angle will necessarily be small; a sloping forehead will have the same effect. Nowadays there are ways of measuring separately the slopes of different parts of the face. Camper's facial angle combines these potentially separate features. Nevertheless the angle was useful to him. He wanted to compare the skulls of various races of man with those of apes and monkeys. In these animals the slopes of the forehead, upper face, and upper jaw all combine to give a very low facial angle.

Camper had already made an anatomical study of the orang-utan,[184, 186] in which he had included his facial line in a drawing of the skull, but in this earlier work he drew the line intended to represent the horizontal plane well below the external auditory meatus and the lower margin of the nasal aperture (though it appears to be parallel to a line that could be drawn through these). In his posthumous book[187] he shows the skull of the orang-utan again, this time with the horizontal plane indicated in his standard way, and he gives the facial angles of this animal, of an unspecified monkey, and of certain races of man. His figures are these: monkey, 42°; orang-utan, 58° (the same figure as he had given before); a young Negro, 70°; a European, 80° (Fig. 3). He considered that the angle between the facial line and the horizontal provided a good index of the appearance of the face, and that in this respect the Negro was closer than the European to the ape.

Camper made various other observations on the anatomy of Negroes. He was aware that in his time many travellers and most naturalists attributed the shape of the nose in this race to artificial deformation, but he knew that a difference from the shape in Europeans was already present before birth.[185] He also mentioned the semilunar membrane at the inner angle of the eye of man, and remarked that it is a little bigger in Negroes than in Europeans; he was of opinion (wrongly) that it was not homologous with the nictitating membrane of animals.[188]

The study of the ethnic problem by the German comparative anatomist and physiologist Friedrich Tiedemann (1781–1861) is closely related to those of Blumenbach, Sömmerring, and Camper. The first edition of Blumenbach's *De generis humani varietate*[106] was published five years before Tiedemann was born, but the latter refers to its author as his friend, and the younger man was well acquainted with the studies of Sömmerring and Camper. In his paper on the brain of the Negro, Tiedemann's main purpose was to discover whether there was any essential difference between this brain and that of the European, and if so, whether the former showed closer resemblance to the brain of the orang-utan.[1059]

Tiedemann's measurements of cranial capacity suggested that the brain of the Negro was no smaller, on the average, than that of the European. His measurements of actual brains gave, on the whole, somewhat smaller figures for the Negro, and he found in particular that the anterior part of the Negro's brain was 'something narrower' than that of most Europeans; but he had not enough material to justify the conclusion that there was in fact any regularly occurring difference. He remarked that Camper's facial angle does not give a measure of the size of the brain, as certain authors had supposed. (It may be mentioned that Camper himself had not claimed this.) He could find no difference in the structure of the brain in the two races, except that the gyri and sulci of the cerebral hemispheres were more regular in their arrangement in the Negro. This was also the only feature in which the brain of the latter approximated more closely than the European's to that of the orang-utan. Tiedemann contradicted Sömmerring's finding that the cranial nerves are thicker in the Negro than in the European.

Tiedemann allowed that many Negroes living in coastal districts of Africa show approximations to the ape in certain structural features. He instanced the greater size of the bones of the face; the projection of the incisor teeth and their alveoli; the prominent cheek-bones; the receding chin; the flat nasal bones; the strong, projecting jaw; the position of the foramen magnum; the long humerus; and the length, breadth, shape, and position of the os calcis. He was of opinion, however, from the reports of travellers, that there were many Negro tribes living in the interior of Africa, in which these features were not evident. He also pointed out that it was unfair to judge the intellectual powers of Negroes by those who had been torn from their native countries and from their families, and subjected to slavery. 'The intellectual faculties of the Negroes', he writes, 'do not in general seem to be inferior to those of the European and other races. . . . The principal result of my researches on the brain of the Negro, is, that neither anatomy nor physiology can justify our placing them beneath the Europeans in a moral or intellectual point of view.' It is not clear why Tiedemann refers here to physiology, since his paper is concerned with the anatomy, not the function, of the Negro's brain.

As knowledge of the anthropoid apes spread gradually during the course of the eighteenth century, the problem of their relationship to man excited a great deal of interest. Explorers were providing more and more information about various human races differing markedly from Europeans in external appearance, and it was realized that some of these peoples lived very simple lives as food-gatherers, without knowledge of agriculture. It seemed possible that the anthropoid apes might also be men. If so, there would be no question, one might think, of the 'equality' of all human races.

Edward Tyson, a physician to the Bethlem Hospital, London, was the first person to make a careful study of the anatomy of an anthropoid ape. He published a book on the subject in the last year of the seventeenth century.|1079| He called his specimen an 'orang-outang', but in fact it was a chimpanzee. It had been captured in the interior of Angola and brought alive to this country. He described the external form, skeleton, and musculature in considerable detail, and gave some account of the viscera and brain. He noticed the presence of an appendix or '*Processus vermiformis*', which he knew to be absent in monkeys, and also the absence of cheek-pouches, which many monkeys possess. He listed 48 points in which his specimen '*more resembled a* Man, *than* Apes *and* Monkeys *do*', and 34 in which it '*differd from a* Man, *and resembled more the* Ape *and* Monkey-kind'. (In these passages he uses the word 'Ape' to mean particular kinds of monkeys.)

The information available to Linnaeus caused him to suppose that the anthropoid apes were not very sharply marked off from man in structure. Strangely enough, he first mentioned the subject in his book on the fauna of Sweden.|668| 'I shall confess', he writes, 'that as a natural historian I have so far been unable to dig up any character by which to distinguish, by the principles of science, between *Homo* and *Simia*,' and he mentions the existence of animals that are 'less *Simiae* than hairy *Homo*'. In his *Systema naturae*|669| he assigns two species to the genus *Homo*, *H. sapiens* (man) and *H. troglodytes* (anthropoid apes). He gives the orang-utan as his example of *H. troglodytes*, but since he says that this species occurs also in Africa, it is clear that some of his information referred to the chimpanzee. (The gorilla was unknown to science at the time.)

Although I brought all my attention to bear on the subject, I could not maintain a genus *Troglodytes*, distinct from *Homo* . . . unless I were to adopt a character of doubtful value, not constant in other genera. Neither the canine teeth, which are scarcely separated from the rest, nor the nymphae of the Kaffir, which monkeys lack, allowed this animal to withdraw to the monkeys. . . . It is not doubtful that the species *troglodytes* is distinct from *Homo sapiens*, however similar the upright posture may be, and similarly one could not imagine it [only] a variety; for instance, apart from anything else, the existence of a nictitating membrane [in *troglodytes*] absolutely denies this.|669|

It is possible that Linnaeus received information from travellers about the stance of the gibbons, for neither the chimpanzee nor the orang-utan holds itself upright in the wild state.

The great French zoologist Leclerc de Buffon saw a living chimpanzee in Paris in 1740. It was a young specimen that had been caught in Gabon and trained to eat at table like a human being. He says that the brain 'is of exactly the same form and the same proportion' as in man, but he rather surprisingly adds, 'and it does not think'.|162| He thought that the 'pongo' of Africa was the same as the East Indian orang-utan, but that the African 'jocko' was perhaps a distinct species. Actually the pongo was probably the gorilla, and the jocko certainly the chimpanzee (cf. Huxley|535|). Buffon remarks of the real orang-utan that the '*Indiens*' (as he calls the inhabitants of the East Indies) 'are to be excused for having associated it with the human species by the name of *orang-outang*, or savage man, because it resembles man in its body more closely than it resembles other monkeys or any other animal'. Nevertheless he denied that the orang-utan was human.

Camper made a careful dissection of a young orang-utan at Groningen in 1770. In his memoir on the subject|184, 186| he once and for all distinguished between this species and the chimpanzee by a precise anatomical description. He also distinguished it sharply from man by several characters, expecially by the shortness of the thumb and the possession of enormous laryngeal air-sacks, which he dissected out and illustrated.

In marked contrast to Linnaeus, Blumenbach overstressed the distinction between man and anthropoid apes. He laid special emphasis on the possession by man of two hands. In the first edition of *De generis humani varietate* he remarks:

> Another peculiarity of man springs directly from what has been said, namely that I attribute two hands to mankind alone, while on the contrary either four or none suit the monkeys; whose big toe, separated from the remaining digits of the foot, applies itself to those functions that the thumbs of the hands fulfil.|106|

In the second edition of the same book he again stressed the fact that man has two hands, while the 'Simiae' (monkeys and apes) are neither *bipedes* nor *quadrupedes*, but use all four extremities as hands in climbing trees.|107| It was only in his third edition of 1795, however, that he introduced the terms that for long affected the classification of the Primates. For him, man stood alone in a division called 'Bimanus', a name provided with a singular ending to denote man's unity as a species, and chosen to indicate that he alone was two-handed; while all the apes, monkeys, and lemurs were lumped together in a single group, the four-handed beasts or '*Quadrumana*'.|108| This arrangement, though long accepted, is not in accordance with modern knowledge. It is customary nowadays to classify man with the apes as a member of the Hominoidea, and to contrast this group with the Cercopithecoidea (Old World monkeys) and Ceboidea (those of the New World).|968| The lemurs stand in a group apart from all of these.

# 3 From Gobineau
## to Houston Chamberlain

SINCE THE thirties of the present century there has existed an almost world-wide movement intended to foster belief in the equality of all human ethnic taxa. There can be scarcely any doubt that the impulse for this movement came from intense feeling aroused by the persecution of Jews under the Nazi regime. Some of those interested in the subject have looked back in history for the origin of the ideas that fructified so hideously in the minds of Hitler and his associates. The belief has grown up that the origin may be found in a book by the Comte de Gobineau. Other authors, writing since Gobineau's time, have been mentioned in the same connection. Unfortunately Hitler himself gave little help to anyone anxious to trace the origin of his thoughts on the ethnic problem. The first volume of *Mein Kampf*,[494] rather strangely subtitled 'A settlement of accounts' ('*Eine Abrechnung*'), was written while he was imprisoned at Landsburg in Bavaria. Here his library facilities were presumably limited, but it is nevertheless surprising that in his chapter on the ethnic problem he mentions only two authorities. He quotes a very brief anti-Jewish phrase of Schopenhauer's, and a little couplet of Goethe's (without mention of the latter's name). Nevertheless, one may gain impressions from various sources, and it is almost certain that some at least of the writers mentioned in the present chapter influenced the thought of some of the Nazi leaders. Whether they should be regarded as in any way responsible for the actions of the Nazis is another matter.

It must be stressed that the present chapter and the next differ from the two preceding ones not only in the period covered (1853–1928), but also in the more limited scope. It is concerned only with the growth of ideas that favoured belief in the inequality of ethnic taxa, or are supposed—rightly or wrongly—to have favoured such belief.

Joseph Arthur, Comte de Gobineau (1816–1882: Fig. 4), was a man of exceptionally wide interests. He was by profession a diplomat, and when the first volume of his work on the ethnic problem was published, he was First Secretary of the French Legation in Switzerland; later he was transferred to the Persian court. In all his writings his meaning is clear, as indeed might be expected of one who was not only a Frenchman but a *littérateur*. He was the author of several novels, novelettes, and books of poems, and he also wrote in the fields of philosophy, history, Oriental studies, and archaeology; one of his books is on cuneiform writing.[412] A useful short biography is given by Redman.[885]

4    *Joseph Arthur, Comte de Gobineau*

Gobineau was the author of what is probably the best known of all works on the ethnic problem,
*Essai sur l'inégalité des races humaines.* [409]
*From a painting in the Bibliothèque Nationale et Universitaire, Strasbourg*

Gobineau's *Essai sur l'inégalité des races humaines* was published in separate parts from 1853 to 1855.[409] Works professing to be translations into English have been published,[410, 411] but in fact they contain no more than *Livre 1* of the original, which constitutes only a part of the first of four volumes. The translation by Hotz[410] was very roughly done, with unnecessary omissions and rearrangements, and at least one surreptitious insertion of an important statement for which there is no authority in the French text.

A selection of Gobineau's writings was published in 1970.[416] The editor of this selection considers it proper that Gobineau 'should have a central place in the history of that pernicious brand of political thinking which culminated in the excesses of the Nazi era'. A small part of Gobineau's novel *Les Pléiades* (in English translation) is included in this selection. The editor says that in this extract various facets of his philosophy 'and of race thinking generally' are 'strikingly epitomized'; he regards it as an example of 'élite morality'. Many readers would be likely to regard the novel itself[413] rather as the work of a man who had exceptional understanding of human nature and was ahead of his time in his insight into the subject of sexual relationships. A full translation into English is available under the title *Sons of kings*.[414]

Gobineau's professional life is reflected in the *Essai*, for his interests are clearly in nations and the events of history rather than in biological or anthropological problems. The book is quietly and effectively written and is obviously the product of a cultured and well-informed person. The problem that he had set himself was not obviously connected with the equality or inequality of races. He wanted to know why great civilizations seemed destined to decay. To resolve this problem he carefully reviews the reasons put forward by others to account for the facts. Decay of religion, fanaticism, corruption of morals, luxury, bad government, despotism—he considers them all and rejects them, on the evidence of history. He cites examples, for instance, to show the moral superiority of certain nations over those that replaced them. Religion sometimes flourished as a nation declined, or a civilization perished when the people were better governed than ever before. The Greeks, Persians, and Romans declined although luxury never reached so high a peak among them as in the France of his own day.

Serious thought on this problem turned his mind to the possibility that the answer might be found in the inequality of races—or rather, in the terminology of the present book, of certain ethnic taxa (p. 4).

The first step towards civilization, according to Gobineau, is the union of several tribes, by alliance or conquest, to form a nation. Certain ethnic taxa seem capable of making this forward stride towards a unit big enough for civilization to develop; others seem incapable. Those that fail do not seem to be prevented by external causes. They are to be found in cold, temperate, and hot climates; in fertile lands and barren deserts; on river-banks, on coasts, and in inland regions.

The allied tribes (presumably closely related) that join to form a nation blend into a homogeneous whole by intermarriage. Cities develop, and as they grow bigger, strangers flock to them. An international society begins to be formed. Among the new arrivals are persons belonging to ethnic taxa that have never shown themselves capable of initiating a civilization. '*Dégénération*' sets in.

I think that the word 'degenerate', applied to a people, should and does signify that this people has no longer the intrinsic worth that it formerly possessed, that it no longer has in its veins the same blood, the worth of which has been gradually modified by successive mixtures; or to put it in other words, that with the same name it has not retained the same race as its founders; in fact, that the man of decadence, whom one calls the degenerate man, is a different product, from the ethnic point of view, from the heroes of the great epochs.

This brief statement summarizes with remarkable clarity the whole underlying idea of Gobineau's thought, which he expounded at such very great length in his book.

Gobineau discounted the importance of environment. 'I want to say that it was not the place that made the worth of a nation, for that never made it and never will make it: on the contrary it was the nation that gave, has given, and will give to the territory its economic, moral, and political worth.' He points out that the great civilizations of India, Egypt, China, and Mesopotamia were not favoured by nature. The people who founded these civilizations had to bring their social systems to high standards before they could profit from such natural advantages as did exist, by irrigation and comparable technological enterprises.

I shall cite the Armenians, shut away in their mountains (in these same mountains where so many other peoples live and die as barbarians), attaining from generation to generation, since very remote antiquity, quite a high level of civilization. Nevertheless these regions were almost sealed off, lacking in any remarkable fertility, and devoid of any communication with the sea.

Gobineau considered that the early civilization of the Jews was derived from that of Mesopotamia, with some Egyptian influence. He attributed their inability to originate a truly independent culture to the fact that they were '*chamatisés*' (that is to say, hybridized to some extent with the *Chamites* (Hamites)). Nevertheless he had a high regard for the Jews. Those who have been inclined to attribute the evils of Nazism to him would be surprised to read what he actually wrote about them. He quotes them as an example of an inherently superior people living and for a time flourishing, like the Armenians, in a somewhat adverse environment.

The Jews . . . surrounded by tribes speaking dialects of a language related to their own . . . nevertheless surpassed all these groups. One sees them as warriors, agriculturalists, businessmen. Monarchy, theocracy, the patriarchal power of heads of families, and the democratic might of the people as represented by assemblies and prophets, balanced one another in a very bizarre manner. One sees them, under this singularly complicated form of government, traversing long centuries of prosperity and glory, and overcoming, by one of the most intelligent systems of emigration, the difficulties opposed to their expansion by the narrow limits of their domain. And once more, what was this domain? . . . In this miserable corner of the world, what were the Jews? I repeat, it was a people capable in all that it undertook, a free people, a strong people, an intelligent people. When, with their arms still in their hands, they lost bravely the position of an independent nation, they furnished to the world almost as many learned men (*docteurs*) as merchants.

Although Gobineau accepted the conventional or 'monogenist' opinion that all mankind had a single origin, he did not hesitate to place certain ethnic taxa on a lower intellectual plane than others. 'The European', he remarks, 'cannot hope to civilize the Negro,' but he hastens to qualify this blunt assertion by insisting that he is here not considering the moral and intellectual aptitudes of individuals taken separately. 'I reject absolutely', he writes, 'the type of argument that consists in saying "Every Negro is foolish," and my principal reason for doing so is that I should be forced to acknowledge that every European is intelligent, and I hold myself at a hundred leagues from such a paradox.' Gobineau also entirely rejects Benjamin Franklin's jibe that the Negro is an animal that eats as much as possible and works as little as possible.

I have denied excessive stupidity or chronic foolishness, even among the most debased tribes. I go even further than my adversaries, because I do not question that a good number of Negro chiefs go beyond the common level to which our peasants, or even our decently educated and gifted townspeople can attain, by the force and abundance of their ideas, the high degree of ingenuity of their minds, and the intensity of their active faculties. Once more and a hundred times, it is not on this narrow terrain of individualities that I place myself. It appears to me too unworthy of science to dwell upon such futile arguments.

Gobineau considered that most scientific observers showed a marked tendency to present an unduly low estimate of primitive human types. 'In the most repugnant cannibals', he claimed, 'there remains a spark of divine fire, and the faculty of understanding can kindle itself at least to a certain degree.'

Gobineau's principal criterion for judging the superiority of a '*race*' was its capacity to originate a great civilization. In his opinion there had been ten such civilizations in the course of history, seven in the Old World and three in America. The seven were those of the Indians, Egyptians, Assyrians, Greeks, Chinese, Romans, and finally '*les races germaniques*'. The American civilizations were those of the '*Alléghaniens*', Mexicans, and Peruvians. It should be pointed out that at the time when Gobineau wrote, it was scarcely possible to realize that the culture of the Assyrians was derived from that of the Sumerians. His Alleghanian civilization was presumably a branch of the ancient 'Mound-building' culture, subsequently recognized as widespread in the United States.

It is clear that by the name '*races germaniques*' Gobineau meant the Nordid subrace. He attributed the civilization of modern Europe to people of this stock, who had intermarried to some extent with Slavs and others without degrading too quickly their natural instinct of initiative. The Germanics were, for Gobineau, a branch of the 'Aryan race', to which he ascribed, in part at least, no fewer than six of the great civilizations of the Old World—all, that is to say, except the Assyrian; for he considered that culture had been brought to China by Aryans of India. The Aryans, in his sense, appear to have been the various peoples who spoke Indogermanic languages, for he did not define them in terms of physical anthropology. He regarded them as the great initiators of civilization.

Gobineau's long book ends on a pessimistic note. Hybridization was destroying the great civilizations of modern times as it had destroyed those of the past. 'Thus mixture, mixture everywhere, always mixture: that is the clearest, most certain, the most durable work of great societies and powerful civilizations.' He recognizes two periods in the existence of man on earth. 'The one, which has passed, will have witnessed and possessed the youth, the vigour, the intellectual grandeur of the species; the other, which has begun, will know the faltering procession towards decrepitude.'

Charles-Henri-Georges Pouchet was only 25 years old when he published his book *De la pluralité des races humaines* in 1858.[853] He was unknown at the time. Subsequently he wrote a large number of papers covering a very wide range of zoological and histological subjects.[856] Apart from a revision of the text of his book for a second edition,[836, 837] he did not revert publicly to the subject of racial inequality, though he continued to show interest from time to time in anthropological topics, in particular the pigmentation of the skin. He became Professor at the Muséum d'Histoire Naturelle in Paris, and was for many years co-editor of the *Journal de l'Anatomie et de la Physiologie*.

Pouchet was acquainted with Gobineau's work, but it obviously made little impression on him and his attack on the problem was quite different. He believed that there was no really fundamental difference, either in bodily structure or in mind, between man and the anthropoid apes, but he stressed the physical and mental diversity of the races of man, some of which—especially the Negro—appeared to him clearly inferior to others in intellectual attainments. He pleaded for the objective study of this problem, without interference by what were supposed to be humanitarian motives. The search for truth should alone guide the investigator. Pouchet denied the origin of races by the direct action of climate or by hybridization, though he thought it probable that all races were potentially fertile with one another. He opposed Blumenbach's theory of their origin by degeneration. The whole book is an exposition of the polygenist point of view—the belief in the separate origin of human races.

The monogenists claimed that man had a single origin; but since the races of human beings were manifestly different, it followed that there must have been evolutionary change (cf. p. 21). Yet those who held this opinion were the very people who opposed most strongly the evolutionary views that were coming to the fore at the time of publication of Pouchet's book. Georges Pouchet himself (who is not to be confused with F. A. Pouchet, the opponent of Pasteur in a celebrated controversy) was a believer in the reality of spontaneous generation, and when he used the word *pluralité* in the title of the first edition of his book, he meant that the several races had originated entirely independently. Darwin's *Origin of species*[254] was published in the following year, and Pouchet's outlook was affected by the ferment of interest in evolutionary biology. In his second edition, published in 1864, he used the word *pluralité* in a different sense. He now believed that a prehuman ancestor gave rise *independently* to several species of man, which were therefore more directly related to their pre-human ancestor than to one another. It follows (though Pouchet did not say so) that convergent evolution must have occurred, for the human 'species' showed resemblances to one another that could not have been shared by their ancestors. This was the germ of an idea that was soon to be more fully developed by Vogt.[1105] (The idea of convergent or parallel evolution from a primitive *human* stock was implicit in a paper published by Peters in 1937,[836] and was interestingly worked out in a much modified form by Coon in his recent work *The origin of human races.*[227])

In the first edition of *The origin of species*, Darwin was very guarded on the subject of the evolutionary history of man. He merely remarked tentatively that as a result of future investigations 'Psychology will be based on a new foundation, that of the necessary acquirement of each mental power and capacity by gradation. Light will be thrown on the origin of man and his history.'[254] These words were slightly strengthened in later editions.[256] As we have just seen, Pouchet entered boldly into this field. If man had originated not by special creation but by evolution, it was perhaps natural to suppose that the human races might represent stages in this process, or the branches of an evolutionary tree. It is therefore scarcely surprising that the next person to make a significant contribution to the ethnic problem was a zoologist.

Carl Vogt was a remarkable man. Radical in his political opinions, he was exiled from his native Germany for his part in the revolution of 1848. While Professor of Natural History in the University of Geneva he was much occupied in 'left-wing' and anti-religious propaganda of a somewhat vitriolic kind,[807] but at the same time he was an important early convert to Darwinism, and his writings were effective in spreading the doctrine of evolution. His most important contribution to this subject, so far as the ethnic problem is concerned, was his book *Vorlesungen über den Menschen, seine Stellung in der Schöpfung und in der Geschichte der Erde.*[1105] This was published in 1863, eight years before Darwin's *Descent of man.*[258] In the latter work reference is made repeatedly, from the first page onwards, to Vogt's writings, especially to the English edition of the *Vorlesungen.*[1106]

Vogt was impressed by the studies of Gratiolet of the brains and brain-casts of monkeys and apes,[430] as a result of which the French anatomist had reached the conclusion that the three great anthropoid apes did not form a natural group. Gratiolet's investigations 'made very probable this proposition, that the gorilla is a baboon and the chimpanzee is a macaque, by the same standard as that by which the orang-utan is a gibbon'.[430] Gratiolet even went so far as to propose that the gorilla should be transferred to the genus *Cynocephalus*, the chimpanzee to *Macacus*, and the orang-utan to *Hylobates*. He knew, of course, that the great apes showed resemblances not shared by the monkeys: he mentions the absence of a tail, the breadth of the sternum, and the habit of walking with the dorsal surface of the manual phalanges directed towards the ground. These features, however, he regarded as much less important than the affinity indicated—so he supposed—by the anatomy of the brain.

Vogt translated Gratiolet's findings in comparative anatomy into evolutionary terms by postulating a process of convergent change. He supposed that there had been no common apelike ancestor of the three great apes, but that each had sprung independently from separate genera of monkeys, and had subsequently come to resemble one another more closely in several respects. It seems possible that this was the earliest clear statement of the principle of convergent evolution, which has been amply confirmed in certain cases by subsequent research (though not in the evolution of the great apes). Vogt uses the analogy of the evolutionary tree, and makes the remark (rather a striking one in view of the novelty of the idea) that the process of improvement (*Vervollkomnung*) 'bent the branches so that their tips came closer again to one another'.

'Does not the history of man show us something similar?' asked Vogt. It was his conclusion that if the various races of man could be traced back to their origins, no single primitive human type would be found; on the contrary, the genealogical tree would lead back to separate groups of apes. 'All these facts', he writes, 'lead us back not to a common stem, to a single intermediate form between man and apes, but to manifold lines of succession, which were able to develop, more or less within local limits, from various parallel lines of apes.' Thus Vogt, like Pouchet, was a polygenist.

It may be remarked that Darwin did not accept Vogt's conclusion about the polygenic origin of man. He allowed, however, that the various races of man were very distinct in their mental characters, chiefly in their emotional but partly also in their intellectual faculties.[258]

Many of the early Darwinists, especially in Germany, were anti-religious and inclined to the 'left' in politics.[807] Ernst Haeckel (1834–1919) had been brought up in an old-fashioned, religious atmosphere, and was at first shocked by Carl Vogt's writings. In later years, when he was one of the chief advocates of Darwinism on the continent of Europe, his outlook had completely changed. He was now anti-Christian, and a radical in politics; Vogt and he found themselves allies. Like Vogt, he considered that the races of man were unequal. He especially admired the rather ill-defined 'Indogermanic race', which, in his view, 'has far outstripped all other races of man in mental development'.[453]

To Francis Galton (1822–1911) the publication of *The origin of species* formed 'a real crisis' in his life. He wrote to its author (a distant relative) that the book 'drove away the constraint of my old superstition as if it had been a nightmare and was the first to give me freedom of thought'.[100] This versatile genius—explorer, meteorologist, geneticist, and founder of eugenics—no doubt became interested in the ethnic problem as a result of his travels in South West Africa, where he came in contact with Bushmen and the very primitive 'Ghou Damup' or Bergdama tribe, as well as the Herero and Ovambo.[378] He was not inhibited by any egalitarian feelings.

It is in the most unqualified manner that I object to pretensions of natural equality. The experiences of the nursery, the school, the University, and of professional careers, are a chain of proofs to the contrary. . . . In whatever way we may test ability, we arrive at equally enormous intellectual differences.[379]

It was Galton who made the first attempt to put the ethnic problem on a mathematical basis. He had been struck by Quetelet's exposition of the law of deviation from an average,[868, 869] though actually the mathematics of the subject had been worked out rather fully in the previous century. The Belgian astronomer studied measurements of various bodily structures on which sufficient data were available. He noted the number of Scottish soldiers whose chest-measurements, to the nearest inch, were 33, 34, 35 inches, and so on up to the maximum of 48 inches. He found that the proportions between the numbers of persons in the various groups could be expressed mathematically, and that the same mathematical expression was valid for measurements of other bodily structures.

An example of Quetelet's principle is shown in Fig. 5, which represents an imaginary case where a million persons have been measured for some particular feature, and counted in groups. In the figure, the number of persons in

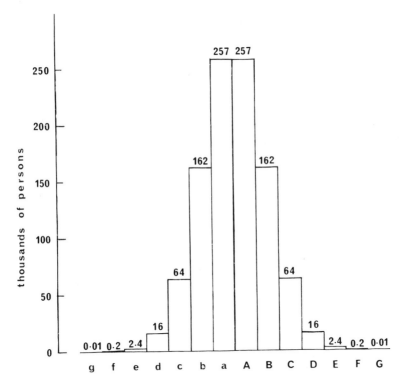

5   *Quetelet's principle of 'the law of deviation from an average'*

A particular feature in a population of one million individuals is supposed to have been measured. It has been decided to recognize fourteen groups or 'grades' in respect of the chosen feature. Each grade represents the same range of the feature measured. The height of each column indicates the number of thousands of persons to be expected, on Quetelet's principle, in each grade. The numbers of persons in the several grades is stated at the tops of the columns in round numbers (e.g. 257 stands for 256,791). The grades are designated by capital and lower-case letters in accordance with Galton's notation. The point on the base-line separating columns **a** and **A** represents the average (mean) of the whole population.
*Diagram drawn from the data of Galton.* [379]

each group is indicated by the height of the columns. One may select arbitrarily the numbers of groups or 'grades': in this case fourteen are taken, seven on each side of the average (arithmetic mean). Each grade differs from the next by the same amount. The general shape of the now familiar figure is commonly similar to that seen in Fig. 5. The grades are here distinguished by letters. The capital letters represent grades of measurements greater, and lower-case letters those less, than the mean.

It occurred to Galton that Quetelet's principle might be applicable to variations in intellect.[379] To test this possibility he made a mathematical study of the marks obtained by candidates in various examinations. He found that the number of candidates falling into various grades according to the number of marks obtained fitted well into Quetelet's scheme. He decided to use fourteen grades in his studies of human intellect, seven on each side of the mean, and he introduced the notation by capital and lower-case letters shown below the base-line of Figs. 5 and 6. He concluded that one person in about 79,000 would fall

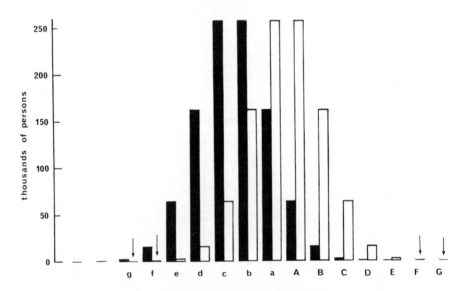

6    *Galton's opinion on the distribution of intelligence among one million Englishmen and one million Negrids*

The letters below the base-line are Galton's grades of intelligence from **g** (imbeciles) to **G** (higher 'eminent' grade), *on the scale applicable to Englishmen.* The black columns represent the numbers of Negrids, the white those of Englishmen. (Arrows indicate columns that should be white but are too short for this to be possible.)                                                                          *Diagram drawn from the data of Galton.*[379]

in the highest grade, **G**, and necessarily the same number in the lower grade of imbeciles, **g**; 1 in 4,300 in grade **F** and in **f**, but one in only four in each of the mediocre grades, **A** and **a**. The two highest grades, **F** and **G**, used in his statistical analysis consisted of persons whom he designated as 'eminent'. He recognized also the existence of a few persons of such outstanding intellect that they were too few for statistical treatment: these 'illustrious' persons he grouped in a grade designated as **X**, and to correspond with it he made another group of complete imbeciles, **x**.

His study—necessarily carried out on incomplete data—suggested to him that the general principle of the distribution of intellect among a population was the same in all ethnic taxa, but that the mean, and therefore the range from **g** to **G**, and so from **x** to **X**, differed. For instance, he was impressed by the number of illustrious Greeks in the free-born population of Attica in the century beginning in 530 B.C. (Pericles, Thucydides, Socrates, Xenophon, Plato, Euripides, and Phidias among them). The number of persons in the highest grades was much greater, in proportion to the total population, than in the England of his day. He concluded that the extent of the range of intellect was the same, but the range was shifted upwards. Thus, for instance, the **A** grade of Attic Greeks should be equated with a grade intermediate between **B** and **C** of Englishmen. Fig. 7 represents the conclusions he reached about the intellectual range of these and other groups of persons. The diagram is not taken from his book, but it exactly represents his conclusions. It shows that in his opinion the Negrids

```
dogs, etc.          x g f e d c b a A B C D E F G X
      Australians          x g f e d c b a A B C D E F G X
        Negroes            x g f e d c b a A B C D E F G X
        English              x g f e d c b a A B C D E F G X
 Greeks of Attica              x g f e d c b a A B C D E F G X
   B.C. 530 - 430
```

7    *Galton's comparison of the range of intellect in various groups of man, and in dogs and other intelligent animals*

The letters **x, g, f,** etc. represent grades of intelligence from **x** (lowest) to **X** (highest). *Diagram designed to illustrate the opinions of Galton.* |379|

stand, on the average, on a lower plane than the English, but with a large margin of overlap. He regarded Toussaint l'Ouverture, the Negrid 'liberator' of Haiti, as an 'eminent' person of grade **F** by English standards, but in the Negrid range he was in the 'illustrious' grade **X**. A Negrid of grade **A** was the intellectual equal of an Englishman of grade **b**. The relative number of persons of each of these two groups supposed to fall into each intellectual grade is shown in Fig. 6.

Fig. 7 shows that Galton placed the Australids (Australian aborigines) one grade lower than the Negrids, but he admitted that he had not sufficient data to enable him to put them with confidence in their correct place.

Galton considered that the 'eminent' grade **F** of dogs and other intelligent species of animals was 'nearly commensurate with the **f** of the human race, in respect of memory and powers of reason. Certainly the class **G** of such animals is far superior to the **g** of humankind.' In Fig. 7 the **F** of dogs is put level with **f** of Englishmen.

Galton's study of ethnic differences in intelligence led him on to a general investigation of the inheritance of mental ability, which resulted in the publication in 1869 of his well-known work *Hereditary genius.*|379| in which the information briefly set out in the preceding paragraphs is presented at greater length. It is perhaps not irrelevant to remark that although he made no special study of the Jews, he does say that 'they appear to be rich in families of high intellectual breeds'.

The step from Galton to Heinrich von Treitschke (1835–1896)—from a retiring British 'gentleman of leisure' to a professional German historian, publicly engaged in political activity—is certainly a long one. In so far as Treitschke was intensely nationalistic, it is possible to represent him as in some sense a forerunner of the Nazis, though it would be unjust to link a man of his character with those who were responsible for the crimes of Hitler's regime. Since, however, he was a famous public figure who wrote and spoke on Jewish immigration, it is necessary to make brief mention of him here.

Those who are not typical of the particular ethnic taxon or the particular nation that has their allegiance are often loudest in their praise of it. Hitler provides an obvious example of this, and Treitschke another. Passionately a German, he was partly of Czech origin, and has been described as 'unmistakably Slav' in physique.[478] This is admittedly a vague expression to anyone interested in the realities of physical anthropology, but the meaning is presumably that his appearance was Alpinid, while the most nationalistic of Germans were inclined at the time to admire the Nordid physique that had characterized the *Germanen* of old. It was Treitschke's fear that the virtues of the German people would be adulterated by the presence of too many or too influential Jews among them. He devoted no major work to the ethnic problem, but in lesser writings he minimized the contribution of Jews to German literature. He was disturbed by their great influence on literary criticism in Germany. Books were praised or abused—so he claimed—according to whether they supported or opposed the Jewish cause. He considered that Jews controlled too large a section of the German press. He did not approve of the massive immigration of Jews from Poland, and deplored the tendency of Jewish pupils to dominate in numbers in the higher classes of Berlin colleges.[478]

Despite all this, Treitschke was opposed to extremist policies on the Jewish problem. His only prescription for the trouble was 'gentle restraint'.[478] In his opinion no sensible person would think of abolishing, or even modifying, the complete emancipation of the Jews; he considered that this would be obviously unjust. So far was he from wishing to interfere with the practice of their religion that he appealed to them not to relinquish it.

It is recorded that the works of Friedrich Nietzsche (1844–1900) 'were obligatory reading for National Socialists and were solemnly presented by dictator to dictator'.[823] Some mention of his message is necessary here, though it is not easy to present in narrow compass any clear indication of the thoughts of this extraordinary, one might almost say incomprehensible, man, whose writings have scarcely anything in common with those of any other writer considered in this or the succeeding chapter. *Also sprach Zarathustra*, published during the years 1883 to 1891,[805, 806] is perhaps characteristic, and less extreme than some of his other works, in which he seems to give indications of his final mental collapse.

*Zarathustra* was not written primarily for academically minded people. 'To the children I am still a learned man,' he wrote; '. . . I am pushed out from the house of the learned, and I have slammed the door behind me.'[804] '*Für Allen und Keinen*'; that is how the author himself saw the book. It is indeed *für Allen*, in the sense that the individual words and the construction of the sentences are intelligible to anybody, but it is also *für Keinen*, for surely no one can interpret with confidence the deeper meaning of everything he says. His style often astounds the reader. 'My tongue', he says, in a typically strange passage, 'is that of the people: I speak too coarsely and heartily for the Angora rabbit. And my words seem still more strange to all ink-fishes and pen-foxes.' One cannot guess why he wrote most of the book in short paragraphs, rather like the verses of the Bible. It is not even clear why Nietzsche should choose to disguise himself as a reincarnation of the Persian thinker; our slender knowledge of the real Zarathustra hardly explains it.

It is at any rate clear that Nietzsche's main purpose was to oppose the spread of thoughtless egalitarianism and to claim special privileges for the *Übermensch*, who was justified—so Nietzsche thought—in disregarding the welfare of lesser men. Compassion he scorns. 'What in the world', he asks, 'has caused more damage than the follies of the compassionate?' Yet with characteristic contempt for consistency, Zarathustra repeatedly goes to the assistance of total strangers in distress. One moment *der Wille zur Macht* absorbs him, or again he says, 'To entice many from the herd—for that purpose I came;' but quite unexpectedly he tells us, 'I lie here willingly where the children play, against the shattered wall, among thistles and red poppy-flowers.' Interspersed with fulminations and quiet sayings there are some rather charming and unexpected paradoxes. 'But if you have a foe,' says Zarathustra, 'do not repay evil with good: for that would disconcert him. But show that he has inflicted some good on you.' Or again, 'And if a friend treats you badly, speak thus: "I forgive you for what you did to me; but that you did it to yourself, how could I forgive you for that?" ' Or yet again, still more unexpectedly, 'It is more distinguished to own oneself wrong than to maintain one's cause, especially if one is right.'

Towards the end of the book Zarathustra seems to be on the verge of pessimism. In his mountain cave, attended by the eagle and snake that are his emblems respectively of power and wisdom, he has gathered together his *höheren Menschen*, to instruct them in his doctrines. Two kings are there, a pope (unemployed through the death of God), an evil magician, a voluntary beggar, a traveller, Zarathustra's own shadow, an old prophet, a spiritually conscientious man, and—strangest of all—the ugliest man. Zarathustra fails, apparently, to transmit his message. And then, at the very end, he seems to spurn them all, and strides off on a new adventure.

Why should National Socialists have been urged to read such a book as this? Nietzsche had no special regard for the German people. Indeed, he even thought of forming an Anti-German League, and he prided himself on his partly Polish descent from the Counts of Nietzki.[641, 57] As for the State, he condemned it through Zarathustra's mouth in no uncertain terms. 'The State is the name of the coldest of all cold monsters,' he exclaims. 'Coldly, too, it lies; and this lie sneaks from its mouth: "I, the State, am the people." ' The book has no direct bearing on the ethnic problem. Jews are only mentioned three times in it, on each occasion very briefly. In one place Zarathustra says that if the peasants were to rule, there would be a 'Mob-hotch-potch [*Pöbel-Mischmasch*], in which everything is confused together, saint and rascal and nobleman and Jew and every beast in Noah's ark'. The second reference is a couplet, offensive to Christians and Jews alike:

> *Rom sank zur Hure und zur Huren-Bude,*
> *Rom's Caesar sank zum Vieh, Gott selbst—ward Jude.*

The third is simply a statement by Zarathustra's shadow that he is not the Wandering Jew.

Nietzsche's real attitude towards the ethnic problem is shown in a much more straightforward way in his *Morgenröthe*,[803, 804] a book that would have surprised the Nazis if ever it had come into their hands. This is a volume of separate 'Thoughts' (*Gedanken*), one of which is devoted to 'The People of Israel'.

> The spiritual and intellectual resources of the Jews of the present day are extraordinary. . . . Their bravery under the cloak of pitiable submission, their heroism in *spernere se sperni*, surpass the virtues of all saints. . . . The way in which they honour their fathers and their children, the reasonableness of their marriages and marriage customs, mark them out among all Europeans. . . . They will be called the inventors and pointers of the way for all Europeans.

One might wish that the whole of Nietzsche's message had been conveyed in such simple terms as these. He would have been less misunderstood.

At the beginning of the Great War of 1914–1918 the Oxford University Press published a number of pamphlets intended to commend the British cause to academically minded people. The Oxford historian, Ernest Barker, contributed to this series an essay, *Nietzsche and Treitschke: the worship of power in modern Germany*.[57] It is perhaps significant that in this little work the author makes no mention whatever of the ethnic problem, apart from a brief quotation from Nietzsche in *opposition* to race-hatred.

Two books on the ethnic problem, not wholly dissimilar in outlook but very unequal in merit, were published in the last year of the nineteenth century. One was written by an extremist, and had little influence; the other, much more moderate in tone, was acknowledged by the theorists of National Socialism as one of the foundations on which their policy was based.

G. Vacher de Lapouge was a man of wide interests in history, sociology, and anthropology. Unlike many students of the ethnic problem, he possessed a good working knowledge of biology and human anatomy. He was a disciple of Haeckel. He translated the latter's booklet on the philosophy of monism into French, and provided an introduction to it.[637]

Lapouge was disturbed by ethnic changes in the population of France, and published a paper on this subject in 1887.[635] In this, he divided the people of his native country into the *endemics*—tall, blond, blue-eyed dolichocephals (Nordids)—and *immigrants*—the shorter, brown-haired brachycephals (Alpinids). He regarded the former as superior, and gave a list of the eminent Frenchmen who appeared, from their portraits or other evidence, to belong to this subrace. He claimed that few French brachycephals had been celebrated in literature, science, or politics. He described in detail the mental characters inherent in each group, even going so far as to say of the Nordid, 'In religion he is Protestant.'

Lapouge expounded these views at greater length in a series of lectures delivered at the University of Montpellier a couple of years later, and brought these together in a book entitled *L'Aryen: son rôle social* in 1899.[635] He explains at the beginning of this work that it is in fact a monograph on the *Homo europaeus* of Linnaeus. In the title he used a word taken from philology simply because there was no generally understood name that would more accurately describe his subject. His intention was to extol the Nordid, but he starts with a careful description of the various subraces of northern and central Europe. He describes them as species and gives them Latinized names. He performs the useful function of attaching the Latin name *dinaricus* to one of the 'species', and defining it accurately.

For Lapouge, each subrace ('species') has very special mental characters, which appear to be inherent, though modifiable by environmental circumstances. He gives reasons for supposing that the fundamental characters of mind exhibited by his *Homo europaeus* have been maintained since ancient times. He does not lay down the law as to whether particular characters that appeared subsequently in history were pre-existent in latent form and were simply revealed by new environments, or whether a certain amount of evolution occurred with the passage of time. He allows that the mental characters of each ethnic taxon are not shared by every member of it.

Lapouge was not content to give his reasons for supposing that one ethnic taxon differed from another in certain broad features of intellectual or emotional make-up. He gives very detailed descriptions of the particular characters of certain groups. He goes to such extremes in this matter, and emphasizes so strongly his belief in the inherent superiority of *Homo europaeus*, that one might almost imagine he was an egalitarian indulging in a lampoon.

The typical *H. europaeus*, for Lapouge, is characterized rather by his reason and will-power than by fertility in ideas, facility in learning, or extent of memory. The Spaniard, Arab, or Hindu has a prodigious variety of ideas, but these succeed one another so rapidly that they cannot arrange themselves, and there is poverty in practical results. In pure intelligence *europaeus* does not greatly exceed the average of humanity, but he applies himself more consistently to mental work and is more capable of breaking with habitual ideas: his tendency, in fact, is towards what is new. His power of reasoning is 'cold' and just. He calculates carefully, draws a conclusion as quickly as is necessary, and acts without indecision. Having once made up his mind, he does not change it without cause. His supreme quality, which characterizes his 'species' and places it above all others, is his precise, tenacious will, which surmounts all obstacles. It is his aptitude for command that gives him dominance over others. He is combative and individualistic, stubborn against authority, but capable of conforming to discipline when necessary.

'The only dangerous competitor of the Aryan', writes Lapouge, 'is the Jew', whom he stigmatizes as arrogant in success, servile in calamity, cunning, a swindler, a great amasser of money, of high intellectual qualities, and yet unable to create. 'He is by nature incapable of productive work. He is a courtier, a speculator; he is not a worker, an agriculturalist. . . . A predator, nothing but a predator, he is a bourgeois; he is not, and does not want to be, anything but a bourgeois.'

Lapouge even defended the institution of slavery, seeing in it 'nothing more abnormal than the domestication of the horse or ox'. He considered that there was a correlation between brachycephaly and servility, and consequently foresaw, in a remarkably prophetic passage, the coming of 'absolute socialism' in Russia.

This summary of Lapouge's opinions on the ethnic problem is given at some length as an example of the most extreme views expressed during the pre-Nazi period.

Lapouge was chiefly interested in the peoples of Europe. It must be mentioned, however, that he had particular admiration for the skill of the Chinese in agriculture, and regarded them as 'not inferior to the majority of Europeans', though different in character.

Those who have particularly admired the Nordids and related peoples have mostly been less precise than Lapouge in defining the ethnic taxon that they meant to praise, in terms of physical anthropology. In this respect Houston Stewart Chamberlain (1855–1927) was no exception, though his *'Germanen'* certainly included the *Homo europaeus* of the French author. His work bearing on the ethnic problem, *Die Grundlagen des neunzehnten Jahrhunderts*, was published in 1899.[201, 202]

Chamberlain was the son of an admiral in the British navy. He was rather weakly as a boy, and his education was undertaken by a German tutor. Subsequently he studied zoology under Carl Vogt in Geneva. He went to live in Dresden and became absorbed in the music and philosophy of Wagner, whose daughter he married. He became imbued with German culture and wrote books in the language of his adopted country. Although educated partly as a scientist and no doubt affected in outlook by his association with Vogt, he was essentially a historian and a biographer. He regarded his life of Immanuel Kant as his most important work.

Chamberlain's outlook, as presented in *Die Grundlagen*, was that of a student of history, interested primarily in Europe and the Middle East. He wanted to picture and explain the nineteenth century in the most general terms, but to do this he found it necessary to go back to the time of the early Israelites and to devote about one-half of the large work to the long period that led up to the century he intended to describe. His main intention throughout was to extol the virtues and emphasize the influence of the *Germanen*. This made it necessary for him to place the origin of the Middle Ages some centuries earlier than is usually allowed, and to lessen the significance customarily attached to the Renaissance. 'The awakening of the *Germanen* to their destiny in world-history', he wrote, 'as the founders of an entirely new civilization and an entirely new culture, constitutes this turning-point: the year 1200 can be designated as the average moment of this awakening.' The 'Middle Ages' that started in A.D. 1200 were not at an end, in his view, at the time of publication of his book. The nineteenth century was only a part of the long period of preparation for a new age that would eventually succeed it.

The people primarily responsible for the advances made in the 'Middle Ages' (in his usage of the term) were the *Germanen*. 'If the *Germanen* were not the only people concerned in the fashioning of history, they were at any rate incomparably the most important.' Unfortunately he uses the word *Germanen* in two separate senses, wide and narrow.

In this book I comprehend under the name *Germanen* the various north-European populations that appear in history as *Kelten*, *Germanen*, and *Slaven*, from whom—mostly in inextricable mixtures—the peoples of modern Europe are derived. It is certain that they were originally one single family—I shall produce the proof of it in Chapter 6, but the *Germane* in the narrower sense of the word, as used by Tacitus, has proved himself so superior intellectually, morally, and physically among his kindred, that we are justified in putting down his name as the essence of the whole family.

Later in the book he hedges slightly on this. 'Indeed, I do not even postulate blood-relationship [between *Kelten*, *Germanen*, and *Slaven*], but I am ... conscious of the appalling complexity of the problem.' He claims, however, that the Slavs were originally similar in physical type to members of the other two groups, and that they gradually evolved into their present form, often so very different from that of the others. He emphasizes that the *Germanen* are not by any means necessarily fair-haired.

There can be little doubt that Chamberlain brought together under the single term *Germanen*, in the wider sense, an arbitrary collection of Nordids, Osteuropids, Alpinids, and Dinarids. It must be allowed that Chamberlain had only a limited knowledge of physical anthropology, and indeed not much interest in the subject, or confidence in its findings.

A considerable part of Chamberlain's book is devoted to an attempt to convince the reader that the Greeks, Romans, and Jews played only a small part in the development of European culture. He deplored the increasing influence of Jews in the government, law, science, commerce, literature, and art of Europe. There is some resemblance to Gobineau's outlook in his insistence on the evil effects of the indiscriminate hybridization of different ethnic taxa. He attributed the downfall of the Roman Empire to what he called its 'raceless chaos', though he did not share Gobineau's pessimistic expectations about the future. The worst example of the indiscriminate mixing of different ethnic taxa, in his view, was the *Völkerchaos* of the ancient Middle East. Nevertheless, he allowed that the intermarriage of what he regarded as closely related peoples—the *Germanen*, *Keltogermanen*, and *Slavogermanen*—was legitimate and indeed beneficial. 'Race', he wrote, 'is not a positive phenomenon, but is created: physiologically by characteristic mixture of blood, followed by inbreeding; psy-

chically by the influence that long-continued historical-geographical circumstances produce on that particular, specific, physiological predisposition.'
It is not clear whether he supposed that environmental factors could affect the
genetic qualities of the 'race'.

Chamberlain regarded the Jews as fundamentally different not only from the
*Germanen*, but also from the Indo-European peoples in general. '*Dieses fremde
Volk*', he writes, '. . . *ewig fremd.*' It is difficult to understand why he should
have taken so much trouble to belittle the intellectual achievements of the
Jewish people. For him there was a 'sanctity of unmixed race' ('*Heiligkeit
reiner Rasse*'). He regarded the Jews as hybrids between *semitischen* (Orientalid), *syrischen* (Armenid), and *indoeuropäischen* peoples, but he admired
them for their efforts to preserve the stock when once it had established itself.
His aversion from the Orientalid and Armenid subraces was too strong,
however, to permit him to make a level judgement. Nevertheless he was far
from having sympathy with the extreme opponents of the Jews. In the long introduction to his book he remarked that the attempt to make the Jew the
general scapegoat for all the burdens of our time was 'obviously laughable and
shocking'. Reverting to the same theme in the body of the work, he asks
whether we should revile the Jews, and answers that to do so would be 'as base
as it would be unworthy and unreasonable'.

There is much of interest and value in *Die Grundlagen*. It is obviously the
work of an earnest and serious-minded person, the possessor of much detailed
historical knowledge bearing on his problem; but he gives much too little credit
to the Mediterranids and Jews for their achievements, and the arbitrary way in
which he links certain subraces together and contrasts them with others is in-
defensible on grounds of physical anthropology. It obviously never entered his
head that the Nordids (that is to say, the *Germanen* in the narrow sense) are in
fact rather closely related to the Mediterranids.

On the outbreak of war in 1914 Chamberlain adhered to Germany's cause,
and two years later he was naturalized as a subject of that country. For his
sake one is glad that he died several years before the Nazis came to power.

A word must be added about Karl Pearson, who stood in relation to Francis Galton
roughly as T. H. Huxley had stood in relation to Darwin: as a younger and more dis-
putatious exponent of the thoughts of a much less obtrusive man. Pearson was a
vigorous supporter of the eugenic movement about the beginning of the present century. His contributions to it are mentioned repeatedly in Dr. C. P. Blacker's *Eugenics:
Galton and after.*[100] Eugenics and the ethnic problem, though related to one another,
are distinct, and Pearson is remembered much more for his work in the former field
than for his controversial writings on the latter subject, which are mostly scattered in
the pages of pamphlets intended for the general reader. His views on it were rather
extreme, since he considered that the advancement of man could only come about by
natural selection between races.[830] Primarily, however, he was a mathematician and a
statistician with special interest in biometry; and his academic work in this field has
been of considerable value to students of human genetics and anthropology. Mention is
made of his statistical work on p. 462 of this book.

# 4  From Kossinna to Hitler

THE GERMAN philologist and archaeologist Gustaf Kossinna (1858–1931) may have assisted to some extent in the growth of Nazi ideas on the ethnic problem, but his activities in this direction seem to have been exaggerated by at least one distinguished authority,[208] to the detriment of Kossinna's reputation as a serious worker in his chosen fields of study. It is true that when the Nazis came to power, after Kossinna's death, they took advantage of some of his writings. For instance, the Reichsminister for the Interior, Dr. Frick, when laying down in 1933 the right lines for education in history in all German lands, spoke as follows:

Let prehistory be named first, because it not only provides the starting-point for the historical development of our part of the world in the mid-European ancestral home of our people, but also is adapted, as no other science is, as 'an eminently national science'—to use Kossinna's expression—a science that counteracts the customary undervaluation of the cultural level of our Germanic forefathers.[522]

It is true that Kossinna used the expression '*ein hervorragend nationale Wissenschaft*' as part of the title of his book on *Die deutsche Vorgeschichte*, the first edition of which was published in 1912.[605] Indeed, he disputed the idea that all science was necessarily international. Army affairs, he pointed out, are a subject for international study, yet each army is primarily national. A genuine *Volk*, he contended, had some proprietary rights over the special concerns of its *Volkstaat* (which he was careful to distinguish from a mere *Nationalitätenstaat*), and these concerns extended to the prehistory of the *Volkstaat*, just as it did to its army. It was his contention that the German people had been a genuine *Volk* since ancient times. (It may be remarked in passing that many archaeologists have taken a lot of trouble to point out the virtues of the remote ancestors of the British peoples, without incurring disfavour on that account.) Most of *Die deutsche Vorgeschichte* is a straightforward account of German prehistory, with descriptions of the various artifacts left behind by the Germanic tribes, but he also sought to show that the manly virtues of these ancient peoples had been inherited by their descendants down to modern times. He mentions in particular the calm self-assurance, the reserve of strength, the willingness to be led combined with an intractable urge towards freedom, the spiritual frame of mind, the serene, sober-minded thought, the high spiritual endowment, and the stern character, which he supposed to have distinguished the German people since prehistoric times. It was these traits—so he thought—that enabled the Germanic people to overrun large parts of Europe as Roman power declined, and everywhere to establish themselves among foreigners as the ruling class. Passages of this sort, however, occupy only a small part of Kossinna's voluminous writings. He did not use his editorship of the *Zeitschrift für Vorgeschichte* (the organ of the German Society for Prehistory) very obtrusively to satisfy the patriotic feelings of his fellow countrymen, and his writings seem to be remarkably free from thoughtless denigration of the many peoples whom he must have regarded as in some degree inferior.

Kossinna had come to archaeology from philology, and he never developed any deep interest in physical anthropology. His classification of Europid subraces, as given in his book *Die Indogermanen*,[606] cannot be accepted as valid. He brings together the 'west-Alpines or Jura-shortheads' and the 'Nordic longheads' to form a 'west-European' group, which he says is 'commonly called Nordic or north-European'. This arrangement enables him to put all Germans in a single group, though he allows that there are many 'Jura-shortheads' and 'Nordic longheads' beyond the confines of Germany.

Though distinguished in his own fields of study, Kossinna was not really a very important figure in the ethnic controversy, and it is doubtful whether he had much to do with the growth of National Socialist ideas.

In intellect and erudition Oswald Spengler (1880–1936) was greatly superior to most of those who have been regarded—rightly or wrongly—as the precursors of Nazism. He was educated as a mathematician and philosopher, but his writings present him as a philosophical historian with a comprehensive knowledge and understanding of the principal civilizations of the world from the distant past to the present century. He was almost unknown until he published the first volume of his famous book *Der Untergang des Abendlandes* in 1918, just before the end of the Great War. The second volume appeared in 1922. One hundred and thirteen thousand copies of the book had already been sold when the definitive edition of both volumes was published in the following year,[997, 998] and many reprints followed.

*Der Untergang* was written for, and read by, the general educated public: indeed, Spengler held 'professional scientific lecture-desk philosophy' in contempt. Yet the book attracted the intense interest of professional philosophers and historians. The first edition contained errors of detail that the specialists were quick to point out, but it was not found so easy to challenge the main conclusions. Spengler's originality and wide-ranging knowledge compel respect. He is long-winded, but even the extensive passages that seem irrelevant to the main thesis are interesting. It was, indeed, an absorbing book, and it retains much of its interest and value today.

Spengler's writings must be considered at some length, partly because of their intrinsic interest and partly because they have been seriously misunderstood, but also because he puts forward an unusual view of the nature of civilization. The ability to create a civilization is generally regarded, naturally enough, as evidence of intellectual capacity, and the subject will be considered in Chapter 27 of the present work; but it is convenient to mention Spengler's unconventional ideas on the subject here.

Spengler's *Abendland* was the whole of Europe west of the River Vistula and the Adriatic Sea, with the addition of North America. He regarded Russia as quite distinct from western Europe and objected strongly to the artificial sub-division of 'continents' by the Ural Mountains. His book is primarily concerned with the decline of the western people as thus defined, but in order to review this subject he found it necessary to consider the origin, rise, and fall of all the best-known cultures of the world.

The reader of *Der Untergang* may well wonder why a book of this sort should be regarded by anyone as having led, however indirectly, to the birth of National Socialism. It is emphatically not propagandist. It does not urge that anything should be done, but only professes to tell what must inevitably happen. There is nothing about the special virtues of Germans or the special defects of Jews. Indeed, much less attention is paid to these two groups of per-sons than to many others. Spengler sets out simply to expound his views on the destinies—the rise and fall—of various peoples throughout history. He recognizes that each great people that has risen and fallen has done so in a dis-tinctive way, but he sees a general similarity in the process, and he thinks that the final fall can never be evaded. In brief, his thesis is that the Land of the Evening has entered the phase of inevitable decline.

Spengler divides the process of rise and fall into four stages or 'spiritual epochs'. At first the population, the '*Urvolk*', is 'rural-intuitive' (*Land-schaftlich-intuitiv*); there are no great cities, but an intellectual ferment has begun. In the western world this period was roughly from A.D. 900 to 1300, though the corresponding stage had already been reached in India (for in-stance) in 1500–1200 B.C. The western thinkers of this epoch were such men as Francis of Assisi, Thomas Aquinas, Duns Scotus, and Dante. To this first beginning there succeeds what Spengler calls the 'Culture-period', during which the people—now a *Kulturvolk*— reach their highest stature. Cities are developing, but they belong solely to the particular culture. 'Traditions' are im-portant at this stage. They involve the recognition of nobleness, the Church, privileges, dynasty; in art, of convention; in science, of the limitations of in-tellectual power. The western peoples were at this phase from the fourteenth or fifteenth century till late in the seventeenth. Some of the names that seemed most significant to Spengler were those of Savonarola, Luther, Calvin, Galileo, Bacon, Descartes, Bruno, Leibnitz, Pascal, Fermat, Newton. Towards the end of this epoch Spengler detects an impoverishment of religion, associated in England with the rise of Puritanism. There succeeds, with some overlap, the 'autumn' or age of reason, as the great cities develop still further. Intellectual creativeness is at its height with Locke, Voltaire, Rousseau, Laplace, Goethe, Kant, and Hegel; but the use of reason—Spengler suggests—is overstressed and religion overrationalized.

There then succeeds—in the nineteenth century, in the case of the western world—the phase that is the main subject of the book. The population loses the feeling of 'we'. The cities are too large, international, no longer representative of the people who created the culture. 'International-urban' (*weltstädtische*) civilization has arrived, which Spengler regarded as destructive of culture. The cities are inhabited by the genuine 'factual man', lacking in tradition, appearing in shapeless, fluctuating masses, irreligious, sharp, unproductive, with a deep antipathy to the peasantry. The spiritual creative force has been lost, and religion begins to be replaced by ethical and practical substitutes that are, in his view, inferior. Abstract thinking degenerates into the 'professional scientific lecture-desk philosophy' that has already been mentioned. Strangely enough Spengler mentions Nietzsche as an example of this tendency—Nietzsche, of whom he has said that he owes more to him than to anyone except Goethe! (He remarks elsewhere that Nietzsche 'arrived at the gate, but remained standing in front of it'.) With Nietzsche he groups a strange collection of thinkers, many of whose names will not sound with a ring of decadence in modern ears. Here stand Bentham, Comte, Darwin, Spencer, Marx, Schopenhauer, Wagner, Ibsen, Gauss. In politics the whole tendency is away from the individual culture that made the people great, and towards internationalism, pacifism, and socialism.

This, for Spengler, is the destiny of all cultures, the final decline.

> Civilization is the inevitable *fate* of a culture. Here the climax is reached. . . . Civilizations are the *most external* and *most artificial* conditions of which a higher kind of man is capable. They are a closing down: they follow, as the *become* follows the *becoming*, as death follows life, as rigidity follows unfolding, as spiritual old age and the stony, petrifying world-city follow the countryside and the soulful youthfulness in which Doric and Gothic reveal themselves. Civilizations are an *end*, irrevocable, but they are always reached at last from intrinsic necessity.

From the point of view of the present book, the most important question is what Spengler means by the word *Volk* when he uses it for the group of men and women who have created a culture. (The original word *Volk* will be used here, because 'people' is too vague, 'nation' and 'race' are inaccurate, and the English word 'folk' is somehow suggestive of feebleness and intellectual poverty.) It is here, surely, that Spengler has been most misunderstood, possibly because his long-windedness has exhausted the patience of some of his readers. One must realize that, contrarily to what one might suppose, he lays very little stress on the ethnic composition of the various *Völker* that have risen to become *Kulturvölker*. He says specifically that *Völker* 'are neither linguistic nor political nor zoological, but on the contrary spiritual units'. He defines *Volk* as 'a society of men that feels itself to be a unit', and in a remarkable statement he claims that it is the *action* of a group of men that turns it into a *Volk*. 'The great events of history', he writes, 'were in fact not carried out by *Völkern*: on the contrary, the great events first produced the *Völker*.'

To make Spengler's outlook on the ethnic problem perfectly clear, once and for all, it is necessary to give rather an extended extract from his book.

> Neither identity of speech nor bodily inheritance is decisive. *Völkerformen* may change their speech, race, name, and country; so long as their soul lasts, they engulf men of any thinkable origin and remodel them. . . . One certainly does not suppose that a *Volk* was ever held together by mere unity of bodily inheritance and that this type of *Volk* could last even for ten generations. It cannot be often enough repeated that this physiological origin exists only for science and never for *Volk*-consciousness, and that no *Volk* has advanced itself for *this* ideal of 'pure blood'. Belonging to a race

[Spengler here means a *Volk*] is nothing material, but something cosmic and ordained, the felt harmony of a destiny.

In 1919—the year after the appearance of the first volume of *Der Untergang* and three years before that of the second volume—Spengler published a strange little book entitled *Preussentum und Sozialismus*.[999] The Weimar Republic had just been set up to replace the empire of Bismarck and the Hohenzollerns. Spengler's object was to weld together the extreme 'left' (the independent socialists and the communists) and the extreme 'right' (the monarchists and conservatives) into a single group that would oppose and destroy the parliamentary government of Weimar. The book is written in a style so different from that of *Der Untergang* that it is difficult to believe that the author was the same person; indeed, I have caught myself turning back to the title-page to find out whether I were reading the wrong book by mistake. Much of it is written in short, jerky sentences; the whole work is propagandist and unintellectual. Spengler was now an advocate of socialism, which he had listed as a mark of decadence in *Der Untergang*; but not many socialists would be likely to call his proposed system by that name. He insisted that everyone defined socialism in such a way as to suit his own purposes. Marxism he condemned; he regarded Marx himself as a destructive critic, not a creator, and only the 'stepfather' of socialism. Only Germans—not Jews—could be genuine socialists. He considered that all real government must be carried out by an élite, but that the opportunity to become a member of the ruling group should be open to all. 'What I hope is that no one shall remain in the abyss, who through his ability is born to command, and that no one shall command, who through his innate talent was not called to it.' He had, however, no respect for the Soviet experiment in socialism. In a passage that is rather characteristic of the book as a whole, he remarks that 'Nothing can be more deplorable than the attempts of a certain type of Protestantism to rub its corpse alive again with Bolshevist excrement.' Under Spengler's socialism, private property and the inheritance of wealth would not be abolished, but industrialists would be forced to act within the framework of rigid rules established by authority. The employer would become, in a sense, a government official. 'Should commerce rule the state,' he asks, 'or the state rule commerce?' There would be no political parties and no elections.

It was Spengler's contention that in so far as the conservatives preserved the true spirit of Prussianism they were socialists (in his sense) without knowing it. 'The old Prussian spirit and socialist conviction, which today hate one another with brotherly hate, are one and the same.' Spengler had great admiration for the Prussian spirit. For him, it was 'a *life-feeling*, an *instinct*, an *inability to be otherwise*'. Frederick William I (father of Frederick the Great) had shown the way by establishing a centralized, bureaucratic state. Spengler's ideal had nothing in common with the pacifist, internationalist outlook of many orthodox socialists.

We need a class of socialist master-natures. . . . socialism means might [*Macht*], might, and ever more might. Plans and ideas are nothing without might. The way to might is indicated: the valuable part of the German working community [will act] in combination with the best upholders of the old Prussian feeling for the State, both determined on the foundation of a rigorously socialist state, a democratization in the Prussian sense.

The true socialists were to ask 'not rights for themselves, but duties from themselves'.

Since Spengler was urging the creation of a nationalistic, socialist state, it was natural enough that he should be regarded as one of the founders of National Socialism; but he was too much of an individualist (though nominally a socialist) to be swept away by party spirit. He never accepted some of the principal Nazi doctrines and he never became a member of the Nazi party. His objection to the Jews was not founded on a belief that they constituted a separate ethnic taxon. He only objected to their cultural heritage, and he wanted to see them integrated into the nation.

So late as the autumn of 1932, in his collected works, Spengler condemned Hitler's policies; but in his *Jahre der Entscheidung*, published shortly after the Nazis came to power in 1933, he revealed himself as somewhat equivocal in outlook.[521] Nevertheless, even mild opposition could not be permitted. The sale of his book was stopped (though not before many copies had been distributed), and the periodical press was forbidden even to mention his name. The Nazis regarded Spengler 'as a precursor gone wrong'.[521]

His final eclipse occurred in curious, almost laughable circumstances. A short book was written by von Leers to demolish the image of Spengler as one for whom a genuine Nazi might have respect.[647] Spengler had gradually developed a rather unexpected antipathy for the various 'coloured' peoples of the world, including the Japanese. The Nazis particularly wanted the friendship of this 'coloured' nation. 'How does Japanese expansion into Manchuria and Mongolia inconvenience us?' asked von Leers; 'it is an entirely Japanese–Chinese–Russian problem.' By a strange irony, Spengler was attacked by this doctrinaire Nazi for his indiscriminate antipathy to 'coloured' people.

Spengler was not molested, but simply disappeared from public view. He died in 1936 from a heart attack. How different might be his reputation today if he had never written *Preussentum* and had died after the publication of the second volume of *Der Untergang* in 1922!

It remains to mention briefly two American authors of far lower calibre than such men as Gobineau, Nietzsche, Chamberlain, and Spengler, and then to attempt a brief summary before we come to Hitler himself.

Madison Grant (1867–1937) was trained as a lawyer, but is known chiefly as an author on various subjects and an amateur zoologist (he was Chairman of the New York Zoological Society). One of his principal works was *The passing of the great race*,[425] published the year before the first volume of *Der Untergang*.

Grant's purpose was to persuade the American people to control more rigorously the ethnic composition of the U.S.A. For Grant, the 'great race' was the Nordid, and he regretted the fact that the proportion of people of this stock in his country had greatly diminished since colonial times. He deplored 'the maudlin sentimentalism that has made America "an asylum for the oppressed"' and was 'sweeping the nation towards a racial abyss'. He was not favourably disposed towards the Jews, but this aspect of the ethnic problem plays only a very small part in his book. Grant seems to have taken almost for granted the superiority of Nordids over others. He claims that they are 'everywhere the type of the sailor, the soldier, the adventurer, and the pioneer'. He considered that their superiority was due to selective influences during their long sojourn in northern Europe.

The climatic conditions must have been such as to impose a rigid elimination of defectives through the agency of hard winters and the necessity for industry and foresight in providing the year's food, clothing, and shelter during the short summer. Such demands on energy, if long continued, would produce a strong, virile, and self-contained race which would inevitably overwhelm in battle nations whose weaker elements had not been purged by the conditions of an equally severe environment. [425]

It is rather difficult to understand Grant's belief in what seems to him the almost self-evident superiority of the Nordids, in view of the virtues that he himself ascribes to other subraces of Europids. He allows that 'The early Alpines made very large contributions to the civilization of the world,' chiefly by introducing the bronze culture into Europe and teaching it to the other subraces, but he considered that their contribution to culture later on, in classical, mediaeval, and modern times, had been small. His praise of the Mediterranids is not qualified, however, in this way. He ascribed to them 'the foundation of our civilization. . . . The mental characteristics of the Mediterranean race are well known, and this race, while inferior in bodily stamina to both the Nordic and the Alpine, is probably superior to both, certainly of [sic] the Alpines, in intellectual attainments. In the field of art its superiority to both the other European races is unquestioned.' One would not suppose that the writer of such words as these would have opposed the massive immigration of Mediterranids into his country.

Grant regarded the Nordids as the only true European ethnic group, the Alpinids and Mediterranids being invaders from Asia (through North Africa in the case of the Mediterranids). It does not appear to have occurred to him that the separation of Europe from Asia is meaningless from any scientific point of view, because the line might well have been drawn somewhere else or (better) not drawn at all. Even if a particular ethnic taxon could be shown to be endemic to some arbitrarily defined territory, this fact could not in itself provide evidence of the superiority or inferiority of that group.

Grant lays considerable stress on the part played by Nordids in spreading Aryan languages throughout almost the whole of Europe and to countries beyond, though he allows the possibility that this speech may have been brought to Europe by Alpinids with the bronze culture.

He was harsh in his schemes for negative eugenics. He considered that 'a human life is valuable only when it is of use to the community or race'. He favoured the forcible sterilization of criminals, diseased and insane persons, and 'worthless race-types', and the enactment of laws against race-mixture.

*The passing of the great race* is not a scholarly book. Grant's opinions are often expressed dogmatically, his classification of the Europid race is greatly over-simplified, and he makes scarcely any references to other authors except in a rough and inadequate list at the end. He makes no mention anywhere of Gobineau, Pouchet, Vogt, Treitschke, Nietzsche, Lapouge, or Kossinna. One might almost suppose that he alone had  considered the possibility that the ethnic taxa of man were in some sense unequal. Yet the book has its merits. He treats in considerable detail the ethnic history of Europe; that is to say, he traces the story from the earliest times onwards in terms of the ethnic composition of the peoples concerned, without consideration of their artificial separation into 'nations'. This part of the book is valuable. It is a line of attack on the ethnic problem that deserves to be followed up in greater detail, and extended to other parts of the world. The historian often seems almost unaware of the taxonomic differences between the peoples of the world, and is content to use undefined group-names, some of which actually stand for arbitrary and temporary associations of unrelated types of mankind, while others are meaningful from the ethnic standpoint.

In his long introduction[426] to Stoddard's book *The rising tide of colour*,[1013] Grant claims that Western civilization is essentially Nordid. The Alpinids and Mediterranids have only been 'effective' to the extent that they have been influenced by Nordid culture. He now[426] seems to allow that the Nordids may have originated partly in western Asia. He claims that the Alpinids are ultimately of Mongolid ancestry, though he had specifically denied this in his own book. He regarded the great conflict of 1914–1918 as a Nordid 'civil war'.

Lothrop Stoddard (1883–1950) was an American author of books for the 'general reader' on political and historical subjects. Like Grant, he had been trained for the legal profession. His style is journalistic; indeed, extracts from newspapers occupy a considerable space in his pages. *The rising tide of colour*[1013] was published after the end of the First World War, before the second volume of *Der Untergang*. It may be regarded almost as a sequel to Grant's book. Unfortunately Stoddard had not sufficient anthropological knowledge to write effectively on the ethnic problem, for his classification of man is oversimplified to the point of crudity, and the book contains nothing profound or genuinely original. He wrote, like Grant, to awaken his fellow-countrymen to what he regarded as the dangers of insufficiently controlled immigration, but he was concerned mainly with non-Europid races.

Stoddard remarked that before the war there had been only nine regions of 'non-white governance' (China, Japan, Siam, Turkey(!), Afghanistan, Persia, Abyssinia, Liberia, and Haiti), and that these covered only 6,000,000 square miles out of the 53,000,000 of non-polar land. After the war the area of effective 'white' control was extended still further, through the domination of Turkey by the French and British and in other ways. People of the 'non-white' races outnumber the 'white' by more than two to one, and multiply more rapidly. Stoddard pointed out the danger that resulted from these circumstances. He was apprehensive about the possibility that 'white' civilization might disappear, by race-mixture or elimination in war. This would be a disaster for humanity, since the greatest creative ability would be destroyed; but he nowhere clearly defined, at any length, what he supposed to be the great inherent virtues of the 'whites'. He admitted that the 'brown' and 'yellow' peoples had contributed greatly to the civilization of the world (the 'brown' being a heterogeneous collection of ethnic groups, from which the Negrids were excluded). Among the 'whites' he particularly favoured the Nordids, 'the best of all human breeds', and he deplored the fact that hordes of Alpinids and Mediterranids were entering the United States along with 'Asiatic elements like Levantines and Jews'. There is, however, very little about Jews in the book: Stoddard, like Grant, seems uninterested in them.

How can one summarize what has so far been said in these two chapters? Are the authors too diverse in outlook to allow of any generalization?

Nietzsche and Spengler may be eliminated at once as irrelevant to the ethnic problem, despite opinion to the contrary and notwithstanding the altogether special interest of their writings. Nietzsche was primarily an anti-egalitarian, but he did not proclaim the inequality of ethnic taxa. Spengler was intensely interested in the *Volk* and its capacity, in certain cases, to initiate a great culture (which would eventually become a civilization and decline); but he makes it abundantly clear that the *Volk* was not an ethnic taxon. Towards the end of his life he showed a mild antipathy to 'coloured' people, but this did not appear in his important writings. His *Preussentum und Sozialismus* does indeed to some extent foreshadow the Nazi movement, but only from its nationalistic fervour and political bias, not from any tendency to favour any particular ethnic taxon.

Of the thirteen authors already mentioned in these two chapters, seven strongly proclaim the superiority of people variously described as 'Nordics', '*Germanen*', '*Indogermanen*', or 'Aryan'. These seven are Gobineau, Haeckel, Lapouge (especially), Chamberlain, Kossinna, Grant, and Stoddard. It is a remarkable fact, however, that none of the authors mentioned in these chapters claims superiority for the whole Europid race: it is only a subrace, or else a section of the Europids not clearly defined in terms of physical anthropology, that is favoured.

Only one of the authors, Lapouge, strongly condemns the Jews. Treitschke is moderately anti-Jewish; Chamberlain, Grant, and Stoddard mildly so; Gobineau is equivocal. The rest show little or no interest in the Jewish problem, apart from Nietzsche, some of whose eulogistic remarks have been quoted. With the exception of Lapouge it is impossible to imagine any of these men participating in or condoning actual cruelty to Jews, though some of them would limit their immigration (with that of certain other peoples), and discourage intermarriage.

No unprejudiced person who had studied the works of all these authors would be likely to suppose that there was no validity whatever in any part of their writings on the ethnic problem. Stoddard was obviously unimportant, Lapouge highly prejudiced; but one cannot lightly dismiss such men as Gobineau and Chamberlain as negligible, and there are passages in the books of most of the others that provoke interest and thought. If one had to choose a single work as the most important of all in presenting one side of the ethnic controversy, it would be reasonable to suggest Gobineau's *Essai sur l'inégalité des races humaines*; but necessarily it is in many respects out of date, and its very great length would deter most readers.

However determined one may be to present an objective account of the ethnic controversy, one cannot altogether avoid a sense of shock and abhorrence as one turns from those who affected the thoughts of men to one who directly and disastrously controlled their actions. Yet Hitler's *Mein Kampf*, published in two volumes in 1925 and 1927,[494, 495] is perhaps a somewhat less violent and emotional book than anyone would be likely to suppose who had only heard him address vast crowds during the 'thirties.

Adolf Hitler (1889–1945) was 36 years old when his first volume was published. The first part of the chapter dealing with the ethnic problem is quite well written and not uninteresting. He starts from the standpoint of biology, by remarking on the tendency of animals to mate strictly with their own kind. He notes the resulting 'internal isolation of the species of all living creatures of this earth'. He intends this to be taken as a guide to human beings to select their mates from among their own ethnic taxa. His biology, however, is tinged with a mystical belief in an innate urge towards the self-improvement of all species under natural conditions. When he turns to his main theme, he discards altogether the attempt to treat his subject scientifically, for he makes no serious attempt to define the two human groups in which he is primarily interested—the 'Aryan' and the Jewish—in terms of physical anthropology; indeed, one is left in doubt as to who *der Arier* may be, and what criteria we should use to identify him. (It is scarcely necessary to remark that the *Germanen* of Tacitus's time would never for an instant have regarded Hitler himself as a potential member of any of their numerous tribes.) He lays great stress, however, on the ethnic separateness of the Jews, and strongly denies that they are simply a religious community.

In the historical part of the chapter, dealing with the gradual increase in Jewish influence in Germany, Hitler traces the way in which they first gained power over the princes through their control of finance, next over the nobility, and then over the bourgeoisie, and how finally they were becoming leaders in the trades union movement, though they lacked—so he claimed—all genuine concern for people of the working class. In particular he deplored their control of the press, and emphasized their astuteness in using it in a clandestine way to their own advantage. In this passage one seems to detect the influence of Treitschke. Hitler suggests that when the Jews talk of the equality of men of all races, they do so simply to conceal their tactics and dupe their victims.

Hitler could not restrain himself from the exaggerated, untrue, and purely abusive remarks that appeal especially to low-grade, vindictive minds. He states that 'the absolutely essential presupposition for a civilized people, the idealistic disposition' was completely lacking in Jews. He reverts several times to their deficiency in *Idealismus*. 'The apparent fellow-feeling (*Zusammengehörigkeitsgefühl*) [among the Jews] is founded on a very primitive herd-instinct, like that which shows itself also among many other living creatures on this earth.' The Jew 'is and remains the typical parasite, a toady, who like a harmful bacillus distributes himself ever more widely, wherever a suitable nutrient soil invites'. Hitler makes dogmatic statements intended to minimize the Jewish contribution to learning and art. Even in the drama, where he seems to allow some success, he says that the Jew is *'nur der "Gaukler", besser der "Nachäffer"'* ('only a buffoon, or better an apelike mimic').

In contrast to this, he makes an absurdly exaggerated claim for the superiority of the 'Aryans' over all others.

> What we see before us today of human civilization, of the results of art, learning, science, and technology, is almost exclusively the creative product of the Aryan. But this fact permits directly the not unfounded conclusion that he alone was, in the main, the originator of the higher man.

It has already been pointed out (p. 33) that in his chapter on the ethnic problem, Hitler quotes only two authorities, Schopenhauer and Goethe. Nevertheless it seems almost certain that he was influenced by Gobineau. His denial that the Jews ever had a civilization of their own is suggestive; so is his use of the name 'Aryan' for the people regarded as the great initiators of civilization (in preference to *Germanen* or *Indogermanen*); and his reference to genetic deterioration through hybridization is almost conclusive. 'All great civilizations of the past', he writes, 'only perished because the original creative race died out from blood-poisoning.'

Anyone who read Hitler's remarks on the ethnic problem in 1925 would be likely to conclude that he was strongly prejudiced against the Jews, to the extent of taking drastic action against their influence in Germany, if ever he could rise to power; but few could guess that the thoughts brooding in his mind would eventually lead on to mass-murder.

In 1928, the year after that in which the second volume of *Mein Kampf* was published, there appeared in the U.S.A. a work entitled *Contemporary sociological theories*. The author was Pitirim Sorokin, Professor of Sociology in the University of Minnesota.[992] The book contains a chapter on the ethnic problem. This chapter is memorable, for it marks the close of the period in which both sides in the ethnic controversy were free to put forward their views, and authors who wished to do so could give objective accounts of the evidence pointing in each direction. From the beginning of the thirties onwards scarcely anyone outside Germany and its allies dared to suggest that any race might be in any respect or in any sense superior to any other, lest it should appear that the author was supporting or excusing the Nazi cause. Those who believed in the equality of all races were free to write what they liked, without fear of contradiction. They made full use of their opportunity in the decades that followed, when nothing resembling Sorokin's chapter appeared in print. He himself supported neither side. All he did was to express, clearly and shortly, the views of both sides in the controversy. Sorokin's chapter is well worth reading today, as a reminder of what was still possible before the curtain came down. In recent years a corner of it has already been lifted.

It was mentioned in the Introduction to the present book that the historical method has been adopted throughout. From this point onwards no attempt will be made to follow the general course of controversy on the ethnic problem, because, for the reason just stated, there has been no general controversy on the subject. Nevertheless, much new knowledge bearing on the problem has been obtained in various branches of science. The historical method will now be pursued in a different way—not by the attempt to present a general view, progressing with the march of time, but by separate accounts of advances made in each particular subject. Special attention will be given to the histories of those subjects that attained first-rate importance later than the others and have therefore been mentioned only incidentally up till now. This applies particularly to the accounts of mental testing and genetics in Chapters 24 to 26, but also to many other branches of knowledge, as the reader will find.

# PART TWO

# The Biological Background

# 5 The meaning of 'species'

'MANKIND IS one:... all men belong to the same species.' These words are taken from the first sentence of a formal Statement issued by a group of social scientists and biologists who assembled in Paris in December 1949, under the auspices of UNESCO, to discuss the ethnic problem.[1080] What exactly does the word 'species' mean?

This question is of such fundamental importance for the subject of the present book that it must be answered in considerable detail. The belief that all human beings belong to a single species is supposed by some to support strongly the opinion that all races should be regarded as 'equal'. Darwin himself foresaw that acceptance of the doctrine of evolution would make this word less clearly definable.

Differences, however slight, between any two forms, if not blended by intermediate gradations, are looked at by most naturalists as sufficient to raise both forms to the rank of species. Hereafter we shall be compelled to acknowledge that the only distinction between species and well-marked varieties is, that the latter are known, or believed, to be connected at the present day by intermediate gradations whereas species were formerly thus connected. ... It is quite possible that forms now generally acknowledged to be merely varieties may hereafter be thought worthy of specific names. ... we shall at least be freed from the vain search for the undiscovered and undiscoverable essence of the term species.[254]

In this important passage Darwin uses the word 'varieties' to mean what the modern biologist calls 'subspecies' or 'races'. This is clear from the context. The question whether the search is actually vain is the first to be tackled in this Part of the present book; it will occupy two chapters. The biological background to the ethnic problem is, however, far wider than that. No one knows man who only knows man. Indeed, that is what Blumenbach and T. H. Huxley implied in their remarks quoted on p. 3. One might almost go so far as to say, in relation to the ethnic problem, that the proper study of mankind is animals.

Many who write or talk about this problem think only of man as he has existed since some of his ancestors gave up being simply food-gatherers and began to develop agriculture and village life, and thus took the first steps towards civilization. To anyone who has studied palaeontology this outlook on man appears so restricted that it cannot provide a basis for true judgement on the nature of man, and especially for an understanding of the ethnic problem. One must see man as the product of his animal ancestors; one must realize that he is still to a large extent an animal and that, palaeontologically speaking, he has only just ceased being exactly that. Let the reader imagine a huge history of the world, covering the whole period from the time when fossils were first being preserved in Cambrian rocks to the present day, written in such a way that the number of lines of print is throughout proportional to the number of years they record. If such a work comprised 120 volumes, each of 500 pages, the history of man from the time when he took the first steps towards civilization to the present day would occupy a little less than the last page of the last volume. Yet man's ancestry stretches back to the first page of the first volume, and indeed far back into pre-Cambrian times; for in the Cambrian period many groups of animals were well established, and no biologist supposes that man's remote ancestors sprang suddenly into existence long after other groups of animals had already evolved to the level exhibited by the Cambrian fossils.

### REMARKS ON NOMENCLATURE

It might be thought pedantic to start an examination of the very interesting subject of the reality or unreality of the idea of 'species', with all its implications for the ethnic problem, by discussing first of all the seemingly dry and un- necessarily formal subject of nomenclature. Readers who are familiar with this subject should skip to p. 69, but it is hoped that others will read these few pages, for much misunderstanding about *facts* can arise from ignorance of the way in which zoologists use their words. What is said here will supplement the very brief remarks already made on this subject in the Introduction (p. 4).

It is widely known that all animals, including man, are divided by zoologists into great groups called *phyla*, of which the Chordata, Mollusca, and Annelida are examples. The Chordata are divided into *classes*, of which the Mammalia are one, and classes into *orders*, such as the Primates, Rodentia, and Car- nivora. These orders, again, are sub-divided into *families*. Three of the families of Primates are Cercopithecidae (Old World monkeys), Pongidae (anthropoid apes), and Hominidae (men). A family usually comprises several *genera*, and some authorities accept *Pithecanthropus* (fossil Java Man), *Sinanthropus* (fossil Pekin Man), and *Homo* (men of modern type) as genera of the Hominidae, though most present-day students of the group allow only the genus *Homo*. A genus consists of one or more species or 'kinds', and the names of the species are written with that of the genus. Thus the common snail (*Helix aspersa*) and Roman snail (*Helix pomatia*) are two species of the genus *Helix*; and *Homo neanderthalensis* and *Homo sapiens* (modern man) have been regarded as separate species of the genus *Homo*, though some authorities con- sider that Neanderthal man belonged to *Homo sapiens* (cf. p. 11).

Confusion would result if each zoologist chose a name at random for each kind of animal. It is a great convenience that rules of nomenclature have been established by international agreement, which make it as nearly certain as can be that there is only one correct name for each species. These rules are set out in detail in a valuable book entitled *The international code of zoological nomenclature.*[1014] It is out of the question to present here even a brief résumé of the rules, for they are extremely (though not unnecessarily) complicated; but a few possible sources of misunderstanding must be mentioned, for the benefit of any readers who may not be acquainted with them.

The system defines objectively what a particular kind of animal shall be *called*; it does not attempt to define how species should be grouped together into genera or larger groups, for that is a matter on which different zoologists may disagree.

The fundamental rule governing nomenclature is the 'law of priority', according to which the correct specific name of any species of animal is the name given to it in 1758 in the tenth edition of Linnaeus's *Systema naturae*,[669] if the species in question is defined in that work; if not (and the vast majority are not), it is the name applied to it, in conformity with Linnaeus's system, in the oldest printed book or journal published subsequently to his tenth edition. The great advantage of this 'law' is that the date of publication is nearly always an objective fact, not subject to argument.

The name is simply a label. It need not necessarily provide truthful information about the animal concerned. For instance, a species called *europaeus* need not be confined to Europe: it might even not occur in Europe (as in fact many plants called *japonica* actually come from China). It must not be supposed that in calling modern man *Homo sapiens*, Linnaeus was under the impression that all human beings are wise. Similarly, the fossil *Homo rhodesiensis* retains his name (for those who regard him as specifically distinct), despite the fact that the country in which his remains were found is now called Zambia. It must here suffice to say that this rule of nomenclature, that a name need not be accurately descriptive, however unfortunate it may appear, is a useful one in practice, and its abolition would cause much more confusion than its retention.

It is important to understand the very special sense in which the word 'type' is used in zoological nomenclature. A particular specimen, in some particular museum, is regarded as the 'type' of a species only in the sense that if it be found that a species is wrongly defined and new knowledge requires it to be split into two (or more) species, the 'type' retains the name and a new name is given to the newly distinguished species. This is a matter on which there is much misunderstanding. The word 'type', as it is used in zoological nomenclature, does not convey that the specimen thus labelled is particularly typical of the group to which it is assigned. It is concerned solely with the proper *naming* of this group. A mistake would only be made if the name of the 'type' were given to a group of animals to which the 'type' does not belong. In any taxon of animals—subspecies, species, genus, family, etc.—there may be forms that are genuinely typical in the straightforward sense that they represent the group well, since they are not strikingly aberrant in any character, while others are so peculiar that no one would consider them typical of the group as a whole. This is an important subject that is discussed in some detail in Chapter 8 (p. 118). Here it must suffice to insist that in zoological nomenclature the word 'type' is used in a special and clearly defined sense, and that the type need not be typical.

So that there may be no doubt as to which animal is referred to by a particular specific name, the person who gave it is often mentioned. Thus modern man may be designated *Homo sapiens* Linnaeus. For this purpose it is permissible to use abbreviations of the names of famous nomenclators, for instance, Linn. or L. for Linnaeus. When there is evidence that a particular species does not fit accurately into the genus in which the nomenclator placed it, it is transferred to another, and a special convention is used to indicate that this has been done. Thus Linnaeus regarded the chimpanzee as a member of the genus *Simia* (in which incidentally he placed all the species of monkeys known to him). It was recognized, however, by the German biologist and philosopher Lorenz Oken, early in the nineteenth century, that the chimpanzee differs sharply not only from all monkeys, but also from its closer relative, the orang-utan, and he defined the differences from the latter with some precision.[810]To emphasize the distinctness of the chimpanzee, he coined for it the generic name *Pan*. The correct name for this species, which was called *Simia satyrus* by Linnaeus, is therefore *Pan satyrus* (Linnaeus). The brackets round the word 'Linnaeus' indicate the fact that Linnaeus himself used a different generic (but the same specific) name. This useful convention is mentioned here because persons not acquainted with the rules of zoological nomenclature sometimes make the mistake of attributing carelessness to authors for the use of brackets in some cases and not in others. They do not understand why one writes '*Homo sapiens* Linnaeus' but '*Homo erectus* (Dubois)'.

When subspecies (races) are concerned, a trinomial replaces the binomial name. Thus the Europid ('Caucasian') race of man is named *Homo sapiens albus*. Once again, there is no need for the subspecific or racial name to be accurately descriptive. Members of the race *H. sapiens albus* never have a skin that is actually white (*albus*), and some representatives of this race in India and Ethiopia are dark-skinned.

Each human race has two separate names: the one conforming in all respects to the international laws of nomenclature (e.g., *Homo sapiens albus*) and the alternative 'trivial' or 'popular' name (e.g., Europid), to which no internationally accepted laws apply but which are nevertheless often useful in speech and writing. A list of human races, showing the correct names in accordance with the laws of. nomenclature and the trivial equivalents used by von Eickstedt[303]and by Peters,[838]is given at the end of this book on pp. 624–5.

The trivial names, like the 'lawful' ones, need not be accurately descriptive. The existence of endemic Europid populations in India and Ethiopia shows this.

It must be clearly understood that there is not universal agreement as to the number or grouping of the races and subraces of man. This subject will be discussed in Chapter 7 (pp. 109–10) by reference to an example taken from animals. It will be shown that there may well be different views on particular points of anatomy, but this by no means invalidates the whole system. Certain arrangements would be nonsensical, while others clearly admit of reasoned discussion. The intention of taxonomists is to approach more and more closely towards a perfect system, in which the relationship of the ethnic taxa would be correctly displayed.

The formal usage of such words as 'class', 'order', 'family', and 'genus' is necessary to establish the hierarchy of taxa: that is to say, to ensure that the word 'order' (for instance) always means a taxon minor to class and major to family. Nevertheless, one cannot *define* what a class, order, family, or genus is, in such a way that one could tell, from objective evidence, that a certain taxon of mammals, a certain taxon of birds, and a certain taxon of reptiles must necessarily all be regarded as orders. It is a mere convenience to fix on particular names, such as 'class' and 'order', to establish a system of hierarchy. The important question arises whether the words 'species' and 'subspecies' ('races') differ from the other names of taxa in not being merely hierarchical. Are species and races realities in a sense in which classes, orders, and the rest are not? If the words 'species' and 'race' have only hierarchical validity, it is open to anyone to affirm or deny at will that all human beings belong to a single species. This is the question with which the rest of this chapter, and also Chapters 6 and 7, are concerned.

The reader's attention is called to a particularly ingenious diagram on p. 125 of Professor A. J. Cain's book *Animal species and their evolution*.[178] This diagram, with the accompanying text, illustrates very clearly the different senses in which the word 'species' is used (though he himself speaks of different 'sorts' of species, to each of which he gives a name, briefly defined on p. 128 of his book).

## THE SPECIES IN THE PALAEONTOLOGICAL SENSE

It is convenient to consider first how the word 'species' is used in the study of evolutionary change. Such change has come about in two distinct ways. On one hand a single kind of animal may give rise, in the course of time, to two or more kinds, and these to yet others, so that one may say metaphorically that the evolutionary tree *branches*; indeed, it may be more like a shrub than a tree. To this type of evolution Rensch has given the name of '*Kladogenesis*'.[894] Change may also come about, however, without any division of one type of animal into two or more. This was already evident to Charles Darwin when he was writing the first edition of *The origin of species*.[254] 'In some cases', he wrote, 'no doubt the process of modification will be confined to a single line of descent, and the number of modified descendants will not be increased.'[254] In this book I shall call an evolutionary change of this kind 'adastogenesis' (from the Greek ἄδαστος, undivided; γένεσις, descent). It is the same as what the Revd. J. T. Gulick, in a very interesting paper published in 1887, called 'monotypic evolution'.[443] Gulick defined it as 'any transformation of a species that does not destroy its unity of type'. He used the alternative terms 'polytypic evolution' and 'divergent evolution' for what Rensch long afterwards called 'Kladogenesis'. The only disadvantage of Gulick's terms is that they are not easily transformed into adjectives.

The word 'anagenesis' has been used[178] with the same meaning as adastogenesis. In introducing the word 'anagenesis', Hyatt defined it as 'the genesis of progressive characters'.[541] It is used in exactly this sense by Rensch,[894] who carefully defined his ideas of evolutionary progress. Neither Hyatt nor Rensch used it with the meaning of adastogenesis.

Adastogenesis is the simpler form of evolutionary change. While it is taking place, the modifications from one generation to the next are so slight that it would not occur to anyone to describe the populations of the two generations as different 'species'. It follows that if a complete series of fossils were left in the rocks in a state fit for study by palaeontologists, it would be an arbitrary matter to decide where a new species began. Let us suppose that a population had been named from specimens taken from a particular geological stratum, which may be distinguished as 'A'. A new species would then be recognized and named by a palaeontologist at the lowest stratum, higher than 'A', at which all the specimens were distinct from those at 'A' (cf. Simpson[969]). This higher stratum may be called 'B'. It follows that if a population in this adastogenetic series had chanced to be named first at some stratum, 'C', lower or higher than 'A', when its characters were slightly different from those at 'A', the next new species would have been named at a level, 'D', at which its characters were distinct from those at level 'C'—*not* when they were distinct from those at level 'A'. The origin of a new species would depend on the chance of first discovery of a population forming part of a continuous adastogenetic series, not on any biological feature of the evolutionary sequence.

In practice the geological record is usually very incomplete, and as a result there are marked differences between the fossils of an adastogenetic series in two different strata, and no intermediates are found between them. If so, palaeontologists would regard the two sets of fossils as different species, to which different names would be given. The definition of the species would depend on the fortuitous circumstances that certain strata survived and fossils were found in them, while other strata were eroded away.

If a complete series of fossils were available, showing the kladogenetic evolution of two forms from one ancestor, the palaeontologist would say that new species had originated at that particular level in the geological strata at which every specimen could be assigned to one or other of the two forms. A problem would, however, remain: had two new species originated—or one? In such cases it is the practice of palaeontologists to say that *two* new species have originated, even though one of them may not differ from the ancestral species.[969] If by chance the other had not been found, no new name would have been given. The problem is not very often posed, however, because the imperfection of the geological record makes it impossible to follow the complete series of evolutionary changes, and favours the discovery of forms that are clearly distinct.

From what has been said it follows that the 'species', in the sense in which the word is used by palaeontologists, is defined by arbitrary criteria. Yet without the description and naming of species, palaeontology would be chaotic. No harm is done by the arbitrary distinction between the 'species' of past times preserved in the rocks, if it is remembered that this is a special usage of the word species. One may refer, if one wishes, to 'palaeontological' or 'fossil' species; but it must be remembered that the meaning of these terms is 'species in the palaeontological sense'. This must be borne in mind in discussions of human evolution as revealed by the fossil evidence. It must also be remembered that the decision whether or not to distinguish two closely similar fossil forms as separate 'palaeontological species' cannot command universal assent.

Some palaeontologists nowadays recognize only two gra(
in the evolution of the genus *Homo*, and the name of '*Homo*
is commonly given to fossil man of the older and more
The specific name *erectus* is taken from Java Man, origi...
*Pithecanthropus erectus* by his discoverer, E. Dubois (1894), who use
adjective to indicate that although the specimen was intermediate between ape
and man, he walked upright. It is argued that the difference between this form
and modern man is insufficient to warrant the use of different generic names,
and *Pithecanthropus* is therefore often (but not invariably) replaced by *Homo*.
Pekin Man, formerly regarded as generically distinct under the name of
*Sinanthropus pekinensis*, was in many respects so similar to Java Man that
many authorities place him in the same species. The majority of later forms, including that which was discovered at Neanderthal, are often grouped with
modern man as *Homo sapiens*.

*Homo* (or *Pithecanthropus*) *erectus* may be distinguished from *H. sapiens* by
several criteria, of which the following are among the most important. In the
median sagittal plane of the skull (the plane that divides the left from the right
side), the frontal and parietal bones are somewhat flattened in *erectus*, bulbous
in *sapiens*; the occipital bone, on the contrary, bulges out backwards in *erectus*,
less so in *sapiens* (though it must be remarked that it projects strongly in
Neanderthal man). The eye-sockets of *erectus* lie largely in front of the brain-
case, in *sapiens* below it. If the skulls are viewed from behind (or better in
transverse section), that of *erectus* appears roughly pentagonal in outline: it is
widest at the base, above which its flat sides slope inwards, and then more
sharply inwards again to meet in a ridge in the middle line on top. In *sapiens*,
on the contrary, the contour is somewhat rounded (even in Neanderthal man),
and the skull is generally widest from side to side far above the base. More important, perhaps, than any of these distinguishing characters is the fact that the
cranial capacity (and therefore the brain) is small (about 775–1280 ml) in *erectus*, large (about 1200–1800 ml) in *sapiens*.

The distinguished human palaeontologist Franz Weidenreich, who did so
much to make Pekin Man known to the world,[1128] was of opinion that human
evolution, from the primitive Java Man to modern man, was in fact what is
here called adastogenetic; for he considered that all known human fossils could
be arranged in a single series, and that no side-branches were produced.[1129]
He appears to have supposed that geographical isolation played little or no part
in human evolution, and that all races, mingled together in space, mated more
or less indiscriminately with one another. Geographical isolation, in his opinion, 'is not and cannot have been a prerequisite for the establishment of
speciations in man'; and he goes on to speak in a contemptuous manner,
strange indeed in a scientific book, of 'the eternal futility of human
isolation'.[1129] (These words appear to mean 'the eternal futility of a belief in
human isolation'.) For these reasons Weidenreich maintained that the whole
series of human fossils belonged to a single species, *Homo sapiens*.

It will be evident to the reader that arguments of this sort carry little weight.
Whether we regard the evolution of the genus *Homo* as kladogenetic or as
adastogenetic, the fact remains that if the skeleton of every human being who

had ever existed were available for study, the series would be complete and no one could possibly define, on objective evidence, the point at which a new specific name should be allowed. If, however, the absence of sudden discontinuity involves the necessity to allow only a single name, then Weidenreich does not go nearly far enough. The subhuman, apelike ancestor of the Pliocene must have the same name, *Homo sapiens*; so must the remote reptilian ancestor of the Mesozoic epoch, so also the amphibian that preceded it in the late Palaeozoic, and the fish that was ancestral to that, perhaps 300 million years ago: for there is no evidence or likelihood that any sudden break ever occurred between one generation and the next.

It is a practical convenience—nothing more than that—to recognize two stages in human evolution, *erectus* and *sapiens*. It does not matter whether we call them species or genera, or whether we recognize different genera (as was formerly done, and indeed still is by some authorities) in what is now usually called the 'species' *erectus*. We can name the ranks in the hierarchy as we please. There is nothing genuinely special about the species when we are studying fossil history.

## THE SPECIES IN THE MORPHOLOGICAL SENSE

The taxonomist in his museum receives from many parts of the world innumerable specimens of animals, usually unaccompanied by information that would enable him to apply any criteria, other than those derived from a study of structure, in distinguishing 'species' from one another. He is in much the same position as the palaeontologist, for he is forced to make somewhat arbitrary judgements as to whether two or more specimens are sufficiently similar to one another to fall into the same species. If no intermediates are known to exist, and the degree of difference is as great as that which usually separates well-known distinct species in the group of animals in which he specializes, he is justified in separating the two forms under different specific names. If he were unwilling to do this, knowledge could not be shared by different taxonomists, because they would not have verbal means of communication. On purely structural or 'morphological' grounds, therefore, a set of specimens is regarded as belonging to a single species, to which a name is given. A species of this sort is sometimes called a 'morphological species', which means a species defined on the basis of structure, without consideration of other criteria, such as its mating habits. A better name would be a 'species in the morphological sense'. Ideally, the naming of species on a purely morphological basis might eventually become unnecessary. Today, and in the foreseeable future, we cannot do without it.

A species in the morphological sense is not necessarily everywhere exactly the same. If it extends over a vast expanse of land, differences are usually observed in different places. Provided that these differences are gradual from each place to the next—less, that is to say, than the differences that usually occur between the recognized species in the particular taxon in question—all the forms are regarded as belonging to a single species. Sometimes there is a noticeable difference among the populations on the two sides of some geographical feature, such as a mountain range or wide river, which partially isolates them; but if there is no absolute distinction between the populations on the two sides that would enable one to determine with certainty from which side of the obstacle every specimen came, the two populations are regarded as belonging to the same species, but to different *subspecies* or *races* of it. The expression 'geographical race' is sometimes used, but the meaning is the same.

A species in the morphological sense might be found, by subsequent research, to be a species also in some other sense; but most species have been defined by the application of morphological criteria only.

## THE SPECIES IN THE GENETICAL SENSE

*Dans la nature, il n'existe que des individus & des suites d'individus, c'est à dire des espèces.*                                             Daubenton, 1754.[260]

According to Blumenbach,[108] the English naturalist John Ray was the first person to state that those animals should be placed in the same species which copulate together and have fertile progeny. I have not found a definite statement to this effect in the works of Ray. The latter discusses what is meant by 'species', in animals as well as plants, in his *Historia plantarum*, published in 1686;[881] but here he only indicates that in deciding whether to regard two forms as belonging to the same species, one should be guided not solely by structural difference or similarity, but by whether they originate from similar parental types: 'for those which differ specifically preserve their species [separately] for ever, and one species does not arise from the germ (*semine*) of another species, or conversely'. In another work[882] Ray briefly mentions the mule, but only asks why 'that hybridous Production should not again generate, and so a new race be carried on; but [that] Nature should stop here and proceed no further, is to me a mystery and unaccountable'.

The Comte de Buffon seems to have been the first to state quite definitely, in 1749, that the criterion of the species was the capacity to interbreed. He remarked that the kinds of animals are easier to distinguish by obvious differences than those of plants, and continued, 'Moreover, there is another advantage in recognizing the species of animals and distinguishing them from one another: this is the fact that one should regard as of the same species those which, by means of copulation, perpetuate themselves and preserve the likeness of this species; and as of different species, those which by the same means can produce nothing.'[159] He goes on to define species more exactly by the test that if members of different species do copulate together, their offspring—if any are produced—are infertile.

Later in the same century the Scottish physician named John Hunter, who has already been mentioned in Chapter 2 (p. 24), put forward a similar but curiously elaborate definition of the word 'species' in the course of his Inaugural Dissertation for the Degree of Doctor of Medicine at Edinburgh University.[524, 525] According to him it was 'A class of animals in which the individuals procreate with one another, and the descendants of which also procreate other animals which either already are, or subsequently become, similar to [other members of] the class'. By this he meant that the parental stocks might differ, but they were of the same species if the progeny of the hybrid offspring and its descendants, mating in each generation with members of one and the same parental stock, eventually produced individuals similar to members of that stock; one of the original stocks had merged with the other, and both were therefore to be regarded as belonging to the same species. It is a very strange coincidence that another Scot also named John Hunter, no less a person than the celebrated surgeon and anatomist of that name, put forward a similar but simpler idea a dozen years later, quite independently. He argued that 'The true distinction between different species of animals must ultimately, as appears to me, be gathered from their incapacity of propagating with each other an offspring capable of continuing itself, by subsequent propagations.'[526] He obtained evidence that the female wolf, and also the female jackal, could mate with dogs to produce a second generation of hybrids. On this evidence he concluded that these three kinds of animals belonged to the same species.[526, 527] Nowadays it is universally allowed that the European wolf (*Canis lupus*) and common jackal (*C. aureus*) belong to different species. The ancestry of the domestic dog (*C. familiaris*) is not known with certainty (see p. 362).

Dobzhansky's definition of the word 'species' is essentially a refined and sophisticated version of the ideas expressed by Buffon and the Hunters. 'Species in sexual cross-fertilizing organisms can be defined as groups of populations which are reproductively isolated to the extent that the exchange of genes between them is absent or so slow that the genetic differences are not diminished or swamped.'[277] One notices at once that those kinds of animals are excluded in which sexual reproduction does not occur; yet these kinds of animals are numerous, and zoologists are unanimous in recognizing species among them. However, man and all his near relatives in the animal world reproduce exclusively by sexual reproduction, and the use of the word 'species' in this different sense, applicable to asexually reproducing animals, need not detain us. A species defined by Dobzhansky's criterion is sometimes called a 'biological species', but this is an unfortunate expression. Any definition of species must necessarily be biological, since biology is the science of life. The term 'genetic species' is preferable, on the understanding that it means a species defined by 'gene-flow', that is to say, the spread of genes from one member of the group to another, but it is more accurate to speak of 'the species in the genetical sense'.

From what has been said, the reader might suppose that the word 'species' has a definite meaning when used in the genetical sense, though not when used in any other. In fact the definition, though useful, is not wholly satisfactory. Its most obvious defect is that it can only refer to a population as it exists during a very limited space of time, almost necessarily the present, and evolutionary history is therefore overlooked.

Strict application of Dobzhansky's definition results in certain very similar animals being assigned to different species. The malarial mosquitoes and their

relatives provide a remarkable example of this. The facts are not only extremely interesting from the purely scientific point of view, but also of great practical
importance in the maintenance of public health in malarious districts. It was
discovered in 1920 that one kind of the genus *Anopheles*, called *elutus*, could
be distinguished from the well-known malarial mosquito, *A. maculipennis*, by
certain minute differences in the adult, and by the fact that its its eggs looked
different; but for our detailed knowledge of this subject we are mainly indebted
to one Falleroni, a retired inspector of public health in Italy, who began in 1924
to breed *Anopheles* mosquitoes as a hobby. He noticed that several different
kinds of eggs could be distinguished, that the same female always laid eggs
having the same appearance, and that adult females derived from those eggs
produced eggs of the same type. He realized that although the adults all
appeared similar, there were in fact several different kinds, which he could
recognize by the markings on their eggs. Falleroni named several different
kinds after his friends, and the names he gave are the accepted ones today in
scientific nomenclature.

It was not until 1931 that the matter came to the attention of L. W. Hackett,
who, with A. Missiroli, did more than anyone else to unravel the details of this
curious story.[449, 447, 448] The facts are these. There are in Europe six different
kinds of *Anopheles* that cannot be distinguished with certainty from one
another in the adult state, however carefully they are examined under the
microscope by experts; a seventh kind, *elutus*, can be distinguished by minor
differences if its age is known. The larvae of two of the kinds can be distinguished from one another by minute differences (in the type of palmate hair
on the second segment, taken in conjunction with the number of branches of
hair no. 2 on the fourth and fifth segments). Other supposed differences
between the kinds, apart from those in the eggs, have been shown to be unreal.

In nature the seven kinds are not known to interbreed, and it is therefore
necessary, under Dobzhansky's definition, to regard them all as separate
species.

The males of six of the seven species have the habit of 'swarming' when
ready to copulate. They join in groups of many individuals, humming, high in
the air; suddenly the swarm bursts asunder and rejoins. The females recognize
the swarms of males of their own species, and are attracted towards them.
Each female dashes in, seizes a male, and flies off, copulating.

With the exceptions mentioned, the only visible differences between the
species occur at the egg-stage. The eggs of six of the seven species are shown in
Fig. 8 (p. 76).

It will be noticed that each egg is roughly sausage-shaped, with an air-filled float at
each side, which supports it in the water in which it is laid. The eggs of the different
species are seen to differ in the length and position of the floats. The surface of the rest of
the egg is covered all over with microscopic finger-shaped papillae, standing up like the
pile of a carpet. It is these papillae that are responsible for the distinctive patterns seen on
the eggs of the different species. Where the papillae are long and their tips rough, light is
reflected to give a whitish appearance; where they are short and smooth, light passes
through to reveal the underlying surface of the egg, which is black. The biological
significance of these apparently trivial differences is unknown.

From the point of view of the ethnic problem the most interesting fact is this. Although the visible differences between the species are trivial and confined or almost confined to the egg-stage, it is evident that the nervous and sensory systems are different, for each species has its own habits. The males of one species (*atroparvus*) do not swarm. It has already been mentioned that the females recognize the males of their own species. Some of the species lay their eggs in fresh water, others in brackish. The females of some species suck the blood of cattle, and are harmless to man; those of other species suck the blood of man, and in injecting their saliva transmit malaria to him.

8    *The eggs of six species of the genus* Anopheles

1, *melanoon*; 2, *messeae*; 3, *maculipennis*; 4, *atroparvus*; 5, *labranchiae*; 6, *elutus.*
*From Hackett and Missiroli.* [449]

Examples could be quoted of other species that are distinguishable from one another by morphological differences no greater than those that separate the species of *Anopheles*; but the races of a single species—indeed, the subraces of a single race—are often distinguished from one another, in their typical forms, by obvious differences, affecting many parts of the body. It is not the case that species are necessarily very distinct, and races very similar.

It is commonly supposed that the species in the genetical sense is distinguished from the race by the fact that the former is cut off from reproduction with other species (in the ordinary circumstances of wild life), while the subspecies or race is not, because interbreeding is known to occur where races of the same species come into contact at the margins of their territories, or the forms pass over into one another by such slight or insensible gradations in the intermediate region that hybridization must be assumed. Yet this distinction between the species and the race is by no means so rigid as these words would imply. The very complicated case of the herring gull illustrates this fact particularly well. It has been thoroughly investigated by independent authors, especially   Stegman,[1005]   Mayaud,[716]   and   Stresemann   and   Timofeeff-

Ressovsky;[1020] and it deserves rather detailed study, because it gives further warning that we should not lay too much stress on the question whether any particular group of related organisms is to be considered as a single species or not.

The Danish writer Pontoppidan was the first to give a specific name to herring gulls. He gave the name of *Larus argentatus* to Scandinavian specimens. When it was discovered that there were many races of the species *Larus argentatus* Pontopp., the Scandinavian race took the name of *Larus argentatus argentatus*, in accordance with the rules of nomenclature, or simply *argentatus* for short in studies of races. The British race of this species,

9    *Species or races?*

A, herring gull (race *argenteus*); B, lesser black-backed gull (race *britannicus* = *graellsii*). *Specimens in the Oxford University Museum, photographed by Mr. J. Haywood.*

*argenteus*, is very similar to *argentatus*. A member of it is shown in Fig. 9A. The back and wings (apart from their black-and-white tips) are silvery or very pale blue-grey; the feet have a somewhat rosy tint, and are usually described as flesh-coloured. Gulls of the same general type may be followed across the Atlantic past Iceland to Canada, and thence across the Behring Straits to Asia and all the way along the northern part of that continent until the circle round the pole is completed by overlap with the habitat of *argentatus* in the White Sea, east of the Scandinavian peninsula. Any zoologist who has followed this route westwards from Scandinavia will have passed through the territories of seven races when he has completed his journey, and will have left on his right-hand side another race in Greenland and yet another in the Hudson's Bay district. During the course of his journey the traveller will have noticed a progressive change in the characters of the seven races. The backs and wings of the gulls will have become pale slate-grey, darker slate-grey, and finally almost blackish; their feet will have passed through intermediate shades to yellow, their wings will have become relatively longer and their whole bodies larger. The gradual transition is attributed to interbreeding at the racial boundaries. A chain of related forms, replacing one another progressively, was given the name of 'cline' by Professor J. S. Huxley.[533] Many examples of clines could be quoted, but a complete circle round the world is exceptional.

On the evidence so far given, no one would doubt that all these races were members of a single species. But *argentatus* and another form *L. argentatus antelius* themselves flatly contradict this supposition; for on meeting in the White Sea they do not breed together (though sexual attraction between some individuals of the two forms has been reported). Thus the zoologist who travelled westward round the world from Norway until he first reached the territory of *antelius* would be inclined to put all the herring gulls he had seen in the same species; but if he had started in the opposite direction he would almost certainly have put *argentatus* and *antelius* in different species as soon as he had reached the White Sea and had observed that the two forms did not merge into one another in their physical characters and did not interbreed.

In Asia a second, more southerly, chain of four races of herring gulls springs from one of the members of the chain of seven, goes through the Caspian and Black Seas to both northern and southern shores of the Mediterranean, emerges through the Straits of Gibraltar as *atlantis*, and spreads southwards along the coast of Africa and also northwards to the Portuguese coast. The Mediterranean race, *michahellesi*, also extends to the Atlantic and breeds as far north as the north-west corner of Spain.

A northerly side-shoot from the first member of this chain of races constitutes yet another race, *omissus*, which enters the Baltic Sea. Here it behaves exactly as *antelius* does in the White Sea: it encounters *argentatus*, but does not breed with it.

In northern Europe, in a zone extending from the eastern end of the Scandinavian peninsula to the British Isles, and also down the Atlantic coast to Africa, there is another group of three races commonly called lesser black-backed gulls, or *Larus fuscus* Linn. These three, *fuscus, intermedius,* and *britannicus,* are rather similar to one another. They tend to be smaller than herring gulls, though there is overlap in size; the feet are yellow and the back and wings very dark slate-grey, almost black. The wings are longer relatively to body-size than in herring gulls. Those races of herring gulls that end the westerly sequences that we have been considering—*antelius* in the White Sea, *omissus* in the Baltic, *atlantis* and *michahellesi* in the Atlantic—are precisely those that reach or approach most closely to the territory of the lesser black-backed gulls *and show the strongest resemblance to the latter*. The lesser black-backed gulls give the impression of being the final members of the series. Stegman says that the British lesser black-backed gull (*britannicus*) is 'amazingly' ('*verblüffend*') similar to the herring gull *antelius*;[1005] but the territories of these two races do not actually overlap. Stresemann and Timofeeff-Ressovsky actually classify *atlantis* with the lesser black-backed gulls in one place (p. 62) in their paper,[1020] though not in other places in the same paper; and they say that interbreeding between *atlantis* and *britannicus* occurs occasionally. (Mayaud, to whom they refer, does not record this.)

Stegman states that *argentatus* forms mixed colonies with *britannicus* on the coast of Holland, and that a certain amount of hybridization occurs, with production of intermediates.[1005] He does not make it clear whether by *argentatus* he here means *L. argentatus argentatus* or *L. argentatus argenteus*. In the Moray Firth, on the east coast of northern Scotland, the British herring gull (*argenteus*) shares a breeding-ground with *britannicus*, but hybridization does not occur.[904]

Seventeen races have been mentioned (though not all of them have been named) in the above account, and another race in Asia brings the total to eighteen. On the evidence of gradation in characters and genetic continuity through occasional interbreeding, all these might seem to constitute a single species. If so, the correct name for it is *Larus fuscus* Linn., since this has priority over the others. The failure to interbreed in certain places has, however, resulted in the suggestion that two species should be recognized: (1) *L. fuscus* (the *fuscus-britannicus* group of three races) and (2) *L. argentatus* (all the rest). It has also been suggested that there are three: (1) *L. fuscus* (as before); (2) *L. argentatus* (the herring gulls of northern Europe, the British Isles, Iceland, Greenland, and Canada); and (3) *L. cachinnans* (comprising the whole of the chain of races that starts on the Asiatic side of the Behring Straits and ends in *antelius*, *omissus*, *michahellesi*, and *atlantis*).

In such cases as this it seems best to discard the idea of species altogether, and to think simply of a group of races, all of which are linked together by insensible or almost insensible gradations in physical characters in such a way that they replace one another geographically, with occasional interbreeding. A group of races of this sort falls into the category called *Formenkreis* (p. 82).*

Another bird, almost as familiar in the interior of Great Britain as the herring gull is on its coasts, presents a curious parallel to what has just been described, though in this case the circle is completed not round the North Pole, but round a huge area comprising the central Asian massif and the deserts of Takla Makan and Gobi to the north of it. The great tit, *Parus major*, has an immense range, extending all the way from the British Isles to Japan, both south and north of the area just defined. A large number of races has been described, but it is not necessary for the present purpose to mention more than three. The European races, typified by *Parus major major*, are greenish on the back and yellow below. As one follows this bird eastwards to Persia and beyond, there is a progressive loss of the yellow pigment in the feathers, until the back has become grey and the belly white (*P. major bokharensis*). Further east, in southern China, a yellow-green patch has appeared on the nape of the neck; this is the race (*P. major minor*) that extends to Japan.[892]

If we now follow the bird from Europe across the continent *north* of the mountainous and desert area, it remains much more constant in colour, and may be regarded throughout as *P. major major*. The narrow tip of its eastern range just reaches the Pacific Ocean and the Sea of Okhotsk, north of the northernmost island of Japan. In one particular area, however, *P. major major* completes the circle by overlapping with *P. major minor*. The overlap occurs in the area partly enclosed by the great northern loop of the Amur River, in Manchuria. This area has been very carefully studied by Stegman.[1004] Although he could not state positively that *P. major major* and *P. major minor* never hybridize in the region of overlap, he could find no evidence of it. Each race maintains its integrity. Just as with the gulls, the two races appear as 'good species' where their ranges overlap. As Stegman mildly remarks, 'On this subject I only want to say that the difference between species and subspecies is not fundamental.'[1004]

Many comparable examples could be quoted of what Stresemann and Timofeeff-Ressovsky[1020] call 'the transgression of subspecific areas without

* For an interesting suggestion about the way in which the Ice Age may have influenced the evolution of the races considered in the foregoing paragraphs, see Schweppenburg.[952]

the formation of intermediate forms and hybrid populations'. These authors quote seven confirmed cases among birds and eleven probable ones. Races that share the territories of other races without hybridizing often avoid one another by occupying different ecological niches within the shared territory, though, as the gulls show, this does not necessarily happen.

Certain non-marine animals that live on oceanic islands, surrounded by a vast expanse of sea, present a problem for anyone who would define the species by the genetical criterion. The sea prevents any effective gene-flow from a continent (though an occasional straggler may arrive, as must have happened in the distant past, when the island was first populated). The isolated population often begins to change in colour or morphological characters, so that one can distinguish the island specimens from members of the typical continental species. In such cases it is customary to make a guess as to whether the two forms would breed together, if they chanced to meet under natural conditions of life. If this is thought probable, the island form is regarded as a race of the continental species.[178] It is clear that the definition of a species in such cases depends not on objective proof of gene-flow, nor even on the likelihood of its occurrence, but only on the probability that such flow would occur if something else occurred which is not known to occur. The same drawback to the definition exists if the island form is not distinguishable from that on the mainland, since no significant gene-flow has occurred. The inclusion of the island form in the same species as the continental is pragmatically useful, because it calls attention to the morphological similarity (or identity) of the two populations, but the use of gene-flow in the definition of the word 'species' loses authority from this practice.

A curiously analogous case is presented by those castes in India that practise strict endogamy. From the time when such castes originated, the exchange of genes with the rest of the population was at an end. A rigidly enforced custom here takes the place of the ocean in isolating a particular class of persons. Strict application of Dobzhansky's definition might cause one to regard the members of such a caste as constituting a separate species of man, even though no morphological character could be relied on to determine whether a person belonged to the caste or not. It may be argued that the absence of structural differences proves that the members of a caste do not constitute a separate species; but if so, the definition rests on a morphological basis, not on the presence or absence of gene-flow.

## REALGATTUNG, FORMENKREIS, AND RASSENKREIS

The writings of Immanuel Kant on the species problem are of extraordinary interest. They belong in part to their time, but here and there the great philosopher seems to have looked far forward into the future.

Kant draws a sharp distinction between 'the description of nature' (*Naturbeschreibung*) and 'natural history' (*Naturgeschichte*).[564] The former, a product of what he rather contemptuously calls the 'academic system' (*Schulsystem*), is a mere description of nature as it now exists, while the latter is literally a history—an account of events in time, *including the origin of races*. To understand him it is necessary to realize that the word *Gattung*, in his writings, means an interbreeding stock, not a 'genus' in the formal sense. He remarks that classification into *Gattungen* 'is based on the common law of propagation, and the unity of the *Gattungen* is nothing else than the unity of the ability to procreate', which prevails widely among animals that show a considerable degree of diversity.

Therefore Buffon's rule, that animals which together produce fertile offspring (whatever differences of form there may be between them) nevertheless belong to one and the same physical *Gattung*, must properly be regarded as the definition of a natural *Gattung* of animals, in contradistinction to all academic *Gattungen* of them. Academic classification extends to *classes*, which it divides according to *resemblances*, while natural classification divides according to *relationships*, by taking reproduction into account. The former provides an academic system for the memory, the latter a natural system for the understanding. The first has as its purpose only to arrange creatures under names, the second to bring them under laws.[564]

It is significant that Kant's thoughts on this subject arose from the fact that it was one of his functions to lecture on physical geography. He recognized that as plants and animals spread over the surface of the globe, each original kind (*Stammgattung*) underwent evolutionary modification (*Anartung*). In his view it already contained the germs (*Anlagen*) that would enable it to transform itself in appropriate ways when it encountered new soils and climates; but the recognizably different forms (*Racen*) retained the capacity to breed with one another and produce fertile offspring. He dispensed with the idea of morphological species (*Arten*) and looked at the whole set of different *Racen* as a 'genuine interbreeding stock' or *Realgattung*, to be distinguished sharply from the academic *Nominalgattung*, in the definition of which no regard was paid to the processes of reproduction. For Kant, then, the grouping of animals was best expressed by the recognition of realities, namely of *Realgattungen*, each of which, spreading widely, might evolve into many geographical races (*Racen*).[565] In dispensing with the species and recognizing as valid only two taxa, the *Realgattung* and *Racen*, Kant was well over a century ahead of his time.

Applying these principles, Kant pronounced that all human beings belonged to 'one and the same natural *Gattung*', which he divided into only four *Racen*, of which three (essentially the Europid, Negrid, and Mongolid) are still recognized today. He thought the Europid was the original stock from which the others had diverged.[565]

Anxious as he was to concentrate on realities, Kant nevertheless allowed himself to theorize on the origin of the *Realgattungen*. He seems to have come to the conclusion that these might have arisen from ancestral forms just as *Racen* had originated from *Stammgattungen* (though he did not state his opinion in exactly this way). His thoughts on this subject are expressed, surprisingly enough, in his celebrated philosophical work *Critik der Urtheilskraft*.[566, 567] He reveals himself here as one prepared to speculate freely about the distant past—or, to use his own quaint expression, to act as 'an archaeologist of nature'. He was even prepared to include man himself in his grand evolutionary scheme. The resemblance of many *Gattungen* to others was due, he thought, to their genuine relationship, and in theory they could be traced back

> through the gradual approximation of one *Gattung* of animals to another ... from man all the way to the polyp ... In this matter the archaeologist of nature, relying on any mechanism known to or conceived by him, is free to imagine that a great family of creatures originated from *Spuren* [? primitive forms] that survived the earliest turmoils*; for one must regard those creatures as a family, if the universal and continuous relationship, already mentioned, is to have a foundation in fact.

He supposed that the earth, developing through these turmoils from its original chaotic state, brought forth 'at first creatures of less well-adapted form, and that these in their turn perfected themselves in adaptation to their place of origin and their interactions with one another'. In a footnote Kant remarks that there must be few scientists to whom such ideas have not occurred.

The idea of the *Realgattung*—though not the revolutionary ideas that inspired the 'archaeologist of nature'—did indeed eventually occur, entirely independently, to another German thinker. It was in the last decade of the following century that Otto Kleinschmidt, a naturalist and at one time a Protestant clergyman, began to expound his *Formenkreis* doctrine, to which he devoted many papers and eventually, more than a quarter of a century later, a book.[592, 593] At first he was unaware that his *Formenkreis* and *Rassen* corresponded closely to Kant's *Realgattung* and *Racen*. When at last he stumbled on the latter's writings, he discarded for a time the use of *Formenkreis* and adopted *Realgattung* in its place. Kant, however, had been interested principally (though by no means exclusively) in the human *Realgattung* and its component *Racen*, while Kleinschmidt had a vastly greater knowledge of animals. Like Kant, he rejected the idea of species (*Arten*) because it represented an unreality. He considered that the word was too much associated with morphology, and too little with actual relationship. In one respect, however, his *Formenkreis* differed from Kant's *Realgattung*. In an early paper, delivered to the German Ornithological Society, he gave in a single sentence the gist of the doctrine to which he was to devote the whole of his energies in the field of science. 'It is not possible', he claimed, 'to distinguish sharply between "good species" and "mere geographical races", because good species may often be geographical representatives of one another.'[591] Thus, wherever two different forms replaced one another geographically, he regarded them as *Rassen* of a single *Formenkreis*, without regard to whether they interbred with one another or not. A single *Formenkreis* therefore often included as *Rassen* many 'good species' of the old systematics, and was thus a much wider term (though he allowed that a *Formenkreis* might in certain cases consist of only a single *Rasse*).

It may be remarked in passing that Kleinschmidt was inclined to place the Neanderthalians and Broken Hill man, and possibly also *Pithecanthropus*, in the same *Formenkreis* as the races of modern man.[593]

---

* Possibly Kant meant revolutions of the earth in the astronomical sense.

The *Formenkreis* resembles 'the species in the genetical sense', but it seems to provide a better representation of reality because it takes some account of the evolutionary history of the forms included in it, instead of being based only on the existence of gene-exchange at a particular time. An important part of Kleinschmidt's doctrine, however, is not acceptable. He considered that each *Formenkreis* had evolved, independently of all others, from a primitive ancestor that had existed in the most remote times. Actual relationship or sharing of common ancestors was thus in his opinion non-existent except within the *Formenkreis*. This implies an incredible degree of adastogenetic parallel evolution. The valuable component of the *Formenkreislehre* is unfortunately impaired by its association with this untenable hypothesis. When he tried to trace his *Formenkreise* back in time, he seems to have been baffled by the same difficulties as are implicit in 'the species in the palaeontological sense', and to have tried to escape them by denying the reality of kladogenesis, except within the *Formenkreis*.

The term *Rassenkreis* was introduced by the German authority on taxonomic principles Bernhard Rensch, who developed his ideas on this subject in a number of papers and books.[891, 892, 894] He found it 'absolutely necessary' to depart from the idea of species as used in the old systematics, and to use instead the idea of '*Rassenkreis* or *Formenkreis*'; and when this was done, he found that all distinction between species and races disappeared.[891] He pointed out that the races of a single *Rassenkreis* often do not differ less from one another than 'good species' do. He allowed, however, that these 'good species' do exist, especially among cosmopolitan or nearly cosmopolitan forms (for instance, certain Protozoa), which seem to be everywhere the same. There are also 'young species', which have not yet had time to spread over a wide area and become diversified, and also 'relict species', somehow cut off in ancient times in a restricted area, from which escape was impossible. For all these he continued, unlike Kleinschmidt, to use the term *Arten* or species. Rensch's writings are more erudite than Kleinschmidt's, but it is questionable whether he could not have expressed his ideas while retaining the latter's terminology (as he did at first), or Kant's.

Unlike Kant and Kleinschmidt, Rensch took cognizance of the fact that animals may become separated in space and gradually develop in several territories into distinct forms that subsequently come together in a shared environment after having diverged sufficiently to be able to avoid hybridity. To this occurrence the term 'disisolation' may perhaps be applied. One does not know whether Kleinschmidt would have included disisolated forms in a single *Formenkreis*. Some of the gastropods (snail-like animals) of Lake Baikal seem to provide a particularly striking example of disisolation. This great expanse of water contains no fewer than 33 forms of the pectinibranch family Baikalidae (related to the very common *Viviparus* of British fresh waters). The members of this family, which are not known to hybridize, occur nowhere else in the world except in the region of Lake Baikal, and it is hard to understand how the ancestral form could have undergone so much kladogenetic evolution without the help of geographical isolation. Some authorities have supposed that the animals of the lake are a relict fauna of what was originally part of the sea, but the evidence against this appears to be conclusive. [667] Rensch supposes that geographical isolation may have played a part in the evolutionary process.[892] His hypothesis is that many of the 33 forms have originated separately as races in waters connected with the lake, and that changes in the inflow and outflow systems, caused by earth movements, provided isolated areas in which these races diverged further, until subsequent geotectonic changes allowed them to come together in the main body of water as 'good species', too distinct to hybridize.

Not only in Lake Baikal, but wherever two or more closely related but distinct kinds of animals live together in the same place and in the same ecological niche in it, there must almost certainly have been isolation followed by disisolation; for otherwise kladogenetic evolution could scarcely have occurred. It cannot reasonably be doubted, despite Weidenreich's opinion (p. 71), that partial geographical isolation played an essential role in the evolution of human races, which, in their typical forms, differ so markedly from one another. The subsequent disisolation which has now been going on for a long time, was caused not by geotectonic changes, such as may have brought together the incipient species of Baikalidae, but by modern inventions. The Victorian anthropologist Dr. J. Beddoe recognized this long ago. 'The ever-increasing rapidity of local migration and intermixture', he wrote in 1885, 'due to the extension of railways and the altered conditions of society, will in the next generation almost inextricably confuse the limits and proportions of the British races.'[69] He was referring to Europe, and should have referred to 'subraces'; but the steamship and now the aeroplane have brought the *races* together in space to an extent never known before. Without these mechanical devices the kladogenetic evolution of human races might possibly have gone further, and produced in the end genetic barriers to hybridity in addition to the psychological ones that have a partial isolating effect today.

# 6 Hybridity and the species problem

EVOLUTIONARY ADVANCE must have been due mainly to the repeated splitting of one species into two or more ('kladogenesis', p. 69), for otherwise there would be no such taxa of animals as genera, families, and orders, but only unrelated stocks. Adastogenesis, or evolutionary change without such splitting, must as a general rule occur temporarily and end in reversion to kladogenesis or in extinction. But kladogenesis implies that one interbreeding stock becomes two or more; and this can only happen when two or more races originate and cease, or nearly cease, to interbreed with one another. Races may originate, for instance, as a result of geotectonic changes, such as the broadening of a river or the uprising of a chain of mountains, with the consequent division of the previously continuous population into partly separated groups. Isolation caused in this way can seldom be sudden and complete. If the races are to evolve eventually into separate stocks ('species'), despite the fact that isolation is incomplete, there must be a tendency towards the mating of individuals that closely resemble one another, and a revulsion against sexual partnership with those that clearly belong to a distinct population. As Broca tritely remarks, 'Animals that live in complete liberty and only obey their natural instincts seek ordinarily for their amours other animals that are altogether similar to their own kind, and mate almost always with their own species.'[139] Sexual revulsion against slightly different kinds is only a particularly sharply marked example of the natural tendency of animals to avoid mating with widely different forms, belonging to different species, genera, families, or orders.

It is thinkable that new taxa might originate without physical isolation, through the tendency of those individuals that chanced to resemble one another most closely in appearance or odour or behaviour to congregate together and select one another as sexual mates; but it is not likely that a tendency of this sort has played any important part in evolution. Partial isolation and evolutionary change must ordinarily come first, before the recognition of 'own kind' steps in to make the separateness of the taxa more complete.

The exceptional occurrence of hybridity between different species of animals living under natural conditions is discussed below (p. 89). Indiscriminate interbreeding between distinct forms, whether 'species' or markedly different races, is not generally beneficial. The defect may show in a change in the sex-ratio of the offspring, probably caused by the early abortion of members of one sex, generally the male in the case of mammals. It is possible for two related forms to occupy the same territory but to avoid mating with one another, because their mating seasons are at different times of the year, or because their habitats within the territory are different; but in many cases isolation is maintained by the marked preference of each form for a mate of its own kind. The nature of the preferences, and the mechanisms by which hybridity is avoided, are widely different in different groups of animals.

In certain fishes a few of the rays of the male's anal fin are lengthened to support an elongated copulatory organ (gonopodium), which is grooved or hollowed out for the passage of spermatozoa to the female. This occurs, for instance, in the guppy, *Poecilia reticulata*, a tropical American species commonly kept as a pet in warm-water aquaria. The male of this species touches the genital papilla of the female with the tip of the organ after an elaborate courtship display.[81, 82] In the fresh waters of its natural habitat in Guyana this fish lives in company with three other species of the same genus. The mechanism by which the four species remain genetically isolated from one another has been investigated in great detail both in the natural habitat and in the laboratory.[666]The facts are complicated and cannot be accurately condensed into a short statement, but the general principle of the isolating or anti-hybridity process may be roughly stated as follows. The males court the females by performing rather elaborate dances, which are different in the different species. The females respond only to the dances of males of their own species. Their responses, though slight, are a necessary stimulus to the male, who discontinues his dance unless stimulated. If stimulated by the correct response, the male perseveres in his display and the female permits the transfer of spermatozoa. The males gradually learn by experience to prefer to display before females of their own species.

Very close association between members of related species is compatible with complete genetic isolation, even in cases where little or no help is derived from differences in the processes of courtship. Two species of gazelle provide an example. *Gazella granti* and *G. thomsoni* live together in mixed herds in the great Ngorongoro crater of Tanzania. The two species are rather similar in appearance, and newcomers to the district almost invariably confuse them.[315]

There are, nevertheless, certain differences in coloration.* The dark stripe along the face is less clearly marked in *granti* than in *thomsoni*, and extends above the eye (instead of stopping short); the dark band along each side of the body is usually rather indistinct in *granti*, while the white area of rump is somewhat more extensive in this species, and sends forward a little projection on each side, in the form of an equilateral triangle, which is absent in *thomsoni*. There is a difference also in height at the shoulder, *granti* being the taller, and its horns are larger and more distinctly lyrate in shape.[690, 954, 315]The scent-glands of the face (pre-orbital glands), which are used to mark out territory by deposit of the secretion on grass, are smaller in *granti*; and the inguinal glands, which produce a musky odour, are present in both sexes in *thomsoni* but absent in *granti*.[315]

No one knows what 'isolating mechanism' prevents copulation between these two gazelles that resemble one another so closely in most respects and live in such very close association. The courting and mating behaviour of the two species is remarkably similar.[315] Possibly the mechanism is visual, but odour from the inguinal glands may presumably play a part. (On the subject of odour, see Chapter 10, p. 161.)

---

* A stuffed male *Gazella granti* is publicly exhibited in the British Museum (Natural History), in the first-floor gallery of the main hall. The markings have faded slightly. The Museum possesses a very fine collection of skins, horns, and skulls of both species.

Skulls play such a large part in human taxonomy that it is interesting to compare those of the two species of gazelles that live in such close association but do not attempt to interbreed. They are remarkably similar, very much more so than those of an Eskimo and a Lapp, for instance, and indeed than those of a typical Nordid and a typical Alpinid, though the two latter are only *subraces* of the Europid *race*. The skull of *granti* is larger, but the only morphological differences are rather trivial.

The skull of *thomsoni* is slightly convex on top in the parietal region, while that of *granti* is nearly flat. In the latter species the facial part of the lacrimal bone is somewhat hollowed out to hold the large pre-orbital gland. This hollow, the lacrimal fossa, extends on to the jugal and maxilla. In *granti* the fossa is shallower, and situated largely on the jugal; it does not extend on to the maxilla. The jugal projects further forward on the face than in *thomsoni*. The paroccipital process of the exoccipital is more sharply pointed in *thomsoni* than in *granti*.[49] The notch in the orbital margin of the frontal, which is present in *granti* and various other gazelles, is scarcely indicated [444] or absent[49] in *thomsoni*. It is doubtful whether any of these differences in the skulls would be noticed by a person untrained in osteology, yet he or she would instantly see how unlike are the skulls of Eskimos and Lapps.

In the distant past these two gazelles (and the others of the same genus) must have had a common ancestor. Since the recognition of difference promotes evolutionary change, it is perhaps not surprising that special adaptations sometimes evolve that have the effect of making recognition easier. If isolation is beneficial, because hybrids are in some way at a disadvantage in the struggle for existence, the process of natural selection may result in the exaggeration of the visible differences, until these suffice in themselves to act as a barrier to copulation, without the necessity for the evolution of distinctive courtship displays. Two species of nuthatches provide a good example of this interesting evolutionary process, which shows clearly the advantage of avoiding hybridity. The two birds, *Sitta neumayeri* and *S. syriaca* (=*tephronota*), are very similar in appearance. *S. syriaca* is slightly the larger, and somewhat paler above; the black stripe along the side of the head, familiar in the British species, is a little broader and extends further down the neck than in *S. neumayeri*.[282] The latter is a western species, ranging from Dalmatia to Iran, while *S. syriaca* replaces it towards the east and does not extend into Europe. They clearly belong to the same *Formenkreis*, since one replaces the other geographically. In parts of Iran, however, the two forms overlap in range, and here a most interesting change occurs in both of them, which has been studied in detail. They have become much more distinctly different in the only territory in which the chance to hybridize could occur.[1088] In Iran the dark stripe is much wider and extends much further back, far behind the head, in *S. syriaca*, while in the other species, in this particular locality, it hardly exists behind the eye, and indeed has become almost obsolete. *S. syriaca* is also a distinctly larger bird in Iran, with a disproportionately larger beak. It must not be supposed, however, that exaggerated recognition marks are usual at the boundaries between one race and another.

In many of the lower marine animals there is nothing that can properly be called selection of sexual partners, for the male and female germ-cells are simply cast into the sea, and the fusion of the spermatozoon with an egg of the same species depends on the selective abilities of these cells, not of the adults that produced them (though restriction of the breeding season may aid the process). Marine vertebrates do not ordinarily cast their genital products indiscriminately into the water. Among the bony fishes it is usual for large numbers of males and females of the same species to congregate together for a communal sexual act. The French have a special word, *la fraye* (not to be confused with *la frai*, spawned eggs), to designate this sexual assembly.[81] There is here mutual recognition of 'own kind', but no pairing-off or selection of particular mates. The males and females simply cast their products into the water in the limited space occupied by the group as a whole.

In some species of bony fishes several males may associate with a single female and cast out their spermatozoa into the water to fertilize her extruded eggs, while in others only one male associates with one female for this purpose. Actual copulation is rather unusual in the bony fishes, but an example has already been quoted (p. 86).

The ancestors of all higher vertebrates are to be sought among the Crossopterygii, a group of fishes that originated in middle Devonian times, some 300 million years ago. A member of this group, the celebrated coelacanth, *Latimeria chalumnae*, still lives in the Indian Ocean, off the coast of Africa, but unfortunately nothing is known about its reproductive habits.[746] No copulatory organ has been described. The lung-fishes (Dipnoi) are an aberrant group, apparently related to the Crossopterygii, that have also lingered on to the present day. In this group also we have no information about the fertilization of the eggs,[824] but since in three of them—the South American *Lepidosiren paradoxa*,[578] and the African *Protopterus annectens*[158] and *P. aethiopicus*[437]—the eggs are laid in nests, it is certain that there is some kind of association between the sexes; and in the two first-named, the male guards the young.

From what is known about the habits of bony fishes in general and of lung-fishes in particular, it seems very unlikely that the ancestral fresh-water Crossopterygii of the mid-Devonian reproduced by random extrusion of spermatozoa and eggs, without *fraye* or actual copulation; and their immediate descendants, the early Amphibia, no doubt also had some form of sexual association, like their descendants of the present day. It follows that from those ancient days onwards till today, throughout their crossopterygian, amphibian, reptilian, and mammalian stages, the ancestors of man needed to recognize their 'own kind' with certainty. One cannot say with confidence, even quite roughly, how many generations there have been in the ancestry of man since the days of early Crossopterygii; but an estimate based on knowledge of the age at maturity and reproductive life-span of various groups suggests that there must have been at the very least sixty million; and in every one of these generations, without a single exception through all those millions of years, the parents recognized their 'own kind' when they performed the sexual act. By 'own kind' is here meant animals sufficiently similar to their own stock—that is, to their actual relatives—to make it possible for copulation to result in a continuous sequence of generations.

The ability to recognize a member of its own kind as an appropriate partner in the sexual act is such an obvious necessity to a vast number of different kinds of animals, including all terrestrial ones, that it tends to be taken for granted by the non-biologist. Yet it is one of the most fundamental characters of all those innumerable animals, of very diverse groups, in which either a *fraye* or an actual copulatory act is a necessary antecedent to reproduction.

## HYBRIDITY UNDER NATURAL CONDITIONS OF LIFE

It is allowed, by those who use the 'genetical' criterion, that members of different species do occasionally mate with one another and produce fertile offspring. It is claimed, however, that there is a sharp distinction between this process on one hand and interbreeding between members of different races (subspecies) of a single species on the other. In the latter case, interbreeding produces offspring showing a smooth gradation of characters, already familiar among the parent stocks, which anyhow cannot be sharply separated; whereas when different species chance to interbreed, markedly strange offspring result, differing sharply from one another and from parent stocks.[178] It was mentioned in Chapter 1 (p. 11) that Neanderthal man and *Homo sapiens* in the narrower sense are thought by some authorities to have interbred in Palestine, and to have produced some strangely diverse forms. This may suggest that the parental populations should be regarded as having belonged to different species.

Nevertheless, doubt must arise as to whether the degree of diversity of the offspring does or does not suffice, in any particular case, to cause the taxonomist to place the parental stocks in different species. The carrion and hooded crows provide an example. It is a familiar fact that these two forms are very different in appearance, for the former is iridescent black all over, while the hooded kind has part of the back and almost the whole of the underparts pale grey. The carrion crow inhabits England, France, part of Spain, western and southern Germany, Switzerland, and the Italian and Austrian Alps. The hooded crow is found in Ireland, northern Scotland, Scandinavia, and central Europe roughly as far west as the River Elbe; its eastern range extends to the Ural Mountains, Asia Minor, and Iran.[732, 802] The territories of the two forms overlap along a strip of country running very roughly south-west to north-east through Scotland (Fig. 10) and north to south through central Europe. The continental strip varies considerably in width, averaging about 65 kilometres. It is thought that the two forms having diverged in past times from a common ancestor, came to occupy separate areas, and then re-established contact in a 'zone of secondary intergradation' or 'hybrid belt',[717] so called because a certain amount of interbreeding occurs in the regions of overlap. The hybrids do not provide a smooth gradation between the parental types, but tend to differ from one another (as well as from both the parental stocks). Anyone who considers the diversity of the offspring sufficient may regard the carrion and hooded crows as different species, *Corvus corone* and *C. cornix*; those who minimize this diversity place the parental stocks in a single species, *Corvus corone*, and make two subspecies or races, *C. corone corone* and *C. corone cornix*. Kleinschmidt, naturally enough, regards them simply as races of a single *Formenkreis*.[593]

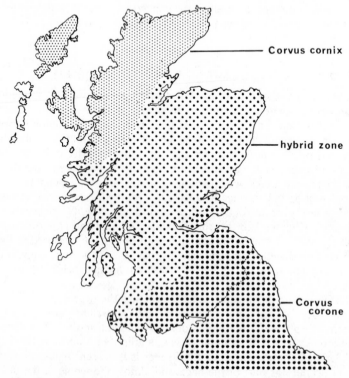

10  *Scotland and part of northern England, to show the 'hybrid zone' between the areas occupied predominantly by hooded and carrion crows.*
Map drawn from the data of Meise. [732]

It has been argued that in cases of this sort the important question is whether the genetic constitution of the two forms is changed *outside* the actual zone of hybridization.[86] It is freely admitted that genes may pass from one species to another in certain circumstances, by interbreeding; indeed, a special term, 'introgression', is used to designate this occurrence. This need not necessarily change either of the species into which the other's genes have introgressed, because the foreign elements may have a disadvantageous effect and as a result be eliminated by natural selection. Nevertheless it is allowed that where hybridity occurs in nature, a sharp distinction between species and subspecies (races) cannot be drawn.[718]

In certain circumstances a species may actually originate in nature by hybridity. The ducks (*Anas*) provide an example. A new species, *A. oustaleti*, was discovered in 1856. It occurs only in Guam and two neighbouring islands of the Mariana group (south of Japan). Careful research has shown that it originated by hybridization.[1163] *Anas poecilorhyncha* is resident in many islands in this part of the world (Caroline and Paulau Islands, Philippines, and Japan). Members of this species must have spread in the past to the Marianas and here interbred with members of the migratory species, *A. platyrhynchos* (mallard), straying outside its usual range. No introgression appears to have occurred: both *A. poecilorhyncha* and *A. platyrhynchos* are perfectly 'good' species wherever they occur outside the Marianas. The hybrid species is somewhat variable, presumably as a result of different amounts of back-crossing with the two parental species. The latter hybridize readily in captivity (like many members of the genus), and their offspring strongly resemble one of the characteristic forms of *A. oustaleti*. Thus one can produce a 'natural' species in captivity. The ocean that surrounds the isolated Mariana Islands has acted rather like the wire of an aviary, if we suppose the wire broken here and there to admit occasional stragglers. As we shall see (p. 97), there seems to be a counterpart to *A. oustaleti* among the manifold forms of man.

One may say, if one likes, that hybridity between species is rare among wild animals, but if so one may be arguing about words instead of the facts of nature. Over a century ago, Broca asked whether in making hybridity the '*pierre de touche*' of species, and species the '*pierre de touche*' of hybridity, one were not turning in a vicious circle.[139]

## HYBRIDITY UNDER DOMESTICATION

'When animals mate with one another by their own nature (*von Natur*), this is an infallible indication that they are one and the same species.' So wrote the German zoologist J. L. Frisch in the first half of the eighteenth century.[362] He seems to have used the words '*von Natur*' to indicate that willingness to mate under natural conditions of wild life was a proof that the participants were of the same species, whereas under domestication or captivity copulation might occur between members of different species. Such was the interpretation put on Frisch's words by Blumenbach.[108] In his work on the birds of Germany, Frisch considered hybridity between captive canaries and their relatives in some detail, without further discussion of the definition of species.[361]

It was Berthout van Berchem the younger who first wrote perfectly plainly on this subject. In a valuable paper on the distinction between species, published in 1789, he wrote:

The first consideration that presents itself is that the rules that serve for wild animals should be different from those that one employs for domestic animals. . . . men have modified and denatured animals while denaturing themselves. . . . In wild animals, copulation is the most certain means one can have for the recognition of species. . . . when copulation does not occur, one can regard them as of different species. If one finds individuals having constant differences between them, which nevertheless do not prevent them from having progeny together in a state of nature, one should consider them as forming different races of the same species.[77]

Berchem insists that different species never mix 'in their state of nature. . . . it is therefore solely the copulation of wild and free animals that must be observed; it is for them alone that it can serve as a guide.' He quotes many examples of hybrids produced by domesticated animals of different species.

Berchem's very clear words on this subject, written not far short of two centuries ago, constituted an important contribution to zoology, though one can scarcely doubt that similar ideas must have been present in other minds than his and Frisch's; for domestication commonly leads to a profound change in habits. A wild animal that is accustomed to scrupulous cleanliness in its native haunts, for instance, may adapt itself to the presence of filth under artificial conditions of life, and substances utterly unlike its natural diet may be accepted as food. Thus the gorilla is strictly vegetarian in nature, but in zoological gardens meat (often horse-flesh) nearly always forms a considerable part of its regular diet.[231, 786] Similarly the capacity for precise recognition of suitable mating partners that has played such an important role in kladogenetic evolution may become so attenuated that two distinctly dissimilar forms may mate together, which would never have accepted one another as sexual partners in the circumstances of wild life. 'Strange as the fact may appear,' wrote Charles Darwin, in *The variation of animals and plants under domestication*,[257] 'many animals under confinement unite with distinct species and produce hybrids quite as freely as, or even more freely than, with their own species'.

Some very strange examples of abnormalities of this sort have been recorded by reputable authorities. Buffon quotes two examples of an '*amour violent*' between a dog and a sow. In one case the dog was a large spaniel on the property of the Comte de Feuillée, in Burgundy. Many persons witnessed 'the mutual ardour of these two animals; the dog even made prodigious and oft-repeated efforts to copulate with the sow, but the unsuitability of their reproductive organs prevented their union.' Another example, still more remarkable, occurred on Buffon's own property. A miller kept a mare and a bull in the same stable. These two animals developed such a passion for one another that on all occasions when the mare was on heat, over a period of several years, the bull copulated with her three or four times a day, whenever he was free to do so. The act was witnessed by all the inhabitants of the place.[164]

Lacépède and the illustrious Cuvier, in their book on the menagerie of the French National Museum of Natural History, record a comparable case.[624] In their description of a captive mandrill (*Mandrillus sphinx*) they write:

We have already had occasion to speak of the sexual love [*amour*] of monkeys for women: no other species gives more lively signs of it than this one. The individual that we describe used to fall into a fit of frenzy at the appearance of certain women, but it was by no means the case that all had the power to excite him to this degree: one saw clearly that he picked out those to whom he wished to express his fancy, and he did not fail to give preference to the younger ones. He distinguished them in a crowd; he summoned them by voice and gesture, and one could not doubt that if he had been free, he would have been carried away to violence.[624]

Darwin made enquiries on this subject at zoological gardens, from keepers and also from a very cautious and sagacious veterinary surgeon employed at one of them. He convinced himself that males of various genera of 'Quadrumani' (monkeys and apes) were in certain cases sexually attracted towards women. He considered that the attraction was caused mainly, though not exclusively, by odour.[258] Georges Cuvier's brother Frédéric, who was in charge of the French Ménagerie Royale, makes some general remarks on the lack of discrimination in sexual matters shown by monkeys and apes in captivity. 'It seems', he writes, 'that the more closely one approaches the human race, the greater enfeeblement there is of the repugnance that separates species from one another and prevents them from mixing.'[400]

Domesticated birds sometimes display similar abnormalities of sexual behaviour. Réaumur records in his characteristic manner a curious example involving a duck in his own possession. 'I have had occasion', he remarks, 'to see every day a duck of the commonest kind that used to squat to receive the caresses of a cock, not always the same one, to which she lent herself with as good a grace as she would have done to those of a drake. The cock, on his part, seemed as ardent for this duck as he could have been for a hen.'[883] The cocks seemed able to perform effectively the functions of a drake. Incidentally the duck had a drake for a husband, with whom she also copulated.

Rare and futile abnormalities such as these are nothing else than extreme examples of the loss of discrimination or sensitivity in sexual matters displayed by animals living under the influence of domestication.

Although, in the definition of species, Buffon failed to draw clearly the necessary distinction between natural and unnatural conditions of life, he contributed very considerably to our knowledge of hybridity under domestication. This subject was in fact carefully studied by Buffon himself and his associates[165] and especially by Broca,[138, 139, 140] during the century and a half that preceded the general recognition of Mendel's discoveries. From then onwards biologists concentrated their attention on such crosses as could be analysed in Mendelian terms, and little attention was paid to hybridity between kinds of animals that differed in so many genes, having cumulative effects, that this type of animal was not applicable. Yet several of the early workers had experimented carefully and thought deeply on the problems of interspecific hybridity.

It was realized that hybridity was not an all-or-nothing affair. Paul Broca, a French surgeon, anatomist, and anthropologist of great distinction, introduced some useful terms by which to distinguish the grades of fertility shown in interspecific crosses.[139] 'Homogenesic' hybridity* may be said to exist where any degree of fertility whatever results from a mating, from the occasional production of a sterile hybrid to the full degree shown by the parental stocks. Broca's degrees of fertility in hybridization are these:

---

* Broca's French terms are here anglicized and slightly simplified. For example, 'homogenesic' replaces 'Homœogénésique'.

*agenesic:*     the hybrids are infertile (the mule is an example);

*dysgenesic:*   members of the F.1 (first filial) generation are infertile among themselves, but occasionally fertile in a back-cross with one of the parental stocks;

*paragenesic:*  the F.1 generation is fertile with one or both of the parental stocks, and permanent stocks of partial hybrids can thus be produced; but an F.2 (second filial) generation is either not produced by mating the F.1 hybrids, or is incapable of repeated reproduction, generation after generation;

*eugenesic:*    members of the F.1 generation are readily fertile among themselves and with the parent stocks; all hybrids may produce permanent stocks.

Modern studies have shown that decreased fertility in paragenesic hybridity tends to show itself by a low ratio of offspring of the heterogametic sex: that is to say, the male in mammals, the female in birds. That the male sex predominates in hybrids between canaries and other species was already known to Buffon, who reported on such crosses in considerable detail.[163] He produced evidence of different degrees of fertility among the hybrids, and his findings can be expressed in Broca's terms, which were introduced much later. He describes the special steps that had to be taken by the aviculturist in some cases to persuade the parents to copulate. He gives particulars showing the possibility of paragenesic hybridity between the female canary (*Serinus canaria*) and males of two species of another genus, *Carduelis*, namely the siskin (*C. spinus*) and goldfinch (*C. carduelis*). With the citril finch (*C. citrinella*) the hybridity actually appears to be eugenesic, although the cross is intergeneric.[139]

These and many similar experiments were performed by others, but Buffon himself supervised experiments on the crossing of sheep with he-goats.[162, 260] The fact that this intergeneric cross is sometimes successful, and that the hybrids are not infertile, appears to be established. It was accepted as true by Broca,[139] who mentions that the French have a special name, *chabin*, for the hybrid. Several examples of the successful outcome of this cross are quoted by Alfred Russel Wallace in his famous work *Darwinism*.[1117] The information he quotes suggests that the hybridity is paragenesic. The cross appears to be what Broca[139] called 'unilateral', since there is evidence that the ram does not produce progeny with the she-goat.[260]

The fact that the domestic goat (*Capra hircus*) has been stated by reliable observers to hybridize in certain circumstances with the domestic sheep (*Ovis aries*) is particularly remarkable, on account of the marked differences between the members of these two forms, which cause them to be placed by taxonomists not only in different genera, but actually in different subfamilies, the Caprinae and Ovinae.[356] Apart from the external features that obviously separate them, there are many others in various parts of the body.

Thus, for instance, sheep have pre-orbital glands on the face, and the facial parts of the lacrimal bones are hollowed out to receive them; there are no such glands in goats, and consequently there is no hollowing of the lacrimal bones. Sheep also have inter-digital glands between the toes of both hind and front feet, while in goats such glands either do not occur or are restricted to the front feet. He-goats possess paired stink-glands below the tail, which the ram lacks. The atlas (first) vertebra is of distinctly different shape in the two subfamilies. The list of differences could be greatly extended.[356, 1122]

Innumerable examples could be quoted of hybridity between species under captivity or domestication. Some examples may be mentioned here, chosen from among species mentioned in the preceding chapter. The *Anopheles* mosquitoes provide a particularly interesting example.[447] When held captive in small cages, the males cannot swarm, and this interferes with the copulatory habits of the females, which refuse to mate with the males of the swarming species. The extraordinary fact is that in these circumstances they depart from their usual custom and mate with males of the non-swarming species, *A. atroparvus*, if present in the same cage, and conception results. No fewer than five species of *Anopheles* will produce hybrid embryos in this way, but the hybridity is agenesic or dysgenesic. In some of the crosses development goes no further than the early stages, but in others (for instance, when *A. melanoon* females are used) healthy adults are produced. The male progeny, however, are sterile. This accords with the rule that sterility usually affects the heterogametic sex of hybrids.

The poecilid fishes, which avoid hybridity in nature by their elaborate courtship arrangements, will breed together in captivity. Agenesic hybrids have been obtained by mating *Poecilia reticulata* with *P. vivipara* and also with *P. parae*.[666]

The species of gulls (*Larus*) interbreed readily in captivity.

The breeding territory of *L. marinus* (the great black-backed gull) overlaps with that of *L. hyperboreus* (glaucous gull), but they do not ordinarily hybridize under natural conditions. In confinement, however, these two species breed together; so do *L. marinus* and *L. argentatus* (herring gull, see pp. 77–9); so also do the latter and *L. canus* (common gull).[952] In this genus, as in so many others, the normal mating behaviour, which made kladogenetic evolution possible, seems to be almost completely broken down by artificial conditions of life.

## HYBRIDITY AND DOMESTICATION IN MAN

The effect of domestication in reducing sensitivity to the recognition of 'own kind' deserves to be carefully considered in relation to the question of species in man.

Blumenbach remarked long ago that man is 'of all living beings the most domesticated'.[108] Berthout van Berchem had already pointed out, in his paper on the effect of domestication in promoting hybridity among animals, 'Men have modified and denatured animals while denaturing themselves'[77] (see pp. 91–2). The human alimentary tract suggests adaptation to a diet similar to that of the anthropoid apes, which do not eat the flesh of mammals under natural conditions[231, 786] (see p. 92); but domestication results in his eating many kinds of food that would not have been accepted by the wild anthropoid ancestors from which he inherited his teeth and alimentary canal. The instinctive attitudes of animals to sex are modified, as we have seen (pp. 92–5), by domestication, and this applies no less to man. Broca pointed out, in his paper on human hybridity,[140] that the loss of sensitivity resulting from domestication has gone so far that from the earliest recorded times it has been necessary to enact laws against bestiality. The ruling of Moses on this subject will be remembered: 'Neither shalt thou lie with any beast to defile thyself therewith: neither shall any woman stand before a beast to lie down thereto' (*Leviticus*, xviii, 23). This rule refers to the extreme of insensitivity in the recognition of sexual partners; but as Broca remarked, 'Man, especially civilized man, is of all animals the least exclusive in his amours.'[140] Examples are quoted in the medical literature of semi-monstrous human beings who have married and become parents. There can be little doubt that the use of alcohol and other drugs has rendered man even less exclusive in this respect than he would otherwise have been, by reducing the capacity for accurate discrimination and judgement, but domestication itself is presumably the primary cause.

The parallel between man and animals in their tendency to indiscriminate mating cannot be exact, since man determines what opportunities shall be available to his domestic animals for the selection of appropriate or inappropriate sexual partners, while he leaves himself free to select partners of either type without comparable restriction.

It is interesting to consider what attitude modern man would have taken towards hybridity today if some of his prehistoric relatives had persisted with little change to the present day. Certainly no normal human being of modern times would willingly copulate with any of the australopithecines (p. 272), and by most of us the acceptance of *Pithecanthropus* (often regarded as a race of *Homo erectus*) as a sexual partner would presumably have been considered as a step across the boundary into bestiality. Broken Hill man (*Homo rhodesianus* Woodward) would probably have been regarded by nearly everyone as too appalling in appearance to be acceptable. Professor Mikhail Gerasimov, the Russian anatomist noted for his work in reconstructing the living appearances of human beings of prehistoric and modern times from study of their skulls, has provided us with a striking portrait of this formidable creature in his book published in English translation as *The face finder*.[401] Most of us, I think, would have drawn the line well on our own side of the typical Neanderthalians, though it is to be remembered that there is some evidence for hybridity between the latter and *Homo sapiens* in the narrower sense (p. 11). Modern Europids would, however, almost certainly have accepted Cro-Magnon man (or woman), if he had survived—as he may in fact have done[48]—from Upper Palaeolithic times. Gerasimov's portrait of him confirms this opinion; indeed, the 'face finder' himself describes Cro-Magnon man as 'in his way good-looking'. Although so much is guesswork in this particular problem, one thing seems certain—that if the complete series of our ancestors could be presented to us, different people would draw the line in different places. The wide acceptance of markedly different partners by some would appear as intolerable and verging on bestiality to others, who would in turn be condemned as 'racialists' by the more permissively inclined. We should remember, however, that some of the 'permissives' would be likely to receive a rebuff from their anticipated mates, who might well be too little domesticated, too 'natural', to view a modern man or woman with anything but revulsion.

It may well be doubted whether any two kinds of animals, differing from one another so markedly in morphological characters (and in odour) as, for instance, the Europid and Sanid (pp. 303–24), and living under natural conditions of wild life, would accept one another as sexual partners. Yet if such acceptance is the result of attenuated sensitivity to the recognition of 'own kind', caused by the degree of domestication to which man has subjected himself, the existence of hybrids cannot be regarded as evidence that Europid and Sanid belong to the same 'species'. Even typical Nordids and typical Alpinids, both regarded as *subraces* of a single *race* (subspecies), the Europid, are very much more different from one another in morphological characters—for instance in the shape of the skull—than many *species* of animals that never interbreed with one another in nature, though their territories overlap (see p. 87).

Although one may well doubt whether two forms so different as the Europid and the Khoisanid would hybridize under conditions that could be regarded as 'natural', yet it is well known that this cross did in fact occur, and gave rise not only to many of the people designated as 'Coloured' in the population of the Cape Province of South Africa, but also to the Griquas and to the Reheboth Bastaards of South West Africa. The events that led to the origin of these hybrids at the Cape are particularly interesting on account of the remarkable analogy with certain occurrences in the animal world, in which hybridity between species was involved (p. 91). When Van Riebeck and his little company of emigrants from the Netherlands landed at Table Bay in 1652, they were met by Hottentot herdsmen belonging to tribes from which the Koranas of the present day are probably descended. Both the Dutch and the Hottentots were in the zoological sense 'stragglers' to this part of the world, for members of the latter group had only recently reached the southern extremity of the continent.[1016] In so far as the land 'belonged' to anyone, it was part of the hunting-grounds of the Bushmen, and the related 'Strandloopers' were present on the coast. The Bushmen held all the great mountain passes and fastnesses on the periphery of the area occupied by the Dutch, and they remained a distinct people, not yet conquered, in the vicinity of the Cape itself.[1016] A certain amount of interbreeding began gradually to occur between some of the Dutch and Hottentots, who thus mingled on soil that was foreign to both peoples. The resulting hybrids were the first members of what eventually became the Cape Coloured population, which was later further hybridized when the Dutch introduced workers from their East Indian possessions.

The Cape Coloured people, despite their hybrid origin, show no sign of reduced fertility. By 1909 their numbers had risen to about half a million, and fifty years later to more than 1,400,000.[26] Nevertheless there is no proof that hybridity among human beings is invariably eugenesic, for many of the possible crosses have not been made, or if they have, their outcome does not appear to have been recorded. It is probable on inductive evidence that such marriages would not be infertile, but it is questionable whether the hybridity would necessarily be eugenesic. For instance, statistical study might reveal a preponderance of female offspring, which would suggest a failure of embryos of the heterogametic sex to develop (p. 94). Again, one would need to prove that the filial generations in the direct line, without back-crosses to either of the parental stocks, retained their fertility. It will be remembered that in crosses between species among animals under domestication, the offspring sometimes show reduced fertility when mated to similar hybrids, but not when mated to the parental stocks (paragenesic hybridity).

When two human races are present in the same country in very disproportionate numbers, the hybrids produced will necessarily tend to intermarry chiefly with members of the more numerous race, and their fertility may therefore be only paragenesic (cf. Broca[139]).

When two human races are present in the same country in numbers that are not very unequal, but one race is more advanced than the other in the scale of civilization, the resultant hybrids are said to differ in their marriage prospects. The female hybrids are said to intermarry frequently with members of the more advanced race, or with other hybrids having a preponderance of the characters of that race, while the male hybrids tend to do the reverse.[140] It follows that many of the marriages are back-crosses to parental stocks. Even if the F.1 hybrids intermarry with others of similar origin, there is no certainty that their descendants will continue to do so, generation after generation, or if they do, that fertility will be fully maintained. In such cases much back-crossing is almost inevitable, and proof of eugenesic hybridity is therefore lacking.

It seems to follow from what has been said in this and the preceding chapter that the facts of human hybridity do not prove that all human races are to be regarded as belonging to a single 'species'. The whole idea of species is vague, because the word is used with such different meanings, none of which is of universal application. When it is used in the genetical sense, some significance can indeed be attached to it, in so far as it applies to animals existing in natural conditions of wild life at a particular time (though even here it ceases to have any quite precise meaning in those cases in which there is interbreeding between what are called 'good species'); but it does not appear to be applicable to human beings, who live under the most extreme conditions of domestication and many of whom have become insensitive in their choice of sexual partners to a degree unknown among wild animals.

# 7 The meaning of 'race'

THE RACE or subspecies has already been mentioned repeatedly in the chapter on the meaning of species. The reader is aware that in following a widely distributed animal over its range, one often notices alterations in its appearance. The changes are particularly evident wherever a partial geographical barrier intervenes, such as a range of mountains, a desert, or a wide river. The populations on the two sides of the barrier are not, however, entirely distinct. Intermediates are found, and there is often direct evidence of interbreeding, though not on a sufficient scale to make the two populations indistinguishable. If the two populations are so distinct that one can generally tell from which region a specimen was obtained, it is usual to give separate names to the two races. If every specimen could be identified with certainty as belonging to one population or the other, it would be evident that no gene-flow occurred between the two, and they would therefore be regarded as different species in the genetical sense of the word, however small the differences might be. It is the fact that intermediates *do* occur that defines the race. The definition of any particular race must be inductive in the sense that it gives a general impression of the distinctive characters, without professing to be applicable in detail to every individual.

For practical purposes it may be found convenient to make an arbitrary decision as to the proportion of intermediates that are allowable, if different races are to be recognized. One may argue that a population 'A' is distinguishable from a population 'B' if $x\%$ of the individuals constituting population 'A' can be recognized as not belonging to population 'B'. It will be understood that the correct value to be assigned to $x$ cannot be discovered by objective means; nevertheless, if a high figure (perhaps 75) is agreed upon by taxonomists, one can scarcely doubt that there is a distinction worthy of recognition as subspecific or 'racial'. Very commonly, however, the differences observed are so evident, and $x$ is clearly so high, that no statistical investigation is necessary to convince other taxonomists that races should be distinguished.

For many purposes it is convenient to regard a whole series of races as a *Formenkreis*, but usually the idea of species is adopted and a system of nomenclature based on that of Linnaeus is then used, the generic and specific names being followed by a third or subspecific (e.g. *Larus argentatus antelius*). This trinomial system has already been explained (p. 68) and used in several places in this book. The naming of races simplifies the discussion of many very interesting problems, without tending—so far as one can see—to mislead anyone by suggesting that the racial differences are greater or of more frequent occurrence than they actually are. Some students of the subject, however, oppose the use of the trinomial system, on the ground that a certain degree of arbitrariness is inherent in the delimitation of races.[148] It is argued that one taxonomist might choose a particular set of distinguishing characters to define two or more races, while some other student of the same group might choose a different set of characters and as a result divide the species differently. It is questionable, however, whether this argument applies more strongly to the race than to other taxa. Universal agreement on taxonomic matters is not to be expected, yet there are many problems in biology that could not be tackled at all without the aid of taxonomists. Students of race are ready to readjust their classifications when sufficient reason is provided.

It is sometimes claimed that the existence of intermediates makes races unreal. It scarcely needs to be pointed out, however, that in other matters no one questions the reality of categories between which intermediates exist. There is every gradation, for instance, between green and blue, but no one denies that these words should be used. In the same way the existence of youths and human hermaphrodites does not cause anyone to disallow the use of the words 'boy', 'man', and 'woman'. It is particularly unjustifiable to cite intermediates as contradicting the reality of races, for the existence of intermediates is one of the distinguishing characters of the race: if there are no intermediates, there are no races. As Kant insisted, those who wish to get right away from the purely academic outlook on animal classification—the *Schulsystem*, as he called it—should use two taxa only in their descriptions of the animal world: the *Realgattung* and its component *Racen* (see pp. 80–81).

Adaptation to different environments often results in the evolution of races, although no clearly defined barriers exist; or the races of a species may be separated from one another by gradual environmental differences in one part of its range and more sharply by clearly defined barriers in another. Sri Lanka (Ceylon) provides many examples. There is a mountainous zone in the centre of the island, and a low-country wet zone in the south-west; the rest of the island constitutes the low-country dry zone. Many species of mammals are represented in each zone by a separate race.[841, 307]

For instance, the leaf-eating monkey commonly called 'wanderoo' (*Presbytis senex*) is represented in the low-country dry zone by a race (*P. senex senex*) distinguished by large size and rather dark coloration, while in the mountains there is a paler, very shaggy, stocky form (*monticola*), sometimes called the 'bear monkey'. The low-country wet zone is divided by a considerable river, the Kalu Ganga, which acts as a barrier in separating the races of certain mammals. North of it one finds the smallest wanderoo (*nestor*), which is grey with a terminal tuft to the tail; south of the river this is replaced by the larger black wanderoo (*vetulus*), which grades into *monticola* in the Adam's Peak district. It should be noticed that one finds gradation in characters as one ascends the mountains, and much sharper change when one crosses the river. It must be mentioned that the differences between the four races, in their typical forms, are far more numerous than the few descriptive words given above would suggest.

It has already been mentioned briefly (p. 83) that races are not necessarily in every case separated geographically: it sometimes happens that two races live in the same territory, but occupy different habitats ('ecological niches') within it. The races and subraces of man seem to have evolved chiefly as a result of (partial) geographical isolation, but here and there one may find examples reminiscent of the 'ecological races' of animals. The pygmies (Bambutids) of Africa, living interspersed among the Negro (Palaenegrid) population, seem to fall into this category. Isolation is not complete, for there is evidence of a certain amount of Bambutid ancestry in the Palaenegrid population.

As T. H. Huxley indicated in the passage quoted on p. 3, almost any widely distributed terrestrial animal could be used to illustrate the facts of race; but some animals are more suitable for this purpose than others, because more is known about them. One wants a common animal that is represented by several races, easily distinguishable (in their typical forms) from one another by morphological features, each caused by the simultaneous action of many genes having cumulative effects ('polygenes'). Preferably there should also be data derived from the analysis of the effects of genes, each of which has an observable effect; and ideally one should also have information about the chromosomal differences between the races. Differences in behaviour or movements are also of special interest in racial studies. In all these respects the crested newt, *Triturus cristatus*, approaches the ideal. It would probably be impossible to choose a better form to illustrate the meaning of race. Great advantage would accrue if everyone who professed to speak or write on this subject would learn something about it from this common denizen of ponds and their environs in many parts of Europe (Fig. 11, p. 102). A rather detailed exposition is therefore attempted here.

The various races of the crested newt are, in general, drably pigmented above, with darker spots, and have a yellowish-orange belly with dark spots on it. There are usually small white spots on the otherwise drab flanks, and the dark throat is also spotted with white in most races. The skin is warty. The racial differences in colour and warts are described below.

With a dead crested newt, an easy way to distinguish the races is to extend the front legs backwards and the hind legs forwards, close beside the body, and then to note how far the tips of the toes reach forward on to the hand or arm; for the races with short bodies tend to have long limbs, so that there is much overlap when this position is maintained, and conversely with races having long bodies and short limbs.[1151] Details of these differences also are given below.

The geographical distribution of the races is shown in Fig. 12. Hybrids occur where the territory of one race merges with that of another. Near Bucharest, for instance, hybrids occur between *cristatus* and *danubialis*,[1151] while in the vicinity of Vienna all intermediate forms are found between these two and between them and *carnifex*.[183]

In captivity F.1 hybrids between these races are vigorous, but F.2 hybrids often fail to survive the larval stage.[183] The hybridity is thus paragenesic. It is perhaps rather surprising that hybrids have been able to establish themselves in nature. There is no actual proof that the hybridity is fully eugenesic under natural conditions, for it does not appear to have been established by experi-

11 *The crested newt*, Triturus cristatus cristatus; *male (above) and female*
From Furneaux. [372]

ment that the natural hybrids can give rise to an indefinitely extended sequence of filial generations.

Members of the race *carnifex*, which inhabit the countries adjoining the Adriatic Sea, are large (up to 150 mm long) and very stocky, with broad heads. The back being short and the limbs long, the tips of the toes reach the elbows, when the newt is put in the position mentioned above.[115] The upper surface tends to have an olive-green tinge, and in the female there is often a broad yellow stripe down the middle of the back (in this sex there is no crest in any of the races).

Thanks to the studies of Spurway,[100] it is possible to analyse certain features of the races genetically. The race *carnifex* is recessive for five easily observable distinguishing features, and this makes it useful in genetical studies, because dominant genes show up in the F.1 progeny when crosses are made. The five genes in question are these:*

*r, r* gives a rather smooth skin; that is, the warts are not very strongly developed;

*t, t* results in the white spots on the throat being rather small, so that this part appears nearly black from the background colour;

*s, s* gives scarcity of white spots on the flanks;

*l, l* causes the dark spots on the belly to be separate from one another, and arranged at random;

*b, b* results in lack of the Prussian blue sheen on the skin, seen in *karelini*.

---

* See opposite, concerning *karelini*, for the significance of the particular letters chosen for the genes described.

The race, *karelini*, which inhabits parts of Greece, Turkey, Georgia, and Iran, may be roughly described from the morphological point of view by saying that it is an exaggerated form of *carnifex*. It is even stockier, the head broad and flat, and the limbs so long in relation to the trunk that the toes may reach as far as the upper arm. The female never has a yellow stripe down the back.

Although the body-form of *karelini* shows it to be closely related to *carnifex*, it happens to carry genes dominant to the five recessives of the latter race:

*Rk, Rk* (meaning *roughness* of the *karelini* type) produces small warts, so arranged as to give the appearance of shagreen;

*Tk, Tk* (meaning *throat* of the *karelini* type) gives an orange-yellow throat, not present in any of the other races (there are sometimes large black blotches on it);

*S, S* gives many white *spots* on the flanks;

*L, L* causes the dark spots on the belly to merge into one another in such a way as to give the impression of irregular, dark, *longitudinal* bands;

*B, B* gives the Prussian *blue* sheen on the skin, not seen in any of the other races.

It goes without saying that this quintuple dominant, when mated with the quintuple recessive *carnifex*, gives an F.1 progeny resembling itself in warts

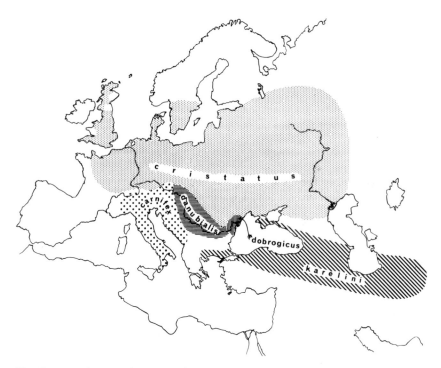

12     *Europe, showing the geographical distribution of the races of the crested newt,*
Triturus cristatus

*Map drawn from the data of Wolterstorff,* |1151| *Mertens and Müller,* |735| *and Smith.* |982|

and colour, and not differing greatly in body-form, since the two races are rather similar in this respect.

In comparison with the other races, the familiar *T. cristatus cristatus* (Fig. 11) of Great Britain and the northerly parts of Europe is neither stocky on one hand nor slim on the other, and the total length of the body (up to 135 mm) is intermediate. The toes reach forward to the base of the hand, and in this respect also *cristatus* occupies an intermediate position among the races.

*Rcr, Rcr* (meaning *roughness* of the *cristatus* type) gives coarse warts on the skin (it is uncertain whether this gene is allelomorphic with *Rk*);

*Tcr, Tcr* (meaning *throat* of the *cristatus* type) gives large white spots on the throat, which therefore appears greyish from a distance (it is uncertain whether this gene is allelomorphic with *Tk*);

*S, S* gives white spots on the flanks like those of *karelini*;

*L, L* gives irregular, dark, longitudinal banding of the belly, as in *karelini*:

*b, b* results in lack of Prussian blue sheen on the skin.

The valley of the Danube is inhabited by another race, *danubialis*, markedly different in form from *carnifex* and *karelini*, but showing some resemblance to *cristatus*. This is a small newt (maximum length 125 mm), slim, with a small head. The limbs are slender, short, and inserted far apart, so that the tips of the toes may not even reach the finger-tips. This newt moves in the water very differently from the others that have been described above, with strongly serpentine bendings of the slender trunk. There is often a yellow stripe along the back of the female.

In its most characteristic form *danubialis* has this genetic constitution:

*Rcr, Rcr* gives coarse warts of the *cristatus* type;

*Tcr, Tcr* gives large white spots on the throat, as in *cristatus*;

*s, s* reduces the white spotting on the flanks to the *carnifex* level:

*l, l* prevents longitudinal banding of the belly by fusion of the darker spots. The latter are rounded, sharply defined, and arranged at random;

*b, b* results in lack of Prussian blue sheen on the skin.

At the eastern extremity of its range, in the region of the Danube delta, *danubialis* gives place to *dobrogicus*, which may be regarded as its exaggerated counterpart, even more slender, but longer and with long fingers and toes.

It follows from the fact that the races interbreed with one another in nature at the boundaries of their ranges, that the genetical constitution of all specimens of a particular race is not the same. Gene-flow between the races probably accounts, for instance, for the fact that *danubialis* is not always *Rcr, Rcr*; *Tcr, Tcr*; *s, s*; *l, l*; *b, b*. Specimens have been recorded heterozygous for genes controlling warts (*Rcr, r*), and others homozygous for the recessive (*r, r*). [1001] The same applies to the genes affecting spotting of the throat. Specimens heterozygous for longitudinal banding of the belly have also been recorded; interbreeding between these would result in the presence of homozygous dominants (*L, L*) among the progeny. The possibility of independent mutation is not excluded.

The four first-mentioned races all have 12 pairs of chromosomes; those of *dobrogicus* do not appear to have been examined. Abnormalities tend to occur in the maturation of the germ-cells of racial hybrids. In normal spermatogenesis the cells in any particular follicle keep pace with one another, so that all are at the same stage of maturation at any given time; but in racial hybrids this synchrony is disturbed, and the pairing of paternally with maternally derived chromosomes is often deranged. This is in part due to the fact that 'translocation' has occurred in the course of evolution; that is to say, in a certain race a part of a chromosome has become incorporated in another chromosome, in which it did not 'belong' ancestrally. When the normal pairing of paternally and maternally derived chromosomes is prevented by irregularities of this sort, strange-looking chromosome complexes ('trivalents' and 'quadrivalents') are produced. Spermatogenesis often does not go beyond the first meiotic division, and those that survive the two divisions often degenerate at the spermatid stage. Nevertheless all male interracial hybrids (so far as is known) produce some spermatozoa.[183]

When *Triturus cristatus* is hybridized with another species, *T. marmoratus*, spermatogenesis is still more abnormal, but the differences are of degree rather than of kind. The racial and specific differences of chromosomal behaviour in the spermatogenesis of hybrids substantiate the degrees of affinity postulated by taxonomists on entirely different evidence.[632]

If matings were made between typical members of the same race taken from widely separated places, it is conceivable that abnormalities might be found in the spermatogenesis of their offspring[1001]; but there is no evidence of this.

While the eggs (primary oocytes) of the crested newt are maturing in the ovary, the chromosomes become enormously long (up to about $\frac{3}{4}$ mm) and assume a very strange form. By examination of these we get a glimpse not simply of racial differences, but of their immediate cause; for the 'genonema' or string of genes is displayed before us in a remarkable way, and we seem to see in action the causative agents that result in the differences of race.

These special chromosomes were first seen in 1878 in the developing egg of the axolotl (*Amblystoma tigrinum*) by the German cytologist Walther Flemming, and were studied by him in collaboration with a medical student named Wiebe; but their extraordinary appearance suggested that they might be artifacts caused by the reagents used in making microscopical preparations. It was four years later when Flemming at last published their results, with some reservations about the possibility that the appearance of the chromosomes might not represent accurately what had been present in life.[342] Meanwhile they had seen similar chromosomes in other Amphibia and in certain unnamed fishes. Ten years later a much more exact study of similar chromosomes in a dogfish (*Pristiurus*) was published by another German cytologist, Rückert, to whom we owe the familiar name nowadays universally applied to chromosomes of this type. 'Very roughly', he wrote, 'one can form a plastic idea of the structure of part of a chromosome if one thinks of a *Lampencylinderputzer*, the threads of which have been distorted by use and matted together.'[922] One of Rückert's drawings is shown in Fig. 13 (p. 106). The name of 'lampbrush' was given from the resemblance—inexact, it is true—to the instrument in general use at the time for cleaning out the glass chimneys of oil-lamps. It consisted of an axis from which bristles projected radially in all directions.

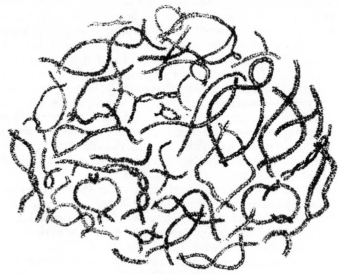

13   *Rückert's drawing of 'lampbrush' chromosomes as he saw them in a developing egg of the dogfish,* Pristiurus

*From Rückert.* [922]

It is now known that lampbrush chromosomes occur in the developing eggs (primary oocytes) of a wide variety of animals in addition to Amphibia and dogfishes. They have been described in certain reptiles and birds, in a starfish (*Echinaster*), in the cuttle-fish (*Sepia*), and in *Anilocra*, a relative of the woodlouse, but parasitic on marine fishes.[180, 182] All the animals in which lampbrush chromosomes are known to occur, have yolky eggs. In the opinion of one of the foremost authorities in this field of research, something corresponding to a lampbrush phase is probably passed through at a particular stage in the maturation of the eggs of all animals, but the appearance is disguised in those cases in which the yolk is scanty.[180]

For our knowledge of the structure and significance of lampbrush chromosomes we are indebted to many independent investigators, but to none more than to Professor J. G. Gall of the University of Minnesota[374, 375, 376] and Professor H. G. Callan of St. Andrews University.[182, 181] It is clear, from studies made by phase-contrast and electron microscopy, that the projections at the sides of the axis are not like the bristles of a lampbrush, but are in fact loops of a continuous thread of DNA (the genetic material, deoxyribonucleic acid) that runs from one end of the chromosome to the other (or part of the way along one chromosome of a pair and the rest of the way along its partner). (See Fig. 14.)

Each object within the nucleus is a pair of chromosomes, roughly parallel with one another, and held together here and there by special connections (chiasmata) (Figs. 13 and 14). Each chromosome consists of two parallel threads (at least over a part of its course), and of the four threads (chromatids)

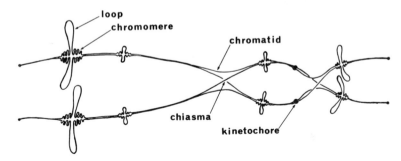

14    *The basic structure of lampbrush chromosomes*

The diagram (not to scale) is intended to represent a pair of these chromosomes. Only four pairs of loops are shown on each chromosome, but actually there are hundreds of pairs on each.
*The structure of the chromomeres is based on Gall's interpretation.* [376]

that constitute the whole object two represent the genetic material derived from the animal's mother and two that derived from its father. The maternal and paternal chromosomes, previously separate, have come together at an earlier stage in the development of the egg (zygotene stage), and each has split longitudinally into two threads (though the split may not be complete at the lampbrush stage). At intervals the chromatids are coiled in such a way as to make little lumps (chromomeres); from each of these a loop projects on each side. In the diagram (Fig. 14) only four pairs of loops are shown on each chromosome; actually several hundreds are present in some of the chromosomes.

It is thought that the loops are the parts of the chromatids that are active, at a particular moment, in synthesizing the gene-products; that is to say, the substances that enable the genes to produce their effects.

The twelve chromosome pairs differ in length and in the number and arrangement of the loops. The number and arrangement are more or less constant in any particular chromosome in all the developing eggs of all the individuals of a race, though there is some variation in different individuals and at different stages in maturation of the egg. The approximate constancy in the number and arrangement of the loops makes it possible to identify each of the chromosome pairs. They are numbered from I to XII, no. I being the longest and no. XII the shortest. The identification of the different chromosomes is rendered much easier than it would otherwise be by the fact that there are a few enormous, very thick loops, which are so helpful in identification that they are called 'landmarks'.

For students of the ethnic problem, the essential fact is that *each* of the twelve chromosomes is very different in the different races of *Triturus cristatus*. This subject has been studied by Callan and Lloyd,[182] who have

described in great detail each of the twelve lampbrush chromosomes in four of
the races of this species.

For the present purpose it must suffice to consider only chromosome-pair
no. X.* Fig. 15A represents this chromosome as it commonly occurs in the
race *carnifex*, but the figure has been simplified by omission of all the loops
except the landmarks, and details of the chromatids and chiasmata are not
shown. One notices at once the 'giant loops' situated towards what is arbitrarily called the 'left' end (LE) of each chromosome. (Fusion of the sides of the
loop makes it look like a shapeless lump.) Callan and Lloyd[182] have prepared

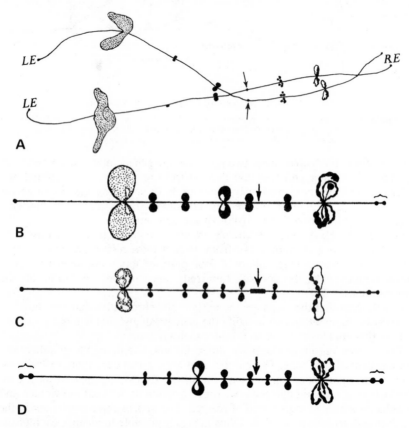

15    *Some of the racial differences in 'lampbrush' chromosomes X of the crested newt,*
Triturus cristatus

Only the 'landmarks' are represented. (See text.) A, a pair of chromosomes X of the race *carnifex*. LE, 'left'
end; RE, 'right' end. B, 'working map' of chromosomes X of *carnifex*; C, ditto, of *karelini*; D, of *cristatus*.
*Diagram rearranged from Callan and Lloyd.* [182]

* This symbol means that the serial number of the chromosome, in respect of length, is *ten*. It
does not refer to an 'X-chromosome' in the sense of a sex-chromosome.

for each chromosome what they call a 'working map' of a typical chromosome of the race. The working map of chromosome X of *carnifex* is shown at B in Fig. 15, and that of chromosome X of *karelini* at C. The general resemblance and the differences are easily noted, especially the much smaller size of the giant loop near the left end in *karelini*, and also the presence of a thickening of the axis ('axial bar') at a particular place on the chromosome in this race. Chromosome X of *cristatus* is shown at D in the same figure. It differs notably from that of *carnifex* and *karelini* in the invariable absence of the giant loop and in several other respects, but some of the landmarks can be recognized as corresponding to those in the other races. The giant loop is also absent from chromosome X in *danubialis*.

The landmarks are not all exactly the same in all members of a race. Comparison of drawings A and B in Fig. 15 gives an impression of the amount of difference that may occur within a race.

The arrows in Fig. 15 indicate the positions of the 'kinetochores', which are concerned in the movement apart of the chromosomes at cell-division. Axial bars of *karelini* are actually situated 'left' and 'right' of the kinetochore, but are not shown separately in the working maps.

Study of the complete sets of working maps representing the lampbrush chromosomes of the crested newt impresses forcibly on the mind the degree of difference in the genetic material of the races, but it is to be remembered that these maps show only the landmarks. If maps could be prepared showing all the loops in all twelve chromosomes, the impression would necessarily be much stronger.

The races of *Triturus cristatus* illustrate a number of important points about racial differences in general. These will now be considered in turn.

(1) A map such as Fig. 12, intended to give an impression of the geographical distribution of races, must not be taken too literally as indicating the exact range of each race. Each differently marked territory simply represents an area *within which* the typical form of the race can be found. The boundaries of these areas are not sharp, as they appear to be on the map, nor do they necessarily remain constant over long periods of time; overlapping of the races occurs, and intermediate forms are naturally commoner near the boundaries than elsewhere. The correct way in which to interpret a racial map should be kept in mind whenever there is occasion to examine one.

(2) None of the racial characters is quite constant. Apart from the immediate hybrids there is a good deal of variation in size, colour, and the proportion of parts; but no one could confuse the extremes, e.g. *dobrogicus* with *karelini*, nor has anyone ever claimed to find a member of either of these races living wild in (for instance) Great Britain or Sweden.

(3) Not everyone agrees on the delimitation of the races. Thus Wolsterstorff[1151] regards *dobrogicus* not as a race but as a subrace ('*forma*') of *danubialis*, while Mertens and Müller[735] regard these as separate races. Similarly, *carnifex* and *karelini* have been regarded as belonging to the same race.[132] It follows that no one can make a definite pronouncement on the number of races in the species *Triturus cristatus*. In the case of man it has been

argued that the whole idea of races collapses, because the number of races cannot be positively stated. The facts that have been given about the races of *Triturus cristatus* show that this is not a valid argument. It is obvious that *dobrogicus* shows closer resemblance to *danubialis* than to *karelini*. It is not of very great importance whether we regard *dobrogicus* as a subrace of *danubialis* or as a separate race; different authorities may properly be permitted, in the present state of knowledge, to differ on this point. A serious error would, however, be made if *dobrogicus* were said to be a subrace of *karelini*, or if these two were regarded without qualification as being of the same race.

Similarly, it does not matter much whether *carnifex* and *karelini* are regarded as racially or subracially distinct, but it would be quite wrong to separate them and then put one of them in the same race as *danubialis*. Again, the Balkan specimens of *karelini* resemble *carnifex* more closely than the Asian ones do. One authority (a 'splitter') might even regard the Balkan and Asian forms as separate races, and another might regard the Balkan form as a subrace of *karelini* and give it a distinguishing name; but it is customary in this case to be a 'lumper' and include them all under the single name of *karelini*. No important error would be involved in any of these arrangements, but it would obviously be wrong to 'lump' the Balkan form with *danubialis*.

(4) Races are in many cases distinguished (in part) by the bodily features that may be referred to by such names as 'stockiness' and 'slimness'. These loose expressions are convenient for certain purposes, but the features in question can be accurately measured and described in statistical terms if necessary. We have noted the stocky newt, *karelini*, and its slim counterpart, *dobrogicus*. One can scarcely fail to be reminded of comparable differences among the ethnic taxa of man. One thinks at once, for instance, of the stocky Palaenegrid of Zaïre and the slim Nilotid of the Sudan, or of the stocky Alpinid and lanky Nordid (though the difference between these two Europid subraces in this respect is not so marked as between the Negrid subraces). There is, however, great variety in these major features of bodily structure. In the newts, for instance, stockiness of the trunk is associated with long limbs, and slimness with short, while the converse is true of man.

It will have been noticed that the features that differentiate the races of newts are of two kinds: those that have been analysed genetically and those that have not. The gross morphological features (shape of body and length of limbs, for instance) do not lend themselves readily to genetical analysis. On hybridizing the races, sharp segregation does not occur in respect of such features as these. Whenever, in cases of this sort, segregation is not observed in the progeny of a cross, but only intermediates appear in succeeding generations of filial descendants, one suspects that the feature under examination is controlled by polygenes: that is to say, by many genes having cumulative effects. Since different sets of polygenes must be assumed to control the shapes of many different component parts of the body (many different bones, for instance, and the muscles attached to them), it is probable that the total number of such genes is in many cases large, in comparison with the number that can be analysed genetically. In trying to determine the relationship of different races to one another, one realizes how unsatisfactory it is to do no more than describe the morphological characters, without being able to analyse the causes that produced them. In a few animals, particularly the fly *Drosophila*, genetic analysis of polygenes is a possibility;[712] but in most cases, and above all in man, where controlled matings cannot be made and reproduction is extremely slow, such analysis is scarcely possible in the existing state of knowledge (though an ingenious start towards it has been made in relation to human skin-colour[1007, 1008](see p. 159)).

The ideal to which one must look forward is a complete analysis of polygenes. Until this ideal can be achieved, a paradoxical situation must exist. The better the evidence of relationship, the less susceptible are the facts to genetical analysis.[57]

(5) When chromosomes can be examined in the extended state as 'lamp-brushes', the numerous differences between the gene-strings (genonemata) characteristic of different races are rendered evident.

(6) Races often differ not only in form and coloration, but also in habits. Some examples are quoted below (pp. 115–17). *Triturus cristatus* does not il-lustrate this type of racial difference particularly well, for the mode of life is, in general, similar; but attention has been called to the very different swimming actions of *carnifex* and *karelini* on one hand, and of *danubialis* and *dobrogicus* on the other. One is reminded of the rather stiff movements of most Europids in walking, and the loose-limbed action characteristic of many Negrids. In the case of newts there can be no doubt that the difference is genetically controlled. In man there may be an element of unconscious imitation in producing the effects that are observed; but it is difficult to see how the differences could have arisen and spread over enormous areas of the globe, unless a genetic element were involved (though it is of course true that members of either race could deliberately copy or avoid the actions of the other, if they wished).

(7) In the study of race, no attention should be paid to the political sub-divisions of the surface of the earth. It would be a waste of time, for instance, to take a random collection of all the crested newts of Romania and describe their average characters. It could be done: the average 'Romanian' among newts could be described. Its body would be of moderate length, neither stocky nor slim, with hind toes reaching to the bases of the fingers; it would neither swim in the serpentine manner of *danubialis* and *dobrogicus* nor paddle like *cristatus*, but make movements of an intermediate kind. Such a creature might well exist in a narrow hybrid zone, but it would be quite unrepresentative of the great majority of crested newts in the country, which would belong to one or other of the three races that occur there. Anyone who wishes to describe the facts accurately would induce, from a mass of information, the distinctive characters of each race, and then plot its geographical distribution. Hybrid zones might be assumed to exist at the racial boundaries, or if they could be ac-curately defined, they would be included on the map (as, for instance, in Fig. 10). It cannot be too strongly insisted that this is the proper procedure, for otherwise important distinctions are necessarily overlooked. The 'political' method is only applicable when all the specimens in a particular country happen to belong to the same race (for instance, *T. cristatus cristatus* in Sweden). Yet over and over again, data (especially genetical ones) are collected

about heterogeneous populations of man, and treated together arbitrarily because at a particular time they chance to be assigned by particular politicians to a particular 'nation'. Information collected in this way tends necessarily to minimize and disguise the true facts about races and subraces.

The chimpanzee, *Pan satyrus* (Linn.), is chosen to provide another example of racial distinctions.[950, 912] The reader may care to note the nature and extent of differences between races in the animal that of all present-day species is perhaps most closely related to man, not only morphologically but also in respect of its blood-groups. The pygmy race (p. 113) is of special interest.

Misunderstandings about the races of the chimpanzee have arisen from the fact that the naked parts are 'flesh'-coloured in young chimpanzees of all races and become blackish or black at the age of 10 or 12 years, for many descriptions refer to immature specimens. The only parts that retain the 'flesh'-colour in old specimens are the penis of the male and the sexual skin of the female. There is a tuft of white hair in the anal region in the young of all races.

The geographical distribution of the races is shown in Fig. 16.

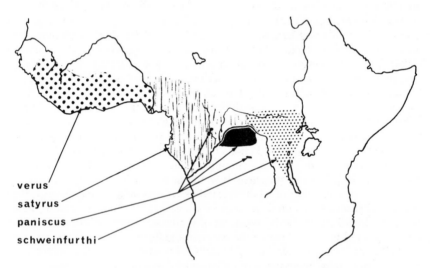

verus

satyrus

paniscus

schweinfurthi

16    *Part of Africa, showing the geographical distribution of the races of the chimpanzee,* Pan satyrus

The black spot north of the Congo River, in the area occupied by the race *satyrus*, indicates roughly the locality in which a specimen of *paniscus* is stated to have been captured. *Map drawn from the data of Rode,* [912] *Coolidge,* [225] *and Urbain and Rode.* [1081]

The 'true' chimpanzee, *Pan satyrus verus*, is a native of West Africa; some authorities have restricted the name of chimpanzee to this race. The skin of the face darkens fairly evenly with age, leaving the lower part pale for a long time. The adult male has side-whiskers and a white beard. The head is hairless along a narrow median strip, giving the impression of a parting. The skull has strongly developed brow-ridges, and the forehead has therefore a markedly concave appearance in side-view. The cranium is high in the parietal region and descends steeply to the occiput.

East of the River Niger *Pan satyrus verus* is replaced by the bald chimpanzee, *Pan satyrus satyrus*, characterized especially by the hairlessness and shining black scalp over a considerable part of the surface of the head. The beard and whiskers are weakly developed. The darkening of the face occurs irregularly in blotches that gradually fuse. In most respects this race resembles *verus*, but the ears are smaller, the back of the skull does not drop away so suddenly to the occiput, and the brow-ridges are strongly developed, especially in the central (glabellar) region. Prognathism is more marked than in *verus*. This race was studied in the wild state by the celebrated explorer, Paul Du Chaillu, who named it *Troglodytes calvus*.* [198, 200] Under the name of *Troglodytes aubryi* it was afterwards studied anatomically in great detail by Gratiolet and Alix, whose well-illustrated description was published more than a century ago. [430]

The race of chimpanzees discovered by the German explorer Schweinfurth in the territory of the Niam-Niam cannibals, on the watershed between the Bahr-el-Ghazal and Ubangi Rivers, is called in his honour *P. satyrus schweinfurthi*. This eastern race, which is now known to extend as far as the vicinity of Lakes Albert and Tanganyika, is more different from *verus* and *satyrus* than these from one another. In describing in great detail the anatomy of this race nearly a century ago, Hartmann remarked that if he had studied it fifteen years earlier, when species-mongering ('*Artmacherei*') was in full swing, he would have made it a new species. [476] The skull is narrower, more elongated, and flatter on top; the profile of the face is noticeably straight. The brow-ridges do not rise up quite so markedly as in the other species. The skin of the face darkens evenly. The fur is very abundant, and the male has well-developed side-whiskers and a beard.

The pygmy chimpanzee, *Pan satyrus paniscus*, was discovered much later than the other races, and only made known to the scientific world in 1929. [949] It had previously been supposed that no chimpanzees occurred south of the River Congo, but in fact this little animal is quite widely distributed in the forested region enclosed by the great northerly bend of the river [947, 225] (Fig. 16). In 1939 an adolescent male was discovered north of the great river, in the Haute-Sangha district; [1081, 913] that is to say, in the territory of *P. satyrus satyrus*. If *paniscus* can really maintain itself in the territory of *satyrus*, this pygmy chimpanzee might qualify as a separate species; but confirmation would be necessary.

*P. satyrus paniscus* is a much smaller ape than *verus*, *satyrus*, or *schweinfurthi*. When adult, it retains many characters, apart from size, that distinguish juveniles in the other races. [949, 225, 1081, 913] Of these the most obvious is perhaps the white anal tuft; the ears are small; the forehead is better developed and the head more convex above than in adults of the other races; the back of the head falls away sharply to the occiput; the brow-ridges are not very prominent and there is not a deep depression behind them; the orbits are nearly circular and close together, so that the frontal sinuses are almost squashed out of existence; prognathism is slight; the canine teeth are small: *all these* are juvenile characters in the other races (though blackening of the facial skin occurs earlier in *paniscus* than in the others).

---

* Both Schwarz [950] and Rode [912] maintain that Du Chaillu's species *Troglodytes koolookamba* [199] was also in fact *P. satyrus satyrus*. This seems improbable. It was more likely to have been a specimen of *verus*.

Since it retains juvenile characters when adult, *Pan paniscus* is an example of what is called a 'paedomorphous' form. This is a subject of particular significance in relation to the present book, for it provides a remarkable counterpart to the small peoples among human beings, such as the Negritids of the Malay Archipelago, the Bambutids (pygmies) of central Africa, and the Sanids (Bushmen of the southern part of that continent). Adults of these three taxa bear about the same size relation to ordinary human beings of other ethnic taxa as *paniscus* does to the other races of chimpanzees, and all of them show juvenile characters, apart from size, when adult. The subject of paedomorphosis is discussed in a general way on pp. 137–8, and Chapter 17 is devoted to the physical characters of the Sanids.

Schwarz[949] considers that *paniscus* is closest in some of its characters to *satyrus*, but Coolidge, in his detailed description, relates it especially to *schweinfurthi*. [225]

The races of chimpanzees differ from one another in the cries that they utter,[947] but wild anthropoid apes do not lend themselves particularly well to the study of racial differences in habit. They are nowhere abundant animals, and study of their behaviour under natural conditions of life is necessarily a slow process requiring great patience. Detailed observations have indeed been made on wild chimpanzees, but there is not much information about differences between the habits of the various races. A few remarks will be made here about certain differences in habit between the races of the gorilla, and attention will then be directed towards those species that lend themselves particularly well to studies of this sort. Carefully planned experiments of the kind that have been carried out with wild deer-mice (pp. 115–16) are unfortunately impossible with man's nearest relatives, the chimpanzee and gorilla.

No fewer than ten species of the genus *Gorilla* have been described, but careful study has revealed that the morphological characters on which this sub-division of the genus was based are in fact very variable from individual to individual.[224] There is great variation in the shape and size of the sagittal crest and brow-ridges and in the shape of the occiput in this animal. It is usual nowadays to recognize only one species, *Gorilla gorilla*, and two races, *G. gorilla gorilla* and *G. gorilla beringei*.[224] The former, the so-called 'coast' gorilla, occupies roughly the same territory as the *satyrus* race of chimpanzees, while *beringei*, the 'mountain' gorilla, is confined to a much smaller area to the west of Lakes Edward, Kivu, and Tanganyika. The typical mountain gorilla has a longer palate and generally a narrower skull than the other; the arms are shorter, the legs longer, and the coat of hair thicker. It has been claimed that only one skull in five can be identified with certainty as belonging to one form or the other. Those specimens of the mountain gorilla that have been tested for blood-groups belong to 'A', those of the coastal form to 'B'.[189] It is probably the overlap in some of the characters that causes zoologists to regard the two forms as racially and not specifically distinct. Since the areas they occupy are not contiguous—indeed, they are nearly 600 miles apart—there is no question of interbreeding in nature, and *beringei* bears much the same relation to *gorilla* as many 'races' on oceanic islands do to their continental representatives. Since gene-exchange cannot occur, literal application of Dobzhansky's definition (p. 74) might cause one to regard these two forms as separate species. It is presumably taken for granted, however, that they would inter-breed if it were possible for them to meet under natural conditions.

The most interesting difference between the two races concerns their habits. The mountain gorilla, occupying as it does an elevated region in the Mitumba range, is adapted for resistance to cold. It is a bulk feeder, and defaecates five or six times a day; it almost invariably fouls its nest. The coastal form eats more fruit, and one might suppose that this would have a laxative effect; but it seldom defaecates more than once a day, or fouls its nest.[786] It would appear from the literature of the subject that these habits are carried over into captive life. In cases of this sort it is often not easy to distinguish with certainty between built-in differences, imposed by genetic constitution, and those resulting directly from environmental effects.

Innumerable instances could be quoted of differences in behaviour shown by the races of a single species. The pipit, *Anthus spinoletta*, will serve as a typical example. The water-pipit, *A. spinoletta spinoletta*, is a bird that frequents the regions of marshy meadows and dwarf trees in the high mountains of central and southern Europe. Its slightly smaller size and thin white stripes above the eyes and at the extreme edges of the tail distinguish it from the rock-pipit, *A. spinoletta petrosus*, which departs so far from the habits of the other race that it confines itself to the vicinity of rocky sea-coasts.[802] The physical resemblance is very close, for the parts corresponding to the white stripes in *spinoletta* are paler than the rest of the body (though not white) in *petrosus*; yet the chosen habitats are entirely different, and the rock-pipit feeds on the marine molluscs and Crustacea of the beach.

The question arises, whether the selection of habitat by members of a particular race is controlled by innate tendencies, or whether the environment of the young imprints on their minds an idea of the 'right' habitat in which to spend their lives. This subject has been investigated experimentally by Dr. S. C. Wecker of the University of Michigan.[1124, 1125] He chose the deer-mouse, *Peromyscus maniculatus*, for his investigations. This species consists of many races, some living in prairies and others in forested areas. Members of the prairie races have shorter ears and tails and are somewhat smaller than those that inhabit woodland. A prairie or grassland form, *bairdi*, and a woodland form, *gracilis*, both occur in the countryside near the University of Michigan, each keeping to its own chosen habitat. Dr. Wecker's object was to discover the immediate cause of the selection by *bairdi* of grassland in preference to woods.

To study this problem he chose the sharp edge of a wood of oak and hickory trees where it abutted on grassland, and fenced off a large pen that included both habitats. Mice were set free in the pen and allowed to choose whichever habitat they preferred. Their movements were recorded automatically by ingenious devices, which need not be described here.[1124, 1125]

Wild mice of the race *bairdi*, when placed in this pen, elected to occupy the patch of grassland in preference to the wood, but this might have been a result of their experience when young. Wild *bairdi* were therefore brought into the laboratory to produce offspring. The latter had had no experience of any natural habitat, but when placed in the pen they showed a very marked preference for the grassland. It follows that prairie deer-mice of the race *bairdi* inherit an innate preference for their natural habitat, and it may be concluded that in this respect they differ from *gracilis* and other woodland races.

The experiments just recorded do not prove, however, that the early environment is altogether without effect. Luckily it was possible to study this subject experimentally. It appears that the tendency of prairie deer-mice to choose the 'right' environment when living in the wild is maintained by natural selection; for when *bairdi* is reared in the laboratory for twelve or more generations, without any experience of a natural habitat of any sort, progeny placed in the experimental pen show no well-defined preference for either habitat, but distribute themselves in woodland or grass at random.

This 'laboratory' stock of mice, in which the selective capacity as regards habitat had become attenuated, provided material for further interesting experiments. Some of them were put with their mothers in a closed pen containing grassland only, before their eyes had opened. After about a month in this environment, the idea of grassland had been imprinted on them; for when transferred to the experimental pen and thus given the choice of grass or wood, they showed a marked preference for the former. This proved that the early environment could exert an effect, but further experiment showed it to be of a limited kind; for when young of the 'laboratory' stock were brought up in a closed pen containing only woodland before being given a choice of woodland and grass in the experimental pen, they showed no particular preference for wood or grass. Thus the attenuated 'laboratory' stock still retained an innate capacity to receive the impression of grassland but not of woodland.

This interesting experiment strongly suggests that a genetical difference affects choice of habitat by races of the deer-mouse, though an element of doubt may arise from the fact that the tendency towards a particular choice is lost after a sequence of only twelve generations in the absence of natural selection of the fittest to survive. The experiment would also have been more demonstrative if it had been repeated with *gracilis*.

Races of animals differ in what might be called temperament, and there is reason to believe that a genetic element is concerned. It has been shown by experiments on rats that genes affecting body-weight, the size of various organs, the dimensions of the skull, and other physical characters, may also influence tameness and docility.[178]

A particularly interesting example of racial differences in innate behaviour-patterns is provided by the honey-bee, *Apis mellifera** Linn. The researches of von Frisch on the 'language' of this animal are well known. Thanks to his remarkable studies it has become a familiar fact that worker bees can tell one another in what direction and roughly how far away a source of food is situated. It is not necessary to describe the 'language', which is very clearly explained in von Frisch's own writings.[363, 364, 365]† It must suffice to say here that a worker bee of the race *A. mellifera carnica*, having found a source of

---

* This specific name is often mis-spelled *mellifica*. The rules of nomenclature require that Linnaeus's spelling should be followed.

† There is an excellent working model, explaining the language, in the Oxford University Museum.

food at some distance from the hive, returns home and performs a particular dance that gives the necessary information to other workers, which fly off and find it. The distance is indicated by the speed at which the dance is performed: the faster, the nearer.

Now another race of this species exists, the 'Italian' *A. mellifera ligustica*, which uses—to speak metaphorically—another dialect of the same language. This differs in two respects. First, *ligustica* uses a *different* dance to indicate direction and distance, when the food-supply is close to the hive. Secondly, for longer distances her dance is the same as *carnica*'s, but her scale is different: to indicate a particular distance, she dances more slowly than *carnica* does. When members of the two races are kept together in the same hive, they confuse one another, because they misinterpret one another's symbols. Worker bees of the race *ligustica* in a mixed hive respond to the message of a *carnica* forager by looking for the food too close to the hive, and conversely a *ligustica* forager sends the *carnica* workers too far away on a useless journey.[365]

There is no evidence that young workers are taught the 'language' by their elders, as children are taught to speak. The capacity to communicate ideas of direction and distance is innate, and the races differ innately in this important component of behaviour.

Although the environment plays such a preponderant part in human language, yet there seems to be no doubt that a genetic element is involved, as Eimer claimed more than eighty years ago.[304] The etymology and grammar of languages are passed on from one person to another in the course of life, but the phonetic element in speech depends in part on inherited characters, which make it easy or difficult to produce certain sounds. This was first established clearly by Professor C. D. Darlington in an article published in a genetical journal,[247, 248] in which he considers the geographical distribution in Europe of people who can readily pronounce the various sounds of the *th* group (as in *this*, *thick*, and the related sound in the Basque language), and those who cannot. He follows the past history of human migrations in relation to changes in the distribution of this capacity, and comes to the conclusion that difficulty in pronouncing these sounds has spread with human populations from the east. Invaders may adopt the languages of their new territories, while retaining their own phonetic capacities or incapacities; the latter may thus be transferred to quite different languages. He brings forward evidence that there is a correlation between a low frequency of the gene for the 'O' blood-group in a population and difficulty in pronouncing the *th* sounds.

Darlington expresses his findings in national instead of ethnic terms; but as a broad generalization (subject to reservations where particular local groups are concerned), one may say that a low frequency of *th*-speakers is found among Alpinids, Osteuropids, and Armenids, while most *th*-speakers are found among Nordids and Mediterranids.

The role of genetic factors in the development of speech-sounds has been treated in some detail by Brosnahan.[146]

# 8 Some taxonomic and evolutionary theories

TYPICAL FORMS

MUCH OF the misunderstanding that arises in discussions of the ethnic problem would be avoided if those who intended to study man would first gain experience of general taxonomy; that is to say, of the principles used in the systematic arrangement of organisms into taxa. These principles are based on studies of animals and plants, and have been secondarily applied to the human *Formenkreis*. In biology the subject exists on a far more extensive basis, for our attention is concentrated not on a single *Formenkreis*, but on all the taxa from the subrace to the phylum, and as a result the principles stand out in much bolder relief. Many students of man have indeed taken a preliminary course in biology; but modern developments in that science have been so wide-ranging and of such great interest that teachers in elementary classes have naturally focused their attention on them, almost to the exclusion of the wealth of knowledge accumulated in earlier times about the variety of organisms and the principles that should guide one in the attempt to gain an impression of a taxon as a whole, and of its history in the distant past. A new generation of teachers has grown up, well equipped to teach certain important branches of biology, but perhaps less so to impart a real understanding of taxonomic biology. Particular organisms are chosen to illustrate particular aspects of animal or plant life, but the study of *the taxon as a whole* is either omitted altogether, or undertaken only by a few of those who make zoology or botany their major subject; and of this limited number, very few indeed become anthropologists. As a result, man and his subdivision into ethnic taxa are often studied in an isolated manner, by persons unacquainted with the massive knowledge and understanding that exist and have not been rendered less true or less relevant by recent advances in particular fields.

Animals are classified into their taxa by their resemblances, and so far as possible by those resemblances that are due to common ancestry. The taxon, whether 'large'—a class, for instance—or 'small', such as a *Formenkreis* or a race, consists of individuals, no two of which (not even 'identical' twins) are exactly alike. The grouping into taxa, large or small, can only be done by persons gifted with the capacity for induction, who are capable of recognizing such resemblances as exist. They will form in their minds an idea of a 'typical' member of the group, and will note the departures, in various directions, from this form. (It will be recollected that the 'type' of a species need not be typical of it. See p. 67.) Some members of a taxon may show specializations adapted to the performance of particular functions; some may be 'degenerate' in the sense of having lost, in the course of evolution, certain structures that were possessed by their ancestors; some may be 'primitive', having never attained the stage of evolution that characterizes the more 'typical' forms. In many cases it is scarcely possible to invent an actual definition of a taxon that will describe every member of it, yet will distinguish it satisfactorily from every other kind of animal; but one markedly aberrant form is often so obviously linked up by intermediates with others that are less aberrant, that the reality of the taxon as a natural unit impresses itself forcibly on the mind. It may be found best not to attempt an all-inclusive definition, but to draw up a description that covers the typical members of the group, and to note the various departures from it.

It is important to realize the limitations of statistical methods in taxonomy. One cannot idealize a 'typical' member of a taxon by simply counting or measuring and then subjecting the figures obtained to statistical analysis. An example taken from the class Gastropoda ('univalves') of the phylum Mollusca will make this clear. Some members of this taxon (e.g., *Trochus*, the common top-shell of our sea-shores) have no specifically genital pores: the spermatozoa or eggs are discharged into the kidney and find their way into the sea through the urinary duct. Others, such as the 'triton trumpets' (*Charonia*, see Fig. 17A, p. 120), have one genital pore, carrying either spermatozoa or eggs to the exterior, according to sex; others again, being hermaphrodite, have two, one to discharge each type of genital product; yet others have these two, and a third to receive spermatozoa from another individual—this occurs in various sea-slugs (Nudibranchia). It would not be sensible to count the number of genital pores in all kinds of gastropods, find the arithmetic mean, and state that the typical form has (say) 1·87 genital pores.

One cannot determine which animals should be included in the Gastropoda and which excluded from it by consideration of metrical data alone. This would be a serious error, yet a comparable one has been made in anthropological writings. For instance, in making a statistical study of all the known Palaeolithic human skulls of Europe, the statistician G. M. Morant took a set of measurements from each, without considering whether the parts measured were those that distinguished various ethnic taxa or not.[765] These measurements, when analysed statistically, might give the impression that all the skulls belonged to members of a single, homogeneous population, and this conclusion has in fact been derived from his data by several anthropologists. Morant himself did not make this mistake. He admitted, in the paper in which he described his findings, that 'the treatment of the series as a sample from a single homogeneous population may obscure some ethnic relations of great importance'. In other words, his work was carried out on the assumption that the population was homogeneous, when manifestly it was not. For instance, the so-called '*négroïdes*',[1094] whose skeletons were found in the Grotte des Enfants, near Mentone, are strikingly different from Cro-Magnon man.[47]

Attention has already been called to this error (pp. 111–12), which might be described as 'political taxonomy'. A certain district, defined by national boundaries, is treated as though it contained a homogeneous population, whether in fact it does or not; this is then compared with another such district,

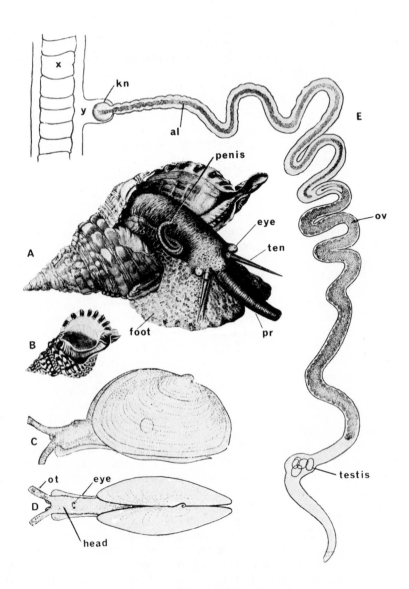

## 17  Typical and untypical gastropods

*Typical:* A, *Charonia nodifera. pr,* proboscis; *ten,* tentacle. B, shell of *Charonia nodifera.*

*Untypical:* C, D, the bivalve gastropod, *Tamanovalva limax,* from the left side and from above. *ot,* olfactory tentacle (rhinophore). E, wormlike gastropod, *Entoconcha mirabilis,* an internal parasite of an echinoderm. *al,* alimentary canal of *Entoconcha; kn,* its knoblike 'head'; *ov,* its ovary. *x,* alimentary canal, and *y,* so-called 'haemal space' of the echinoderm, *Synapta digitata.*

A, *from Poli;*[850] B, *from Reeve;*[887] C *and* D, *from Kawaguti and Baba;* [572] E, *from Müller.* [780] *Lettering by the author.*

treated in the same way. This procedure has been adopted on a large scale in the study of blood-groups in Europe. That it is not a reliable method of exposing biological truths is demonstrated by the fact that no one adopts it when ethnic differences are so obvious, even to those untrained in morphological anthropology, that they cannot be overlooked. Thus, no one studying blood-groups in Australia 'lumps' the aborigines (Australids) with persons of European origin; clearly one would only confuse the results by so doing. In taxonomy one must use common sense, morphological insight, and evidence from palaeontology, too, if this is available, to discover which animals (or men) fall into a natural group or taxon, and to gain an impression as to which members of it may properly be regarded as typical, which primitive, and which specialized.

The various taxa of animals—the phyla, classes, orders, and the rest—provide almost unlimited scope for illustration of these ideas, but there is perhaps no group better adapted to the purpose than the very large class of Gastropoda. This includes the familiar garden snail, *Helix aspersa*, but no one acquainted with its anatomy would choose this species as typical of the group as a whole. Its reproductive system is very complex, and its nerve centres concentrated in a small region of the head instead of being distributed in various parts of the body, as in so many members of the group. The spirally coiled shell is, however, characteristic of very many gastropods.

In choosing such a large and diverse assembly of animals as a class to illustrate the ideas of typical, specialized, degenerate, and primitive members of a taxon, I am simply using an extensive canvas to show in bold outline what will appear again in miniature, but nevertheless distinctly, when in subsequent chapters the taxon under consideration will be a single *Formenkreis* and the human races that compose it. The ideas are fundamental and must be grasped from a preliminary study of easily interpreted material, before the facts of physical anthropology can be properly appreciated.

In seeking a typical form, one must avoid those that are primitive, for these are in certain respects untypical, since they possess features that are not represented in most members of the class, and lack others that occur in many or most. Different authorities would no doubt choose somewhat different forms, but one cannot go very far wrong in selecting an unspecialized member of the order Pectinibranchia, such as the 'knobbed trumpet triton', *Charonia nodifera* (Lamarck) (often called *Triton nodiferus*); indeed, this is precisely the form chosen by Parker and Haswell for rather detailed description, as characteristic of the class as a whole, in their *Text-book of zoology*.[820] This large marine gastropod (Fig. 17A, B) has been recorded from British seas and is common in the Mediterranean; members of the genus occur in the Red Sea and off the coast of South Africa, and their range extends across to the South Pacific Ocean, where the shells are bored near the tip by the natives of the New Hebrides and other islands to form trumpets for long-distance communication.

In a book such as this, a detailed description of the anatomy of *C. nodifera* would be out of place, but anyone who is at all familiar with the gastropods can see at a glance, by looking at the text-figure, that there is nothing highly specialized about its external characters; and the internal ones are such that a student who has examined them is in a favourable position to understand the anatomy of almost any gastropod that is not markedly specialized or aberrant. *C. nodifera* has a spirally coiled shell, protecting a corresponding coiled visceral hump; a 'mantle' or fleshy fold hanging down from the hump; a flat foot on which the animal moves; a 'tongue' (radula) provided with teeth, and an alimentary canal ending in an anus; eyes, and a statocyst or gravity-organ; a complicated nervous system, consisting of paired nerve-centres (ganglia), joined by nerves called commissures and connectives; and a single genital gland (testis or ovary, as the case may be, for the sexes are separate).

No one who wished to name a typical gastropod would choose one of the cowries (*Cypraea*) for the purpose. The shell of these animals is very untypical of the group as a whole, for each succeeding whorl almost entirely covers the preceding ones, so that it could scarcely be guessed that the structure had ever been spiral. Beyond this, the part of the shell that separates the successive whorls is gradually absorbed, so that even internally the spiral structure is removed; and the aperture of the shell, instead of being rounded, is flattened to a slit. Yet the anatomy of the soft parts is not very abnormal, and *Cypraea* falls into the same order as *Charonia*. Another untypical gastropod is *Umbrella*, a Mediterranean form, in which the shell is flattened and resembles the object to which the generic name refers; no trace of spiral structure persists in it. Other gastropods, again, have lost the shell altogether in the course of evolution. The strange planktonic form, *Pterotrachea*, is an example: not only the shell, but the visceral hump also has disappeared; so have the tentacles; and a long thread-like appendage hangs out from the posterior end of the body.

These animals, however, are only untypical to a moderate degree; there are far more astonishing departures from the characteristic gastropod form. One of the most extraordinary was only discovered quite recently. A glance at the shell shown in Fig. 17C and D, would convince almost anyone that the animal was a bivalve—that is to say, one of the Lamellibranchiata and not a gastropod at all. This curious animal was discovered in Japanese seas in 1959.[572] Unlike the lamellibranchs, however, it has a head and eyes and olfactory tentacles. A study of its internal anatomy shows conclusively that despite its bivalve shell it is a gastropod, belonging to the subclass Opisthobranchia.

In the course of evolution certain animals have become simpler in structure than their ancestors were, generally as a result of their restriction to a very limited habitat. Very untypical, 'degenerate' forms often originate in this way. The gastropods provide some excellent examples. It will be allowed that no one, not already acquainted with the facts, could possibly suppose that the wormlike creature shown in Fig. 17E was a gastropod. This is *Entoconcha mirabilis*, and the specific name does not exaggerate its peculiarity. The animal is a parasite in the body-cavity of the marine holothurian *Synapta digitata* (related to the 'sea-cucumber', *Cucumaria*, and to *bêche-de-mer* or *trepang*). It was discovered by the German physiologist and comparative anatomist Johannes Müller[780] in the course of his study of the holothurian. It lives attached to a haemal or 'blood' vessel on the wall of its host's intestine (seen on the left of Fig. 17E). The reader may find it instructive to compare the following description with that of the typical gastropod, *Charonia*, given above. In its adult state *E. mirabilis* has no spirally coiled shell, nor indeed any shell at all; no visceral hump, no mantle, no foot, no radula, no anus, no eyes, no statocyst, no nervous system—but two genital glands (an ovary and a testis)! One may well ask how such an animal can be called a gastropod, for we have here an extreme example of departure from the typical. Yet it is universally allowed by zoologists that *E. mirabilis* belongs to this class, and indeed to the same order (Pectinibranchia) as *Charonia*. Its position in the classification is determined partly by a study of its development, and *partly by comparison with an interesting series of intermediate forms that connect it with typical members of the group.*

From what has been said it will be understood that there are gastropods that may be called 'typical', because they represent so well the group as a whole, and others so specialized or degenerate that they can only be called untypical. It will be realized that it is almost impossible to frame a definition that will include all gastropods and exclude all animals that are not gastropods; for if it were to cover the extremely aberrant forms, it would necessarily be so vague and all-inclusive as to conjure up no clear idea in the mind, and it would in fact be useless. If, however, one learns the characters of the typical forms, and then studies the progressive departures from the norm until such extremely aberrant offshoots as *Entoconcha mirabilis* are reached, one can delimit the class with confidence. The idea of the typical is valuable in taxonomy; and it is inescapable, because anyone who looks will see it, even though the perfectly typical form may not be found. The idea is applicable to all taxa, at any rate from the class downwards, although naturally the extremes of divergence are not to be expected in the minor range of the taxonomic hierarchy, among the genera and species. But even among the races, in man as in animals, the idea is valid and indeed manifest, though intermediates produced by hybridity may make the proportion of typical forms lower than it would otherwise be.

There are some who argue against the idea of the typical, claiming that this is a mere abstraction, without reality; yet anyone who thinks it necessary may choose a particular *individual* as his type. This is precisely what the philosopher, Sir William Hamilton, did in respect of man.

The class *man*\* includes individuals, male and female, white and black and copper-coloured, tall and short, fat and thin, straight and crooked, whole and mutilated, &c., &c.; and the notion of the class must, therefore, at once represent all and none of these. It is evident, therefore, though the absurdity was maintained by Locke, that we cannot accomplish this; and, this being impossible, we cannot represent to ourselves the class *man* by any equivalent notion or idea. All that we can do is to call up some individual image, and consider it as representing, though inadequately representing, the generality. [464]

It is unlikely, however, that many zoologists, in forming their ideas about typical members of a taxon, do actually think of a single individual. They are more likely to discard temporarily from their minds all extremely primitive, specialized, or aberrant animals that clearly belong to the taxon but do not adequately represent it; they then build up the idea of the taxon from what remains, and regard any form as typical if it falls within the scope of the idea.

\* It is scarcely necessary to remark that Hamilton does not use the word 'class' in the sense in which it is used in the taxonomy of animals.

It would be possible to carry out an experiment to determine whether the idea of the typical is valid. In teaching comparative anatomy it is usual to select one species of a taxon and make an exact study of every part of its body and then proceed to a much less detailed review of the structure of other members of the taxon, including those that depart most significantly from the form that has been chosen for special study. It would be possible to arrange that one half of the class used *Charonia nodifera* as the example chosen for detailed study, and the other half *Entoconcha mirabilis*. The whole class would then join for the general review. At the end, the same examination on the anatomy of the Gastropoda would be set to both halves of the class. It is scarcely possible for any comparative anatomist no doubt that those who had studied *Charonia* would gain significantly higher marks (unless, indeed, the students of *Entoconcha* had surreptitiously studied some more typical form before joining the others, as they would be severely tempted to do); and those who had studied *Charonia* would also be at a great advantage when the time came to study the remaining classes of the Mollusca.

PRIMITIVE FORMS

Some memorable words taken from a contribution by Sir Ray Lankester to the *Encyclopaedia Britannica* will serve to introduce the idea of the 'primitive', as that word is used in biology. He is here considering not just the class of gastropods, but the phylum Mollusca as a whole. He constructs

a schematic Mollusc, which shall possess in an unexaggerated form the various structural arrangements which are more or less specialized, exaggerated, or even suppressed in particular members of the group. Such a schematic Mollusc . . . may be taken as more or less coinciding with what we are justified, under present conditions, in picturing to ourselves as the original Mollusc or archi-Mollusc.[631]

It will be noticed that in this passage Lankester goes back in imagination far beyond the typical forms to a primitive ancestor common to all members of the phylum.

In many taxa of animals one need not use imagination to find a primitive form. Studies in comparative anatomy will reveal that certain members of a class are simpler in many respects than others, but show no sign of degenerative changes; and these forms often resemble, more or less closely, the comparable simple members of other classes of the same phylum. Further, if fossils have been left in the older sedimentary rocks, it may be found that the forms supposed to be primitive on grounds of comparative anatomy are in fact very similar to animals that existed in far-off times, before the 'typical', 'specialized', and 'degenerate' representatives of the group had evolved. It happens not very rarely that a living animal, previously unknown, is discovered which closely resembles the members of a primitive stock till then known only from its fossil remains in ancient rocks. Such forms are often called 'living fossils'.

The facts related in the preceding paragraph can be well illustrated by reference once again to the gastropods.

In the typical form, *Charonia*, there are many organs that occur only on one side of the body; but in other species, simpler in structure but not degenerate, these organs are seen to be paired, left and right. A study of all the relevant facts indicates that in the ancestral gastropod these organs were represented by an equal left and right pair, like the kidneys, for instance, in our own bodies; but in the course of evolution the strange spiral twisting of the body had gradually resulted in the reduction and finally in the elimination of the organs that were originally on the left side, but were twisted to the right; while the organ of the other side, brought over to the left, remains large. The twist can be seen to occur at an early stage in embryonic development. In the account that follows, the words 'left' and 'right' refer to the final situation of the organs in adult animals.

In *Charonia* and in an enormous number of other species of gastropods, only the left-side organs remain. This applies to the following:

the gill (ctenidium) or respiratory organ;

the organ of chemical sense (osphradium), which tests the water entering the gill-chamber (mantle-cavity);

the mucous (hypobranchial) gland, which secretes a substance that keeps the gill-chamber clean by sticking together faecal and other particles;

the vessel (auricle) that brings blood to the main contractile organ (ventricle) of the heart;

the renal or excretory organ.

In a few gastropods, however, the ancestral condition is retained, for all these organs are still present on both sides of the body, though the left and right members of a pair are commonly unequal. A good example of such a creature is the 'ormer', *Haliotis tuberculata* (Fig. 18A, p. 126), which occurs off the coasts of the islands in the English Channel, and indeed is sufficiently abundant there to form the basis of an industry, since the flesh is edible. Other species of the genus occur in Californian, Japanese, and East Indian seas. In California the local species is known as the 'abalone'. Many who are familiar with *Haliotis* as an article of food are probably unaware of its special scientific interest as a primitive gastropod.

*Haliotis* is specialized in certain respects (as many primitive animals are). It is flattened from above, and the spiral form of the shell is greatly reduced; indeed, there is little of it left except the enormous last whorl, which contains almost the whole of the animal (Fig. 18A). As a result, the shell shows some resemblance to a human ear, and it is this that gives rise to the name of 'ormer' (a contraction of the French *oreille de mer*), by which the animal is known in the Channel Islands; the scientific name of the genus has exactly the same meaning. *Haliotis* would be an almost ideal example of a primitive gastropod if only its visceral hump and shell took the form of a gradually expanding spiral.

The left gill of *H. tuberculata* is decidedly bigger than the right; the left hypobranchial gland is very much larger than the other; the left auricle is slightly, and the left kidney considerably, *smaller* than the right. [232] The osphradia are about equal. Another primitive form, *Fissurella*, which occurs in British seas, is remarkable in having exactly equal left and right gills (Fig. 18B), but this is perhaps a secondary condition, consequent upon the assumption of a somewhat limpet-like shape.

Wherever in a taxon of animals we find a primitive form, we may expect to see in it *resemblances to members of related taxa.* We may therefore look among other classes of Mollusca for features in which *Haliotis* resembles them; and we shall certainly not be disappointed, for this animal is a good example of a form that has retained many characters which must have been possessed not only by ancestral gastropods but also by the ancestors of all the classes of Mollusca, but which have been lost in the course of evolution by all the gastropods except the primitive ones.

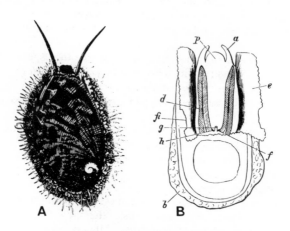

18    *The primitive gastropods* Haliotis tuberculata
*(A) and* Fissurella *sp. (B)*

The mantle of *Fissurella* has been cut longitudinally and turned aside to the right (*e*) and left to show the two equal gills (ctenidia), *d. a*, tentacle; *b*, foot; *fi*, hole in mantle; *g*, anus; *h* and *f*, openings to exterior of left and right kidneys; *p*, head.
*A. from Fischer;* [334] B. *from Lankester.* [631]

Brief mention must be made here of other molluscan classes, for the benefit of those readers who have not made a study of this great phylum. Of these classes the most familiar is the Lamellibranchiata or 'bivalves', of which the mussel and oyster are examples. Everyone has also seen or read about the squid and octopus, and perhaps also the pearly *Nautilus.* The symmetrically wound spiral shell of the latter is rather similar to that of the ammonites shown in Fig. 21 (p. 133); it is sometimes displayed as an ornament. These three—squid, octopus, and *Nautilus*—are representatives of the class Cephalopoda.

The other classes of Mollusca are much less likely to be known to those who have not studied zoology. One of them indeed, the Monoplacophora, was not known to anyone, except as a misunderstood group of fossil shells, until 1952, when a few specimens of a single species (*Neopilina galatheae*) were obtained by trawling in the depths of the Pacific Ocean, west of Costa Rica. [651] While still known only by their fossil shells, the members of this group had been regarded as aberrant limpets—that is, as gastropods; but their soft parts showed them to be quite different in structure, and very remarkable for the serial repetition of some of their organs. The Polyplacophora or chitons, not wholly dissimilar, are another primitive group, their most obvious feature being the presence of eight calcareous shells strung out in a line along the upper surface of the body. Both these and the Monoplacophora are known from early Palaeozoic rocks. (The other main taxa of molluscs, the Aplacophora and Scaphopoda, are not particularly important in connection with the subject under consideration here.)

Apart from the gastropods, all molluscs that possess ctenidia show symmetry in respect of these organs, the right and left ones being equal in size on the two sides of the body. *Haliotis* thus shows resemblance to members of other classes, since its right and left ctenidia are not very different in size. The ctenidia of *Haliotis* are bipectinate; that is to say, they have projections on both sides of an axis and thus resemble bipectinate hair-combs, while in the great majority of gastropods that have ctenidia, the projections are on one side only, as in the ordinary domestic hair-comb. (*Fissurella* resembles *Haliotis* in this respect, as can be seen in Fig. 18B.) It is particularly interesting that in this respect *Haliotis* resembles *Nucula* (a primitive lamellibranch), *Nautilus* (a primitive cephalopod), and *Neopilina* (a member of the primitive group Monoplacophora—though in the latter case the projections are unequal on the two sides). Again, *Haliotis* is primitive in that the living tissues of its eye form a hollow cup, whereas in the vast majority of gastropods the edge of the cup grows across and joins up, so that the lens is totally enclosed. Now *Nautilus* has the same type of eye as *Haliotis*, but is still more primitive, for the cup is devoid of lens and filled with sea-water. *Haliotis* also has a blind spiral tube (caecum) projecting from its stomach; in this it differs from the great majority of gastropods, except the primitive ones; but a corresponding structure occurs in most cephalopods.

There are yet other ways, besides these, in which *Haliotis* differs from most gastropods but resembles members of other classes. The most striking of all is in the nervous system. In all gastropods except the most primitive this system consists of two distinct elements: numerous brainlike *ganglia* (containing aggregations of nerve-cells) and nerve-fibres (devoid of cell-bodies), which connect the ganglia and innervate all parts of the body. In *Haliotis*, however, this sharp distinction does not exist. There are no demarcated ganglia, for the nerve-cells are distributed all along the chief nerve-trunks, and there are not swollen regions to which the cell-bodies are restricted. This applies equally to the nervous systems of the two most primitive groups of molluscs, the Monoplacophora and Polyplacophora; and although ganglia occur in *Nautilus*, the commissures that connect the corresponding ganglia of the two sides of the body contain nerve-cells as well as nerve-fibres.

*Haliotis* is thus in most respects a primitive gastropod. Its organs are for the most part unspecialized and such as one would expect to find in an ancestral form. It shows several striking resemblances to primitive members of other classes, and thus seems not to have diverged very far from the ancestor from which all molluscs must originally have sprung. It is probable, however, that the early gastropods had large, spirally coiled visceral humps, and a shell widening evenly from the tip to the open end. It has already been mentioned that *Haliotis* is in these respects specialized, for its body is compressed dorso-ventrally and little remains of the spiral shell except the enormous last whorl. Is it possible to find a gastropod that possesses the primitive characters of

*Haliotis*, but lacks these specializations?

Certain fossil shells were already known long ago which appeared to have belonged to forms related to *Haliotis*, but were of unspecialized spiral type. The genus *Pleurotomaria*, familiar to palaeontologists, belongs here; its range in time extended from the Triassic to the Miocene.[1137] Many genera of the family Pleurotomaridae are, however, much more ancient, going back perhaps 430 million years to the early Ordovician, and related genera about 90 million years further back still, to the lower Cambrian.[1137]

The fossil shells could not provide positive evidence that *Pleurotomaria* and similar gastropods were genuinely primitive in the absence of any knowledge of the soft parts. In 1856 a remarkable discovery was made. A collection of molluscs from the French West Indies had been sent to France for study. Among them was a shell of *Pleurotomaria*, with the coloured cuticle still intact and a few fragments of the soft parts of the animal still attached.[335] It had been obtained in deep water off the island of Marie-Galante. Hopes that the complete 'living fossil' would be discovered were naturally aroused, and before the end of the century a number of specimens had been obtained at various times off Barbados;[242, 133] but although some of them had been alive when caught, not very much was learnt about their internal organs, apart from the nervous system and radula. Eventually, however, a specimen of the genus was obtained off the coast of Japan and was still alive when examined by a Japanese zoologist, who preserved it excellently for anatomical and histological study.[749] This specimen, with others from Japanese seas, was carefully examined by M. F. Woodward of the Royal College of Science, London, to whom we are indebted for most of our knowledge of the anatomy of this interesting genus.[1154]

Apart from having a slit in it, through which the respiratory current is expelled with the faeces and excreta, the shell (Fig. 19A) is a simple, regularly enlarging spiral and contains a normal visceral hump. In those respects in which the organs differ from the corresponding ones of *Haliotis*, they are even more primitive. In particular, the eye is simpler, for the lens does not fill the

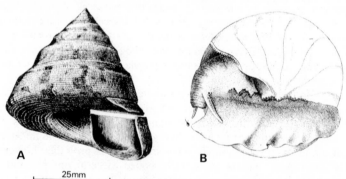

A                                B

25mm

19    *The 'living fossil'* Pleurotomaria

A, the shell of *Pleurotomaria quoyana*; B, *P. adansoniana*, crawling.
*From Dall.* [242]

open cup, as it does in *Haliotis*, and sea-water enters the organ freely, as it does in *Nautilus*. A few other gastropods are more primitive in particular respects, but no other member of the group shows so many ancestral characters so well. Not only is *Pleurotomaria* a primitive gastropod: in certain respects it approaches Ray Lankester's ideal of the 'archi-mollusc', except in the spiral twisting of the body that is one of the most characteristic features of the great majority of the class to which it belongs.

The gastropods have been chosen to illustrate the ideas of the typical and the primitive, because they happen to be particularly well suited for the purpose. Many other taxa would have served nearly as well, and indeed a closer approach to human affairs could have been made by using the Mammalia instead. In the latter group the so-called 'tree-shrews' (Tupaiidae) are probably as good examples of typical forms as one could choose, while the duck-billed platypus (*Ornithorhynchus anatinus*) and spiny anteaters (*Echidna* and *Zaglossus*) are primitive in several respects, since they retain certain characters that associate them with the reptilian ancestors of the group (though they cannot be regarded as very close to the ancestral form from which the higher mammals (Placentalia) arose[435], and they are much more specialized in particular features than *Pleurotomaria* is among the gastropods). The manatees (*Trichechus*) and dugongs (*Halicore*) are obviously highly specialized in relation to their marine habitat.

It is hoped that the foregoing brief remarks, intended to introduce the ideas of the typical and the primitive to readers who have not studied morphological and taxonomic zoology, will be found useful when the occasion arises in Chapter 16 of this book to discuss these ideas in relation to a much smaller and less diverse taxon than a class, the *Formenkreis* of man.

## THE RECAPITULATION THEORY

In judging whether a particular organism is to be regarded as primitive in certain respects, one is naturally inclined to rely primarily on evidence derived from comparative anatomy and palaeontology. The question arises whether embryology may not also provide a clue. The theory of recapitulation suggests that it does. The word 'recapitulation', in this context, means that the individual, in the course of its development, tends to re-enact the evolutionary history of the race. The matter is important for the ethnic problem; for if it were true, one could draw conclusions about the 'primitiveness' of certain groups of mankind from studies in human embryology.

Foreshadowings of the recapitulation theory can be detected in eighteenth-century writings, and more definitely in those of the first half of the nineteenth. In 1811 the German comparative anatomist J. F. Meckel wrote a 'Sketch of a demonstration of the parallel to be found between the embryonic states of the higher animals and the permanent states of those of lower rank'.[727] Meckel presented his ideas on this subject at considerable length, and a part of what he says is valid. He points out in some detail, for instance, how the heart, major blood-vessels, and brain of the higher vertebrates at the embryonic stages of their development show resemblances to the corresponding organs in adults of animals in the lower groups. In the next decade these ideas appear to have been widely accepted, for von Baer[42] referred to

the ruling idea that the embryo of higher animals passes through the permanent forms of the lower animals.... Few statements of affairs in the organic world have found so much approbation as this, that the higher forms of animals, in the several stages of development of the individual from its first origin to full maturity, show correspondence with the forms that remain behind in the animal series; that the development of individual animals follows the same laws as that of the whole series; and that the more highly organized animal, in its individual development, thus passes through what are more or less the same as the permanent stages of those which stand below it in the series.

Having now said the same thing four times (and actually he goes on to say it once more in the same sentence), von Baer might be thought to have accepted the idea of recapitulation, but in fact this great embryologist had done nothing of the sort—for he gives no indication that he has any idea of evolution in his mind.

The Swiss-American zoologist and palaeontologist Louis Agassiz carried these conclusions rather further by comparing the embryonic stages of modern animals with the forms of life that had existed in remote geological ages.

In my researches on fossil fishes I have often made allusion ... to the resemblance that one can remark between embryonic forms and the characters of the most ancient representatives of this group in the geological epochs. This latter analogy corresponds to another important principle: that the order of succession of the geological types in time agrees with the gradual changes that the animals of the present day undergo during their metamorphoses.[11]

Agassiz illustrates this theme by examples chosen from diverse groups of animals.

One might well suppose that Agassiz's words, quoted in the preceding paragraph, did not simply foreshadow but actually stated the theory of recapitulation. This, however, was not so; for Agassiz never accepted the doctrine of evolution, though he lived till 1873. It was Charles Darwin who first put it forward, tentatively and not very clearly, in the first edition of the *Origin*.[254] He argued that, as a general rule, the modifications of structure that distinguish a species from its ancestors appear in the offspring 'at a not very early period of life', and that 'at whatever age any variation first appears in the parent, it tends to reappear at a corresponding age in the offspring ... the embryo is the animal in its less modified state; and in so far [as this is so] it reveals the structure of its progenitor'. Thus 'we can clearly see why ancient and extinct forms of life should resemble the embryos of their descendants—our existing species'.

These ideas were powerfully reinforced by Fritz Müller in his little book *Für Darwin*, published five years later.[775, 776] One of the early followers of Darwin, Müller not only spread the latter's doctrine, but also made important contributions to it, especially in the field of mimicry. *Für Darwin* is essentially an exposition of the recapitulation theory, based on a study of the development of Crustacea.

Müller's main thesis was that the various larval forms known in this group gave a general impression of the ancestral history of the class. He was much struck by the fact that a shrimplike creature, *Peneus* (or a member of a closely related genus), though belonging to one of the most highly evolved groups of Crustacea, started life as a free-swimming larva of the type called 'Nauplius', the characteristic larva of many of the most primitive forms (Fig. 20). He

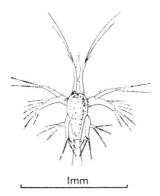

20    *The Nauplius larva of* Peneus
*From Müller.* |775|

remarked that this developed into another very distinctive type, called 'Zoea', a characteristic larval form of many of the *higher* Crustacea, and this again into a third kind of larva, closely resembling the *adults* of the family Mysidae, another group of shrimplike forms, regarded as somewhat more primitive than *Peneus*. 'The shrimp', he wrote, 'that we accompany from the Nauplius through the Zoea and *Mysis*-like stage up to the form of a long-tailed crustacean, at present appears to be the animal which, within the group of the higher Crustacea (Malacostraca), gives the most complete and truest information about its ancestral history.'

In the fourth edition of the *Origin*, published in 1866|255|, Darwin referred several times to Müller's contributions to the recapitulation theory, and recorded the latter's conclusions about the ancestry of *Peneus*. He still only accepted the theory rather tentatively, however, and in the latest edition published during his lifetime|256| he still remarked, in reference to the supposed 'law' requiring that ancient forms should resemble the embryos of existing species of the same class, '... we may hope hereafter to see the law proved true'—almost the same words as he had used in the first edition, thirteen years earlier.

The wide acceptance of the recapitulation theory must be ascribed neither to Darwin nor to Fritz Müller, but to Ernst Haeckel. This strange man, fantastic though some of his writings were, had a remarkable capacity for exposition, and probably did more than anyone else except T. H. Huxley to popularize

Darwin's doctrine of evolution by natural selection. He briefly summarized the recapitulation theory in his *Generelle Morphologie*. 'Ontogenesis', he wrote, 'is the short and quick recapitulation of phylogenesis.'[451] This appears to be the first use of the word 'recapitulation' in connection with the processes of development. He also coined the term '*Biogenetisches Grundgesetz*' as a more dogmatic name for the recapitulation theory. This theory has probably never been more clearly explained than in the following remarks taken from *Anthropogenie*, his work on the development and evolution of man.

> These two parts of our science—on one hand ontogeny or the history of the embryo and on the other phylogeny or the history of the stock—stand in the closest possible relation, and one cannot be understood without the other. The relation between the two is not of a merely apparent or superficial, but of an intrinsic, causal nature. This knowledge is, of course, an achievement of very recent times, and even now the *fundamental law of organic development*, based on it, is still often doubted, and not acknowledged even by famous men of science. This '*fundamental biogenetic law*', to which we shall repeatedly come back again, and on the acknowledgement of which all genuine understanding of the developmental process depends, may be expressed in the statement, 'The history of the embryo is an epitome of the history of the stock;' or in other words, '*Ontogeny is a short recapitulation of phylogeny;*' or in somewhat greater detail, 'The series of forms through which an individual passes during its development from the egg-cell to its adult state is a short, compacted repetition of the long series of forms that the animal progenitors of the same organism (or the ancestral forms of its species) have passed through from the earliest times of so-called organic creation up to the present day.'[452]

Ideally, to reach certainty on this subject one would need a complete series of fossils at all stages of individual development through a long sequence of geological strata. As a general rule adult animals stand a better chance of being fossilized than young ones, because they usually possess harder constituent parts, less liable to decay before the process of petrification has set in. When fossil embryos or larvae are found, it may be difficult to associate them with the correct adults. The Ammonoidea (ammonites) circumvent these difficulties to some extent. They constitute an extinct order or suborder of cephalopod molluscs, numbering many thousands of species; they are found as fossils in Palaeozoic and Mesozoic rocks, and are extremely abundant in the latter. Some were minute, but there were giants with shells up to two yards in diameter. In this group the shell has a general resemblance to that of *Nautilus*, the characteristic form being a flat spiral (Fig. 21). As in *Nautilus*, growth began at the centre. The initial chamber was formed by a very young animal, and each succeeding part of the spire was added by the same individual at later and later stages of its life. Thus the adult carried about with it a record of its own life-history; for ridges and tubercles developed on its surface, and these formed distinctive patterns at different ages (see Fig. 21A). By searching back into older and older rocks one could find slightly different forms that seemed to represent an ancestral series.

The American palaeontologist Alpheus Hyatt, who was a distinguished authority on this group of animals in the second half of the nineteenth century, claimed that the evidence provided by the ammonites supported the theory of recapitulation, for he found a correlation between the developmental history of the individual and the evolutionary history of the stock to which it

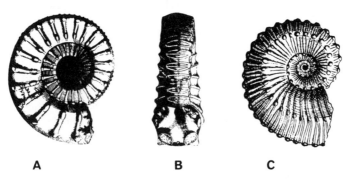

**A**                              **B**                          **C**

21    *The ammonites* Peltoceras *and* Cosmoceras

A. *Peltoceras athleta* (from the Jurassic of Normandy), viewed from the right side. The change in the external sculpturing with age is well shown. B. *P. athleta*, from in front. C. *Cosmoceras ornatum* (from the Jurassic of Baden-Wurtemberg), viewed from the right side. The orientation of these fossil shells has been altered from the original illustrations to accord with the modern interpretation.    *From Zittel.* [117]

belonged.[541] It seemed that the structure of the parts of the shell formed by geologically ancient ammonites when they were *adults* resembled parts formed by more recent species (their supposed descendants) when they were *young*.

Hyatt's conclusions could scarcely have been more directly contradicted than they were by the researches of the Russian palaeontologist Pavlow on the ammonites in the Lower Cretaceous strata of his country.[828] The facts he observed are interesting and relevant; the conclusions he drew from them can only be described as astonishing. Pavlow examined the internal, intermediate, and external whorls of the shell in certain ammonites that appeared to form an evolutionary series, ascending from *Kepplerites* in the lower (earlier) strata to *Cosmoceras* in the upper (more recent). So far was he from obtaining confirmation of Hyatt's results, that he found the exact opposite. 'It seems more accurate', he wrote, 'to say, not that the internal whorls of *Kepplerites* repeat the characters of the immediate ancestors of this genus [as the theory of recapitulation would require], but that they announce the characters of the descendants [*Cosmoceras*] of this genus: there is not an atavistic phase but a prophetic one'! Pavlow found comparable series of forms in various groups of ammonites and coined the term '*précession des caractères*' to indicate his belief that developmental stages might actually foreshadow the future.

One can only suppose that modifications in the external characters of the shells in various lines of descent over long periods of time chanced to give appearances suggesting recapitulation in Hyatt's cases and *précession* in Pavlow's. This is borne out by the statistical studies made later by Brinkmann on Jurassic ammonites and reported by him in a massive contribution to a scientific journal, longer than many books.[137] He found no evidence of any *general* tendency for the parts of the shell formed by the animals when young to resemble the parts formed by adults of related species occurring in more ancient rocks. In some cases a resemblance of this kind existed, in others it did not; no rule could be applied.

Up till the end of the first quarter of the twentieth century the theory of recapitulation was widely accepted, and it was applied by Haeckel and others to the ancestry of man. It was argued by the anthropologist Klaatsch that since the skulls of young orang-utans and gorillas resemble that of adult man more closely than do those of adult apes, it followed that the common ancestor of apes and man must, when adult, have had a skull like adult man's, from which that of adult apes subsequently diverged.[588, 589] Klaatsch considered that the ancestral anthropoid apes were much more like man than were their descendants, the apes of the present day. Only the foot, he thought, was markedly different from that of man. He based this conclusion on embryological, not palaeontological evidence. It is strange that he made no actual reference to the theory of recapitulation or the biogenetic law.

These ideas of Klaatsch were developed independently and at much greater length by a Canadian anthropologist, Hill-Tout[491, 492], who based his opinions firmly on

> that great biogenetic principle sometimes called Baer's law. . . . Now it must follow from Baer's law that the skull-forms of the young of the anthropoids and the young of man must represent very closely the original skull-form of their common progenitor. . . . in his head form and general cranial characters man has remained practically unchanged from the period when he and the anthropoids first set forth upon their divergent careers.

Hill-Tout concluded that in the common ancestor of apes and man, the forehead rose steeply above the orbits, and that the great brow-ridges and sloping foreheads of *Pithecanthropus*, the Neanderthalians, and Australids evolved quite independently of the similar features in the apes. He would not allow that *Pithecanthropus* was even a semi-human forerunner of man; he denied that it belonged to the family Hominidae.

If the conclusions of Klaatsch and Hill-Tout could be substantiated by evidence supporting the theory of recapitulation, a new light would be thrown upon the ethnic problem; for certain features in the skulls of Australids and others, long regarded as evidence of primitiveness, could no longer be attributed to retention from an apelike ancestor. Hill-Tout did allow, however, that the receding chin, characteristic of certain ethnic taxa, was a genuinely primitive character.[491]

As Darwin had foreseen[254], the theory of recapitulation gave a great impetus to embryological research. Objections to it soon arose, however, which have never been satisfactorily answered. One might well imagine than von Baer would have supported the theory, which has often been wrongly attributed to him as a result of what he wrote in 1828.[42] In fact he opposed it strongly.[43] The main opposition started, however, in the twenties of the present century, and has grown into a large literature, which appears to have resulted in the rejection of the whole idea of recapitulation. The fact that very different animals have similar larvae is interpreted in another way. From the fact that the sessile barnacle and the free-swimming *Peneus*—utterly unlike one another in appearance when adult—start life as very similar Nauplius larvae, the conclusion is no longer drawn that the common ancestor of both, in its adult state, resembled a Nauplius. On the contrary, it is supposed that the common ancestor must have had a Nauplius larva. It is recognized also that one takes too narrow a view if one regards the phylogeny of an animal as simply the evolutionary history of the series of *adults* from which it is descended. On the contrary, all stages in individual development are subject to evolutionary change, and phylogeny, properly understood, is a description of events that have affected all stages in the lives of ancestors. A well-adapted and therefore successful larval form, such as the Nauplius, may persist in two or more groups of animals that are now widely different in their adult stages, and are therefore placed far apart in the system of classification; in other groups, more closely related to one another, very different larval forms have sometimes evolved.

A particularly striking instance of what has just been said may be quoted. It involves what would be an impossibility under a rigorous application of the biogenic law. *Lineus gesserensis*, an unsegmented marine worm belonging to the phylum Nemertini, occurs off the coast of Brittany in two forms, regarded as subspecies and named *L. gesserensis gesserensis* and *L. gesserensis ruber*. The adults differ from one another in no feature, so far as is known, except the minor one of colour, *L. g. gesserensis* being green and *L. g. ruber* red. Cocoons are laid, each containing many eggs. The young of the green form is of the type commonly called 'Desor's larva', in honour of the Swiss-American who first described it;[270] but the name is ill-chosen, because the object to which it is applied is an embryo, not a free-swimming larva. This embryo transforms itself gradually, and the animal that eventually escapes from the cocoon is a little worm. There is no need here to describe the process of development; it is enough to say that the embryo is sluggish and has a small mouth. The red form develops, surprisingly enough, from a very different embryo.[943] It is active and has a large mouth and oesophagus, which it uses to good purpose: for the great majority of the embryos die when they are no more than groups of undifferentiated cells, and these are greedily consumed by the embryos that survive.

It is remarkable enough that two very different processes of development should be undergone by animals that are indistinguishable as adults, except by colour; but that is not all. Another species of the genus, *Lineus lacteus*, develops in an entirely different way, characteristic of many nemertines. The young form of this species is a free-swimming, planktonic larva, called 'Pilidium' from its resemblance to a small hemispherical felt cap with lappets to cover the ears (Greek πιλίδιον). No one would be likely to guess that this organism and the embryos of the green and red worms would all three develop into closely similar nemertine worms. The theory of recapitulation might be thought to imply that the *adult* ancestor of *L. lacteus* resembled a Pilidium, while that of the green kind was like Desor's embryo, and the red one's ancestor like the egg-eater. It is, however, incredible that such similar adults as the modern forms could each have an entirely different ancestor; all must be descended from the same stock. It must be supposed that the common ancestor was a wormlike creature when adult, quite unlike any of the three youthful forms. The evidence suggests that the young of this ancestor was a Pilidium, and that in the course of evolution of the green and red worms this Pilidium larva was transformed into the two embryonic forms that have been mentioned.[419]

The conclusions of Klaatsch and Hill-Tout are not supported by more recent studies. Acceptance of the theory of recapitulation would suggest that the ancestors of modern dogs had skulls with bulging foreheads and short, weak jaws, like those of the Pekinese; for that is the form of the skull in the young embryos of all dogs. If, however, the ancestry of the Canidae is followed in the fossil record, no adult skulls resembling those of the Pekinese are found. On the contrary, there is a gradual evolution towards the type of skull found in the jackal and wolf, and in what appear to be the least modified forms of domestic dogs.[434] The form of the skull in mammalian embryos throws no light on its structure in adult ancestral forms. It is quite usual for mammalian embryos to have skulls showing some resemblance to those of adult modern man. This was recognized by von Baer nearly a century before Klaatsch and Hill-Tout expressed their views. 'The pig and dog', he wrote, 'are at first very similar to one another and have short, human faces (*Menschengesichter*).'[42] As the American palaeontologist W. K. Gregory pointed out, the feebleness of jaws and lack of bony ridges for the insertion of jaw-muscles in immature skulls of man and apes are not evidence that their common ancestors had feeble jaws and lacked bony ridges when adult, but only that at the suckling stage strong jaws would have been purposeless. 'To suppose that the remote common ancestor of man and anthropoids had a vertical forehead without brow ridges is to invent an entirely hypothetical group and to disregard the series of existent inter-grading conditions from that of the lower mammals on the one hand to that of man on the other.'[434] It need not be supposed, however, that in the common ancestor of man and apes the brow-ridges were developed to the excessive degree that we see in the male gorilla and in that strange, isolated human fossil, Broken Hill man, discovered in 1920 in what is now Zambia.[866, 1136, 48] A certain amount of convergent evolution has occurred in this respect in the two stocks.

A mass of evidence has accumulated in opposition to the theory of recapitulation. One of the most interesting general attacks on it was written by Garstang[388] at a time when the theory still received support from influential biologists. The much later work by de Beer *Embryos and ancestors* includes a valuable critique of the whole subject.[71] Neither of these authors was primarily concerned, however, with the relevance of the subject to the problem of primitiveness in man. In this connection it must suffice to say that there is no biogenetic 'law' requiring that the ancestor of man should resemble the human embryo; but since this embryo resembles that of the anthropoid apes, there is every reason to believe that the common ancestor of apes and man developed, generation by generation, from an embryo of similar form. We shall not find out which are the most primitive ethnic taxa of modern man by looking for those that retain youthful or embryonic characters when adult. On the contrary, we must look for those that retain characters shared by adult anthropoid apes, though not necessarily by those rather unrepresentative members of this group that happen to have survived to the present day. It will be necessary to revert to this subject in Part 3 of this book (Chapter 16).

## PAEDOMORPHOSIS

It follows from what has been said that Darwin was wrong when he argued (see p. 130) that the modifications of structure that distinguish a species from its ancestor appear in the offspring 'at a not very early period of life', and that, as a result, 'the embryo is the animal in its less modified state; and in so far it reveals the structure of its progenitor'. The *opposite* process does, however, sometimes occur: the adult retains to some extent what had been embryonic or larval characters in its ancestors, and what had in the past been adult characters no longer appear.

Some animals are capable on occasion of becoming sexually mature while still retaining larval characters, or in other words the larval stage is stretched out so as to include sexual maturity. The word *Neotenie* (Greek νέος, young; τείνω, stretch out, extend) was coined in 1885 by Kollman, who had noticed that if he kept amphibian larvae of various species as prisoners in water, after the time when they would ordinarily have metamorphosed into the adult form and become terrestrial, they retained their larval characters even when at last given the opportunity to escape on to dry land.[604] He mentions cases in which the crested newt, *Triturus cristatus*, passed the winter in the larval stage and become sexually mature in the following summer, while still retaining the larval form and without ever having passed through a terrestrial phase. In the same paper he refers to the case of the axolotl in Mexico.

It is nowadays a familiar fact that the axolotl (*Amblystoma tigrinum*) often retains the larval form of a salamander, respiring by external gills, when sexually mature. Sometimes, however, it metamorphoses into a form resembling that of the adult salamander, lacking gills and breathing by lungs. Related forms, such as *Necturus* and *Proteus*, have altogether lost the capacity to metamorphose. They remain throughout life in the larval condition, except in the development of their reproductive organs.

The great influence that neoteny may have on the process of evolution was emphasized nearly half a century ago by the British zoologist Professor Walter Garstang, who claimed that many of the major taxa of animals derive their characters not from the adults but from the larvae of remote ancestors.[388] His contention was that in many cases the ancestral adult form was discarded during the course of evolution. This was the reverse of the theory of recapitulation. He expressed his views in a neat epigram, 'Ontogeny does not recapitulate Phylogeny: it creates it,' and he introduced a new word, 'paedomorphosis' (Greek παῖς, παιδ-, boy; μόρφωσις, shaping) to extend the idea of neoteny. He defined it very briefly as 'the influence of larval characters upon adult organization'. The mere retention of larval characters by some individuals of *Amblystoma tigrinum* scarcely suggests a fundamentally important process, affecting the major taxa of the animal world. By paedomorphosis Garstang meant something more significant—a new principle underlying evolutionary changes. This idea was seized upon and extended by A. C. Hardy, who saw in paedomorphosis a method by which animals had gained release from close adaptation to particular circumstances of life and thus enabled themselves to branch forth freely in new variety. He called this the 'escape from specialization'.[468]

The fundamental principle of paedomorphosis need not be restricted to animals that have a distinctive larval form that must undergo sudden and dramatic metamorphosis in order to assume the structure of the adult. In very many animals there is no such distinctive free-living form, to which the name of larva can properly be applied. The embryo develops gradually into the infantile, juvenile, and adolescent stages and so to the adult, without any sudden or profound changes in structure; yet throughout the process gradual modifications have been occurring. Although there is no larva, animals that develop gradually may undergo evolutionary change of the same type as that to which Garstang gave the name of paedomorphosis; for it may happen that adults resemble the infantile or juvenile stages of their ancestors, except in the maturity of the reproductive organs. It seems legitimate to extend the meaning of paedomorphosis to cover such cases. This has been done, for instance, by G. R. de Beer, in *Embryos and ancestors*.[71] The pygmy chimpanzee (pp. 113–14) is clearly a paedomorphous subrace of *P. satyrus*.

Paedomorphosis is highly relevant to the subject of this book, for modern man himself shows some paedomorphous traits, and certain human taxa have gone much further than others in this respect. Chapter 17 is devoted to a paedomorphous subrace of man.

## ORTHOGENESIS

Some analogy has often been supposed to exist between the processes of individual development on one hand, and those of evolutionary advance on the other. Indeed, the theory of recapitulation reflects one aspect of this idea. Another aspect is represented by those theories that have a central theme in common, namely, the belief that there exists a 'force' or mechanism or influence of some sort, that directs the course of variation and thus evolution. Those who accept this central theme are united in believing that evolution is not due, as Darwin claimed, to random variation coupled with the better chance of survival possessed by those individuals that happen to be the best fitted to survive.

The name of 'orthogenesis' is commonly applied to theories of evolution based on the central theme mentioned in the preceding paragraph. The fact that the word 'orthogenesis' was introduced by a man named Haacke is mentioned by a few writers, but I have never seen a quoted statement of what he meant by it. Johann Wilhelm Haacke of Darmstadt, traveller and biologist, coined the term in 1893, in a book written primarily to oppose the opinions of August Weismann, as expressed in the latter's celebrated work, *Das Keimplasma*[133, 134], which had been published in the preceding year. Haacke made perfectly clear what he meant by his new technical term. The first sentence in which it occurs is this: 'But in accordance with our earlier considerations we have first to ask whether variability occurs in all directions or whether it follows a prescribed direction—whether we can establish amphigenesis or orthogenesis.'[446] The name 'amphigenesis' for random variation has disappeared; 'orthogenesis' has remained. Haacke meant by it that the 'prescribed' (*vorgeschrieben*) direction caused evolution to proceed in such a way that *reversal* did not occur (with certain minor exceptions). Whether one examined the evolutionary history of a particular organ (the eye, for instance) or of a great group of animals, such as the Mammalia, one never found a *return* to an earlier condition. Apart from single reverse mutations, which do in fact occur but do not significantly influence the course of evolution, Haacke was right in this contention. He was well aware that degenerative changes do occur, especially in the circumstances of parasitism, but he knew that earlier stages in the evolutionary history did not reappear during the process. In brief, he considered that evolution took place through a process of variation that did not occur at random and did not result in 'reversal' or repetition of earlier states; and that is what he meant by orthogenesis.

Since Haacke's time, however, the term orthogenesis has generally been used to mean not only that variation is what he called 'prescribed', but also that evolution tends, as a general rule, to proceed in a 'rectilinear' manner; that is to say, in such a way as to cause continuous progress in the same direction. Examples of the parallel but independent evolution of related stocks are quoted as evidence of this. As we shall see, some biologists have attributed rectilinear evolution to an unexplained cause, residing within the organisms; others (but not many) to the action of the environment in influencing the course of variation.

In considering the ethnic problem, one is concerned with the inborn potentialities that may manifest themselves, in suitable environments, by intellectual achievement. Just as there are 'slow developers' among human beings, so also—it is widely believed—certain ethnic taxa that have not yet shown much evidence of intellectual attainment are 'slow developers' in the evolutionary sense, and will eventually, of necessity, reach the same standard as the rest. The American palaeontologist G. L. Jepsen has remarked that it 'is a favorite pastime of popular writers' to predict the course of evolution; and anthropologists—so the same author says—have assumed that orthogenesis has been demonstrated by palaeontologists and is still held in high esteem by them.[552] The Dutch anatomist L. Bolk in his pamphlet on human evolution makes a definite statement implying that the less advanced races of man must inevitably evolve as others have done in the past.[120]

Striking evidence of rectilinear evolution was provided by the Austrian palaeontologist, M. Neumayr, who made a study of certain highly fossiliferous freshwater deposits in the Pliocene of what is now northern Yugoslavia, and published a detailed account of them in 1875.[795, 794] Species of the familiar genus of pond-snails, *Viviparus*, usually known as *Paludina*, occur so abundantly in this geological formation that some of the strata are called *Paludinenschichten*. Passing from earlier to later deposits, Neumayr found what he regarded as an evolutionary series of forms. In the early ones the shell was smooth, and the whorls evenly rounded; corrugations with intervening furrows began to appear in slightly later forms, becoming progressively more marked in still later deposits, till eventually the corrugations broke up into tubercles. Neumayr's illustrations of the gradual change of form through the ascending strata are impressive.

Careful study of Neumayr's report [795] reveals that the sequence was not in fact quite regular. In *Viviparus sturi* the tubercles were even more highly developed than in *V. hörnesi*, though the former occurred in a lower stratum. Slight corrugations, in addition to the major ones, occurred in some of the species. These, too, reveal departures from strictly rectilinear evolution.

From his study of ammonites, already mentioned on pp. 132–3, Hyatt came to the conclusion that evolution was controlled by internal causes, and not primarily by natural selection. [541, 542] In the early stages of the evolution of an ammonite stock, the change of form in the shell was 'progressively direct' (i.e. rectilinear); it then became 'progressively indirect', as aberrant forms appeared; finally there was a 'retrogressively direct' stage, as the stock declined towards the phylogenetic counterpart of senility. Hyatt stressed the parallel between ontogenetic and phylogenetic change—between individual development and evolution—and attributed both to internal causes.

The Swiss botanist Carl von Nägeli was another early exponent of the idea of an internal force affecting the direction of variation. Like Hyatt, he was unable to believe that natural selection of random variations could be the cause of evolutionary progress. His book on the subject [785] is, however, very different in outlook from the writings of Hyatt and also from those of Neumayr, though the ideas of all three were to fall subsequently into the as yet unnamed category of orthogenesis. Nägeli distinguished between the influences of the environment (*die äusseren Ursachen*) and the internal ones (*die inneren Ursachen*), the former producing only temporary modifications that were not inherited, while the latter resulted in continuous changes and originated new varieties and species. [785] These internal causes were molecular forces associated with the genetic material, which he named *Idioplasma* (corresponding to the deoxyribonucleic acid of modern science). The chemical composition of this *Idioplasma* was such that it entailed a perfecting principle ('*Vervollkom-nungsprincip*'). He disavowed any mystical interpretation of his beliefs, which he described as a 'mechanical-physiological theory of the origin of species'; but he did not base this theory firmly on evidence that could be tested by the observations or experiments of others.

In the long and devious history of orthogenesis, no one seems to have been so frequently mentioned or so much misunderstood as the Swiss zoologist G. H. T. Eimer, Professor of Zoology and Comparative Anatomy at Tübingen, who was the first to adopt Haacke's term and make it widely known. Nordenskiöld, in his *History of biology*, says that Eimer followed the lines laid down by Nägeli and accepted the idea of an 'inner force'. [807] Actually Eimer considered Nägeli a teleologist and in this respect specifically disclaimed any association with him. 'I want to know nothing of a particular, internal evolutionary force,' he wrote; 'in my view everything happens in evolution by altogether natural processes, altogether materialistically [*ganz materiell*], altogether physically.' [304, 305] He attributed variation to the direct effect of the environment on the organism (*not* to the effects of use and disuse).

According to my conception the physical and chemical modifications which organisms undergo during life through the influence of the environment, through light or the lack of it, air, warmth, cold, water, humidity, nutriment, and so on, and which they transmit [to their descendants], are the first means for shaping the manifoldness of the world of organisms and for the origin of species. From the material fashioned in this way the struggle for existence makes its selection.

These words are not in accord with Locy's remark, in his *Biology and its makers*,[677] that Eimer was 'radically opposed to the belief that natural selection plays an important part in evolution'.

Eimer considered that, over certain periods of time, the effect of the environment (aided by natural selection) was to produce more or less rectilinear evolution, and it was for this reason that he stressed the reality of orthogenesis. Some members of a group, at any particular time, had moved further forward in a certain direction than others, and it was therefore possible to witness the orthogenetic stages by observations on related animals at the present day. His first studies were on lizards; afterwards he made a very large series of observations on the Lepidoptera, and devoted the second volume of his book[304] to this group. Since the ionizing radiations present in the natural environment do in fact increase slightly the amount of mutation that occurs in the germ-cells of organisms, and natural selection does sometimes result in rectilinear evolution over a limited period of time (see p. 143), it must be allowed that Eimer's views were not wholly at variance with modern knowledge.

The philosophical biologist Hans Driesch may be regarded as an orthogeneticist, though he had little in common with those, Eimer among them, who sought materialistic explanations of rectilinear evolution. As a matter of fact he was not very much interested in evolution (or 'descent', as he insisted that it should be called). He pointed out weaknesses in Lamarck's and Darwin's explanations, and put instead the idea of 'entelechy', which he defined as 'a something in life phenomena "which bears the end in itself"'.[284] He took the word from Aristotle's ἐντελέχεια, but denied that he used it in the latter's sense. Driesch's views, frankly teleological and vitalistic, do not seem to lend themselves readily to scrutiny by observation or experiment. One is reminded of the '*Vervollkomnungsprincip*', though Nägeli himself would not have admitted any sympathy with Driesch's opinions if he had lived long enough to have heard of them. Driesch, for his part, dismisses Nägeli with the dry remark that he does 'little more than state the mere fact that some unknown principle of organization must have been at work in phylogeny'.[284]

Some similarity to Driesch's opinions is detectable in a book, *Nomogenesis*, written by Professor L. S. Berg, though the latter denied that vitalism could help in the understanding of purposive adaptations, and rejected the idea of entelechy. An authority on fishes in the State University of Leningrad, Berg was a friend of the very distinguished Russian geneticist, N. I. Vavilow, who helped him in the preparation of the English edition of the book, published in 1926.[78] That this is a serious work is indicated also by the fact that Professor D'Arcy Thompson wrote an Introduction to it (without committing himself to its author's views). Like so many others, Berg was impressed with the idea of a fundamental similarity between development and evolution (or between 'morphogenesis' and 'transformism' or 'descent', as Driesch would have said). Like the other orthogeneticists, Berg could not accept the doctrine of evolution by natural selection of random variations (which Driesch, fairly enough, had called 'the elimination principle').

The laws of development of the organic world are the same both in ontogeny and phylogeny. . . . Neither in the one nor in the other is there room for chance. . . . New characters, both in the course of ontogenetic and phylogenetic development, arise not at random, but in a certain sequence and in such a manner that, knowing the preceding stage, we may foretell the following.[78]

Berg used the term 'Nomogenesis' to indicate his belief that evolutionary change is somehow predetermined or subject to laws, 'the modes of which we see and measure, the causes of which we do not and may never understand, but nevertheless laws and not fortuities or chance happenings'.[78] He repeatedly uses the word 'orthogenesis', and it is not obvious why he felt it necessary to coin another name. He insists that internal forces control the evolutionary process, though he allows that natural selection accounted for the *extinction* of ammonites, pterodactyls, dinosaurs, and many other groups.

Several noted palaeontologists of more modern times, the American H. F. Osborn among them, have followed Hyatt in upholding orthogenetic views. They were impressed, like many others from Neumayr onwards, by series of fossils that appeared to show rectilinear evolution in successive geological strata.

Osborn, who was chiefly interested in mammalian palaeontology, distinguished between two modes of evolution. On one hand there was a gradual change in the proportions of the constituent parts of the skeleton: on the other there was the origin of new structures of which no rudiment had been observable in the fossils of older rocks. To the elaboration of these new structures into complicated organs, Osborn gave the name of 'aristogenesis'—the origin of the best. He did not consider that the origin of these organs was predetermined, in the sense that they must necessarily evolve, and he therefore denied the truth of entelechy; but he insisted (perhaps unnecessarily) that there was an inherent potentiality in organisms to evolve and elaborate new structures of particular kinds. He made no claim, however, to explain the cause of aristogenesis. His theory was clearly orthogenetic. 'The process is continuous,' he wrote, 'gradual, direct, definite in the direction of future adaptation.'[812]

Anyone who believes in the inevitable intellectual advance of backward ethnic taxa of men, and bases his belief on the principle of orthogenesis, has a wide variety of conflicting opinion to which to look for support. He may accept the opinion of Eimer that environmental factors enforce rectilinear evolution; or he may suppose that something intrinsic to the organism itself makes necessarily for progressive evolution. If the latter alternative appeals to him, he may postulate, with Nägeli, a materialistic, mechanical-physiological 'perfecting principle', acting on the germ-plasm, generation after generation; he may suppose, in accordance with the ideas of Hyatt, that man is at the 'progressively direct' stage of evolution; he may homologize development with evolution, and find, like Berg, a similar but unknown and perhaps unknowable cause for both; he may rely on the palaeontological evidence of Osborn for the existence of an unexplained, internal, aristogenetic principle; or he may fall back on vitalism, and accept the entelechy of Driesch. Whichever view appeals to him, he should study the evidence for it in the works of the authors that have been named, which are representative of the chief varieties of orthogenetic theory.

Those who accept the doctrine of orthogenesis lay stress on the supposed tendency of organs to go on enlarging or becoming more complex in the course of evolution, even when the enlargement or extra complexity seems useless or disadvantageous. The analogy of 'momentum' has often been used to describe or explain the facts underlying these changes. Fuller study seems, however, to weaken the case for orthogenesis that the facts seem at first sight to support. The extinction of the giant deer *Megaceros giganteus* ('Irish elk') is often attributed to the fantastic growth of the antlers of the male. Similarly the enormous development of the upper canine teeth of the sabre-toothed cats, *Machairodus*, is thought by some to have contributed to their eventual extinction, after they had been abundant for a very long time (even by geological standards) over a large part of the world. It has been pointed out, however, that the antlers of *Megaceros* may have enlarged through the action of sexual selection (that is, female preference), not orthogenesis, and as a matter of fact no one knows the cause of its extinction; and as for *Machairodus*, there was no increase in the size of the canine teeth, in proportion to that of the skull, after the end of the Oligocene, though these strange animals did not finally die out until the Pleistocene, nearly 30 million years later.[552, 971]

At the outset of any attempt to evaluate orthogenetic theories, it is important to realize how insecure these must be if they are based on belief in the fundamental similarity between individual development on one hand and evolution on the other. It is obvious that internal causes (*die inneren Ursachen* of Nägeli) are concerned in the development of an embryo, and it is not absurdly far-fetched to postulate that a perfecting principle (Nägeli's *Vervollkomnungsprincip*) is at work during the process. But modern studies in the field of experimental embryology and genetics have enabled us to get away from vague terms like these; and although much remains to be discovered, there exists today a wealth of information about the factors that control the course of development.* It must be emphasized that in all this mass of knowledge there is nothing that would suggest the possibility that comparable processes control the course of evolution.

The palaeontological evidence for the reality of orthogenesis is much stronger than the embryological, because cases can be quoted in which, over a limited period of time (seldom exceeding a million years[971]), particular stocks seem to have exhibited rectilinear evolution, as we have seen (pp. 139–40). But under nearly uniform conditions of life, natural selection might well be expected to produce something of the sort. The term *'Orthoselection'* was coined by L. Plate, Professor of Zoology at Berlin University, to describe this process. His introduction of the term was rather strangely worded: he defined it as 'Evolution in the sense of the selection theory, [occurring] because the external factors act very unequally on the members of a species, so that selection determines the direction of evolution'.[847] He used these words because he thought that rectilinear evolution resulted not only from orthoselection but also, in

---

* Readers who are unfamiliar with this subject may like to consult a useful paperback booklet by J. D. Ebert.[297]

some cases, from the action of the environment, without any important con- tribution from selection; for this he adopted Haacke's term '*Orthogenesis*'. He thought, however, that orthoselection and orthogenesis should not be separated too sharply, since both might act simultaneously. Nowadays, those who use the term 'orthoselection' are probably unanimous in rejecting orthogenesis.

The accumulation of an immense store of new factual knowledge in palaeon- tology has undermined the credibility of much that was previously accepted, and the attack on orthogenesis has come largely from this direction. Thus the branch of knowledge that had been thought to provide its strongest support has turned against it. Important contributions to this subject have been made by G. L. Jepsen, Professor of Geology at Princeton University,[552] and by G. G. Simpson of the American Museum of Natural History,[971] among others. It is easy in many cases to find evidences of continuous evolution if one works backwards from particular species existing at a particular time, but if one starts in remote antiquity and attempts to follow the divergent progeny of ancient forms, a very different picture is presented. Wrong ideas have spread from oversimplified accounts of certain evolutionary histories that happen to be par- ticularly familiar.

Almost every elementary introduction to the subject of evolution includes an account of the ancestry of the horse. The student learns about the gradual in- crease in size, the reduction in number of digits in fore and hind limbs, the lengthening of the face, the adaptation of the teeth and neck to grazing, and so on. Looking at the pictures and reading the text, he might well invent orthogenesis without ever having heard of it. When, however, one looks in some detail at what is known about the past history of the whole group to which the horses belong, one sees a very different picture. If one were to draw an ancestral 'tree', it would not consist of a stem like that of a palm, beginning with *Hyracotherium* at the base in the Lower Eocene and passing at ascending levels through *Orohippus*, *Miohippus*, *Merychippus*, *Protohippus*, and *Pliohip- pus*, to burst forth at last into the group of leaves at the top, representing the Equidae of the present day (zebras, asses, and horses). On the contrary, the genealogical diagram would not be a tree at all, but a bush, from one side of which a branch would extend sideways at a level representing the Upper Miocene, divide repeatedly at Pliocene and Pleistocene heights, and leave one twig to straggle upwards to the highest level of all (cf. Simpson[970]).

Detailed study of the ancestors, direct and collateral, at any one geological level, reveals strange modifications that simply will not fit into any orthogenetic scheme. A single example may be quoted to illustrate this fact.

During the Upper Miocene, at the base of the 'side-branch' that led on eventually to the horses of the present day, a curious structure developed on the face in the genus *Merychippus* and related forms. This is seen on each side of the skull as two depressions or fossae, situated in front of the eye. Their size and position in relation to one another varied considerably from one species to another; in one species the larger was 9 cm long. There has been dispute about the significance of these pre-orbital fossae, which have been carefully investigated.[1023, 432, 714, 970] It would appear that they did not house scent-glands, like the rather similar depressions on the faces of gazelles (pp. 86–7) and sheep (p. 94). The evidence suggests that the lower of the two fossae served for the posterior attachment of a muscle (*levator labii superioris*) from which a tendon passed forward, joined with the corresponding one of the other side, and then descended from above the nostrils to attach itself to the upper lip. A similar muscle exists in the tapirs, which are remote relatives of horses. The facts suggest that in *Merychippus* the upper lip was prolonged into a snout or short trunk, like that of the tapir. Faint indications of a fossa corresponding to this one can just be detected in the remote ancestors of horses that lived right back in Eocene times, [1023] but there are none in the modern horse. The upper fossa, not represented in earlier members of the stock, probably held a greatly enlarged diverticulum of the nasal cavity. This organ still exists in the modern horse, as a blind·pouch opening into the nostril, [974] but it is not large enough to require a special depression to lodge it. The significance of the *diverticulum nasi* is obscure. It is large in the tapirs, and the fossa in which it is situated is a striking feature of the skull (especially in the Malayan species, *Tapirus indicus* [49]).*

Detailed studies, such as those briefly described in the preceding paragraph, reveal no rectilinear trends; organs enlarge, become variously modified in different species and genera, and then dwindle or disappear in some of their descendants. In the ancestry of the horses there has been no constantly prevailing trend in size of body, in length of tibia in relation to femur or of radius in relation to humerus, or in the structure of the teeth. [971]

In rejecting orthogenesis (in its widest sense) as a cause of evolution, one is saying that there is no known automatic, internal mechanism in organisms that will cause variations to appear in determinate order, generation after generation, so as to result necessarily in step-by-step rectilinear progress. Mutation is regarded as a 'random' process in the sense that the modifications that result from it may be harmful, neutral, or beneficial, in association with the particular gene-complex in which they first make their effects apparent or with other gene-complexes with which they may be associated in subsequent generations through sexual reproduction. Selection then plays its role, in the way that Darwin described. 'As many more individuals of each species are born than can possibly survive; and as, consequently, there is a frequently recurring struggle for existence, it follows that any being, if it vary however slightly in any manner profitable to itself, under the complex and sometimes varying conditions of life, will have a better chance of surviving, and thus be *naturally selected*.' [254] Later, Darwin himself freely admitted that his expression 'natural selection' was metaphorical [256], but it is unlikely to be misunderstood today, as it was when his first edition was published.

Selection may be 'natural', that is to say, operative under the conditions of wild life, or, in the circumstances of domestication, it may be either 'methodical' or 'unconscious', [257] according to whether man improves his domestic animals by deliberate selection of his breeding stocks, or merely as an unplanned consequence of his desire to possess the best specimens of a breed. The only domesticated animal to which man does not apply selection, either methodical or unconscious, is man himself. It follows that we cannot look for any advance in inborn intelligence, except in so far as talented people may tend

---

* According to Matthew, [714] this fossa in tapirs serves as the base of attachment of the muscles that move the proboscis, but this appears to be incorrect; cf. Flower [347] and Gregory. [432]

to intermarry and thus give rise to an intellectual aristocracy; and any ethnic taxon that may be backward in the sense that it possesses a lower proportion of innately gifted persons than certain other groups, will remain so unless it adopts eugenic methods.

## NON-ADAPTIVE EVOLUTION

Nearly a century ago a British clergyman pointed out that selection need not in every case be responsible for evolutionary change. The Revd. John Gulick had been struck by the extraordinary profusion of species and 'varieties' of land snails belonging to the pulmonate family Achatinellidae in Oahu, one of the Hawaiian Islands.[442] Sharp ridges radiate from the main mountain range of this island, dividing it into valleys. The climate and vegetation of these secluded areas are all closely similar, yet in many cases only a single form (either species or 'variety') is found in a particular valley. Gulick considered that in this case selection had played no part in evolution. Immigration and variation had taken place at random. A bird might have chanced to carry a leaf bearing only two individuals to a previously untenanted valley, and these had become the ancestors of nearly all the individuals that eventually populated it. There was no mechanism to ensure that small groups of snails in newly occupied valleys would vary in exactly the same way as those in the valleys from which they had come. If selection had been the cause of evolution, it would have resulted in uniformity throughout the island. Gulick makes the interesting comment that 'Natural selection is as efficient in producing permanence of type in some cases as in accelerating variations in other cases'.

In the present century there has been much controversy among biologists about the way in which differences in gene-frequency may have arisen. The random drifting of these frequencies may indeed be responsible for cases such as those described by Gulick, but there is rather general agreement nowadays that non-adaptive variation, without any influence from selection, has played only a minor role in evolution. Indeed, there are those who would deny that it has played any part at all. Opinion has been affected by an important study of evolution in action by the British geneticists R. A. Fisher and E. B. Ford. The investigation in question was concerned with the frequency of a gene affecting wing colour in an isolated colony of the moth *Panaxia dominula*. Fisher and Ford followed the evolutionary change in this frequency over a long period of years, and obtained strong evidence that in this particular case natural selection was the sole cause of the change.[338]

There is reason to believe, however, that what is here called the Gulick effect may play a part in evolution, in collaboration with other factors. This idea has been put forward particularly by Sewall Wright, Professor of Genetics at Wisconsin University. Wright lays stress on the necessity to consider not only natural selection and the Gulick effect (or 'drift', as he calls it), but also recurrent mutation, the action of modifying genes, and the movement of genes from one population to another through migration. Modifying genes are those that are without significant influence on the individual in which they occur unless that individual happens to possess in addition a major gene the effect of which they are able to modify. Sewall Wright's views cannot be adequately expressed in a short statement, but the following paragraph will give an impression of them.

In Wright's opinion, evolution tends to occur most rapidly in a large population of a species, dispersed in a number of semi-isolated populations. The Gulick effect appears in the existence of differences between these populations in the frequency of genes that are capable of modifying a particular major gene which does not occur initially, however, in any of them. If, in one of these semi-isolated populations, there happens to be a very high frequency of genes that are able to modify this major gene in such a way as to favour the natural selection of individuals that possess it, and if this major gene arrives in that population (either by mutation or by immigration of an individual that carries it), it will spread rapidly as a result of the advantage conferred by the new gene complex in the struggle for existence. Increase in the population may result in emigration and the spread of the new gene complex to other semi-isolated populations, and possibly eventually to the whole species.[1159, 1160, 1161, 1162]

The Gulick effect may have played a part in human evolution in Palaeolithic times, when man appears to have lived to a large extent in isolated communities. Genes controlling blood-groups may have established themselves in different frequencies in some of these, without direct control by selection. At any time in human history the isolation of a small community (e.g. the Todas, pp. 221-3) might result in unusual gene-frequencies. It is characteristic of the Indianids (American 'Indians') that the great majority of them (in many cases more than 90%, in some cases whole tribes) are members of blood-group 'O'; yet less than half the population of the Blackfoot tribe of central North America[1353]—perhaps only about one-quarter of it[383]—belong to 'O'. One is tempted to suggest that at some time in the past a particular group of persons, who happened to be unrepresentative of Indianids as a whole in their blood-group frequencies, somehow became isolated. The Blackfeet, however, are in other respects rather typical members of the Silvid subrace. It is unlikely that a group of people differing from their relatives in a multitude of genes affecting the structure of various parts of the body happened to become isolated and thus gave rise to a new race or subrace of man, without the directive pressure of selection. Partial isolation combined with selection, in accordance with Sewall Wright's theory, may, however, have played a part in human evolution.

# 9 Colour

Colour is generally esteemed by the systematic naturalist as unimportant.

Darwin[257]

THE EMPHASIS placed on the colour of the skin in popular speech and writing, and the genuine significance of pigmentation as one among very many factors that must properly be considered in the classification of man, make it necessary to describe in some detail what this colour actually is, how its intensity is controlled, and what its biological significance may be. These are subjects of considerable complexity, and they require some understanding of the structure of human skin. It will be helpful to readers who have not studied histology to be provided with a description of the minute anatomy of this part of the body. Everything that is not necessary for an understanding of skin colour will be omitted from the brief remarks that now follow.

If, in imagination, one takes a large number of microscopic bundles of parallel threads and arranges these bundles in a criss-cross manner so as to form a layer, one will have a rough impression of the sheet of connective tissue that forms the *dermis* or internal part of the skin, and attaches it everywhere to what lies beneath. The threads may be taken to represent the fibres of the protein called *collagen* that are the most important constituents of the layer. Between the bundles one may imagine branching and anastomosing tubules, representing the little blood vessels of the skin, which are confined to the dermis.

The bloodless external cellular layer or *epidermis* is situated, as its name implies, *on* the dermis. A vertical section through this layer in a region of the body in which it is particularly thick is shown in Fig. 22A. The specimen was taken from the sole of the cat's foot, but human skin is very similar. A sheet of cells, one cell thick, constitutes the basal layer (*Ba. Schi*), which is attached to the surface of the dermis. The cells of this layer have some resemblance to bricks in shape; they stand upright on the dermis (which is not shown in the figure). Above this sheet comes a thick mass of cells, which receives the name of the Malpighian layer (*Ml. La*) because it was first described by the Italian biologist, Marcello Malpighi, who distinguished it from the overlying layer in two short papers published in 1665.

The first of these dealt with the skin of the tongue, [699] the second with that of the surface of the body. [698] He remarked that this lower layer was '*mucosum*'. By this he meant only that it was soft and sticky, unlike the dry external '*cuticula*'; he did not mean that it contained what we now call mucus. He also gave it the unsuitable name

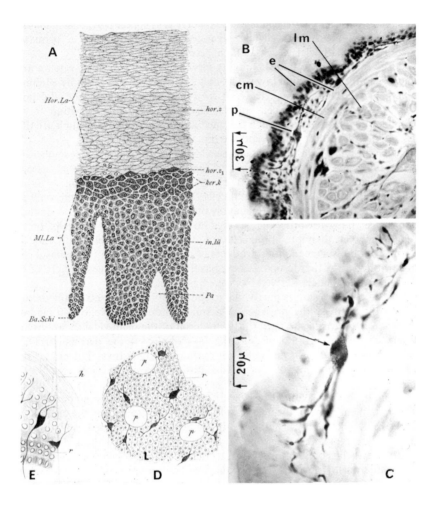

## 22   The skin and its pigment cells

A, the structure of thick mammalian skin (sole of cat's foot), as seen in a vertical section. *Ba. Schi*, basal layer; *Hor. La*, stratum corneum; *in. lü*, artificial space between cells; *ker. k*, interstitial cells; *Ml. La*, Malpighian layer; *Pa*, space occupied in life by connective tissue.

B, transverse section through the superficial epithelium (skin) and underlying layers of the freshwater leech *Piscicola geometra*, to show *p*, the branched pigment-cell lying in the epithelium; *cm*, circular muscle layer; *e*, external and internal limits of the epithelium; *lm*, longitudinal muscle.

C, the same branched pigment-cell as in B, at higher magnification.

D, E, branched cells (melanocytes) in the skin of man. D is a horizontal section through the skin of the finger; E, a vertical section through that of the forearm. *h*, stratum corneum; *p*, space occupied in life by connective tissue; *r*, cells of the Malpighian layer. The melanocytes have been treated with a solution of a gold salt to blacken them.

A, *highly magnified drawing from Schneider;* [954] B *and* C, *photomicrographs by the author (not previously published);* D *and* E, *highly magnified figures from Langerhans.* [629]

of 'rete' or net, by which it is often known at the present day; but it is better to call it simply the Malpighian layer. The cells that compose it press against one another and their apposed surfaces are thus flattened, so that the cells appear polygonal in thin sections; but they are usually slightly separated from one another in permanent preparations, with artificial spaces (*in. lü*) in between.

A large number of flattened, roughly circular cells are piled on one another externally to the Malpighian layer. The name of *cuticula* was given by Malpighi to this layer of dying, horny cells (*Hor. La*), but nowadays it receives the name of *stratum corneum*. The cells of this layer that are in apposition to the Malpighian layer are not so much flattened as the external ones, which are thin, hard, dead scales; these fall off and are replaced from below.

Between the typical cells of the Malpighian layer and the stratum corneum there is a thinner layer of cells (*ker. k*) that are in some respects intermediate in character between those of the two main layers. These cells may be called interstitial.

Of the various kinds of epidermal cells that have been mentioned, only the basal cells are capable of multiplication by division. Some of the products of this process pass towards the surface to become first of all cells of the Malpighian layer, then interstitial cells, and then horny cells, till finally they are cast off from the surface. Other products of the multiplication of the basal cells remain attached to the dermis as new basal cells. Thus all these layers of the epidermis are ultimately derived from the basal cells.

The colour of the skin is partly due to the blood in the vessels of the dermis. It is also affected by the presence of a small amount of a yellowish pigment (*carotene*) dissolved in the *lipid* (fatty) material of the dead cells that compose the stratum corneum, and also in the fat-globules of the dermis.[92] These colours, however, are not distinctive of particular ethnic taxa. The colour that plays such an important part in popular discussions of the ethnic problem is *melanin*.

Although, in dark-skinned persons, nearly every cell of the epidermis may contain pigment, none of the cells that have been mentioned has the capacity to synthesize it. These cells, whether (in crude terms) brick-shaped, polygonal, or scale-like, are typical *epithelial* cells; that is to say, cells of the kinds usually found in epithelia, or membranes that bound a surface (whether external, as here, or internal). Now cells that produce pigment in animals are commonly of quite a different kind. They are usually spheroidal or ovoid, with long, branched processes extending from them, and they are usually situated not in an epithelium but in connective tissue.

Up to the 1850s, no one had ever seen a branched pigment-cell in the skin epithelium of man or any other animal. Then in 1857 a German histologist, Franz Leydig, described (but did not figure) typical branched pigment-cells in the superficial epithelium (skin) of the little freshwater leech *Piscicola geometra*, which feeds on the blood of fishes.[664] The photomicrographs reproduced in Fig. 22B and C are possibly the first that have been published of these interesting cells in the skin of *Piscicola*. It will be noticed that these cells, with their curious branched processes, lie wholly within the superficial epithelium, which is very simple in structure in comparison with the elaborate skin of man and many other animals. The pigment (which is not melanin) occurs in the form of tiny spheres (just visible in Fig. 22C) within the cells. Under the microscope the individual granules appear brownish-yellow. Leydig, who had no means of identifying the pigment, called the cells '*die verzweigten Pigmentfiguren*'. He also described branched pigment figures in the lower layers of the skin of the frog (*Rana*) and lizard (*Lacerta agilis*).|664|

The cells that produce pigment in the skin of mammals are called *melanocytes* because the pigment is the substance called melanin. They were first seen in human skin by the Swiss zoologist Kölliker in 1867.|603| He found them interposed among the cells of the basal layer of the epidermis. He called them '*sternförmige Körper*'. He remarked that they resembled spots of pigment, but he misunderstood their nature, regarding them as nerve endings. Next year they were described by a medical student in Berlin, Paul Langerhans,|629| who was the first to recognize the melanocytes of the epidermis as cells (Fig. 22D and E). He noted their resemblance to the kinds of pigment-cells with which he was familiar, because they had the same branching form, but he did not notice the pigment-granules in them.

It has been suggested that the cells he saw were actually effete melanocytes, on their way to be ejected on the surface of the body. |87|Langerhans was the same young man who, in the following year, in his Dissertation for a degree at Berlin University, described for the first time the little heaps of cells ('*Zellhäuflein*') in the pancreas that are to this day known to every histologist and medical man as the islets of Langerhans.|630|

Melanocytes were first recognized as pigment-cells in the superficial epithelium of a mammal by Heinrich Müller, who described them in 1860 under the name of '*ramificirte Pigmentzellen*' in the conjunctiva of the rat, near the edge of the cornea or white of the eye. He claimed in two separate papers that he saw similar cells in the epidermis of the sturgeon before Leydig first described them, but he does not appear to have published this observation at the time.|777, 778|

The melanin granules of human skin vary in diameter from $0 \cdot 1$ to $0 \cdot 4 \, \mu m$ (that is to say, from one-tenth to two-fifths of a thousandth of a millimetre).|285| Even in the Negrid each single granule is deep golden, not black. It is the piling up of many such granules that results in the absorption of most of the incident light of all colours, and the consequent appearance of dark brown or an approximation to black.

The melanocytes of vertebrates have a very curious origin, quite different from that of the epithelial cells of the epidermis. They originate as part of the nervous system, from the left and right ridges (neural 'crests') that project from the sides of the embryonic spinal cord.|296, 880| The cells leave these ridges and migrate to the dermis of the whole body. Some of them pass from the dermis to the basal layer of the epidermis, where they insinuate themselves between the basal cells. They now undergo a peculiar metamorphosis. Their branching processes grow out and make contact with the external ends of the basal cells, so that there is continuity between the protoplasms of these two very different cells. This continuity has been definitely established by electron microscopy.|286| The melanocytes secrete granules of melanin and pass them along their processes to the tips, and thence into the basal cells. Here they collect, on the side of the nucleus that faces the surface of the skin. In Europeans the melanocytes do not make many granules, and only a few pass into the basal cells; but in persons of dark-skinned races and subraces they are very active, and granules continue to pass through the tips of the processes until they have spread to all parts of the basal cells except the nuclei.[87, 88, 89] In the Negrid embryo, melanin granules are present in the melanocytes of the skin late in the fourth or early in the fifth month of pregnancy, and transfer to the basal cells begins late in the latter month.[1170] More than three centuries ago Thomas Browne knew that the skin of Negrids darkens long before any ray of light has touched it. In his work generally known as *Vulgar errors*, which he himself called by the grander title of *Pseudodoxia epidemica*, he remarked of Negroes that 'not onely their legitimate and timely births, but their abortions are also duskie, before they have felt the scortch and fervor of the Sun'.[150]

The melanocytes, like the basal cells, are capable of multiplication by dividing in two. It would appear that some of the products of their division pass towards the surface as effete cells. Presumably they are sloughed off with the scales of the stratum corneum.

Melanocytes are not easily seen in routine microscopical preparations. It is for this reason that they are not usually shown in drawings intended to reveal the structure of skin. This applies to Fig. 22A.

Melanin is a complex substance that occurs commonly among very diverse groups of animals.[619, 656, 710] Plants do not produce it, but they produce a familiar substance of rather similar composition. Everyone has seen how an apple, if cut across and left exposed to the air, becomes brown on the new surfaces. The formation of the brown pigment provides a simplified illustration of the way in which melanin is produced in the bodies of men and other animals. The precursor of the brown substance in the cells of the apple is a phenol. The reaction by which this colourless substance becomes coloured is caused by an enzyme, polyphenol oxidase, in the presence of the oxygen of the air. The monophenol is first oxidized to a diphenol, and this to a quinone. It is characteristic of quinones that they are coloured. In the structural formulae shown here, the symbol 'R' is used to represent any of several possible groups of atoms.

*monophenol*          *diphenol*          *quinone*

In animals, including man, melanin is produced from the amino-acid tyrosine (hydroxy-phenyl-alanine), which is abundantly present in the body as a constituent of most proteins. It is a colourless monophenol. Under the influence of the enzyme tyrosinase it is oxidized first to a diphenol and then to a quinone. The diphenol is DihydrOxy-Phenyl-Alanine, commonly shortened to *dopa*, and the coloured quinone is called dopaquinone. During these changes the basic structure of the amino-acid (shown in the diagrams by the chain of atoms orientated at 45° to the sides of the page) remains unchanged. Further changes (not involving tyrosinase) result in the elimination

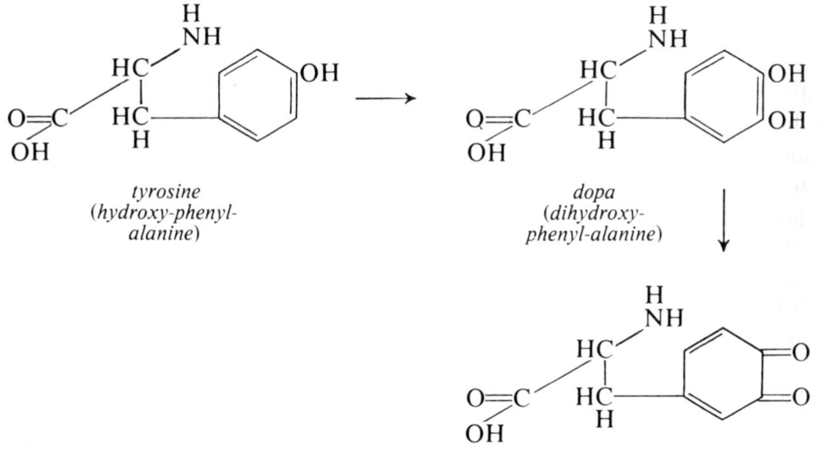

tyrosine
(hydroxy-phenyl-
alanine)

dopa
(dihydroxy-
phenyl-alanine)

dopa-quinone

of the acidic $O{=}C$ group from this basic structure, and the linking up of the OH
nitrogen atom to the phenyl ring. This produces the dark-coloured substance, indole-quinone, which is chemically related to the familiar coloured plant-product, indigo (nowadays also manufactured synthetically).

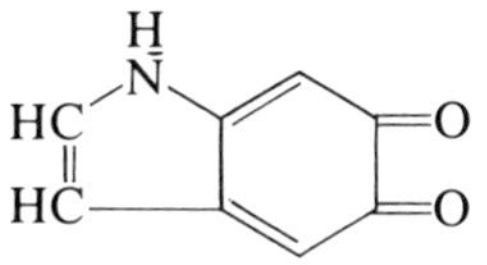

indole-quinone, the
basis of melanin

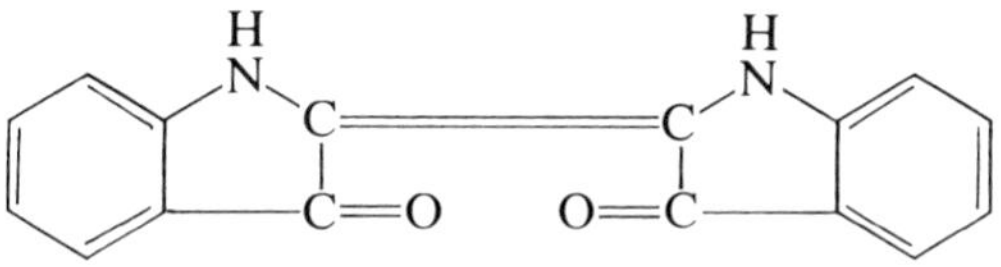

indigo (indigotin)

Indole-quinone *polymerizes* (that is, the molecules associate together in groups to form larger molecules), and the polymer attaches itself to protein. The final result is the familiar pigment melanin, the 'colour' referred to by writers on the ethnic problem. Melanin is not exactly a single chemical substance, because the degree of polymerization and the protein-content may vary; but so far as is known, all races have essentially the same melanin in the skin. The colour depends on the amount present.[657]

Melanin gives colour not only to skin but also to hair. The clump of cells from which a hair grows out contains melanocytes that are very similar to those of the skin. They pass melanin granules into the cells that will be transformed into the dead cells of hair. The coloured substance of hair, whether golden, auburn, 'mousy', brown, or nearly black, is melanin, the shade depending on the amount of pigment present. The only exception is so-called 'red' hair, which owes its colour to a slightly different substance called *phaeomelanin.* Unfortunately the extraction of this pigment for chemical analysis is liable to cause change in its composition.[799] The amino-acid tryptophane appears to replace tyrosine as the starting-point for the production of phaeomelanin.[341] Ordinary melanin is sometimes called dopa-melanin to distinguish it. Phaeomelanin is not important in the study of the ethnic problem, because red hair is not characteristic of any ethnic group. It occurs among particular individuals of various subraces.

It might be supposed that the pale-skinned subraces of man have fewer melanocytes in the epidermis than the dark races, but this is not so. Even albinos have the same number of melanocytes as dark-skinned people.[66] The differences depend on the activity of the melanocytes, not on their number.

It has been shown that the melanocytes in the skin of the pale subraces of man contain the whole system for the production of melanin; it is not lack of tyrosine or of tyrosinase that causes the amount of melanin to be so small.[33, 192, 88, 619] The tyrosinase system is somehow *inhibited* and dormant in most parts of the body, though less so in the skin of the nipples and certain other areas.

It has been proved by experiment that pale human skin contains a substance (or substances) that reduces the rate of formation of melanin. The mechanism of inhibition does not appear to be fully understood, but there is evidence that the sulphydryl groups (—SH) of proteins may possibly be involved. Experiments performed outside the body have shown that substances which interfere with the reactions of sulphydryl groups increase the amount of melanin formed when tyrosinase acts on tyrosine. [917]

The lack of colour in the skin, hair, and other parts of human albinos appears to be due to the complete *inhibition* of tyrosinase, but it is the *absence* of this enzyme that causes the white patches on black-and-white guinea-pigs. [87, 56]

A hormone called MSH (the melanocyte-stimulating hormone), produced by the pituitary gland below the brain, in some way increases the amount of melanin in the skin of both pale and dark-skinned human beings. Its release from the pituitary gland is inhibited by a hormone secreted by the cortex or outer part of the *adrenal* gland (situated, as its name conveys, beside the kidney). If this cortex is damaged by disease, the pale skin of a European may become dark. The connection between disease of the adrenal glands and darkening of the human skin was first suggested by Thomas Addison, a London doctor, in 1849.[8] In his very brief and tentative remark on the subject, amounting in all to 39 words, he made the mistake of supposing that the discoloration of his patients was caused by escape of blood from the vessels of the dermis ('purpura' is the medical name for this condition). He corrected his mistake six years later, in a book devoted to disease of the adrenal glands. He now realized that the 'dingy', 'smoky', 'amber', or 'chestnut-brown' colour was due to pigmentation of the skin itself, not to darkening by escaped blood. His book is illustrated by large coloured portraits.[9]

The intramuscular injection of MSH darkens the human skin. Experiments were performed on so-called American 'Negroes', but it is evident from the published pictures that the subjects were partly of European ancestry. The skin began to darken after a day or two from the first injection; it returned to its original colour some weeks after the last. The evidence suggested that persons whose skin was particularly dark before the injections started, showed the strongest response.[658] There does not appear to be any conclusive evidence as to whether MSH or the inhibiting hormone of the adrenal cortex may play a part in determining the normal skin-colour of the races and sub-races of man.

It has been proved by direct experiment that the pigment in the epidermis of man reduces the amount of ultraviolet light that passes through.[1049] The skin of Europeans and Negroes was blistered by the action of *cantharidin* (a vesicant material obtained from the blood and accessory reproductive organs of certain beetles). This substance causes the stratum corneum to separate from the Malpighian layer of the skin as a blister, and it can then be painlessly cut off with scissors. It was shown that there is no significant difference between Europeans and Negroes in the thickness of the stratum corneum, but this layer taken from Europeans transmits $3\frac{1}{2}$ times as much ultraviolet light as the corresponding layer taken from Negroes. Pieces of the stratum corneum of European and Negro skin were placed over living pale human skin and exposed to the Nigerian sun. It was found that the dark stratum corneum of Negro skin gave better protection than the other against the *erythema* of sunburn (that is to say, against the reddening due to the congestion of the blood-vessels in the superficial part of the dermis). The difference is caused by the presence of melanin granules in the dead cells of this layer in the Negro's skin. The melanin granules absorb the ultraviolet rays and also scatter them, so that further absorption occurs by other melanin granules, and also by the proteins of these cells.[105] No doubt the abundant melanin of the Malpighian layer and basal cells of Negroes acts in the same way, and greatly reduces the transmission of ultraviolet light.

The darkening of a pale skin in sunlight is a protective response against the effect of too much ultraviolet light, which not only causes an inflammatory condition in the superficial layer of the dermis, but also damages the living cells of the epidermis. It is often mistakenly supposed that this darkening is a sign of health. Indeed, persons with pale skins are sometimes said to be 'etiolated'. The word is taken from botany, where it is used to mean the state of a plant that has failed to produce the green pigment of leaves because it is grown in darkness. The cases, however, are fundamentally dissimilar. The green pigment (chlorophyll) is absolutely necessary for the normal life of the plant, and the plant can only produce it in the presence of light. The melanin of skin, on the contrary, only plays a defensive role in protecting the skin from the damaging effect of ultraviolet light.

The chief danger of overexposure to the ultraviolet light of the sun is the production of cancers (carcinomas) of the epidermal cells.[105] In the temperate zones the light from the sun has to traverse a longer course through the ozone of the upper atmosphere than in those regions in which the sun is more nearly overhead. Ozone absorbs ultraviolet light strongly. Skin-cancers occur very much more frequently among European residents in subtropical countries than among the dark-skinned inhabitants.[105] They occur especially on the face and other exposed parts. A curious case is that of long-sighted people who wear bifocal spectacles outdoors in parts of the world where the sunshine is intense.

The carcinogenic rays are unfortunately able to penetrate the glass, and the lower lens concentrates them on a particular area of skin below the eye; cancer not infrequently results.[1181]

It is well known that ultraviolet light is absorbed by nucleic acids and can cause mutations in the genes. It seems highly significant that melanin granules are directed by the ultimate branches of the melanocyte to the side of the nucleus of the basal cell that is nearest to the surface of the skin—the side, in fact, from which the light comes: for the nucleus contains the deoxyribonucleic acid (DNA) of the genes. A little pile of melanin is built up here to form a cap over the illuminated side of the nucleus. The nuclei of the basal cells constitute the source of all the nuclei of the epidermal layer, except those of the melanocytes themselves. In dark-skinned persons so many melanin granules enter the basal cells that eventually the nucleus may be surrounded by them.

The basal cells of the epidermis are not the only cells that are protected by melanin from damage caused by excess of ultraviolet light. The fibroblasts, or cells of the dermis that produce the connective-tissue fibres of that layer, are also liable to be harmed by intense sunlight. They contain no melanin; but if there are enough granules in the basal layer of the epidermis, and in the more superficial layers, they are protected. This probably explains the crowding of melanin granules in the basal cells in members of those ethnic taxa that are adapted to subtropical and tropical environments. The bases (basic chemical groups) that form an important constituent part of the genetic material (DNA) are subject to transformation by ultraviolet light. The fibroblasts contain a system of enzymes that have the remarkable capacity to extract the altered bases and replace them by the correct ones, so that the proper genetic material is maintained. Some persons, however, are very sensitive to ultraviolet light. They lack a part of the genetic replacement system, and the damage caused by light is not put right.[212] Such persons are said to suffer from *xeroderma pigmentosum*. The damaged cells proliferate and spread to various parts of the body, where they continue to multiply and produce malignant tumours.

Experiments carried out in Germany just after the First World War proved that in certain circumstances ultraviolet light was by no means necessarily harmful to human beings.[111] It was shown that exposure to this light would prevent the development of rickets in children. Soon afterwards a surprising discovery was made. Certain oils, linseed among them, have no capacity to protect against rickets when taken into the body as food, but they develop this capacity if exposed to ultraviolet light, and indeed develop as powerful an anti-rachitic property as that of cod-liver oil itself. Finally it was shown that the substance in these oils that became antirachitic when irradiated was *ergosterol*, which became converted to vitamin D, the antirachitic vitamin. It was concluded that ultraviolet light prevents rickets when it shines upon the skin by converting the ergosterol, already present in the body, to vitamin D.

The following hypothesis seems to account rather satisfactorily for the varying degrees of pigmentation of the skin among the races and subraces of man in different latitudes. It is thought likely that man evolved in the warm regions of the globe. As the hair coat inherited from his ancestors gradually became reduced, the pigmentation of his skin would presumably be retained or increased, by the natural selection of those persons who were best protected from the ultraviolet rays of the intense sunshine. When, on the retreat of the ice, huge new areas of fertile land were exposed for human habitation, natural selection would act in a different way. The filtering off of the ultraviolet light from the slanting rays of the sun would make protection less necessary; meanwhile it would become more and more valuable to catch some remnant of this light, to provide a source of vitamin D. Selection would now act in the opposite direction, tending to favour persons in whom the melanin-inhibiting factors chanced to be strongly developed. Paleness of skin would result in those subraces, especially the Osteuropid and Nordid, that penetrated far towards the north.

This hypothesis is supported by evidence that there is a tendency to rickets among the children of immigrants from the West Indies to Great Britain, where the disease has almost disappeared among the fair-skinned native population.[859] It seems that in the tropical environment there is sufficient sunlight to penetrate the Negrid skin and act upon ergosterol, or enough vitamin D in the food; but in England the sunlight does not always suffice, and if the diet is deficient in the vitamin, rickets results. The evidence would only be conclusive, however, if the two groups of children—dark-skinned and fair—were known to have similar diets and to expose the same area of skin to the light.

Since pigmentation of the hair is controlled in essentially the same way as that of the skin, there would be some tendency for those who became very pale-skinned in the course of evolution to become fair-haired at the same time, even though those with fair hair might gain no practical advantage from the possession of this particular character. Fair hair reached its extreme (apart from sporadic albinism) in the Osteuropid subrace, seen today in parts of Poland and north Russia.

The eye-colour of man is due to melanocytes in the *stroma* or connective-tissue layer of the iris. These have the same origin as the melanocytes of the skin, but do not act in quite the same way. They are 'continent'; that is to say, they do not extrude their melanin granules into other cells, as those of the skin and hair do, but retain them within themselves. If they produce abundant melanin granules, they give a brown or almost black colour, just as they do in the skin. If the granules are sparse, they act in quite a different way. The red light (and light of long wavelengths in general) passes through with little scattering, and is absorbed at the back of the iris. The light of shorter wave-lengths is selectively scattered (diffracted) by the melanin granules and thus passes from one to another, and some of it forward, out of the eye. The light that emerges is therefore blue or bluish, though no blue pigment is present.[1091] The pure blue eyes of the Osteuropids and many Nordids is due to this 'Tyndall effect'. The blue skin on the muzzle of the male mandrill (*Mandrillus sphinx*) is also due to a Tyndall effect produced by sparse melanin granules.

Not all the melanocytes derived from the neural crests reach the epidermis.

Every biological student has seen them in the connective tissue surrounding the nerves and blood-vessels of the frog. They occur in many animals in the connective tissue of the dermis. It is stated that in the baboons (*Cynocephalus*) and macaques (*Macacus*) the colour of the skin is entirely due to dermal melanocytes, but in the chimpanzee (*Pan satyrus*) and orang-utan (*Pongo pygmaeus*) melanocytes occur in both dermis and epidermis.[4] Dermal melanocytes occur also in man, especially in the lumbar region and on the buttocks in late embryonic life and in the early years after birth. Here the melanin granules are often abundant enough to produce visible spots, sometimes an inch or more across. There is usually not enough melanin to produce a dark brown or black colour, and a bluish Tyndall effect may result from sparse distribution of the granules. The melanocytes of the dermis are always continent, like those of the iris.

When the attention of the scientific world was first called in the 1880s to the existence of these marks, it was supposed that they constituted a diagnostic feature of the Mongolid race[713], but in fact they occur fairly commonly in most races and subraces, so far as is known.[217, 390] In the pale-skinned subraces of the Europid race they only appear sporadically,[6] though it seems that dermal melanocytes are always present at a late stage of embryonic life. It has been claimed that these marks never occur among the Ainuids of Japan,[104] but it is questionable whether a sufficient number of babies has been examined to prove that this rather isolated Europid subrace is exceptional in this respect.

The marks are presumably to be regarded as an archaic feature inherited from ancestors that had abundant dermal melanin, like the chimpanzee and orang-utan.

The inheritance of skin-colour is complex. Albinism is very simple genetically, but it is not relevant here, because no ethnic taxon consists of albinos. There are people of blond subraces who are scarcely able to respond to ultraviolet light by the development of melanin in the skin, while those of certain other subraces (for instance, the Mediterranids and Nordindids) are able to become noticeably dark in the exposed regions of their bodies, though rather pale-skinned in parts that are protected from the sun. The skin of Negrids is dark in certain protected parts, though it may be capable of further darkening by ultraviolet light. These different characters and potentialities are presumably under separate genetic control. As always in the study of human heredity, progress is retarded by the impossibility of making the crosses that reason would suggest, and by the long intervals between generations.

The evidence suggests that the colour of human skin is controlled by *polygenes*; that is to say, by many genes, having additive effects. Studies of this problem have been made on American 'Negroes', who are in fact a hybrid population, descended mainly from Negrid and Europid ancestors. There is a very wide range in skin-colour among them. If intermarriage occurs between two of them, different but not extremely so in colour, the offspring are commonly intermediate in colour, and if these offspring intermarry with persons differing somewhat in colour, once again the offspring are commonly intermediate. (Studies of Negrid-Europid hybrids in Liverpool suggest that there may be a slight tendency towards dominance of a pale skin, if the parents are very different in colour.[474]) The production of intermediates, generation after generation, is strongly suggestive of the action of polygenes. In such cases the genetical interpretation must rest on a special type of statistical analysis. It appears that about five pairs of genes, all additive and nearly equal in effect, must be concerned.[1007, 1008] At each of the five loci on the chromosomes, both of the genes might be for pale skin, or one for pale and one for dark, or both for dark. Europeans would not necessarily possess exclusively the 'pale' genes: one, two, or three might be 'dark'. Unfortunately a statistical analysis of this sort cannot take account of complications such as ability to respond to ultraviolet light.

There is no evidence that any gene concerned in the control of skin-colour has any effect on the mental capacity of human beings. In the course of evolution particular races or subraces might evolve to higher average levels of intelligence than others; but if so, there would be no necessary correlation with the colour of the skin. It might happen, nevertheless, that selective influences would result in the production of a particular skin-colour (whether dark or pale) in a certain race or subrace, and that selective influences of another kind would independently result in the acquisition by this race or subrace of a high average level of intelligence (or of a high proportion of persons of exceptional intelligence). This would be an example of the coexistence in a particular race or subrace of two or more characters controlled by two independent sets of genes (for instance, brachycephaly and the rather broad, slightly concave nose in the Alpinid subrace).

In the classification of animals, zoologists lay little emphasis on differences of colour, which are commonly caused by the accumulation of coloured granules within cells, or by the existence of extremely fine parallel striations on cuticles. They pay far more attention to differences in grosser structure. Such differences result when particular cells in two or more taxa of animals arrange themselves in different ways, so as to form aggregates that are markedly different, or when the cells produce skeletal matter (bones, for instance, or the external skeletons of insects) that are obviously different in shape. It is therefore surprising to a zoologist that such very great emphasis should be laid on colour in popular discussions of ethnic problems.

There are marked differences of a structural or 'morphological' kind between the races, and to a less extent between the subraces of man. Some of these will be described in considerable detail in Part 3 of this book. Here it need only be remarked that there are races of man so different from the Europid (for instance in the breadth of the nose, the thickness of the lips, the degree of projection of the jaws, and the length and texture of the hair), that it must seem strange indeed to any zoologist or physical anthropologist that a mere difference of colour should be the feature that seems most important to anyone.

Nevertheless, people do commonly make remarks about those non-white races that are in fact very different in morphological characters, to the effect that 'the only thing that distinguishes them is the colour of their skin'. It scarcely seems possible to believe that anyone who has seen an Australian aborigine, a Melanesian, a Bushman, or a Negro could accept such words as true. They are directly contrary not only to the established facts of physical anthropology, but also to ordinary observation.

An albino Melanesid (Melanesian) or Negrid, who is fairer than any non-albino European, appears even more unlike a European than a normal Melanesid or Negrid. This fact was pointed out (with reference to Negrids) by the French mathematician Maupertuis more than two centuries ago.[715] The association of a pale face and straw-coloured hair with the features of a non-Europid race brings out strongly the great differences that in fact exist. This is perhaps partly because darkness of the skin interferes with clear vision of the face. Indeed, if the skin were actually black (which it never is), it would be impossible to see any features, apart from the lips, gums, teeth, and whites of the eyes, except in profiile.

The relative unimportance of colour in comparison with morphological features is witnessed by the fact that there is no race of man, in the sense of the word adopted in this book (pp. 99 ff.), that is characterized by the possession of a pale skin. Most of the subraces of the Europid race have pale skins, but the Nordindids (Indo-Afghans) and Aethiopids have not. The Sikhs and other Nordindids become pale brown in the exposed parts of the body, and members of the Aethiopid subrace are very dark—darker, in fact, than certain Negrid tribes. If a Nordindid were slightly paler, it would not be easy to distinguish him from a Mediterranid. Indeed, some authorities regard the Nordindids as constituting a local form of the Mediterranid subrace.[1085]

In view of these facts, it is surprising that unrelated groups of persons are often classified together in common speech as 'coloured', as though this implied genetic affinity. It results that an Indian, who may show close resemblance to many Europeans in every structural feature of his body, and whose ancestors established a civilization long before the inhabitants of the British Isles did so, is grouped as 'coloured' with persons who are very different morphologically from any European or Indian, and whose ancestors never developed a civilization of their own. Those who group human beings in this unscientific way would not think of applying the same classificatory principle to animals. They would not predicate anything about the virtues or defects of the ordinary types of Labrador retrievers, Scottish terriers, and schipperkes merely on the basis of their black pigmentation, and they would be well aware that a golden Labrador retriever is very similar in most respects to a black one.

# 10 Odour

'THOSE WHO have travelled in foreign lands must readily have noticed that all peoples have an odour that is peculiar to them. Thus one distinguishes without difficulty the Negroes, Malays, Chinese, Tatars, Tibetans, Indians, and Arabs.' Thus wrote the French missionary and explorer Évariste Huc, more than a century ago.[520] The present chapter is concerned with this curious and difficult subject.

## TYPES OF SCENT-ORGANS

Many animals have special glands for the production of substances that can be detected by other animals through the organs called *chemo-receptors* that detect and discriminate between chemically different substances. The secretions produced by the special glands have varied functions. Some, such as those produced by the stink-glands below the tail of the skunk (*Mephitis mephitis*) and by the wax-glands (*ceruminous glands*) of the human ear, act as repulsive agents against intruders, but most of them are attractive towards members of the same species.

The attractive scents fall into two main categories: those that tend to keep members of a herd together, and those that are specially related to the sexual function. The scents that belong to the former group (the species- or herd-recognition scents) are produced by similar organs in both sexes. There are not many different kinds of organs of this sort that can be quoted as perfectly typical examples, but the metatarsal brushes of certain species of deer will serve as well as any other. These are areas of skin provided with special glands and stiffly projecting tufts of hair, in some cases of a distinctive colour, situated on the outer sides of the lower parts of the hind limbs. They brush against the undergrowth through which the deer passes and leave a scent that is recognizable by members of the species.[1122] There is reason to believe that metatarsal brushes occur most commonly in gregarious species of deer.[689] The scents produced by the metatarsal glands of certain species of deer are examples of what are called *pheromones*; that is to say, substances secreted by one individual that pass to another individual (commonly through the air) and elicit in it responses of an adaptive nature.

It often happens in the most diverse animals that hairs or hairlike structures are associated with scent-organs. They distribute the scent, either by acting mechanically as brushes, or else by increasing the area from which the smelly substance may volatilize.

The pre-orbital glands of many of the Bovidae, especially certain species of antelopes, goats, and sheep, seem to fall into the same group of scent-producing organs as the metatarsal brushes of deer; that is to say, the group that produces species-recognition scents. These organs of the Bovidae are elongated patches of skin in front of the eyes, bearing the openings of many small glands. The patches are sunk into depressions of the lacrimal bone, easily visible on inspection of the skull. In some cases they can be everted, so as to volatilize the scent more readily. They occur in both sexes, like typical scent-organs adapted for species-recognition; but they seem not to belong wholly to this category, for they are more active in the sexual season and as a general rule are better developed in the male sex. In the duikerbok (*Cephalopus* spp.) of tropical and southern Africa the secretion of the male is highly scented; that of the female cannot be detected by the human nose, and, unlike that of the male, is coloured blue. It is clear that the pre-orbital glands of the Bovidae, or at any rate some of them, merge into the second category of sexually alluring scent-organs.

The sexually alluring smells are usually different, and produced by quite different organs, in the two sexes, or they may be produced by members of one sex only. The scents produced by female animals are often *directive* rather than immediately stimulating; that is to say, they lead the male to where the female is, but are not an immediate stimulus to copulation. The most astonishing examples for directive scents are provided by certain moths. It has been proved that the males of certain species belonging to two different families (Lasiocampidae and Lymantriidae) are capable of being attracted towards a female situated a mile or more away.[352] It is a strange fact that none of the directive scents produced by female Lepidoptera can be detected by man.[351]

The scents produced by male Lepidoptera do not direct a female towards him, but stimulate her to copulate. These *stimulating* scents can be detected by human beings, and almost all of them are pleasant to our sense of smell.[351] The scent-organs of male Lepidoptera occur on various parts of the body in different species—on particular parts of the wings, on the front (*prothoracic*) or hind (*metathoracic*) legs, or at the base or top of the abdomen. They are often accompanied by hairlike structures, reminiscent of the metatarsal brushes of deer. In some cases there are elaborate arrangements for the conservation of the scent in repose, and its dispersion when the occasion arises.

The common fan-foot moth (*Herminia barbalis*) may be cited as an example. [543] In this species, which occurs in southern England and in parts of Europe and Asia, the scent-hairs of the male are borne on the joints called *tibia* (*tb*) and *femur* (*fe*) of the prothoracic legs (Fig. 23A). There are two tufts of scent-hairs (*tbl* and *tbk*) on the tibia and one (*fb*) on the femur. These long hairs give the moth its vernacular name, though 'brush-leg' would be more appropriate. Organs of this kind ensure that females copulate with males of their own species, even when, as in this case, [769]there are several closely related species occupying similar ecological niches in the same districts.

Sexually alluring odours are produced by certain female Primates. This has been shown experimentally by a small-scale experiment with the rhesus monkey, *Macaca mulatta*.[740] A male was placed in a cage, so arranged that

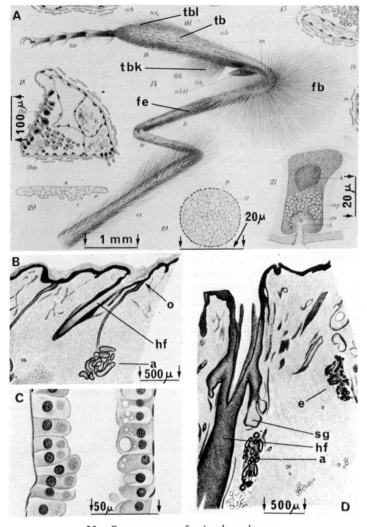

## 23  Scent-organs of animals and man

A, an anterior (prothoracic) leg of the moth *Herminia barbalis*, to show the large scent-tuft (*fb*) on the joint called the femur (*fe*) and the two smaller tufts (*tbk* and *tbl*) on the tibia (*tb*).

B, vertical section through the skin of a pig, to show the place (marked by an arrow) where an *a*-gland (*a*) opens into the upper part of a hair-follicle (*hf*).

C, longitudinal section through the secretory part of an *a*-gland in the armpit of a Europid woman. Some of the cells contain spherical masses of granules at the ends directed towards the cavity of the tubule; others are vacuolated in this region. Several show projections into the cavity, and an ovoid body near the lower right-hand corner of the figure gives the impression that a projection has been separated from a cell.

D, vertical section through the skin of an Australid, from the cheek near the ear. The *a*-gland (*a*) opens (not in this section) into the hair-follicle (*hf*) above the sebaceous gland (*sg*). *e*, *e*-gland.

A, *magnified drawing from Illig;*|543| B, C, *and* D, *highly magnified drawings from Schiefferdecker;*|941|*with scales and lettering added by the present author.*

by pressing repeatedly on a lever he could gain access to a female, by the automatic opening of an intervening door. When he had discovered this fact, his nasal olfactory area was plugged with gauze impregnated with a special paste that rendered him incapable of smelling. He now no longer worked the lever, but resumed the habit when the gauze had been removed. Only two males were used in this study, and the evidence would have been more conclusive if control experiments had been carried out with omission of the anti-olfactory substances from the paste; but there seems to be little doubt that the sex instinct of the males was in abeyance if they could not smell their females. The source of the sexually alluring substances was not determined.


MUSK

A familiar example of a sexually alluring odour is the musk produced by the male musk-deer (*Moschus moschiferus*), which inhabits mountainous districts in Asia. The musk is secreted by a large gland that opens in the middle line of the belly, in front of the preputial opening.[299, 1122] (It does not open into the preputial cavity, as is often stated in writings on the subject.) There is no trace of a corresponding organ in the doe.[348] The gland consists of a pouch of inturned skin. The secreted product constitutes the musk of commerce, from which the cosmetic scent is prepared. More than one scented substance exists in the contents of the pouch, but the principal one, to which the odour is mainly due, is *muscone*. This was first isolated as a chemical individual at the beginning of the present century, but its exact composition was not determined until 1934, when the identical substance was synthesized in the laboratory.[923]

Muscone may be regarded as based on a molecule that is a paraffin chain joined end-to-end to form a ring. The ring contains fifteen carbon atoms and is called *cyclo-pentadecane*. The synthesis started from the closely related substance *cyclo-pentadecene*. It will be noticed that the muscone is a *ketone*; that is, it contains the group $O=C-R$, where R and R' are radicles such as $-CH_3$ or $-C_2H_5$; or derivatives of
$\overset{|}{\underset{R'}{}}$
these.

cyclo-pentadecane          cyclo-pentadecene          muscone

Several ketones related to the cyclic paraffins, and therefore closely similar to muscone, are used as scents in the cosmetic industry.[70] They are of animal origin. It is a most remarkable fact that these substances, so similar in chemical composition, are produced by different organs belonging to particular species of different orders of mammals. The scent-gland of the civet-cats (*Viverra* spp.) resembles that of the musk-deer in opening by a longitudinal slit in the middle line of the body, but it occurs in both sexes and opens in a different place: in the male between the testes and the penis, and in the female between the anus and the vulva (that is to say, *behind* the genital opening in each case).[428] The musk-rat (*Ondatra zibethica*) produces a similar scent, but by a large organ that surrounds the anus in both sexes.[429] The evidence suggests that this organ is not homologous with the circumanal glands of man. In all these cases the principal scents are cyclic ketones (or in the case of the musk-rat, two such ketones and also the alcohols related to them).

Near relatives of these animals have similar glands and a similar smell, and it is very probable that the scented substance is chemically similar. It would appear that the capacity to produce scented cyclic ketones from diverse organs is widely spread among mammals.

It may be mentioned that several synthetic substances, chemically unrelated to musk and not known to be secreted by any animal, have a remarkably similar smell and are used in the cosmetic industry.[822]

## GLANDS OF THE AXILLARY TYPE (*A*-GLANDS)

In the skin of the axilla of men and women there is a flat, oval organ, commonly some 5 cm long and about 3 to 5 mm thick, which produces a smelly sweat. This *axillary organ* consists of very numerous, separate, but contiguous glands. Each separate gland (cf. Fig. 23B) is a little tube, rolled up in an irregular fashion at one end, so as to form a little rounded object. The end of the tube within the rounded part is closed off. In this part there are short branches from the tube, some of which join the main tube, so as to produce a loose meshwork. The part that has been described is that which produces the odorous secretion. The other end of the tube is a duct, leading towards the exterior. The (unbranched) sweat-glands of the general surface of the body open directly by spirally wound (corkscrewlike) ducts on the surface of the epidermis; but each of the nearly straight ducts of the axillary glands opens, as a rule, into the little pit or follicle from which a hair grows out. The rounded, secretory parts of two or more glands are in many places so crowded together as to form apparently composite glands, big enough to be visible to the naked eye, but their ducts open into separate hair-follicles. The axillary glands originate in the embryo from the linings of the hair-follicles, and most of them retain this association. Thus the axillary sweat pours on to the hairs of the armpit.

The restriction of the body-hair in man to particular areas, and its abundance in these regions, are significant. The hairiness and warmth of the armpit are both conducive to the evaporation of the smelly substance when the arm is raised, yet the organ is almost closed off when the upper arm is held beside the body. The whole arrangement is similar in principle to the male scent-organ of the fan-foot moth, though each constituent part is fundamentally different. The hairs of man, for instance, consist of horny (keratinous), dead cells, while the hairlike structures of the moth consist of a hard substance that is not keratin (a protein), but chitin, a complex substance (mucopolysaccharide) related to the sugars. The 'hairs' of insects do not consist of dead cells, but of chitinous material extruded from the surfaces of cells.

The liquid substance produced by the axillary gland of man is regarded as a form of sweat, because it exudes on the surface of the skin, but the glands that produce it are different from those that produce the sweat of the greater part of the body. It was a German anatomist, Krause, who first drew a distinction, in 1844, by remarking on the very large size of the axillary sweat-glands in comparison with those of the rest of the body.[610] A much more precise distinction was drawn the following year by a French histologist, Robin, who remarked that whereas the sweat-glands of the rest of the body are clearly separate, the secretory parts of the axillary glands are often associated to form the visible groups that have already been mentioned. He also remarked that whereas the ducts of the other sweat-glands are coiled like a corkscrew, those of the axillary glands are nearly straight. Robin realized clearly that the axillary glands are the ones that produce the odour of the human body. He did not name them, but simply remarked that they were sweat-glands '*d'un espèce particulière*'.[908]

Sweat-glands of this special type were studied in detail by Schiefferdecker, [940, 941] who discovered a great deal about them, but was mistaken about the way in which the glandular cells secrete. Unfortunately he called them '*die apokrinen Drusen*', to emphasize his erroneous belief. He knew that certain gland-cells, ordinary human sweat-glands among them, produced their secretion in the form of a fluid that oozed through the intact cell-membrane into the cavity or lumen of the gland and thence to the exterior. He designated such glands '*die ekkrinen Drusen*'. He thought that Robin's glands produced their secretion in a different way, by the nipping-off of the ends of the cells into the lumen, and he gave the general name of *die apokrinen Drusen* to all glands in any part of the body that produced their secretion in this way (Fig. 23c). The usual spelling of the two adjectives in English is 'eccrine' and 'apocrine'.

The cells of the axillary glands of man differ sharply from those of the sweat-glands of the general surface of the body in containing large, brownish-yellow, globular secretion-products.[754, 513, 205, 753] These contain lipid (fatty) material (phospholipids and cholesteryl esters).[787] This lipid material can also be demonstrated in the duct of the gland[787], but the evidence seems conclusive that the globules themselves are not cast out as such into the duct. The free end of the cell is devoid of globules at all times. Apparently the secreted material passes out in solution through the intact cell-membrane.[754, 753] It is therefore unfortunate that the adjective 'apocrine' has stuck so obstinately to sweat-glands of the axillary type. Certain gland-cells (such as those of the pancreas that produce digestive enzymes) are in fact apocrine, but the cells of Robin's glands are not.

Schiefferdecker himself[940, 941] suggested that the two kinds of glands should be called '*a-Drusen*', and '*e-Drusen*', and these names (or the English equivalents) are convenient if new meanings are attached to '*a*' and '*e*'. The '*a*' may well stand for glands of the *axillary* type, the '*e*' for those that open directly on the general surface of the *epidermis*, and have no connection at any stage with hair-follicles.

There are *e*-glands among the *a*-glands in the axillary organ of man, but it is very improbable that they contribute to the odour of the secretion.

Since the sweat of the axillary glands is yellowish, one would naturally and perhaps correctly attribute the colour to the material in the large globules, but the suggestion has been made that it may be due to the action of bacteria in the exuded sweat.

Sweat-glands of the characteristic '*a*' type are not confined in man to the axillary organ. Robin reported their existence '*au creux dë l'aisselle*' in his paper of 1845.[908] In 1867 the presence of glands of this type in the anal and genital region was very briefly mentioned by Kölliker.[603] An excellent account of the *a*-glands that surround the anus was given four years later by Gay, a physiologist of Vienna University, who named them the *Circumanaldrusen*.[394] He stated that they were situated in a ring round the anus, the inner limit being 1 to $1\frac{1}{2}$ cm from the latter. Neither he nor Kölliker realized that these glands are outgrowths from hair-follicles. Schiefferdecker[941] considered that the *a*-glands of this region were sufficiently aggregated to constitute a *Circumanalorgan*. It must be mentioned that since Gay's time circumanal glands and organs have been described in very many different kinds of mammals, but the great majority of these are not homologous with those of man, because their histological structure is quite different.[935]

Certain other glands of the genito-anal region of man (scrotum and root of the penis in the male, and *labia majora* and *mons veneris* in the female) are of the *a*-gland type. They were mentioned by Kölliker in his century-old paper.[603] They combine with the circumanal, so far as is known, to produce the odour of this part of the body. Kölliker also noticed similar glands in the skin of the nipples and surrounding areas. There are certain regions of the body in which *a*-glands occur in some races of man but not in others (pp. 170–71), but the principal odour-producing parts of the human body are the *a*-glands of the genito-anal region and of the axillary organs, especially the latter.[5]

There are also two highly modified types of *a*-glands that occur in all races, so far as is known. These are certain glands in the eyelids, called Moll's glands after their discoverer,[750] and the ceruminous glands that produce ear-wax. The latter is said to be sometimes smelly,[5] but its function is to repel insects by action on their taste-receptors. (Certain mites (Acarina) specialize in this habitat and are not repelled. [941])

Non-functional vestiges of *a*-glands occur in the embryo in parts of the body where they no longer exist in the adult.[5]

In most mammals the *e*-glands are restricted to the parts of the body that are devoid of hair, such as the foot-pads of dogs and cats. The *a*-glands commonly occur wherever there is hair[940, 941], but the smell they produce is generally not so strong as that which comes from localized scent-organs. Since most mammals are hairy over the greater part of the body, the sweat is usually produced mainly by *a*-glands. In horses and certain other animals these glands seem to play a part in the control of body-temperature, like the *e*-glands of man.[941] The tufted scent-organs of many species of deer and antelopes contain both *a*- and *e*-glands.[513]

Monkeys (*Cynocephalus* and *Cercopithecus* spp.) differ from other mammals in the distribution of *e*-glands, for these are not confined to the bare areas, but occur over a large part of the surface of the body, as in man.[940, 941] Hairy axillary organs occur in the chimpanzee (*Pan satyrus*). Each consists of a glandular area, with a tuft of hair, situated in the deepest part of the armpit; it is surrounded by an almost hairless zone of skin.[136] The organ occurs in both sexes, and no sexual difference has been reported. A similar organ occurs in the gorilla (*Gorilla gorilla*), but there is not a bare area round it. There are no *e*-glands in the axillary organs of the chimpanzee or gorilla.[941] In the orang-utan (*Pongo pygmaeus*) and gibbon (*Hylobates leuciscus*) there is no gland in the axilla, and in the former this part of the body is almost hairless.[136] In the evolution of man, the reduction in body-hair has resulted in the restriction of *a*-glands to a few special regions. As Schiefferdecker has remarked, most mammals are '*a*-gland animals', monkeys are 'mixed-gland animals', and man is essentially an '*e*-gland animal', with the *a*-glands restricted to a few small areas.[940, 941]

## THE SECRETORY PRODUCT OF THE *A*-GLANDS

The sweat produced by the *a*-glands of man is 'oily'. It has already been mentioned that the secretory products in the ducts of the *a*-glands contain lipid (fatty) material. This has been proved by histochemical tests.[787] There is here a strong contrast with the *e*-glands. It is commonly believed that the general sweat of the body is fatty, but this is not so. More than 99% of the sweat produced by the *e*-glands is water. Of the other constituents, only sodium chloride, urea, and lactic acid are present in more than very minute amounts.

The chemical identity of the smelly substances in the secretion of the *a*-glands of man is not known. This is unfortunate, but perhaps should not cause surprise. Despite the fact that man's sense of smell is very much weaker than that of many animals, his nose is able to detect the presence of one ten-millionth of a gram of certain substances. It often happens that a substance can be detected by smell when the most sensitive instruments cannot analyse and thus identify it, or indeed even record its presence.[17] The axillary secretion is available only in minute quantities, and is difficult to collect.[962] One may hope that greatly improved methods for the isolation, recognition, and assay of the odorous components of the secretion will eventually be devised.

It has been suggested that there is a constituent in the *a*-gland sweat of man that has some resemblance in smell to musk. Muscone and related scents are soluble in lipids, and it is possible that the lipids secreted by the *a*-glands of man serve as vehicles for a related scent—if indeed one of these ketones is present in the axillary sweat. It is obvious that the odour is not simply that of musk in most cases, since there is a component that can be described as fetid, which musk is not. When first exuded on the surface of the skin, the secretion of the gland is sterile and whitish, grey, or tinged with yellow.[962] After a time bacteria multiply in it, and it becomes distinctly yellowish. Both the colour and the odour have been attributed to the action of bacteria.[843, 753] If the odour is really due to the bacteria, it must be supposed that the function of the *a*-glands is to provide a nutrient material for them, and also a precursor or '*Odorigen*'[547] for the odoriferous substance or substances. A special scent may, however, be present from the start, the fetid component being merely a contaminant originating by bacterial action. In a remarkable book on the nervous diseases of women, written more than a century and a quarter ago, an

English doctor named Thomas Laycock made a very similar suggestion. He noted that the odour 'in some is very pleasant; perhaps it would seldom have that disgusting suffocative effect peculiar to it, if due attention were paid to cleanliness'.[644] One has, indeed, the subjective impression that two *separate* odours are present (at any rate among Europids), one fetid and the other fragrant. The existence of the former is hard to explain. The early hominids were almost certainly more sensitive to smell than modern man is, since their nasal cavities were larger, and there has no doubt been a progressive diminution in the relative size of the olfactory regions of the brain since man branched off from his pongid ancestors. We can have no certainty that the particular strain of bacteria that produces the fetid smell was in existence when the sense of smell was more effective in sexual selection than it is today. In the evolution of man, sight has become increasingly important, and this must have affected the process of sexual selection. In modern civilized life the axillary odour has tended to become repulsive, or perhaps only attractive when sexual desire has been aroused in other ways.[309]

It seems certain that in some cases at least, or under certain conditions, there is in fact a sexually alluring component in the axillary secretion. The retention of a strong growth of hair in the armpit, when such a large part of the body has become nearly hairless, suggests that the axillary organ is a scent-gland that has a functional significance, or was of functional significance to man's ancestors. It has already been mentioned (p. 165) that the hairiness and warmth of this region, combined with the protection from useless evaporation of the sweat unless the upper arm is held away from the body, would seem to be adaptations to the function of a scent-organ.

It is regarded as significant that an important scent-organ of man is situated at a level above the ground not far from that of the nose of other members of the species.[940] A scent-organ in the metatarsal region, like that of deer, would be ill-adapted to a tall, upright animal, that never holds its head near the ground when approaching another member of its kind, or following a trail.

It is also regarded as significant that the *a*-glands of the axillae and genito-anal region only become functional at puberty.[733] In his important work *Geschlecht und Geschlechter im Tierreiche*, Meisenheimer[733] says that the characteristic smell produced by the axillary organ of man has an influence on the sexual life that is 'absolutely indisputable'. He remarks that human beings have 'mutually alluring' scent-organs. Schiefferdecker also considered that the odour produced by these glands in the axillae and genito-anal regions appeared to act as a strong sexual stimulant; their scent, he said, is a '*Geschlechtsgeruch*'.[940, 941] Adachi stated that the axillary gland is a sex-organ, producing an odour that is sexually stimulating to persons of the same race.[5] If all this is true, the stimulus must be of the intermediate kind, for it is not nearly powerful enough to be 'directive' in the sense defined on p. 162.

In discussions on this subject, stress is sometimes laid on the musklike constituent of the axillary odour, and on the sex-stimulant effect of musk. 'The musk odour', wrote Laycock,[644] 'is certainly the sexual odour of man.' 'The perfume which is of all perfumes the most interesting from the present point of view', wrote Havelock Ellis in his *Sexual selection in man*,[309] 'is certainly musk. . . . [it] is a very frequent personal odor in man. . . . Musk is the odor which not only in the animals to which it has given a name, but in many others, is a specifically sexual odor.'

A very curious and significant sidelight is thrown on the relation between sex and smell in human beings by experiments carried out with a substance nicknamed 'exaltolide'. When the chemical structure of muscone had been established,[923] a considerable number of synthetic substances were produced, roughly similar to the natural product in composition and odour. Exaltolide is one of these. Men were found to be incapable or scarcely capable of smelling it, and so were girls before puberty; but women varied in their response, some saying that they found the the smell feeble, while others described it as intense or even 'violent'. It appeared that this depended on the stage of the menstrual cycle at which the test was made. Women who had found the smell feeble during menstruation became more sensitive to it in the course of the following days, their response reaching a maximum 7–9 days before the next menstruation; that is to say, at about the time of ovulation.[696] When a female sex-hormone (oestradiol benzoate) was injected into a man, his sensitivity to exaltolide was markedly increased.[697] It is to be hoped that these experiments, performed on a small number of persons, will be repeated on a larger scale, and with other substances related to muscone.

## RACIAL DIFFERENCES IN THE DISTRIBUTION OF $A$-GLANDS

The account that has been given in this chapter of the distribution of $a$-glands over the surface of man's body refers to their situation in Europids, who provided the material for all early studies of the subject. Further research has shown that they are not developed to the same extent in all the races of man.

In some Negrids (and probably Europid–Negrid hybrids) $a$-glands are present in the skin of the chest (away from the nipples).[509] They do not appear to have been reported in this situation in Europids. They have also been found in the skin of the abdomen of several Negroes, among the few who have been examined for this peculiarity; they occur both above and below the navel.[940, 509] The abdominal skin of a very large number of Europids has been examined microscopically with this subject in view,[5] but $a$-glands have been reported in only three, in each case below the navel.[509, 940]

Schiefferdecker reported the presence of $a$-glands in front of the ear of an Australian aborigine (Fig. 23D).[940, 941] They occur in this region in the monkeys Cercopithecus and Cynocephalus,[940, 941] but have never been found there in any other adult human being. Reports have been made on the $a$-glands of the anal region in only two Australids, in both of whom they were powerfully developed and constituted an 'anal organ', comparable with the axillary organ.[1156] It has been claimed that the $a$-glands of these two Australids were similar to those of Europids described by Krause in 1876,[611] but actually the latter devoted less than three lines to this subject, and his description is not sufficiently detailed to act as a basis for interracial comparison. The $a$-glands of the mons pubis and nipple area are normal in the Australid.[1156] Further study will be necessary to establish whether differences occur regularly between

Australids and Europids in the distribution and degree of development of the *a*-glands.

From the racial point of view the most striking fact about the *a*-glands is their weak development in the Mongolids. There is not necessarily a correlation here with the partial suppression of body-hair in Mongolids, for Negrids have little of it, yet their *a*-glands are well developed. In the weak development of both body-hair and *a*-glands the Mongolids have advanced furthest from the ancestral prehuman condition, represented today (in much modified form) by the apes and monkeys. The subject has been very thoroughly investigated by Japanese workers, especially Adachi.[5] They have naturally carried out their most extensive investigations on their fellow-countrymen, and this is rather unfortunate, because the Japanese are a somewhat heterogeneous and partly hybrid people, who cannot be neatly assigned to a single subrace. Fundamentally the type is Palaemongolid (the southern subrace of the Mongolids), but there has been intermarriage with immigrants from Korea and elsewhere, and in particular with the indigenous population of Ainuids, who are an offshoot of the Europid race. Among the Koreans, who are chiefly Sinids of the local form called by Liu[675] 'Huanghoid' (see Appendix 1, p. 538), the reduction of the *a*-glands has gone further than in any other people, so far as is known. In the axilla of the Koreans the glands do not touch one another so as to make a composite organ; indeed, it appears that in about half the population there are no *a*-glands in the armpit at all.[5] Among the Japanese the *a*-glands are more numerous in this situation than they are in the Koreans, but they are usually too sparse to touch one another, and there is no axillary 'organ' visible to the naked eye when the skin is viewed from the inner side. The glands are rarely present on the *mons pubis* and *labia majora*.[5] In these characters there is a striking difference between Mongolid and Europid. There is, however, no sharp difference in the development of the circumanal glands. There are no glands on the chest (apart from the nipples) in the Japanese.[5]

The presence of *a*-glands has been reported in the skin of the *mons pubis*, chest, and abdomen of a Chinese (presumably Sinid).[940] As in the Europids, non-functional vestiges of *a*-glands are found in Mongolid embryos in situations where they do not occur in the adult.[5]

There is a remarkable correlation between the degree of development of the axillary organ and the type of wax produced by the ceruminous glands. In those races, such as the Negrid and Europid, in which the axillary organ is well developed, the ear-wax is generally soft and sticky ('*klebrig*') (though dry ear-wax does occur in some Europids). In the Mongolid race, in which the organ is scarcely or not at all developed, the ear-wax is dry.[5] It will be remembered that the wax is produced by modified *a*-glands (p. 167).

RACIAL DIFFERENCES IN BODY-ODOUR

Only the endogenous odour—that produced (directly or indirectly) by the secretory processes of the body itself—is considered here. The smell in question is that which originates from the *a*-glands of the axillary organ and the genito-anal region. The odour of semen is also endogenous, but there does not appear to be any information about racial differences in it in the scientific literature. The exogenous smells are not pertinent here. Their causes are manifold, and the different customs of people in various parts of the world result in diversity. Food decays between the teeth or in carious cavities in them, and the smell of the breath is also affected by excretion through the lungs of products of decay in the alimentary canal. Opium and tobacco have their distinctive effects, and so do external objects adhering as 'dirt' to the surface of the body or to clothes. Beyond these are the innumerable substances deliberately applied to the body for the sake of their odour. All these are irrelevant to the subject under discussion, because they are not caused by genetic differences between races (or if it is conceivable that in the case of some of them there may be a genetic cause, it must be so indirect in action that no one could be sure of its reality).

The distinction between endogenous and exogenous personal odours is usually not difficult. Many exogenous ones, such as those of tobacco or opium, are so familiar in the parts of the world where they are used that no one would make the mistake of attributing to them an endogenous origin. The wood-smoke of native huts, adhering to hair or clothing, cannot be mistaken for body-odour. The various smells that contaminate the breath may vary with the customs of different peoples, but one cannot fail to note that they emerge from the mouth. Decaying skin between the toes announces the place of its origin, far from any $a$-gland. Conversely, the location of axillary odours in the armpit region of discarded clothing can be detected easily enough. The fact that axillary secretion is usually poured out most freely in circumstances that promote the secretion of ordinary sweat (from $e$-glands) also helps to confirm that the source is endogenous. Doctors who concern themselves with the elimination of body-odour (p. 173) can determine the place of origin of the axillary secretion with certainty, by bringing the nose near the surface of the bare body.

Most cosmetic scents, especially those that smell like flowers, could not be confused with endogenous products. The only exceptions that might mislead are scents that contain musk or substances with similar fragrance; but males seldom anoint themselves with these, and the axillary secretion usually has additional components that are not included in cosmetic preparations. There are many remote parts of the world, too, where endogenous body-odour exists, but the cosmetic scents of commerce do not.

The subject of ethnic differences in endogenous body-odour is necessarily subjective, in view of our ignorance of the actual substances that produce the smell. Nevertheless, despite the fact that the nose cannot undertake reliable chemical *identifications*, it can often *discriminate* with extraordinary accuracy (p. 168). This is a faculty in which people differ greatly. There are those whose sense of smell has always been poor, while others who could at one time smell acutely have damaged their olfactory receptors by smoking. If they give up this habit and the organ recovers its original sensitivity, they may re-enter an almost forgotten world of experience—not a very pleasant one on all occasions.

Persons whose sense of smell is acute are aware of axillary odour, and of differences in its quality and intensity in different persons (and indeed in the same person at different times, especially in relation to the menstrual cycle). In a few persons the acuity is astonishing, though probably it never approaches that of the dog. A case was reported long ago of a monk at Prague who could recognize people by smell as others do by sight.[23] An ornithologist, Dr. Julius Hoffmann, is said to have demonstrated his ability to distinguish by smell alone between carrion and hooded crows, which are commonly regarded as races of a single species (see pp. 89–90).[547]

There are certain points that should be borne in mind in any consideration of ethnic differences in odour. Since the a-glands respond to warmth by pouring out their secretion, the native inhabitants of a tropical country might give the impression of being exceptionally smelly, although the same persons, if living in a cool climate, would not call attention to themselves in this way. Also, no one can give off an axillary smell the instant after he has washed off the secretion of the a-glands with a suitable detergent, such as soap; but the inhabitant of a tropical country, however cleanly in his habits, would begin to become smelly more quickly after washing than a person living in a cool climate, if the odour of the axillary secretion were equally strong in both cases. These remarks, however, refer only to the intensity, not to the distinctive characters of the smells.

There is, naturally enough, a correlation between the development of the axillary organ and the smelliness of the secretion of this gland (and probably this applies also to the a-glands of the genito-anal region). Briefly, the Europids and Negrids are smelly, the Mongolids scarcely or not at all, so far as the axillary secretion is concerned. Adachi, who has devoted more study to this subject than anyone else, has summed up his findings in a single, short sentence: 'The Mongolids are essentially an odourless or very slightly smelly race with dry ear-wax.'[5] Since most of the Japanese are free or almost free from axillary smell, they are very sensitive to its presence, of which they seem to have a horror. About 10% of Japanese have smelly axillae. This is attributed to remote Ainuid ancestry, since the Ainu are invariably smelly, like most other Europids, and a tendency to smelliness is known to be inherited among the Japanese.[5] The existence of the odour is regarded among Japanese as a disease, *osmidrosis axillae*,[513] which warrants (or used to warrant) exemption from military service. Certain doctors specialize in its treatment, and sufferers are accustomed to enter hospital.

It might be supposed that Adachi and other Japanese scientists who have written about the absence or feebleness of axillary smell in the Mongolid race might have deceived themselves by possessing the particular odour themselves, and thus tending to notice it less in others of their own race. The finding is confirmed, however, by Europids who have lived among them. For instance, a lecturer in Japanese at Cambridge University, a Europid of British nationality, writes as follows: 'An example of how little the Japanese smell is that when I underwent a week's initiation in a mountain sect in which one of the austerities was not washing, I experienced no discomfort although I was sleeping in a room with seven [Japanese] men.'[1176]

The Tungus and Kalmuks (Tungid subrace of Mongolids) are said to be devoid of axillary smell, almost without exception.[5] The lack of axillary smell in the Tungus is all the more remarkable since they are said to be very careless about cleanliness;[5] the same has been said of the Koreans.[275]

There do not appear to be many records in the scientific literature about the axillary smell, if any, of the 'typical' Chinese ('Changkiangids' of Liu;[675] see Appendix 1, p. 538). Adachi claims that only 2% or 3% of 'Chinese' have any axillary smell.[5] Huc states that they have a distinctive odour of musk.[520] This is accepted by certain authorities.[268, 309] Musk, if unaccompanied by any other odour, would be agreeable to Europids. Havelock Ellis quotes a Chinese drama in which a young lover addresses a poem specifically to the odour of his betrothed's armpits.[309]

The lack or feebleness of axillary smell among the Tungus, Kalmuks, Koreans, and Japanese seems to be shared by the Sibirids (northern Mongolids). Georg Steller, the naturalist who accompanied Bering in the exploration of the Straits that bear the latter's name, remarked on the freedom from smell of the inhabitants of Kamchatka (Itelmes or Kamchadales), who belong to the Sibirid subrace. In his book published in 1774, Steller wrote of them, 'They are not disposed to perspiration, and consequently are without any of the usual smell of sweat.'[1006]

There can be no doubt that to persons of certain other races, the axillary smell of Europids is strong and unpleasant. Adachi has written, '*Vor allem riecht der Korper der weissen Rasse*,'[5] but it must be mentioned that he did not himself study all the major races of man. In the New Hebrides, the native inhabitants (Melanesids) had no inhibition about speaking to me of 'smell belong white man'. There is a curious statement by Le Cat, the French physiologist of the eighteenth century, to the effect that the Negroes (presumably slaves) living in the Antilles could distinguish the smell left behind by a Frenchman from that left by Negroes, and could thus determine whether a Frenchman or a Negro had passed by.[192] There would not appear to be any information in the scientific literature about the repulsiveness or attractiveness of the Europid axillary odour to Negrids.

Huc says that the Chinese detect a special odour in Europeans, but that this is less noticeable to them than that of other peoples with whom they come in contact. When travelling in remote parts of their country in Chinese disguise he himself was never recognized as a foreigner except by dogs, which must have been aware of the strangeness of his smell, for they barked at him incessantly.[520] The native inhabitants of Peru (Andid subrace of South American 'Indians') are said to distinguish the odour of Europeans from that of Negroes and from their own, and to have a special word for each of the three smells.[22]

The German anthropologist von Eickstedt considered that the Europid smell was particularly strong in people of the Nordid subrace and other subraces of northern and central Europe. He remarked that the smell was pleasant to persons of the same race, but that to the Japanese it seemed 'pungent and rancid'.[302]

It has already been mentioned that all persons of unmixed Ainuid stock have axillary odour.[5] The Galla, dark-skinned Europids of the Aethiopid subrace (pp. 225–6), have no trace of the special smell of the Negrid.[579]

There seems to be general agreement that Europids find the smell of Negrids strong and markedly different from their own. The authors of earlier centuries remarked on this subject with greater freedom than those of the present day. Thus Henry Home, in his *Sketches of the history of man*, refers to the 'rank smell' of Negroes.[508] In a work published in the same year (1774), *The history of Jamaica*, Long says that the Negroes are distinguished by their 'bestial or fetid smell, which they all have to a greater or lesser degree. . . . This scent in some of them is so excessively strong . . . that it continues in places where they have been near a quarter of an hour.'[678] A doctor named Schotte, living on an island near the mouth of the River Senegal in West Africa to attend to the soldiers of a French garrison, wrote at some length on the same subject. He describes the sweat of the native inhabitants during the rainy season as 'remarkably fetid', and mentions also the 'foul and nasty vapours' arising from the skin of most of them. He notes that they were continually washing themselves, and that the smell could only be due to the sweat itself. The 'fetor' of the Europeans on the island was 'not to be compared to that of the blacks'.[946]

Sir Harry Johnston, traveller and colonial administrator, remarks that the smell of the Negro 'is sometimes offensive to an appalling degree, rendering it well nigh impossible to remain in a closed room with him'. He notes that the smelly secretion comes from the armpits and is more oily than ordinary sweat.[555] Similarly the explorer Du Chaillu writes of certain villagers (Palaenegrids) in Gabon, 'Almost every day a party of men and women crowd into my hut to see my stuffing operations, and scarcely are they there than I have to leave it, the odour is so unsufferably sickening.'[200]

Havelock Ellis, in *The psychology of sex*, says that the powerful odour of Negroes is well known, and has been described as 'ammoniacal and rancid; it is like the odour of the he-goat'.[309] It is stated by Adachi that all Negroes are smelly to the Japanese, and that the smell is very repulsive to them.[5]

Certain anthropologists have made similar observations. Deniker simply remarks that Negroes have their 'specific odour', which is not abolished, so he says, even by scrupulous cleanliness.[268] Professor W. Joest studied the so-called '*Buschneger*' of Guiana; that is to say, the descendants of imported Negro slaves, living in freedom in the primeval forest. He commends them highly, remarking that the worst evil with which he could reproach them '. . . *ist ihr Geruch: sie stinken furchtbar!*'[554] He lays emphasis on their cleanliness. The smell, he says more mildly, is 'not congenial' to Europeans. Joest mentions that Negroes (some of them presumably hybrids) living in Haiti, Washington, and Berlin smell to him like those of Guiana. Many records of the strong smell of Negroes to persons of other races are quoted by the German anthropologist Andree.[22] He mentions that the Masai of East Africa, who belong to the Aethiopid subrace of the Europids and are thus quite distinct from typical Negroes, find the smell of the coastal natives '*verhaszt*' (odious).

Tnere is little information about the differences between the axillary smells of the various subraces of Negrids. The natives of Angola (Palaenegrid subrace) have been stated to have a particularly strong smell, while those of Senegal (Sudanid subrace) have been described as less smelly to Europeans than other Negroes.[678] This seems to conflict with the evidence of Schotte,[946] unless the latter was referring to labourers imported to his island from other parts of Africa. Emin Pasha claimed to be able to distinguish different Negro tribes by smell.[309]

One must remember that all these comments on the axillary odour of Negroes are subjective and were made by persons belonging to other races. There can, however, be scarcely any doubt that the characteristic odour of Negrids is different from that of Europids. Even Ludwig Wolf, who denies that the natives of Angola emit an unpleasant smell, allows that Negroes in general have a particular odour that differs from that of Europeans and also from that of Indianids (American 'Indians').[1146]

The smell of the Australids (Australian aborigines) is said not to be very strong (see, however, p. 296). Horses, cattle, and dogs appear to distinguish it from that of Europeans. If unaccustomed to it, they are reported to show signs of restlessness when approached by an unseen aborigine.[22]

When all this has been said, there remain certain unresolved problems about the endogenous odours of man. Further research is needed, especially on the differences in the distribution of $a$-glands, and in the chemical composition of the scented substances they produce, in the various ethnic taxa of man. It might be possible, by the use of bacteriostatic agents, to find out whether the non-fetid component of the scent differs in chemical composition in the several races and subraces. These are matters for the future; but it may not be unprofitable to suggest the direction in which the evidence at present available points.

It seems strange that the odour produced by men and women of the same ethnic taxon should be the same and that it should have a sexually alluring effect. One might, indeed, think it an analogous case, if men were attracted by bearded women; but one must remember the strong evidence that musk possesses a general property of stimulating sexual instincts, and that the non-fetid component of the axillary scent of man is thought by many to smell like musk. Civet-cats of both sexes produce the smell; so do musk-rats; so (more or less) do men and women of the same ethnic taxon (except that there is in some cases a special smell in women at the menstrual period, not necessarily originating from the $a$-glands). The facts suggest that in all three cases something in addition to sexual allurement may be involved. The axillary odour may perhaps act rather like the substances produced by the metatarsal glands of deer, as ancillary guides to the recognition of 'own kind'.

I have already mentioned some of the reasons for supposing that the axillary odour of man was formerly much more noticeable than it is today. Not only were facilities for personal cleanliness less readily available than they are now, but sensitivity to smell must have been more widespread when the smoking of tobacco had not yet been introduced. One must also remember that the skulls of fossil hominids show that there has been progressive diminution in the capacity of the nasal cavities and in the size of the olfactory centres of the brain. These considerations make it likely that the axillary odour was more important in the sexual and social lives of our remote ancestors than it is today; and differences in the odour between one group of mankind and another may have played a part in the avoidance of miscegenation and therefore in the evolution of the ethnic taxa.

# PART THREE

# Studies of Selected
# Human Groups

# 11 Introduction to Part 3

SEVERAL GROUPS of human beings have been selected for special consideration in this Part of the book, each to illustrate a different aspect of the ethnic problem. A certain amount of physical anthropology will enter into most of the chapters of this Part, and some of them will be concerned with nothing else. It is necessary to consider here the relevance of this branch of anthropology to the ethnic problem.

There has unfortunately been a tendency for physical and social anthropologists to draw somewhat apart, as though the interests of one set of students did not impinge directly on those of the other. This tendency has increased in recent years, but it is by no means new. It was recognized and regretted by T. H. Huxley long ago. He complained that those ethnologists

who have been least naturalists . . . have most neglected the zoological method, the neglect culminating in those who have been altogether devoid of acquaintance with anatomy. . . . it is plain that the zoological court of appeal is the highest for the ethnologist, and that no evidence can be set against that derived from physical characters.[536]

In Chapter 9 emphasis was laid on the relative unimportance of skin colour in the distinction of human taxa (pp. 159–60). The subject needs re-emphasis at this point, for one repeatedly finds mankind divided into 'white' and 'coloured' in popular speech and writing, and sometimes it is actually stated that there is no difference between races except in the colour of the skin. Nevertheless, it is obvious that such statements are untrue. Novelists, untrained in physical anthropology, often provide vivid thumbnail sketches that pick out some of the characters, apart from the colour of the skin, that distinguish persons belonging to particular *sub*races. For instance, in his novel *A nest of gentlefolk*, Turgenev gives a description that leaves one in no doubt that Lavretsky bore the essential physical features of an Osteuropid. The novelist evidently considered this subrace as especially characteristic of Russia (as indeed it is, over a considerable part of the country), for he writes of Lavretsky's 'red-cheeked, typically Russian face, with large, white forehead, rather fat nose, and wide, straight lips. . . . He was splendidly built and his blond hair curled on his head as on a youth.'[1071] Turgenev mentions also that his eyes were blue. Lavretsky was born on his family's estate in Byezhetsk, in the typically Osteuropid region, and both his mother and his paternal grandmother were local women.[1071, 1070]

Lermontov was as perceptive as Turgenev of the physical features that most evidently characterize certain subraces of the Europid race. In his semi-autobiographical novel *A hero of our time* he gives a brief physical description of Lieutenant Vulich, the fatalist who risked his life for a bet in a variant form of 'Russian roulette'. His words strongly suggest a Dinarid, for he remarks on Vulich's 'tall stature and the swarthy complexion of his face, his black hair, black piercing eyes, and large but straight nose, typical of his nation'.[655, 654] Serbia is populated principally by Dinarids, and the physical anthropologist is not surprised to read that the gambler was a Serb.

The question arises, why so many people say or imply that the races differ only in skin-colour, when this is obviously untrue. Those who minimize racial differences, by speaking as though the only distinction between a European and (for instance) a Chinese or a Negro were one of skin-colour, appear unwittingly to admit that recognition of the more fundamental differences that actually exist might affect people's views on the ethnic problem; for it might be regarded as unlikely that such differences could coexist with exact similarity in the parts of the body concerned with thought and feeling.

This idea would be strengthened by the well-known fact that 'identical' twins—those who develop from the same fertilized ovum and therefore carry the same set of genes—usually show marked resemblances to one another not only in physical but also in mental characters. This subject has been studied in great detail in the U.S.A. by H. H. Newman and his colleagues, who made a statistical investigation of the resemblances and differences between members of pairs of identical twins, in comparison with the resemblances and differences between members of those pairs of twins, called 'fraternal', who originate from separate ova and therefore do not resemble one another more closely than ordinary brothers or sisters, except in age. This study was carried out on fifty pairs of fraternal twins (each member of a pair being in every case of the same sex) and fifty pairs of identical twins. The members of each pair had been brought up together in the same environment. It was found that identical twins often differ from one another in the rather ill-defined character called 'personality'. For instance, it was found quite usual for one of the pair to show more initiative than the other in dealing with strangers. In intelligence and educational achievement, however, identical twins were found to be much more like one another than fraternal ones. In these and certain other respects (such as quality and speed of handwriting) 'it is obvious that the twins who have the same inheritance are the more alike. . . . This conclusion seems clearly warranted.'[798] It follows that the physical similarity of the identical twins (established by elaborate criteria) was correlated with similarity in important mental attributes. It is particularly to be noted that Newman and his colleagues were studying variations within families. Fraternal twins, like ordinary brothers and sisters, inherit many of the same genes from their parents, and therefore tend to be more like one another than unrelated persons. If the resemblances and differences between members of pairs of identical twins had been compared with those between unrelated persons, the tendency towards mental similarity, resulting from the possession of the same genes, would have revealed itself even more clearly. The reader is referred to Chapter 24 (pp. 459–67) for a much closer study of the role of the genetic element in determining mental characters.

The idea that the existence of manifold physical differences between certain ethnic taxa makes it probable that there are also inborn differences of mental potentiality, is by no means confined to persons untrained in biological science. As Professor H. J. Muller has written, 'To the great majority of geneticists it seems absurd to suppose that psychological characteristics are subject to entirely different laws of heredity or development than other biological characteristics.... Psychological comparisons of fraternal and identical twins have provided one type of empirical evidence in support of this conclusion.'[779] Very similar ideas have been expressed by Professor Sir Ronald Fisher:

> It appears to me unmistakable that gene differences which influence the growth or physiological development of an organism will ordinarily *pari passu* influence the congenital inclinations and capacities of the mind. In fact, I should say that... 'Available scientific knowledge provides a firm basis for believing that the groups of mankind differ in their innate capacity for intellectual and emotional development,' seeing that such groups do differ undoubtedly in a very large number of these genes.[337]

It is, indeed, scarcely possible to believe that two ethnic taxa, differing from one another in many genes affecting various parts of the body, could be identically similar in all those genes that affect the development and function of the nervous and sensory systems. For this reason it is relevant to the ethnic problem to consider the extent to which the taxa of man differ in their physical characters. Some general indications of the nature and extent of the physical differences between the taxa of man are therefore provided in Chapter 12.

As a concrete example of the physical characters that distinguish a human race, the Europids are considered in some detail in Chapter 13. Two of the Europid subraces are also compared, to give an impression of the extent of subracial differences. Hybridity between the subraces, and between the Europid and other races, is also discussed.

To clarify more exactly what is and what is not an ethnic taxon of man, attention is next turned to group-names that are often used but do not qualify as names of taxa. Certain categories of human beings are named in common speech, and even described under terms—such as 'race'—that would suggest a taxon, when in fact they are nothing of the sort, but only groups of people associated by nationality, territory, language, religion, or customs.* To make this clear, the Jews are studied in Chapter 14. It is shown that although some Jews belong to various ethnic taxa, a large proportion of them have many physical characters in common that place them in a particular taxon that also includes many who are not Jews.

The same theme is pursued in Chapter 15. It is shown that the word 'Celt' has been used with several different meanings. The *'Celtae'* of Julius Caesar can indeed be referred to a particular subrace, but the name of Celt has also been used to mean those who practised a particular culture in past times, or occupied a particular territory, or speak a particular language (or formerly spoke it). Emphasis is placed on the fact that groups of human beings throw no light

---

* It is true that certain named territories are inhabited principally by people of a particular ethnic taxon (for instance, Serbia by Dinarids, or the New Hebrides by Melanesids); but it seldom happens that the taxa in question are restricted to such territories.

on the ethnic problem unless they constitute ethnic taxa recognizable by the criteria of physical anthropology.

In Chapter 16 the Australids (Australian aborigines) are subjected to rather close scrutiny for the light they may throw on the question whether any human taxon, still surviving at the present day, shows in its physical characters any traces that would indicate closer links with man's remote, semi-human ancestors than those shown by other taxa.

The subject of paedomorphosis has already been introduced in Chapter 8 in preparation for a discussion of its relevance to man in Chapter 17, in which the very remarkable anatomical peculiarities of the Bushmen, and especially of the Bushwomen, are described and illustrated.

The physical characters of the Negrids are mentioned only briefly. Members of this race are studied in Chapters 18–21 mainly from the point of view of the social anthropologist interested in their progress towards civilization at a time when they were still scarcely influenced, over a large part of their territory, by direct contact with members of more advanced ethnic taxa.

# 12 Physical differences between the ethnic taxa of man: Introductory remarks

A CONSIDERABLE section of Chapter 8 of this book was devoted to the meaning of the expression 'typical forms', used in descriptions of the taxa of animals. It was pointed out that the almost infinite diversity of form encountered in animals makes definitions of taxa vague and useless if they cover every individual, but that the process of induction makes it possible to recognize the more typical forms of each taxon, and then to appreciate the smaller and greater deviations from the typical.

There are, however, also certain characters in which the ethnic taxa exhibit dimorphism; that is to say, some members of a particular taxon show a certain character that is lacking, and replaced by another, in other members of the same taxon. The dimorphic forms live and breed together in the same area. In a sense, the two sexes might be regarded as dimorphic forms, but it is not customary to extend the meaning of the word to cover this very special case. There are often several characteristic forms of the same ethnic taxon; if so, one speaks of polymorphism. In certain species of butterflies the males all resemble one another, while the females are polymorphic, showing characteristic differences in the shapes of their wings and in the patterns on them. In man, however, the same polymorphic forms occur in both sexes.

Polymorphism often exhibits itself not in externally visible characters, but in the chemical properties of the blood and other body-fluids. An example from man, concerned with racial differences, may be quoted by way of introduction to this important subject.

The fluid part (plasma) of human blood contains substances called *haptoglobins* that have the capacity to combine chemically with haemoglobin, the substance inside the red corpuscles that gives the colour to blood and carries oxygen from the lungs to all parts of the body. The haptoglobins may be obtained from the serum when blood has been allowed to clot. The significance of the haptoglobins is rather obscure. They cannot ordinarily come in direct contact with haemoglobin; but if a red blood-corpuscle is damaged or decays, the haemoglobin will escape into the plasma and the haptoglobin will combine with it and prevent it from being excreted by the kidneys. There are two chemically distinct types of haptoglobin in human blood, called Hp 1 and Hp 2. The former is due to the possession of the gene $Hp^1$, the latter to $Hp^2$. Each human being may possess $Hp^1$ in double dose, or $Hp^2$ in double dose, or single doses of $Hp^1$ and $Hp^2$. Some people have no haptoglobin in their blood, apparently as a result of the presence in double dose of a recessive suppressor gene, which prevents the synthesis of both types of haptoglobin. Thus there are four types of persons as regards the presence of haptoglobin in the plasma of their blood. Some have Hp 1 only, some Hp 2 only, others both Hp 1 and Hp 2, yet others have neither.

The percentage of people of these four types differs significantly in different races. A group of Europids (British), for instance, was compared in this respect with a group of Nigerian Negrids of the Yoruba tribe (*Pan 2*—see pp. 328–9 and 331–3—modified by hybridization with Hausa).[13] The percentage in each category is expressed (to the nearest unit) in the table shown here.

|  | Hp 1 only | Hp 2 only | both | neither |
|---|---|---|---|---|
| Europids | 10 | 32 | 55 | 3 |
| Negrids | 54 | 3 | 11 | 32 |

The differences in gene-frequency, resulting in the figures tabulated above, may be described as 'characters' of the races, but they cannot be used to *define* them, in the sense of determining which persons belong to one race and which to the other. It is necessary to use criteria of a different sort to distinguish Europids from Negrids; then, the distinction having been made, one may discover interesting facts about the distribution of certain genes among people belonging to each race. The characters that permit distinction of the various taxa may be called 'primary', while the designation 'secondary' may be applied to those characters that cannot ordinarily be used for the original distinction, though they may be used in certain cases for confirmation of distinctions, or for evidence of hybridity.

A great deal of information has been obtained in recent years in the field of 'biochemical anthropology'. A valuable review of this subject is available.[621, 622] The blood-groups are really only a familiar but special case of this much wider phenomenon—the existence of chemical differences between persons belonging to the same ethnic taxon and indeed often to the same family, and of differences between one taxon and another in the *proportions* of people possessing particular biochemical characters. An immense amount of knowledge has been obtained about the gene-frequencies concerned with blood-groups in different populations. Tables of these frequencies are printed in many text-books. There is a particularly convenient one, for instance, in Schwidetzky's *Die neue Rassenkunde*.[953]

In a few cases, the great majority of people in a particular ethnic taxon belong to the same blood-group. This applies, for instance, to certain aboriginal inhabitants of Ecuador studied by Santiana.[929] This work had the great merit that ethnic taxa were first recognized by morphological characters, and the gene-frequencies then determined. Santiana investigated the ABO blood-groups of 8,112 persons belonging to the Andid subrace of Indianids (American 'Indians'), and found that no fewer than 7,707 of them belonged to group 'O'.

Instead of stating the number or percentage of persons belonging to each of the groups 'A', 'B', 'AB', and 'O', it is preferable for some purposes to state the frequency of the genes responsible for the production of the observable (phenotypic) characters.

Each reproductive cell (spermatozoon or ovum) can only carry one of these genes: a gene making for 'A' or one for 'B' or one for 'O'. It will be understood that a person belonging to group 'AB' has received the gene for 'A' from one parent and that for 'B' from the other. One might express the facts by the percentages of the reproductive cells carrying each gene, but it is customary to state the 'gene-frequencies' in figures adding up to 1·0 instead of 100. These frequencies can easily be calculated by the application of simple algebraical equations, if the percentages of persons belonging to each of the four blood-groups is known.[870, 472] The frequency of the gene for 'A' is represented by the symbol $p$; for 'B' by $q$; and for 'O' by $r$. Gene-frequencies will be quoted here and there in this book.

The frequencies of the genes responsible for the ABO blood-groups of the Ecuador Andids studied by Santiana worked out at these very unusual figures: $p$, 0·019; $q$, 0·007; $r$, 0·974. The case is remarkable, even for a subrace of Indianids, among whom a high percentage of persons belonging to group 'O' is quite usual.

The very strange gene-frequency in the ABO blood-groups of Andids almost persuades one to regard group 'O' as a primary character of the subrace. One cannot fail to notice the striking difference in this respect from most other ethnic taxa, in which there is no question of any particular blood-group being a primary character. For instance, among the Sikhs (Nordindid subrace of Europids), the following percentages of persons belonging to groups in the ABO series have been reported: 'A', 25·2; 'B', 30·6; 'AB', 8; 'O', 35·3.[1953] It is obviously impossible to say to which group a typical Nordindid belongs, or to use the blood-group of an individual as evidence of his subrace. As soon, however, as the gene-frequencies of Nordindids have been determined, by study of many individuals referred to this subrace on the evidence of morphological characters, they may be recognized as a significant *secondary* character of the subrace (of which most Sikhs are particularly typical examples).

Blood-grouping can be used negatively in some cases to make it practically certain than an individual does *not* belong to a particular ethnic group. If, for example, one knew nothing about someone except that he (or she) belonged to the group 'A2' in the ABO series and to '$r$' (=cde/cde) in the Rhesus, one could exclude the possibility that he was an Andid. (He might well be a Laplander, for these rather unusual blood-groups occur fairly commonly among the Lappids.)

Some of the human blood-groups are found in apes; and as J. B. S. Haldane remarked many years ago, 'Hence comes the paradoxical fact that it may be no more dangerous to have a transfusion of blood from a chimpanzee than from your own brother.'[459] Another very curious similarity between particular human beings and particular chimpanzees may be quoted. It concerns the sense of taste.

Dr. A. L. Fox, working in an industrial chemical laboratory in Wilmington, Delaware, had occasion to prepare a quantity of phenyl-thio-urea. This is a colourless substance, crystallizing from hot water in the form of needles. A colleague working in the same laboratory complained of the bitter taste of the dust. Dr. Fox repudiated the complaint; he found the crystals of his preparation tasteless. His colleague tasted them and found them 'extremely bitter'. Many peoples of both sexes, various ages, and different races were then tested.

Some of them were found to be 'tasters' of phenyl-thio-urea, others 'non-tasters'—the latter being persons unaware of the presence of the substance when dissolved at concentrations that produced unpleasant bitterness for the 'tasters'.[355] (It is a remarkable fact that the substance is chemically related to another used as a commercial sweetening agent.)

In the same year (1932) in which Dr. Fox published his results, two independent papers appeared, reporting on the genetics of the capacity to taste phenyl-thio-urea.[986, 102] The deficiency of taste appeared to be a simple recessive character, though there were certain minor complications due to the age and sex of the subjects tested and the range of concentrations at which the tests were performed. These early reports were substantially correct. Inability to taste phenyl-thio-urea, when dissolved at a carefully selected concentration, is in fact a simple recessive character.[736] In countries where Europids predominate, 30% or more of the population are commonly non-tasters.[736, 953]

It was discovered by experiments carried out in zoological collections at Edinburgh, London, and Whipsnade, that chimpanzees (probably of the race *Pan satyrus verus*) are also divisible into tasters and non-tasters.[339] Of the 27 specimens of both sexes that were tested, seven (26%) were non-tasters. It is presumed that the gene concerned is the same as that which controls the tasting of the substance by man.

The ease with which the test can be applied has resulted in the supply of information on the subject from almost every part of the world. Among Sinids (Chinese), examined in their own country and in various parts of the world, the proportion of non-tasters is usually less than 10%. Among the Chinese of Taiwan (Formosa), for instance, only about 6·4% are non-tasters.[197] Some of the aboriginal tribes of the same island, who appear to belong to the Palaemongolid subrace, show an even lower percentage of non-tasters. In the Paiwan tribe they amount to only 2% (ten persons among 300 women and 199 men).[197] It is obvious that in respect of taste-deficiency, the Europids are much closer to the chimpanzee than to the Sinids and Paiwan people; yet no one would claim that this resemblance gives a true representation of relationship. The morphological resemblances between human beings of diverse groups altogether outweigh the trivial evidence provided by the frequencies of a pair of allelomorphic genes controlling a polymorphic character.

The Paiwan tribe occupies the southernmost part of the island. It is a curious but unexplained fact that as one goes north in the island, one finds in general a higher and higher proportion of non-tasters among the aboriginal tribes.

The subject of dimorphism and polymorphism involving pairs or larger groups of allelomorphic genes is so important that yet another example will be given. It is well known that a disease called 'sickle-cell anaemia' is common among Negrids over a wide tract of tropical Africa.[973] It is characterized by a tendency of the red blood-corpuscles to assume a crescentic shape, and the red colouring matter in them is very slightly different from the normal in chemical composition. The condition is determined by a gene which may be present in single or double dose. If the latter, the person usually dies in childhood, but in single dose (that is, if both the normal and abnormal genes are present) a certain degree of resistance to malaria results. In 1952 sickle-cell anaemia was reported from southern India among a tribe known as the Irula, a jungle people practising a simple culture. The trait was observed in no fewer than 30% of those whose blood was examined.[649] The Irula are Weddids; that is to say, they are of the same taxon as the Veddahs of Ceylon. To account for the presence of this peculiarity among a very different people, it has been suggested that this stock spread in ancient days to Africa, and that it was they who introduced the sickle gene into the Negrid population of that continent, by intermarriage.[649] Singer, who has made a comprehensive study of the distribution of the sickle-cell trait, thinks it just as likely that the Negrids brought it to India; but he allows that it may have arisen independently in more than one place.[973] This, indeed, seems the most likely explanation. One must always be on the look-out for the possibility of independent mutation, whenever two apparently unrelated ethnic taxa resemble one another by the fact that some individuals in both groups reveal the presence of the same gene. It is quite possible that the sickle gene appeared by mutation in Africa and independently in southern India, and was maintained by natural selection in certain malarious districts. The Weddids are very different morphologically from Negrids. The nose is wide, but this is so in various unrelated ethnic taxa of man.

Evidence from blood-groups does not support the suggestion of genetic relationship between Weddids and Negrids. The gene-complex cDe of the Rhesus system is frequent among Negrids, but did not occur at all in the Weddid populations studied by Lehmann and Cutbush, who included 100 Irulas in their investigation. [949] CDE, on the contrary, is unknown among Negrids, but was found in five of the Irulas.

There is no doubt that a gene can spread widely through a population, even if actually harmful. That which causes the disease known as hereditary variegate porphyria provides a striking example. It produces an inborn error of metabolism.

A substance called uroporphyrin III plays an essential role in the synthesis of haemoglobin in the normal human body. A very small amount of a closely related substance called uroporphyrin I is present as well, but plays no part in the process. In some persons, however, this type of uroporphyrin is formed in large amounts. Unable to participate in the synthesis of haemoglobin, it is excreted by the kidneys and gives rise to coloured substances that make the urine look like port wine.[265, 1044]

Hereditary variegate porphyria occurs among the Europid population of South Africa. Patients commonly suffer from severe colic and sensitivity of the skin to light; they tend to become acutely anxious. Paralysis may supervene, resulting in some cases in death.

Thousands of people have inherited this disease from a single common ancestor who married at the Cape in 1688. The gene expresses itself as a Mendelian dominant. The facts have been established by the painstaking medical and genealogical studies of Dr. G. Dean.[265] If mutation were to produce the same gene in some other ethnic taxon, it might give rise to a misleading impression that the two taxa were closely related, since they possessed this secondary character in common. Care must be taken in human taxonomy to avoid errors arising from independent mutation.

When once a taxon has been defined on the evidence of primary characters, the frequency of the genes that control blood-groups, haptoglobins, and other biochemical properties of individuals may be stated as secondary characters of that taxon; but one does not know among which people to count the genes, until the taxon has been defined. For instance, one might count the genes among 'Russians', and this has indeed been done; but the count would not serve to define any taxon. The peoples of Russia are very diverse, including as they do not only several subraces of Europids (Osteuropids, Alpinids, Dinarids, Armenids, and others), but also two subraces of Mongolids (Sibirids and Tungids). It is true, of course, that since few representatives of these taxa exist in Holland (for instance), one finds a sharp difference between the frequencies of blood-group genes in Holland and Russia (see p. 243); but one cannot reasonably lump together all the diverse peoples of Russia, simply because they all happen to live in the same country. It has been claimed that 'To the geneticist, a race is a population which differs from other populations in the frequency of its genes.'[29] If this were so, the Russians would be one race, the Dutch another, despite the fact that the Europid Russians are obviously much more closely allied to the Dutch than they are to the Mongolids of Russia. The mistake would be comparable to the one mentioned in Chapter 7, of lumping together all the crested newts of Romania and taking the average of their characters, when in fact three subraces exist in that country, and two of them extend widely outside it.

Each of the differences that enable one to distinguish all the most typical individuals of any one taxon from those of another is due, as a general rule, to the action of *polygenes*; that is to say, to the action of numerous genes, having small cumulative effects. If members of two ethnic taxa are mated together, and the offspring again mated, it is usual to find that the distinguishing primary characters of the parental types do not 'segregate' or reappear separately among the progeny, but that intermediates are produced, generation after generation. Whenever this occurs, one may suspect that polygenes control the distinctive characters of the parental taxa. The genes that control the blood-groups and other polymorphic characters are readily analysed by the conventional techniques of genetics, but polygenes present great difficulties. I have remarked elsewhere on this unfortunate paradox, that the better the evidence of relationship or distinction between ethnic taxa, the less susceptible are the facts to genetic analysis.[47] In animals, where appropriate matings can be made, genetic and chromosomal analysis of polygenes is in some cases a possibility,[712] but in man the difficulties are very great and can rarely be surmounted, and then only by unusual genetical techniques.[1007, 1008] (See pp. 158–9.)

Because polymorphism lends itself so readily to genetical analysis, the geneticist is almost forced to concentrate his attention on genes that are *shared* between different taxa, and differ from one taxon to another only by their frequency. Thus by concentrating his attention on the genes of polymorphism, he may tend to underestimate the differences between taxa. Polygenes, on the contrary, affect morphological characters that *distinguish* the taxa, and are only accessible to genetical analysis in particular cases and by special methods.

The whole vast system of animal taxonomy, from species upwards through genera, families, and so on till finally the phylum is reached, is based mainly on evidence derived from morphological studies. At present it is almost impossible to institute a genetical analysis of the causes that underlie the differences between the various higher taxa, because the necessary experiments would require interfertility between members of these taxa, which generally does not exist. This fact, however, does not invalidate the mainly morphological basis of taxonomy. The principles on which the classification of animals has been built up do not suddenly become invalid when one passes down from the species or *Formenkreis* to the race. This would indeed be unthinkable, since, as we have seen in Chapter 5–7, there is no sharp line of demarcation that distinguishes the race from the next higher taxon.

Nothing that has been said here is intended to disparage the genetical analysis of polymorphism. Where gene-frequencies have been studied in ethnic taxa that have already been established on the basis of primary characters, they have often added a wealth of valuable information. Damage is only done when obviously heterogeneous populations are treated by geneticists as though they were homogeneous. It is very much to be hoped that methods will be devised to analyse genetically the polygenes that are the underlying cause of the primary characters by which typical members of the various ethnic taxa are distinguished. Indeed, one hopes that eventually it will be possible, through some technique that cannot at present be imagined, to analyse the differences between all the taxa of animals from the subrace to the phylum, in terms of the genes that must constitute the underlying cause.

It is far from being true that the type of polymorphism studied by geneticists is alone in providing the secondary characters of the various ethnic taxa of man. Many characters, well known to physical anthropologists but not analysed genetically, occur in a certain percentage of persons belonging to particular taxa, but are rare or unknown in other taxa. For instance, the arrangement of the bones at the sides of the head in the region called the *pterion* in some cases shows a resemblance to that characteristic of the gorilla and certain other apes. This arrangement is much commoner among Australids (Australian aborigines) than among Europids, but the majority of Australids resemble the Europids in this respect. A tendency for the 'simian' or anthropoid arrangement to present itself is thus a *secondary* character of the Australids (see p. 298). Similarly, about 15% of Sinids (Chinese) have a bony swelling or *torus* on the inner (lingual) side of the lower jaw (mandible), generally reaching its largest size in the vicinity of the canine or 1st premolar tooth.[227] Since this swelling is rare in several other ethnic taxa, the tendency to produce it is a secondary character of the Sinids.

The torus is a secondary character in most of those ethnic taxa in which it occurs, but we would perhaps be justified in saying that the *typical* Eskimid has this peculiar bump on his mandible. If so, it would seem to be a primary character of the taxon, and comparable, in a wide sense, with the blood-group 'O' among the Andids. It is to be noticed that the distinction between primary and secondary characters, though valid in most cases, is not necessarily absolute.

## THE SKULL IN TAXONOMY

There are several reasons why the skull provides primary characters that are particularly valuable to the taxonomist in his task of distinguishing the ethnic taxa of man. The external features of the body do indeed supply useful evidence, but they are subject to the disadvantage that the deposit of adipose tissue, especially in the face, may hide distinctive characters that would otherwise be obvious. All the soft parts of the body, being subject to decay, require the permission of relatives and immediate skilful treatment, if they are to be made available for study. Bones are much more readily obtainable, not only from graves and ossuaries, but also, in fossil form, from more ancient sources; and they provide the greater part of all the direct evidence we have of man's evolution. Of the various parts of the skeleton, the skull is the most valuable to the physical anthropologist, not only because it is more commonly found and made available in museums than the rest, but also because it consists of so many bones and teeth, many of which are of distinctive form in different taxa. The only disadvantage of this part of the skeleton, from the point of view of the taxonomist, is the fact that certain peoples are accustomed to deform it artificially during childhood; but reasonable care should prevent the possibility of error arising from this cause.

More than three centuries have elapsed since Dr. Thomas Browne, already well-known as the author of *Religio medici*, remarked on the fact that one could readily distinguish the skull of a Negro. He made this observation in a little book, *Hydriotaphia or urne-buriall*, published in 1658, in which he discussed the conclusions that may be drawn about the appearance of persons when alive, from study of the skeletons found in their graves. 'A critical view of bones', he wrote, 'makes a good distinction of sexes. Even colour is not beyond conjecture; since it is hard to be deceived in the distinction of *Negro's* sculls.'[151] Unfortunately Browne did not enumerate the criteria by which he made the distinctions, nor did he in the second edition,[152] nor in that of 1669.[153] In the Everyman edition of a selection of Browne's writings,[154] a footnote is added, apparently attributed to Browne himself, to the effect that the skulls of Negroes were distinguishable by the thickness of the bones; but other differences are so much more obvious that this is perhaps an interpolation by some other hand. In the next century Blumenbach made an observation to the same effect as Browne's. 'It is so evident', he remarked, 'that an intimate relation exists between the external face and its underlying bony structure, that even a blind man, if only he had some notion of the very great difference by which the Mongolian face is distinguished from the Ethiopian, would undoubtedly be able, by touch alone, to distinguish the skull of a Kalmuk from that of a Negro.'[108]

Within any particular taxon there are naturally variations in the form of the skull, but valuable generalizations can usually be made about the differences in this respect between one taxon and another. It would scarcely be possible to write better sense on this subject that did Blumenbach himself (though it might be wished that he had composed this passage in less clumsy Latin, lending itself more readily to literal translation into English):

It is certainly obvious ... that the shapes of skulls, not less than the colours of the skin and other variations of this sort in individual persons, are occasionally deceptive, and one shape melts, as it were, with others through gradations and by imperceptible transition; nevertheless, as a general rule there exists in them an untainted and striking constancy of characters that are very closely related to the features of the racial stock and correspond exactly to the appearance[s] appropriate to the nations.[108]

There are several different ways in which skulls may be compared with one another. First of all there is the classical method of human anatomy and physical anthropology, by which the individual bones and their positions in relation to their neighbours are minutely described. Although this method does not lend itself readily to the mathematical expression of resemblances and differences, it provides valuable information for the physical anthropologist. Another method is to choose particular points on the skull and simply measure their distances from one another. Sixty-nine such points are used in craniometry. For instance, one may define the *glabella* as that point in the median sagittal* plane of the frontal bone that lies above the root of the nose, between the eyebrow ridges, and projects furthest forward, while the *opisthocranion* is the point in the median sagittal plane of the skull that is most distant from the glabella. The *length* of the skull is defined as the distance in a straight line between these two points. A measurement not involving defined points is that which states the *breadth* of the skull. This is defined as the greatest breadth at right angles to the median sagittal plane, wherever this may be.†

When *measurements* have been obtained, *indices* may be derived from them by expressing one as a percentage of another. Physical anthropologists recognize no fewer than 173 indices, some of them further subdivided into minor categories by the selection of slightly different points for one or both of the measurements. The breadth of a skull, expressed as a percentage of the length, is called the *cranial index*. Technical terms are widely used to give general impressions of various indices, without the necessity to state the percentages exactly on every occasion. Some of these terms are used so frequently in this book that readers who are unfamiliar with them would do well to commit them to memory. A skull that is neither very broad nor very narrow is called *mesocranial*. All skulls are included under this term if the cranial index is 75·0% or more, but less than 80·0%. Skulls that are broader than this (index 80·0% or more) are called *brachycranial* (short-skulled); those that are narrower (index less than 75·0%) are *dolichocranial* (long-skulled). Terms such as *hyperbrachycranial* and *hyperdolichocranial* have been introduced to express more exactly the breadth of a skull in relation to its length, but will seldom be used in this book. It is to be remarked that the sign for percentages is usually omitted in the statement of indices.

---

* A *sagittal* plane is that which divides the body into right and left halves, or any plane parallel with this.

† For the sake of accuracy it must be mentioned that if the greatest breadth happens to lie between two ridges called the supramastoid crests, the distance between these ridges is disregarded and the breadth is determined elsewhere (cf. Martin and Saller [708]).

Two dissimilar skulls might have the same cranial index, because the glabella of one and the occiput of the other happened to be particularly prominent, and indices necessarily suffer from this type of defect; nevertheless they generally give some idea of the shape of a skull or of a part of it. Their only major disadvantage is that they may cause certain anthropologists to overlook striking differences between one skull and another, in features too elaborate in detail to make measurement and mathematical expression a practical proposition. This applies, for instance, to the structure of the anterior nasal aperture (apertura pyriformis), the lower border of which shows marked differences in structure in the various taxa (see pp. 282–6). These differences can be noticed at a glance, and each main type expressed by a single word; but it would be such an elaborate task to describe them in terms of three-dimensional geometry that no one has ever attempted to do so.

The general form of the head can be measured on the living subject in such a way as to provide an approximation to the cranial index. For this purpose the length is taken as the distance from the most prominent point in the median sagittal plane between the eyebrows to the most distant point in the same plane at the back of the head, and the breadth as the greatest distance from one side to the other above the ears, at right angles to the median sagittal plane. The measurements are made to the surface of the skin, without depression of it by the instrument used. The breadth, expressed as a percentage of the length, is called the *cephalic index*. A rough approximation to the cranial index can be obtained by subtracting two units from the cephalic index. It is unfortunate that confusion often results from the use of the term 'cephalic index' when 'cranial index' is meant. The habits of life (especially over- and under-nourishment) naturally influence all such indices, but living human beings present the advantages that they are much more numerous and much more readily available than skeletons, and sex can be determined with certainty. X-rays can be used effectively for taking several of the standard measurements of skulls and thus obtaining indices; but in the more remote parts of the world, where observations would be particularly interesting, facilities are not available.

In addition to measurements of distances and the indices derived from them, *angles* are useful in the description of skulls. These may be measured between two straight lines joining (or extending beyond) defined points, or between a particular line and a defined plane. This method was used nearly two centuries ago by the Dutch anatomist, Petrus Camper,[186, 187] who set up the skulls of men and apes in a defined position, and measured the angle subtended with the horizontal by a line (his celebrated 'facial line') touching the front surface of a first upper incisor tooth and the median plane of the forehead (see pp. 28–30 and Fig. 3). Modern physical anthropologists use fourteen different angles in their descriptions of skulls (one of them appearing in the literature in no fewer than nine variant forms, in accordance with differences in the definitions of the precise positions of the lines and planes).

Studies of skulls, by the methods briefly indicated above, probably provide the most important of all the various kinds of evidence on which the taxonomy of man can be based, though it goes without saying that every available fact bearing on the subject should be considered. In studying the skull it is important to supplement the purely metrical techniques by those of classical morphology. Particular skulls and the individual bones that compose them must be examined in detail. Without this control, the statistical treatment of measurements, indices, and angles may in certain circumstances mislead.

Those who rely wholly on statistical methods for the distinction of ethnic taxa have devised complicated mathematical formulae for determining—so it has been supposed—the degree of resemblance or distinction between different skulls. In these studies it is usual to pay no particular attention to the obvious differences between one skull and another, but to pay just as much attention to numerous features, arbitrarily chosen, in which they do not differ. Further, they sometimes treat a heterogeneous set of skulls from a particular locality as though they all belonged to a single taxon, when deciding whether a particular skull should be regarded as belonging to it. For instance, it has been *assumed* that all Upper Palaeolithic skulls of Europe form a natural group, and various particular skulls are compared with the mathematically assessed characters of the group.[765] The error involved in this procedure is of the same kind as that which invalidates the grouping of persons by nationality in studies of blood-groups (p. 190). It is important to record that Morant, the statistician who grouped together all the Upper Palaeolithic skulls of Europe for mathematical treatment, himself recognized the possibility of this error. 'The treatment of the series as a sample from a single homogeneous population', he wrote, 'may obscure some ethnic relations of great evolutionary importance, but a treatment of that kind appears to be the only *statistical* one which can usefully be employed at present.'[765] For certain purposes in his statistical studies Morant found it best to use figures representing ten selected indices and angles. He makes the astonishing admission that the 'brachycephalic European races are not distinguished in this way from Negroes, Australians, and other primitive types'. It is conceivable that he wrote 'brachycephalic' by mistake; but even if he meant 'dolichocephalic', or rather 'dolichocranial', the inadequacy of his statistical method is shown by the fact that anyone trained in physical anthropology could at once distinguish a typical Europid from a typical Negrid or Australid skull.

Despite Blumenbach's remark, quoted above (p. 192), it might be thought that detailed study would be necessary before anyone could recognize the characteristic differences between one type of human skull and another by cursory inspection. It is true that some of the features that are distinctive of particular ethnic taxa need to be pointed out. The border of the anterior nasal aperture is an example. Certain features of this sort, which may be called 'minor' because they do not affect the gross shape of the skull, are indeed of particular interest, but the major differences are in many cases so obvious that no one could fail to notice them. The skull of the Eskimid is strikingly different from most others. A child of six years, provided with a number of Laplander and Greenland Eskimo skulls of various sizes, could separate them correctly into two groups without the necessity for any previous instruction (see Fig. 24, p. 196). It is to be remarked that Laplanders, though of low stature, have quite large skulls, only about one-tenth less in circumference, on the average, than those of other Europeans,[402] and the child would therefore not be guided merely by size.

The skull of the Eskimid is high, very long, and narrow (cranial index about 71), while that of the Lappid is short and wide (index about 85). The former is described as 'scaphoid', because the sides slope upwards like those of an upturned boat towards the keel. The inward slope starts in the Eskimid skull not far above the external auditory meatus, in a region where that of the Lappid bulges outwards. The brain-case of the Lappid is rounded except posteriorly, where it descends abruptly to the occiput. In the Eskimid the temporal lines on each side of the skull, marking the boundary of the area

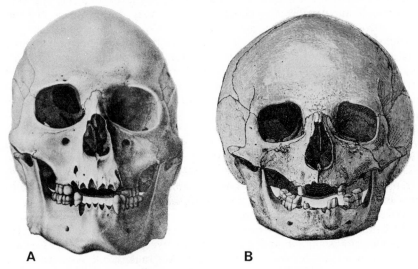

**A**                    **B**

24     *Skulls of Eskimid* (A) *and Lappid* (B)
*From Quatrefages and Hamy.* [867]

from which the temporalis masticatory muscle and its associated fasciae arise, curve upwards so as to approximate more closely to the top of the skull than in any other taxon of man surviving to the present day, and the area of insertion of the muscle is very large. In the Lappid, on the contrary, this area is not particularly large.

The zygomatic bones of the Eskimid are very large, and their lower borders project outwards to an exaggerated degree, thus greatly widening the face. The zygomatic arches of the Lappid spread outwards to give a wide face, but they are rather slender.

The orbits are higher and closer together in the Eskimid than in the Lappid. The whole face and jaws of the former project forward to the degree described as mesognathous, while the Lappid is orthognathous. The nasal bones are reduced in the Eskimid to narrow slips (not clearly outlined in Fig. 24), and their upper parts project forward less than those of the Lappid. The anterior nasal aperture (apertura pyriformis) is probably narrower in relation to the length of the nose (from nasion to nasospinale) than in any other taxon of man. That of the Lappid, on the contrary, is rather wide in relation to the length of the nose.

One of the striking features of the Eskimid skull is the massive size of the maxilla. If the two skulls are placed in frontal view, with the orbits at the same level, the rows of teeth are seen to be far lower in the Eskimid, as a result of the great vertical depth of this bone. Where it is hollowed out in other ethnic taxa to form the so-called 'canine fossae', there is only a slight depression in the Eskimid.

The mandible of the Eskimid is powerful, with strong ascending rami, and the angles (gonia) flare outwards. The areas on it for the insertion of the masticatory muscles are strongly marked. In the Lappid, on the contrary, the mandible is notably small and the gonia do not project laterally. [263, 293, 402, 512, 895, 896, 897, 1062]

Complicated mathematical methods, much more elaborate than Morant's algebraical equations, are available to the investigator who wishes to compare skulls with one another. These methods may be traced back to the German painter and engraver Albrecht Dürer, [295] who in the sixteenth century introduced a technique that subsequently became very much more exact. His method was to inscribe many vertical and horizontal lines through particular points on a drawing: for instance, in side-views, vertical lines through the back of the head, the hinder edge of the ear, and the front surface of the eye; horizontal lines through the top of the head and of the ear, and the lowest point of the nose (to mention only a few). By changing the distances between the lines, or drawing the lines so as to cut one another at angles other than a right angle, or making one set of lines radiate from a distant point, and then filling in the details of the head or other part with lines passing through the rectangles or other shapes that corresponded to those imposed on the original drawing, he was able to transform the face as he wished, so as to produce a wide variety of appearances. Dürer himself made no study of the skeleton or any other internal part of the body by this technique.

Well over a century ago it was proposed by G. T. Fechner, the German author of works on physics, psychology, and philosophy, that mathematical methods might be used to characterize the races of man. [324] He was dissatisfied with the separate linear measurements used by physical anthropologists, and suggested that mathematical approximations should be found to the curves seen in transverse sections of human skulls. For instance, an ellipse or an oval might serve for a particular part of a skull, and the equation that represented it might be used for comparison with another representing the corresponding part in a skull from another race. He realized that an exact mathematical description of every part of a skull was unthinkable, but he remarked that geographers had had no hesitation in making a first approximation to the shape of the earth as a sphere, and then improving on this by describing it as an elliptical spheroid, only capable of being expressed mathematically by the use of a complicated formula; yet they recognized that a mathematical account of every rock, and then of every roughness on the surface of every rock, was unthinkable. '*So kommt man nie zu Ende,*' he wrote.

Nearly seven decades later D'Arcy Thompson hit on essentially the same idea, without knowledge of Fechner's priority. [1041, 1042] By an extraordinary coincidence he used the same geographical simile as Fechner's, in claiming that mathematical analysis of organic forms was desirable, even though it would not be possible to achieve absolute exactitude in this way. He used what was essentially Dürer's method, except that the vertical and horizontal lines imposed on the original drawing were always equally spaced so as to form a grid of small squares. He next transformed the grid in a number of different ways. For instance, the distance between the horizontal lines could be increased, so as to transform the squares into rectangles of unequal sides; and the increase might be uniform over the whole drawing, or might increase logarithmically from the top to the bottom; or the co-ordinates might be made oblique instead of forming right angles with one another, so that each element of the grid became like a playing-card diamond; or one of the co-ordinates might radiate from a focal point, or the straight lines might become logarithmic spirals or more complex curves. In each case one could draw a skull or other part in such a way that the lines of the drawing passed in comparable manner through the corresponding elements of the grid. Thompson showed that *in selected cases* the drawing of a skull of one animal was transformed into the likeness, more or less exact, of another. Indeed, the side-view of a human skull (his drawing cannot be referred with certainty to any particular taxon) could be transformed, by the change of the straight lines of the grid into complicated curves, into that of a chimpanzee. One must realize, however, that if an Alpinid skull (for instance) had been used instead of the unspecified one illustrated by Thompson, quite a different mathematical expression, and probably a much more complicated one, would have been required for the conversion.

Thompson's results gave rise to the impression that the differences between the skulls of different races of man might be due to minor causes, affecting the growth-rates of the different parts in rather simple relation to one another, so that the diversity of type was due to much fewer separate causes than the physical anthropologist had supposed. It must be remarked that in the half century since Thompson wrote, no one has ventured to express the mathematical differences between the skulls of different races in terms of the precise genes that cause each difference; nor have we any reason to believe that the genetic basis would be a simple one, even so far as the appearance of the skull, projected on a plane surface, is concerned. Thompson's drawings of skulls show only features that are visible externally, and with one exception (the extinct rhinoceroses) only a single view of the skull is considered. The mathematical complications are greatly increased when account is taken of a front and back view, as well as that from the side; and if the appearance from above and below were also considered, the difficulties would be very great indeed, even though no attention were paid to any part not visible on the surface, and all the minor external irregularities were disregarded. One would require proof that the relationship between one ethnic taxon and another, established by a study of side-views and expressed mathematically, could be confirmed by views from front, back, above, and below.* It would be much safer, however, to apply Fechner's method of sections through the skull, for the taxa differ in the internal as well as the external parts. It must be remembered, too, that certain external features, not gross enough to be included in Thompson's

_____

* It would be possible to record the whole surface of a skull, as seen from any selected point of view, by the process known as 'photogrammetry'. Contours are automatically represented on paper. See Jerie.[553]

drawings, are particularly important in the differentiation of one race from another; for instance, the lower border of the anterior nasal aperture (pp. 282–6). Such evidence as is at present available suggests that the differences between the skulls of the different races of man are due to very complex causes. Thompson himself evidently realized that his own account of what he called 'deformation' by changes of co-ordinates was oversimplified, for he remarks, '. . . we must be prepared for very much more recondite methods of comparison and analysis, leading doubtless to very much more complicated results.'

The application of Thompson's method led him to certain strange conclusions, in particular to a belief that the horses and their allies (Perissodactyla) are closely related to the rabbits and hares (Lagomorpha); more closely, indeed, than they are to the even-toed 'ungulates' (Artiodactyla), and also than the Lagomorpha are to the Rodentia. It is true that the Perissodactyla and Artiodactyla are not nearly so closely allied as was generally believed in Thompson's time, and the rabbits and hares, formerly regarded as rodents, are now separated from that taxon; nevertheless, it is not likely that anyone today would support his conclusions about the relationships of these animals (cf. Simpson[1968]).

The need for 'very much more recondite methods of comparison and analysis', recognized by D'Arcy Thompson, has been to some extent met by an elaborate method devised by P. H. A. Sneath.[1985] The fundamental difference between the latter's method and Thompson's is that when two skulls are to be compared, Sneath represents both of them on the same rectilinear grid, bearing sets of equidistant lines placed at right angles to one another; in fact, on ordinary graph paper. A general impression of Sneath's method, which he explains in great detail, may be obtained from the following condensed account.

In his example, Sneath selects particular points in the median sagittal plane of a skull of modern man (*Homo sapiens*), and compares the relative positions of these with those of corresponding points in the skull of a chimpanzee. He inscribes the selected points on similar pieces of graph paper, and finds for each skull the point ('common mean point') that is the mathematically exact middle point, as revealed by the situation of the selected points. Next, he changes the size of the chimpanzee's skull (as represented by the points) to that of the human skull, by measuring the distance from the common mean point to each point in turn, and using mathematical calculation to find the uniform adjustment of all these distances necessary to make the chimpanzee's skull (as represented by these points) of the same size as the human. He then superimposes the two sets of points on the same piece of graph paper, with coincidence of the common mean points. It then only remains to rotate the whole set of points representing the chimpanzee's skull until the distances of these points from the corresponding ones in the human skull are as short as possible. These distances represent the differences between the two skulls, as revealed by the selected points; and they are very much easier to handle mathematically than the curved lines of Thompson's 'deformations'. Sneath uses his method to obtain mathematically exact figures representing the degrees of difference between the human skull and those of *Pan satyrus* ('*troglodytes*'), *Pithecanthropus erectus*, and *Australopithecus* sp. (? *africanus*), as represented by the selected points.

Sneath's method is objective and valuable, but it serves only to compare skulls or other parts of the body by reference to particular points, and these may not be the ones that reveal most clearly the degree of difference or similarity between two organisms. Sneath freely allows that although the skull of *Australopithecus* sp. is shown by his method to be very unlike that of *Homo sapiens*, the difference between them would have appeared much less if he had studied the pelvis or foot instead of certain points in the median sagittal plane of the skull. The taxonomist must be willing to take into consideration every part of the body that is available for study and can throw light on his problem. Whether one is dealing with major taxa or with minor ones such as races and subraces, classification can only be achieved satisfactorily by induction and the recognition of typical forms, with subsequent extension of the taxa by the inclusion of other forms that are obviously related. The subject has already been treated rather fully in Chapter 8, and it is only necessary to re-emphasize here the importance of this principle when concentrating the attention, in this part of the book, on the ethnic taxa of man.

Ideally one would like to be able to subject the skull, in all its various forms, to the usual processes of genetic analysis; and in certain cases there has, indeed, been some suggestion that a particular character is controlled by a single pair of allelomorphic genes.

For instance, in certain ethnic taxa there is often a small conical projection of the enamel on the lingual side of the first permanent upper molar teeth. This cusp, which occurs occasionally on the second or third permanent molars and also in the milk dentition (see pp. 208 and 210), is called 'Carabelli's tubercle' from the name of its discoverer. It is partly surrounded by a groove that makes the projection more noticeable. The degree to which it projects varies considerably. In some cases the cone is quite small, while in others it actually disappears and is represented by nothing more than a little pit, the remnant of the groove. When present, the tubercle or pit is usually found on both sides of the mouth, and nearly equally developed on both sides. It is always either present or absent in both members of a pair of identical twins.

Studies pursued through four generations suggested that the development of Carabelli's tubercle was controlled in a very simple way, by a pair of allelomorphic genes.[609] It appeared that in the double recessive (cc) there was no sign of the tubercle, while in the double dominant (CC) it was fully developed. Even this apparently straightforward case, however, was not so simple as would appear at first sight. The evidence suggested that there were modifying genes that caused the varying degree of development of the structure, from well-formed cone to pit, in heterozygotes (Cc).

This, however, was not all. The tooth in question was examined in 100 nine-year-old Europid children, all from a single locality in the U.S.A. They were selected at random as healthy representatives of the Europid children of the district, not requiring dental treatment. The age of nine years was chosen because the first permanent upper molars would not have been in use long enough to make it likely that the tubercle or pit would have been effaced by abrasion. It is claimed by the investigators that every one of the 200 teeth showed the tubercle or pit.[734] More than half of the children showed the cusp or pit in the condition supposed to be heterozygous. If the 100 children were at all representative of the Europid population of the locality where the observations were made, the simple explanation given above is untenable; for intermarriage of heterozygotes would necessarily have resulted in the production of homozygous recessives, yet not one of the children lacked the cusp or pit in some form or other.

If one looks closely at records of this sort, one receives the impression that simple explanations do not cover all the facts. The genetic control of the structure of the skull seems to be complex, even in those cases in which the early observations suggested that only a single pair of allelomorphic genes was concerned in the production of a particular character. There is reason to believe that in most cases polygenes play a part and that genetical analysis therefore presents difficulties that might be thought insuperable. Not only is one faced by the problems inevitably involved in the genetic analysis of polygenes; there is also the impossibility of arranging the matings one would like to make, and the slowness of human reproduction is an added difficulty. The skull, moreover, presents special barriers to analysis. The teeth of parents and their children may indeed be studied, for the crowns are open to direct inspection, and extraction makes the whole object available (though often partly decayed); but with this exception it is scarcely ever possible to obtain cranial material from a succession of generations. The necessary information can only be obtained by the use of X-rays, with the limitations thereby imposed.

Special methods must be adopted to determine the relative roles of nature and nurture in the control of those physical characters that may legitimately be supposed to develop under the influence of polygenes, and which therefore do not lend themselves to the ordinary processes of genetical analysis. In the early years of the present century the American anthropologist Franz Boas attacked what was essentially this problem (though the term 'polygenes' was not in use at the time) by studying changes in the sizes of many parts of the body among various peoples who had emigrated from Europe to the U.S.A. He divided members of each immigrant people into two categories, 'foreign-born' and 'American-born', and obtained numerical data on their physique. A few examples from his extensive studies, relating to the form of the head, will give an impression of his mode of attack on the problem.

Males born in the U.S.A. to Neapolitan parents showed, at nearly every age from four years to eighteen, a mean cephalic index exceeding that of foreign-born Neapolitans of the same ages by amounts varying from 0·1 to 1·8 units. Similarly, male offspring born in the U.S.A. to Sicilian parents showed, at nearly every age from five years to eighteen, a mean cephalic index exceeding that of foreign-born Sicilians of the same ages by amounts varying from 0·1 to 3·3 units. Data for East European Hebrews appeared, however, to show an opposite effect of the American environment. Their sons born in the U.S.A., at each age (with one exception) from five years to nineteen, showed a mean cephalic index *less* by 0·9 to 3·4 units than that shown by foreign-born immigrants of the same ages. [113]

Another American anthropologist, N. D. M. Hirsch, obtained data on immigrant Russian Jews that supported Boas's conclusions about the effects of the American environment on members of the same people who had immigrated from various countries of Eastern Europe; but Hirsch's study of immigrant Swedes showed that in their case the cephalic index was changed insignificantly or not at all by the new environment. [493]

It is not easy to account for these conflicting data, which appear to show that the environment may produce opposite effects, or none at all, in different cases. Sufficient information for full analysis is not available. The possibility must be borne in mind that the true parentage was not in all cases correctly stated. There is no proof that all the foreign-born and American-born persons described by such names as 'Neapolitans' were closely similar in genetic make-up. The East European Hebrews were probably a rather homogeneous group, but careful statistical analysis would be necessary to establish the significance of the differences between their foreign-born and American-born offspring. Boas himself allowed that the history of the British in America, the Dutch in the East Indies, and the Spanish in South America favoured the assumption of 'a strictly limited plasticity'.[112]

In more recent times the intensive study of twins has proved a much more reliable method for solving problems of this sort. One may measure a particular feature in monozygotic (identical) and single-sexed dizygotic (fraternal) pairs of twins, and note whether the members of the identical pairs resemble one another in respect of this feature more closely than the members of the fraternal pairs do, and if so to what extent. Statistical study of the data makes it possible to determine the extent to which genetic as opposed to environmental factors are involved in controlling the development of the feature.

Twin studies of this sort are almost necessarily carried out on living subjects, because skeletal material is seldom available in sufficient quantity. It is here that X-rays are of special value to the physical anthropologist. They were used by Lundstrom in his study of the skulls of fifty pairs of monozygotic twins and the same number of single-sexed fraternal pairs.[683] In each case five measurements were taken of the distances between points recognized in classical craniometry, and records were also made of nine angles subtended between lines joining these points. It was shown that in all these measurements of distances and angles, the monozygotic twins resembled one another more closely than the dizygotic. The results showed clearly that the proportions of the skull are largely under genetic control.

A comparable study was published by Osborne and George in 1959.[813]The twins were adult American Europids. Many parts of the body were measured, but we are concerned here only with the head. The work was done with calipers instead of X-rays, and data on the skull itself were therefore not obtained; but many parts of the head owe their form mainly to the shape of the skull. This study was of particular importance on account of the rigorous statistical analysis to which the data were subjected. The differences between the measurements of any particular feature in members of the two sets of twins (monozygotic and single-sexed dizygotic) were expressed by comparing the mean variance of one set with the mean variance of the other. The degree of difference between the two variances was expressed by dividing the mean variance of the dizygotic by the mean variance of the monozygotic pairs. The quotient provided a convenient index of the relationship between the genetic and environmental contributions to the measurement concerned. The breadth of the head in the region of the vault was shown by this method to be predominantly under genetic control, since the quotient obtained was no less than 18·22; the upper facial height and nasal height were also shown to be little affected by the environment. The length of the head in males, though not in females, was shown to be greatly affected by environmental influences. This result was attributed by the authors to the sporadic growth of bony projections in the region of the opisthocranium in males.

It remains for the geneticists of the future to evolve a technique that will disentangle the individual polygenes that make the genetic contribution to the manifold shapes of the human skull, and thus to provide an expression in genetical terms of the differences between typical skulls of the various ethnic taxa. Meanwhile the skull furnishes us with some of the best evidence for taxonomic distinctions and some of the worst obstacles to ordinary genetical analysis. Those features in man that are most readily available for such analysis unfortunately give an inadequate impression of the diversity of the ethnic taxa.

# 13  The Europids

IT IS likely that most of the readers of this book will be Europids, and it therefore seems appropriate that this race should be chosen to provide a general impression of the physical characters by which typical members of one race may be distinguished from those of other races, and to give some idea of the nature of subracial differences, by the use of selected examples. The Europids also exemplify well the phenomena of hybridity, both subracial and racial, and advantage will be taken of this fact in the present chapter.

## THE NAME OF THE EUROPID RACE

What is here called the 'Europid' race, in conformity with the nomenclature of von Eickstedt[303] and Peters,[836] was distinguished as the *Varietas prima* in the second edition (*Editio altera*) of Blumenbach's *De generis humani varietate nativa liber*.[107] It was in the third edition of this book, published in 1795, that he used for the first time the expression *Varietas Caucasia*.[108] He stated clearly that he gave this name for two reasons: first, because the neighbourhood of the Caucasus mountain range, especially its southern slopes, was the home of what he regarded as the most beautiful stock (*stirps*) of human beings; and secondly, because in his opinion mankind probably originated in this region. He reached this conclusion about the original home of mankind because he considered that the skull of the Georgians was of an intermediate variety, from which other types diverged by gradations in two chief directions, until the extremes—Mongolian and 'Aethiopian' (by which he meant Negrid)—were reached. In forming this opinion he was also influenced by the fact that the pale skin of persons of his 'Caucasian' variety readily became brown, while brown skin was not easily transformed to white.

It has been stated repeatedly that Blumenbach gave the name 'Caucasian' to the Europid race because he happened to possess a particularly beautiful skull of a Georgian woman. Even such distinguished authorities as T. H. Huxley,[536] W. Z. Ripley,[905] F. H. Garrison,[387] and E. von Eickstedt[302] have made this remark, but it is not correct. Blumenbach did possess a female Georgian skull and he did regard it as beautiful, but his naming of the race depended on much wider considerations.

Blumenbach did not formally introduce *Caucasia* as a subspecific name of the Linnaean species *Homo sapiens*. If he had wished to do so, he would simply have added the masculine of his adjective to Linnaeus's name for the species.

Instead he used the adjective *Caucasia* to qualify the noun *Varietas*. It follows that under the *International code of zoological nomenclature*,[1014] *Homo sapiens caucasius* is not the name of any subspecies (race) of man. Curiously enough, the correct name of the subspecies under the rules of nomenclature seems to be uncertain. If it were accepted that the 'type-specimen' of man was a Europid, the name of the subspecies would be *Homo sapiens sapiens* Linnaeus, 1758;[669] but no one can point to the type-specimen in any museum. Some authorities think that the name should be *Homo sapiens europaeus* Linnaeus, 1758,[669] but careful consideration of the arguments suggests that *Homo sapiens albus* Gmelin, 1788[671] is probably preferable. The reader is reminded that the use of the adjective *albus* does not imply that all members of the race have skin of the colour to which the description 'white' is applied in common speech (see p. 68).

The *Trivialnamen* ('common' names) of the races of man are not subject to any international code, and one is free to make one's choice. In his standard work *The races of Europe* Ripley refers to the 'utter absurdity' of the misnomer 'Caucasian'. 'It is not true', he remarks, 'that any of these Caucasians are even "somewhat typical".... It is all false; not only improbable, but absurd.'[905] It would, indeed, be hard to choose a less suitable name for the race; for the inhabitants of the Caucasian region are very diverse, and few of them are typical of any large section of Europids. If it were thought desirable to call the Europid race by a name relating to any particular area in which some of its members live, it would be better to call it the Punjabi than the Caucasian; for the majority of the inhabitants of East and West Punjab are indeed in many respects rather typical of a considerable part of the Europid race. It is better, however, to choose a larger area inhabited by a wider variety of characteristic types. The only complete and consistent system of *Trivialnamen* for the races and subraces of man is that which was proposed by von Eickstedt[303] and adopted with small modifications by Peters.[836] This system has been adopted in the present work, and in accordance with it the name 'Europid' has been and will be used throughout. It is not intended to convey the idea that Europids are confined to Europe, or that those who happen to live there are more significant than other members of the same race whose ancestral home is elsewhere; for the native inhabitants of large parts of Asia and Africa belong to this race. But the name is as suitable as any other that can be suggested, since the great majority of the inhabitants of Europe are Europids, and most of the subraces are well represented in this so-called 'continent'. The suffix *-id* is to be regarded as a contracted form of the Greek *-ίδης*, meaning 'of the family of' or 'associated with', so that a Europid receives this name because he resembles or is a European (with the reservation that a small proportion of Europeans are not Europids).

## THE PHYSICAL CHARACTERS OF THE EUROPID RACE

The reader may remember that the idea of 'typical' forms has already been considered at some length in Chapter 8 (pp. 118–24). The general idea of the typical can scarcely be better expressed in a few words than it was by

Helmholtz, in the course of his remarks on Goethe's contributions to natural science. It would be difficult, or probably impossible, to find another example of a genius in science assessing the work of an amateur, himself a genius in a different field. Goethe did in fact make contributions to morphology—the very word is his—and Helmholtz's tribute is deserved, however mistaken the poet's ideas on certain other branches of science unquestionably were. 'The special character of the descriptive sciences—botany, zoology, anatomy, and so on,' wrote Helmholtz, 'is occasioned by the fact that they have to collect, sift, and above all to bring into a logical arrangement or system, an enormous stock of separate facts.' (Writing in 1853, himself a physiologist and physicist, Helmholtz can almost be forgiven for calling these sciences 'descriptive', without qualification.)

> So far, their work is only the dull one of a lexicographer; their system is a bookshelf on which the mass of records is so arranged that anyone can find what he wants in an instant. The intellectual part of their work and their proper interests begins when they try to trace out the scattered features of order (*Gesetzmässigkeit*) in the disconnected mass and from these to produce a synoptic general picture, in which each separate object retains its place and its right, and gains in interest through the connection with the whole.[485]

He attributes to Goethe the idea 'that the diversities in the anatomical structure of different animals were to be interpreted as modifications of a common structural plan or type'. From the 'enormous stock of separate facts' that constitutes our knowledge of Europid physique, the attempt is made in this chapter to induce what Helmholtz would have called a '*Bauplan oder Typus*' of the race. The 'bookshelf'—to use his simile—must be a considerable one.[30, 41, 237, 238, 245, 281, 293, 405, 512, 519, 573, 609, 614, 660, 734, 801, 827, 832, 862, 909, 953, 980, 1061, 1062, 1065, 1073, 1074, 1075]

All the primary characters listed below are ones that distinguish typical Europids from typical members of certain other ethnic taxa. Any person who exhibits a high proportion of the listed primary characters is a Europid, but reliance must not be placed on the possession of any one of them, taken by itself. To prevent the necessity for repetition, the reader is asked to take for granted the phrase 'in comparison with the corresponding part in other ethnic taxa', wherever these words are clearly required. For instance, when it is said that the mandibular fossa is deep in typical Europids, the words must be understood to mean that it is shallower in typical members of certain other ethnic taxa. The statement that 'The percentage of persons belonging to blood-group "A" is rather high' means that it is rather high in relation to the percentage of this group in other taxa (*not* that it is high in relation to the percentage of persons belonging to group 'O'); and the principle implied in this example should be applied wherever it is applicable.

Emphasis is laid throughout mainly on the skeleton and external characters, because these are so very much more readily available for study than the soft internal parts.

The reader who prefers not to study in detail the list given below of the primary and secondary characters of the Europids may nevertheless care to cast a glance over it, so as to gain (if he does not already possess) some impression of the characters by which typical members of one race may be distinguished from those of other ethnic taxa. He may also find it helpful to turn back to these pages from time to time for comparison, when studying the chapter (16) concerned with the physical anthropology of the Australids.

PRIMARY CHARACTERS

*Skull.*—The brain-case is large and 'well-filled'; that is to say, it is smoothly rounded on top and at the sides, without markedly flattened or sunken areas. Viewed from above it presents the shape known in craniology as 'ovoid', though the shape of the frontal bone makes the 'egg' much blunter at the narrow end than most birds' eggs are (those of the osprey and golden eagle represent it fairly well). The forehead is not bulbous, nor does it recede strongly. The brow-ridges are not very strongly developed. The temporal lines are widely separated from the median sagittal plane, and not strongly marked. The mastoid apophyses are large. The plane of the occipital foramen (foramen magnum), prolonged forward, meets the face about the middle of the nasal aperture (apertura pyriformis).

The facial skeleton is small in relation to the brain-case, but long in proportion to its breadth. The zygomatic bones are rather small; and when the skull is viewed from above, the arches of which they form a part are only just seen, or are not seen at all.

The outer edges of the orbits are not bevelled off by curves of large radius, but are rather sharply demarcated. Within the orbit the lacrimal bone has a long suture with the lamina papyracea of the ethmoid. The apertura pyriformis is narrow or of moderate width (leptorrhine or mesorrhine); it is shaped like a narrow ace of hearts, turned upside down. It has a simple, sharp border. This is a particularly important character of the Europids, fully discussed on pp. 282–6. The anterior nasal spine is well developed. The nasal bones are long and wide, but narrower above than below; they are sharply inclined to one another (except towards their junction in the middle line). The 'total profile-angle' (*Ganzprofilwinkel*) is high and the skull is therefore orthognathous.

The mandibular fossa of the temporal bone is deep.

The ascending rami of the lower jaw are well developed, with deep sigmoid notches; the chin does not recede.

The styloid process is long.

The teeth are of moderate size. The incisors project forward only slightly or not at all; the upper ones overlap the lower. The crowns of the upper incisors continue the direction of their roots (instead of being bent slightly backwards). The outer (lateral) and inner edges of these teeth are not reflected backwards (towards the cavity of the mouth) in such a way as to give the whole tooth the form of a scoop or shovel. The roots of the permanent upper molar teeth are long and tend to be somewhat splayed outwards rather than convergent; the 'body' of these teeth (the region between the cemento-enamel junction and the level at which the roots diverge) is short (in other words, there is no tendency to taurodontism). The permanent upper first molar tooth of one side or both, when first erupted, bears at least some vestige of Carabelli's cusp (see p. 200).

*Skeleton apart from the skull.*—The curves of the spine are strongly marked. It is particularly noteworthy that the bony centra of the lumbar vertebrae are so shaped as to accentuate the forward convexity of this region, which is due primarily to the wedge shape of the intervertebral disks (see pp. 290–91). The sacrum of the male is decidedly wide in relation to its length; this is partly due to reduction of the length by strong curvature. The scapula is rather narrow in proportion to its length. The distance from the anterior to the posterior spine of the ilium, expressed as a percentage of the total length of the innominate bone, gives a low figure. The combined length of the humerus and radius, expressed as a percentage of the combined length of the femur and tibia, gives rather a high figure, but the radius is comparatively short.

*Internal organs other than skeleton.*—The ceruminous glands of the external auditory meatus generally produce a soft ear-wax (p. 171). The axillary glands are well developed and their secretion gives a rather strong odour (pp. 173–4). There is no cartilage in the plica semilunaris of the eye (Fig. 26).

The brain is large, averaging about 1,410 g in adult male European members of the subrace.[1062] The convolutions (gyri) of the cerebral hemispheres are very tortuous. At the occipital pole of each hemisphere the visual area striata does not push round from the medially facing to the external surface in such a way as to produce on that surface a large, operculate sulcus lunatus (pp. 292–5).

*External characters.*—The typical Europid is rather tall. The shoulders are wide. The 'calf' is prominent and reaches below the middle of the lower leg. The buttocks of the female are prominent, but not excessively so.

Axillary and pubic hair is well developed in both sexes. In the male, facial hair is abundant and general body-hair moderately or strongly developed. The limit of insertion of the scalp-hair sweeps backwards on each side of the middle line more markedly than in certain other races. The scalp-hair is wavy and flexible. Its length, when uncut, differs in the sexes, seldom exceeding 40 cm in the male but averaging about 70 cm in the female. In transverse section each hair is oval or rather widely elliptic; the follicle from which it grows is straight and oblique to the surface of the head.

The skin of young children is pale.

Below the eyebrow the skin is tucked backwards and then folded forwards over the eyeball to form the upper eyelid, instead of descending almost vertically, without a distinct fold (Fig. 25A and B). The upper and lower lids meet at an acute angle at the inner (nasal) as well as at the outer side of the eye; that is to say, the inner corner of the eye is not rounded off by a *Mongolenfalte* or plica naso-palpebralis superior (for an illustration of which see Fig. 25C). The space between the lids is approximately horizontal. When a Europid looks straight forward, the white of the eye is symmetrically disposed on both sides of the iris. The eyelashes are long and divergent (compare A and B in Fig. 25). The plica semilunaris (Fig. 26) is small.

The nose projects rather strongly, its right and left sides tending to form an acute angle with one another (except where they converge to meet at the middle line). The nostrils are narrow laterally and elongated in the antero-posterior

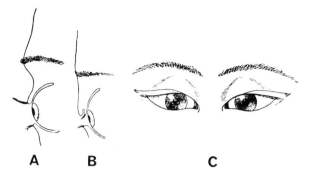

**A**      **B**          **C**

### 25   *Europid and Mongolid eyes*

A, diagrammatic view of Europid eye; B, ditto, of Mongolid eye; C, Mongolid eyes in front view.             *From Baelz.* [41]

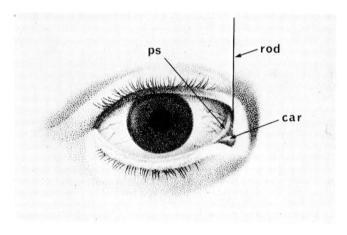

### 26   *A right human eye, to show the 'third eyelid'*   *(plica semilunaris)*

*car*, caruncle; *ps*, plica semilunaris; *rod*, rod holding the upper eyelid aside to reveal the plica.
*From Demours;* [267] *lettering by the author.*

direction (Fig. 27A, p. 210), though they may tend towards a kidney-shape, with the posterior ends turned laterally (Fig. 27B). The lips are moderately or very thin, with little eversion. The ear is large, and long in relation to its breadth; the helix is a well-formed fold; the lobule is large.

### SECONDARY CHARACTERS

The frontal bone seldom articulates with the squamous part of the temporal at the pterion (perhaps only in 1% of all persons: see Fig. 28C and pp. 298–300).

Congenital absence of the lower permanent first or second incisor teeth is

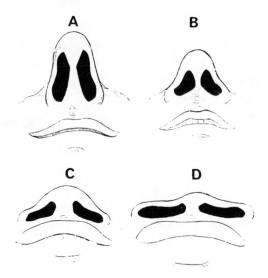

27  *Europid and Negrid noses, viewed from
below to show the shapes of the nostrils*

A, B, types of noses found among Europids. The nostrils of
most Europids are intermediate in shape between those
shown in the two drawings. C, D, types of noses found
among Negrids.                          *From Topinard.* [1061]

very rare. It is a strange fact that Carabelli's tubercle occurs much *less*
frequently on the second upper molar of the milk (deciduous) dentition than in
certain other taxa in which its presence on the permanent upper first molar is
rare. (These are the two chief sites of the tubercle.)

There is a third trochanter on the femur of about 30% of all persons (that is to say,
much more commonly than in certain other races). The hepatic and pancreatic ducts
open separately into the duodenum only in about 35% of all persons. (In certain taxa
the ducts open separately in the majority.)

Full sets of finger-prints show, on the average, about 62% of 'loops', 33% of
'whorls', and 5% of 'arches', though variation is considerable. (The Europids show an
intermediate condition in this respect, for higher and lower percentages of all three
types of prints occur in other ethnic taxa.)

The Europids are exceptional in the fact that blond hair, pale skin, and blue
eyes occur commonly among the adults (as well as children) of certain subraces.

About 30% of all Europids are unable to taste phenyl-thio-urea in concentrations at which the remaining 70% find it very bitter. (The number of non-
tasters is very high in comparison with the number in certain other races.) The
percentage of persons with both haptoglobins (Hp 1 and Hp 2) in their blood
plasma is very high (commonly 45–50% in most Europid subraces). As in
most (but not all) other ethnic taxa, very few (3% or less) have neither Hp 1 nor
Hp 2.

The percentage of persons belonging to blood-group 'A' is rather high (generally 32–48% in most subraces). In comparison with most other races the percentage belonging to group 'B' is high, but it varies widely (commonly 8–24%; higher among Nordindids). In the Rhesus series of blood-groups the frequency of the gene-complex CDe $(=R_1)$ is moderately high, of cde $(=r)$ very high, in comparison with most other ethnic taxa.

## EUROPID SUBRACES

More than a dozen subraces of Europids are recognized by some authorities, but nothing would be gained by reciting the characters of each here. A list of the ones mentioned in this book will be found at the end of it. It is important, however, to provide some idea of the extent to which subraces may differ from one another, and for this reason two—the Alpinids and Nordids—have been chosen for rather detailed study, and a brief description of the Mediterranids is also given. The reader will find a fairly full account of the Armenids in Chapter 14 (pp. 238–43). Various other Europid subraces have been and will be mentioned here and there.

It will be remembered that the existence of hybrid intermediates is one of the characters of a race, and subraces merge into one another even more extensively than races; so much so, indeed, that there has been a tendency to doubt the reality of the subrace. It is said that many anthropologists have discarded the idea of the subrace partly because it is reminiscent of Hitler's activities, and partly because it has been used to designate selected individuals of extreme types rather than populations.[228] These reasons, however, should not cause us to close our eyes to a reality. Scientists should not be affected in their opinions by the activities of politicians; and any undue emphasis on extreme types can be corrected without disregard for the fact that less extreme but nevertheless recognizable types do exist. It is true that one member of a family of subracial hybrids may show a somewhat closer resemblance to a typical specimen of a particular subrace than his brother does; but when it is claimed that a typical Mediterranid, a typical Nordid, and a typical Alpinid may be the progeny of one man and his wife,[383] it is necessary to say clearly that no evidence of such an extremely unlikely occurrence has ever been verified, so far as I am aware. It may be remarked that those who lay stress on the supposed appearance of 'types' by chance re-assortment of genes, are among those who use the genes of polymorphism as the main basis for the classification of man; yet it is precisely the polymorphic phenotypes that do in fact occur very frequently among members of the same family of brothers and sisters.

Hybrid intermediates do indeed exist, and a section of this chapter is devoted to them (pp. 223–31); but this fact no more extinguishes the reality of the subrace than the existence of mongrels makes the various breeds of dogs unreal. It has already been pointed out as a general principle that the existence of connecting links does not necessarily cause real entities to vanish (p. 100). In many parts of the world where there have not been any large movements of population over a long period, the reality of subraces is evident enough. Anyone who doubts this should spend a week among the indigenous population of central Sweden, then move on for a brief sojourn in the valley of the Rhine, near its source (W.S.W. of Chur); and end up with a visit to Sardinia (avoiding the tourist centres). He will not go home with the impression that the populations of the three districts were indistinguishable from one another, every person the result of a random assortment of genes. If he has any knowledge of human osteology, let him enter the Beinhaus beside the Catholic church in Hallstatt, Austria, and examine the remarkable collection of skulls taken from local graveyards, century after century, to leave room there for the newly dead. He cannot fail to recognize that the physical types represented there in such profusion could not be paralleled if any comparable collection had been made in Sweden or Great Britain. If circumstances do not permit such a visit, he may peruse Sauser's book on the similar ossuaries of the Ötz valley, near Innsbruck.[932] It would scarcely be possible to read this scholarly and detailed work, yet retain the impression that the population of this valley has been and is a random collection of Europids.

The fact that subraces do exist is perhaps most forcibly brought home to people of a pragmatic turn of mind by the need that has been felt, even in such an ethnically mixed population as that of the U.S.A., to take note of it in the practical affairs of everyday life. It was found desirable in American colleges, schools, and associations of young people, to obtain information about the average measurements of Europeans of various ages, so that remedial exercises might be introduced into gymnasia to improve the physique of those who did not conform to the average type. This action on the part of the educational authorities was opposed by an anthropologist. 'If we happen to measure an individual belonging to the Central European [i.e. Alpinid] type,' he wrote, 'we must compare his measurements with the ideal Central European type. It would, evidently, be wrong to compare him with the standard obtained from measurements of North Europeans [i.e. Nordids].' It will probably surprise many readers to learn that the author of these words was none other than Franz Boas.[114] It follows necessarily from what he wrote that in his opinion the subrace was not a mere figment in the minds of certain anthropologists, as so many who quote certain other passages from Boas's writings would have us believe.

Examples of particularly uniform populations are given later in this chapter (pp. 221–3).

THE ALPINID SUBRACE

The Alpinid subrace has received many names. Most of them refer to districts in which this ethnic taxon is particularly well represented. The following have been used: *la race cévenole* or *auvergnate*, Celtic, Celto-Ligurian, Ligurian, *'Homo alpinus'*,[636] Rhaetian, Alpo-Carpathian, Celto-Slav, and Slav. The confusion caused by the application of the name 'Celtic' to this subrace will be mentioned in Chapter 15 (p. 269). In its most characteristic form the subrace extends from the Cévennes Mountains and central massif of France through Switzerland, Bavaria, Austria, Slovakia, and southern Poland into Ukraine and other parts of Russia. It has been claimed that the most typical examples of all are to be found in Switzerland, in the valley of the Rhine near its source (the '*Disentistypus*' of Reicher[1889]).

The following are the characters by which the typical Alpinid may be recognized.[128, 269, 450, 503, 512, 636, 682, 889, 890, 905, 932, 953, 1085]

PRIMARY CHARACTERS

*Skull.*—(See Fig. 28A and B, p. 214.) The typical Alpinid skull is markedly brachycranial, the average cranial index being about 85. The maximum breadth is far back on the parietals. The whole brain-case is well rounded apart from a small flattened area immediately behind the obelion, which is the region where the descent towards the occiput begins in this subrace. The brow-ridges are scarcely marked. The forehead rises steeply above the orbits. Even in its narrowest part it is remarkably wide in relation to the greatest breadth of the whole skull, and also in relation to the greatest distance between the outer margins of the orbits (i.e. the fronto-biorbital index is very high).

The height of the skull (basion to bregma) varies. In general, it is less high in the western part of the Alpinid range, and higher in the eastern and more northerly part, beyond the River Danube. The high skull seen in Fig. 28A is from Bohemia.

The bizygomatic breadth (the extreme distance between the zygomatic arches) is great, giving a wide face. The height of the face (from prosthion to nasion) is not low, but it is low in relation to the bizygomatic breadth.

The upper edge of the orbit projects somewhat further forward than the lower, when the skull is placed in the standard horizontal position. (This character is weakly developed in the skull shown in Fig. 28A, which is typical in most respects.) The orbits are widely separated.

The nose is rather wide in comparison with that of most Europids (commonly in the mesorrhine range, though tending to leptorrhiny). The nasal bones project strongly.

The face as a whole is orthognathous, but there is a slight tendency to prognathy below the nose (alveolar prognathy). This is well seen by comparing A and C in Fig. 28. The Nordid skull (C) shows no alveolar prognathy.

The palate is moderately wide. The gonial angles of the lower jaw project laterally.

*Internal organs other than skeleton.*—See comparison with Nordid on pp. 217–18.

*External characters.*—The stature of the typical Alpinid is medium or rather short, adult males averaging about 164 or 165 cm. The body-build is thickset, with short, thick neck, broad shoulders, deep chest, and short limbs.

The characteristic appearance of the Alpinid head is well shown in Fig. 29A (p. 215), which represents Nikita Krushchev. Marshal Zakharov, seen in Fig. 29B, is a more extreme example of the subrace. The general form of the head follows from that of the skull. Fig. 29A shows well the high head, typical of eastern members of the subrace. The great breadth of the brain-case and face is particularly apparent in Fig. 29B. The face is low in relation to its width, and is surmounted by a steep, wide, high forehead, without noticeable brow-ridges. The chin, too, is wide. The nasal profile of Alpinids tends to be slightly concave, especially in women; the nose widens markedly below, and the tip, often upturned, is fleshy. The shape of the nostrils tends towards that shown in Fig. 27B (p. 210).

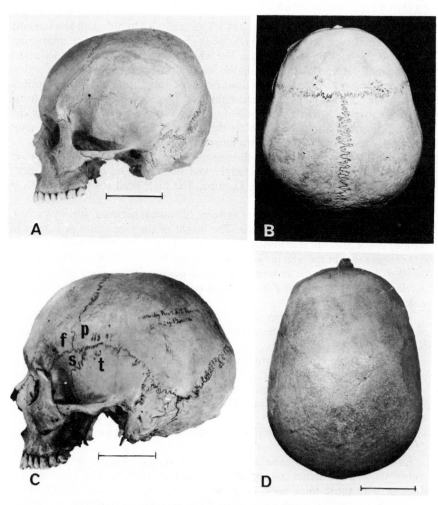

28    *Alpinid and Nordid skulls*

A and B, lateral and vertical views of an Alpinid (Bohemian) skull (cranial index 86·4); C and D, skulls of Nordid form (cranial indices 72·4 and 72·3 respectively). The scales represent 50 mm. *f*, frontal bone; *p*, parietal; *s*, sphenoid; *t*, temporal (see p. 209).
*The skulls are in the Oxford University Museum with these markings: A and B, 980; C, 'X'; D, 'Z'. A shows the* right *side of the skull; the photograph has been reversed for easy comparison with C.*

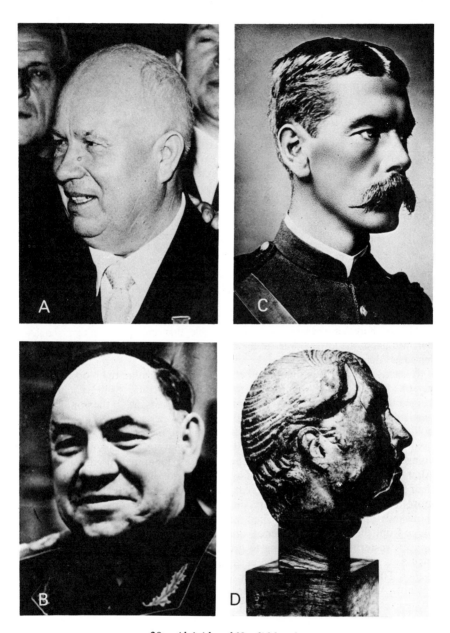

### 29   Alpinid and Nordid heads

A, a normal Alpinid (Nikita Krushchev); B, an extreme Alpinid (Marshal Zakharov); C, a normal Nordid (Lord Kitchener); D, another Nordid (a sculpture of the third century B.C., representing a 'German' warrior).

A, *Press Association;* B, *Associated Press;* C, *Bassano and Vandyke Studios;* D, *Les Musées royaux d'Art et d'Histoire, Brussels.*

The complexion is somewhat tawny.

The scalp-hair varies from dark to pale brown. The iris is brown, often with a greyish tinge. Facial and body-hair are strongly developed in the male. (Clean-shaven subjects have been chosen for the photographs, to show more clearly the form of the face.)

## SECONDARY CHARACTERS

There is conflicting evidence about the frequency of variations in the structure of the lower border of the nasal aperture (apertura pyriformis) in the Alpinid skull. The types of structure found in this part of the various ethnic taxa of man will be described in the chapter on Australids (pp. 282–6). It must suffice here to say that the types called amblycraspedote and bothrocraspedote are unusual in most Europid subraces. In his detailed report on the apertura pyriformis in 52 skulls from Tyrol and the adjoining province of Carinthia, Holl[503] stated that in no fewer than 28 of them there were sulci praenasales or fossae praenasales, and only 16 showed the usual Europid structure (oxycraspedote). The 28 were what are now called ambly- or bothrocraspedote. Sauser's study of well over a thousand skulls from the ossuaries of the Ötz valley in Tyrol gave results in marked contrast to Holl's. The skulls were mostly those of Dinarids, Alpinids, and Dinarid-Alpinid intermediates. Well over half of them were complete apart from the lower jaw, but among all his specimens only nineteen were ambly- or bothrocraspedote.[932] It is desirable that more information should be obtained about the lower border of the apertura pyriformis in skulls separately determined as Alpinid.

It seems that no attempts have been made to determine the blood-groups of persons classified as Alpinids on the evidence of their primary characters. Huge numbers of blood-group tests have been carried out on the populations of particular nations; but since the boundaries between states are determined by political, not ethnic considerations, the data obtained are not very helpful in taxonomic studies. If a physical anthropologist were to designate a group of villages and the surrounding countryside as inhabited predominantly by Alpinids, and if the blood-groups of as many as possible of the inhabitants were then determined, information of great taxonomic value would be obtained—far more than could be derived from similar studies carried out on many tens of thousands of persons distinguished only by their nationality. So far as one can judge from the available evidence, one can only say that rather a low proportion of western Alpinids belong to group 'B', in comparison with the Europid race as a whole, but among the eastern group the proportion is considerably higher. There would not appear to be any clear distinction between western and eastern Alpinids in the proportion of people carrying the various gene-complexes of the Rhesus group.

## THE NORDID SUBRACE

The Nordid subrace, like the Alpinid, has received many names—'*Homo Europaeus*',[636] *la race germanique, kymrique, galatique, aryenne, nordique, die Germanen, die teutonische Rasse, die Nordrasse*, and the English equivalents of some of these, such as Nordic. It is to be noted that some French and German authors use the words for 'race' when what is here called 'subrace' is intended. The names *la race germanique* and *die Germanen* must not be confused with the English word 'Germans'. The latter is a political term meaning the inhabitants of Germany, most of whom do not belong to the Nordid subrace.

The most typical Nordids live in the part of the Netherlands north of the Rhine, in Germany along the north coast from East Friesland to Schleswig-Holstein and beyond the Elbe to Mecklenburg, in Denmark, Norway (except the south and south-western coastal districts), Sweden, the Åland Islands, and the coast of Finland; also in the Faroe Islands and Iceland. The population of Great Britain is largely of Nordid origin, but there was considerable admixture of Mediterranid (or possibly Mediterranid-Aethiopid) stock in ancient times, and the proportion of quite typical Nordids is not very high (see pp. 264–9).

In the following account of the physical characters presented by typical members of the Nordid subrace, attention will be focused chiefly on those that distinguish Nordids from Alpinids.

PRIMARY CHARACTERS

*Skull.*—The brain-case is typically either dolichocranial or just within the mesocranial range. The striking difference between many Nordid and Alpinid skulls in this respect may be realized by comparing D with B in Fig. 28. The skull shown in D has a cranial index of 72·3. The parietal eminence is not strongly marked in Nordids, and the skull appears well-filled and smoothly arched above, whether viewed from the side or in front. The occiput projects, and the inion is a distinct eminence.

The zygomatic bones tend to bend inwards from the places of their articulation with the processes of the temporals, so that the front of the face is narrow; narrower, in fact, than in any other Europid subrace except the Dinarids. The facial skeleton as a whole is high in relation to its width. The orbits are large, well-rounded above and at the corners, and high in relation to their width; the interorbital distance is moderate.

The nose is leptorrhine, with strongly projecting nasal bones.

Modern Nordids are orthognathous, both as regards the facial skeleton as a whole and in the alveolar region (cf. Fig. 28C), but there was a tendency towards prognathy (especially in the alveolar region) in some of the ancient 'Germanen'.

The chin projects forwards. The gonia of the lower jaw do not flare outwards.

*Internal organs other than skeleton.*—The general form of the human brain and its lobes is adapted to that of the skull, although the correspondence is not exact. It follows that the brain of a Nordid has not the same shape as that of an Alpinid. The gyri and sulci are stated to be somewhat differently placed in dolichocranial and brachycranial persons. The position of the upper end of the central sulcus (Rolando's) in relation to the form of the skull can be determined as follows. A mark may be made on the scalp of a corpse over the glabella and another over the inion (in the occipital region), and a line may then be drawn on the skin over the top of the head, in the median sagittal plane, to connect the two. This line may then be divided into 100 equal parts, numbered from the glabella. If the skull is then dissected to reveal the position of the sulcus in question, the position of the upper end of the latter can be expressed numerically by reference to the subdivisions of the line joining glabella and inion. [470] It is stated that the number of subdivisions of this line representing the position of the upper end of the sulcus is *less* in dolichocranial than in brachycranial persons, and indeed—rather surprisingly—that the distance is absolutely less in dolichocranials. [354] Unfortunately these results do not seem to have been established by studies of persons positively identified as Nordid and Alpinid.

It is stated that the vagina and cervix of Nordid women are longer than those of Alpinids. [636] Further evidence is necessary before these statements can be accepted.

*External characters.*—The typical Nordid is considerably taller than the Alpinid, the average height of the adult male being about 173 cm, or perhaps more; many men greatly exceed this figure. The limbs, especially the legs, are long. The body tends to be slim, and here again there is a contrast with the stocky Alpinid.

Typical examples of the Nordid head are shown in Fig. 29C and D. The upper picture represents Lord Kitchener, one of those Englishmen who happen to show the unexaggerated Nordid features particularly well. The lower picture represents a statue of the third century B.C., in the Musées d'Art et d'Histoire, Brussels. It has been partly restored, but the restorer is thought to have been guided by broken parts of the original during the process. In describing it, Cumont remarks that anthropological exactitude was one of the characters of the art of the period. [236] It represents a Nordid warrior, probably dying or dead in battle. The arrangement of the hair suggests that the man was one of the Bastarnae, a tribe of *Germanen* that occupied the region between the Carpathians and the Black Sea at the time in question. [573] The Nordid type seen in this statue is more extreme than that represented by Lord Kitchener, but unfortunately the shape of the back of the head is hidden by the long hair. The projecting occiput of Nordids is one of the most obvious differences from Alpinids.

The brow-ridges and somewhat sloping forehead; the narrow front of the face; the straight or slightly convex nose, with compressed alae and narrow tip—all these characteristic Nordid features are seen clearly in the two illustrations.

The complexion tends to be florid and easily freckled by bright sunlight.

The eyes are not set very far apart. In advanced age there is a curious tendency for the upper eyelid to sink at its outer side. Characteristically the iris is blue or pale grey, but sometimes pale brown. (Kitchener's were described as 'blue as ice', [314] and are pale blue in the painting by Herkomer in the National Portrait Gallery.) The scalp-hair of Nordids is not very abundant, and there is a tendency to baldness in males. The hairs are fine and flexible. Too much stress has been laid by some authors on the colour of the scalp-hair in Nordids. It is commonly ash-blond (the 'platinum blonde' of women), golden, golden brown, pale brown, or reddish-brown. Many adult Nordids whose hair is darker than any of these colours had golden locks when they were children.

Gradual darkening is quite usual. (For instance, Kitchener's scalp-hair is light brown in the portrait mentioned above, painted when he was 40; his moustache was honey-coloured. Both scalp-hair and moustache were considerably darker when another portrait (in the same gallery) was painted by C. M. Horsfall nine years later.)

It is often supposed that blondness is an indication of Nordid ancestry. Taken by itself, it is nothing of the kind. The Dalofalids, for instance, who inhabit Westphalia and the province of Kopparberg in Sweden, are as blond as the most typical Nordids; so are the Osteuropids of north-eastern Europe, who are very unlike Nordids in appearance, and seem to be an offshoot of the Alpinids, adapted to a more northerly habitat by greater body-size and reduction in pigmentation of the skin (pp. 156–7), with consequent paleness of the hair. The suggestion is sometimes made that the Osteuropids are Alpinid-Nordid hybrids, but there is no convincing evidence of Nordid ancestry. Fair hair and blue eyes also occur sporadically among the Kabyles of northern Algeria and the Kurds of northern Iraq and the adjacent parts of Turkey and Iran. The original inhabitants of the Canary Islands, the Guanches, were fair-haired and blue-eyed.[1092, 1093]

The hair in the armpits of Nordids is generally from ash-blond to reddish-brown; it is fairly abundant. Pubic hair (somewhat scanty in the female) is of the same colour as the axillary.

The claim has been made that typical Nordids and Alpinids differ as much from one another in the external genital organs of the female as in the skull.[636] It is stated that these organs are situated lower and more posteriorly in Nordids than in Alpinids, and that the labia—both majora and minora—are larger. It is also stated that the male Nordid has a larger penis with a particularly long prepuce.[636] It is difficult to obtain reliable measurements of these parts of the body, and statements about subracial differences in them must not be accepted without confirmation. (The undoubted peculiarities in the external genital organs of Khoisanids will be described and illustrated in Chapter 17 (pp. 313–19).

The ease with which Nordids pronounce the *th* sounds has already been mentioned on p. 117.

SECONDARY CHARACTERS

The Nordids do not appear to possess any special characters falling clearly into this category. The lower border of the apertura pyriformis is always or nearly always oxycraspedote, and the blood-groups resemble those of western Alpinids. For remarks on the lack of precise information about the blood-groups of the latter subrace, see p. 216.

The various subraces of the Europid race, in their typical forms, are not equally different from one another. For instance, the Nordid and Mediterranid subraces are close to one another in morphological characters,[343, 302] much more so than either is to the Alpinid. It is not always very easy to distinguish a

Nordid skull from a Mediterranid, though anyone could distinguish it from an Alpinid.

In external characters, however, the typical Mediterranid of southern Italy and the western Mediterranean islands differs from the Nordid in several respects. He is much shorter; indeed, the mean stature of adult males is said to be only about 161 or 162 cm.[269, 331, 450] He is perhaps slightly more dolichocephalic, on the average, than the modern Nordid; the forehead is slightly steeper, and tends to run with less interruption into the slope of the nose, which does not project quite so much, and is somewhat wider (though still leptorrhine). The continuity of the forehead with the nose was much admired by the classical sculptors, who exaggerated it to produce the so-called 'Greek profile'. In actual fact, continuity of the two slopes, with no alteration of slope or sunken region in the vicinity of the nasion, is unknown in any ethnic taxon of man (though well exhibited, for instance, by the Bornean leaf-monkey, *Presbytis rubicundus rubidus*[49]). The face of the Mediterranid is oval, perhaps tapering below more than that of the Nordid. The ears tend to be smaller, the lips somewhat thicker. The differences between the sexes are more marked, the hips of Mediterranid women being relatively wider. Apart from these morphological differences, the scalp-hair is very dark brown (commonly called black), and the iris also very dark.

From the very short descriptions of ethnic taxa that are given in some anthropological text-books, one might well imagine that something of very special importance has been said about a skull when it has been described as brachycranial—as though all brachycranial skulls were similar. This is far from being true. There are brachycranial Europids and brachycranial Mongolids, and the two types of skull are in fact very different. This subject was studied especially carefully by the Swiss anthropologist M. Reicher, who made a detailed comparison of the skulls of Alpinids and Tungids.[889, 890] The latter, often called 'Mongols', are perhaps to be regarded as the most typical representatives of the Mongolid race. They occupy (though not to the complete exclusion of others) a huge area extending from the Arctic coastline to about 40°N. latitude, where they abut on the Sinids (Chinese), and from 80°E. or thereabouts at the westernmost limit of their main range to the seas of Okhotsk and Japan. There is an isolated group of them on the north-western shore of the Caspian Sea, and many other small ones in various places west of the main range. Reicher's studies were carried out on the skulls of Buriats, Kalmuks, Torguts, and Telengets. His Alpinid skulls were obtained in Bavaria, Switzerland, and Tyrol. In his investigation he concentrated his attention entirely on lengths, indices, and angles. The differences between the two sets of skulls would have appeared even greater if he had also examined the characters that do not lend themselves readily to measurement and statistical analysis (for instance, the structure of the lower border of the apertura pyriformis).

Although the cranial indices of the two taxa do not differ significantly, the part of the skull where the greatest breadth occurs is not the same. In Alpinids the most distant points are almost always on the parietal bones, in Tungids on the squamous part of the temporals The Alpinids (even the western ones, studied by Reicher) have skulls that are considerably higher, and wider in the frontal region. In this taxon the inion (the most prominent point on the external occipital protuberance) is situated higher up on the occiput.

It is in the facial region, however, that the chief differences occur. The zygomatic bones are less powerfully developed in the Alpinids, and do not project so far forward. The bizygomatic breadth is also less in this taxon. The face is less high (both absolutely and relatively to other parts). Both taxa are orthognathous as regards the face as a whole, but the Alpinids tend to alveolar orthognathy (though not so much as the Nordids), while the Tungids tend to be prognathous in the subnasal region. The Alpinids have narrower aperturae pyriformes, tending towards leptorrhiny, while the noses of Tungids are considerably wider, tending towards chamaerrhiny; and in Alpinids the nasal bones project forwards very much further. The palate is narrower in Alpinids.

The orbits are much further apart in Alpinids. The entrances to the orbits slope downwards and backwards towards their outer edges much more than in the Tungids, in whom they are almost horizontal and scarcely slope backwards laterally. It has already been mentioned (p. 213) that in typical Alpinids the upper borders of the orbits overhang the lower considerably, while in Tungids they are almost directly above.

These differences impress on the mind how misleading the description of a skull as brachycranial may be, if it gives the impression that fundamental similarity is necessarily implied. The cranial index is useful only if its limitations are recognized. It is scarcely necessary to add that the differences between Alpinids and Tungids are very evident when characters apart from the cranium are taken into consideration.


## ISOLATION AND UNIFORMITY

When members of one of the minor ethnic taxa (subraces or local forms) have lived for a long time in more or less complete isolation, the population may exhibit remarkable uniformity in physical characters (apart from differences between the sexes). The isolation may be due to physical causes, such as the sea that surrounds an oceanic island, or to the unwillingness of the people concerned to hybridize with members of other ethnic taxa (or to the converse of this). The celebrated French anthropologist, Paul Topinard, regarded the Negritids of the Andaman Islands as the extreme example of uniformity among human populations.[1062] These little people, the Minkopis or Andamanids, owed their uniformity primarily to the surrounding ocean, which enabled them to live in isolation. Their pygmy stature and unusual appearance may have exerted an additional isolating effect when people of other taxa came to live on their islands.

The Todas of the Nilgiri Hills in southern India provide an example of a Europid stock that has avoided miscegenation and remained very uniform in physique as a result. Their existence was first made known to Europeans by a Portuguese missionary who penetrated their territory in 1602 and spent two days among them, but more than two centuries elapsed before they were seen again by any European.[906] The lofty plateaux that constitute their homeland are indeed somewhat inaccessible and uninviting to the lowlanders of the surrounding country, but the physical uniformity of the Todas is not due solely to geographical isolation. There are several other tribes in the Nilgiri Hills, but miscegenation does not occur. Major Ross King, who lived for three years in these hills, wrote of the Todas in 1870:

> Totally distinct in aspect, mould and bearing from any of the various races of the low country, and as markedly different from the rest of the tribes immediately around them, their exceptional and striking appearance at once arrests the eye of the most unobservant. . . . the Todas never contract marriages with the other tribes, though living together on most friendly terms. That there never has been any mixture of the races, is sufficiently evident from the strongly marked distinctions that continue to exist between them.[581]

Syphilis was introduced by Europeans and has spread among the Todas,[1052] but the presence of hybrids has not been reported. The avoidance of hybridization is all the more remarkable since they shared the Nilgiri Hills with no fewer than four other tribes—the Badaga, Kota, and two Weddid groups (Kurumba and Irula). When they were first discovered by the Portuguese missionary in 1602, the Todas were already in touch with the Badagas.[906] They developed a special mode of salutation for members of the Weddid groups, and a more elaborate one for Badaga headmen.[906]

Lieut.-Col. W. E. Marshall, in describing their physical appearance in 1873, emphasized their similarity to one another in appearance, and mentioned 'the remarkable uniformity of cranial development'.[703] 'Whoever has seen one Toda has seen the whole race,' he remarked[704]—though it must be admitted that it would be advantageous to have seen two Todas, one of each sex. Thurston, the authority on Indian anthropology, is quoted as having said that the Todas 'are so inbred that they look like members of one family'.[1053] The geneticist and anthropologist R. Ruggles Gates, who visited them in 1959, confirms this statement.[392]

The Todas are to be regarded as what would be called in zoological literature a 'relict fauna'—a group left behind and isolated on the retreat (or in some cases the partial extinction) of a taxon that had been more widely distributed in earlier times. Their physical characters show them to be Nordindids (Indo-Afghans).[268, 302] Indeed, when von Eickstedt first saw a Toda, he actually thought he was looking at a Sikh. (The absence of a turban must surely have surprised him, for the Sikhs are as rigorous about wearing their headdress as the Todas are about leaving their scalp-hair uncovered.) Rivers's very tentative suggestion that the Todas may be related to the Nambutiris of Malabar[906] cannot be substantiated.

Two separate studies of Toda blood-groups have been made, involving altogether 282 persons.[816, 650] The two sets of figures are somewhat discordant, but if one adds them together and calculates the frequency of the genes responsible for the ABO groups, the following results emerge: $p$ (frequency of gene for 'A' group), 0.179; $q$ (ditto, for 'B' group), 0.347. $p$ is close to the figure for the Sikhs (typical Nordindids), but $q$ is considerably higher—in fact, one of the highest ever recorded. The blood-groups of 86 Kotas were also studied.[650] These people are the closest neighbours of the Todas. Not a single person belonging to groups 'A' or 'AB' was found among the 86. This confirms the strong evidence that the Todas have avoided miscegenation.

Another example of isolation may be quoted. In 1929 there occurred an 'Armenian Diaspora' from Turkey. Some 10,000 of the emigrants settled in Marseilles and adjacent parts of Provence, adding themselves to the small group of Armenians already present in the district. A study has recently been made of the ABO blood-groups of 7,943 persons belonging to this Armenian community.[800] The numbers in each blood-group, expressed as percentages of all who were tested, are shown in the accompanying table, with figures for 3,816 Armenians of Tiflis (Georgia) for comparison. (The figures for Tiflis are from Martin and Saller.[708])

|  | 'O' | 'A' | 'AB' | 'B' |
|---|---|---|---|---|
| Armenians in Provence | 31·3 | 47·1 | 7·9 | 13·0 |
| Armenians in Tiflis | 31·2 | 48·5 | 6·5 | 13·8 |

The agreement between the two populations is remarkable. A special feature of the Armenid subrace, in comparison with most other Europid subraces, is the high percentage of persons belonging to group 'A'. In those European countries in which many non-Armenid persons have been tested, the figure is mostly about 42%, and in some places considerably less. Wherever Armenians have been tested, the percentage is high. (The figures on which the left-hand column of Fig. 35 (p. 243) is based show an even higher frequency of the gene for group 'A' than those for the Armenians of Tiflis or Provence.)

The facts show clearly enough that there are peoples who isolate themselves genetically, even though there is no geographical barrier to separate them from others.

EUROPID HYBRIDS

In the modern world the degree of uniformity shown by such peoples as the Minkopis and Todas is unusual. Isolation and local uniformity were probably more usual in the remote past than they are today. The various subraces and races have merged together to a considerable extent by hybridization. In some cases new taxa, more or less homogeneous in composition, have originated in this way; in others the result has been a shading-off of one taxon into another, with all intermediate gradations. Increase in population due to the introduction and improvement of agriculture must have had considerable effect in bringing different ethnic taxa into contact. Wars, with resultant transfer of prisoners from one population to another, also favoured hybridization. The facts can scarcely be better expressed than they were nearly a century and a half ago by Bory de Saint Vincent, in his remarks on the early history of his native country of France:

From the flux and reflux of so many tribes ... there could only result a mixture of blood, which, blending more and more the characters of each of the types that had become mixed together, produced those particular varieties of which the western population is today composed—a population in which the traits of the typical forms, transmitted through one another, reappear here and there on our faces, but blend on them insensibly.[128]

This fusion has indeed occurred on a large scale in France, for a considerable part of the population is composed of Nordid-Alpinid hybrids, with Mediterranid elements added in certain localities. It has already been mentioned (p. 84) that Beddoe long ago foresaw the influence that the railway would have on miscegenation,[69] but writing as he did in 1885 he could not have guessed what rapid advances in means of transport lay ahead, with all their effects on human life.

Some writers, however, have tended to exaggerate the extent of hybridization. Otto Ammon was particularly influential in this respect. It is necessary to make it clear that although he called his short paper on this subject '*Zur Theorie der reinen Rassentypen*',[16] in his main study he was not in fact concerned with races at all, but with what he called the *Nordeuropäischer Typus*, the *Alpiner Typus*, the *Mittelländischer Typus*, and intermediates;[15] in other words, with Nordids, Alpinids, Mediterranids, and their hybrids. The investigation was carried out in the Grand Duchy of Baden, situated in the south-western corner of Germany, where that country abuts on France and Switzerland. The persons subjected to study were nearly thirty thousand conscripts and secondary-school children. (A small group of Jews was considered separately.) Ammon and his collaborators used cephalic index, stature, and colour of eyes, head-hair, and skin as criteria by which to judge whether each person could justifiably be regarded as belonging to one or other of the three types. They concluded that only 1·45% of them could be classified as belonging to the *Nordeuropäischer Typus*, 0·39% to the *Alpiner*, and 0·09% to the *Mittelländischer*. Ammon's contention was that true types do not exist in a hybrid population (*gekreuzte Bevölkerung*); and one could hardly choose a place where long-established hybridity was more likely to occur than here. The three subraces, as he pointed out, had been living in the Grand Duchy for three hundred years; and he remarked that, in these circumstances, if one were to take into consideration every character by which the three types could be distinguished, one would expect to find no 'pure race' (*reinrassige*) individual at all, or only sporadic examples with perhaps a few more in secluded places. He thought that all populations were to some extent hybrid, and that the degree of hybridity was probably greater in Europe, and especially Central Europe, than anywhere else in the world;[16] and Central Europe is where his investigation took place. One must remember that the whole native population of the Grand Duchy was *reinrassige* in the strict sense of the word, for all the people belonged to the Europid race.

It appears to have escaped notice that the investigators must have hugely underestimated the number of people who should have been assigned to the *Alpiner Typus*, for the criteria they used for this purpose were open to serious objection. In particular, they regarded no one as an *Alpiner* unless his hair was black or brownish-black (see pp. 209, 9–10, and 128 of Ammon's book[15]); and this criterion would in fact *exclude* every typical Alpinid.

It is true, of course, that there are many examples of hybridity between Europid subraces. Armenid-Orientalid hybrids are mentioned in Chapter 14, and the participation of Nordid and Mediterranid ancestors in the origin of the British people in Chapter 15. It is perhaps doubtful whether any Europids of the present day, apart from the Todas and a few other isolated peoples, are descended exclusively from ancestors who belonged to a single *subrace*. In many cases, however, the preponderance of one subrace in the ancestry is obvious enough, and it is this fact that justifies the recognition of subraces. In any group of subracial hybrids that has not become inbred to a sufficient extent to reach homogeneity, random assortment of genes may bring together in a single person a set of them that will give a closer resemblance to one ancestral form than to another, and the chance of this is obviously greater if members of one subrace predominated in the ancestry.

When members of several Europid subraces have colonized a previously underpopulated country, intermarriage between them may result in confusion of subraces, so that eventually the word no longer has meaning in that part of the world, so far as the majority of the population is concerned. Members of such a population who have not seen typical members of various Europid subraces in their native habitats may even be inclined to doubt the reality of the subrace as a valid ethnic taxon.

Hybrid populations may originate not only by intersubracial, but also by interracial miscegenation. An interracial hybrid population may give rise to a recognizable new ethnic taxon by intermarriage within itself, generation after generation. Such taxa generally (but not always) originate where the natural habitats of two races abut on one another, and therefore only two ancestral races are concerned. One of these has usually provided the majority of the ancestors, and if so it naturally has a predominant effect on the physique of the hybrids. As a result the latter are commonly regarded by anthropologists as belonging to the predominant race, and as constituting a somewhat aberrant subrace of it.

Europids have participated in the production of several interracial hybrid taxa to which their contribution has been predominant, so that the hybrids are grouped within the Europid race. The Turanids ('Turki'), for example, are Europid-Mongolid hybrids, among whom the physical characters of their Europid ancestors generally predominate over the Mongolid. They occupy a huge territory extending from the eastern shore of the Caspian Sea to the borders of Mongolia, and a narrow tongue of Turanid territory stretches north of the Caspian to the Black Sea coast. The Mongolid element in their features becomes progressively less towards the western limit of their territory.[573]

The Aethiopids ('Eastern Hamites' or 'Erythriotes') of Ethiopia and Somaliland are an essentially Europid subrace with some Negrid admixture. Typically these are slender people of medium stature, dolicho- or mesocranial; the face is more or less of the Europid form, with rather narrow, prominent nose; there is no prognathism (Fig. 30B, p. 230). Various parts of the body give evidence, however, of Negrid influence. The skin is reddish- or blackish-brown. The dark brown or black scalp-hair is neither long, like that of most Europids, nor very short, as in Negrids. It is variable in texture in different local forms, but as a rule it is not wavy, like that of typical Europids, nor wound into many tight spirals (what the French call 'cheveux crépus') like that of Negrids, but of the intermediate condition described as 'frizzy' ('cheveux frisés'), in which each hair curls into several ringlets, the spiral having a diameter of 1 cm or more. The ears are rather small. Both upper and lower lips are rather thicker than in typical Europids, but not much everted. Other indications of Negrid participation in the ancestry are the wide shoulders associated with narrow hips, long forearms, weakly developed calves of the legs, and scantiness of all hair except that of the scalp. It must be remarked that since the Negrid ancestors were presumably Nilotids, prognathism would not be expected in the hybrid taxon (see p. 329).

It is not possible to state with confidence which Europid subrace was chiefly responsible for the non-Negrid contribution to this hybrid taxon, and indeed this may well have varied in different local forms. Some authorities lay stress on the predominance of one Europid subrace, others on another. It is probable that there were both Orientalid ('Arab') and Mediterranid (or Proto-mediterranid) ancestors, and the Orientalid ancestors may perhaps have been hybridized with Armenids, as in so many places they are.[1024, 302, 1085, 228]

The Aethiopids have hybridized secondarily with Nilotid Negrids to give rise to tribes referred to under the general title of Niloto- or Nilo-Hamites (or sometimes Half-Hamites). In these the Negrid characters are somewhat more evident. Among the nomadic pastoralists called the Masai, who inhabit the Kenya–Tanzania borderland, the further hybridization has been so slight that some authorities classify them as Aethiopids.[302] The same applies to the Latuko (Lotuko) and Turkana of the grassland between the Bahr-el-Jebel and Lake Rudolf.

The Wahima (Bahima) of south-western Uganda are another group of very tall pastoralists, in this respect resembling the Turkana, but the evidence suggests that they are Aethiopid-Kafrid, not Aethiopid-Nilotid hybrids; whether this is so or not, the Aethiopid character greatly predominates among these people.[1024, 573, 450] The Kafrids are themselves a group of Aethiopid-Negrid hybrids, among whom, however, the Aethiopid element is much smaller, so that they are classified as Negrids (see p. 333).

It was remarked long ago by the French anthropologists Collignon and Deniker that 'The word "Moor" should be banished from ethnographic terminology, like so many others of which the meaning is vague and badly determined.'[218] Unfortunately there is no other name for the 'true' Moors, of hybrid Europid-Negrid stock, who live in Mauritania (formerly Mauretania) and the adjacent countries.

In one sense the word 'Moor' means the Mohammedan Berbers and Arabs of north-western Africa, with some Syrians, who conquered most of Spain in the eighth century and dominated the country for hundreds of years, leaving behind some magnificent examples of their architecture as a lasting memorial of their presence. These so-called 'Moors' were far in advance of any of the peoples of northern Europe at that time, not only in architecture but also in literature, science, technology, industry, and agriculture; and their civilization had a permanent influence on Spain.[1123, 860, 472] They were Europids, unhybridized with members of any other race. The Berbers were (and are) Mediterranids, probably with some admixture from the Cromagnid subrace of ancient times.[302, 47] The Arabs were Orientalids, the Syrians probably of mixed Orientalid and Armenid stock. The skin of Orientalids and of some Berbers darkens readily under the influence of sunlight, and many of them become quite dark in the exposed parts of the body. The association of dark skin with the name of 'Moors' resulted eventually in the same term being applied to Negrids. This mistake was made even by scientists—for instance, by Sömmerring (p. 27) in 1784, in the first edition of his important work on the anatomy of Negroes;[987] but in the second edition he changed *Mohr* to *Neger*.[988] Kant, writing in the previous decade, had made no such mistake. For him, the Europids ('*die Race der Weiszen*') included '*die Mohren (Mauren von Africa)*' as well as Arabs in general (and also Persians and certain other Asian peoples).[569] The Tuareg (Fig. 30A) are Islamized Berbers.

The area inhabited by the 'true' or racially hybrid (Europid-Negrid) Moors includes Mauritania, with the adjoining part of Mali and Rio de Oro; it extends southwards to the River Senegal and then roughly along lat. 15°N. to the Niger. Well over three centuries ago Dr. Thomas Browne noted the southern boundary of the tawny Moors in his *Pseudodoxia epidemica*. He remarked on the inconsistency of those who attributed the blackness of Negroes to the direct action of the sun,

> ... for whilst they make the River Senega [Senegal] to divide and bound the Moores, so that on the South-side they are blacke, on the other onely tawnie; they imply a secret causality herein from the ayre, place or River, and seem not to derive it from the Sunne; the effects of whose activity are not precipitously abrupted, but gradually proceed to their cessations.[150]

At one time the range of the true Moors extended a short distance south of the River Senegal, but the French excluded them from Senegalese territory.[218]

One of the first to give an adequate account of the physical characters of the true Moors was the French natural historian Michel Adanson, who went to Senegal as a young man and lived there for five years.[7] The fullest description is that by Collignon and Deniker,[218] who brought together the scattered information on the subject and carefully examined a few Moors who had come to Paris in 1895—the first ever seen in France. They reached the conclusion that the true Moors are hybrids between Berbers and West African Negrids (that is to say, Sudanids), the Berber contribution predominating. This conclusion was accepted by Eickstedt.[302] The French authors remark on the 'prodigious' resemblance to Ethiopians and related peoples of the eastern side of Africa. It is clear, however, that the Moors must not be placed in the same ethnic taxon as the Aethiopids, since their origin is different.

In western just as in eastern Africa one can note a transition from hybrid peoples, such as the true Moors, in whom the Europid element predominates, to others in which the reverse is true. The nomadic 'pastoral Fulbe' of West Africa are intermediate; the 'sedentary Fulbe' admit Negroes to their settled communities and show more strongly developed Negrid characters. The Europid element in the Fulbe, as in the Moors, is probably derived from the Berbers. [450] The Hausa, who number some eight millions and may be said to have achieved a dominating position in northern Nigeria, are essentially Negrids of the Sudanid subrace, with a small but varying proportion of Europid admixture. The latter is ascribed by different authors to Mediterranid (Berber), Orientalid, and Aethiopid ancestors; [573, 450, 268] possibly all three have contributed.

Most of the hybrid taxa mentioned above are examples of what Gedda has called 'border' or 'Type A' hybridization. [397] Another kind, called by Gedda 'colonialistic' or 'Type B', results from the deliberate emigration of members of one taxon into the territory of another—often into the interior of it, with resulting miscegenation between the colonists and the endemic population. This occurred, for instance, when Europids entered the Indianid territories of South America, with the resultant production of a largely hybrid population. In some cases two colonizing taxa have independently entered an underpopulated (or unpopulated) country and mated together to produce a new hybrid taxon. Many of the 'Coloured' population of South Africa (Europid-Khoid) originated in this way (see p. 97). Gedda also distinguishes a type of hybridization resulting from the use of force by members of one taxon to cause members of another to enter into an underpopulated (or unpopulated) one to serve as slaves—and some of their women as mistresses. He calls this 'slave' or 'Type C' hybridization, of which the most familiar example has resulted in the production of a huge number of Europid–Negrid hybrids in both North and South America.

Hybridization does not rapidly produce a homogeneous population. The F.1 progeny may mate with a similar hybrid or with one of the parental types. In former times it was the custom in various parts of America to use particular names for each degree of hybridity. In Mexico, for instance, an extraordinarily precise system of nomenclature was developed, to distinguish different degrees of hybridity. [845] For instance, if a Europid man married (or mated with) a Negrid, their daughter was a '*Mulata*', who on marrying a Europid would produce a '*Morisca*'; the latter on marrying a Europid would produce an '*Alvina*', who, if she repeated the process, might give birth to a '*Tornatras*'. Other special terms were invented to cover various possibilities of intermarriage between Europids, Negrids, Indianids, and hybrids.

In the United States of America the so-called 'Negro' population is largely hybrid. This must, indeed, be evident to anyone who has travelled widely among the Negrids of Africa before entering the U.S.A. Fortunately it has been possible to assess rather precisely the extent of Europid admixture with Negrids in the U.S.A. When the Rhesus blood-groups of persons regarded as 'Negroes' in that country were investigated, it was found that the frequency of cDe was generally about 45%.* This was an astonishingly high figure, because it was known that among the Europids of the U.S.A. (and elsewhere) this was an unusual type, with frequency only about 2·6%. Since it was obvious, from other evidence, that the so-called 'Negroes' were Europid-Negrid

---

* The frequencies of the various gene-combinations of the Rhesus system are commonly expressed as percentages.

hybrids, the first reaction to this discovery was one of surprise that the 'Negroes' showed such a high frequency of cDe. The facts were soon explained when figures for the frequency of Rhesus blood-types were obtained for actual Negrids in Africa. The frequency of cDe was found to be considerably higher in them than among the hybrids constituting the 'Negro' population of the U.S.A. The Sudanids gave a frequency of 64%, Kafrids 63%. It was at once evident that the figures, if confirmed, would provide means of discovering the proportion of Europid ancestry in the hybrids.

A statistical investigation of the subject was undertaken by Glass and Li,[407] who took into consideration not only the Rhesus blood-group, but also the ABO and MN. Their purpose was to discover the extent of the Europid contribution to the genetic make-up of the 'Negroes' of Baltimore, of whom they were careful to obtain a random sample. They concluded that the accumulated amount of Europid admixture was about 30%. It was subsequently found, however, that this figure was too high. An elaborate mathematical study of the whole subject of gene-flow from one population to another was made at Oxford and Leeds by Roberts and Hiorns.[907] These authors used the principles that resulted from their theoretical investigation to make estimates of the European contribution to the genetic constitution of the American Negro. Using evidence from different sources and making different assumptions, they obtained five figures, not widely divergent from one another, as follows: 23·2%, 23·4%, 26·0%, 26·1%, and 26·3%.

In reaching the figure of 26·1%, Roberts and Hiorns made use of the 'Duffy' blood-group system (in addition to several others), without laying any special emphasis upon it. This system had been discovered in 1950 (just half a century after the discovery of the ABO system) in the course of work carried out under the auspices of the British Medical Research Council.[239] It was found that the blood corpuscles of many Europeans were agglutinated (clotted) by the blood serum of a person named Duffy, and that the reaction had nothing to do with any previously known blood-group system. The gene responsible for the property that makes the corpuscles agglutinable by serum of the Duffy type was named by its discoverers $Fy^a$, and the allelomorphic gene (not having this effect) as $Fy^b$. The gene-frequency of $Fy^a$ in Europeans is about 0·43, but among the Negroes of West Africa, which was the original home of most of the slaves transported to the U.S.A.. it is extremely low, about 0·02. Dr. T. E. Reed of the University of Toronto recognized that this gene would be of particular value for estimating the contribution of Europids to the genetic constitution of the American Negroes, not only because its frequency in Africa had been very thoroughly investigated, but also because it has no harmful effect and there could therefore be no question of evolutionary changes in its frequency arising through the action of natural selection.[886] (Duffy himself was a haemophiliac, but this had nothing to do with the blood-group system to which he gave his name.) Basing his study on the frequency of this gene, Reed reached the conclusion that the European contribution to the genetic composition of the Negro population of Oakland (California) was about 22%, of Detroit 26%, and of New York about 19%. Much lower figures were obtained in the southern states; in Charleston (South Carolina) the Europid contribution

30　*Mediterranid, Aethiopid, and 'Negro' heads*

A, a Tuareg Berber (Mediterranid); B, a Somali (Aethiopid); C, an American described in nationally distributed British newspapers as a Negro;[28, 725] D, another American described in a nationally distributed newspaper as a Negro. [27]

A *and* B, *from Hutchinson, Gregory, and Lydekker;* [530]C *and* D, *Associated Press.*

amounted to less than 4%. The much lower proportion of Europid genes in southern Negroes should be borne in mind when the results of cognition testing in the U.S.A. are considered (pp. 471–82 and 484–5).

It goes without saying that in any particular person of Negrid-Europid ancestry, the proportion of the Europid contribution may be great or small. Unfortunately it is usual in the U.S.A. to apply the name of 'Negro' to everyone who shows any evidence of a Negrid element in his ancestry, and this practice is copied by British journalists when reporting American affairs. For instance, the man shown in Fig. 30C was described as a Negro, without qualification, in at least two nationally distributed British newspapers.[28, 725] It is clear from the photograph that there is a Negrid element in his features, but anyone with any knowledge of physical anthropology would know that this man was a hybrid, and probably as much Europid as Negrid. A much more extreme case is seen in Fig. 30D; for this photograph gives no morphological evidence of Negrid ancestry, yet the person depicted was described un-equivocally as a Negro in the article accompanying the photograph, which also appeared in a nationally distributed British newspaper.[27] Without the opportunity to examine the whole body one cannot deny the possibility of some Negrid admixture, but it is most misleading to describe a predominantly Europid person simply as a Negro—or perhaps one should say that it would be most misleading, if the contrary evidence presented by the photograph were not conclusive.

Even in scientific journals one often finds the same tendency as in the popular press to classify as 'Negroes' all persons who are in fact Americans of Europid-Negrid ancestry. This is regrettable, because it may result in the drawing of conclusions about Negrids that could not be substantiated by data derived from persons actually of that race. No one who wished to obtain general information of any kind about Europids would select Niloto-Hamites or Moors (in the strict sense), or even Aethiopids, as the principal subjects of his research.

It is hoped that the examples quoted in this chapter will suffice to give an impression of the part that hybridization has played in the late stages of human evolution. Some authors have stressed the effect of this process in increasing the diversity of mankind.[797, 893] Nevertheless this effect cannot be extended indefinitely: for if all human beings in the whole world were able and willing to mate at random, without consideration of ethnic taxa, a tendency towards uniformity would gradually result. Random assortment of genes might, indeed, occasionally produce marked prognathy or extreme pigmentation of the skin,[1007] or some other particular distinctive character developed to a high degree; but the person who bore such a character would probably be a more or less generalized human being in many other respects, showing no other marked peculiarities. There would be few individuals in the world who differed from one another in so many physical characters as a Nordid does from a Bushman, for instance, or a Tungid from a Negrito.

# 14 The Jews

THE MIND can only adapt itself to serious thought on the ethnic problem if the great complexity of the subject is recognized. A sentence, even a phrase, may seem plain enough; yet when its meaning has been thoroughly examined, the intricacies and errors that were hidden in apparent simplicity are startlingly revealed. This chapter is concerned not with a sentence or a phrase, but with the single word 'Jews'. There is no question of attempting to give here, even in brief summary, a general history of the people called by this name. The primary intention is only to review those aspects of the subject that throw the vividest light on the complexities and misunderstandings that may lurk behind a single word, supposed to be descriptive of a particular group of persons.

It is appropriate that the Jews should have a chapter to themselves in this book. The terrible persecution of a large section of this people under Hitler's regime probably did more even than the evils of Negro slavery to bring the ethnic problem to the attention of humane people all over the world. The importance that many Jews have attached to endogamy is also relevant. In any serious study of the superiority or inferiority of particular groups of people one cannot fail to take note of the altogether outstanding contributions made to intellectual and artistic life, and to the world of commerce and finance, generation after generation, by persons to whom the name of Jews is attached.

Who, then, are Jews? It is often said that they are those who adhere to the Jewish religion. For instance, in the *Statement on the nature of race and race differences* drawn up by a group of physical anthropologists and geneticists assembled in Paris in June 1951 under the auspices of UNESCO, one finds these words: 'Muslims and Jews are no more races than are Roman Catholics and Protestants.'[1080] This contention needs to be examined.

In various parts of the world today there are communities that practise the Jewish faith in one form or another, but are ethnically distinct from the Jews of Europe and North America. These will now be considered.

The Falasha or 'black Jews' of Ethiopia are members of the Aethiopid sub-race, a hybrid taxon that has already been briefly described in Chapter 13 (pp. 225–6). It is claimed by some that a certain facial resemblance to the Jews of Europe can be detected among the Falasha,[530] but this would not appear to be borne out by studies in physical anthropology.

In classical Ethiopia the word 'Falasha' means 'immigrants', and indeed Judaism must obviously have been introduced from without; but many of the local people eventually adopted the new religion. According to tradition, their conversion was brought about through the agency of the Queen of the

Sabaeans or 'Sheba'; that is to say, of the people whose country is now called Yemen. James Bruce, the explorer of Ethiopia in the 1770s, was told by the Falasha themselves that the Queen of the Sabaeans visited Jerusalem, became a convert to Judaism, and bore a son to Solomon; the boy, Menilek, was educated at Jerusalem and returned to found a colony of Jews on the opposite side of the Red Sea to the country of the Sabaeans, in Ethiopia. The whole of the country was converted to Judaism, but most of the inhabitants subsequently adopted Christianity, the Falasha being those who did not.[156] Such was the legend. The underlying facts remain obscure. It appears that some of the rulers of Ethiopia from the tenth to the thirteenth century A.D. were Jewish by religion, and Jewish rulers maintained themselves in the north of the country until 1617, when a massacre ended the independence of the Falasha. Bruce considered that there were still half a million of them in his time. There were 200,000 left in the nineteenth century, but today the number is reduced to 25,000, scattered in small country districts in the north, with a few in Eritrea.[325] The Falasha are endogamous and practise a peculiar version of the Jewish religion, in which the Talmud is not recognized.[545]

The 'Cochin Jews' are another isolated group of persons who practise the Jewish faith in a distant part of the world. They live in the town of Cochin and three neighbouring villages in Kerala State, in south-west India. It has been claimed that the religion was brought there by Jews fleeing from their country after the distruction of Jerusalem by the Romans in A.D. 70. Some of the local people must have adopted the new faith, for the 'Cochin Jews' of today are indistinguishable in physical characters from the rest of the Indian population of the district. They wear similar clothes and speak, like the others, the Malayalam language. Only a few can speak Hebrew, though this is used in prayers. Migration to Israel is rapidly depleting the two thousand or thereabouts that still remain.[325] A few European Jews, with Spanish or German surnames, live in the same district, but appear not to mix with the others.[545, 325]

Further north, in the neighbourhood of Bombay, there is another group of religious Jews, more numerous than those of Kerala. These people, the Bene-Israel, resemble the local Indian population in appearance and dress.[325] They claim to be able to trace their origin to the period that followed the destruction of Jerusalem by the Babylonians in 586 B.C.

There does not appear to be any reliable account of the origin of the 'Tsung' of China.[545] These distant Jews are said to have lived in that country since remote times and at first to have avoided intermarriage with the Chinese, but eventually they became almost purely Mongolid in physical characters.[477] Since the beginning of the communist regime in China they have mostly emigrated.[325]

It is evident that the Falasha, 'Cochin Jews', Bene-Israel, and 'Tsung' are ethnically distinct from the Jews of Europe and America, the only connection being through religion. They constitute, however, a very small proportion of all Jews. Towards the end of the nineteenth century they only amounted to about 1%,[545] and the proportion is unlikely to have increased since then, despite the mass murder of European Jews by the Nazis.

Mention must be made here of a group of Jews who lived in Europe but were distinct in physical type from all the European Jews of today. The Khazars or Cozars were a community of so-called 'Tatars' (or 'Tartars') who were converted to Judaism in the eighth century and established a kingdom, Jewish in the religious sense, in the region between and to the north of the Caspian and Black Seas. Their ethnic position is uncertain, since the word 'Tatar' cannot be precisely defined in terms of physical anthropology, but it is clear that they were not related, except by religion, to any modern group of Jews. They are said to have been 'perfectly un-Jewish' in appearance, and scarcely to have intermarried with other Jews.[545] Their kingdom was destroyed by the Russians in the tenth century.[149]

A very strange community of so-called Jews was brought to the notice of the scientific world by a German expedition to the west coast of Africa about ninety years ago.[61, 21] A special 'caste' of Negroes was found to inhabit separate villages near the coast, some 20 to 30 miles south of Loango (north from the mouth of the River Congo). These people were called 'Judeus' or 'Judeos' ('Jews') by the local Portuguese. They were obviously Negroes, though a German artist thought he could detect a slight suggestion of 'Jewishness' in their faces. The non-Jewish Negroes of the district claimed that they could distinguish the Bavumba, as they called them, by the restlessness of their eyes and certain lines on their hands. The Judeus achieved a dominating position by their skill in trade, but were nevertheless despised by other Negroes. No exact information is available about their religious practices, but they are said to have observed the Sabbath so strictly that they would not speak a word on that day. Their customs differed markedly from those of the other Negroes of the district. Thus they did not use fetishes, and they constructed their graves of masonry and decorated them with figures of snakes and lizards. Their origin was unknown. It is related that when the Jews were expelled from Spain in 1492, some two thousand of their children were sent to the island of Sao Thomé in the Gulf of Guinea; but there is no proof that the Judeus were hybrid descendants of these exiles. We thus have the curious circumstance that a name meaning 'Jews' was attached to a group of persons who did not practise a distinctly Jewish form of religion and were not Jews in the ethnic sense of the word.

Those who have written about the native inhabitants of this part of the West African coast in recent years do not appear to have mentioned the Judeus.

From the traditional religious point of view, a Jew was a person born of a Jewish mother,[1177] but this formula suffers from the defect that the defined word is included in adjectival form in the definition. The same flaw occurs in part of the new definition enacted by the Israeli Parliament in March 1970, according to which a person is a Jew if he or she is the offspring of a Jewish mother or has been converted to the Jewish faith by the Orthodox Rabbinate or by the Rabbis of the Jewish Reform Movement or by the Rabbis of the Jewish Conservative Movement.[33, 1174] Anyone who wishes to do so may accept the UNESCO doctrine and refuse to regard a person as a Jew unless he or she practises the Jewish religion; but there can be no doubt that many people in Europe and America who do not practise this religion are regarded by others as Jews and have no hesitation in agreeing that this description is correct.

Joseph Jacobs, who described himself as a Jew, was the author of important articles on Jewish problems. He drew up a valuable list of the most renowned Jews who had reached the age of 50 years in the century beginning in 1785.[546] He divided them into categories, corresponding to those devised by Francis Galton in his *Hereditary genius*.[379] It may be remembered that Galton distinguished his highest category as **X** and the next as **G** (see pp. 42–3). Jacobs considered that four of the Jews in his list fell into the group of 'illustrious' persons of category **X**, namely Disraeli, Heine, Lassalle, and Mendelssohn-Bartholdy. It is relevant to consider whether these men were Jews in the sense defined by the UNESCO *Statement*. The facts are as follows. Disraeli was baptized a Christian at the age of 12.[826] Heine had himself baptized at the age of 27, and on that occasion adopted 'Christian' as one of his names.[826] Mendelssohn's father added the extra surname 'Bartholdy' in order to distinguish his branch of the family from that which retained the ancestral faith, and he brought up his children, including Felix, as Protestant Christians.[826] Lassalle practised the Jewish religion as a boy. It does not appear to be possible to determine when he renounced the faith. When he was 29 he was no longer restricting himself to the diet of religious Jews, and at the age of 35 he said definitely, in a letter to Sonia Sontsev, that he was no longer a Jew in the religious sense.[350]

It would be tedious to consider the religious beliefs of all the 26 persons whom Jacobs placed in the 'eminent' category (Galton's **G**). Some, like Meyerbeer, adhered to the Jewish faith.[76] Others were equivocal about their religion. The actress Rachel, for instance, permitted forbidden food on her table and rarely attended a synagogue,[320] but she allowed a Rabbi to minister to her on her deathbed.[903] Others were definitely not Jews by religion. The German political writer Ludwig Börne started life as Lob Baruch. At the age of about 32 he was baptized and changed his name to that by which he is known.[826] The philosopher Solomon Maimon was a rationalist and sceptic. The president of the religious court by which he was divorced from his wife described him as a 'damnable heretic'.[79] Karl Marx, influenced by the writings of Feuerbach, had become a materialist by the age of 27 and remained one from then onwards.[652] He did not observe the rules that deny certain foods to religious Jews.[625]

It follows from what has been said that if Jacobs had restricted his interpretation of the word 'Jew' so as to exclude all who did not practise the religious rites of Judaism, he would not have been able to name a single 'illustrious' Jew among those who lived in the century covered by his studies, and the number of 'eminent' Jews would have been considerably reduced. In fact, however, his very careful analysis led him to the conclusion that a higher proportion of Jews than of non-Jewish Englishmen rose to become illustrious or eminent.

If anyone who wished to adopt the Jewish faith were free to do so after receiving the necessary instruction, and if any considerable number of persons did so wish, the word 'Jew' might be used as the words 'Roman Catholic' are, to denote the adherents to a religion, though in this case it could not be applied to anyone who had first accepted and then rejected the religion. In fact, however, there is no close resemblance between Judaism in the religious sense and a proselytizing religion such as the Roman Catholic. A person not born a Jew can only be accepted into the faith if he or she can satisfy the requirements mentioned on p. 234, and conversions are rare.

There is a widespread impression that those Europeans who are commonly called Jews tend to conform to an ethnic type distinguished by facial features, so that a Jew can be recognized without any need to apply a religious test, which would, indeed, be irrelevant. It is necessary to consider carefully whether this impression is soundly based. Some readers of this book would probably welcome a few words on the scientific study of the head, before embarking on this particular problem, and a brief digression is made here for their benefit. Those who are familiar with the terms used in physical anthropology are asked to skip to p. 238. In the digression a few terms are introduced that are not immediately relevant here, but may nevertheless be useful to readers of the rest of the book.

The head shown in Fig. 31A (which is not that of a Jew) has been placed in the *standard horizontal plane*. To achieve this, it was necessary to determine the position of the orbitale by feeling through the skin. This term refers to the lowest point on the lower margin of the bony orbit. The position of the orbitale was marked on the overlying skin. The tragion (trn in Fig. 31A) is the notch above the small flap of skin and cartilage, called the tragus, that is situated immediately in front of the aperture of the ear. The head was held in such a position that the most anterior point of the tragion was in the same horizontal plane as the orbitale. This plane, the standard horizontal, should also pass through the most anterior point of the tragion of the other ear, but for most purposes it suffices to make sure that the head does not incline noticeably to left or right. The standard horizontal plane is indicated in Fig. 31A by a line passing horizontally across the figure.

The height of the head may be measured in different ways. It is convenient for some purposes to consider the distance of the vertex, or highest point of the surface of the skin in the median sagittal plane, from the standard horizontal plane.

The measurement of the breadth and length of the head, and the derivation of the cephalic index from the figures obtained, have already been explained on p. 194, where it was mentioned that an approximation to the cranial index could be obtained by subtracting two units from the cephalic index.

The nose is generally very inadequately described in popular writings. It is often said to be 'long', but this gives little indication of shape, because one is not told the position of the point from which the measurement is supposed to be taken. Does a 'long' nose project a long way *downwards* or *forwards*? The first requirement is to fix two definite points in the median sagittal plane. The uppermost is the sellion, the deepest point in the defined plane in the depression at the root or upper extremity of the nose (sel in Fig. 31A). The lower is the subnasale (sub), which is the point in the median sagittal plane at which the skin of the upper lip meets that of the nasal septum, or cartilaginous partition between the two nostrils. It is best to use the latter term to mean the two air-passages leading into the cavities of the nose. The wings or alae limit the nostrils laterally, and are separated on their outer sides from the rest of the nose by a groove, the shape of which is characteristic of certain ethnic taxa. The word 'nostril' is often applied loosely to the ala, but this is confusing.

The shape of the nose may be described in part by considering the projection of the tip of it in relation to a plane, parallel to the standard horizontal plane, passing through the subnasale. In Fig. 31A the tip does not reach this plane, but in some types of face it

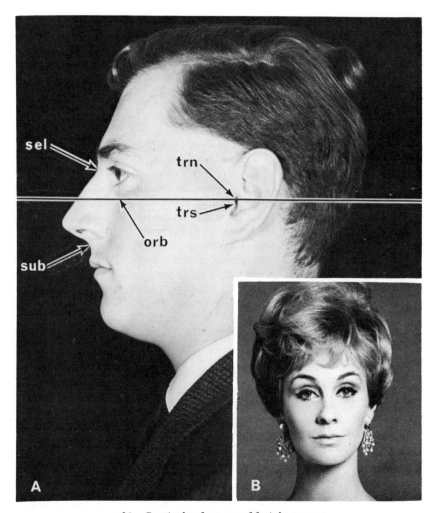

31    *Particular features of facial anatomy*

A, a head held in the standard horizontal plane (indicated by a line drawn right across the figure); B, face of a young woman, to show a Europid nose of non-Armenid character. *orb*, orbitale; *sel*, sellion; *sub*, subnasale; *trn*, tragion; *trs*, tragus.
A, *photograph by Mr. J. Haywood;* B, *Daily Telegraph (photograph by Mr. Murray Irving).*

projects considerably below it, and the nostrils can then not be seen in full face by a person holding his eyes in the plane of the subject's subnasale, if the subject holds his head in the standard horizontal position.

The breadth of the nose is greatest in the region of the alae. The maximum breadth in this region may be expressed as a percentage of the distance from the sellion to the subnasale. Expressed in this way, the breadth is very different in the various ethnic taxa of man. The condition is said to be *leptorrhine* if the percentage is less than 70; *mesorrhine* if 70 or more but less than 85; and *platyrrhine* if 85 or more.

The shape of the nose above the groove shows characteristic differences. In some faces (Fig. 31B) it is narrow, and in full-face view each side appears to form a curve that joins smoothly with that of the eyebrow above and with the outer edge of the ala below, the groove above the ala being so slight as to be inconspicuous from in front.

There are two groups of European Jews, the Ashkenazim and the Sephardim, who differ in physical characters. When it is said that a person has a Jewish appearance, the speaker usually has persons of Ashkenazic stock in mind. The members of this group are the typical Jews of Russia, Poland, and England, and they constitute the great majority, perhaps 90%, of all the people in the world to whom the name of Jews is applied (cf. Jacobs[545] and Ripley[905]).

Persons of Ashkenazic stock can generally be recognized by certain physical characters that distinguish them from other Europeans. It will be understood that not every member of this group exhibits all the distinctive characters, but many of them show most of the ones that will now be described. The description will apply in particular to the adult male.[49, 302, 331, 477, 545, 905, 925, 1085]

Typically the Ashkenazim are brachycranial, though some of them fall within the range of the mesocranial. The relative breadth of the skull is produced in a special way. In several ethnic taxa the brachycranial condition arises simply from the fact that the head is particularly broad, but this is not so here. It is caused by the head being very *short*, the cranial capacity being maintained by the unusual height of the vertex. The shortness of the head is due to the suppression of the occipital region. A skull of this type is said to be *hypsibrachycranial*. An example is shown in Fig. 32B, which should be compared with the skull in Fig. 28C. In some cases the impression is given in side view that the back of the head has been sliced off by a vertical cut (cf. Fig. 33B, p. 240). The forehead is special in two respects. It tends to recede rather noticeably (Fig. 33B), and also to be rounded in the horizontal plane (Fig. 32A), instead of being squared off on each side, as it is in certain types of head, in which the forehead is almost rectangular in horizontal section. Thus in the Ashkenazim the front and sides of the head tend to curve smoothly upwards to a high vertex. In front view the face is seen to be rather wide above and narrow at the rounded chin, which somewhat recedes.

The upper and lower eyelids, especially the latter, tend to be somewhat puffed out. The iris is large. The ear is large, wide in its upper part, and provided with a large lobe.

The mouth is large. The lower lip is everted so as to appear thick, but it is not swollen out like that of a Negro; on the contrary, it tends to be rather flattened (Fig. 33A). The flattened area is formed mainly of the 'transition zone', or *Lippensaum* of German authors.[796] This is the reddish zone of modified skin—the lip in the narrower sense of the word—that separates the ordinary skin of the face from the mucous membrane of the mouth. In Ashkenazim this zone of the lower lip is sometimes rather sharply marked off

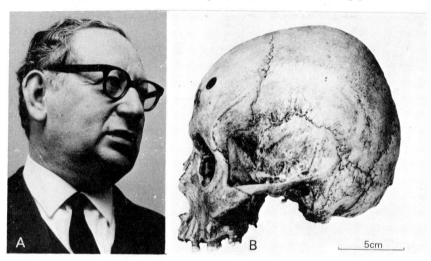

32    *A typical Armenid head* (A) *and a typical Armenid skull* (B)

A, *Link Information Services;* B, *British Museum (Natural History), skull no. E.504, photographed by the author.*

from the facial skin by being raised somewhat above it. This gives a curious appearance in black-and-white photographs, especially when the lip is strongly everted; for the ordinary facial skin bordering the transition zone may be mistaken for the transition zone itself, and the latter for the mucous membrane of the mouth, or even for the tip of the tongue (Fig. 33D).

It may be remarked that in all ethnic taxa, so far as is known, the change in histological structure from the transition zone to the mucous membrane is gradual, while that from the facial skin to the transition zone is abrupt; but in most of the Europid subraces there is not a change in level where the abrupt change in histological structure occurs.

The nose (Figs. 32A and 33A, B, and C) is large in all dimensions. It is in some cases straight in profile, in others somewhat convex. It is wide at all levels, especially towards its lower end, and is sharply divided by the deep grooves that separate the alae from the rest of the organ. The alae are thick ('fleshy') and generally curved out widely at the sides. The part of the nose above the grooves generally has rather flattened sides, instead of presenting a curved surface from cheek to cheek, as in many Europid subraces. It follows from this that when the face is viewed from in front, the sides of the nose are seen to follow an irregular course, rather straight above the groove and markedly curved out below them. This gives a very different appearance from

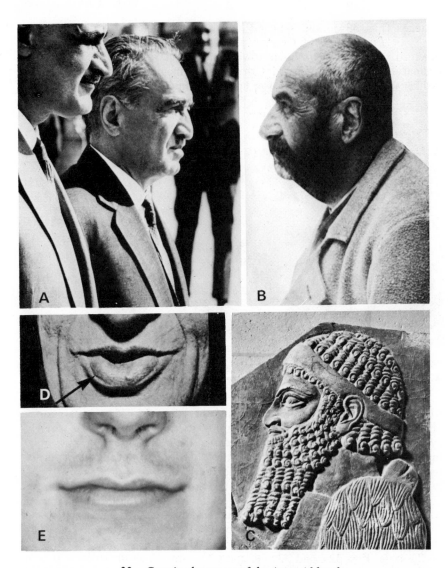

**33    Certain characters of the Armenid head**

A, President Mikoyan (the central figure in the photograph); B, an Armenian of Kayseri (Césarée), Turkey; C, part of an Assyrian alabaster relief of about 700 B.C., from Chorsabad-Dûr, Surrukin, showing the head of a subjected mountain-dweller; D, lips of Armenid type (the arrow, added by the present author, points to a groove mentioned in the text); E, lips of non-Armenid type, for comparison with D.

A, *United Press International (U.K.);* B, *from Chantre;* [204] C, *Palais du Louvre, Paris;* D, *Hermann Luchterhand Verlag;* E, *photograph by the author.*

the smooth curve seen, for instance, in Fig. 31B, extending all the way from the eyebrow to the lower extremity of the ala.

In the typical Ashkenazic nose the distance from the sellion to the tip is longer than that from the sellion to the subnasale, with the result that the tip projects downwards below the horizontal plane passing through the subnasale. It follows that an observer who holds his eyes in the plane of the subject's subnasale, while the latter holds his head horizontal, may not be able to see the nasal septum, for it may be hidden by the tip. In some cases one cannot see the nostrils at all in these circumstances. It is quite usual, however, and indeed rather characteristic, for the alae not to extend downwards so far as the septum does (see especially Fig. 33C, and the central face in Fig. 33A). In this case the lateral parts of the nostrils can be seen from in front, and a considerable part of the septum can be seen when the face is viewed in profile.

The breadth of the nose, as expressed by the nasal index, does not necessarily reach a high figure, because the distance from the sellion to the subnasale is great; but the absolute breadth is considerable, on account of the thickness of the alae. This is a particularly distinctive character.

Joseph Jacobs, whose article on illustrious and eminent Jews has already been mentioned, refers in another paper to a particular character of the type of nose often seen in Jews, which he illustrates diagrammatically in the sketch here reproduced as Fig. 34A.[545] It results from the facts already mentioned

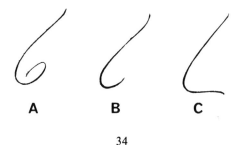

**A**     **B**     **C**

34

Three noses, showing diagrammatically the characteristic appearance of this organ among Ashkenazim (A) and in other types of persons (B and C).
*Sketches from Jacobs.*[545]

that when the nose is viewed from the left side, its edge, continuing as a curve into the edge of the nasal septum and thence into the deep groove already mentioned, forms a figure resembling an italic 6. As Jacobs remarks, when the part of the figure that is twisted round is omitted (Fig. 34B), the characteristic form to a large extent disappears, while if the part representing the edge of the nasal septum is drawn horizontally and the groove is not shown (because weakly developed in the subject), the whole character of the organ is changed, and it no longer resembles the nose of a Jew (Fig. 34C).

The skin is rather swarthy. The scalp-hair is generally (but not always) very dark brown or almost black; it is more wavy than is usual in Europid subraces.

The facial hair of the male is abundant, but there is not an unusual amount of body-hair.

The legs are rather short, and the total height is therefore moderate or rather short. The shoulders are broad and the form is thick-set, with some tendency to corpulency in elderly persons.

The characters that have just been described are very close to those of the Armenid subrace of the Europid race. Facial characters of Armenid type are illustrated in Figs. 32A and 33. The Armenians themselves, from whom the name of the subrace is derived, are of remarkably uniform physical type.[685] A good description of the Armenians was published by Chantre in 1895.[204] Essentially the same type was represented in ancient times by the Hittites[685, 925] and Assyrians;[466] indeed, the type was named Assyroid by Deniker.[268] The fact that there are strong resemblances between many Jews and the Armenians was pointed out at a meeting of the Royal Anthropological Society in 1885[323] and is generally accepted.[268, 302, 450, 1085]

It is thought, however, that another subrace besides the Armenid enters into the composition of the European Jewish stock, and perhaps entered into that of the Hittites and Assyrians. This is the Orientalid subrace, which includes many of those commonly called by the vague name of 'Arabs'. It is seen in its most typical form in the interior of Arabia, but also among the population of Syria and Iraq. The Orientalids are slender people of moderate stature. In certain respects they differ markedly from the Armenids, for they are very dolichocranial, with prominent occiput, and the nose is narrow, with compressed alae. The sellion is situated high up towards the forehead. The profile of the nose is sometimes straight, but often somewhat aquiline (that is to say convex, with a nearly straight or slightly concave border to the nasal septum). The face is long and narrow, and tends to appear oval in front view. The lower lip is not everted. The slit between the lids of the open eye is wide on the side towards the nose, so that the visible part of the eyeball has the form of an almond; the iris is black. The hair is almost black, the skin rather swarthy.

The evidence from blood-groups bears on the theory that the Ashkenazim have both Armenids and Orientalids for ancestors. Fig. 35 is a diagram in which the frequency of the gene responsible for blood-group 'A' is represented by black rectangles, and that for group 'B' by dotted ones. On the left side of the diagram the frequency of these genes in certain Jewish communities is compared with that found among Bedawin (a typical Orientalid group) and Armenians. The Jews represented here were immigrants of Ashkenazic stock to Tel Aviv, and Russian and Polish Jews; it may be assumed that all, or nearly all, were Ashkenazim. It will be noticed that the Jews were intermediate in their blood-group genes between Armenians and Bedawin. It must be borne in mind, however, that an intermediate position in a diagram of this sort does not by itself indicate a double origin; it can only support evidence from other sources.

The right-hand part of Fig. 35 shows that Jews living among Gentiles retain their characteristic blood-group genes. The Dutch Jews and Russian Jews resemble one another in this respect and differ from the Gentiles among whom they live. The frequency of the gene for 'A' is about the same in Dutch

Jews as in the Dutch population as a whole, but there is a big difference in the gene for 'B'; and Russian Jews differ widely in both these frequencies from the Russian population as a whole.

As a broad generalization one may say that on the evidence of morphological characters alone, as opposed to that from blood-groups, people of Ashkenazic stock show a much closer relationship to the Armenid than to

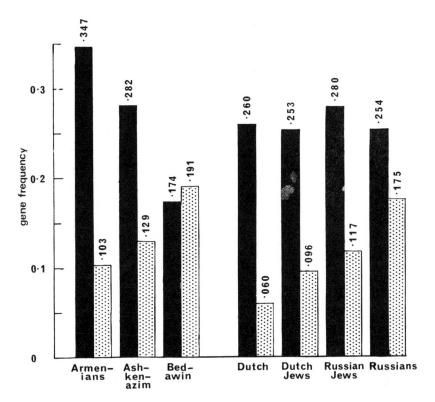

35    *The frequencies of the genes for blood-groups 'A' and 'B' in Jewish and other communities*

Blood-group 'A', black rectangles; 'B', dotted. The figures are based on the following numbers of persons: 3,166 Armenians; 3,793 Ashkenazim (Russian and Polish Jews, and Ashkenazim of Tel Aviv); 642 Bedawin; 14,483 Dutch; 705 Dutch Jews; 1,475 Russian Jews; 57,122 Russians.
*The frequencies shown in this diagram were calculated from information collected from various sources by Wiener.* [1140]

the Orientalid subrace. This is not true of the Sephardim, many of whom are not very different in physical features from Orientalids, though Armenid features are not lacking.

It does not seem possible to reach certainty about the origin of Near Eastern and European Jews. From the account in *Genesis* xi it would appear that Abram's family lived in the great city of Ur in southern Sumeria, near the northern extremity of the Persian Gulf. It has been argued, however, that 'Ur of the Chaldees' should properly have been described as 'Ur of the Khassedites', and that in fact Abram's family lived in the Ur of northern Syria, some 600 miles away.[395] An interesting hypothesis about the ethnic origin of the Jews has been founded on this argument, which deserves careful consideration. On the whole, however, it seems more likely that the patriarch's family started its travels from the Sumerian Ur. The influence of Sumeria on the writer of *Genesis* xvi is clear enough. The incorporation into the Bible story of Sumerian myths, interestingly recounted by Kramer,[608] points in this direction. The behaviour to one another of Abram, his wife Sarai, and the latter's handmaiden Hagar, as recounted in *Genesis* xvi, was in exact accordance with Sumerian custom.[1158] These facts, however, do not imply that Abram was a Sumerian. It seems best to accept the common opinion that if the Hebrew patriarchs could be seen today, they would be taken for Bedawin;[450] that is to say, they belonged to the Orientalid subrace. When the lower delta of Mesopotamia began to dry up, the new expanse of land was occupied not only by Sumerians, with their highly developed culture, but also by Accadians (Orientalids) coming from the north, and by a much less advanced Orientalid people who entered the eastern extremity of the 'Fertile Crescent' from the west. The latter seem to have established themselves before the Sumerians came, and to have survived under Sumerian domination.[1158] It is to this stock that we must look, in all probability, for the origin of the Jewish people.

The question now arises, when did the amalgamation with the Armenid stock occur? Even the patriarchs themselves were not endogamous, for Abram's second wife, Hagar, was an Egyptian, and the angel of the Lord promised that her progeny would be multiplied exceedingly (*Genesis*, xvi, 10). When the Hebrews returned from Egypt to Palestine, they almost certainly found a large Armenid element among the population of that country, for the Hittites and Assyrians were Armenids, and there were no rigidly fixed national boundaries that would prevent the interpenetration of ethnically distinct types. There is much evidence in the Bible that the early Jews intermarried with people of other stocks. Solomon, it will be remembered, 'loved many strange women', including Hittites (I *Kings*, x, 1). Conquering nations in this part of the world were accustomed to remove whole populations and replace them with their own nationals. This happened, for instance, when the Assyrians brought a new Armenid stock to Samaria after removing most of the inhabitants (the 'Lost Tribes') to Mesopotamia in 722 B.C. It is noteworthy that the Jewish prisoners of the Assyrians at this period, as represented in Assyrian sculptures, were already 'thoroughly Jewish' (that is to say, partly Armenid) in appearance.[925]

The hybridization of the early Jews is not surprising, for at first they were not denied the opportunity of intermarriage with 'proselytes of righteousness'. Nevertheless, during the exile in Babylon (586–538 B.C.), that frenzied prophet Ezekiel attributed the downfall of Judah largely to the wrath of God at the intermarriage of the Jews with strangers. The Lord instructed him to tell the people of Jerusalem, '. . . thy father was an Amorite, and thy mother an Hittite. . . . Thou hast played the whore with the Assyrians' (*Ezekiel*, xvi). It is particularly interesting that two Armenid peoples, the Hittites and Assyrians, are mentioned in this passage. Nevertheless, those who were not taken away to Babylon are thought to have intermarried freely with the non-Jewish inhabitants of Palestine, and intermarriage continued after the return from exile (*Ezra*, x, 11; *Nehemiah*, xiii, 23). There thus arose a people of mixed Orientalid and Armenid stock, united principally by religious and nationalistic bonds.

At the 'Golus' or 'Diaspora' that followed the sacking of Jerusalem by the Romans in A.D. 70 and continued for more than a century, two principal routes were used, one northwards towards the part of Europe adjacent to Asia Minor, the other to the southern shores of the Mediterranean. It is sometimes claimed that the Sephardim have retained the original (mainly Orientalid) physical features of the Jews, while the Ashkenazim are descended from those who had intermarried extensively with Armenid peoples in ancient times. This would imply that the Ashkenazim and Sephardim were already separate communities before the Diaspora. There is no direct evidence of this.[792] It seems much more likely that the Jews had become a mixed Orientalid-Armenid community before the Diaspora, and that the Sephardim subsequently became modified by intermarriage with Mediterranids.[925]

The fates of the two streams were different. Those who followed the northern route necessarily passed at first through Armenid territory. Hauschild attributes the Armenid character of the Ashkenazim to the consequences of this migration.[477] The extent to which the Armenid composition of the people was increased during this slow migration cannot be determined, but there can be no doubt that those who eventually found their way by this route into Russia, Poland, Germany, and other parts of Europe were ethnically much more Armenid than Orientalid.

The Jews had already been established for a long time in a colony at Alexandria. Those who fled to Africa at the Diaspora spread widely along the north African coast[477] and seem to have intermarried with the Mediterranid peoples of this area; that is to say, with people of the same general physical type as those of Southern Italy and Spain today. Jews entered Spain freely during the period of Moorish domination, some presumably from Africa, others from elsewhere, including a group descended from those who had remained in Babylonia or had gone to Mesopotamia after the exile.[149, 915, 925] The Jews flourished at first in Spain under the Muslim regime, but eventually every unconverted Jew was expelled in 1492, when Christianity had reestablished itself and the Inquisition had done its work. The exiles or 'Sephardim' (Hebrew for Spaniards) established themselves at first in north Africa, Asia Minor, the Balkan states (where they were called 'Spagnuoli'), and Italy; some also in Holland and elsewhere.

The Sephardim are distinguished from the Ashkenazim by physical characters. No full analysis of the blood-groups of Sephardic Jews would appear to have been undertaken, but it is clear from morphological evidence that the Armenid element is much less evident in them than in the Ashkenazim. Intermarriage either in north Africa or in Spain or in both places produced an approximation to the Mediterranid type.[477, 925] The Sephardim are typically more slender than the Ashkenazim. They are mostly mesocranial; an index of

78·1 has been quoted.[477] It is sometimes said that they are actually doli-chocranial, but this is denied by Jacobs.[545] The head-hair is less wavy than that of the Ashkenazim,[21] and almost always dark;[925] the irises are particularly dark. The nose is narrower,[21, 477] and there is less tendency to convexity in this organ.

The Sephardim are frequently seen in Rembrandt's paintings. This is not surprising, because from early times there were members of this community in the cities of Holland. He painted 34 portraits of Jews, as well as very numerous illustrations of Biblical scenes, and only a minority of all these paintings show the features of the Ashkenazim in their most typical form. The 'Portrait of an old Jew in an armchair' (Leningrad, Hermitage) is an example. Many of the rest are representations of rather untypical Ashkenazim, or else of Sephardim. The wearing of hats unfortunately conceals the hypsibrachycranial feature of the Ashkenazim, and thus makes positive identification more difficult in some cases. A good example of Sephardic features is seen in the 'Portrait of a young Jew' in the Van Horne Collection (Montreal). This young man appears to have been the model for many of Rembrandt's numerous portraits of Christ,[135] none of which shows the features of the Ashkenazim.

The present-day Sephardim of Asia Minor became somewhat less typical by intermarriage with the Ashkenazim of that country,[477] but elsewhere there is, or was for a long time, a tendency for the two groups to remain separate. This was fostered at first by the fact that the Sephardim spoke Ladino (Spanish-Hebrew), the Ashkenazim Yiddish (German-Hebrew). At the end of the nineteenth century the Sephardim held themselves entirely aloof from the Ashkenazim both in London and in Amsterdam.[905] In America each group built its own synagogues.[149]

It would not appear that any estimate of relative numbers has been made recently, and no doubt the distinction is less rigid than formerly; but, as has already been remarked, the great majority of all Jews in the world today are probably of Ashkenazic stock.

The reader who has studied the evidence presented in this chapter will agree that the meanings of the word 'Jews' cannot be satisfactorily summarized: the subject is too complicated. Nevertheless, certain conclusions do stand out. Various communities scattered over the world are Jews simply in the sense that they adhere to a particular religion (in various forms); they are not definable on an ethnic basis. These communities, however, comprise only a very small proportion of those who call themselves and are regarded by others as Jews. The great majority are persons of Ashkenazic stock. Many of these do not practise the rites of the Jewish religion. Whether they do or do not, they show in their physical characters a genetic relationship to the Armenians, and they must be associated with the Armenid subrace, even though there has been an Orientalid element in their remote ancestry. They are thus related to the Assyrians and Hittites of antiquity, as well as to the modern Armenians. They do not *constitute*, and never have *constituted*, a subrace of their own, because there are and always have been persons who do not call themselves Jews and are not regarded by others as Jews, but who belong to the Armenid subrace.

It may be added that the contribution of the Armenid subrace to civilization will bear comparison with that of any other. The contributions of the Assyrians, Hittites, and Armenid Jews are too well known to require emphasis here. The achievements of the Armenians themselves are perhaps less familiar. Almost continuously their country has been the scene of struggles for mastery by much greater powers. Nevertheless they had developed a civilization while many European countries were still illiterate. Early in the fifth century A.D. they had devised and standardized an alphabet to meet the special needs of their language. A curious feature was that every consonantal sound, whether simple or compound, was represented by a single letter. Thus, for instance, a single letter represented *ts*, though there were also letters for *t* and *s*. Remarkable contributions to scholarship, the arts (especially architecture), and Christian theology were made from the seventh century onwards, until the Armenian nation was shattered by the Seljuk Turks in the eleventh, never to become independent again. Some of their early illuminated manuscripts and other works of art are beautifully reproduced in a recent book on the achievements of the so-called 'Dark Ages'.[790]

# 15  The Celts

THIS CHAPTER has two purposes. Like the preceding one, it is partly concerned with the different meanings that have been attached to a single word, and with the complexities and misunderstandings that have resulted. The other main purpose is to correct certain erroneous statements concerning people to whom the name of 'Celts' has been applied. One of these relates to the degree of civilization attained by the early Britons before the Roman occupation; the other, to the extent of hybridization in the ancestry of the modern British people.

The Danube basin was for long the centre of an industry and an art that may be regarded as representing the early stages of what became known as the Celtic Iron Age culture. Unfortunately for the anthropologist, many of the people who made the objects found in the ancient graves had the custom of partly burning the bodies of their dead, and the skeletons are therefore often unsuitable for detailed study. Luckily, however, this practice was not invariable. In the valley of the River Amper, a remote tributary of the Danube in Upper Bavaria, a great necropolis of the Early Iron Age was situated in what later became the Royal Forest of Mühlhart. Here, in one of the tumuli, there was found a well-preserved cranium. This was carefully examined and described by a versatile pathologist, biologist, and anthropologist of the nineteenth century, Richard Virchow. The cranial index was 74·2; the forehead was somewhat sloping, the brow-ridges rather strongly developed, the face high and narrow, the nasal bones prominent, the nose narrow, the eye-sockets large and appearing nearly rectangular in front view. The cranium was orthognathous; the lower jaw was unfortunately not found.[1104] Virchow's description provides clear evidence of the association of a rather typical Nordid cranium with artifacts of the early Iron Age.

The grave-goods buried in the tumuli of Mühlhart belong to the same general type as others found in various parts of the Danube basin. The most famous of these sites is near the Austrian village of Hallstatt, on the west side of a little lake about fifty kilometres south-east of Salzburg. The ground rises sharply behind the village. One can walk up the hill to the ancient site in three-quarters of an hour, or make a funicular ascent from the neighbouring village of Lahn. The graves were dug near the lower end of a narrow, gently rising valley, on the southern side of a little stream. Beyond the valley the ground ascends to the dominating heights of Mt. Plassen (Fig. 36); below, it falls away to the lake, giving an extensive view of the mountains that lie on the other side. Here, in

**36  *The ancient cemetery near Hallstatt, Austria, a famous Iron Age site***

The corpses (many of them incinerated) were buried in the field (Gräberfeld) on the left side of the path, and in the adjoining region (now wooded) above it. The entrance to the salt-mine (not seen in the photograph) is just beyond and to the left of the most distant houses. The mountain in the background is Mt. Plassen.

*Photograph by the author, 1966.*

this remote valley, some 2,500 corpses were buried over a long period of centuries in the distant past.

Excavation of the graves began in 1846. It revealed one of the world's archaeological treasures, perhaps the finest collection of early Iron Age art. The burial-site, or *Gräberfeld*, consists today of meadow-land near the stream and a wood on the adjacent higher ground. It is about 260 yards long and varies irregularly in width from about 50 to 130 yards. The grave-goods buried with the corpses are representative, in a general way, of a culture that spread over a vast area of Europe. Archaeologists speak of the Hallstatt culture and the Hallstatt period without any thought of restricting the meaning of these terms to a little valley hidden away in the highlands of Austria.

The buried treasure of the Gräberfeld consists of articles of bronze, iron, gold, amber, and ivory. An earlier and a later Hallstatt period are recognized, the former (with much bronze but not much iron) extending from about 900 to 700 B.C., and the latter from then onwards till 400 B.C. There are brooches in profusion, neck-bands, bracelets, finger rings, figures of animals, needles, lance-points, daggers, swords, and highly decorated scabbards, as well as pottery. The geometrical decorations, so characteristic of what is commonly called Celtic art, are particularly well seen on the chased girdle-clasps. Many of these articles are today in the excellent little museum in Hallstatt itself, others in the Landesmuseum at Linz; the finest collection is in the Natural History Museum in Vienna.

An immense amount of knowledge has accumulated about certain aspects of the material culture of the Hallstatt people, but little is known of the men and women who made the objects that decorate the museums today. Why did a little community live, century after century, in such a remote place? There can be scarcely any doubt that the reason was the existence of a huge supply of common salt in the immediate vicinity. The salt-mine of this valley is said to be the oldest in Europe, and it is still in active production today. It appears that in early times the valley was primarily an industrial settlement. The tools of the miners, marvellously preserved, have been found in the ancient underground galleries. One can still see their wooden shovels and wedges, hafts for bronze pickaxes, tubs for carrying salt, leather shoes, and fragments of garments made of skins and cloth, even the chips of burnt wood that had been used for torches. All these articles are thought to date from the Hallstatt period. The amber from northern Europe, gold from southern Germany, and ivory from Africa must have been obtained by barter for the precious product of the mine.

Many of the corpses in the Gräberfeld were burnt and only the ashes remain; fortunately others were inhumed. It has been supposed that there were two classes of persons in the little community, the cremators and the inhumers. It is claimed by some authorities,[497] though denied by others,[771] that the most splendid grave-goods were buried with the ashes; and the opinion has been expressed that the cremators were the '*Bergherren*'. Whether this was so or not, weapons are more usually found with the cremated remains. It may be supposed that soldiers were necessary to protect the priceless treasure of the mine itself. Many of the soldiers were buried with an *Antennendolch*, a special variety of dagger provided with two projections from the hilt, resembling the antennae of an insect. We know nothing of the physique of the cremators, but seven skeletons of the inhumers are exhibited in the Hallstatt Museum. The occiputs projected sufficiently to bring these people into the dolichocranial range; the forehead receded somewhat; the face was long and somewhat prognathous; the men must have been about 170 cm (5′ 7″) tall.[497] The skulls are remarkably similar to the definitely Nordid ones found in the 'graves in rows' (*Reihengräber*) of southern Germany, though they are not quite so flat on top. It must be remembered, nevertheless, that the skulls of Nordids are not very markedly different from those of Mediterranids, and the suggestion has been made that the inhumed people may possibly have been of the latter subrace.[905]

The skulls of the Gräberfeld contrast very strongly with those of the modern population of this part of Austria, and of their ancestors of recent centuries. It is a striking experience to pass from the local museum to the charnel-house (*Beinhaus*) beside the Catholic church of Hallstatt, where, over a period of some three and a half centuries, human skulls and long bones have been stored from lack of space in the churchyard (see p. 212). There are said to be 1,300 skulls in the house,[771] and nearly all appear to be brachycranial or in the broader-headed range of the mesocranial. One cannot tell whether the cremators of the Gräberfeld were brachycranial like the present population of the district or dolichocranial like the skeletons in the graves.

We now come to the crucial question. What name should be given to the people who made and buried the art-treasures of Hallstatt? According to the Swedish archaeologist Montelius, Hallstatt with the neighbouring part of Austria, Switzerland, southern Germany, and Belgium was all occupied throughout the Hallstatt period by '*la même race celtique*'.[758]

Moritz Hoernes, Professor of Prehistoric Archaeology in the University of Vienna, who made a special study of the Hallstatt period,[499] did not use the word 'Celtic' in quite the same sense. He recognized four great groups of people who practised the Hallstatt culture in somewhat different styles, so that their works of art can be distinguished. These were the *illyrische Gruppe*, occupying the east Adriatic region from Herzegovina to Carinthia; the *ostkeltische* in Upper and Lower Austria, southern Bohemia, and Moravia; the *germanische* of northern Germany from the Elbe to the Oder; and the *westkeltische* of south and west Germany, eastern France, and northern Switzerland.[499, 500] Thus the Celtic peoples extended over a broad territory from France to Moravia. Hallstatt itself lay near the boundary between the west and east Celtic groups, but its culture approximated more closely to that of the former.

At one time Hoernes had been slightly equivocal as to whether it was legitimate to regard the Celts as an ethnic taxon,[499] but seven years later, in his book,[500] he makes it clear that for him the Celts were those people who occupied a particular geographical area and made objects that could be recognized as essentially similar (though slight differences warranted the recognition of a western and an eastern sub-area). The Celts, in his view, were not people of any particular nation or any particular ethnic taxon.

During the fifth century B.C., particularly from about 450 B.C. onwards, certain objects of another culture, that of La Tène, began to infiltrate into

37   *An ornamental bronze disk from a tumulus*
*at Glasinac, Yugoslavia*

The disk is 155 mm in diameter. The decoration is
characteristic of an early stage in the development of the art.
*From Fiala.* [328]

Hallstatt;[499, 772] and at the turn of the century, especially about 390 B.C., a
profound change occurred. *'Die keltischen Völker treten auf den Schauplatz.'*
So says Friedrich Morton, an authority on the Gräberfeld. The Hallstatt period
in the strict sense was at an end in Hallstatt itself; that of La Tène had replaced
it in the upland valley. The Celtic people had arrived with their own
culture—the Celts, who had been there for centuries, if we accept the opinions
of Montelius and Hoernes! So now a new period had started at Hallstatt, that
of La Tène. It lasted into the century before Christ.

There were certainly big changes. The pottery began to be made of clay
heavily impregnated with graphite, and the *Vollgraphitton-Scherben* mark
clearly the beginning of the La Tène period at Hallstatt.[771] The potter's wheel
came into general use. Jugs were made with spouts drawn out like beaks; some
of these were decorated in polychrome. Gold coinage was introduced. Persons
of both sexes wore torques with thickened end-pieces round their necks. Iron
brooches were inset with coral and enamel. Finger rings were made of coloured
glass. Swords became long, double-edged, and adapted to the cutting instead of
the thrusting stroke. Some of the scabbards were elaborately decorated with
figures of men and horses. There would be no point in extending the list. A new
culture had certainly been brought to Hallstatt. But by whom? Morton speaks
of *'Der Einbruch der Kelten'*—but were those who brought this culture *by
definition* the Celts? Must one define these people by the products of their art?

It is perhaps appropriate at this point to step aside from the strictly Celtic zone of
Hoernes to take a sidelong glance at the people of the neighbouring *illyrische Gruppe*
at Glasinac.

A road from Sarajevo to Višegrad in Bosnia-Herzegovina was under construction in 1880. About forty kilometres east of Sarajevo it passed across a plateau, some 800 metres above the sea and several miles across. This eerie place, called Glasinac, is almost surrounded by mountains, on the slopes of which are innumerable mounds. These are in fact ancient tumuli, made by the piling up of stones. The workmen engaged in building the road found them a convenient source of material for their purpose. Under the stones they began to discover the implements and ornaments of a remote age. It was found that a huge area had been set apart for the burial of the dead. There were 20 or 30 cemeteries, each containing several hundred graves covered by tumuli. The contents of the graves have been thoroughly investigated. [328, 781, 983] It is thought that burials went on here almost continuously from the Bronze Age through the Hallstatt period and beyond. Most of the objects are of Hallstatt types. The bronze disk, ornamented with a simple geometric pattern (Fig. 37), might be taken as an example of early Celtic Iron Age art.

The special interest of the burials at Glasinac is that many of the bodies had not been cremated. Before the end of the nineteenth century, 38 skulls had been obtained, which, though broken by the overlying stones, could be fitted together sufficiently well to provide information about the shape of the cranium. [1132] The lower part of the face was unfortunately in all cases too much damaged to permit study. Of the 38 skulls, 11 were dolicho-, 14 meso-, and 13 brachycranial. Some of the skulls were extremely elongated, one of them showing a cranial index of 63 and another of 64. These figures contrast strongly with those representing the modern Serbo-Croat (Dinarid) population of the region, which is predominantly brachycranial (Fig. 38). It is evident that the Iron Age culture of Glasinac existed in an ethnically mixed population. Both dolichocranial and brachycranial skulls were sometimes found in the same tumulus, and when they were in separate tumuli, they were accompanied by similar grave-goods. [1132] It is

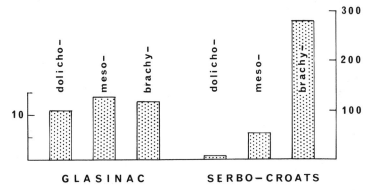

38    *A graphical comparison of Iron Age skulls from Glasinac with those of nineteenth-century Serbo-Croat soldiers from the same region*

The heights of the columns represent the proportions of dolicho-, meso-, and brachycranial skulls in each of the two groups of persons. The data for the soldiers are adjusted from measurements taken in life. The scales at the sides show the numbers of skulls or heads on which the heights of the columns are based, in each of the two groups.
*The diagram is constructed from the data of Weisbach.* [1132]

39   *The north-eastern end of the Lake of Neuchâtel, to show the position of La Tène*

The famous Iron Age site is marked by an oblique arrow. The vertical arrow points to the former River Thiele, now converted into a canal. The photograph was taken from Chaumont, in the hills above Neuchâtel.                                                                         *Photograph by the author, 1966.*

impossible, however, to tell whether people of more than one ethnic taxon were engaged in *making* the goods.

Whoever the artists and technicians of Glasinac may have been, they eventually adopted the Celtic art-styles of La Tène, though they did not produce any masterpieces in this genre. For these one looks naturally to the fountain-head itself.

From Chaumont, on the high ground above the city of Neuchâtel in Switzerland, one may look down on one of the most celebrated sites of Iron Age culture, and picture to oneself a hive of splendid industry on the lake-shore below (Fig. 39). The distant view is best, for on the site itself one sees little more than a modern bathing-beach, revealing no trace of former glories.

The axis of the long, narrow Lake of Neuchâtel extends from south-west to north-east. The River Thiele flows in at its south-western end and used to flow out at the north-eastern, into the Bielersee; the latter is connected through the River Aare with the Rhine at Koblenz. The short stretch of the Thiele between the two lakes has been replaced by a canal in roughly the same position. All the way along the north-western side of the two lakes and of the river that connected them, there formerly lived Iron Age people of the *westkeltische Gruppe* of Hoernes. During the Hallstatt period they made objects typical of their group and buried some of them with their inhumed or cremated dead. Some of these objects are good examples of the art of the period. In the Cantonal

Museum of Archaeology at Neuchâtel there is, for instance, a fine girdle-plate from near Bussy, some three or four kilometres from Neuchâtel; it is decorated with an elaborate geometrical design. It was in the neighbourhood of this city that a later upsurge of originality in design produced a novel art and technology that eventually replaced those of Hallstatt, even in Hallstatt itself.

Just beside the outflow of the Thiele from the Lake of Neuchâtel, on its left (north-western) bank, was (and is) La Tène (Fig. 39), famous throughout the civilized world for the development of a culture that everyone seems to agree on calling Celtic. The archaeological exploration of the site was begun in 1856 by Col. Schwab of Bienne; its area was extended some twenty years later by the artificial lowering of the water-level of the lake. It is supposed that the people who produced the industry and art of La Tène migrated from the basin of the Danube to this tributary of the Rhine soon after 500 B.C.; the culture persisted in the same place until well into the first century B.C., though the latest products were inferior in design. Although the majority of the people concerned in the industry may perhaps have come from Danubian territory, yet there is reason to suppose that the features of the La Tène culture that distinguish it from those of Mühlhart and Hallstatt spread hither from the middle region of the Rhine Valley, for the earliest examples are seen in the war-chariot graves of this region. La Tène art is perhaps to be regarded as part of an aristocratic culture derived from this source,[857] but its full development was attained beside this remote lacustrine tributary of the great river.

La Tène appears to have been a workshop and an art-centre, a repository for manufactured goods, and a military frontier-post (for the culture is not represented on the other side of the river). Many of the treasures obtained at this site are in the Cantonal Museum of Archaeology at Neuchâtel, others in museums in various parts of Switzerland, France, and Germany. In the Cantonal Museum one may see axes and adzes, scythes and sickles, large iron cooking-pots hung on chains, an excellent saw resembling a modern bread-knife, gouges and chisels of various sizes, knives, spring-scissors, bits closely resembling modern snaffles, metal parts of harness, a waggon- or chariot-wheel (iron-shod, with wooden spokes and a hollow wooden centre for the axle), lances of various kinds, swords and scabbards (some of the latter with very beautifully worked geometrical and other designs), and articles of personal adornment such as brooches and bracelets. The special skill of the artists was in the use of gold and bronze. The designs used in their decorations were mostly abstract and geometrical rather than naturalistic, though with occasional allusions to natural forms; curved lines usually predominated, and strict symmetry was avoided as a general rule. Their art can be recognized wherever it is found. It is legitimate, from a purely archaeological point of view, to give the name of Celts to those who produced it, and perhaps to those who brought it to the neighbourhood of the Lake of Neuchâtel from elsewhere.

The La Tène culture spread very widely. From a large area of northern Switzerland and part of Germany a massive migration of 'Celts' swept westward into France, where they occupied the territory extending from the River Garonne to the Seine.

The taxonomic position of the people in what is now France whom Julius Caesar called '*Celtae*' has given rise to endless discussion. A large part of the country was occupied in Caesar's time by people who spoke a language that is called Celtic. The more northerly group of these people, the '*Germanokelten*' of Höfler,[502] were essentially Nordids, differing little from the Germani in physical characters, but speaking a very different language. Their neighbours to the south, called by Höfler the '*Gallokelten*', were Alpinids, who spoke the same language as the *Germanokelten*, though perhaps a different dialect of it. The territory of the *Germanokelten* overlapped to some extent that of the *Gallokelten*, and some hybridization probably occurred. In the regions of overlap, the former were the dominant group. The most northerly of the *Germanokelten* were a separate people, called by Caesar the '*Belgae*', whose territory extended to the lower Rhine. They may possibly have mixed and hybridized with *Gallokelten*, but if so, to a much less extent than their southern neighbours.[505] The language of the Belgae was said by Caesar to have been different from that of the Celtae, but probably this difference also was only one of dialect.[141, 505, 857]

Much of the misunderstanding arose from Caesar's casual remark that the people who called themselves '*Celtae*' were called '*Galli*' by the Romans ('*Qui ipsorum lingua Celtae, nostra Galli appellantur*').[626] This suggests that members of only one ethnic taxon were present in the territory in question, whereas in fact there were two taxa, whose territories overlapped. Caesar and his officers would have been in touch with the dominant *Germanokelten*.

It has been argued that only the dominant people would have called themselves Celts, and that the Romans made a mistake in ascribing to the Celtae the name (Galli) of those whom they had subjugated.[462] This, however, was strongly denied by certain French anthropologists of the nineteenth century,[626, 243] and especially by the celebrated Paul Broca.[141] These authorities insisted that the true '*Celtes*' were the short, brown-haired, brachycephalic people (Alpinids, in fact) who occupied a huge area from the Danube across southern Germany and central France to Basse-Bretagne, and some of whose descendants form a considerable part of the modern French population. Contemporary Greek statues show clearly that the *Gallokelten* of ancient times were Alpinids, and indeed their resemblance to modern Auvergnats has been remarked by several authors.[502]

French anthropologists adopted the name '*race kymrique*' for the physically very different 'Germanic' invaders from the north-east (that is to say, the *Germanokelten*). This name (spelled '*race kimrique*') had been used by the French historian Amédée Thierry[1040] for the martial people who inhabited both banks of the lower Rhine and the neighbouring littoral region; he included the '*Belges*' (Caesar's '*Belgae*') as part of this '*race*'. Thierry himself did not give any description of the physique of these people. It is evident that the French anthropologists applied the name '*race kymrique*' to those Nordids who spoke a Celtic language.

The question next arises, 'What were the physical characters of the invaders who brought the Iron Age culture to Great Britain, and whom Caesar called Celtae and Belgae?' This can best be answered by a study of the skeletons that their descendants left in the graveyards of the Romano-British period. The skulls have been subjected to very careful study, with full statistical analysis, by Morant.[762] It is clear that those Celtae and Belgae who established themselves in Britain were essentially Nordid. Indeed, it is shown in the table on p. 82 of Morant's paper that their skulls scarcely differ from those of the Anglo-Saxons who subsequently dominated them, except in one particular character, namely, that the skull is slightly (but significantly) lower in the Iron Age man than in the Anglo-Saxon. Beyond this there are some minor differences that might be noticed if it were possible to put a typical Iron Age man of Romano-British times beside an Anglo-Saxon.[226] The skull might be meso- rather than dolichocranial, and not only lower, but rounded on top instead of slightly keeled; the cranial capacity would be a little less. The distance between the level of the lower teeth and the chin would probably be less than in the deep-jawed Anglo-Saxon. The build would tend to be slighter, with less massive long-bones moved by less powerful muscles. One thing is certain. The Celts who came to Britain were not the Celts of Broca, Lagneau, and Dally. They were *Germanokelten*, not *Gallokelten*; essentially Nordid, not Alpinid. It follows that in all probability they were mainly fair-haired, though some of the Celtae who had Alpinids among their ancestors may have had pale brown hair, and exact uniformity in this respect would anyhow not be expected.

Diodorus, writing in the last half-century B.C., stated that the natural hair-colour of the Γαλάται was ξανθός.[274] The meaning of ξανθός is yellow, though it was sometimes applied to auburn or chestnut hair.[665] Oldfather [274] translates Γαλάται in this passage as 'Gauls', but Diodorus used Κελτοί (Celts) in the immediately preceding paragraph without any obvious difference of meaning, and it seems almost certain that he was referring to people whom Caesar would have called Celtae or Belgae (though it must be admitted that the Greeks were very loose in their use of the word Γαλάται, as Anderson[20] has pointed out). Hörnes uses the German word '*blond*' for the hair-colour of the '*Kelten*',[498] and Höfler refers to the '*blondgelben Germanokelten*'.[502]

A special Celtic ancestry is sometimes postulated for British populations in which red-heads are unusually numerous, on the supposition that an ancient people called 'Celts' had been red-haired. Some casual remarks made by Tacitus (A.D. c. 55–c. 120) seem to have originated this idea. Hoernes, in his work *Die Urgeschichte des Menschen*,[498] in commenting on the physical resemblance between the ancient Gauls (*Gallier*) and modern Auvergnats, says that their kindred to the north 'were already at the time of Tacitus of such lanky, red-haired (*rothhaarige*) aspect, that the historian ascribed to them a Germanic origin'. It is important to notice the word used by Tacitus for blond hair. In describing the Germani, he refers to their '*rutilae comae*'.[1033] Gerber and Greef, who made an exact study of the meaning of every word used by Tacitus, translated his '*rutilus*' as '*rötlich, goldgelb*'.[403] Lewis and Short, in their Latin dictionary, give 'red (inclining to golden yellow)' as the meaning, and remark that the word was used to describe the Golden Fleece, and that gold was called the *rutilus* metal.[663]

The *Gallokelten* liked to consider themselves closely related to the *Germanokelten*, and for this reason sometimes dyed or bleached their brown hair in an attempt to make it blond.[502] Gauls taken prisoner by the Romans were required to do this in order to represent Germani at the triumphal procession of Caligula.[498] According to Pliny (born A.D. 61 or 62), they were accustomed to use a special soap, made from goat fat and beech ash, which has the effect of making the hair reddish. [848] This soap, sometimes called '*sapo Batavorum*', appears to have been an invention of the tribe called Chatti (probably an offshoot of the Belgae). The dyeing or bleaching effect of this substance is not explained by what we know of its chemical composition. Diodorus remarks that it was used by the Γαλάται although their hair was already blond. [274] In his Epigram XXVI, Martial (died A.D. *c.* 104) recommends Roman women to use it, to improve the lustre of their wigs made from the locks of German slaves. [705]

During the fifth century B.C. the people of the Hallstatt culture had already moved onwards into Great Britain and started working iron in South Wales, [480] but the characteristic La Tène culture did not reach the island until about 250 B.C. [481] It was these early invasions of Iron Age people that brought the 'Q-Celtic' speech to the British Isles. It eventually spread from Ireland to the Isle of Man and parts of Scotland, but was replaced in most of Great Britain by 'P-Celtic', which has left so many place-names beginning with 'P' in Wales. The Belgae had already established themselves on a small scale in Great Britain in the last decade of the second century B.C. [1064] Pressure from Germani on the east caused the continental Belgae to move westward and eventually to invade Great Britain on a large scale about 75 B.C. and at later times. The Celtae of Great Britain practised the Iron Age 'B' culture, the Belgae the 'C'; but these were both modifications of La Tène, and in the following brief account it is legitimate to consider them together.

At the time of Julius Caesar's invasions in 55 and 54 B.C., skill in ironwork had made it possible to clear the forest over large areas. Some of the country people were primarily pastoralists, but the cultivation of food-crops was well advanced and the heavy plough was in use. The limits of arable fields are still recognizable in various parts of the country as lynchet banks, some of which date from a very remote period. In the agricultural districts most of the houses were oval or circular huts, but a good start had been made here and there towards greater elaboration in urban life. The pastoralists naturally made use of skins in preparing their clothing, but well-constructed implements for weaving were available. The designs of the woven clothes are not known, beyond the fact that the wearing of trousers had long been usual among the Celtae. The wheel was in use not only in chariots, but in the high-speed potter's wheel, the rotary quern for grinding corn, and the lathe for turning wooden vessels.

Hill-top forts of simple construction had already been built in Great Britain by the Hallstatt people; but when the sling became an important instrument of warfare about 100 B.C., it was found convenient to make a series of parallel ditches and ramparts following contour-lines on the hills. The distances apart of these fortifications depended upon the effective range of the slings. The intention was to use one defensive ring round a hill-top after another, if necessary. Some of the multivallate forts cannot have been constructed without considerable skill in the organization of manpower. No one who has seen the so-called Maiden 'Castle' in Dorset (Figs. 40 and 41, pp. 259–60) can fail to be impressed by its grandeur and the complexity of the two entrances. There were four ramparts on the southern side, with three ditches between; the innermost rampart originally towered about 60 feet above the ditch, which has gradually become partly filled in with fallen rubble. The distance round the outside of the outermost rampart is about a mile and a half. It is interesting to look at the sling-stones in the Dorset County Museum at Dorchester and to reflect that these ancient bullets were the logical cause of the whole design of the fort. The multiple ramparts and ditches were constructed by Iron Age 'B' people, but the fort was eventually occupied by Belgae, who modified it and left behind some of their artifacts. Among these are pots made on the wheel, now in the County Museum.

The Iron Age 'B' people used bars of definite weight for exchange. Gold coinage was brought to Great Britain by the Belgae at their first entry to the country towards the end of the second century B.C. The decoration on them was probably derived from the ancient coinage of Philip II of Macedon, though this has been disputed.[1064] Minting in a copper-tin alloy and in gold soon began in Britain. There was at first a marked deterioration in the design, for the craftsmen appear to have been very careless or clumsy in copying the imported coins. The decoration of coins continued subsequently to be affected, but not dominated, by classical models.

40    *Maiden 'Castle', a hill-fort of the Iron Age*

The letters A, B, *x,* and *y* are explained in the legend to Fig. 41. The arrow marked N gives roughly the direction of the north, which cannot be indicated exactly in a photograph taken obliquely.
*Photograph in the Ashmolean Museum, Oxford, taken from the air by Major G. W. G. Allen; lettering by the author.*

41  *Maiden 'Castle', to given an impression of the circumvallate fortification as seen from the ramparts*

A, taken from the point indicated by the arrow marked A in Fig. 40. The point *x* is labelled with the same symbol in the latter figure. B, taken from near the point indicated by the arrow marked B in Fig. 40. The point *y* is labelled with the same symbol in the latter figure. The arrows in Fig. 40 show the directions in which the two photographs of Fig. 41 were taken.                    *Photographs by the author.*

In their decoration of metal objects the pre-Roman people of Iron Ages 'B' and 'C' brought their culture to a very high level. Indeed, La Tène art is considered to have reached its climax in Britain (Figs. 42 and 43, p. 263). The enamelling of metal was invented and perfected by people regarded by the classical writers of antiquity as barbarians; and nowhere did the La Tène artists show greater skill than in the works of art produced in Great Britain,

42    *A small shield of gilt bronze, one of the finest examples of British Iron Age art*

The shield was probably made between 25 B.C. and A.D. 50. It was found in the River Thames at Battersea. The 27 small circles were all enamelled in red, and each was decorated with an anti-clockwise fylfot in brass (bright in the photograph). The gilding has not survived.
*British Museum.*

chiefly for the princes and nobility. The style of decoration had become freer, though still moderated by the classical tradition derived ultimately from the Mediterranean peoples. There resulted what has been described as 'one of the most masterly arts which Europe has known'.[481] Toynbee says that its 'glory' was 'the flowing, curvilinear, abstract, and often amazingly intricate designs adorning the splendid *de luxe* products of the metal-worker's craft. . . . No other group of late La Tène objects manifests more resplendently the creative genius of the British artist.'[1064] Navarro says of this art that 'at its best it was unsurpassed, and in independence and imaginative power unexcelled by the finest La Tène masterpieces which the continent has to show.'[788] J. and C. Hawkes[481] go so far as to say of the La Tène settlers in Yorkshire and Lincolnshire that they 'were responsible for the growth of a British school of decorative art which is one of the outstanding episodes in the story of our civilization'. The actual objects must be seen to be appreciated to the full. A fine example is reproduced in colour as the frontispiece to the old British Museum guide;[983] a photograph of the same object is shown here as Fig. 42. Good photographs of other specimens of the art are readily available in several books (see, for example, Plates XIII and XIV in *Prehistoric Britain* by J. and C. Hawkes[481]).

Such, then, was the state of affairs over a considerable part of Britain, in particular the south-east, when Julius Caesar landed.

An account of the history of these times has been provided by one of the authors who lay special stress on the influence of environment on human progress, and who minimize or deny the importance of ethnic differences. He tells us[36] of the primitiveness of the inhabitants of Britain when Julius Caesar landed in A.D. 52 and 'opened up ... the opportunities for cultural development'. If he had not done so, we are told, their development would have been greatly delayed. The Britons had been isolated from the main 'cultural fertilizing agents' until Caesar arrived, but all was now well and 'development followed with great rapidity'. Within a hundred years of his landing 'these selfsame savage Britons were well on the way toward the development of a civilization'. It is necessary to revise the impression conveyed by this account.

It will be remembered that Julius Caesar made his landings in Britain in 55 and 54 B.C., not in A.D. 52 (by which time he had been dead for 95 or 96 years). On the first occasion he landed with about 10,000 men somewhere between the sites where Walmer and Deal Castles now stand, on the coast of Kent. The Belgae put up an effective opposition. Caesar's men were unnerved—as he himself tells us—by the novel tactics of the defenders, who sent their cavalry and chariots in advance. Caesar was obviously much impressed by the charioteers. He remarks that they exhibited the mobility of cavalry combined with the steadiness of infantry. His first invasion was really a reconnaissance in force and he soon withdrew.[504]

On the second expedition, in 54 B.C., Caesar evidently intended to establish Roman authority in Britain. His army consisted of five legions and 2,000 cavalry, probably about 25,000 men in all. Eight hundred vessels set them ashore a few miles north of where he had previously landed. As he moved inland he found himself opposed by the formidable Belgic chief, Caswallon (Caesar's '*Cassivellaunus*'), and noted his adversary's tactics with respect. He tells us that the Britons did not fight in massed formation, but in groups separated by wide intervals; reserves were arranged, who relieved the combatants when necessary. The British soldiers stained themselves with a blue dye, presumably to incite fear in close fighting, rather as modern soldiers sometimes use horrific cries. Caesar's own words on the subject, in what is supposed to be the most accurate text, are as follows:[501] *'Omnes vero se Britanni vitro inficiunt, quod caeruleam efficit colorem, atque hoc horridiores sunt in pugna aspectu.'* ('All the Britons actually dye themselves with woad, which produces a blue colour, and from so appearing they are more terrifying in battle.') It is supposed by some authorities that the use of woad was general among the Britons,[1012] but in fact it seems probable that in this passage Caesar was referring only to the soldiers.

43　*A bronze mirror with handle, an example of British Iron Age art at its fully developed stage*

The photograph shows the back of the mirror, decorated with a typical curvilinear geometrical design. The mirror, which was found in a quarry at Desborough, Northamptonshire, was probably made about A.D. 15–20.
*British Museum.*

Caesar tells us that the people of Kent were the most civilized of the Britons. He nowhere states that any of the Britons were savage (*immanis*), nor does he speak specifically of their ignorance (*ignorantia*), though he does twice mention their indiscretion (*imprudentia*) in parleying.[501] He was under the impression that it was the custom among the Britons for a group of ten or twelve men to share a number of women as wives. It is not impossible that some of the hybrid communities (not Celtic or Belgic) in remote districts may have had a custom that gave rise to Caesar's statement. It has been supposed by some authorities that he may have been confused by the occurrence of matriarchy. The Belgae, who were the dominant group in the country invaded by Caesar and the people with whom he came into direct contact, did not practise group-marriage or polyandry.[506]

Caesar indicates that most of the people of the interior did not cultivate grain, but this means no more than that they were primarily pastoralists, and as a result naturally used skins for clothing.

On this expedition Caesar was able to penetrate beyond the lower Thames, but once again his stay was short. Some of the tribes opposed to Caswallon made submission, but the latter adopted guerilla tactics, and the invaders were insecure. Caesar was disturbed by serious news from France. He decided to relinquish his attempt at establishing himself in the island, and before the end of the summer his army had retreated to the ships and left its shores. Caesar never returned. His invasions had no effect on the culture of Britain. There had been Mediterranean influences on Iron Age culture centuries before Caesar was born, and they continued in Britain, on a limited scale, after he had gone; indeed, they were encouraged by the later Belgic kings;[1064] but Caesar himself achieved nothing in Britain for Rome apart from the imposition of a tribute that soon lapsed, and nothing at all for the inhabitants. Rome was without direct influence in the island until the Emperor Claudius came as conqueror in A.D. 43.

One effect of the submission to Rome was a severe setback to British art. Hawkes sums it up pithily: 'With the Roman conquest (from A.D. 43) the art became altered and diminished. . . . never quite extinguished even in Roman Britain, it was revived in new forms in post-Roman times.' The art of Roman Britain is described and lavishly illustrated in Toynbee's book;[1064] a convenient source for the post-Roman period is Chadwick's.[196]

The Iron Age invaders of Great Britain transmitted the dialects of their Celtic language to the more ancient Britons whom they found in possession of the land. They pushed back these less advanced peoples towards the west and north as they themselves spread across the country. To this day there is evidence of ethnic peculiarities in those who occupy the districts to which the dispossessed people were confined by the advance of the invaders. One of the most obvious distinctive features of these people is the colour of the hair. The geographical distribution of hair colour in the British Isles was studied in some detail towards the end of the nineteenth century by John Beddoe, who had devised a useful (if somewhat arbitrary) 'index of nigrescence'.[69] The index expresses in rather a roundabout way the proportion of dark-haired to light-haired people of the country, in his time. He prepared a detailed map, illustrating the distribution of hair-colour. It shows clearly that the tendency towards the possession of dark hair was much more marked in Wales than in England, and still more marked in the western districts of Ireland.

The general accuracy of Beddoe's map is confirmed by an investigation carried out some seventy years later,[1029] by methods involving the use of a recording spectrophotometer to establish the colours of a thousand specimens of hair, and substitution of modern statistical techniques for Beddoe's somewhat arbitrary method for translating his visual impressions into numbers. The latter's map of 1885 and Sunderland's of 1956 agree remarkably well, and both show clearly the high incidence of dark hair in Wales. The only sharp difference between the two maps reflects the ever-shifting population of London. Beddoe was mistaken in supposing that the peoples of Great Britain would become 'inextricably confused' in a single generation.

It is worth remarking that there is rather a high proportion of people with red hair in Wales, and that no fully satisfactory explanation of this fact has been provided.

Hair colour is only one indication among many that a Mediterranid element has persisted in Great Britain since Neolithic times. That this persistence has been particularly obvious in Wales was emphasized more than half a century ago by Fleure and James in a very long and detailed paper on the physical characters of the people of that country.[344] One need not suppose that any Welshman is descended from Mediterranid ancestors exclusively. It is evident, however, that genes of that subrace are more frequent in Wales than in most parts of Great Britain, and random (or more or less random) assortment of those genes will more often bring them together in a single individual, to produce a close approximation to a Mediterranid, in Wales than elsewhere. Plate I (Figs. 2A and B) in Fleure and James's paper provides a striking example of a Welsh Mediterranid head.

Recent work on blood-groups confirms the evidence about special elements in the ancestry of the Welsh people. In studies of this kind it is best to count the number of people belonging to each group in a random sample of the population and to calculate the gene-frequencies from the figures obtained (see pp. 186–7). For some purposes it is convenient to divide the frequency ($r$) of the gene making for the blood-group 'O' by that ($p$) of the gene for the group 'A'. For instance, in a particular population one might find these frequencies: $p$, 0·270; $q$, 0·082; $r$, 0·648. The quotient just mentioned, $r/p$, would then be 2·4. If the gene for 'O' is high and that for 'A' low, a high figure would necessarily result.

In most parts of England the quotient is about 2·4, but in north-western Wales the gene for 'O' shows a high frequency,[773] while that for 'A' is low.[774] The quotient thus rises to between 3 and 3·5. In the extreme south-west of Ireland it rises even higher, to more than 5·5. These figures give an indication of the extent to which a Neolithic population has transmitted its genes to the present-day population of these parts of the British Isles. The facts are well exhibited in a map of these islands showing the geographical distribution of the quotient. As the Swedish anthropologist Lundman remarks, '…it is obvious from this map that the old population-groups (those with high quotients) have been forced away into remote marginal zones'.[680] There is a remarkable (though not exact) correspondence between Lundman's and Beddoe's maps.

The gene for 'A' has a low frequency in many Mediterranean lands, especially North Africa, Corsica, Sardinia, the southern half of Italy, and Sicily. In some of these countries, especially Corsica and Sardinia, the gene for 'O' shows a very high frequency.[774, 72] The quotient in these parts of the world is therefore similar to that in north-western Wales. The results obtained in modern studies thus support the opinion that has long been entertained on other grounds, that the Neolithic population of Great Britain was of the Mediterranid subrace, and that people still living in north-western Wales and certain other parts of the British Isles have inherited a particularly high proportion of their genes from this ancestral stock.

At or near the beginning of the Bronze Age a very distinct new type appeared. These 'Beaker Folk' were taller, markedly brachycranial, and broad-faced, with rather wide noses. It seems impossible to place them with confidence in any of the existing subraces, though they were certainly Europids, and they have been regarded by some authorities as Dinarids.[512] The evidence from the round barrows of the Bronze Age suggests that they intermarried to some extent with their Neolithic forerunners, to produce at last a hybrid type having a skull strangely similar to that of the Iron Age invaders (Celtae and Belgae), though differing from it in the greater height of the cranium and wider face.[516]

It is often supposed that the Celtae and Belgae almost exterminated and replaced the population over a considerable part of Great Britain.[762, 510] It seems more probable, however, that Mediterranids and Mediterranid/Beaker Folk hybrids survived to form part of the modern British population, though the unhybridized descendants of the Celtae and Belgae continued to predominate greatly in certain places, especially the south-eastern part of England.[516]

At one time it was widely believed that the Iron Age people of Great Britain (the descendants of the Celtae and Belgae, intermixed and hybridized with Mediterranids and Mediterranid/Beaker Folk hybrids) were in their turn driven out to remote districts or slaughtered by the Anglo-Saxon invaders; but opinion has changed. It is considered that too much stress was laid by the historians of the past on the partial dying out of the Celtic place-names and language. Modern historians allow that while some withdrew to more remote districts and some were indeed killed by the Anglo-Saxons, others merged with the latter.[496] Physical anthropologists, relying on evidence provided by the skulls of ancient and modern times, consider that the descendants of Iron Age people of Romano-British times continued to occupy the country during the period of Anglo-Saxon domination, and were so far from being driven away or exterminated that it might almost be said that it was they who eventually absorbed the Anglo-Saxons, while adopting the language of their conquerors. On this view the present-day population of England and much of Scotland is to a very considerable extent derived from the Celtae and Belgae of the Iron Age.[640, 762, 510, 175, 516]

That the Anglo-Saxons were not simply exterminators of the people they found in this country is indicated by the strange evidence of a graveyard at East Shefford in Berkshire, which dates from the latter half of the fifth century A.D. This contained the skeletons of elderly Anglo-Saxon males, elderly females of a distinctly different ethnic taxon, and youthful intermediates. It seems almost certain that the elderly people were the parents of the intermediates. The skulls of the elderly females suggest that they were of the ancient Mediterranid/Beaker Folk stock.[829]

It has been claimed that the British people are 'one of the most mongrel of all the strains of the human race'.[1147] It is appropriate to examine this statement here.

Apart from some of the recent immigrants, who do not appear to have hybridized to any important extent with the native population of the country, the ancestors of the British people of the present day are Europids who have come in successive waves. Some of the minor incursions have been of little importance, for they cannot have left enough descendants to have had any significant effect on the genetic make-up of the British population as a whole. This applies, for instance, to the brachycranial people who arrived in advance of the main Bronze Age invaders. The Jewish immigrants of recent centuries, again, have not had very much genetic effect on the rest of the population, partly because they have not been very numerous, partly because they have tended to practise endogamy.

It has been stated that the English were 'a truly multiracial society' because there were Angles, Saxons, Jutes, Normans, Belgics, and 'flamboyant Celts' among their ancestors.[1179] The reader should note that all these peoples were not only of one race (Europid) but of one subrace (Nordid). Incidentally it is doubtful whether the Angles and Saxons were different peoples in any sense.[101]

It follows from what has been said that the English are far from being 'one of the most mongrel strains of the human race'. The facts can perhaps be best represented by use of a rough analogy. Let us suppose that a dog-breeder has been specializing in harriers (hounds for hare-hunting, an ancient breed). Let us suppose further that it occurs to him to mate some of his harriers with bloodhounds. He keeps his stock of harriers and makes a new hybrid breed of bloodhound-harriers. He gives some of each stock to a master of foxhounds. The master incorporates them in the breeding stock of his pack, and later introduces some otterhounds as well. Interbreeding for several generations eventually produces a varied but roughly homogeneous pack, all the ancestors of which were hounds of the long-eared group that hunts by scent.

No one, on seeing the pack, would say that these hounds were one of the most mongrel of all the strains of dogs. The man-in-the-street would simply say that they looked rather like foxhounds, while a huntsman would remark on the differences from typical members of the breed. The inexpert and the expert would *agree*, rightly, in describing a cross between a bull-dog and a greyhound, or between a Pekinese and a beagle, as a genuine specimen of one of the most mongrel of all the strains. Comparable examples could be quoted from mankind, but since the word 'mongrel' is disparaging when applied to man, it is far better to avoid it.

In the analogy just related, the Neolithic (Mediterranid) people are represented by the harriers; the Beaker Folk by the bloodhounds; the Iron Age invaders (Celtae and Belgae) by the foxhounds; and the Anglo-Saxons and other northerners by the otterhounds. Only the Beaker Folk were markedly different from the rest (though of the same race), just as the bloodhounds were among the dogs (though of the same group of breeds).

The people of a large part of Wales would be represented, in an analogy of this sort, by a pack of foxhounds to which the breeder of harriers had made a much bigger contribution of his unhybridized stock to the master of foxhounds than he did in the case just considered.

It is a remarkable fact that those in the British Isles who spoke a language derived from the dialects of the Iron Age invaders forgot the origin of their speech. They did not realize that it had been handed down to them from the people whom Caesar had called Celtae and Belgae, and for more than a millennium and a half it did not occur to anyone to call the language (in its various forms) 'Celtic', or the people who spoke it 'Celts'. It was a strange Scottish Latinist and humanist, George Buchanan (1506–82), at one time a prisoner of the Spanish Inquisition, who first revealed the facts. By studies of the classical authors, but especially of place-names, he reached the conclusion that the 'Galli' or people of central France in ancient times must have spoken a language similar to that used in his own country by particular groups of people. The salient passage in a long and detailed argument is this:

Iam tandẽ eò ventũ est, ut ex oppidorum, fluminũ, regionũ, & alijs id genus nominib' linguæ inter Gallos, & Britãnos cõmunionẽ, atq; ex ea veterem cognationem demõstremus. Lubricus sane locus, & diligẽter examinãdus.[157]

These words may be translated thus: 'Now at last it comes to this, that from the names of towns, rivers, districts, and so forth, we may demonstrate a fellowship of speech, and from that an ancestral relationship, between the Gauls and the Britons. To be sure, this is a slippery topic, to be examined with care.'

Buchanan uses the word 'Galli' to refer to those among the people of ancient France who spoke a Celtic language. However slippery the topic might be, he and his successors (notably the antiquarian Edward Llwyd in the next century) made their case secure enough. As a matter of fact, there is no reliable evidence that any of the Iron Age invaders of the British Isles called themselves Celts when they had established themselves there;[857] the dominant people in Great Britain were anyhow the Belgae, who would not have used the name of another nation. Nevertheless, after the studies of Buchanan and others had revealed the origin of languages used in certain parts of Britain, the romantic tendencies of the eighteenth century produced a fellow-feeling among those groups of persons, of whatever ethnic origin, who spoke a Celtic tongue. They began to call themselves Celts and to believe that they shared certain peculiarities in addition to their speech.[857] It is not necessary to stress the cultural differences that in fact existed and still exist.[214]

The Belgae and other related people who spoke the Brythonic or 'P-Celtic' tongue spread over most of the southern half of Great Britain, and where they met the more ancient inhabitants of the country they imposed their language upon them, with strange consequences. The ancient Neolithic or hybrid stock had no very close taxonomic relationship with the Brythonic-speaking invaders. To this day the ancient stock, more or less intermarried with Nordids, constitutes what Fleure and James called the 'fundamental type' of the Welsh population.[344] As Coon has pointed out, it is these people, the least Celtic—in the ethnic sense—of all the inhabitants of Great Britain, that have clung most obstinately to the language that their conquerors first taught them two thousand years ago.[226] In an interesting lecture on 'Genetics and prehistory', largely concerned with the ethnic evidence derived from blood-groups, the late Sir Gavin de Beer remarked, 'In ... Ireland, Wales, and Scotland, are found people with dark eyes and jet-black hair who have, completely erroneously, been spoken of as "Celtic".'[72]

The Brythonic speech and literature that still survive in the Basse-Bretagne district of Brittany are not to be regarded as a direct local relic of the language of Caesar's Celtae. The language appears to have been brought there by refugees from south-west England, fleeing from the Anglo-Saxon invaders. It resembles the Cornish more closely than the Welsh dialect.[767]

It will be clear from what has been said in this chapter that the word 'Celts' has been used with very different meanings. The archaeologist, basing his opinion on the objects buried with corpses or ashes, may apply the word to all or nearly all those who practised the Hallstatt culture, or to those who developed particular styles within that culture; or, on the contrary—and this is more usual—to those who developed and spread the culture of La Tène. The historian may use it for a nation that inhabited a part of what is now France, in ancient times; this is a political application of the term. The linguist may mean by it the very diverse peoples who use or have used a particular language or group of related dialects. The anthropologist may apply it to those people of the Alpinid subrace who formed part of the population of ancient France, or even to the Alpinid subrace in general; or, on the contrary, to those Nordids (perhaps slightly intermixed with Alpinids) who spoke a non-Germanic language, or to the people of a particular local form of the Nordid subrace, some of whom brought certain Iron Age cultures to the British Isles before the Roman occupation of Great Britain.

No one has the right to insist that the word 'Celts' must be used with the particular significance that happens to have his approval. In the anthropological sense—as opposed to the archaeological, political, or linguistic—it seems best to use it for the people who brought a culture of the Iron Age to Great Britain before the Belgic invasions, and to the continental stock from which they sprang. These people, like the Belgae, belonged to a 'local form' of the Nordid subrace (probably with some slight modification due to limited hybridization with Alpinids). The modern population of Great Britain probably derives mainly from the 'Celts' (in this sense) and Belgae, though a more ancient stock has left its mark rather clearly in certain parts of the country, and the Anglo-Saxons and other northerners made an additional Nordid contribution later on.

This book is not concerned with the question whether groups of persons practising particular arts, or speaking particular languages, or constituting particular nations, or occupying particular territories, are superior or inferior to others. It is concerned with the differences between the ethnic taxa of man, and with the ethnic problem.

## Epilogue

### VOLTAIRE ON THE BRITONS OF THE IRON AGE

'When Caesar crosses into England, he finds this island still more savage than Germany. The inhabitants scarcely covered their nudity with a few skins of beasts. The women of a district belonged equally to all the men of the same district. Their houses were huts made of reeds, and their ornaments were shapes that the men and women imprinted on the skin by pricking it and pouring on to it the juice of herbs, as the savages of America still do.'[1107]

# 16 The Australids
## (Australian aborigines)

INTRODUCTION

IN THE course of evolution a group of interbreeding individuals may become isolated from the rest of their kind. Their descendants, cut off from others of the same stock, may in certain cases fail to evolve further, or may make only limited advances. If they survive without much change, generation after generation, they may serve as a reminder of a stage in the evolution of more advanced forms. The problem of primitiveness in animals has already been discussed (pp. 124–9), in preparation for its application to human affairs in the present chapter. We are concerned here with the question whether there are any physical features in the Australian aborigines that suggest a stage in the evolution of more advanced taxa of modern man.

The subject is one that demands serious attention. Nothing would be gained by a superficial glance at a few features of Australid anatomy that might suggest relationship with prehuman ancestors. A considerable amount of detail is unavoidable if anything is to be attained, and this chapter is more technical than any other in the book. Nevertheless the intrinsic interest of the subject will perhaps make the presentation acceptable even to those who do not claim any special knowledge of human anatomy. It is hoped that the attempt to write intelligibly will not make the chapter tedious to others who have gained a solid background in the anatomical departments of medical schools. They may find interest and surprise in looking at a form of human life very different in many respects from the specimens ordinarily studied by medical students—and different in particularly significant ways.

Readers may find it helpful to refer occasionally to the abbreviated classification of the Primates in Appendix 2 (p. 540). It will be understood that all such classifications are provisional and subject to modification as knowledge advances. Different authors do not exactly agree on any particular arrangement, but the broad outlines of the classification used here would be generally approved in the existing state of knowledge. It must be remarked that the term 'anthropoid apes' is used by many authors as a non-technical term for the family Pongidae. The reader should note that it does not correspond to the Anthropoidea, which is a much more comprehensive taxon (a suborder). One must distinguish, too, between the hominoids (apes in the narrow sense, and men) and hominids (men).

Reference will be made repeatedly in this chapter to the primitive fossil hominids commonly known as 'ape-men', 'Java Man', and 'Pekin Man', because it will be necessary to consider whether there are any anatomical features in the Australids that suggest a closer relationship to these ancient forms than that shown by most races of modern man. Ideally one would begin by giving rather a full description of these fossils; but many readers in zoological and anthropological departments will already have the necessary knowledge, and some idea of the anatomy of the primitive hominids will anyhow emerge from the comparisons with Australids given in the present chapter.

Many readable accounts of the primitive hominids are available to those who want more information about them. For the Australopithecinae ('ape-men') one may turn to the popular account given by one of the foremost research workers on the subject, Dr. R. Broom, in his book entitled *Finding the missing link*,[144] or to the very clear account by Sir Wilfrid le Gross Clark in his *Man-apes or ape-men?*,[210] which has the rare merit of being readable by expert and non-expert alike. It must suffice at this point to say that the australopithecines were African hominids, whose long muzzles and small brain-cases made their heads very pongid (ape-like) in appearance, but who undoubtedly belong with the rest of us to the family Hominidae.

Java Man and Pekin Man, so called because their remains were found in the island and near the city bearing those names, were closely related to one another and much less primitive than the australopithecines. They are particularly important in relation to the subject of the present chapter. Readers who are unfamiliar with their anatomy (so far as it is known from their fossil bones) will be able to pick up a certain amount of information about them from remarks scattered through this chapter; but anyone who wants a short, consecutive description, with illustrations, may find it in an article in the *Scientific American*.[517] The British Museum (Natural History) provides a postcard showing front and side views of Pekin Man's skull, as restored under the direction of the foremost authority on the subject, Franz Weidenreich. The pictures are taken from the latter's very detailed monograph on the subject.[1128] One of Weidenreich's collaborators in China, Dr. G. H. R. von Koenigswald, has provided a short and informal but reliable and first-hand account of both Java Man and Pekin Man in his book *Meeting prehistoric man*.[602]

Many of the best authorities consider that Java Man and Pekin Man are sufficiently similar to one another and to modern man to be regarded as merely two races of a single species, *Homo erectus*.[972, 719, 227, 517] Others regard them as generically distinct from modern man and specifically distinct from one another, under the names of *Pithecanthropus erectus* (Java Man) and *P. pekinensis* (Pekin Man). This, however, is a matter of opinion, like many other problems in the taxonomy of fossil forms (see p. 70). As Ernst Mayr has remarked, in relation to the nomenclature of hominids in general, '. . . a taxonomist with a different viewpoint might arrive at a different classification'.[719] In what follows, the word *Pithecanthropus* will be used wherever reference is made to characters shared by Java Man and Pekin Man.

It follows from the discussion in Chapter 8 that a taxon is regarded as primitive if it retains physical characters that were possessed by remote ancestors but have been lost in the course of evolution by most members of the taxa that are related to it.

The fact that primitiveness is a relative term does not seem to have been kept in mind by all writers on human evolution. Thus, objection has been taken to the use of the term 'primitive' for pongid and cercopithecid characters possessed by certain ethnic taxa of modern man, on the ground that the Pongidae and Cercopithecidae are rather specialized mammals in some respects.[1153] There can, indeed, be no doubt that the Prosimii (lemurs and their allies), and especially the family of this taxon known as the Tupaiidae ('tree-shrews'), are much more primitive. Nevertheless, the objection cannot be sustained; for one might as well go back to the reptilian ancestors of the mammals and deny that the Tupaiidae are primitive, because their remote ancestors were more primitive still. In this chapter *degrees* of primitiveness will be recognized, and it will not be denied that any character is primitive merely because animals that were still more primitive did not possess it.

A very brief sketch of the probable ancestry of man will clarify the ideas expressed in the preceding paragraph. It will be understood that despite the remarkable advances made recently in ancient chronology, one can only give approximate statements of the periods that have elapsed since the various stages in the evolution of modern man were reached. The rough estimates of the periods will be expressed in years and enclosed within parentheses, with the accepted expression 'B.P.' (before present). ('B.C.' would suggest a far more exact knowledge of the periods than can possibly be attained in the present state of knowledge.) The reader will realize that anything concerned with the remote ancestry of man must be related rather dogmatically, if wordy reservations about debatable points are to be avoided. A long dissertation on the subject of man's evolution would neither clarify the special point at issue, nor serve the general purposes of the book.

It is probable that the Pongidae (pongids, anthropoid apes, or apes in the narrow sense) evolved from a group of Cercopithecidae (Old World monkeys) early in the Oligocene epoch (B.P. nearly 40 million). One cannot say with certainty which pongid fossil represents most nearly the ancestral form of man, but there is general agreement that *Dryopithecus, Ramapithecus,* and related forms were close to the ancestor. This group—the 'dryopithecine complex' of Simpson[972]—was first made known to the scientific world by Édouard Lartet (father of Louis, of Cro-Magnon fame[639, 47]). Fossil remains of an ape, probably larger than a chimpanzee, had been discovered in Miocene deposits at Saint-Gaudens in Haute-Garonne, southern France, and sent to É. Lartet for study. Only a humerus and three fragments of a lower jaw were available, but in describing it in 1856 Lartet had the prescience to remark that in the order of replacement of the teeth, it occupied an intermediate position between modern apes and man.[638] He considered it to have been arboreal, and therefore gave the generic name of *Dryopithecus* (meaning tree-ape). Seventy-one years later the American palaeontologists Gregory and Hellman, in a study of the dentition of *Dryopithecus,* traced back the human dentition to this ancient form, which they regarded as close to the common stem from which, in their opinion, modern pongids and man separately evolved.[436] Most members of the dryopithecine complex are known, like Lartet's *D. fontani,* only from lower jaws and other fragments, but a few relatives of the group, such as *Proconsul africanus* (from Kenya), have left more complete remains. Whether an intermediate form related to the chimpanzee may have intervened between these and the australopithecines is uncertain; but the latter subfamily of hominids appeared in early Pleistocene times, (B.P. $1\frac{1}{2}$ million), to be followed by *Pithecanthropus* (B.P. 1 to $\frac{1}{2}$ million) or some as yet unknown but closely related form (or forms), ancestral to modern man.

If, now, it appears that an ethnic taxon of modern man retains characters that were possessed by *Pithecanthropus* but are not retained by other taxa of modern man, the former taxon is to be regarded as *primitive* in that respect, whether or not the characters in question were shown by australopithecines or by more remote ancestors. It will be understood that such characters were

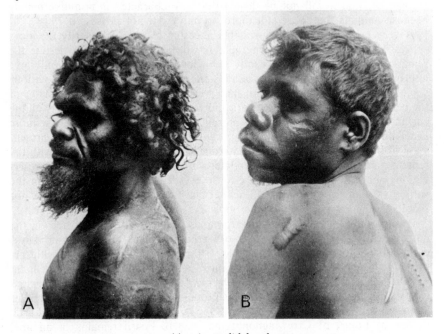

44   *Australid heads*

The photographs represent aborigines of the Gilbert River district, northern Queensland.
*Photographs from Hutchinson, Gregory, and Lydekker.* [530]

formerly possessed by the ancestors of all the more advanced taxa of modern man, but have been lost by them in the course of evolution. Certain taxa of modern man do in fact show characters that are no longer retained by more advanced taxa, but were possessed by pongid and even cercopithecid ancestors. These characters are clearly evidence of a *greater degree* of primitiveness than those that only extend back to the pithecanthropine stage. The facts may be expressed thus. If two ethnic taxa of modern man differ in this respect, that one of them retains pithecanthropine, australopithecine, pongid, or cercopithecid characters that are no longer possessed by the other, the former taxon is *primitive* in relation to the latter. A taxon may also be primitive in the more limited sense that it frequently (though not usually) exhibits primitive characters that are seldom or never exhibited by another taxon. which is more advanced in this respect.

It is sometimes easier to recognize pongid and cercopithecid than pithecanthropine and australopithecine characters in modern man, because perfect skeletons of present-day apes and monkeys are readily available, whereas the fragments of fossil man are incomplete and often imperfectly preserved, so that the finer details of their structure (such as the exact course of the sutures between the bones of the skull) are difficult to determine. Another difficulty with fossil men is that there are not enough of them to give us a clear picture of the frequency of secondary characters, some of which, found among the Australids, are of special interest. Again, we have no knowledge of the soft parts of *Pithecanthropus* or *Australopithecus*, except where they have left their impress on the bones; but all parts of the anatomy of apes and monkeys are available for comparison with those of Australids.

It is appropriate at this point to call attention to an aspect of human evolution that has tended to be overlooked. It is believed that modern man originated from *Pithecanthropus*, but two different opinions are held about the way in which the change came about. In the opinion of some authorities, one of the species of *Pithecanthropus* (or, in other words, one of the races of *Homo erectus*) evolved into *Homo sapiens*, which subsequently split up into the races of modern man. According to the other view, which has been marshalled in a most interesting way by Coon, [227] the various races of modern man originated from different species of *Pithecanthropus* (or, in Coon's terms, from different races of *Homo erectus*); and they came to resemble one another by *independent* evolution of those characters that distinguish the races of modern man from his remote ancestors. Thus, for instance, it is argued that Java Man gave rise to the Australids, and Pekin Man to the Mongolids. If this were true, the resemblances between the Australids and the Mongolids, which cause taxonomists to place them in the single species *Homo sapiens*, must be due *not* to the inheritance of the shared characters from a single ancestral form, but to *parallel evolution from separate stocks*, neither of which possessed the characters that they eventually came to share. This is not a subject on which it is desirable to dogmatize in the present book, though it is perhaps not irrelevant to mention that I myself doubt whether parallel evolution has in fact occurred in this case. If, however, there are ethnic taxa of modern man that possess in common certain characters that were not inherited from a common ancestor, but evolved separately in the several stocks by independent evolution, then it would be contrary to the rules of nomenclature that are universally accepted by zoologists to group them all under a single name, *Homo sapiens*; for the members of a taxon are placed in that taxon *because* their shared characters are thought to be derived from a common ancestor *which possessed them*. The zoologist is always on the look-out for examples of parallel, independent evolution, and he immediately divides a taxon into new taxa with different names, as soon as it has been clearly shown that similar groups of animals have actually evolved separately.

An example of parallel or convergent evolution that is particularly well known among zoologists is provided by the marine gastropods familiarly known as 'sea butterflies'. In these molluscs the 'foot'—primarily a crawling organ—is drawn out on each side of the body into a flat lobe, which is flapped like a wing in swimming. The gastropods that possessed these wings were formerly grouped together as 'Pteropoda' (wing-feet). Many of them were obtained by the naturalists of H.M.S. *Challenger* during the oceanographic voyage of that vessel in the years 1873–6, and Paul Pelseneer, an authority on the Mollusca, undertook to describe them. Careful examination showed clearly enough that 'wings' had evolved independently in two separate taxa of the order Opisthobranchia, and the remarkable resemblances between them were not due to inheritance from a common ancestor. 'The Pteropoda', he wrote, 'are polyphyletic in their origin.... they have not a common origin.... Henceforth, therefore, we should abstain from making a distinct class of the Pteropoda, but should rather distribute the animals which have been called by this name among other groups, according to their natural affinities.'[833] He did this, and his conclusions have been accepted ever since. The 'Pteropoda' have disappeared, except in writings on the history of zoology.

## THE TAXONOMY OF THE AUSTRALASIDS

Several distinguished anthropologists classify the Australids in a taxon that includes the Melanesians and Papuans, and also—though with some hesitation—the extinct Tasmanians.[293, 302, 227] It is thought probable that the Australids represent best the original stock from which the others may have diverged by hybridization, though the ancestry of the divergent groups remains obscure. A Mongolid element has been suggested on evidence from blood-groups,[227] but little support for this view can be gained from anatomical studies. It remains to be discovered how the Melanesians and Papuans came to possess quite a high frequency of the gene for the 'B' blood-group, which is altogether lacking in Australids (except in those local forms that are thought to have hybridized in the past with Melanesians or Papuans). The anatomy of the Australids will be considered in some detail below, and it will suffice here to mention very briefly some of the characters that are shared with the other minor taxa. The Tasmanians seem to stand somewhat apart from the others, and are not brought so easily under a single definition.

As a general rule the members of the major taxon are dolichocranial, platyrrhine, and prognathous, with narrow, retreating forehead and large supra-orbital ridges; the skull as a whole is 'ill-filled', being flat-sided and somewhat keeled on top (Fig. 51, p. 297). The sphenoid bone makes only a short suture with the parietal, or the two bones are separated by junction of the frontal with the temporal (see Fig. 28 and pp. 298–300). The lower border of the apertura pyriformis is commonly orygmo-craspedote or amblycraspedote (pp. 282–6).

The nasal bones are particularly characteristic (Fig. 45A). The naso-frontal suture is curved (generally more so than in the photographed specimen), with the convexity upwards; and both the frontal and the nasal bones are turned inwards in the immediate vicinity of the suture, so that the latter seems to lie at the bottom of a little trench. This makes the vicinity of the suture a striking feature of the skull, even when the latter is viewed from a distance. A few millimetres below the suture the nasal bones are narrowed and below this widened out again, so as to give the two bones together an appearance that has been compared to that of an hour-glass (though it would be a very wide-waisted one). The nasal bones project forwards more than they do in Negrids.

The stature is moderate. The black scalp-hair is neither very long, like that of Europids, nor very short, as in Negrids and Sanids (Bushmen). It is usually either curly or 'frizzy', but typically not 'woolly' like that of the two last-mentioned peoples. The skin is dark brown.

In the Rhesus system of blood-groups the complex CDe ($R_1$) is very high (one of the very marked differences from the Negrids).

There are obvious differences between most Australian aborigines and most Melanesians in external features, especially in the characteristic form of the hair, the former being mainly wavy-haired and the latter provided with a mop of frizzy hair; yet even in this respect there is overlap, some Australids having hair that verges on the frizzy, and some Melanesians having more loosely curled locks than the rest. The skulls are remarkably similar. Anyone, after a few minutes' instruction, could tell a Nordid's skull from an Alpinid's; but even an expert would hesitate to say that he could always tell an Australid's from a Melanesian's at a glance, or even, in some cases, after careful study.

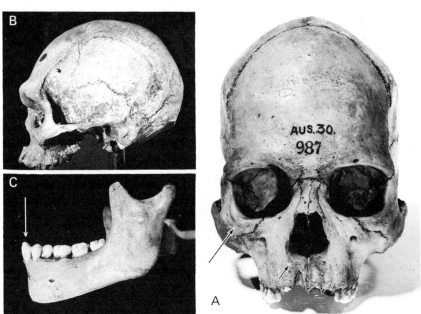

45   *Australid skulls*

A, facial view, to show especially the roof-like cranial vault, the rounded outer margin of the orbit (long arrow), and the orygmocraspedote lower border of the nasal aperture (short arrow). B, lateral view; the specimen was chosen to show the strongly developed brow-ridge and very receding forehead. C, lower jaw, to show the vertical (not projecting) chin and the large teeth. (The projecting canine tooth (arrow) of this specimen is referred to on p. 289.)
*The specimens are in the British Museum (Natural History). A is no. AUS.30.987; B, AUS.440; C, AUS.50.994. Photographs by the official Photographer of the Museum.*

The peoples whose most obvious common characters have been briefly mentioned above form a taxon sufficiently distinct from other human taxa to
qualify as a subspecies (race), but it would not appear that anyone has definitely applied to this taxon a name in the Linnean system that obeys the *International code of zoological nomenclature*.[1014] The rules are rather difficult to
apply in this particular case, but *'australasicus* Bory, 1825' is used in this
book. For the common name I suggest 'Australasid'. The reader is referred to
Appendix 3 (p. 541) for an account of the reasons for regarding *australasicus*
as the correct name for the race, and for dividing it into three subraces, namely
*australasicus* (common name Australid, the Australian aborigines), *melaninus*
(Melanesid, the Melanesians and Papuans), and *tasmanianus* (Tasmanid, the
Tasmanians). The two latter subraces are seldom mentioned in this book. (See
also the table of races and subraces at the end of the book.)

It is generally agreed by all who have studied the question that the
Australids scattered over a vast area of Australia (New South Wales, Victoria,
and South Australia, with the adjoining parts of Queensland, the Northern
Territory, and Western Australia) are very uniform in their physical
characters. Certain authorities, however, recognize special 'types' in other
parts of the range. They assign the Australids of the region designated above to
'type A', and separate off as 'type B' those who inhabit the northern parts of
the Northern Territory and the adjacent region of Western Australia.[763]
Others, who also recognize 'type B', regard the aborigines of the coastal districts of Queensland as sufficiently different from the others to be distinguished
as 'type C'.[326] There are, indeed, peculiarities in these regions, almost certainly
caused by hybridization with Melanesids, and perhaps others; but there are no
generally accepted names for the three 'types', and the differences are so small
that the Australids may be regarded as essentially homogeneous.


THE PRIMARY CHARACTERS OF THE AUSTRALID SUBRACE

An attempt will now be made to describe the 'typical' Australids, from the
point of view of the physical anthropologist.

Except where the contrary is stated, the description will refer, throughout the
chapter, to the adult male. The reader is asked to keep this in mind. The male
sex has been chosen because among the Australids, as among most other
ethnic taxa of man, it reveals the differences from other taxa more clearly than
the female.

Our knowledge of Australid anatomy is 'patchy'. About some parts of the
body the wealth of information is formidable. This applies in particular to the
skull, which has been described in great detail. One author alone, for instance,
has reported very minutely, and obviously very accurately, the results of his
researches on 1,182 Australid skulls.[326] Many other authorities who have
examined very large numbers of Australid skulls will be quoted in the general
description given below. A good deal is known about the rest of the skeleton,
the blood-groups, and the external characters; but our knowledge of the soft internal parts is very incomplete. It might perhaps be desirable to offer rewards

to Australids who would bequeath their bodies for anatomical study, if this suggestion could be made without causing them offence.

In describing the ethnic taxa of man, authors usually begin with an account of the external appearance; but the skull is much more important in human taxonomy, because it provides more information of a precise and varied nature, and allows detailed comparison with the same part of the body in fossil forms. The human skull was described first in the chapter on the Europids, and the same arrangement will be adopted here. Many Australians and most others have never seen an Australid, and although the reader has probably seen photographs of them, he may find it convenient at this point to refresh his memory by examining Fig. 44A and B. The external characters are described on pp. 295–8 and 301–2.

*Skull.*—The description of the skull given here is based on a full study of the original authorities, with some additions of my own.[49, 166, 167, 276, 518, 586, 587, 613, 692, 707, 708, 742, 743, 763, 1062, 1072, 1076, 1152]

The *brain-case* is massive. The bones of the cranial vault (frontal, parietal, temporal, and occipital) are probably thicker, on the average, than those of any other ethnic taxon of modern man. They often reach 10 mm and more, while in most other races the thickness is generally about 5 mm. In this respect the Australids equal *Pithecanthropus*. Not only are these bones thick; they are particularly heavy, because the spongy part (diploë) in the interior of each bone (between its outer and inner surfaces) is largely replaced by compact bone. As Klaatsch remarked, 'The thickness and sometimes wonderfully developed strength of the cranial bones, offer such resistance against violence as to astonish every investigator.'[587]

The capacity of the brain-case is small, about 1,290 ml on the average. The corresponding figure for the skulls of the Anglo-Saxon invaders of Great Britain was about 1,540 ml;[762] of Pekin Man about 1,075 ml; Java Man's is estimated at only 860 ml.[1128]

The skull generally appears long-ovoid when viewed from above; there is often an occipital bulge, similar to that of Pekin Man. The cranium is 'ill-filled'. In facial or occipital view one notices the elevated sagittal ridge running longitudinally along the top, and the flat surfaces on each side of it, falling away like the low-pitched roof of a house; below this roof the sides are flat and vertical, like walls (Fig. 45A). In many cases the greatest breadth of the cranium is situated very low, so that the flat 'walls' actually slope outwards below. This is a typically pithecanthropine character, unusual in modern men of other races.

One of the most obvious features of the Australid skull is the strong development of ridges on the external surface of the brain-case. The brow-ridges (superciliary ridges) are usually prominent and often continuous with one another across the glabella. Rather strong transverse ridges are present in the occipital region. The superior nuchal line and occipital protuberance are sometimes so powerfully developed as to constitute what is called an 'occipital torus',[742] but this is unusual. As a rule the superciliary and occipital ridges are less developed in the female, but huge development of them has been described in a skull known to have been that of a woman.[166] The supramastoid crest is also strongly marked in Australian aborigines. The temporal lines and all the muscular impressions, especially those on the occipital bones, are well developed. The general ruggedness of the brain-case, and above all the prominence of the superciliary ridges, are reminiscent of *Pithecanthropus*, and indeed of the larger pongids.

Some authorities have suggested that superciliary ridges evolved separately in pongids and hominids, from more primitive forms that lacked them altogether. This belief was fostered by the discovery in the Transvaal in 1925 of the first australopithecine, to which Professor Raymond Dart gave the name of *Australopithecus africanus*;[250] for this young specimen lacked the ridges. When the skulls of adult australopithecines were found, they were given a new specific name, *transvaalensis*, and some students of the subject put them in a new genus, *Plesianthropus*. Nowadays, however, it is usual to regard the forms previously known as *Plesianthropus transvaalensis* as adults of *Australopithecus africanus*. The ridges are well seen, for instance, in an illustration published by Dr. Robert Broom,[143] who had been the first to find adult australopithecines. They are even larger in what appears to be another species of the same genus, *A. robustus*. It seems, therefore, that the large brow-ridges of Australids should be regarded as one of the many primitive characters that link them through *Pithecanthropus* and the australopithecines with some of the larger apes.

It has already been mentioned that *Dryopithecus* and most of its close relatives are known only from lower jaws and teeth. The skull of one of them (*Proconsul africanus*), however, is complete in the front part of the brain-case, and it is known to have lacked brow-ridges; but this was a small, lightly built ape, and one cannot assume that it was typical of Miocene and Pliocene hominoids. [209]

Particularly huge superciliary ridges evolved independently in the male gorilla among apes and in Broken Hill man[866] among human beings, but this does not exclude the probability that less developed ridges were present in the remote common ancestor, at any rate in the male.

Despite the projection of glabella and occiput, the Australid skull is not exceptionally long, as a rule, the mean length being about 188 mm; but its narrowness results in a cranial index of only 71, on the average. This is nearly but not quite what is called a 'hyperdolichocranial' figure. Cases of extreme dolichocephaly have from time to time been reported. Turner measured an Australid skull 200 mm long and only 123 mm broad.[1072] This gives the astonishing figure of 61·5, which is well beyond the limit of the hyper-dolichocranial and ranks as 'ultradolichocranial'. It does not, however, constitute the most extreme example of dolichocephaly known in the subrace. Miklouho-Maclay,* a reliable observer, described an Australid skull, stated by him not to have been artificially deformed, that was 204 mm long and only 119 mm wide.[743] Thus the cranial index was 58·3, one of the lowest ever recorded in any human taxon. Pekin Man had a cranial index of about 72, and Java Man was also dolichocranial. The Australids have retained the primitive

---

* Miklouho-Maclay's name was spelled thus in papers written in English, but 'Miklucho-Maclay' in those written in German.

character of dolichocephaly, and so, indeed, have many other ethnic taxa of modern man, including the Nordids and certain other Europid subraces, though generally to a lesser degree.

The mean height of the skull is rather low, but not excessively so. In this respect the Australids do not approach the condition in *Pithecanthropus*. The forehead recedes markedly, however (Fig. 45B), and in this respect the Australid skull is nearer to the pithecanthropine condition.

The frontal region of the skull is narrow.

The distance between the left and right asterions, expressed as a percentage of the breadth of the skull, is greater than that of any other living taxon of man. [763] This is no doubt related to the fact that the skull is wide below and relatively narrow higher up—a primitive character.

The mastoid processes are rather small. This is sometimes described as a primitive character, because these processes are lacking in most pongids, and when they do occur in rudimentary form, they contain no air-cells. [1002] However, their small size in Australids can scarcely be regarded as primitive, since they were not particularly small in Pekin Man. [1128] In this ancient form, however, the mastoid processes projected downwards and inwards instead of directly downwards, as is usual in most taxa of modern man. There is a tendency to this inward direction in the mastoid processes of the Australids.

The sutures of the brain-case are rather simple, especially the pars obelica of the sagittal (which tends to be simpler than the others in all taxa). Wormian bones are frequent, especially in the lambdoid suture.

The temporal fossae are deep. The greater wings of the sphenoid bone give the appearance of having been scooped out deeply with a finger-tip.

The *zygomatic arches* give the impression of projecting widely (Fig. 45A). The mean bizygomatic breadth is slightly greater than the greatest breadth of the brain-case, and when one looks down on the skull from above, one sees considerable spaces between the frontal bones and the arches. The facts are attributable, however, to the narrowness of the brain-case, especially in the frontal region, rather than to particularly wide separation of the zygomatic arches from one another.

The *facial part of the skull* is characterized by marked prognathism. This is an easily observed primitive feature, possessed also by *Pithecanthropus* and to a still greater degree by the australopithecines and pongids.

For many purposes the best measure of prognathism is the *Ganzprofilwinkel,* that is to say the angle made with the standard (Frankfurt) horizontal plane by a line joining the nasion to the prosthion. The mean figure for Australids quoted by Martin and Saller is 76·8°. [708] This is the lowest (i.e. represents the greatest degree of prognathism) of all the figures quoted for total prognathism by these authors among the various ethnic taxa of man. The prognathism of the region below the nose (alveolar prognathism) averages 66·6°, so that this part projects even more acutely than the upper part of the face.

It was claimed by Thomson and Randall-Maciver at the beginning of this century, in their study of ancient Egyptian skulls, that the basion–nasion line is a better basis for the measurement of prognathism than the standard horizontal plane. [1046] The 'nasion angle' subtended at the nasion by the lines joining this point to the basion and the prosthion, was used by Morant in various biometric studies,[762, 763, 764] and was strongly recommended as a measure of prognathism by Weidenreich, who used it in his classical work on Pekin Man.[1128] The *greater* this angle, the higher the degree of prognathism. He gives 100° as the average for modern pongids; 81° for Java Man; 72° for Pekin Man. Morant found 72·1° from his measurements of 44 Australid male skulls of the typical 'A' group.[763] He found the mean nasion angle in skulls from 15 western European ethnic taxa to be 65·0°;[764] in those from sixteen Anglo-Saxon burials in England and Scotland, 62·1°.[762]

The canine fossa of the maxilla is deep in Australids (though not deeper than in some Nordid skulls).

The *nose* is one of the most interesting parts of the Australid skull. A deep depression at the root is very characteristic. It is emphasized, but not wholly caused, by the projection of the glabella. The nasal bones are short, and do not project very far; they are concave in profile view and thus present roughly the shape of a saddle. They are slightly wider at their upper and lower ends than in the middle. The pair of them together thus gives the characteristic 'hour-glass' appearance, already mentioned (pp. 276–7), (Fig. 45A).

The nasal aperture (apertura pyriformis) of the male Australid is on the average 27·3 mm from side to side at its widest part, and the height of the nose (measured in the standard way) is 48·8 mm.[518] These figures give a nasal index of 56, which places the nose in the chamaerrhine category, and not far from the hyperchamaerrhine. The nose of Pekin Man was a little wider still (30 mm) but also higher (52·5 mm);[1128] this gives a nasal index of 57·1, close to that of the Australids and still just within the chamaerrhine range. The upper (wider) limit of the narrow (leptorrhine) nose, characteristic of many Europids, is only 46·9. The broad nose is one of the more obvious primitive characters of the Australids.

It must be remarked that the height of the nose, on which the nasal index depends, is taken by some authors from the nasion to the nariale, by others from the same point to the subspinale; but the difference between the two measurements is so small as to be negligible for most purposes.

There are astonishing features about Morant's statistical data on the width of the nose in relation to its height. He measured the standard height (Frankfurt nasal height, nasion to nariale) of only *three* male Australid skulls, and obtained a mean (52·3 mm) that is considerably above the average for male Australids as a whole; and beyond this he made a mathematical error in calculating the nasal index from this figure, thus obtaining an even lower nasal index (49·2) than his figure for height would have given.[763] Hrdlička measured the nasal heights of 2,384 male Australids from all parts of Australia and obtained the mean given above (48·8 mm); this, taken in conjunction with his measurements of the breadth of the nose in 1,333 specimens, gave the index quoted (56).[518] It is scarcely credible but nevertheless true that Morant also made an error in calculating the nasal index of male Anglo-Saxon skulls.[762] From his figures it would follow that both Australids and Anglo-Saxons were mesorrhine, whereas in fact the former are chamaerrhine and the latter were leptorrhine. These serious errors seem not to have been pointed out previously.

Even more obvious than the relative breadth of the nose, to anyone looking even casually at an Australid skull, is the lower border of the nasal aperture (apertura pyriformis). This feature is so important in relation to the subject of primitiveness that it is necessary to discuss it at some length. It is one of the skeletal characters that have been called 'non-metrical'*.[1153, 326] The reader who does not want to study it in great detail may at least glance at the photographs labelled A, C, and D on Fig. 46 (p. 284). They represent the nose and surrounding parts of the skull of a Nordid (A), an Australid (C), and an orang-utan (D). The photographs were taken at an oblique angle, because it shows the significant features particularly clearly. In the Nordid, the sharp lateral edge of the nasal aperture is continued across at the bottom of it as an upstanding ridge that joins the projecting anterior nasal spine (*ans*) in the middle line, and thus distinctly separates the nasal cavity (*nc*) from the sloping surface of the maxilla (alveolar slope, *as*) that runs down towards the teeth. This arrangement, which occurs in the great majority of Europids (pp. 207 and 216), is called *oxycraspedote*[693] (Greek ὀξύς, sharp; κράσπεδον, border). Fenner[326] never found the oxycraspedote arrangement in his study of 1,182 Australid skulls.

In the Australid skull represented in photograph C, there is no such sharp separation. The lateral edge of the nasal aperture fades out as it reaches the level of the bottom of the nasal cavity. The region where the separating ridge exists in the Europid appears to have been excavated and eliminated. This condition is called *orygmocraspedote* (Greek ὄρυγμα, excavation). The nasal floor flows, as it were, into the alveolar slope, without any clear line of demarcation. The Australid skull represented in Fig. 45A is also orygmocraspedote. This type of lower border is characteristic of most pongids and cercopithecids, and occurred also in the ape-man, *Australopithecus africanus*.[250] It is well seen in the orang-utan skull represented in Fig. 46D.

The anterior nasal spine is generally feebly represented in Australids, and double at its tip (Fig. 46C, *ans*). Cases have been recorded of its complete absence in skulls of this subrace.[465, 538] It is present in Java Man, but not in Pekin Man[1128] nor in young *Australopithecus africanus*.[250] It is 'quite distinct', though small, in adults of what is probably the same species ('*Plesianthropus transvaalensis*').[145] In pongids there is usually no spine, but it is sometimes present in rudimentary form, with double tip.[465, 662, 418, 930] The rudimentary condition can be seen in the orang-utan's skull shown in Fig. 46D.

It has frequently been stated that the orygmocraspedote structure is correlated with prognathism, but among Australid skulls one can find specimens that are orygmocraspedote though not prognathous. It has also been stated that the nasal spine

---

* The expression 'non-metrical' does not mean that the feature in question cannot be measured, for objects of every conceivable shape are capable of being measured, and the results expressed in mathematical terms that define the shape exactly. In fact, however, there are certain anatomical features that differ strikingly from one ethnic taxon to another, but which would require an enormous expenditure of time and energy for their full expression in numerical form. If anyone wishes to do so, and has the necessary mathematical knowledge, he can express the facts about the lower border of the nasal aperture in that form; but no one has done so, because it seems that nothing would be gained when the facts are so obvious and so easily and effectively expressed 'non-metrically'. Those who use non-metrical methods are as ready as anyone else to measure, wherever this process does not involve waste of time. Those who rely solely on measurements often overlook obvious differences between one ethnic taxon and another, because they concentrate their attention on those parts of the skeleton that happen to be the most easily measured.

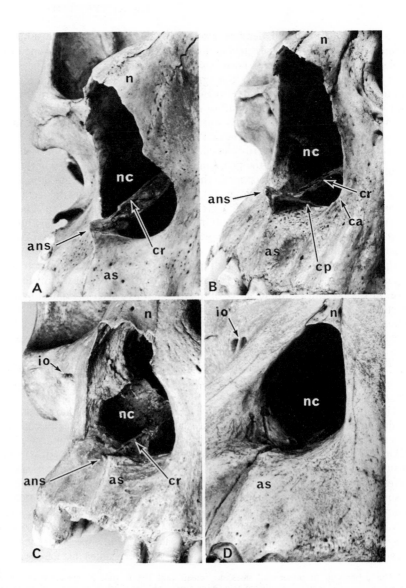

46   *The structure of the lower border of the nasal aperture (apertura pyriformis) in human and pongid skulls*

A, Nordid form (oxycraspedote); B, Australid (amblycraspedote); C, Australid (orygmocraspedote); D, orang-utan (orygmocraspedote). *ans,* anterior nasal spine; *as,* alveolar slope; *ca,* crista anterior; *cp,* crista posterior; *cr,* nasal crest of maxilla; *io,* infra-orbital foramen; *n,* nasal bone; *nc,* nasal cavity.
A, B, *and* D *are in the Oxford University Museum and* C *in the Department of Human Anatomy at Oxford.*
A, *skull marked 'Z';* B, *836b;* C, *AUS.20.2. Photographs by Mr. J. Haywood.*

is only fully formed in orthognathous skulls, but some Australids show a well developed spine despite strong alveolar prognathy. Examples are quoted in Appendix 4 (p. 543).

One might take leave of the lower border of the apertura pyriformis at this point, and say that Europids are usually oxycraspedote, while Australids tend to resemble pongids and cercopithecids in being orygmocraspedote; but the facts are so significant, and yet so incapable of complete expression in such simple terms as those, that some readers will be glad of the more precise presentation that now follows.

In some Australids there are are no cristae at the lower border of the apertura, and in this respect there is a resemblance to the orygmocraspedote condition; but the horizontal floor of the nasal cavity ends rather suddenly at the top of the alveolar slope, instead of merging gradually into it. The floor then looks rather like a parapet surrounding a fort. This structure, not previously named, may be called *epalxicraspedote* (Greek ἔπαλξις, parapet) From Weidenreich's descriptions (1943) it would appear that both Java Man and Pekin Man had epalxicraspedote skulls.

Another type, the *bothrocraspedote* (Greek βόθρος, trench) is found in several taxa of man, especially the Mongolids, and above all among Malayans. This type is illustrated by the nose of a Sumatran, shown in Fig. 47. Here the floor of the nasal cavity is separated from the alveolar slope by two ridges, called by von Bonin[124] the *crista posterior* (*cp*) and *crista anterior* (*ca*), with a trench or *fossa praenasalis* (*fp*) [1172] between them. The crista posterior, which looks like a lateral outgrowth from the nasal spine, runs obliquely backwards and outwards in a curve to join the turbinal bone at the lateral wall of the nasal cavity. It is sometimes double (two parallel cristae, very close to one another). The crista anterior is an inward continuation of the lateral edge of the apertura pyriformis. It runs across in a wide curve to join the nasal spine.

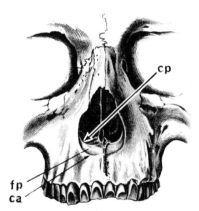

47    *Facial skeleton of a Sumatran, to show the bothrocraspedote lower border of the nasal aperture (apertura pyriformis).*

*ca*, crista anterior; *cp*, crista posterior; *fp*, fossa praenasalis.
*From Zuckerkandl;*[1172] *lettering by the author.*

Among various ethnic taxa of man one frequently finds skulls in which the lower border of the apertura pyriformis has maintained into adult life the form that is usual in embryos or infants of most human taxa. This form is related to the bothrocraspedote, but the crista posterior extends only a short distance outwards from the spine, fading out on the floor of the nasal cavity, and the crista anterior reaches only a short distance inwards towards the middle line, fading out on the alveolar slope. This stunted or incomplete arrangement of the cristae is called *amblycraspedote* (Greek ἀμβλύς, blunt). It occurs in some adult Australids, and is shown in Figs. 46B and 48A. Indications of it can be detected in some skulls that must be classified as orygmocraspedote (Fig. 46C).

In the true oxycraspedote form the lateral border of the apertura pyriformis turns towards the middle line as a sharp, upstanding crest that joins the medial part of the crista posterior and thus links up indirectly with the nasal spine. About one-fifth of all Australid skulls possess what has been called a 'pseudo-European' lower border,[326] but will here be called *pseudo-oxycraspedote*. This differs markedly in appearance from the other, because the continuation of the lateral border towards the middle line is not a crest but a low ridge that sweeps round in a wide curve, generally making direct contact with the nasal spine without any intervention of the crista posterior. The latter in fact, nearly vanishes.

The orygmocraspedote, amblycraspedote, and bothrocraspedote types merge into one another by intermediates. The bothrocraspedote has occasionally been recorded in pongids,[930] and, strangely enough, in two species of seals (*Phoca*). [708]

Of the 111 Australid skulls (complete and incomplete) in the British Museum (Natural History) and the Departments of Zoology and Human Anatomy at Oxford, the structure of the lower border of the apertura pyriformis could be determined in 98.[49] The results of the investigation showed that the great majority are orygmo-, ambly-, or epalxicraspedote; that is to say, there are no ridges separating the nasal floor from the alveolar slope, or if there are any, they are very imperfectly developed. This is a pongid and cercopithecid character. For full analysis of the 98 specimens, see Appendix 5 (p. 544). (See also Appendix 4, p. 543.)

The *orbits* are interesting in several respects. Professor William Turner, in his *Challenger* Report,[1072] seems to have been the first to remark on the unusual form of their outer (lateral) borders in Australids. He noted 'a peculiar breadth and curvature of the malar [zygomatic] bone where it formed the boundary [of the orbit], which wanted the sharpness one sees in crania generally, so that in taking the transverse diameter of the orbit there was a difficulty in deciding on the exact point on which the calipers should be placed'. This characteristic feature of the adult Australid male is well seen in Figs. 45A (long arrow) and 47A. The outer border of the orbit is not preserved in any of the parts of Java Man's skull that have so far been discovered, and the zygomatic bone of Pekin Man is only known from three fragments of it. Weidenreich's description and illustrations suggest that the outer margin of the orbit was rather sharper than it is in typical male Australid skulls, for the latter usually show a smooth curvature in this region, strongly reminiscent of the corresponding part in australopithecines and pongids.

The orbital plate (lamina papyracea) of the ethmoid bone, forming part of the inner (mesial) wall of the orbit, is notably shallow in vertical height, especially in front, where it makes a short suture with the lacrimal bone (Fig. 47A). The ethmo-lacrimal region is

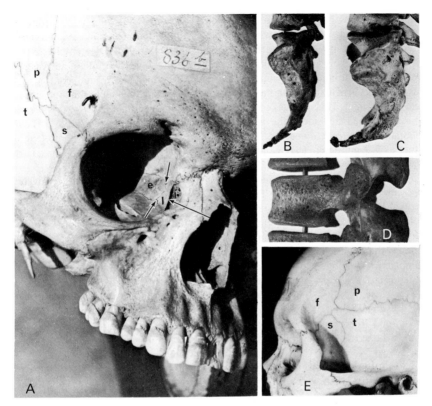

48   *Skulls and vertebral columns, to illustrate special points in the anatomy of Australids*

A, the skull of an Australid, to show especially the ethmolacrimal suture and the posterior lacrimal crest.

B, sacrum (with coccyx) of an Australid. C, ditto, of a Europid, for comparison with B. D, the third lumbar vertebra of an Australid, viewed from the left side.

E, skull from Celebes (thought to be of the Toala tribe, regarded by some as 'Australoid'), to illustrate the fronto-temporal pterion. *e*, ethmoid; *f*, frontal; *l*, lacrimal; *p*, parietal; *s*, sphenoid; *t*, temporal.

In A the short arrows indicate the ends of the ethmo-lacrimal suture: the long arrow points to the edge of the posterior lacrimal crest.

*All the specimens shown in this figure are in the Oxford University Museum. A is no. 836b; B, 987a; C, 988; D, 987a; E, 775. Photographs by the author (A), Mr. D. Turner (B, C, and D), and the official Photographer of the British Museum (Natural History) (E.).*

very fragile, and no part of the skull is more frequently found to be broken in museum specimens. One hundred skulls of Australids of both sexes in the collections of the British Museum (Natural History) and the Departments of Zoology and Human Anatomy at Oxford were examined to find the mean length of the ethmo-lacrimal suture. Of the 200 left and right sides of these skulls, only 44 were sufficiently intact for the accurate measurement of the ethmo-lacrimal suture. The lengths were taken in a straight line, from one end of the suture to the other. The mean length was only 7·9 mm (standard deviation of mean, 2·1; extremes, 3·2 mm and 12·8 mm).[49] In certain cases, however, more extreme reduction of the anterior end of the orbital plate of the ethmoid bone has been recorded. Turner described three Australid skulls, from Victoria and Western Australia, in which the plate actually terminated in a point anteriorly, so that the ethmoid barely articulated with the lacrimal. [1072] He emphasized the apelike nature of this arrangement. Duckworth [293] gives a photograph of an Australid skull in the Anatomical Museum at Cambridge in which the frontal bone actually makes a short articulation with the maxilla in this position, thus separating the ethmoid from the lacrimal. This happens commonly in the chimpanzee and gorilla. In a drawing (to scale) of the inner side of the orbit of an adult ape-man, *Australopithecus africanus* ('*Plesianthropus transvaalensis*'), Broom and Robinson represent the ethmo-lacrimal suture as 7·9 mm long. They emphasize the variable arrangement of the bones in this region among pongids. [145]

The posterior lacrimal crest does not appear to have been mentioned previously in descriptions of Australid skulls. This is the vertical bony ridge that projects from the lacrimal bone and forms the posterior support of the tear-sack (saccus lacrimalis). In various ethnic taxa of man it often extends only a short distance upwards from the lacrimal hooklet (hamulus lacrimalis). It is commonly broken in museum specimens. Among the skulls of both sexes that were examined for peculiarities in the ethmolacrimal region of the orbit, only 68 sides were sufficiently intact for study of the posterior lacrimal crest. In 58 of these it extended right up to the fronto-lacrimal suture, or very close to it (Fig. 48A). [49] The crest has not been described in *Pithecanthropus*. The drawing of the skull of *Australopithecus africanus* ('*P. transvaalensis*') given by Broom and Robinson suggests that in this form it extended nearly to the top of the lacrimal bone. [145] Among the pongids it is very variable, but in many cases poorly represented.

The *palate* of Australids is very long, no doubt in relation to prognathism. Its area is greater than that of any other ethnic taxon of man except the extinct Tasmanians.

The *lower jaw* (Fig. 45C) is rather massive, exceeding in weight that of an average Englishman by about one-tenth, but it does not approach the bulkiness of Pekin Man's. The chin scarcely projects, but does not usually recede strongly, like Pekin Man's.

For comparison with fossil specimens it is best to express the angle of inclination of the chin by measurement of the angle subtended by the incision-gnathion line with the alveolar line (since fossil mandibles do not usually form part of skulls that are sufficiently intact for the establishment of the Frankfurt horizontal). In the baboon, with very receding chin, this angle is only 40°; in recent pongids, 44°–54°; in Pekin Man and Heidelberg Man, about 60°; in Australids, 74·5°. In other races of modern man it sometimes exceeds a right angle. [1127] (It is to be remembered that the most prominent point of the chin is usually far in front of the gnathion, and the chin may therefore project strongly when the angle measured in the way described is considerably less than a right angle.)

In the Primates the recession or projection of the chin varies with age. [1121] In monkeys (both Ceboidea and Cercopithecoidea) it recedes when first laid down in the embryo and remains in this condition throughout life. In the young pongid, on the contrary, it is nearly vertical to the horizontal plane of the skull, but recedes in the adult. In most taxa of modern man it is nearly vertical at first, but projects in the adult. It is significant that in Pekin Man the chin angle (measured as in the preceding paragraph) is greater in the young than in the adult. [1127] The chin of Australids is primitive, since it usually does not project or scarcely projects in the adult, but in this respect it is not nearly so primitive as in the australopithecines and Pekin Man, especially the latter, in whom it recedes strongly.

It is a curious fact that in some specimens of the siamang, *Symphalangus syndactylus*, a pongid of the Malay Peninsula and Sumatra, the chin does not recede in the adult, but remains nearly vertical. [121]

In Heidelberg Man and Pekin Man the lower border of the horizontal part or 'body' of the lower jaw is more nearly parallel with the upper or alveolar border than in modern man, and the ascending part or ramus more nearly vertical (that is to say, leans backwards less, from its junction with the body). In both these respects the typical Australid inclines somewhat towards the primitive condition. In Heidelberg Man the mandibular notch (between the coronoid and condylar processes) is very shallow; it is rather shallow also in Pekin Man and the Australids.

The *teeth* of Australids are large. It is stated that in adult Australid males the mean area of the crowns in the upper jaw is 1,536 square mm, and that the corresponding figure for Englishmen is only 1,286. [692] The large size of the teeth is one of the primitive characters of the Australids, shared by the early hominids. So also is the position of the lower incisors in relation to the upper, when the mouth is shut. In the typical Australid (though not in every specimen) the upper and lower incisors meet one another without overlap, as in cercopithecids, pongids, *Australopithecus*, and *Pithecanthropus*, whereas the upper incisors project forward beyond the lower in most ethnic taxa of modern man. The incisor teeth are commonly somewhat procumbent in Australids.

In Australids, as in australopithecines and *Pithecanthropus*, the canine teeth do not ordinarily project beyond the level of the others. It is stated, however, that those of the upper jaw have very long roots. [586] On the occasional projection of canine teeth in Australids, see Appendix 4 (p. 543) and Fig. 45C.

The *hyoid arch* of Australids does not appear to have been very fully described. The stylohyal cartilage usually ossifies as a styloid process that becomes attached, as in other races of modern man, to the pars tympanica of the temporal bone. Generally, however, this process is rather small or even rudimentary in Australids, and more fully ensheathed by an outgrowth of the temporal bone than is usual in other races. (See p. 300.)

A list of particularly interesting Australid skulls in certain British collections is given in Appendix 4 (p. 543).

*Skeleton apart from skull.*—Two British anatomists of the nineteenth century, Professor D. J. Cunningham and Professor Sir William Turner, made outstanding contributions to our knowledge of the postcranial skeleton of the Australian aborigines, especially of the vertebral column, which is the part of greatest interest in connection with the question of primitiveness.

It had long been supposed that the vertebral column of apes differed from that of man in showing no forward curvature in the lumbar region. This had been stated by Goodsir in 1862, in a lecture given to the anatomy class in the University of Edinburgh, and subsequently published. [420] T. H. Huxley knew that in skeletons of young gorillas and chimpanzees, prepared without removal of the ligaments, the lumbar part of the spinal column was, in fact, slightly convex forwards;[535] but the whole question of the supposed differences between man and apes in this respect, and the structure of this part of the body in the Australids, required to be cleared up. Cunningham and Turner reached essentially the same conclusions, and each published two articles on the subject in 1866.

Instead of relying on prepared skeletons, Cunningham froze a number of corpses of Europeans, apes, and monkeys, and divided them in the median plane with a saw.[237, 238] He at once saw that the curve of the spinal column in the lumbar region was not, in itself, a distinctive feature of any particular taxon; the forward curve was manifest, for instance, in the chimpanzee.

The main or central part of each vertebra is the *centrum,* which is essentially a thick disk of bone, with two nearly flat surfaces. These, however, are seldom quite parallel with one another in hominoids, for the centra are generally thicker either dorsally or ventrally; that is to say, on the side directed towards the back or towards the belly. The thickness of each vertebra may easily be measured at its dorsal and ventral sides, and the departure from parallelism of the two flat surfaces thus established. If the upper and lower surfaces of the intervertebral disks were parallel to one another, and the dorsal and ventral measurements of the centra were the same, the vertebral column would necessarily be straight; but if the dorsal side of each vertebra were thinner than the ventral, there would be a convexity of the column towards the ventral side, and conversely.

Cunningham realized that the actual shape of the vertebral column, in the lumbar or any other region, did not by any means depend wholly on the parallelism, or lack of it, between the two flat surfaces of each centrum; for the intervertebral disks differed sufficiently in the thickness of their dorsal and ventral sides to affect and even reverse the curvature that the bony centra alone would have produced.

To determine the contribution of the bony centra towards the curvature of the spinal cord in the lumbar region, Cunningham measured the thickness of each of the five lumbar centra on the ventral side, and added these thicknesses together; he then did the same with the dorsal sides, and expressed the sum of the latter as a percentage of the former. He named the resulting figure the 'lumbovertebral index'. If it were 100, the vertebrae would cause no tendency towards ventral or dorsal convexity; if less than 100, the centra would tend towards convexity of the vertebral column in the lumbar region on the ventral side; if more, on the dorsal.

In the vertebral columns of 76 Europeans, he found the lumbo-vertebral index to be 95·8, on the average; in other words, it was clear that the shape of the centra contributed towards the ventral convexity of the spinal column in the lumbar region. In the pongids he measured the five vertebrae above the sacrum in the same way, for comparison with man, and obtained these mean figures: 4 orang-utangs, 107·1; 9 chimpanzees, 117·5. Since even in these pongids the lumbar convexity of the spinal column as a whole was *ventral,* despite the fact that the lumbo-vertebral index exceeded 100, it was clear that the thickness of the intervertebral disks on the ventral side was sufficient to outweigh the superior thickness on the dorsal side, which, if they had been separated from one another by parallel-sided disks, would have produced a dorsal convexity. Thus in the pongids the shape of the centra *detracted from* (but did not abolish) the ventral convexity of the lumbar part of the vertebral column.

We come now to the crucial point. Does the lumbar region of the Australid spinal column show any resemblance to that of the apes? Cunningham was able to examine the lumbar vertebrae of seventeen Australian aborigines. His mean figure for the lumbo-vertebral index was 107·8. In his own words, '. . . the European lumbar vertebrae are moulded in accordance with the curve [of the lumbar region of the spinal column], while the corresponding vertebrae of the low races are not'.[237] He refers also to 'The striking manner in which the European stands apart in this respect [lumbo-vertebral index] from his lower brethren, and also from the anthropoid apes'.[238] The third lumbar vertebra of an Australid is viewed from the left side in Fig. 48D. The upper and lower flat surfaces of the centrum of this vertebra are 22·6 mm apart on the ventral side (at the left of the photograph) and 24·8 mm on the dorsal. Thus the lumbo-vertebral index of this vertebra (without reference to the others in the series) is 110.

Turner made some similar observations when on a visit to the Oxford University Museum. He was shown an Australid skeleton that had been mounted by a technician, Charles Robertson, in 1873. The latter had articulated it by reference to the shape of the centra only, without thought of the intervertebral disks, and as a result it showed ventral concavity in the lumbar region.[1075] The specimen (no. OC 836 *a*) is still in the Department of Zoology at Oxford, exactly as Robertson mounted it. In his *Challenger Report* Turner gives the mean lumbo-vertebral index of twelve Europeans as 96·0, and of five Australids as 106·0.[1073] It will be noticed that these figures agree well with Cunningham's. The high lumbo-vertebral index of the Australids thus appears to be a primitive (pongid) character, in the sense of the word 'primitive' explained on p. 273. (The pongids are not primitive in this respect in relation to their own ancestors.)

The sacrum of the Australids is as interesting as the lumbar part of the vertebral column. As in man, so also in the chimpanzee, gorilla, and orang-utan, the sacrum consists of five coalesced (anchylosed) vertebrae; but in these pongids it is much narrower in proportion to its length, and less concave on the ventral side. It was noted by Richard Owen in 1862 that the sacrum of the Australid is less concave ventrally than that of Europeans, but more concave than that of apes.[815] The form of the Australid sacrum was more fully studied by Turner, who measured its breadth and length and expressed the former as a percentage of the latter.[1074] In European males this 'sacral index' was known to be about 112, but the sacra of the Australid males measured by him were considerably narrower in relation to their length. His mean figure for these was 98·5; for orang-utans, 87; chimpanzees, 77; gorillas, only 72. Lateral views of Australid and Europid sacra are shown in Fig. 48B and C, to show the more pronounced concavity of the latter (C).

It has been suggested that, in races regarded as primitive, the spines on the cervical vertebrae are not bifid at their tips, like those of Europeans.[293] This would be a pongid character. The vertebrae in question are presumably the unspecialized ones, nos. 3–6. Actually one can find Australid skeletons in which some of these spines are bifid and others not, and exactly the same state of affairs in skeletons of Europeans.[49] There does not appear to be any reliable distinction in this respect.

The length of the radius of the arm in Europeans, expressed as a percentage of that of the humerus, is about 73·4 (mean of many measurements by several authors). The radius of Australids is proportionately longer, giving a radio-humeral index of about 76·5,[1074] but there are other ethnic taxa (Negritos, for instance), in which the index is still higher.

It is claimed that the talus, calcaneus, and cuboid bones of the foot are less developed in Australids than in certain other races of man, regarded as more advanced.[1019] If so, this would be a pongid character; but the facts do not seem to have been established by observations on a sufficient number of specimens.

*Internal organs other than skeleton.*—It has already been mentioned (p. 278) that our knowledge of the internal organs is very incomplete.

The *brain,* like the skull, is a particularly significant part of the body in the study of human taxonomy, because it is of such definite and complex form that it gives many opportunities for the discovery of anatomical differences between ethnic taxa. Rather formless or diffuse organs, such as the pancreas, are unlikely to provide many independent characters by which the ethnic taxa can be distinguished (unless, indeed, such characters can be discovered at the histological or cytological level). Unfortunately not very many Australid brains are available for study. Until more material has been obtained, the possibility must remain that a considerable part of the following account would have fitted more appropriately into the part of this chapter that deals with secondary characters. It is at least clear, however, that the brain is smaller than that of Europids, for this follows from the relative cubic capacities of the skulls. Australid brains that have been weighed amount to about 85% of the normal Europid organ.

The gyri (convolutions) of the cerebral hemispheres are said to be simpler in arrangement[914] and less tortuous[293] than those of Europeans.

It appears to be quite usual for the central sulcus to approach very closely, or actually to join, the lateral sulcus (either directly, or through a branch joining the postcentral).[744, 914] This is very rare in Europeans.

Very interesting peculiarities have been described in the occipital lobes of the cerebral hemispheres of Australids, though more specimens must be examined before it can be stated with confidence that the typical Australid possesses them. In some of the Cebidae, and apparently in all the Cercopithecidae and Pongidae, there is a very evident crescentic furrow, the sulcus lunatus, visible in the occipital lobe of the cerebral hemisphere (Fig. 49A). This is produced by the extension of the visual area, on each side of the calcarine sulcus, round the posterior end of the hemisphere from the mesial to the lateral side of the brain, and then forward in such a way as to push the visual area over and

beyond the position of the original sulcus and thus convert it into a sulcus operculatus. This overgrowth, which has been compared to part of the rim of a
mushroom,[980] leaves a deep, crescentic furrow between itself and the more
anterior part of the occipital lobe. Since this was thought to be one of the
striking features that distinguished the brains of apes and monkeys from that of
man, it was called the *Affenspalte* (monkey-cleft).

Gustav Retzius, neurologist son of the Swedish physical anthropologist,
claimed that an 'analogy' to the *Affenspalte* could be found in the brains of certain Europeans,[898] and Elliot Smith[979] claimed that seven of Retzius's
drawings support the latter's contention; but examination of the particular
figures specified by Smith does not confirm this, with the single exception of
Retzius's Plate XLVIII, fig. 4. The lunate sulcus does indeed occur in the
brains of Europeans, but as Sir Arthur Keith remarks, when it is recognizable
at all it is always placed considerably further back than in the apes;[576] or, to
put the matter in other words, the visual area does not extend nearly so far
round the posterior end of the occipital lobe on to its lateral surface. The visual
area is marked by a thin layer of white fibres, and its limit can therefore be easily determined on dissection. The external characters of the human cerebral
hemispheres are somewhat variable from one individual to another, but in an
attempt to provide a drawing of a typical arrangement of the sulci in the brain
of a European in lateral view, it would be appropriate to omit the lunate sulcus,
or to include a small one situated far back, as in Fig. 49C.

Elliot Smith himself made a detailed investigation of this subject, using the
brains of Fellahin (Aethiopids) and Negrids as his research material. Among
these he found a remarkable range in structure, culminating in the well
developed sulcus lunatus operculatus of the pongid type. Although he found
that a remnant of the pongid and cercopithecid condition was 'a fairly constant

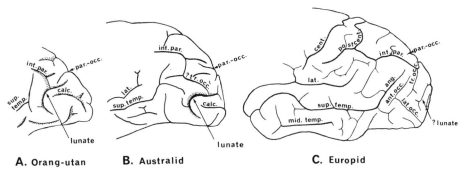

**A. Orang-utan**    **B. Australid**    **C. Europid**

49    *The posterior parts of the cerebral hemisphere of an orang-utan* (A), *an Australid*
(B), *and a Europid* (C)

*ang.*, angular sulcus; *ant.occ.*, anterior occipital; *calc.*, calcarine ('retrocalcarine'); *cent.*, central (Rolando's);
*int.par.*, intraparietal; *lat.*, lateral (Sylvius's); *lat.occ.*, lateral occipital; *mid.temp.*, middle temporal; *par.-occ.*,
parieto-occipital; *postcent.*, postcentral; *sup.temp.*, superior temporal; *tr.occ.*, transverse occipital.
A. *after Smith,*[980] *redrawn and lettered by the author; B. after Duckworth,* [293]*ditto; C. original, drawn
from specimen no. 913 in the Department of Zoology, Oxford. A represents part of a right hemisphere; the
drawing has been reversed for easy comparison with B and C.*

feature' in these brains, he allowed that a dwindling of the operculate condition was carried to an extreme degree in the brains of most human beings, and indeed that in many cases the area striata was 'wholly relegated to the mesial surface' of the hemisphere.[979] This will be confirmed by anyone who looks at a random collection of pongid and European brains in a museum. The sulcus lunatus is a striking distinguishing feature of the former.

For the structure of the brain in fossil hominids one must rely on evidence from endocranial casts. It is claimed by von Bonin that in man the occipital lobe is so closely invested by membranes that it would be impossible for any cast of the cranial cavity to reveal the situation of the sulci in this part of the brain, and for this reason he rejects the claims that have been made to describe the lunate sulcus in australophithecines and *Pithecanthropus*.[125] Nevertheless, those who have studied the casts have felt fairly confident that the positions of the chief sulci can be determined. Professor Raymond Dart claimed to detect the lunate sulcus in *Australopithecus africanus*, 'thrust backwards towards the occipital pole by a pronounced general bulging of the parieto-temporo-occipital association areas'. He reached this conclusion from his study of a deposit inside the skull, which had taken the form of an endocranial cast.[250] Sir Arthur Keith, however, considered that Dart had identified the sulcus incorrectly. In Keith's opinion the lunate sulcus was further forward, in the pongid position.[576] Schepers, working on an artificial endocranial cast of an adult *A. africanus* (called by him *Plesianthropus transvaalensis*) reached a conclusion similar to Dart's. The indentations in the parieto-occipital area suggested to him that the sulcus lunatus lay 'well back to the cerebrum'.[939]

Endocranial casts appear to have revealed the presence of a lunate sulcus on the right side of the brain in Java Man, but unfortunately the wording of the reports does not make the position perfectly clear. According to Eugène Dubois, the discoverer of Java Man, it was situated 'above the internal asterion';[290] Kappers says that its position 'corresponds with the top of the lambda suture'.[570] These statements seem to indicate that the sulcus in question was situated in the vicinity of the upper part of the lambdoid suture; that is to say, further back than in the apes, but anteriorly to the position it usually occupies when it occurs in modern man.

The reader will have surmised that the lunate sulcus has been treated rather thoroughly in the preceding paragraphs because it is of special significance in Australid anatomy, and this is indeed so, though the available information on the subject is sparse. Four brains of Australids in the Cambridge University Anatomical Museum were examined by W. L. H. Duckworth, who reported on the occurrence and position of this sulcus in considerable detail.[293] A sulcus lunatus of typical pongid type was found in two of the four specimens. One of them, copied from Duckworth's drawing, is represented in Fig. 49B. The resemblance to Fig. 49A (orang-utan) is obvious. A small but distinct operculate lunate sulcus was identified in another specimen.

In one of the specimens the sulci in the occipital lobe could not be identified with certainty. In another, which was poorly preserved, a small sulcus lunatus operculatus could be distinguished on the left side. In a third, the occipital lobe was damaged on the right side, but a perfectly clear sulcus lunatus, pongid in size, position, and operculation, was present on the left (Fig. 49B). In the remaining brain there was a similar sulcus lunatus on both sides.

It is desirable that as many Australid brains as possible should be examined to find out whether the *Affenspalte* occurs in the majority of the Australid population, and may thus be listed with confidence as a primary character of the taxon.

If a new supply of Australid brains became available, it would be useful also to make a special study of the insula of Reil. In most human brains this area is covered over by the lips of the lateral sulcus; but in some Australids it is exposed to view, as in pongids.[293] There is not enough evidence to show whether this is a primary character.

The *a*-glands of the Australid skin have already been mentioned briefly in Chapter 10 (pp. 170–71). These glands are so small that they have been studied mainly by histologists rather than anatomists. It is possible that further study will reveal interesting differences between the ethnic taxa of man at the histological level, but the most promising material for preliminary studies is certainly provided by organs that are visibly complex. Eventually, however, gross structure will give place to the excessively minute; for some of the most important differences between one ethnic taxon and another are likely to be discovered in the distant future at the ultrastructural (electron microscopical) level.

*External characters.*—The account of the external appearance given here is based on the writings of several authors, but the important contributions of Howells[516] and Abbie[2] must be specially mentioned.

The average stature is about 165–170 cm. The trunk is short and the legs exceptionally long, with the result that the sitting height, expressed as a percentage of the stature, is remarkably low.[261] The body is slender, as a rule; the shoulders and the hips (of women as well as men) are narrow. The buttocks are small, the upper leg slender, and the 'calf' of the lower leg feebly developed.[1019]

It is stated that the big toe and the 'ball' under the metatarsal-phalangeal joint are small, and that the lower surface of the foot is not strongly arched on the inner side, so that the whole of the sole tends to be planted flat on the ground in walking. These features are regarded as adaptations to enable the foot to be used effectively in climbing and grasping.[1019] Whether this is so or not as a general rule, it appears that Australids do use the foot for grasping to an extent that is unusual in other races.[560]

The 'third eyelid' or plica semilunaris is represented in Europids by a small fold beneath the caruncle at the inner angle of the eye (Fig. 26, p. 209). Vogt stated in 1863 in his *Vorlesungen über den Menschen* that this structure is larger in Australids, and similar in relative size to the corresponding part in apes.[1105] Darwin called attention to this in his book *The descent of man*.[258]

The breasts of Australid women are said to be of the type called 'primary', *'Euterbrüste'*, or *'mammae areolatae'*;[1019] that is to say, the areola or modified region surrounding the nipple does not conform to the curve of the rest of the breast, as it does in Europids and Mongolids, but is raised up into a projecting dome (cf. Fig. 50, p. 296).

The appearance of the head is shown in Figs. 44 and 51. The great eyebrow-ridges, the sunken orbits, and the deep notch at the root of the nose are well seen in Fig. 44. The prognathy and retreating forehead are best seen in Fig. 44B. The mouth is wide, but the lips not particularly thick. The nose is also wide, and the nostrils transversely elongated. The ear is large (Fig. 51), but provided with a rather small lobe.

50    *The breast of a Caroline Islander (Micronesia, Western Pacific)*

A pronounced example of the 'primary mamma' (Martin and Saller)[708] or 'mamma areolata' (Stratz den Haag).[1019]    *From Finch.*[329]

The flattened sides of the head sloping up to the mid-line like the roof of a house are well seen in the photograph of the hairless man (Fig. 51). This was taken in 1880 by Miklucho-Maclay,[741] who made a laborious journey into the interior of Queensland to find and study him and one of his two hairless sisters. Miklucho-Maclay carefully washed him all over, but could find not a single hair anywhere on his body except four in one nostril and a few short eyelashes, widely separated. Unfortunately no reliable pedigree was available to throw light on the genetics of this extraordinary family, the members of which were normal in every other respect. The man, named Aidanill (meaning 'go back'), was rewarded for his patience under detailed examination, but resolutely refused to permit a specimen of his skin to be taken for microscopical examination, even under general anaesthetic. He was so apprehensive on the subject that Miklucho-Maclay promised that he would not take a specimen. In the evening Aidanill spent his reward on alcoholic refreshment, and became so drunk that a fragment of his skin could easily have been obtained; but Miklucho-Maclay kept his promise. It would have been interesting to know whether there were any hair follicles (without hairs) in Aidanill's axillae, in view of the fact that both he and his sister had strong body-odour (see Chapter 10).

Typically, the scalp-hair is wavy (Fig. 44A), but in some cases nearly straight and in others 'frizzy' (cf. p. 277). It is oval in section, the least diameter amounting to about 70% of the greatest. In these respects, and also in area of cross-section, the hair resembles that of Europids and differs from that of Negrids and Mongolids.[1068] In the form of their scalp-hair the Australids and

Europids are primitive. The fact that the latter are pongid in the character of their hair was brought home very effectively to the African explorer Du Chaillu, the first European to study the gorilla in its native habitat. He had often jokingly told his Negrid companions that they shared their black colour with the apes; but one day, when a young chimpanzee had been captured, they neatly turned the tables on him by pointing out with roars of laughter that its face was white and its hair straight, like his.[200] Pruner-Bey, the first person to undertake a detailed study of the shape of human hair in transverse section, more than a century ago, remarked on the strong resemblance between a young gorilla's and that of Europids.[862]

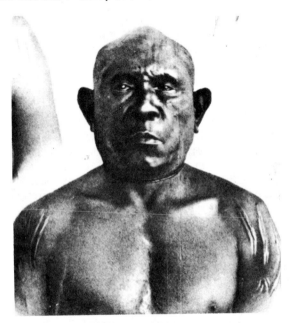

51   *A hairless Australid of southern Queensland*

*Photograph from Miklucho-Maclay.* [741]

It is often wrongly supposed that Australids have abundant body-hair. Some elderly males are hirsute, but this is unusual.[2] It is uncommon for Australids to have hair on the chest or hands. The facial hair of the male is similar in abundance to that of most Europids (Fig. 44A).

The colour of the hair is typically dark brown or black. True albinism is unknown in the taxon.

The skin is generally dark brown, but a tinge of colour from the blood may be observable. In naked infants full pigmentation is reached at the age of three years, except in the mucous membrane of the mouth and in the glans penis, which darkens later.[2] Skin that has been protected from the sun throughout life is not much darker than that of many Europeans. F.1 hybrids between

Australids and Europeans scarcely differ from the latter in skin-colour;[391] and when these hybrids intermarry with Europeans, their progeny are indistinguishable from Europeans in this respect.[393] Australids differ markedly from Negrids in most of the features mentioned in this paragraph.

The iris of the eye is dark brown or nearly black, the sclera somewhat yellowish. Dark spots on the skin caused by dermal melanocytes (p. 158) have not been observed.

The finger-prints of Australids (all digits combined) show a high percentage of whorls and a very low percentage of arches. Whorls actually reach 77·6% in Arnhem Land (Northern Territory),[235] but the figure is lower in Western and Central Australia.[874, 875] Among the Australids as a whole, the number of arches expressed as a percentage of the number of whorls is probably lower than in any other taxon of mankind.[235] It is considered by some authors, though not by all, that complexity of finger-prints (that is to say, a high percentage of whorls) is a primitive character in man.


SECONDARY CHARACTERS

*Skull.*—The pterion is the region at each side of the brain-case where parts of the frontal, parietal, temporal, and sphenoid bones are close to one another. Readers who are not familiar with the anatomy of this part of the body may care to refer to Fig. 28C, where the sutures separating these bones are clearly seen. Differences in the arrangement of the sutures at the pterion in the various races of man and in other Primates are the subject of a large literature.[30, 31, 34, 219, 220, 326, 873, 930, 1061]

It happens occasionally that the four bones meet at a point to produce a 'point-type' pterion, but this is so rare that it need not detain us. In the great majority of mankind the greater wing of the sphenoid bone articulates with the parietal at the pterion, and thus prevents the squamous part of the temporal from touching the frontal. This arrangement, which is seen in Figs. 28C and 48A, is called 'spheno-parietal'. In other human beings, especially among ethnic taxa regarded as primitive, it sometimes happens that the pterion is 'fronto-temporal'; that is to say, the squamous part of the temporal articulates with the frontal and thus separates the sphenoid from the parietal (Fig. 48E).

Most of the fossil skulls of early hominids were not excavated in a sufficiently complete and well-preserved condition for accurate study of the pterion. In skulls nos. XI and XII of Pekin Man the arrangement was spheno-parietal;[1128] but far more material is necessary before one can form any judgement about the presence of a fronto-temporal articulation as a possible secondary character.

The fronto-temporal pterion occurs invariably (so far as is known) in the Sumatran orang-utan, very nearly always in the gorilla, and nearly always in the chimpanzee; but curiously enough, the spheno-parietal is commoner among the orang-utans of Borneo.[219] Both types of pterion are to be found among the gibbons (*Hylobates*) and cercopithecids.

Reports have been made on the arrangement of the bones at the pterion in an enormous number of skulls of many ethnic taxa of man. The figures in the accompanying table will serve as examples. The evidence suggests that the frequency of the fronto-temporal pterion may be highest of all among the Melanesians of the western Pacific Ocean, and indeed in the island of Malekula (Mallicolo) there may perhaps be more fronto-temporal than spheno-parietal skulls;[293, 930, 34] but it is probable that artificial deformation of the head in infancy plays a part in this particular island.[34] The Papuans of New Guinea are often quoted as presenting an extremely high proportion of fronto-temporal skulls, but the very extensive data of Anutschin*[31] and Ranke[873] do not support this. Abundant information is available about the pterion of Australids and Negrids. These races show much higher frequencies of the fronto-temporal arrangement than most other taxa. There is no evidence that artificial deformation plays any part here. The fronto-temporal pterion is rarer in Europids than in any other race of man. The figures given in the table suggest that it occurs more than seven times as frequently in Australids as in Europids. The question naturally arises whether this secondary character is to be regarded as a pongid survival.

*Table showing the occurrence of the fronto-temporal pterion in certain races of man*

| Race | Number of skulls examined | Number of skulls with fronto-temporal pterion on one or both sides | Percentage of skulls with fronto-temporal pterion on one or both sides |
|------|---------------------------|--------------------------------------------------------------------|------------------------------------------------------------------------|
| Europids of Europe | 20,867 | 326 | 1·56 |
| Australids | 1,688 | 191 | 11·3 |
| Negrids | 2,115 | 256 | 12·1 |

Note.—The figures for the Australids were obtained by adding together the data of Anutschin,[31] Ranke,[873] Collins,[220] Ashley-Montagu,[34] and Fenner;[326] the others from those of the two first-named only.

The whole question of the morphology of the pterion in Primates has been considered in great detail by Ashley-Montagu, who recognizes no fewer than sixteen different types.[34] His work deserves careful consideration by everyone interested in the subject. He has regarded the problem of the human pterion partly from the embryological point of view (as indeed Ranke [873] did, long before). The pterion arises in the region occupied in the embryo by soft tissue, the anterior fontanelle. Into this space between bones the orbitosphenoid often detaches a separate fragment, which grows into a bone called epipteric. Among Europids it is the fusion of this accessory bone with the squamous plate of the temporal that causes the (rare) fronto-temporal articulation; and this occurs predominantly in *brachycranial* skulls, which are very *broad* in the temporal region.

Among the races regarded by Ashley-Montagu as 'lower', 'less developed', or 'more primitive', the fronto-temporal pterion arises in a different way. Here it is associated

* Anutschin's name is spelled thus in his papers written in German, but 'Anoutchine' in those written in French.

with the *dolichocranial* condition, and especially with *narrowness* in the temporal region; and often it exists without participation of an epipteric. Ashley-Montagu claims that in such cases it is the constriction in this region that causes the frontal and the squamous part of the temporal bone to approach one another. He remarks that almost any Australid skull will show this constriction clearly, whether actual contact occurs between the two bones or not. He suggests a correlation between this arrangement of the bones and poor development of the fronto-temporal region of the brain.

Ashley-Montagu[34] distinguishes the fronto-temporal pterion that occurs occasionally in man (type XVI) from the 'spheno-fronto-temporal' (type XII) found in the great majority of chimpanzees, but the differences seem to be unimportant.

Several authors have remarked on the frequency of separate epipteric bones in skulls of Australids. It often happens that they are so placed as to prevent the sphenoid from touching the parietal, and also the frontal from touching the temporal. In such cases it might be said that there is no pterion, in the usual sense of the word. Among 82 Australid skulls examined for this feature in the collections of the British Museum (Natural History) and the Departments of Zoology and Human Anatomy at Oxford, no fewer than fifteen presented the 'no pterion' arrangement on one side, and six on both.[48] Epipteric bones are unusual in modern pongids, and very rare in cercopithecids. It is to be hoped that sufficiently abundant and complete dryopithecine material will eventually be found to throw light on the structure of the pterion and the presence or absence of epipterics in the common ancestor of apes and man.

Attention was called by Dixon long ago to the grooves on the squamous part of the frontal bone, occupied in life by branches of the supra-orbital nerve. [276] He drew attention to the wide differences between the ethnic taxa of man in the frequency of occurrence of these grooves. He reported their presence in a small percentage of Australid skulls, but it would appear that they never occur in aborigines who have no non-Australid ancestors.[326]

An anomaly occurs not infrequently in Australid skulls at the place where the infra-orbital nerve (a branch of the maxillary) emerges from below the floor of the orbit to open on the front surface of the maxilla and supply sensory fibres to the skin of the face. In man, the nerve normally emerges through a single aperture, the infra-orbital foramen. In pongids, on the contrary, the aperture is usually double or multiple. The double aperture is marked *io* in the photograph of part of an orang-utan's skull in Fig. 46D. In 5% of Australid skulls the aperture is double (or in one case triple), and in a further 17% there is a single main aperture and a small accessory one.[326] In other cases, again, the foramen is single, but divided internally by a partition. It is a strange fact that the foramen was single in australopithecines,[145, 210] though there are indications that it may have been divided internally. There does not appear to be any precise information about the infra-orbital foramen in Pekin Man. In his reconstruction of the skull, Weidenreich put one large aperture on each side, and a smaller one at some distance from it on the outer side (apparently on the zygomatic bone).[1128]

Styloid processes are lacking in nearly one-quarter of all male Australid skulls.[326] This is a pongid character. It has already been mentioned (p. 289) that when present, it is often (though not always) small or even rudimentary.

*Skeleton apart from skull.*—It happens not uncommonly in man that the second sacral vertebra is much narrower laterally than the first or third. The indentation thus formed on each side has received the name of 'simian notch', because it is characteristic of the pongids. It occurs in nearly one-third of all Australid and Europid sacra, but is much more frequent in Negrids, among whom it appears to be a primary character.[825]

*Blood-groups.*—There is strong reason to believe that all Australids, apart from hybrids, belong to blood-groups 'A' or 'O'.[213, 953, 585, 2] The 'A' is always 'A$_1$', 'A$_2$' being unknown in the taxon.[2] The percentage of persons belonging to group 'A' is perhaps the highest among all the ethnic taxa of man. Figures exceeding 60% have been reported. Blood-group 'B' does occur among the aboriginal population of Queensland and the Northern Territory, but this is attributed to hybridization with Melanesians, Papuans, and perhaps Negritos and others. It is an astonishing and apparently inexplicable fact that on Bentinck Island, near the southernmost extremity of the Gulf of Carpentaria, the aboriginal population consists solely of persons belonging to blood-groups 'O' and 'B'.[585]

In the Rhesus system the most frequent complex among Australids is CDe (=R$_1$). cde (=r) has not been reported.[953, 585]

It has been suggested that the blood-groups of the Australids, apart from those in the peripheral regions where hybridization is suspected, are those that may have characterized the people of Europe before 'B' and cde were imported into that part of the world.[2]

*External characters.*—Several authors mention the occurrence of light-coloured scalp-hair among Australids.[515, 585, 2] It is noted especially among children, of whom Abbie gives some striking photographs. The colour is described as yellow-brown or straw-coloured. In Melanesia the hair is often artificially bleached, but this is not the cause of blondness among Australids.[515] There is some evidence that it may be due to a partially dominant gene, but the genetics of this feature has not been worked out satisfactorily.[585]

A curious secondary character of the Australids is hairiness of the flap or auricle (or pinna) of the ear.[1, 3] This has no connection with the 'ear-tufts' that commonly grow in the vicinity of the external aperture of the ear (actually from the tragus and antitragus) in males of many ethnic taxa of man, nor yet with the fine 'down' present on the auricle in young children. The anomaly in question, generally called 'hairy pinna', occurs in about 20% of non-hybrid male Australids aged 20 or over; the incidence increases beyond the age of 40. In this taxon the hair on the auricle is dark brown or black and usually grows from below the inturned margin of the ear (or, in technical terms, from the scaphoid fossa below the helix), but also, in some cases, from the external surface of the helix, and occasionally even from the lobe. 'Hairy pinna' has been known for some time among Europids. It appears to be especially frequent among the Sinhalese of Sri Lanka, but it has been reported also among Indians, Iranians, Iraqis, Israelis, and Europeans (unfortunately without precise information as to the subraces concerned, in most cases).[287, 976] The descriptions suggest that the exact site may differ in the various subraces. There is strong evidence, not amounting to proof, that hairy pinna in a particular Indian family is due to a gene carried on the Y-chromosome.[287] It seems probable that the hairy pinna of Australids is the same character as that which bears the same name among Europids, but no genetical data are available about the anomaly in the former taxon.

*Unclassified characters.*—A small percentage of Australids are deficient in haptoglobins (phenotype HpO, which is rare also in Europids). Most Australids belong to phenotype Hp2-2, but the gene $Hp^1$ does occur, with frequency generally between 0·13 and 0·26. Roughly one-half of the aboriginal population are tasters of phenyl-thiourea. The percentage of red-green colour-blind persons is significantly lower than among Europids. Among males, the figure is 2·3%; no colour-blind female has yet been reported.

In concluding this chapter on the physical characters of the Australids, it is desirable to mention a statement of Morant's that might otherwise be misunderstood. At the end of his well-known statistical paper on the skulls of Australids and Tasmanids he remarks, 'The view advocated by some writers that the two races are distinguished from all other modern races on account of their ultra-primitive characters can receive no support whatever from a comparison of these measurements.'[763]

First, it must be observed that Morant makes no statement to the effect that the Australids are not primitive. From what he says in the statement quoted it follows only that there may be other ethnic taxa of modern man that are still more primitive in some of the particular characters that he chose for statistical study.

Secondly, the characters that he chose are the ones that lend themselves most readily to description by simple measurement, and these are by no means necessarily those that throw the clearest light on the problem of primitiveness. In the whole of the paper in which the statement occurs, Morant says nothing about the thickness of the bones of the cranial vault, the prominence of ridges in the occipital region, the structure of the apertura pyriformis at its lower border, the size of the anterior nasal spine, or the rounding of the outer orbital margin; he does not mention the pterion or the infra-orbital foramen or the ethmo-lacrimal suture or the teeth or the lower jaw or the styloid process. One cannot form a valid judgement on the question of primitiveness without considering these features.

Thirdly, although the skull is the most important single part of the body in matters relating to human taxonomy and evolution, anyone interested in the problem of primitiveness must consider also the evidence from the postcranial skeleton and soft parts of the body.

In most ethnic taxa of man one can point to a few primitive characters, not possessed by certain other taxa. The Europids, for instance, are primitive in the shape of the scalp-hair as seen in transverse section (though not in its length), and some of the Europid subraces are primitive in their dolichocephaly; but the Australids are exceptional in the number and variety of their primitive characters and in the degree to which some of them are manifested. In this chapter twenty-eight such characters have been mentioned. It is questionable whether any other ethnic taxon of modern man shows so many resemblances to *Pithecanthropus* and to more remote ancestral forms.

# 17 The Sanids (Bushmen)

TWO REASONS underlie the choice of the Bushmen of southern Africa as the subject of a chapter in this book. First, they are very different in physical characters—indeed, in certain respects astonishingly different—from both Europids and Australids, and thus show particularly clearly how wrong it is to suggest that there are few differences between races, apart from skin-colour. Secondly, the Bushmen provide a good example of the influence of paedomorphosis (pp. 137–8) in the evolution of certain ethnic taxa of man.

The pygmy chimpanzee, *Pan satyrus paniscus,* has already been described as an example of an animal that in its sexually mature form resembles in several respects the young of its closest relatives (pp. 113–14). Paedomorphosis of this type has been of great significance in human evolution, for modern man as a whole shows clear evidence of being a paedomorphous form; and some human ethnic taxa, the Bushmen among them, are more paedomorphous than others.

The idea that modern man as a whole is paedomorphous seems to have been put forward clearly for the first time by the Dutch anatomist, L. Bolk, in an address given to the German Anatomical Society at Freiburg in 1926. The audience seems to have been bewildered. The chairman closed the meeting with the remark, 'The wide range of the subject cannot be grasped clearly, and I am afraid that the discussion went off readily into extravagance.'[119] Bolk subsequently amplified his address and published it as an independent pamphlet.[120] One might expect that he would have started with some remarks about neoteny, for this had been a familiar word among zoologists for half a century; but almost throughout he writes instead of *Fetalisation* or *Fetalisierung.* His mention of the word 'neoteny', more than half-way through the pamphlet, gives the impression of having been an interpolation into the original manuscript, for he remarks at the beginning, 'I intend to explain to you the origin of man on the basis of an evolutionary principle that until now has found no application in biology.'

Bolk listed a number of characters that are found in the embryos of other Primates, but do not persist into the adult form except in man himself. 'In other words,' he remarked, 'structural characters or relations that are transient in the embryos of other Primates are stabilized in man.' Among these he mentions orthognathy, hairlessness, the form of the outer ear, the central position of the foramen magnum in the skull, the relative size of the brain (made possible by the slow fusion of the embryonic cranial sutures), and many others. Two of his most striking instances of fetalization concern the cranial axis and the position of the female reproductive aperture. In mammalian embryos, including those of Primates, the base of the skull—what T. H. Huxley[540] called the 'basi-cranial axis'—is bent so as to form roughly a right angle with the vertebral column. In nearly every case this 'cranial flexure' is straightened out during development; but in man, as Bolk pointed out, it persists in the adult. A flexure at the opposite end of the body reveals the retention of another fetal character. The caudal or posterior end of the body is curved forward in primate embryos. This is shown in Fig. 52A, which represents part of a longitudinal sagittal section through a human embryo 26 mm long, viewed from the left side. The arrow gives a general impression of the curvature of the body in this region. A

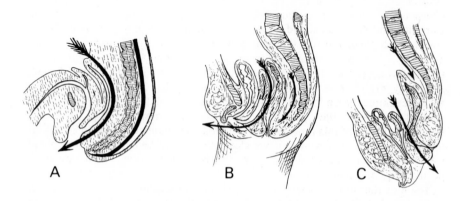

A                    B                    C

52    Caudal flexure in a human embryo and in a girl, and the lack of it in a chimpanzee

The posterior parts of the body are seen in left-side views of median sagittal sections of A, a human embryo 26 mm long; B, a girl aged two years; C, a half-grown chimpanzee.        *Diagram from Bolk.* [120]

similar representation of the corresponding parts in a two-year-old girl shows that the ventral flexure is maintained (Fig. 52B); it results in the final position of the vulva in women. In pongids, on the contrary, the curve straightens out during development, so that it is lost or even turned in the opposite direction, and the vulva therefore has quite a different position. This is shown by the figure of the corresponding parts in a half-grown chimpanzee (Fig. 52C). It is the human being that retains the fetal state in this respect, as in so many others. As Bolk remarked, 'To some extent we represent the infantile form of our ancestral stock.'

The idea of fetalization occurred to Émile Devaux, a *Médecin-Colonel* of the French army, independently of Bolk. He was apparently in complete ignorance of neoteny and paedomorphosis, for he never mentions either of these words in his book, which was published seven years later than Bolk's pamphlet. [272] He remarked that 'Anthropoid [pongid] babies have a human appearance, a human skull, a human brain,' and he gave a certain amount of evidence supporting this statement; but his contribution to the subject does not bear comparison with Bolk's. It contained nothing on the subject of fetalization that would be useful to anyone who had read the latter's pamphlet.

So much, then, for the significance of paedomorphosis in the evolution of modern man from his remote ancestors. Bolk may have carried his ideas too far, but he made a significant contribution to our understanding of human evolution. But when he tried to apply his ideas to the origin of human races, he was less successful. Indeed, it has to be admitted that his remarks on this subject, in his pamphlet[120] and in a paper entirely devoted to it,[122] contain little that is of any value. His *Fetalisations-hypothese* is in fact applicable to the origin of some of the ethnic taxa of man, but he himself did not realize how it should be applied.

In the tropical and subtropical parts of the world, often in remote districts, there live human beings of small stature, who seem in many cases to represent the aboriginal populations of countries subsequently invaded and dominated by taller peoples. Small stature originated independently among several ethnic taxa of man. The Laplanders provide a familiar example, exceptional in their northerly habitat. Among the little men of warm climates one may mention the Negritids (Negritos of the Andaman Islands, Malay Peninsula, and East Indies); the Weddids (Veddas of Ceylon; Kurumba and related peoples of India; Senoi of the Malay Peninsula, Toala of Celebes); Bambutids (African pygmies); and the Sanids (Bushmen) of southern Africa.

There is no reason to suppose that ancestral man was particularly small, and the independent origin of low stature in several human taxa in the hot regions of the world suggests that the need to maintain correct body-temperature may have played a part in their evolutionary processes. The importance of intellect in the self-preservation of man, and the deleterious effect of high temperature on mental activity, might well be supposed to result in the natural selection of small human beings in hot climates; and there would be no easier way in which such selection could act, than by the permanent prolongation of the juvenile form. While as yet there were no larger people in the territory of the aborigines, little disadvantage would result from small stature. Many of the small peoples of the tropical and subtropical regions of the world do in fact possess a number of juvenile characters in addition to the obvious one of small size, and the Bushmen serve well as an example. It must be mentioned, however, that there are pygmies in the Zaïre forest and other parts of the world who are not typical paedomorphs. There is also some evidence that paedomorphous characters may have evolved before reduction in size. Fossil remains have been found over an immense area from the Transvaal to places along the south coast of Africa from near Cape Town to near Port Elizabeth, which show strong evidence of relationship to Bushmen, yet belonged to men of large stature. The South African anthropologist M. R. Drennan has stressed the paedomorphous character of these skulls.[279]

The Sanids or Bushmen constitute one of the two subraces of the Khoisanid race. The other is the Khoid, comprising a number of tribes usually grouped together as Hottentots, and also, according to most authorities, the Korana; but it has been suggested that the latter might more correctly be placed with the Bushmen.[1060] Certain Europid–Khoid hybrid taxa, the Griqua among them, are probably best included among the Khoids.

The Khoids differ from the Sanids in several respects, especially in being taller and having longer, higher heads; the prognathous face, very wide in the zygomatic region, narrows below to a pointed chin, giving a triangular appearance in front view. They are almost certainly themselves a hybrid taxon, of Sanid and Negrid (Kafrid) ancestry; and since the Kafrids show evidence of an Aethiopid strain, it is not surprising that this appears also in Khoids (though there may have been direct hybridization between Sanids and Aethiopids, when the former were more widely distributed). The Khoids have been cattlemen since remote times, and in this respect differ from the food-gathering Sanids.

The Sanids present no evidence of descent from a hybrid stock, though some of their tribes have hybridized with Negrids or Khoids. Formerly they had a very wide distribution in southern Africa. Their artifacts, rock art (see Appendix 6, pp. 545–9), place-names, and skeletal remains show that they originally extended from the Zambesi to the southernmost extremity of Africa, and one tribe of them, called by the Dutch 'Strandlooper' (coastal rangers), adapted themselves to life on the seashore in the vicinity of the Cape. These people have been regarded by some authorities as belonging to a separate ethnic taxon, and it is true that they were taller than typical Bushmen, had larger cranial capacity, and were more decidedly orthognathous;[706] but they seem not to have been sufficiently different from the rest to merit taxonomic separation. They are now extinct.

The sad story of the encroachment of stronger foreigners on the traditional hunting-grounds of the Bushmen in fertile parts of Africa has been told in great detail by G. W. Stow in his large work *The native races of South Africa*.[1016] The Hottentots came first, probably about the beginning of the seventeenth century, sweeping down the west coast of the continent. The very name of 'San', which they bestowed on the Bushmen, shows that they recognized the latter as the rightful owners of the land, for *San* means natives.[103] The Bushmen knew nothing of farm animals, and they preyed on the Hottentots' cattle. War was inevitable, and depopulation of the endemic tribes began. In the great periods of Negrid expansion to the south, and especially about the end of the eighteenth century, the Bushmen's land was invaded from the north and east; the Dutch and then the British pressed from the south. Only the more inaccessible regions were eventually left to the pitifully small remainder, amounting in recent times to some 53,000 persons in all.[1060]

The Bushmen of the present day live chiefly in the north-eastern part of South West Africa, with the contiguous region of southern Angola, and in the northern and central parts of the Kalahari Desert,[936] but some of them still have their homes in the south, even beyond the Orange River.[1060] Apart from isolated remnants, the subrace reaches its eastern limit in the vicinity of the southern part of the frontier between Botswana and Rhodesia.

The rest of this chapter will be devoted almost entirely to the subjects mentioned in the first paragraph, namely the anatomical peculiarities of the Sanids and the evidences of paedomorphosis. The anatomy of these little people is particularly interesting, and an attempt will be made to present the principal facts in a form acceptable by those who do not profess to be experts in physical anthropology. Many of the most important bodily features of the Sanids can be described without the necessity to rely on much previous knowledge of anatomy. A few words addressed to physical anthropologists will be inserted here and there between parentheses, but nearly all the more technical aspects of the subject will be relegated to a separate section near the end of the chapter.

It is intended to present here a general account of the physical anthropology of the Sanids. The subrace comprises several tribes of 'local forms', but these will not be separately considered. Tobias, an authority on the Bushmen, has made a detailed report on their anatomical differences.[1060]

In this chapter measurements will be given in both metric and British units. Whichever is printed first will be the figure given by the authority quoted. Measurements converted from one unit to the other will be stated in round figures.

Since one of the main purposes of this chapter is to display a human taxon that differs very markedly from the Europids in physical characters, it is well to call attention to the minor role of colour in taxonomy by remarking at the outset that this can scarcely be regarded as one of the distinguishing features of the Bushmen. The skin is only slightly darker than that of the Mediterranids of southern Europe,[849] and paler than that of many Europids whose ancestral home is in Asia or Africa. The skin-colour of the Bushmen is pale brown, usually tinged with yellow;[1100, 849, 281] some of them are more distinctly yellowish.[936]

Right back in 1886, Virchow had stressed that the Bushmen showed few apelike structural features. 'Similarity to the younger developmental states of man', he wrote, 'obtrudes itself upon us much more than similarity to animals';[1101] and he lists a number of what we should now call their paedomorphous characters, starting with small stature. Males are commonly only 140-144 cm in height (4' 7"–4' 9"), and females not much less, if at all; indeed, Fritsch actually maintained that the women were taller than the men.[366] In the northern part of their range the people are taller. In Angola most of them are said to reach about 152–9 cm (5'–5' 2½").[936] and among the !Kun of South West Africa a male 171 cm tall (5' 7½") has been recorded;[956] but even in this tribe the mean weight of adult males is only 40·4 kg (6 stone 5 lbs). We are dealing here with a diminutive people. Pöch, one of the best authorities on the physical anthropology of the Bushmen, considered that statures exceeding 150 cm (4' 11") were to be attributed to hybridity with Negrids or Khoids.[849]

The very small size of the hands and feet attracted the attention of early observers,[349] and was regarded as an infantile character.[1101] This is one of the respects in which there is strong contrast with the Negrids. The shortness of the hands combines with that of the upper arms[1101, 281] to make the upper extremities very short; indeed, they are said to be shorter than those of any other taxon of mankind.[281] The legs, too, are short, in proportion to the trunk. This feature of the lower extremities is also regarded as infantile.[302] The 'calf' of the leg is fully developed,[1101, 1102] unlike that of the Negrids.

The fatty layer of the dermis is very poorly developed,[849] and as a result the skin has a strong tendency to wrinkle. This is not restricted to elderly people, though in some of the latter it is excessive. Good feeding tends to reduce the wrinkles,[706] but malnutrition cannot be the primary cause, since they occur in people who accumulate enormous amounts of fat in particular parts of the body (pp. 317–18).

The scalp-hair is black and of the extreme *crêpue* variety of Pruner-Bey,[862] often called 'woolly' in English, though the resemblance to wool is not very close. Each hair is fine, and narrowly elliptical in transverse section, the lesser axis of the ellipse being rather less than half the greater, on the average.[293] The hair is very short. If pulled out straight, some of the hairs may extend to 6" (15 cm),[349] but in their natural state they are tightly coiled in close spirals. They are aggregated in tufts, often separated in such a way that the skin can be seen between them (Fig. 54C, p. 310). This is not due to scarcity of hair-roots on the apparently bare areas, for they are as abundant there as below the tufts. This fact was made known by Flower and Murie in 1867,[349] and rediscovered by Wolff nearly two decades later.[1148] The hair-follicles are curved[367] and the hairs, emerging obliquely from the skin, twist of their own accord into tufts. The spiral of each individual hair has a radius of only about 0·8–1·5 mm (0·03"–0·06"), and the coiling is so tight that the tufts are often only 15 mm (0·6") long,[706] though Flower and Murie[349] found some measuring $1"-1\frac{1}{2}"$ (25–51 mm) on the top of the head, where they are longest. If a tuft is artificially divided, it may spontaneously twist into two or more.[1148]

The facial hair of the male is very weakly developed,[1100, 1102, 706, 936] and so is that in the axillae and genital regions of both sexes.[349, 1101, 849] These are regarded as infantile characters. Such hairs as exist in the axillae are spirally coiled.[349, 1101]

The shortness of hair on the scalp and its scantiness on the face of the male reveal the general outlines of the skull. It will be convenient to describe the latter before turning to the more superficial features of the head as seen in life.

Drennan has remarked that 'The usual description of the infant human skull found in text-books of anatomy epitomizes the salient features of the Bushman skull'.[279] The reader may care to compare the skulls of a European child and man, as represented in Fig. 53, in order to confirm the remarks about paedomorphous characters in the description of the adult Sanid skull that now follows.

It is a paedomorphous character of the Sanids that it is particularly difficult to determine the sex of an unidentified skull; and there are hardly enough specimens that belonged to persons who were known when alive, to warrant any statement about the relative cranial capacities of males and females. The statistics tabulated by Martin[706] suggest that the cranial capacity of males is greater and that female skulls are shorter and wider, but some skulls may have been regarded as female partly at least because they were smaller than others. It is safest to say simply that most adult Sanid skulls are small, having a capacity between 1,250 and 1,330 ml.[1072, 964, 849, 706, 281] In comparison with most skulls of Mongolids, Europids, and Negrids, the capacity is low; but in proportion to the size of the body it is not, and the average capacity is about the same as that of Australid males, despite the very much greater stature of the latter.

The forehead is rather wide, but the projections of the parietal bones (parietal eminences), situated far back, are so strongly developed that the hinder part of the skull is much wider. Viewed from above, the sides appear flat between the parietal eminences and the front of the skull; and since they converge forwards, a wedge-shaped (sphenoid) appearance is given. Behind the eminences, the sides tend to be flattened once more where they converge towards the occiput. A particularly good example of this type of Sanid skull is no. Af. 63.420 in the British Museum (Natural History).[49] Other Sanid skulls appear rounded behind the eminences, when viewed from above. The strong lateral projection of these parietal eminences is regarded as an infantile character.[1072, 1101] It results in a cranial index of about 74–76; that is to say, near the dividing line between the dolicho- and the mesocranial.[1072, 1101, 964, 293] Skulls that are conspicuously dolichocranial are probably those of hybrids between Sanids and Negrids or Khoids.[849]

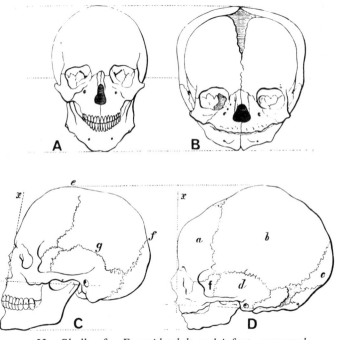

53    *Skulls of a Europid adult and infant, compared*

Facial views of A, adult, and B, infant; lateral views of C, adult, and D, infant. The total height of the skulls has been made the same in adult and infant. *x*, Camper's facial line.                      *From Langer.*[628]

Since the parietal eminences are situated high up on the skull, the latter is rather flat on top in its hinder part.

The frontal bone rises steeply, giving an almost vertical forehead, and the brow-ridges are only slightly developed. These features of the skull, which can be readily observed on the living subject (Fig. 54) are regarded as infantile (Fig. 53; compare D with C).

The face is broad because the cheek-bones (zygomatics) project laterally, and it is remarkably flat because these bones extend far forward and then turn sharply inwards towards the nose. The flatness of the face is accentuated by the fact that the nose projects very little (Figs. 54C and 55A, especially the second man from the left). It looks, as Virchow remarked, as though it had been mechanically compressed.[1101] The root is extraordinarily flat. If one views the skull from the side, one can scarcely see a nasal bone at the root of the nose. This, and the fact that the two nasal bones are often fused together, are among the few pongid characters of the Sanids.

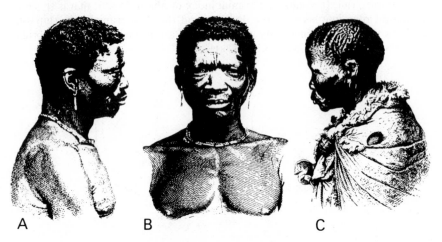

A                        B                        C

54    *Portraits of male Sanids* (A *and* B) *and of an elderly female*
(C) *of the same taxon*
From Fritsch.[366]

The nose is very wide (Fig. 54B), and the nostrils flattened. Its width is perhaps best represented by the nasal index, obtained by measurements made on the skull. The Sanids not only fall into the extreme (hyperchamaerrhine) category in width of nose (in relation to length), but are exceeded in this respect, so far as is known, by no other groups of mankind except the Khoids and women of the Fan tribe (*Pan 3,* see pp. 331–3)—and only marginally by these.[708] It is uncertain whether in this particular case the exceptional width of the nose is to be regarded as a paedomorphous or a primitive character; but the former possibility seems the more probable, since the Sanids give so little indication of anatomical primitiveness. The breadth of the nasal aperture (apertura pyriformis) in the skulls of the European child and adult is shown in Fig. 53B and A.

Thomson and Buxton found that the mean relative breadth of the nose in various groups of mankind in different parts of the world was positively correlated with the mean annual temperatures and relative humidities of the atmosphere to which they were exposed outdoors.[1045] Measurements of both living subjects and skulls were taken into consideration. Weiner, using Thomson and Buxton's data, found a closer correlation with the mean annual vapour pressure of the atmosphere than with the temperature taken in conjunction with the relative humidity. [1130] The correlations found by these authors would almost certainly have been considerably lower if they had not used so few data relating to Indianids, whose noses tend to be rather narrow or of only moderate width. One tribe of this race does reach chamaerrhiny, though only a very low degree of it, and there does not appear to be any record of an Indianid tribe reaching hyperchamaerrhiny (cf. Martin and Saller [708]). If the correlations were everywhere applicable, the extremely wide noses of the Sanids would suggest that these people were adapted to a very hot and moist climate, or to a very high atmospheric vapour pressure. It is true that the Sanids of former times did not experience such exceptionally dry climates as most of their descendants do today; still, the ancestral habitat was not a particularly wet one. It was presumably savannah and steppe, like much of Africa south of the rain-forest zone at the present time. If Thomson and Buxton's correlations had held true for the Sanids, the latter would have stood somewhere in the middle of the mesorrhine range.

The face as a whole is orthognathous or nearly so,[628, 964, 849] and any tendency towards prognathism is entirely confined to the region below the nose.[293, 849] In the literature one comes across references to the existence of a *'museau'* or muzzle, and David Livingstone makes the extraordinary remark that Bushmen are in some degree like baboons;[676] but this is quite wrong, for

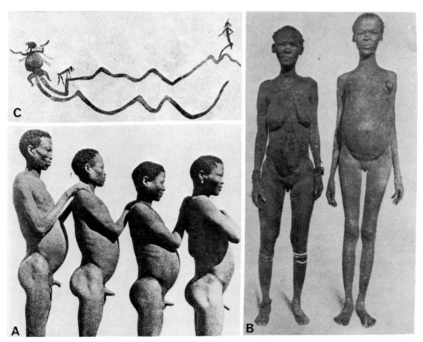

55   *Bushmen (A) and Bushwomen (B), with a specimen of Sanid rock art (C)*

The pendent labia minora are well shown in B. In C there is a fanciful representation of them, enormously enlarged.    A *and* B, *photographs from Seiner and Staudinger;*[956] C, *photograph from Summers.* [1025]

a muzzle is the projecting part of an animal's head that includes the mouth *and nose,* and there is no projection of the face of a Bushman at the level of the nose, but only below it. Orthognathy is a paedomorphic character shown by many human ethnic taxa besides Sanids (cf. Fig. 53D).

The height of the upper facial part of the skull, from the mouth to the root of the nose (prosthion to nasion) is low in relation to the breadth of the skull in the zygomatic region. This is a salient character of the infantile skull (compare B with A in Fig. 53).

The lower jaw is slender, but wide at the articulation with the rest of the skull. The chin scarcely projects or actually retreats. It is not possible to state whether the 'weak' chin of Sanids is infantile (cf. Fig. 53D) or primitive.

The lips, in the narrower sense of the transitional zones between the skin of the face and the mucous membrane of the mouth, are not much thicker than in many Europids, and are not bulbous like those of Negrids. They are well shown in Fig. 54B. Both upper and lower lips project in what looks like a pouting position (Figs 54A and 56A). It is this, no doubt, that has given rise to the mistaken references to a 'muzzle'. It is caused in part by the tendency to subnasal prognathy.

The eyes present many remarkable features. They are set wide apart, as in infants (Figs. 53B and 54B). The upper lid is thickly distended with fat, so that there is scarcely any infolding below the eyebrow. It usually presents a horizontal outfold, which extends inwards towards the nose and outwards towards the cheek. A fold of this sort (but not the fatty distension) is quite usual among Europids who have passed middle age,[1206] but in Sanids it exists from early life onwards. In these people it has often been mistaken for the eyelid-fold that occurs in many Mongolids (Fig. 25B and C, p. 209), but in fact it is very different. This was emphasized by Aichel, who made a detailed study of folds in the upper lids of various ethnic taxa of man.[12] He calls the fold in question *'der seitliche Deckfaltenüberhang',* and contrasts it strongly with the *'Mongolenfalte'.* The latter is a very definite fold of two adpressed layers of skin, turned over sharply at their junction, while the former is a more amorphous projection (*Überhang*). Further, the *Mongolenfalte* turns downwards at the nasal side, and often covers the canthus or inner corner of the eye, while the inner fold or projection of the Bushman's upper eyelid is nearly horizontal and never covers the canthus.[849, 706] The external or lateral part of the fold does not rise upwards, as it does in Mongolids, so as to give an appearance of obliquity to the eye: on the contrary, it passes straight outwards, or droops as in some elderly Europids.

A very characteristic feature of the Sanid eye is that the edges of the eyelids are almost straight, parallel, and close together, so that the eyeball can be seen only through a narrow slit (Fig. 55B). The eyelashes on the upper lid are very short, those on the lower scarcely perceptible.[349]

The iris is dark brown,[1101] sometimes mottled.

The external ear is seldom usable as a distinctive feature in physical anthropology, but the Sanids are peculiar in this respect. Their ears distinguish them not only from members of other races, but even from Khoids. Great stress was laid by Luschan on the ears of Bushmen, as one of the characters that distinguish them from Hottentots. He remarks that the latter have the European type of external ear, but 'all the Bushmen I have seen, without one single exception, have entirely different ears'.[684] In its most typical form the structure is as follows.[1102, 849] The auricle or pinna is small. There is no trace of a lobe, and the lower extremity extends forward, gradually fading out as it merges into the cheek. The forward extension of the lower part in some cases gives the impression that the ear is set obliquely on the head (Fig. 55A, second man from left). The upper edge of the ear is often nearly horizontal, passing almost straight back from the place of attachment to the head (Fig. 54A and C). The reflected edge (helix) is broad at the top of the ear, but narrows quickly in the descending part. The tragus is small or scarcely exists[360] (Figs. 54A and 55A; cf. Fig. 31A, trs).

Unquestionably the external genitalia and secondary sexual characters of the female are the strangest features of Sanid anatomy.

The earliest records on this subject are rather vague, and uncertainty results from the fact that there was a tendency to call both Bushmen and Hottentots by the latter name, so that one is often at a loss to know whether the descriptions refer to a Sanid or a Khoid. This is not, however, a matter of much importance in the present context, since the peculiarities of female anatomy that are about to be described are very similar in the two subraces. In the early days of European colonization at the Cape of Good Hope, the Hottentots were in much closer contact with the newcomers than were the Bushmen, and the facts to be recounted were probably first noticed in Khoids. There seems to have been some reticence at the start in referring to the matter in print. Dapper, writing on Hottentot women in Dutch in 1668, remarked mildly that 'The lining of the body appears to be loose, so that in certain places part of it dangles out'.[246]

Many of the subsequent reports were misleading, and it is therefore all the more remarkable that a description published only eighteen years after Dapper's was very accurate. Wilhelm ten Rhyne, a physician of the Dutch East India Company, referred to the subject in a book written in Latin and published in 1686. The women to whom he refers must have been Hottentots, not Bushwomen, since they were among a group of cattle-dealers. 'They have to themselves this peculiarity from other races', he wrote, 'that most of them possess finger-shaped appendages, always double, hanging down from the private parts; these are evidently nymphae.'[900] ('Nymphae' is another word for the labia minora.) Rhyne derived his information from a surgeon of his acquaintance, who had lately dissected the body of a Hottentot woman who had been strangled to death.

It is curious that this correct account, published both in Latin[900] and not long afterwards in English,[901] was for a time overlooked, and a totally wrong description, published in 1708, accepted as true. François Leguat had been in charge of a party of French Protestants forced to leave their country by the persecutions that followed the revocation of the Edict of Nantes. He was told of the peculiarities of Hottentot women when his ship called at Cape Town on the return journey from Mauritius to Europe. He mentions the clothing of

Hottentot women and remarks, 'They would not need this to cover that which bits of skin, hanging like a flounce (*Falbala*) from the upper part, would conceal sufficiently from the view of passers-by. Several people have told me that they have had the curiosity to see these veils, and that one can thus satisfy one's eyes for a piece of tobacco.'[648] A crude picture accompanying Leguat's account shows a female Hottentot with a semicircular fold of skin hanging from the lower part of her abdomen and covering her external genitalia.

Although Leguat himself did not use the word, it was probably his report, and in particular the picture accompanying it, that gave rise to the idea of a *'tablier'* or apron of skin, hanging down from the abdomen; and the word has persisted to the present day. Captain James Cook (then Lieutenant), on the homeward voyage of his first circumnavigation of the world, called at Cape Town in 1771, and took the opportunity to investigate what he called 'the great question among natural historians, whether the women of this country have or have not that fleshy flap or apron which has been called the *Sinus pudoris'*. A local physician declared that he had examined many hundreds of Hottentot women, and 'never saw one without two fleshy, or rather skinny appendages, proceeding from the upper part of the Labia, in appearance somewhat resembling the teats of a cow, but flat; they hung down, he said, before the *Pudendum*, and were in different subjects of different lengths, in some not more than half an inch, in others three or four inches'.[223] This passage of Cook's was known to Blumenbach, who relied on it in the first edition of *De generis humani varietate nativa liber* as the basis for what might be regarded as an understatement of the peculiarity of Khoisanid women. (See p. 26 of the present work.) 'The most recent testimony of travellers', he wrote, 'commands us to put the cutaneous *ventrale* of female Hottentots (the existence of which was asserted by the early travellers) in the same category as the human tail, and in like manner to relegate it to the fables.'[106] He added in a footnote, 'The pendulous labia seem to have deceived the early observers.'

The first thorough investigation of the external genitalia of female Khoisanids resulted indirectly from an expedition sent out by the French government in 1800, at the instigation of the Institut de France, to make scientific observations in Australia and Tasmania. Few such enterprises have met with so many misfortunes.[653] Many sailors and scientists had already deserted the ships before they had left Mauritius; violent tempests caused changes of plan; at one stage illness reduced the effective crew of one of the ships to four men; the other was eventually seized by the British on its return journey, and taken to England. Only two of the zoologists who had set out, Péron and Lesueur, remained with the expedition throughout. On the way back to France their ship called at Cape Town, where they took the opportunity to study the anatomy of Bushwomen.

Even when both ships had at last reached France, the ill luck of the expedition was not at an end. The two zoologists prepared a full account of the external anatomy of Bushwomen, accompanied by the excellent coloured engravings of Lesueur (two of which are reproduced here in black-and-white in Fig. 56C and D), and their paper was read by Péron at a meeting of the Institut in 1805. It was then referred to Cuvier and Labillardière, both of whom without delay pronounced it suitable for publication; but for some unexplained reason the opinions of these authorities were disregarded.[103] It may have seemed incredible that there should descend from the vulva an object, $8\frac{1}{2}$ cm (3·3″) in total length, extending 4 cm (1·6″) below the vulva, and somewhat resembling a penis (Fig. 56C). The object was in fact the two labia minora, enormously lengthened, and adhering (as they usually do in Khoisanids) to look like an unpaired organ. Spread out, when a woman lay on her back, their appearance was quite different (Fig. 56D). It may have been supposed that the

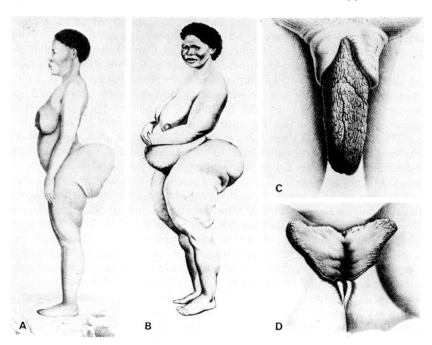

56   *Khoisanid female anatomy*

A, a Bushwoman (the famous 'Hottentot Venus'); B, a Korana woman; C, the external genitalia of a Bushwoman, standing upright; D, the same, of a Bushwoman lying down with the labia minora separated and turned aside.
A, *from Cuvier;*[241] B, *from Friedenthal;*[359] C *and* D, *copies of coloured engravings by Lesueur, reproduced by Blanchard.*[103] *The latter made the mistake of saying that the organs were those of a Hottentot.*

report of Péron and Lesueur was inaccurate or exaggerated, or that they had examined monstrosities and represented them as normal, or perhaps the subject may have been regarded as indelicate. In fact the only errors made by Péron and Lesueur were their denial that the *'tablier'* represented any part present in Europeans, and their statement that only Bushwomen, not Hottentots, possessed it. Yet 78 years elapsed before their most interesting paper was at last published in 1883.[835] Much of the scientific work of the expedition suffered a similar or worse fate. Most of the records of anthropology and zoology were dispersed and remained unpublished, though as many of them as possible were eventually collected and preserved with Péron and Lesueur's in the Museum at Le Havre, the port from which the ill-fated expedition had set out in 1800.

Meanwhile investigation of the subject had by no means stood still, for Sanids had begun to appear in Europe, and to allow themselves to be examined by anatomists. In 1804 there was great shortage of food among the Bushmen living in the northern part of Cape Colony, and one of them, who happened to be personally acquainted with the Governor, asked the latter to take care of his son, aged about ten years. The boy was sent to Cape Town and eventually found his way to Paris, where he was examined by Georges Cuvier. A Sanid girl of about the same age found her way to Cape Town in similar circumstances, and evidently lived there for many years. She married a Negro and had two children. An Englishman eventually persuaded her that she could make a great fortune if she visited Europe and exhibited herself, and she travelled to Paris. Here she was heartlessly abandoned to a showman of animals and exhibited under the misleading description of 'La Vénus hottentote'. This was in 1814, when she was about 26 years old. In the spring of the next year she had the 'complaisance' to remove her clothing so that she could be examined by Georges Cuvier. She was painted in the naked state on this occasion, in front and lateral views. Bushwomen are accustomed to tuck their labia minora into the vagina in such circumstances,[288] and this is evidently what she did, for the famous anatomist did not see them on this occasion, and they do not appear in the paintings. She died at the end of the year of some unspecified inflammatory disease, after everyone who wished to see her enormous buttocks and other physical peculiarities (apart from the *tablier*) had had an opportunity to do so. Her corpse was made available to Cuvier for more exact study. He described her anatomy before an audience in 1817, and on this occasion took the opportunity to exhibit her external genital organs, prepared in such a way as to leave no doubt as to their true nature. He confirmed the general accuracy of Péron and Lesueur's unpublished account, but stated correctly that the organ projecting from the vulva consisted in its upper part of the prepuce of the clitoris, while the whole of the rest of it represented the greatly enlarged labia minora. Thus the true facts were established on the authority of Cuvier.[240] It is to be remembered, however, that Rhyne had given the correct interpretation, though with extreme brevity, 131 years before. Cuvier's paper was republished in 1824 by his brother Frédéric and Geoffroy-Saint-Hilaire, at the very beginning of their enormous *Histoire naturelle des mammifères*.[400] It was in Volume 1 of this book that the two paintings of the Bushwoman that had been made nine years before were at last published. The lateral view is reproduced here in monochrome in Fig. 56A.

The conclusions of Rhyne and Cuvier were confirmed by many investigations carried out during the second half of the nineteenth century. There were some who studied Bushwomen in their native territories;[1100, 366, 367] others examined in life those who had been brought to Europe;[1101, 1102] autopsies were carried out on the corpses of those who had died there.[349] It was soon apparent that the strange structure of the female external genitalia was normal among Khoisanids, though Fritsch, a distinguished authority on South African peoples, understated the hypertrophy of the labia minora, and considered (wrongly) that those of the 'Hottentot Venus' had been monstrous.[366] It was observed that while the prepuce of the clitoris was enlarged, the latter organ itself was not.[349] Virchow noted that the organs in question did not resemble the female genitalia of apes.[1101] Péron and Lesueur's paper was at last published in 1883,[835] and immediately followed in the same journal by an important paper on the female anatomy of Khoisanids by Blanchard, only marred by the fact that in reproducing Lesueur's engravings, he described them as representing the organs of Hottentots.[103] He remarked that the hypertrophy of the labia minora is already noticeable in infancy. Blanchard gave 20 cm (7·9") as their maximum length in adult Khoisanids; Vincent,[1100] referring to Bushwomen, said 18 cm (7·1"). These were presumably measurements of the labia minora from the uppermost point of their emergence from the vulva to their lower extremity when the subject was standing and the organs pendent. Blanchard's maximum figure may refer to Hottentot women, among whom they are in some cases particularly large.[849]

In the present century our knowledge of the female genitalia of Bushwomen has been extended chiefly by studies carried out on living subjects in southern Africa by Pöch,[849] Drury,[288] and Villiers.[1099] All these authors agree that there is no evidence of artificial elongation of the labia minora. These are already enlarged and protrude from the vulva in young girls, and increase in size at puberty. Their average length in Bushwomen is much less than the maximum given by Vincent.[1100] The organs assume different forms in different districts. In South West Africa, for instance, each labium is flattened and broadened to form a winglike object, when laid out flat (cf. Plate 25D); this is known as the 'butterfly' type. In Botswana and the Cape Province of South Africa the width is reduced and the anterior part thickened, and this results in an object resembling the wattle of a turkey-cock. The 'wattle' type is commonly 3–4" long (7½–10 cm), the 'butterfly' 1½–2" (3·8–6·3 cm), according to Drury and Drennan;[288] Villiers gives a maximum of 9 cm (3½") for the 'butterfly'.[1099] The women shown in Fig. 55B probably had organs of the latter type, but they are shown in the pendent (penis-like) position.

It is said that in former times Bushwomen deliberately exposed the labia minora to the view of men in the course of erotic dances.[288] What appear to be enormously elongated labia minora are represented in many examples of Bushman rock art (Fig. 55C). Although the artists were experts at the naturalistic representation of animals (see Fig. 82, p. 547), and also produced tolerable likenesses of Negrids and Europids, their representations of members of their own taxon, both male and female, were highly stylized and fanciful.

The enormous size and strange form of the buttocks in the female sex are among the most striking peculiarities of the Khoisanids. They are characteristic of Bushwomen, Korana, and Hottentots alike. Perhaps they reach (or reached) their maximum among some of the latter, but if so the Bushwomen (Fig. 56A) and Korana (B) run them close. Very large buttocks occur sporadically among Sudanid, Aethiopid, and Europid women, and were depicted by

Palaeolithic artists in European caves; but their form is rounded in these people, whereas it is particularly characteristic of the Khoisanids that the shape of the projecting part is that of a right-angled triangle, the upper edge being nearly horizontal while the hypotenuse slopes at about 45° (Fig. 56A). Internally the female buttocks of Sanids (and probably of the other Khoisanids) consist of masses of fat incorporated between criss-crossed sheets of connective tissue,[241, 1100] said to be joined to one another in a regular manner.[687] Some of the Wolof women of West Africa (Sudanid Negrids) have greatly enlarged buttocks, but in them there is a mere accumulation of fat between two of the gluteus muscles (maximus and medius).[511] It has been suggested that the term 'steatopygia' should be used only for the specialized type of buttocks characteristic of Khoisanid women.[359] Many Kafrid women have large buttocks, and since there is strong reason to believe that there was a Khoisanid element in the ancestry of the Kafrid subrace (p. 333), it is possible that the term 'steatopygia' is applicable to them; but this does not seem to have been proved by anatomical study.

The degree of steatopygia is recorded as the shortest distance between the deepest point in the hollow of the back and a plane, placed at right angles to the median sagittal, just touching the most posterior point of the buttocks. In her work among the Kalahari Bushwomen, de Villiers found an average of 7·8 cm (3″) and a maximum of $11\frac{1}{2}$ cm ($4\frac{1}{2}$″) in adults before middle age;[1099] 3–6″ ($7\frac{1}{2}$–15 cm) has been quoted as the range in Bushwomen of the Cape Province.[288]   If, as seems probable, the painting here reproduced as Fig. 56A was accurate, the steatopygia of the 'Hottentot Venus' must have amounted to about 19·3 cm (7′ 6″).[49]

It is improbable that the enlarged buttocks of female Khoisanids represent a storehouse of nutriment on which the body may call in times of scarcity. The Hottentots, Korana, and Bushmen are not to be regarded as people adapted by natural selection to desert life. The great authority on the history of the Khoisanids, George Stow, has written, 'In the days of undisturbed occupation by the early Bushmen, the country literally swarmed with game, both large and small.'[1016] It is far more likely that the buttocks became enlarged in response to sexual selection. This is what Darwin implied in the case of Hottentot women, in whom 'the posterior part of the body projects in a wonderful manner'.[258] He mentions the admiration felt for this peculiarity by the males of their tribe. This should indeed not have surprised him; for he wrote his work on sexual selection at the time when bustles were in fashion in England, and he must have realized that the women who wore them were under the impression that this change in their appearance increased their charms for members of the opposite sex. The admiration for this particular feature of feminine anatomy must, however, have been much more lasting among the Khoisanid males, for the remarkable results achieved suggest selection over a long period.

Steatopygia is often accompanied by the accumulation of fat in the thighs (*steatomeria*) (Fig. 56B).

It is not unusual for the breasts of Sanid women to be situated near the armpits (Fig. 55B, right-hand figure). In women who have borne several children they become very long and hang downwards.[288] The dark areas round the nipples (mammary areolae) are very large (Fig. 56A). The nipple is short, and tends to be sunken at its base.[1102]

The anatomy of the male Sanid is in some respects as peculiar as that of the female. The penis, when not erect, maintains an almost horizontal position (Fig. 55A).[849, 706] This feature is scarcely ever omitted in the rock art of the Bushmen, in their stylized representations of their own people. The prepuce is very long:[366, 1101] it covers the glans completely and projects forwards to a point.[288] The scrotum is drawn up close to the root of the penis, giving the appearance that only one testis has descended, and that incompletely (cf. Fig. 55A, second figure from right). These characters are clearly paedomorphous, and they are less marked in old men.[288]

The buttocks of male Sanids are often enlarged, even in boys,[1101] but this is by no means always so (compare the four figures in Fig. 55A). There does not appear to be any evidence that the male ever shows true steatopygia, as defined above.

The brain of the 'Hottentot Venus' was preserved, but Cuvier himself did not examine it. Tiedemann (p. 30) reported on it briefly in 1836, and was thus the first person to describe a Sanid brain.[1059] Gratiolet, a distinguished French neurologist of the time, gave a more detailed description of the same brain in 1854, nearly forty years after the woman had died.[430] He found the gyri on the external surfaces of the cerebral hemispheres simpler than those of any other normal human being he had examined. He gave a good lateral view of the whole organ, with that of a Europid (French) for comparison. (Tiedemann had already given a good drawing of the brain, viewed from above.) The simplicity of the gyri and sulci is certainly striking, but it might be supposed that some of the lesser folds had disappeared through inadequate preservation over a very long period. Ten years later, however, a whole Sanid head was very carefully preserved by a doctor in Cape Town. The arteries supplying the brain were injected with alcohol in preparation for special study of that organ. The head was sent to England and the brain examined at University College Hospital by Dr. J. Marshall, who reported that 'The numerous secondary sulci and convolutions, which so complicate the larger ones in the European brains, are everywhere decidedly less developed in the Bushwoman.'[701] He found the brain similar to that described by Gratiolet, but very slightly more advanced. It is particularly interesting that in his paper, published more than a century ago and 21 years before Kollmann[604] introduced the idea of neoteny, Marshall makes this comment: 'Undoubtedly both brains show an infantile or foetal leaning.' (For further remarks on the Sanid brain, see p. 322.)

A high percentage (61·4) of Sanids belong to blood-group 'O'; the percentage belonging to group 'A' (34·2) is near the average for human beings as a whole; 'B' (3·5) is low. It chanced that there was no one belonging to group 'AB' in the series of tests from which the percentages given here are quoted.[1131] The figures would not be a very strange set for a small population of Europids, though among them 'A' would probably be lower and 'B' higher.

Even if the idea of Mongolid or Negrid elements in Bushman ancestry were not contradicted by morphological evidence, the low figure for 'B' would make it rather unlikely.

*Particular points in the physical anthropology of the Sanids, more technically treated*

*Rhesus blood-groups.*—In this system there is some resemblance to the general Negrid pattern, for cDe is high and cDE low. [1131] The high frequency of cDe contrasts strongly with the situation in Mongolids.

*Haptoglobin.*—Bushmen are remarkable for the comparative rarity of the haptoglobin gene Hp'. Barnicot and his colleagues reported a frequency of only 0·29; [58] Jenkins and Steinberg, 0·31. [550] (In the calculation of the latter figure, a few HpO phenotypes were disregarded.) These frequencies compare with 0·51 for Hottentots and 0·53 for Zulus. The latter, like other Kafrids, may have a Sanid element in their ancestry. This would account for the fact that the frequency of the Hp' gene among them, though much higher than among the Bushmen, is significantly lower than in Sudanid Negrids, among whom there is no reason to suspect former hybridization with Sanids. The low frequency of Hp' would suggest the possibility of a Mongolid element in the make-up of the Sanids, if there were any strong morphological evidence for this (which there is not) or resemblance in blood-groups.

*External characters.*—The breadth of the head in the region immediately below the zygomatic arches is often exaggerated by the particularly large size of the parotid glands. [706]

It will be remembered that the position of the vulva was particularly stressed by Bolk as a paedomorphous character of women in general (see p. 304 and Fig. 52). It seems that the Sanids have gone further than others in this respect, for according to Eickstedt the vulva of Bushwomen is situated further forward than in any other human ethnic taxon. [302] Unfortunately he quotes as his authority a paper by Luschan in which there is no mention of the subject. If Eickstedt's statement could be confirmed, it would be an interesting example of paedomorphosis, since in other taxa the vulva is situated further forward in young girls than in adults.

The finger-prints of 345 members of the !Kun* tribe have been examined. The !Kun inhabit a large area in the north-eastern corner of South West Africa, and in the contiguous parts of Angola and Botswana. Over most of their territory they have avoided hybridization with Negrids. [445] Their prints are remarkable, for arches reach the exceptionally high figure of 13·0% in males and even 19·4% in females, and whorls, which are much more abundant than arches on the fingers of nearly all races except Khoisanids, sink to 15·1% and 17·1% respectively. [234] In this respect (though not in most others, apart from low stature) the !Kun resemble Bambutids (African pygmies). The contrast with Australids (p. 298) is particularly striking. An offshoot of the !Kun who live in the narrow band ('Caprivi Strip') of South West African territory that runs to the Zambian border, entered long ago into association with Negrids, and the resulting hybridization shows itself manifestly in their more evident morphological characters. [445] It is therefore particularly interesting to note that the finger-prints of these people, who call themselves Barakwengo, fall within the Negrid range. Arches are here down to 5·2% in males, and whorls up to 30·7%. [234]

*Skull.*—This presents a number of rather interesting characters, judged unsuitable for mention in the brief account given above (pp. 308–12).

---

* The exclamation mark represents a sound not used in European languages.

The sutures are on the whole simple. Wormian bones are uncommon, and epipterics very rare. The pterion is normal (spheno-parietal), apparently without exception. [964] There is a long backward extension of the greater wing of the sphenoid. In these features there is particularly strong contrast with the Australids.

Metopism does not appear to have been recorded. This would have been an infantile character. It is a curious and inexplicable fact that grooves on the frontal bone, occupied in life by branches of the supra-orbital nerves, occur much more frequently in the Khoisanids than in any other race of man. Indeed, their presence may perhaps be regarded as a primary character of the race.

The occipital bone is only very slightly marked by muscular impressions. [964]

The foramen magnum is generally (but not always) long and narrow, and in some cases rhomboid. [49]

The mastoid processes of the skull are small. [293, 574, 281] Their small size is regarded by Keith[574] as an infantile character, but it might be primitive. The mastoid notches (posterior digastric fossae) are unusually well-cut. [964] It is worth remarking that the celebrated Boskop skull, regarded as 'pre-Bushman', has exceptionally large and deep mastoid notches. [865]

The sigmoid notch of the lower jaw is shallow. [1072, 964, 281] This is an infantile character.

The wide separation of the eyes, well seen on the living head in Fig. 54B, is due to the breadth of the frontal processes of the maxillae. The nasal bones (or bone) are narrow in this region.

In two out of seven skulls examined by Turner,[1072] the orbital plate (lamina papyracea) of the ethmoid bone failed to articulate with the lacrimal (in one or both orbits), and the frontal bone articulated between them with the maxilla. This is a pongid character that has been recorded among the Australids (p. 288).

The lower border of the apertura pyriformis of Sanids has not been accurately described in the literature. The specimens I have examined have mostly been orygmocraspedote, with indications of the ridges characteristic of the bothrocraspedote condition.

The anterior nasal spine is usually weak or inconspicuous,[964] but this is not always so, and it is well formed in the Strandlooper skull in the British Museum (Natural History).[49]

There is evidence that the Sanids show a peculiarity in the order of eruption of the permanent grinding teeth. In Europids the 2nd molars of the permanent dentition usually erupt after the 2nd premolars, but in Bushmen the few available records show that this sequence is reversed.[280] In this respect the Bushmen resemble most pongids (chimpanzee, orang-utan, and gibbons (*Hylobates* spp.)), [612] and also Neanderthal man.[280] The 3rd molars appear late, or may fail to erupt. [1101] Edge-to-edge clenching of upper and lower incisors has been recorded. [1076] This occurs commonly in Australids (p. 289).

*Post-cranial skeleton.*—The olecranon fossa of the humerus is very frequently perforated.[103] This pongid character was noted by Cuvier in the skeleton of the 'Hottentot Venus'.[241] It appears that the shortness of the hands is due to that of the metacarpals, not of the phalanges. [706]

Both Cunningham[238] and Turner[1074] reported a high lumbo-vertebral index (about 106·5). New-born children show a high index, but it is not possible to be sure whether the Sanids are paedomorphous or primitive in this respect. The index is almost the same in Sanids and Australids (p. 291). In the latter it is regarded as a primitive character.

The strong forward convexity of the lumbar part of the spine in Sanids must necessarily be due to the wedge shape of the intervertebral disks, since the convexity would be backwards if their upper and lower surfaces were parallel. Several authors have claimed that the projection of the buttocks in Bushwomen is caused in part by the lumbar curvature, for it causes the sacrum to assume an almost horizontal position, and thus to tilt the pelvis.[1359, 849, 706, 302] The projection of the lower part of the abdomen (Fig. 56B) is also attributed partly to this cause. It is pointed out that if (as in fat Europeans) there is much adipose tissue in the buttocks but no special orientation of the pelvis, the particular form of the posterior part of the body characteristic of the Khoisanids does not result.[1359] Again, if lumbar convexity does tilt the sacrum and pelvis, but an excessive amount of fat does not accumulate in the buttocks, there is no steatopygia. Bambutid pygmies provide an example of this. However, as we have seen, something more than accumulation of fat and tilting of the pelvis is necessary to produce true steatopygia.

The sacrum is only very slightly curved in Sanids,[1293] and both sacrum and pelvis are narrow and long.[849]

*Internal organs other than skeleton.*—In discussing the brain of the *'Vénus hottentote'*, Gratiolet mentioned that in Europeans the Sylvian (lateral) sulcus is widely open at the moment of birth; and he inferred, without definitely saying so, that it remained open in the adult Bushwoman.[430] This certainly is the interpretation placed on his words by Marshall,[701] who confirmed it on his own specimen, in which the insula of Reil was exposed to external view.[701] Marshall regarded this as one of the foetal characters of the brain.

Gratiolet stressed the remarkable simplicity of the gyrus labelled $c'c'$ in his illustration. This is clearly the superior frontal gyrus, which is much convoluted in Europeans. Vogt (see pp. 39–40) was particularly struck by the simplicity of the sulci in the temporal lobe, as represented in Gratiolet's drawing.[1105, 1106] It must be mentioned, however, that Luschka, who reported on the third Sanid brain made available for study, denied that the gyri were poorly developed.[687]

Gratiolet recognized nothing corresponding to an operculate sulcus lunatus in the brain of the *'Vénus hottentote'*. He was familiar with it in pongids, but denied its existence in man.[430] Duckworth, however, noticed what he called a 'distinct vestige' of it in Gratiolet's figure of this brain, in the right hemisphere only.[1293] One can see the sulcus to which he refers in Gratiolet's drawing. Duckworth also examined the brains of two Sanids preserved in the Museum of the Royal College of Surgeons. One was the brain described by Marshall (see p. 319), the other possibly that of the woman whose body was studied by Flower and Murie.[349] He described and figured a well-marked sulcus lunatus on both sides of both these brains.[1293]

Giacomini claimed that Harder's gland occurs in a rudimentary form in the Bushman. His original paper on the subject cannot be traced, since it does not occur anywhere in the journal that he quotes in his 1897 paper.[406] It is extremely unlikely that this gland actually exists in Sanids, since it is unknown in any other ethnic taxon of man, and indeed in pongids. Bartels gives strong evidence that Giacomini saw only the glands of the plica semilunaris (*Nickhautdrüse*).[59]

That the Sanids show certain paedomorphous characters is agreed by most physical anthropologists who have written about them, and has been denied—so far as I know—by only one. Dreyer is exceptional in claiming that the Sanid is *less* like an infant of other races during the first few years of his life than he subsequently becomes.[283]

Dreyer bases this conclusion on only two features, both in the skull. The first is orthognathism. His argument is that the Sanid is prognathous when new-born and gradually becomes very orthognathous at the age of six years; subsequently he becomes somewhat less so. There are several reasons for not accepting this as evidence against paedomorphosis. First, the number of infantile skulls studied by Dreyer was very small. Secondly, he discarded the Frankfurt horizontal as the plane by reference to which prognathism was to be measured, thus making it impossible to compare his results with the great majority of those available from other sources. Thirdly, and most importantly, he recorded no measurement of alveolar (subnasal) prognathism, though it is an important character of adult Bushmen that they tend to be orthognathous as regards the upper face as a whole (*Ganzprofilwinkel*) but prognathous below the nose. Lastly, neoteny and paedomorphosis are names for the stretching out of a younger stage into adult life, but not necessarily the stretching out of the earliest stage.

Dreyer's second argument concerns changes with age in the relation between the *chord* from nasion to opisthion and the *arc* from the nasion over the top of the skull and round the occiput to the opisthion. Dreyer's own data show that this relation remains nearly constant in Sanids from the age of five or six years onwards, and his few figures from new-born and very young infants do not seem to throw any clear light on the problem of paedomorphosis.

Although Dreyer's arguments do not appear to invalidate the many clear examples of paedomorphosis mentioned in this chapter, one may readily agree with him on the existence of deep-seated differences separating the Sanids (as the less hybridized or more typical subrace of Khoisanids) from other races of man. One can, indeed, pick out characters here and there in which they resemble Negrids or Mongolids; but the older anthropologists had sound reasons for rejecting decisively the idea of any close relationships. Fritsch, for instance, one of the early students of Bushmen in their native land, was outspoken against another author who had proposed to call them 'Cape Negroes' (*Capneger*), to indicate their true affinities. He remarked that this would be like calling Germans 'European Chinese', and he claimed that Germans were in fact closer to Chinese than Bushmen to Negroes.[367] More than half a century later, in 1934, Eickstedt remarked with equal emphasis (and some exaggeration), 'It is worth remarking that we cannot establish a single unequivocally Negrid character!'[302] Pöch, who went to southern Africa to complete the observations of Fritsch and others, wrote with greater restraint but no less cogency. He gave his reasons for believing that the Bushmen had originated early as a separate race of mankind and had given rise to the Hottentots by hybridization, but were unrelated by ancestry to both Mongolids and Negrids. The evidence brought together in this chapter tends to support his view; for modern studies have on the whole confirmed the conclusions of earlier workers, though some distant relationship with the Negrids cannot be ruled out. No one has suggested any special relationship with the Australasids or Europids, from whom the Sanids are particularly distinct. Here and there hybridization with Negrids has occurred, to produce modified forms such as the Barakwengo (p. 320), or in more remote times and on a much larger scale to give rise to the Hottentots and others; but the bulk of the Sanids remain a distinct branch of humanity, illustrating well the significance of paedomorphosis in the evolution of certain ethnic taxa.

Although mankind as a whole is paedomorphous, those ethnic taxa (the Sanids among them) that are markedly more paedomorphous than the rest have never achieved the status of civilization, or anything approaching it, by their own initiative. It would seem that when carried beyond a certain point, paedomorphosis is antagonistic to purely intellectual advance. There were, however, some very skilful artists among the Sanids of past times, before the culture of these little people had been disrupted by the incursion of Hottentots, Negrids, and Europids into their territory. This has already been mentioned in the present chapter, and Appendix 6 (pp. 545–9) is devoted to the subject. It appears significant that among Europid peoples artistic talent commonly manifests itself early in life.

# 18 The Negrids (Negroes)
## I. Introduction

IT WOULD be much easier to solve the ethnic problem if whole races of man had lived in complete isolation until their cultures could be studied and recorded by qualified persons from the outer world. Isolated tribes have indeed existed which have been studied before any important changes in their culture had been caused through external influence; but tribes do not lend themselves to the solution of the problem. Small, isolated populations may remain primitive in their mode of life simply as a result of their isolation. In any community the number of persons of high intellect and character, capable of initiating advances in culture, constitutes only a small proportion of the whole. The smaller the isolated group, the less chance there is that there will be a sufficient number of such persons in it to lead the rest towards civilization. This may be so even though the isolated group is genetically as capable of *adopting* a civilized mode of life as the great majority of their relations in the larger community, among whom higher standards have resulted through the initiative of the few. The capacity or incapacity of a race to initiate a civilization can only be judged if there exists a very large number of men and women who have been uninfluenced or only slightly or indirectly influenced by cultures brought in from outside.

Anyone who wishes to obtain evidence bearing on the ability of a race to initiate a civilization must first of all consider whether the extent of foreign influence can be assessed. For this purpose he must find out as exactly as he can what contacts have been made with people of other races, in what ways and to what extent the indigenous culture has been affected by these contacts, and whether a sufficiently large number of people has been so slightly influenced that a study of them will yield information on the primary problem. The Negrids have been selected for an investigation of these problems in this book. An attempt will be made in Chapter 20 to present evidence bearing on the primary problem. The necessarily circuitous approach to it will occupy this chapter and the next.

THE PHYSICAL CHARACTERS OF THE NEGRIDS

It is necessary first of all to establish who the people are with whom we shall be concerned; in other words, to distinguish them by their physical characters. The distinction will not be made here in an elaborate manner, for we have reached a turning-point in this book and are about to leave the technicalities of physical anthropology aside until the final chapter of the book is reached. In the attempt to characterize the Negrids in the present chapter the human body will be considered only in so far as it can be seen without dissection and described in non-technical language.

First of all, however, attention must be called to the possibility that neither the Negrid race as a whole nor its subraces are capable of being distinguished.

The non-Europid peoples of Africa south of the Sahara have been somewhat differently classified by different students of the subject. This is in accordance with the usual state of affairs in taxonomy, for opinion in these matters is not determined by authority, but by careful consideration of the weight that should be accorded to different opinions. Dr. Jean Hiernaux, however, has suggested that all the proposed classifications are invalid; for he claims that the people in question cannot be separated into taxa by objective criteria.[489] It would follow that there are no such races as the Negrids and Khoisanids, and that the proposed minor taxa of these peoples are also unreal (with some rather insignificant exceptions). Hiernaux urges anthropologists to abandon all classification of the populations of sub-Saharan Africa into large subdivisions. He considers that if they would agree to this, they would liberate their thought from an 'iron collar' (carcan).

Hiernaux's case merits serious consideration, for it is carefully argued and the conclusions he reaches follow from the established facts on which he bases them. He chooses thirty-three sets of data on which he will rely. Some of these are blood-group frequencies; others are arithmetical means of certain measurements and of percentages derived from these (for instance, stature, length of front limbs and of head, breadth of head, greatest width of skull in the regions of the brain-case and of the zygomatic arches, and the length of the radius expressed as a percentage of the length of the humerus).

It must be objected to Hiernaux's conclusions that many of the data on which he relies are not those that in fact separate particular races and subraces from one another. This objection can be explained most readily by taking an extreme example of the same error from the animal world. If one wished to discover whether the Monotremata (the duck-billed platypus and spiny anteaters of Australia and New Guinea) were significantly different from other mammals, one might decide to rely on the means of particular measurements. Perhaps one might choose total body-length (corresponding very roughly to stature) and the rest of the measurements mentioned above, all of which are applicable. The study would be entirely objective. Inevitably one would find that Monotremata were not different from other mammals, since there are great numbers of members of this taxon that are significantly longer and many others that are significantly shorter than the Monotremata, and many have significantly longer and shorter front limbs, and so on in each case. One's conclusion would, however, be false, for in reaching it one would have overlooked the fact that the Monotremata, unlike other mammals, have only a single aperture in both sexes for discharge from their genital, urinary, and digestive systems; their right and left oviducts are separate throughout; they reproduce by laying eggs; they have no nipples; the shoulder girdle has an astonishingly close resemblance to that of reptiles; and there is no corpus callosum in the brain. For these and other reasons zoologists group them together and place them in a separate taxon from all other mammals.

It may be argued that one would not have chosen body-length and the other measurements mentioned, in seeking to determine whether to place the Monotremata in a taxon separate from the rest of the Mammalia. But *why not*? The reason is that one would have noticed the significant differences. Hiernaux admits this principle when he allows the possibility that the set of data on which he relies may not include those that discriminate best between Bushmen and Hottentots on one hand and other sub-Saharan African populations on the other. In all cases one should look at all parts of the body, so far as possible, to find the significant distinguishing features and those that link different peoples together. Some of the frequencies, measurements, and percentages used by Hiernaux are useful for certain purposes, others for other purposes in taxonomic studies; but by themselves they do not suffice as bases for sound conclusions in human (or any other) taxonomy.

As we shall see, there are certain large areas of sub-Saharan Africa in which there live various hybrid groups of mankind, and this fact is in part reflected by some of Hiernaux's results.

The first Negrids to become known in Europe were probably inhabitants of West Africa. It happens that these show in extreme degree most of the characters that distinguish the Negrids from other races of man. It is interesting to note how European artists represented these strangers in their sculptures and drawings, made when Negroes were not so familiar in Europe as they are today. The artists' attention was naturally drawn to the distinctive features of Negrid physiognomy. The sculpture of a Negro's head, shown in Fig. 57A, was discovered by a French peasant in 1763, buried with other ancient statues, presumably Roman, near Chalon-sur-Saône, soutn of Dijon.[195] Albrecht Dürer's excellent drawing (Fig. 57B), dating from 1528, is one of the many figures in the work already mentioned (p. 197) in which he attempted to represent the human form by what may be roughly described as a

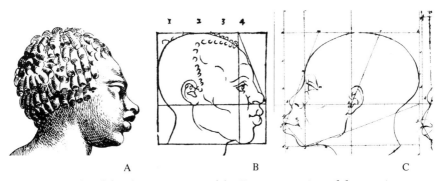

A           B           C

57   *Sudanid heads, as represented by European artists of former times*

A, sculptured head, probably Roman, found near Chalon-sur-Saône, France, in 1763; B, drawing by Albrecht Dürer, published in 1528; C, by Camper, published in 1791.
A, *from Caylus*;[195] B, *from Dürer*;[295] C, *from Camper*.[187]

system of coordinate geometry.[295] So also may Camper's sketch (Fig. 57C), published in 1791 in his *Dissertation physique* on the faces of men of different countries[187] (see pp. 28–30). In these figures one cannot fail to note the elongated head, prognathous face and jaws, weak or receding chin, small ear (B), and greatly swollen lips. An attempt is made in the sculpture to represent the tightly coiled, somewhat fleecelike scalp-hair of the Negrids. In this race the hair is very much shorter (in both sexes) than in Europids.

The models for these portraits clearly belonged to the Sudanid subrace, described by Eickstedt as 'the most Negrid of all Negrid forms'.[302] The word *Sudan* is here used in its original sense to mean the part of Africa extending from the southern limit of the Sahara through the grassland towards the region of rain-forest; but the Sudanids occupy only a westerly part of it, and their range is far distant from the politically defined state of Sudan (see map, Fig. 58). They are tall, powerful people, with slender neck, wide shoulders, long forearms, narrow hips, and very dark brown skin. Beyond the facial characters visible in side-view (Fig. 57) one may mention the rather prominent cheek-

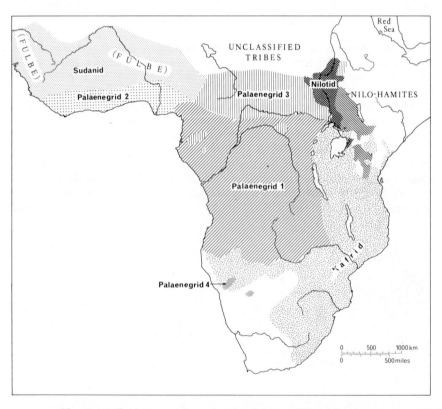

58    *Part of Africa, to show the distribution of Negrid subraces*

Attention is called to remarks on p. 109 relating to maps intended to show the distribution of races. The remarks apply also to subraces.                                                                                    *Original map.*

bones, extremely wide, flat nose with particularly large alae, sharply marked off from the rest of the organ; the nostrils are transversely elongated (Fig. 27c and D, p. 210). The 'calf' of the lower leg is somewhat better developed in the Sudanids than in the other Negrid subraces.[302]

Four subraces of Negrids are recognized in this book, the Sudanid, Nilotid, Palaenegrid, and Kafrid. They will be distinguished where abbreviation is desirable by use of the conventional symbols *Su, Ni, Pan,* and *Ka,* introduced by Eickstedt.[303]

The Nilotids occupy the region of the upper Nile (Fig. 58). They are a homogeneous taxon, and can readily be described by noting their differences from the Sudanids. They are tall and slim, with very long limbs (Fig. 60A, p. 332). It is characteristic of the Negrids in general that the forearm is long, but this feature is emphasized in the Nilotids. The lower leg is thin and (as in most Negrids) almost devoid of a 'calf'. The Negrid tendency towards a projecting heel is pronounced in this subrace.

The penis is very long and rather thick when not erect,[302] but this may perhaps be a general character of Negrids. From observations made while dissecting Negroes, the French anthropologist Paul Topinard confirmed the impression that this organ, in its flaccid state, was longer than that of Europeans,[1061] but he gave no indication of the subrace to which the corpses belonged. That Negrids have large penes is sometimes questioned, but those who doubt it are likely to change their minds if they will look at photographs nos. 8, 9, 20, 23, 29, and 37 in Bernatzik's excellently illustrated book, *Zwischen weissem Nil und Belgisch-Kongo.*[80] These represent naked male Nilotids, and appear convincing.

The skull of Nilotids is long and narrow, with bulging occiput, and the brow-ridges are feebly marked; but in most respects the face is very unlike that of Sudanids. The Nilotid is not prognathous (Fig. 60B), the chin is well developed, and the nose has quite an upstanding 'bridge', so that it is not altogether unlike that of Europids except that the alae are widely spread and more sharply marked off from the rest of the nose and from the cheeks. The lips are strongly everted, but tend to be flattened, as though compressed from in front (Fig. 59, p. 330), not bulbous as in Sudanids.

Dark as the Sudanids are, the Nilotids excel them in this respect; indeed, they are among the darkest of all the ethnic taxa of man. The cornea of the eye is somewhat brownish, and even the tongue is spotted with brown.

In studying the classification of animals one often remarks that a particular major taxon includes some minor taxa that are very distinct and others that are not easy to define. This applies also to the Negrids. The characters of the Sudanids and Nilotids can be enumerated without much difficulty, but the other two subraces, Palaenegrid and Kafrid, are much less easily defined, because they are more diverse and linked to one another by many intermediate tribes that cannot be assigned with confidence to one taxon rather than the other. There are, indeed, Palaenegrid tribes (such as the Balunda) that could not be regarded as Kafrid, and Kafrid tribes (such as the Wanyoro) that could not be regarded as Palaenegrid; but in the intermediate territory one may easily be puzzled. In the present work most of the doubtful tribes have been included in the Palaenegrid subrace. This may be justified on evolutionary grounds, for there is some evidence that the Palaenegrid should be regarded as the most unspecialized (primitive) of Negrid subraces, from which the others have sprung in the distant past,[302, 757] while no one has suggested that the Palaenegrid subrace as a whole has sprung from Kafrid ancestors.

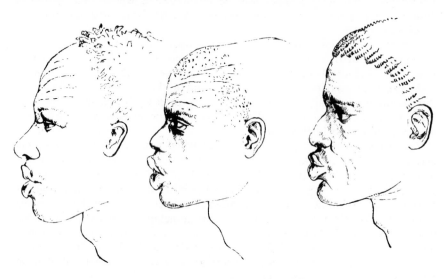

59    *Nilotid heads (Dinka tribe)*
*From Schweinfurth.* [951]

The appearance of typical Palaenegrids makes on many Europeans an impression conveyed by such subjective terms as *grob*[302] and *grossier*.[757, 1085] Livingstone had lived and travelled for years among Kafrids before he entered Palaenegrid territory, and it is evident that the difference in the appearance of members of certain tribes belonging to the latter subrace made a strong and unfavourable impression on him, which he expressed in no uncertain terms. He remarks of the Basinje that

> they seem to possess more of the low negro character and physiognomy [than certain other Negrid tribes]; their colour is generally dirty black, foreheads low and compressed, noses flat and much expanded laterally. ... their lips are large.... They make a nearer approach to a general negro appearance than any tribes I met.[676]

Two other Palaenegrid tribes, living in the vicinity of the Zambesi downstream from the Victoria Falls, also appeared unprepossessing to him.

> The Batoka of the Zambesi are generally very dark in colour, and very degraded and negro-like in appearance.... Though all [the Batonga] have thick lips and flat noses, only the more degraded of the population possess the ugly negro physiognomy.[676]

If the subjective elements in these comments are disregarded, they give an idea of how a typical Palaenegrid would be likely to appear to a Europid who had seen no Negrids except Kafrids. It will be understood that there may be many ethnic taxa of men to whom the Palaenegrids would apply words in their own language no less indicative of disfavour than Livingstone's.

The typical 'Forest Negro' or Palaenegrid is short and thickset (*'gauchement trapue',* according to Montandon[757]), with long back and short limbs, contrasting extremely in these respects with the Nilotid. The neck is short. The head is shorter than in the Nilotids, for the occiput scarcely projects and there is a tendency to mesocephaly. The brow-ridges overhang to give the impression that the eyes are sunken. The face is short and wide. The nose, flattened almost to extinction at its root, widens out greatly below to assume the form described by German authors as *trichterförmig* (funnel-shaped). Facial and body-hair are more strongly developed than in the Sudanids. Certain of the characters of the latter subrace appear in less extreme form among the Palaenegrids. Thus the alae of the nose are not so strongly demarcated, the lips are less swollen, the degree of prognathy is less, and the skin is generally paler.

Ludwig Wolf, who made a study of the physical anthropology of the Baluba tribe, remarks that 'As a general rule the male organ in its relaxed state is astonishingly strongly developed;' but he was informed by Negresses who had cohabited with both Negrids and Europids that, when erect, the organ is of about the same size in the two races.[1146] Topinard had claimed that though the penis of Europeans was smaller than that of Negrids when flaccid, it was larger than theirs when erect.

It is possible that typical Palaenegrids owe some of their characters to hybridization with the pygmies of central Africa (Bambutids).

It follows from what has been said that it is not easy to delimit the territory of the Palaenegrids on a map. All the more typical ones fall well within the area marked 'Palaenegrid 1' in Fig. 58. The inhabitants of the Guinea coast (here called 'Palaenegrid 2') are grouped by some authorities with the Sudanids[268] and separated by others as a fifth subrace,[1085] but it seems best to follow Eickstedt[302] in placing them with the Palaenegrids. The Guinean seen in Fig. 60C shows the *trichterförmig* nose particularly well. Not being extreme in any respect, the Palaenegrid 2 group may be regarded as rather typical of the Negrid race as a whole.

To the north of the Palaenegrid 1 area there is another, marked 'Palaenegrid 3' on the map, inhabited by Negrids having a strong tendency towards brachycephaly, or at least towards the brachycephalic end of the mesocephalic range. The tribes are very diverse, and many of them obviously much hybridized. They do not fit conveniently into any scheme of classification. They are put by Eickstedt[302] with the Sudanids, but it is difficult to justify this arrangement. The group seems nearer to the Palaenegrid 1 than to any other taxon.

Further north again, in the region that includes Lake Chad, the tribes are so diverse and so hybrid that in the present state of knowledge they appear to defy classification.

Far to the south, the Haukhoin (otherwise known as Ghou Damup or Bergdama[1089]) appear to represent a primitive, long-isolated group of

60  *Negrids*

A, a Nilotid (Nuer tribe), showing a stance often adopted by members of this subrace: B, a young Nilotid woman (Nuer tribe), to show the orthognathous jaws and face, and tufted hair; C, a Guinean Palaenegrid (Yoruba tribe), showing particularly well the *trichterförmig* nose.

*A and B, photographs from Bernatzik;*[180]*C, photograph from Hutchinson, Gregory, and Lydekker.* [530]

Palaenegrids, here provisionally designated 'Palaenegrid 4'. Bergdama is an unsuitable name, for although it is true that they live on high ground, they do not seem to be closely related to the Damara (Ovaherero). Haukhoin and Ghou Damup are names bestowed on them by other tribes (see pp. 425–6). It is unfortunate that they appear to have no name of their own.

It would hardly be justifiable to call the four groups of Palaenegrids 'local forms', partly because three of them are spread over such huge areas that the word 'local' is scarcely applicable, and partly because the people composing them (especially the Palaenegrid 3 group) are more diverse and harder to define satisfactorily than most local forms are.

In what follows, the names of the four groups will be written *Pan 1*, *Pan 2*, *Pan 3*, and *Pan 4* wherever abbreviation seems desirable.

The Kafrids occupy an enormous territory in the eastern part of Africa, from just north of the equator to the southern coast, and they extend across the continent in a narrow strip almost to its western fringe (Fig. 58). The subrace as a whole is a hybrid one, and the various tribes are hybrid to different degrees. Miscegenation has occurred not only with Aethiopids, but also with Sanids. The Aethiopid influence shows itself particularly clearly among the Zulu of eastern Africa and the Ovaherero (Damara) of the west. Characters of the skull suggest that the Tswana (of what is now Botswana) possess the largest share of Sanid ancestry.[252] It has already been remarked that the Kafrids merge with the Palaenegrids, so that it is particularly difficult to decide where to draw the dividing-line on the map. It would have been legitimate to expand the area assigned to the Kafrids, at the expense of the Palaenegrids. Still, the typical Kafrid differs significantly enough from the typical Palaenegrid, for he lacks those characters of the latter that appear *grob* or *grossier* to a European eye. In general, the stature is somewhat greater, despite the rather short legs; the head is higher and longer, the prognathy less marked; and the nose, though still rather broad, approximates more closely to the Europid form. The chin is more prominent than that of the Palaenegrids. Facial and body-hair is moderately developed in the male. The scalp-hair of adults in some cases tends to twist into separate tufts. This is a common occurrence among youthful Negrids, but not in adult Palaenegrids (nor Sudanids).

The inclination of the lumbar region and pelvis produces in some cases, especially among women, a particular posture with 'hanging' abdomen that is reminiscent of the Sanid. The broad shoulders, narrow pelvis, thin 'calf', and short, flat foot are common Negrid characters. The skin of Kafrids is particularly variable in colour in the different tribes, but often paler (and in some tribes much paler) than that of most Palaenegrids. The iris of the eye is brown.

Such, then, are the Negrids, with two very distinct subraces, the Sudanids and Nilotids, and two that are much more diverse and more hybridized, the Palaenegrids and Kafrids. The tribes that will be most frequently mentioned are listed and classified in their subraces in Appendix 7 (pp. 550–51).

The Nilo-Hamites (p. 226) and Fulbe (pp. 227–8) are too diverse in ancestry to constitute a taxon in the zoological sense, and they cannot be regarded without qualification as forming parts of the Negrid race. They will not be considered in what follows, but their distribution is roughly indicated in the map (Fig. 58).

## FOREIGN INCURSION INTO NEGRID AFRICA:
## A HISTORICAL SKETCH

The purpose of this section of the chapter is to explain the selection of the material on which Chapters 19 and 20 are based.

For the present purpose the vast territory of Negrid Africa may be considered in two parts. One of these corresponds roughly with those marked 'Sudanid', 'Palaenegrid 2', and 'UNCLASSIFIED TRIBES' in Fig. 58; the other comprises all the rest of the shaded areas except that marked 'NILOHAMITES', with which we are not concerned here.

The first of these two areas is that into which foreigners penetrated deeply and from many directions many centuries ago. Unfortunately they did not leave adequate accounts of the indigenous culture of the Negrids as it existed at the time of their entry. It is evident that they profoundly affected the lives of the native inhabitants by the introduction of some of their own customs and beliefs, and as a result this part of Africa is less suitable than the other for studies of the capacity of Negrids to build up cultures of their own; for the interior of the other area was entered much later and much less extensively, and the influence on native culture was therefore far less, with the result that we can gain an impression of the indigenous mode of life from the reports left by the European explorers who entered the country in the nineteenth century.

Since we shall not be concerned with the first or 'penetrated' area of Negrid Africa in Chapters 19 or 20, and shall be only partly concerned with it in Chapter 21, the history of foreign incursion into it will here be sketched in very brief outline.

Trade across the Sahara had begun to develop in the Greek and Roman periods of North African history, and the general directions of some of the caravan routes of those early times are known.[582] Salt, cloth, copper, and ornaments were carried south to the Negroes of the region of the Niger and Lake Chad in exchange for gold and slaves.

In the great area of savannah that separates the Sahara from the forests further south, large states or 'empires' began to develop under the influence of non-Negrid invaders from the north. As early as the fourth century A.D., Berbers and Jews seem to have established peaceful dominion over these states, but subsequently the foreign rulers were overthrown and the Negrids became masters in their own territories. What would have been the ultimate fate of these states if they had been left to their own devices can never be known, for the rise of Islam transformed the cultural life of northern Africa. The enthusiasm of the adherents to the new faith made itself felt right across the continent to the Atlantic coast and also southwards, deep into the land of the Negroes.

In the eleventh century Ghana was conquered by Berber followers of Ibn Yasin. The Negro rulers of Mali became Muslims, and by the fourteenth century their empire extended over 10° of latitude. The trade with the north brought such riches to this state that in 1324 the ruler made a magnificent pilgrimage to Mecca with 500 slaves, showering gold upon the Egyptians as he went. [582] By the next century a part of what had been Mali territory had fallen to the Songhai empire, which also engaged energetically in trade with the Mediterranean area. Here again the ruler was a Muslim who made a pilgrimage to Mecca.

A Europid people, the Fulbe or Ful, had found their way into Hausa territory by the end of the thirteenth century,[957] and although they did not actually take possession of the country, they soon established themselves over wide areas as members of a ruling class. The Fulbe intermarried with the Negroes, but most of them—especially those in settled communities—retained the Islamic faith. They distributed themselves here and there over West Africa and no doubt made foreign ideas familiar to many Negroes who were not actually converted to Mohammedanism.

Among the important Sudanid tribes that to a large extent adopted Islam were the Wolof[957] and Malinke.[1268] Of the hybrid tribes the ones chiefly affected were naturally those living furthest north, among them the Songhai, Haussa, Kanuri, Baghirmi, and Fur.

The extent of Moorish, Arabic, and European influence in the first or 'penetrated' area is well revealed in Mungo Park's account of his expeditions into Sudanid territory in 1795–7 and 1805.[818, 819] Far beyond the limits of previous exploration by Europeans, Mohammedan culture was well established among a considerable proportion of the Negrid population. At various places situated from nearly 60 to 220 miles beyond these limits, Park found a Mohammedan schoolmaster who possessed not only the Koran but books of commentaries on it; there were Negroes who possessed Arabic versions of the Pentateuch, Psalms of David, and Book of Isaiah, and who could tell biblical stories in their own (Mandingo) language as a result; and in one place in this area there was a Negro who possessed a large collection of Arabic books. At another place in the same area Park came across a Negro who practised the art of making gunpowder, using sulphur imported by Moors from the Mediterranean region, and at yet another there was a Mandingo merchant who possessed houses built in the style of English architecture as seen on the lower reaches of the River Gambia; his food was served on pewter dishes. Park's experiences were thus very different from those of the European explorers who entered the second, more secluded area in the middle part of the nineteenth century.

It was the Portuguese who first brought European influence round the coast of West Africa into the Gulf of Guinea and thus into Palaenegrid 2 territory. Cape Bojador in lat. 27°N. remained for a long time the limit of European exploration of the West African coast, but in 1434 one of the ships sent out by Prince Henry of Portugal rounded this point and opened the way to the south. Small quantities of gold were obtained not long afterwards and provided a great stimulus to further exploration. By 1475 it was known that the metal was available in large quantities round the bend of the coast in Ghana. The development of active trade between Portugal and the Guinea coast made foreigners and foreign customs familiar over a large part of the area inhabited by those Sudanids and *Pan 2*s who lived beyond the reach of Mohammedan influence.

In the 'secluded' part of Negrid Africa, lying to the east and south of the 'penetrated' part with which we have been concerned, the external influence was mainly non-existent or very slight, except in certain places on or near the coast; and Europeans knew little about the inhabitants of central Africa before the middle of the nineteenth century. It is significant that in Labouret's book *L'Afrique précoloniale*,[623] more than seven times as much space is devoted to the penetrated as to the secluded area, despite the fact that the latter was considerably larger. Yet it is to the latter area that our attention must be almost wholly directed, since our object is to assess the capacity of Negrids to advance towards a civilization of their own. It follows that the evidence on which conclusions are to be based must be derived mainly from observations made in the huge area occupied by the Nilotids, Kafrids, *Pan 1*s, and *Pan 3*s, in the pre-colonial period.

In presenting information about the history of the secluded area, it will be convenient to start at its north-eastern or Nilotid corner (see Fig. 58) and from there to pass down the east coast, round the southern tip of the continent, and finally up the western coast until the limit of the area is reached at the junction of *Pan 1* with *Pan 2* territory. Mention will be made of the journeys made by traders into the interior from various points on the coast, and of the depots they established in remote districts. They themselves left little information about their own contacts with the natives, and we must rely on the accounts of the nineteenth-century explorers for our knowledge of the extent to which Negrids in this area had already been affected (if at all) by foreign incursions (see Chapter 19).

In the map (Fig. 61) and also in the text of the chapters on the Negrids, the names of the tribes and places are spelled nearly or exactly as the original authors spelled them, so as to make it easy to confirm the accuracy of what is recorded here. (See Appendix 7, pp. 550–51.)

The Nilotids remained for a long time almost free from external influence. The ancient camel-routes across the Sahara passed well to the west of them, and the Nile itself was far from providing a convenient approach. Direct passage up the river from Egypt was made difficult not only by the cataracts in the lower part of its course, but even more so further upstream by the periodical accumulation of enormous masses of entangled aquatic vegetation. For long ages this *sudd* constituted a formidable barrier between the Egyptians and the Negrid tribes to the south.

Traders in slaves and ivory, loosely called 'Turks' and 'Arabs' in the history of exploration, eventually established a trading-post at Gondokoro in the southern Sudan, a little downstream from a series of waterfalls that prevented any further passage by boats. The fierce Baris of this district made travel by land precarious, but trade was carried out by armed parties over a limited distance. When Speke[996] passed northwards from the region of the great lakes in 1862, the furthest outpost of the traders was at Faloro in Acholi (*Ni*) territory, nearly 120 miles south of Gondokoro and to the north-east of Lake Albert. They had not yet penetrated into Unyoro (*Ka*) at that time, but a party of them did so immediately afterwards, just in advance of Baker.[51] Some of the traders who were in Unyoro at the same time as Baker were literate persons, accustomed to communicate with one another by letter; but they were concerned with their trade and not in the least with the propagation of economic, intellectual, ethical, or any other ideas. When Schweinfurth[951] penetrated into the district of the Bahr-el-Ghazal (*Ni* and *Pan 3*), to the west of the upper White

## 61 Part of Africa, to show the explorers' routes

The places where they met members of certain tribes are also shown (not necessarily at the centres of tribal territories). The names of tribes are written in italics. For explanations of 'X', 'Y', and 'Z', see text.
*Original map.*

Nile, he found conditions similar to those encountered by Speke and Baker to the east of the latter river. There were a few widely separated trading-posts, mostly under the control of 'Arabs' sent out by merchants resident in Khartum.

Before the nineteenth century a large proportion of the Kafrids and *Pan 1* Palaenegrids developed their own cultures with only indirect interference from the outside world, but it is necessary to consider such foreign influence as did in fact exist over the enormous area of Africa occupied by these peoples (Fig. 58). No attempt will be made to treat the subject comprehensively, but the examples given, representing the state of affairs in various parts of the country, may suffice to give a general impression.

Centuries before Christ, sailors were already accustomed to make voyages from Egypt to beyond the Red Sea. The discovery of the trade winds by the Alexandrian merchant Hippalus in A.D. 45 gave a great stimulus to the exploration of the African coasts of the Indian Ocean. A number of foreign settlements were founded along the east coast of Africa, especially from the seventh century A.D. onwards, and by the end of the tenth or thereabouts Arabs and Persians had established trading-posts as far down the coast as Sofala.[582] Several of these settlements were built on islands near the shore, such as Mombasa, Zanzibar, and Kilwa Kisiwani (Fig. 61), presumably for safety from raids by coastal natives. Slaves, ivory, and gold were exported, and in return there were imports of beads, cloth, and other articles valued by the Negroes. The influence of the foreigners was not, however, very great, because they did not attempt to take possession of any wide strips of territory, though no doubt the traders often went inland with their goods.

The Portuguese were the first Europeans to gain knowledge of these outposts of the Muslim world. Towards the end of the fifteenth century Diaz had rounded the Cape of Good Hope, but had not reached the Arab settlements. Shortly afterwards Covilha left Aden in an Arab ship and passed down the east coast to Sofala. He reported to the Portuguese authorities from Cairo in 1491. Vasco da Gama brought the first European ships to this part of the world in 1498. Passing round the Cape of Good Hope he missed Sofala and came first into port at Kilimane. Here the Portuguese found a town with streets, shops, tall stone buildings, and mosques.[463] They passed on to the large Arab town of Mozambique and then to Mombasa and Malindi, before continuing their historic voyage that opened direct commerce between Europe and India. It was chiefly to protect their trade with India that the Portuguese established colonies on the East African coast, though they were interested also in the gold exported from Sofala. Early in the sixteenth century they already controlled the whole of the East African coast from south of Sofala to north of Malindi. The Arabs paid tribute and continued their trade. The chief settlements of the Portuguese were at Sofala, Mozambique, and Kilwa Kisiwani. Forts and churches were built; slaves were exported, as they had been for centuries past by the Arabs; beads and cloth were brought in.

Arabs and other eastern Europids gradually established themselves inland at a few places on the main trade-routes between the east coast of the African continent and the interior. The most notable of these were at Ujiji, on the eastern shore of Lake Tanganyika, and at Kaze, south of Lake Victoria.

Kaze, nowadays called Tabora, is no less than 430 miles in a direct line from the sea at the nearest point, and 525 by the route that was actually followed from the coast opposite Zanzibar.[32] When Speke was there in 1861 he found a considerable town, with Arab and Indian merchants permanently in residence.[996] He describes it as 'the great central slave and ivory merchants' depot'. A 'whole conclave' of Arab merchants came to call on him here. There were several little settlements further on, in Karagwe. The most remote had been at Ngandu, west of Lake Victoria and north of the Kagera River, but this was no longer occupied at the time of Speke's visit. Strangely enough, a Beluchi had formerly made his home in what is now southern Uganda, and Arab merchants had often visited Mutesa, the king of Buganda, at his palace. Apart from the slave trade, which will be considered briefly in the next chapter (pp. 364–5), the foreign merchants who penetrated to central Africa in these regions had scarcely any effect on native beliefs or customs. A few Negrids in the immediate vicinity of the Arab establishments may have become nominal Muslims, but it is doubtful whether genuine conversion to Islam occurred at the inland depots.

When Livingstone reached Zumbo (Fig. 61) in 1856 on his journey across Africa from west to east, he found the ruins of a Portuguese church and of eight or ten stone houses. The place was 395 miles from the coast, and a much greater distance along the windings of the Zambesi. The Portuguese had left behind them no living trace of their culture; the explorer described the natives of this region as 'savages'. Tete was at that time the outpost of permanent Portuguese settlement in the interior of Africa; here Livingstone found a little community of soldiers and civilians, with a fort and some thirty houses built in European style. Formerly, however, the settlement had been larger.

The Portuguese had long been in touch with the natives of the gold-producing country that is now Rhodesia, and one of their missionaries is believed to have lived at Khami, west of the present city of Bulawayo,* at some time during the seventeenth century or perhaps even earlier.[910] The stone cross still preserved at No. 2 Hill Ruin (the 'Cross' Ruin) at Khami is supposed to have marked the site of his grave, but the evidence for this is slender. There was also at one time a Jesuit mission at Mt. Gorongoza, between Sofala and Tete, but this was no longer occupied in Livingstone's time.[676]

Foreigners had penetrated individually or in small parties to certain districts of central Africa in advance of Livingstone. An Italian had gone beyond Zumbo into Batonga (*Pan 1*) territory and reached the point marked 'Y' on the map (Fig. 61).[676] About the end of the eighteenth or beginning of the nineteenth century a former commandant at Tete, Dr. Lacerda, accompanied by another Portuguese, had explored so far as Kasempa (Kazembe), in what is now the north-west corner of Zambia.[676] Livingstone found a party of half-caste Portuguese traders at Linyanti and another at Naliele, far up towards the source of the Zambesi (Fig. 61). The leader of the latter party had actually sent letters by an Arab from Naliele to Mozambique. Since the Portuguese was himself based on Loanda, the continent had thus in fact been

---

* Not the Bulawayo shown near the south-east coast of Africa in Fig. 61.

spanned by foreigners from coast to coast before Livingstone's great journey. (Galton[378] remarks that a Portuguese, Pereira, had crossed Africa from Mozambique to Benguela well before his or Livingstone's time, but this seems to lack confirmation.) Livingstone mentions the presence of another group of half-caste Portuguese traders at Shinti, north of Naliele, but the chief here had never seen a full Europid before Livingstone's arrival. A party of Arab traders reached the vicinity of Naliele from Zanzibar while Livingstone was there.

The Portuguese established themselves at Delagoa Bay in the eighteenth century. The local chief, Dingiswayo, probably began to trade with them about 1800. The natives (*Ka*) brought their goods to the coast, for the Portuguese did not penetrate inland from here. The English trader Fynn was the first European to visit the Zulu capital.[373] This was in 1824, when Chaka had succeeded Dingiswayo. Fynn was an associate of Lieuts. Farewell and King in the foundation of the little European settlement at Port Natal (later Durban) in that year. Further information about this remarkable man is given on pp. 344–5.

About 1825 there was a Christian missionary at Buntingville, at the southeast extremity of Africa.[373] Along all the 480 miles from here to just south of Delagoa Bay, in country occupied by the Amapondo (*Ka*), Zulu (*Ka*), and other tribes, no foreigner had made his home.

In the south-eastern part of Africa very little was known about Europeans before the beginning of the nineteenth century. About that time a European (probably a Dr. Cowan) had come on horseback from Boer territory. His appearance had caused astonishment, and marvels were still related about him in later years.[373] His hat, though known to be removable, was supposed to be part of his head; he was mounted on an unknown animal capable of great speed, and he carried a pole that spat fire and thunder and killed wild animals at a distance. This unfortunate man was put to death in the belief that he was an unnatural animal.

About this time very extraordinary notions about Europeans were entertained by some of the natives of this part of Africa.[373] It was supposed that they were not actually men at all, but marine creatures that traversed the ocean in large shells. Their food was the tusks of elephants, which were laid on the shore for them to take away. In return they brought beads, which they had collected from the bottom of the sea.

The Scottish missionary Robert Moffat established himself at Kuruman in Bechuana (*Ka*) territory in 1826. Here he was joined by Livingstone in 1840. The latter soon made expeditions to the north, then extended them as far as Lake Ngami, and subsequently undertook the explorations of central Africa that made him famous throughout the world.

The Dutch East India Company established itself at Table Bay in 1652 to supply its ships engaged in trade with the east. A very large part of what is now the Cape Province was uninhabited by Negrids when Europeans founded their settlements here and along the south coast. The native population, like that of much of South West Africa, consisted of Hottentots and Bushmen. The Kalahari Desert, very sparsely populated, stood between the Europeans of the Cape and the Negrids of central Africa. It was not until towards the end of the eighteenth century that the European colonists of South Africa first came into close contact with the Kafrids, during the course of the latter's great migration towards the south. The meeting took place in the region of the Great Fish River, beyond Grahamstown. There was no immediate settlement among Negrid populations, because the two peoples wished to extend their territories in opposite directions, and the resulting hostility led to a succession of Kaffir Wars.

Climatic conditions long interfered with penetration into Africa along the southern part of the west coast. Not far north of Cape Town the so-called 'Mediterranean' vegetation is replaced by desert steppe and then by actual desert, which extends all the way to the southern border of Angola. The infertility of the coastal region and the low density of population further inland saved such natives as there were in this part of the continent from the slave trade and to a large extent kept them free from contact of any sort with the outside world. In the middle of the nineteenth century only a few isolated Europeans had made their homes inland from Walvis Bay. Galton reports that a Russian missionary was living with his English wife at Barmen in 1850, and the next year he came across a Dutchman living in extreme isolation from other Europeans at the point marked 'Z' on the map (Fig. 61). A few Europeans had penetrated overland from the south and lived at Rehoboth in Hottentot country.[377]

Further north, where the coastal climate was more genial and capable of supporting a considerable population, the Portuguese had already made contact with the natives in the distant past. The capital of the king of Congo, situated a hundred miles from the coast, had actually received Portuguese visitors in 1491. This potentate, whose realms extended from the River Congo to the Kwanza, agreed to send some of his subjects to Lisbon for instruction, and the Portuguese transformed his town into a city with a cathedral, churches, and other stone buildings.[623] San Salvador, however, did not retain its splendour. A grandson of Diaz laid the foundation of Loanda in 1576, and when eventually slaves began to be exported from the Portuguese West African possessions to supply the sugar plantations of Brazil, the port supplanted the inland city, which was gradually deserted by its European population and fell into ruins.

On his journey from central Africa to the west coast, Livingstone found the extreme limit of Portuguese authority some 380 miles inland from Loanda, where he met a half-caste Portuguese sergeant of militia.[676] At Kasanje, about fifty miles further towards the coast, he came to a little settlement of male Portuguese, unaccompanied by any Portuguese women. Here Easter Day was celebrated not only by the Europeans, but also by some of the native population.

The French established themselves in Gabon in 1839, but it was not necessary for them to penetrate far inland in search of trade, since the coastal natives (Mpongwe, *Pan 1*) were active intermediaries with the inland peoples in this respect. As a result there was little penetration of the interior by foreigners until exploration was undertaken by Du Chaillu in 1856.[200]

What has just been said may be summarized as follows. When explorers entered central Africa in the nineteenth century, Arab and Portuguese settlements had long been established here and there on the coasts and neighbouring islands, and foreign traders had set up depots far inland at Kaze, Ujiji, Tete, Kasanje, and a few other widely separated places. In most of these, however, no attempt had been made to convert or educate the native inhabitants. Here and there a very small number of foreigners was scattered at wide intervals along the main trade-routes, some of them in permanent residence. In the region of the upper Zambesi valley there had been only a few occasional visitors—mostly half-castes—from the outside world, and in many other parts of the interior there had been none at all. Even certain coastal districts had not yet been visited by foreigners.

As a result of these circumstances, the explorers saw the Negrids before their modes of life had been much changed by foreign intervention. There had, however, been certain modifications. The extent of these is discussed in Chapter 19, in preparation for the attempt made in Chapter 20 to give some impression of the indigenous culture of the Negrids and thus provide a basis for the assessment of their capacity for unaided progress towards civilization.

# 19 The Negrids
## II. Foreign influences on culture

IT HAS been shown in Chapter 18 that in the early part of the nineteenth century, over a huge area of inland Africa occupied by Nilotids, Kafrids, and Palaenegrids, there had been little opportunity—and in most places none—for the direct inculcation of ideas that had originated in more advanced countries of the external world. Yet foreigners did in fact exert some indirect influence even on remote districts. These effects of other cultures are the subject of the present chapter.

To obtain information about the life of Nilotids, Kafrids, and Palaenegrids (*Pan 1, Pan 3,* and *Pan 4*) in the pre-colonial period, it is necessary to turn to the works of the explorers of Africa in the nineteenth century. It would scarcely be possible or rewarding, however, to try to consider critically all the many reports handed down to posteriority by these men. It has seemed best to select a limited number of those who visited the country during the half-century beginning about 1820, and to make a careful study of their findings. It was important that the explorations should cover many different parts of the huge territory, and that the chosen men should be acute observers, interested in native customs and as unprejudiced as possible. They should preferably be persons with markedly different characters and backgrounds, so that uniformity of outlook caused by similar upbringing could not give a misleading impression.

The men chosen with these principles in view are listed below, with the dates of the explorations that will be considered in what follows. Some of their observations have already been recorded in Chapter 18.

| | |
|---|---|
| H. F. Fynn[373] | 1824–34 |
| D. Livingstone[676] | 1840–56 |
| F. Galton[378] | 1850–51 |
| B. P. Du Chaillu[200] | 1856–9 |
| J. H. Speke[996] | 1860–63 |
| S. W. Baker[51] | 1862–5 |
| G. Schweinfurth[951] | 1869–71 |

Wherever in this book information is attributed to any of these seven men, it is derived from the books referred to in the above list by the numbers that follow their names, unless some other book of theirs is quoted.

The first edition of Galton's book was published in 1853.[377] The 1890 edition, used in the preparation of the present work, is almost identical in most respects, but the map is much more accurate. It is to be noted that the page references given in Chapter 20 apply to the 1890 edition. The earliest edition of Schweinfurth's book was used; that is to say, the English edition, published in 1873.[951] The first German edition was published in the following year.

The routes followed by the selected explorers are shown in Fig. 61. The name of each is written beside the place on the map from which he set out, and his route is indicated by a distinctive line. The tribes on which they made most of their observations are named. They are listed in Appendix 7 (pp. 550–51), with the names of the explorers who visited them. The majority of the tribes were visited by only one of the explorers, and it is therefore unnecessary to give a reference to the authority for each statement; a glance at Appendix 7 will give the information.

It has already been mentioned that the names of most of the tribes are written in this book nearly or exactly as the explorers wrote them, so as to make it easy to find them in their books. Alternative names, most of them more accurate or according better with modern phonetic principles, are given in Appendix 7.

The choice of the seven explorers was necessarily to some extent arbitrary. Isaacs[544] might have been chosen instead of Fynn, the Pethericks[839] instead of Schweinfurth; other possibilities will suggest themselves to students of African exploration. The seven were chosen as fulfilling best the requirements that have been mentioned. It is improbable that a very different picture would have been presented if another set of explorers had been substituted, or a full study made of the writings of a larger number of explorers. A certain amount of information relating to particular areas not visited by the chosen seven is given, however, in Chapter 21.

A brief note on each of the explorers now follows.

Henry Francis Fynn was the first person to make a detailed study of the group of Kafrid tribes that were welded together, by Dingiswayo and especially by Chaka, under the collective name of Zulu. Fynn did not penetrate nearly so far inland as the other six explorers, but he travelled throughout in territory almost entirely unknown to Europeans. He had been supercargo on a ship engaged in an unsuccessful attempt to open trade with the natives of St. Lucia Bay, when he chanced to meet in Cape Town two Lieutenants of the Royal Navy, G. F. Farewell and J. S. King, just as they were planning to found a settlement at Port Natal (afterwards Durban) with the intention of trading with Chaka (see pp. 389–90). Fynn entered into partnership with them.

Fynn was a man of extraordinary character, combining fearlessness and capacity for endurance with common sense, modesty, and sensitiveness to the feelings of other people of whatever race. Isaacs, a trader who went into partnership with him afterwards in Zululand, wrote of him:

He was highly beloved by the natives, who looked up to him with more than ordinary veneration, for he had been often instrumental in saving their lives, and, in moments of pain and sickness, had administered to their relief.[544]

Fynn himself wrote:

A long residence, the author is not ashamed to confess, had endeared the people to him, but he has adhered strictly to plain matter of fact in describing their persons, manners and customs.

He had had, no doubt, less formal education than the other six explorers, and indeed he put his diary into the hands of more literate persons that it might be presented to the public in an acceptable form; yet none of the others made so detailed a study of any particular tribe (or group of tribes) as he did of the Zulu. Stuart, one of the editors of his diary, wrote of him:

The fact is that Fynn stood and still stands in a category of his own, and it is this freely and unanimously accorded precedence which straightway invests almost everything from him about the earliest days of Natal and Zululand with a distinction and quality of its own.[1021]

Fynn was a good linguist and became fluent in the Zulu tongue during his ten years' residence in the country. On leaving Natal at the end of 1834 he became Headquarters Interpreter to Governor Sir Benjamin D'Urban on the outbreak of war with the Xhosa tribe.

The demonstrable inaccuracies in Fynn's diary are so trivial as to be scarcely worth mentioning. When he wrote of 'wolves' he must have intended to refer to the African hunting-dog (*Lycaon pictus*). Unlike the other explorers, he did not survey his routes, but his descriptions leave no doubt about where he went. Although the coast of Natal runs roughly N.E. and S.W., and indeed more nearly N. and S. than E. and W., yet he adopts the strange convention that it runs E. and W. Thus, when he wishes to say that he travelled along the coast from Port Natal in the direction of Delagoa Bay, he says that he is going 'east', and in the opposite direction 'west'.

It is well known that David Livingstone undertook his stupendous journeys of exploration partly because he believed that Christianity would be most easily introduced into central Africa if convenient trade-routes to the coast could be established; yet it is obvious from his own writings that he had an intense urge to explore and to carry out geological and biological investigations. One cannot fail to be astonished at the brevity with which he explains his reasons for deciding to explore a route from central Africa to the west coast; but more extraordinary still is the economy of words with which he records his decision, made when at last he had reached that coast, that the route was not suitable for trade (because of the taxes imposed by the native chiefs), and that he must therefore turn round and travel the whole way back through central Africa and then on again to pioneer a way to the Indian Ocean. He makes no more fuss about the necessity to become the first European to cross the continent, than many a motorist would make if he found a road closed to traffic and had to make a short detour. Throughout his book he gives the impression of being an exceptionally unemotional person, tending to minimize rather than to exaggerate. 'The Boers,' he remarks laconically, 'by taking possession of all my goods, have saved me the trouble of making a will.' (To prevent misunderstanding it should be mentioned that he refers here to a particular group of persons. Of the Boers in general he remarks that they are 'a sober, industrious, and most hospitable body of peasantry'.)

An amusing instance of Livingstone's capacity to glide smoothly from religion to science is provided by the following passage. 'Walking down to the forest, after telling these poor people [Batonga, *Pan 1*], for the first time in their lives, that the Son of God had so loved them as to come down from heaven to save them, I observed many regiments of black soldier ants, returning from their marauding expeditions'—and he goes straight on to devote more than three pages to the habits of ants and related topics of natural history. In another place he gives an interesting account of the careful experiments he performed in an attempt to find out whether the larvae of Cercopidae (froghopper insects) obtain the fluid for their 'cuckoo-spit' from the atmosphere or from the sap of the plants on which they live. Livingstone also made a noteworthy contribution to evolutionary theory, which appears to have been overlooked by historians of biology. (See Appendix 8, p. 552.)

It scarcely needs to be said that Livingstone, as a medical missionary, adopted a humane and enlightened attitude towards the Negroes. Of his carriers he writes, 'I speak to them and treat them as rational beings, and generally get on well with them in consequence.' He makes generous reference to the kindness shown to him by people of certain tribes. 'I earnestly long to return, and make some recompense to them [Barotse, *Pan 1*] for their kindness.' 'After long observation, I came to the conclusion that they [Makololo, *Ka*] are just such a strange mixture of good and evil, as men are everywhere else. . . . by a selection of cases of either kind, it would not be difficult to make these people appear excessively good or uncommonly bad.'

The reliability of Livingstone's record of events can scarcely be challenged. He surveyed his routes accurately by astronomical observations. One can seldom find a slip of any kind in his book. His classification of Negro tribes is, however, rather illogical, and he is not consistent in his usage of tribal names. In one place, for instance, he equates the Makololo with the Basuto; in another he treats them as separate. In common with others of his time, he sometimes writes 'alligators' for crocodiles.

It is a far cry from Livingstone to Galton—from the missionary to the rather cold intellectual. Not everyone thinks of this remarkable and most versatile man as an explorer. Galton's fame rests chiefly on the achievements of his later life in the fields of meteorology, eugenics, and criminology. Yet his adventures when he was travelling as a young man in South West Africa were remarkable enough. He penetrated a considerable distance through unknown territory towards the part of the continent where Livingstone was then at work. He tells his story drily in the main, with only occasional attempts to entertain the reader. The most striking exception occurs when he is confronted by the enormous buttocks of a Hottentot woman and is torn between his desire to record their measurements with scientific accuracy and his delicate consideration for the modesty of their possessor. 'I was perfectly aghast at her development,' he writes. Luckily he was able to resolve his difficulty by taking observations with his sextant and then measuring the distance to where the woman had stood. Finally he 'worked out the results by trigonometry and logarithms'.

Galton is perhaps the severest and least sympathetic of the seven, but there is nothing to suggest any prejudice against the native inhabitants; he distributes praise or blame as it appears to have been deserved. Though not warm-hearted, he had the capacity for humane feelings. He was incensed by the brutal behaviour of an exploring expedition that entered South West Africa long after he had returned home. He wrote of Ovamboland (*Ka*) as 'the happy country of a noble and a kindly negro race, which has now, for the first time, been confronted and humbled before the arrogant strength of the white man'.

It would be strange indeed if one could impugn the accuracy of such a meticulously careful person, and indeed the honesty of the reporting is transparent. Still, it must be admitted that he does make a few slips. 'Alligators' appear several times, and on one occasion he thinks he has seen 'deer'. It seems probable that the use of these words was laxer in his time than it is today.

Du Chaillu was an American, a trader and the son of a trader in western Africa. His post was on the right bank of the Gabon River near its mouth. His explorations did not carry him very far inland, but he penetrated farther up the Muni, Ogowe, and Rembo Rivers than anyone of European ancestry had ever gone before. Although he traded to some extent on his numerous exploring expeditions, it is clear that this was not his main purpose in going inland. He was an enthusiastic amateur naturalist, with a considerable knowledge of birds; but he was animated above all by a determination to be the first white man to study the gorilla in its native haunts—in fulfilment of which he was eminently successful. He laid no claim to be an anthropologist, but his descriptions of the natives and their customs appear to be factual, objective, and unprejudiced. He accumulated extensive collections of objects made by the people through whose territory he passed, and many of these are illustrated in his book.

He gives the impression of having been a warm-hearted, enthusiastic, truthful, but not very intellectual traveller. He minimizes rather than exaggerates the rigours of African exploration. He was a religious man, genuinely concerned with the welfare of native peoples. A few extracts will demonstrate his lack of prejudice against them.

> I met everywhere in my travels men and women honest, well-meaning, and in every way entitled to respect and trust; and the very fact that a white man could travel alone, single-handed, and without powerful backers, through this rude country without being molested or robbed, is sufficient evidence that the negro race is not unkindly natured.

> I shall never forget the kindness of the women [Bakalai, *Pan 1*] to me while I was sick. Poor souls! they are sadly abused by their task-masters [husbands]; are the merest slaves, have to do all the drudgery, and take blows and ill-usage besides; and yet at the sight of suffering their hearts soften just as in our more civilized lands.

> Women [Apingi, *Pan 1*] are ever kind and ready to help the helpless even in brutalized Africa.

Du Chaillu relates that on one occasion he and his party, nearing starvation, came unexpectedly upon some Negroes of the Ashira [*Pan 1*] tribe. These people, to whom his party were total strangers, and who must have regarded Du Chaillu himself almost as an apparition from another world, at once provided them with food.

When Du Chaillu first reported his experiences, especially those with the gorilla, he was met with a good deal of incredulity. Time has proved the essential truth of what he wrote, though he was not so accurate as the other explorers. He nowhere reveals his survey methods, and although he gives a detailed map, one cannot be quite certain of his routes. He mentions a river running 'easterly', when obviously it flowed towards the west. He shows little concern for the correct names of animals. He writes of deer, tigers, vampire bats, 'touracaw', toucan, and humming-birds, none of which are names properly applicable to animals inhabiting the Ethiopian zoogeographical region. It seems incredible that anyone so much interested in birds as he was, and so knowledgeable about them in some ways, should not be aware that what he called a 'toucan' was in fact a hornbill. Carelessness, not ignorance, surely provides the explanation.

Speke, a Captain in H.M. Indian Army, ranks with Livingstone and Baker as one of the greatest African explorers. When he undertook the journey with which we are concerned in this book, he had already made two expeditions to Africa with Burton, on the second of which he had discovered the Victoria Nyanza. He now set out with Grant from the mainland opposite Zanzibar, to pass clockwise round the lake until he should find the outflow of the Nile. He gives the impression of having been a rather typical army officer of his time—brave, persevering, just (though rather harsh in his dealings with delinquents), on the whole warm-hearted, and generous to those who dealt faithfully with him. He writes in a straightforward style, but with a strong tendency to long-windedness. The details he gives of the taxes or *hongo* paid to various chiefs through whose territories he had to pass are almost intolerably tedious.

He was a careful observer of native life. 'I profess accurately to describe native Africa,' he writes, '—Africa in those places where it has not received the slightest impulse, whether for good or evil, from European civilization.' He points out frankly the deficiencies he found in the people of certain tribes, but he is clearly unprejudiced. 'To say a negro is incapable of instruction', he remarks, 'is a mere absurdity; for those few boys who have been educated in our schools have proved themselves even quicker than our own at learning.'

Speke's accuracy is beyond reproach. One cannot find in his book any little slip similar to those already mentioned in the accounts of the other explorers. When he returned to England he was strongly attacked by his former companion, Burton,[173] and certain other geographers, who were unprepared to accept his account of the source of the Nile. It was arranged that he should confront Burton at a meeting of the British Association for the Advancement of Science, but on the very morning of the day appointed for this purpose he tripped at a stile when out shooting, and was killed by the discharge of his gun.

Subsequent explorations confirmed the accuracy of Speke's geographical researches. His map and Burton's are put conveniently side by side in the latter's book.[173] One can see at a glance that Speke's was essentially correct, while Burton's was entirely wrong.

When Speke reached the little trading-post of Gondokoro, after having proved that the Nile flows from Lake Victoria, he found Samuel Baker and Florence von Sass, who had set out in the opposite direction with the intention of discovering the source of the river, and Baker left for the south to study the still unknown regions. Baker proved—as Speke had suspected, from native reports—that the river flows from the Victoria Nyanza into another large lake, the Albert Nyanza, before turning northwards as the definitive White Nile.

Baker travelled largely to satisfy his love of adventure. He had formed a fixed resolve—communicated, when he left civilization, to no one but Florence von Sass, who was his companion throughout and subsequently became his wife—to solve the mystery of the Nile sources. The book is remarkable for the full credit he gives to Speke and Grant, from whose achievement he never tries to detract one iota. He was the best writer of the seven, a master of clear, direct English, capable of expressing facts in all their stark reality, yet with humour and pathos. His obviously genuine grief at the deaths of some of his faithful companions of various races is touching even at this distance of time. He was a keen and accurate observer of the native populations of the countries through which he passed. 'I will exhibit a picture of savage man precisely as he is,' he justifiably claims, 'as I saw him; and as I judged him, free from prejudice.'

Baker's writings are as devoid of errors due to carelessness as Speke's. He seriously misjudged the extent of Lake Albert in the part to which he did not penetrate, but his survey of nearly the whole of his route is remarkably accurate, despite the great difficulties under which he worked. His main geographical discoveries have all been confirmed.

George August Schweinfurth was born in Riga and refers in his book to 'my Livonian home', but he was in fact a German, and studied botany at German universities. The main purpose of his expedition of 1869–71 was to study the vegetation of the country traversed by the Bahr-el-Ghazal and its tributaries. Although a botanist by training and profession, he was well equipped for observations in zoology and anthropology. As a surveyor he was not in the same class as Livingstone, Speke, and Baker, but he was able to make some notable contributions to geography. He was the first European to penetrate from the north beyond the Nile–Congo watershed, and the first also to give a full account of the Azande or 'Niam-Niam' cannibals (*Pan 3*). His writings are eminently accurate, but rather dry and humourless (though in one place he does say of certain Arab women that they were 'little accustomed to keep alive the sacred fire of Vesta'). When he gives particulars, in the text itself, of the width and depth of every trivial stream he has to cross, he is even more tedious—if that is possible—than Speke on *hongos*; but the book is enlivened by his excellent drawings, which are finished works of art that did not require the hand of a professional artist to fit them for publication. Of his humanity there can be no question, for there are many evidences of it. He describes the slave-traders as 'incarnations of human depravity'. Of the death of little Tikkitikki, the pygmy (Bambutid) whom he adopted, he remarks:

> Never before, I think, had I felt a death so acutely; my grief so weakened and unmanned me that my energies flagged entirely. Since that date two years have passed away, but still the recollection of that season of bitter disappointment is like a wound that opens afresh.

These, then, were the seven men on whom I rely for the information given, in this chapter and on the next, about Negrid culture in the secluded area. They had not the training or expertise of modern social anthropologists, but they belonged to no particular school of thought, and I think the evidence is indisputable that they reported what they saw and gave a reliable general impression of many aspects of the Negrid life of their times, in the remoter parts of Africa.

The foreign trade-goods most frequently noticed by the explorers were beads, which had already spread nearly everywhere. The cannibal Fang tribe (*Pan 3*) of the interior of Gabon were already using imported beads when the first European explorer reached them; they had almost become a 'necessity' in their lives. It is easily understandable why these objects were particularly favoured. They were more ornamental than the comparable objects of native manufacture; they were hard and not subject to spontaneous decay; and their size and weight were small in relation to the value placed upon them. They were the standard small change of barter. In East Africa they were imported mainly from Venice, though the red ones (*kadunduguru*) came from India.[996] The eastern trade was mostly in the hands of the Indian merchants (Banyans) of Zanzibar. In the middle of the nineteenth century no fewer than four hundred varieties of beads were available. It was important for the traveller to know in advance precisely which varieties were favoured in particular districts. Explorers were thus at a disadvantage as soon as they entered territories where the local taste was not yet known by the traders on the coast. The use of imported beads does not appear to have altered the thought-processes of the native inhabitants to any marked extent, or upset their endemic institutions.

Foreign cloth was exchanged in more important transactions. It was valued for its intrinsic worth rather than traded repeatedly from hand to hand as a substitute for money; but the native chiefs of East Africa made large demands for particular varieties of foreign cloth as part of the *hongo* required from travellers for permission to pass through their territories,[996] and stores of it no doubt constituted part of their wealth.

American sheeting (*merikani*) and red Indian stuffs (*kiniki*) were among the favoured cloths in East Africa, but there was a remarkable demand for British goods towards the central part of the continent. Livingstone found the territory between Tete and Zumbo abundantly supplied with English cotton goods, which were, indeed, carried still further from the coast by Babisa traders to just beyond the confluence of the rivers Kafue and Zambesi. He found 'Manchester goods' at the extreme north of Barotse (*Pan 1*) territory, near the frontier with the Balunda (*Pan 1*); the place is marked 'X' on the map (Fig. 61). These goods had been brought by enterprising Mambari traders. The explorer's Makololo (*Ka*) carriers, who had not seen such stuffs before, could not believe them to be the work of mortal hands. 'To Africans our cotton mills are fairy dreams,' he wrote. A little further along, on his journey towards the west coast, Livingstone found about a hundred women belonging to a Balunda chief 'clothed in their best, which happened to be a profusion of red baize'.

Firearms had not yet reached the central part of the continent. They were unknown, too, at Kamurasi's palace in Unyoro when Speke first arrived there. Chaka knew nothing of them, and was at first unwilling to believe that they could be more effective in warfare than the assagai. In many places, however, the knowledge of these weapons spread inland well in advance of the white man himself. Du Chaillu was surprised to find guns and powder 'not at all uncommon' among the Bakalai (*Pan 1*) of Gabon, some 90 miles from the coast; indeed, they were the chief articles of trade in this previously unexplored district. They were used here in hunting. In the region of the watershed between the Zambesi and the Kasai, at the western limit of the Balunda tribe, Livingstone found it difficult to obtain food except in exchange for gunpowder. The people had cleared most of the district of big game by shooting with firearms. In general, however, the difficulty or impossibility of obtaining a regular supply of bullets and powder set a limit to the use of muskets, except near trading-posts.

Several of the musical instruments of the Negrids were clearly of foreign invention. Schweinfurth mentions two used by the Azande that will serve as examples. He calls one of them a mandolin and the other 'something between a mandolin and a harp'. Both of these seem to fall into the category of *harpes arquées,* by Hickmann's definition.[488] Instruments of this general type consist of a resonating chamber to which one end of each string is attached; the other is fixed to a solid curved shaft that forms an extension of the chamber. The difference from the true harp is that the shaft is not turned back over the resonating chamber, but forms an obtuse angle with it. Arched harps similar to those of the Azande were in use in Sumeria three thousand years before the birth of Christ.[1111] A number of specimens from ancient Egypt, preserved in the Cairo Museum, are described and illustrated in Hickmann's book.[488]

The *robaba* or *rabala* of the Mittu and Obbo peoples will serve as an example of those musical instruments that can neither be claimed nor disclaimed with confidence as inventions of the Negrids. The name suggests the *rahab* of Arab countries, but the latter was a different instrument, played with a bow. The *robaba* was essentially a lyre, with a large hollow base and few strings (five in the Mittu version, eight in that of Obbo). The Nubians (Aethiopids) certainly possessed it and called it *robaba*, but whether it diffused to or from them seems to be uncertain. One has the impression that whoever first made it must have previously seen a typical lyre.

. The objects so far mentioned fall into three categories, as follows. (1) Those, such as beads, that serve only for ornament or exchange. (2) Those (firearms, for instance) that can be used for practical purposes but do not lend themselves to being copied by the people who receive them, or to the making of anything else. (3) Those that can be used and also copied, but again do not serve to produce any other object or substance (the arched harp is an example). The objects classified in categories (1) and (2), and possibly those in (3) also, are likely to have less effect on ideas and culture than contrivances that are useless in themselves, but valuable for what they can make, if the recipient will learn to use them. These contrivances are of two kinds: those that make a decorative or practically useful *object*, and those that have as end-product a *substance* that can then be fashioned for decorative or practical ends. In the present context the two kinds are best represented by the loom and the smelting-furnace respectively.

There can be scarcely any doubt that weaving was introduced into Negrid Africa from the north. Livingstone points out that the method of spinning cotton and the construction of the simple looms he saw were the same in Angola and south-central Africa as those represented on the monuments of ancient Egypt. More complicated looms than those described by Livingstone were observed by Du Chaillu further north, among the Apingi (*Pan 1*) and Ashira (*Pan 1*) tribes. Two sets of 'dividers' were incorporated in these instruments, to separate the warp and admit the shuttle. The fibre used by the weavers of these two tribes was a local product, derived from the leaf of an unstated species of palm. The Ashira cloth was described by Du Chaillu as 'of very fine and tolerably even texture'. Men were the weavers here, women in Angola. Speke says that the Wanyamwezi (*Ka*) were expert in the weaving of cotton on their looms. It must be remarked, however, that the explorers seldom mention weaving by members of the very numerous tribes through whose territory they passed. Schweinfurth attributes the fact that the Monbuttu did not weave to the lack of any intercourse with Muslims or Christians.

The practice of smelting iron from its ores and forging it into weapons and tools is thought to have been brought to the Sudanids by Berbers at some time during the first five centuries of the Christian era.[207] Knowledge of these techniques may have spread from the west to all parts of Negrid Africa, but one cannot rule out the possibility that it came to the east and south along the Nile from the ancient civilization of Meroe.[207] The smelting of iron was probably practised in most parts of Negrid territory by the tenth century, except in districts where the ore was lacking.

Baker watched and sketched the smelting of iron by men of the Lotuko tribe (variously regarded as Aethiopid and 'Nilo-Hamite', see p. 226) at Tarangole, east of the White Nile, near the southern extremity of what is now the state of Sudan. The bellows were made from two pots each about a foot deep. Their mouths were covered with very pliable leather, and to the centre of each covering was attached an upright stick, about four feet long. From the bottom of each pot there extended an earthenware pipe about two feet long, the extremities of the two pipes being inserted in a charcoal fire laid on the ground. The bellows-blower worked the sticks rapidly up and down, in alternation, and thereby produced a powerful blast. The ore was laid on the charcoal. It is interesting to place side by side Baker's drawing, on p. 205 of Vol. 1, and Du Chaillu's, on p. 91 of his book. The close resemblance between them is remarkable, for the latter's were made in Fang (*Pan 3*) territory, about 1,550 miles away. The only differences are that the pots and pipes of the Fang were made of wood, and the pipes tipped with iron; a system of valves is mentioned and vaguely indicated in the drawing. The similarity makes a single origin scarcely questionable.

Among the Monbuttu (*Pan 3*) leather was replaced by plantain leaves, simmered in hot water until silky; no valves were provided. The Bongo (*Pan 3*) and Dyoor (*Ni*) made conical furnaces of baked clay, instead of simply placing the charcoal and ore on the ground or in a trench, as other tribes did. The Dyoor put airpipes at the bottoms of their furnaces, but did not use bellows. The Zulu (*Ka*) used square bags made of bullocks' hides as bellows and worked them with horizontal sticks, moving their thumbs and middle fingers to act as valves; the pipes were bullocks' horns. However, they seldom smelted iron from the ore, since they found it easier to take it by force from their enemies.

Du Chaillu described the iron of the Fang as superior to that brought by traders to Africa for sale to the Negroes, and Schweinfurth claimed that the Bongo metal was 'quite equal to the best forged iron of our country' (Germany), even though they did not understand how to prepare good charcoal.

Baker, Du Chaillu, Livingstone, Speke, and Schweinfurth are all lavish in their praise of Negrid skill in forging iron into tools and weapons. Indeed, there was perhaps no other art in which they excelled to quite the same degree. The tribes mentioned for their particular expertness in this respect were the Wanyoro (*Ka*), Wanyamwezi (*Ka*), Banyeti (*Pan 1*), Bongo (*Pan 3*), Fang (*Pan 3*), and above all the Monbutto (*Pan 3*). The Zulu and Bongo blacksmiths used a stone for an anvil. The latter sometimes used simple iron hammers, not provided with handles. Though Schweinfurth does not specifically say so, it seems probable from his account that they made these themselves. If so, it would be an example of the construction of tools designed to help in the manufacture of other kinds of tools. Thomas Carlyle long ago attributed to his hero, Professor Diogenes Teufelsdröckh, the statement that 'Man is a Tool-using Animal (*Hanthierendes Thier*),'[190] but actually there are a few species of animals that not only use but make tools. The construction of a tool designed to make other tools seems, however, to be a purely human achievement, and one not attained by every ethnic taxon of man.

The chief tools made by Negrid blacksmiths were hoes (especially the heart-shaped variety called *molote*), knives, and choppers, but they were also capable of making delicate instruments, such as razors; and the Zulu and Wanyoro were skilful enough to make iron needles. The Wanyoro did not bore the eye, but pointed the eye-end, turned it back, and hammered it into the shaft, in which a small cut had previously been made to receive it. Another very delicate instrument was made by the Bongo for a purpose that would astonish Europeans, for they were designed to pluck out the eyebrows *and eyelashes* of the women. Such instruments, made by Negrids, are often called 'pincers', but this name is incorrect, since there was no pivot, the points having been directly joined by a springy piece of iron. 'Tongs' is the right name. The masterpieces of the Monbuttu were ornamental chains, of which Schweinfurth remarks that 'in refinement of form and neatness of finish [they] might vie with our best steel chains'.

Particular interest attaches to the roughly shaped *molote* called *loggoh kullutty*, which was made and used as a medium of exchange by the Bongo and many other tribes in the region of the upper Nile and its tributaries, and indeed further afield, to the west. The article in question must have originated by the use of an ordinary *molote* in bartering for other goods; but it is evident that in the course of time its primary function was lost and it was passed from hand to hand as currency. Eventually it could no longer be used as a hoe or spade. It became nearly circular instead of heart-shaped, and was often decorated with a double hook at what should have been the pointed end. Strangely enough, a fitting for a wooden handle survived uselessly at the other end, reminding one of what zoologists call a 'rudimentary organ'. Schweinfurth remarks that the *loggoh kullutty* was the only equivalent of money in central Africa; but he must have meant the only equivalent that was *made* in central Africa, for as we have seen, imported beads served the same purpose over a very wide area.

The chief weapons made of iron by the Negrids were war-knives of various designs, the heavy thrust-spear or assagai, and lighter spears commonly referred to by the explorers as 'lances'. Some of the heads for the lighter spears were extremely elaborate and obviously demanded a high degree of skill in forging (Fig. 62A). The assagai was a weapon of the Berbers (the name is a corruption of theirs), but its use and manufacture spread through Africa right down to the territory of the Zulus, whose success in battle under Chaka was largely due to its use. The harpoons used by the Wanyoro in hunting the hippopotamus were of precisely the same pattern as those used by the Hamran Arabs of Ethiopia. A remarkable weapon called the *kulbeda* may, however, be a Negrid invention, originating with the *Pan 3* Palaenegrids or their neighbours, the hybrid tribes living in the vicinity of Lake Chad. It was a complicated missile dagger, with three blades, of very constant design over a huge area. Specimens made by the Azande (Fig. 62B) not far west of the Nile were of essentially the same form as those made by the Fang in Gabon, more than a thousand miles away (C).* It is noteworthy that the Fang are an isolated group of *Pan 3* living in an enclave of *Pan 1* territory.

The explorers do not mention the use of any iron device of what might be called a mechanical nature, in which the motion of one part would cause another part to move in a particular direction to achieve an intended result.

Some of the Negrid tribes, in particular the Bongo (*Pan 3*), were primarily cultivators of the soil; others, the Wanyamwezi (*Ka*) and Zulus (*Ka*) among them, were both cultivators and pastoralists on a large scale; the Ovaherero (*Ka*) and most of the Nilotid tribes were mainly pastoralists. With the possible exception of the Nilotid tribe called by Baker 'Kytch', all the Negrids visited by the explorers cultivated plants to a greater or smaller extent. Even the Haukhoin (*Pan 4*), despised and regarded as primitive by the Negrids and Khoids with whom they came in contact, were in fact agriculturists and pastoralists, not merely food-gatherers.

The crops most frequently cultivated in the secluded area were dhurra (especially), telaboon, maize, sugar-cane, yam, plantain, cassava, ground-nut, and sweet potato. A list of all the identifiable cultivated plants mentioned by the explorers is given in Appendix 9 (p. 553), with the scientific and common names of each.

The cultivation, improvement, and export of certain plants as food-crops goes so far back into antiquity that it is in some cases difficult to determine where the wild prototypes originally lived and by whom they were first cultivated; but when the explorers reached the interior of Africa, several undoubtedly exogenous crops were already under cultivation on a very large scale. Maize, cassava, and ground-nut were almost certainly brought to the African coast from South America by the Portuguese; sugar-cane originated in Asia, but at least some of it was imported into Negrid Africa from the West Indies.[373]

* A specimen of the Fang *kulbeda* is exhibited in the British Museum, and another in the Queen Victoria Museum, Salisbury, Rhodesia. Both are closely similar to the one illustrated by Du Chaillu (Fig. 62C).

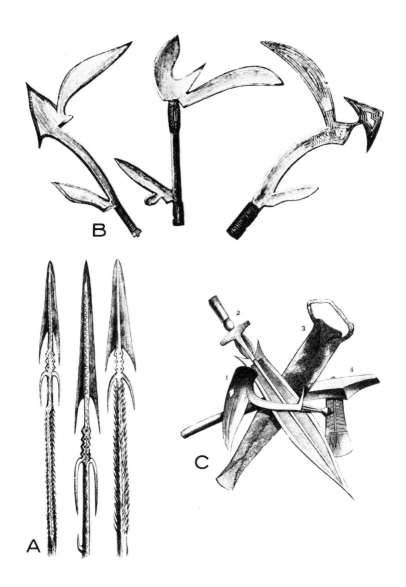

62  *Negrid (*Pan 3*) weapons forged in iron*

A, Bongo lance-heads; B, three missiles (*kulbeda*) of the Azande; C, Fang weapons; 1, *kulbeda*; 2, war-knife (and 3, its sheath); 4, war-axe.          A *and* B, *from Schweinfurth;* [951] C, *from Chaillu.* [200]

Although, superficially at least, the introduction of cultivated plants from abroad made the lives of Negrids more similar to those of the inhabitants of the countries from which they were imported, yet this external influence was remote, for foreign advisers on agricultural methods did not travel inland with the crops. One must suppose that seeds or young plants passed from hand to hand into the interior, and that to a large extent the Negrids adopted their own methods of cultivation, and modified their lives to suit the new conditions.

Some of the introduced plants became the principal food-crops of particular tribes. Cassava and ground-nuts attained this status among the Balunda (*Pan 1*), and the Fang (*Pan 3*) relied principally on the former for the vegetable part of their diet. Some of the tribes, however, showed initiative in cultivating a considerable number of foreign and indigenous food-plants.

The Abanga (*Pan 3*), neighbours of the Azande and Monbuttu, cultivated at least sixteen species of food-plants. It is difficult to be quite sure of the identity of some of the species listed by Schweinfurth, but the sixteen were almost certainly these: cassava, ground-nut (*Arachis hypogaea*), butter-bean, Catiang bean, horse-bean, Bambarra ground-nut, sweet potato, sesame, kendee, yam, bajra, telaboon, maize, sugar-cane, taro, and plantain. The Abanga also cultivated a bark-cloth tree (probably *Ficus natalensis*, but named *Urostigma Fotschyana* by Schweinfurth) and Virginian tobacco.

South American tobacco (*Nicotiana tabacum*) had already penetrated to the central part of the isolated area before any of the explorers had reached it. It is a strange fact that this species was everywhere known as *tab* or *tabba*, while the North American species (*N. rustica*) received various names in different native dialects. Schweinfurth (1873) concluded from this that *rustica* was indigenous, but this cannot be accepted. Smoking was introduced to Negrid Africa by foreigners. The Batonga (*Pan 1*), Makololo (*Ka*), and certain other tribes of central Africa were much addicted to smoking hashish, and Livingstone attributed the 'very degraded' appearance of the former partly to their indulgence in this habit. Indian hemp, the source of the drug, is indigenous to central Asia, and was probably brought to Africa from Persia or India.

Some of the animals introduced from the outside world affected the rules, ceremonies, superstitions, and tabus of native life very much more than the plants we have been considering. In many places cattle became as important as anything else in tribal life, and indeed among some tribes came to dominate the thoughts of the people. Foreigners thus had a very great effect, but an effect of an entirely different kind from the introduction of, for instance, a new religion. What was introduced was not a new idea, but an alien self-reproductive object, about which new ideas would originate locally. It is necessary to consider the domestication of animals in some detail, partly because of their importance in tribal life, and partly because it is necessary to know whether the Negrids relied wholly on the import of already domesticated species, or whether they showed any aptitude for the actual process of taming wild animals. We must take leave of the explorers for a while and turn our attention to some problems of geographical distribution and domestication.

Among the striking negative characters of the Ethiopian zoogeographical region of Wallace[1116]—that is to say, the whole of Africa from the southern part of the Sahara to the extreme south of the continent—is the absence from the indigenous fauna of certain animals that have long been domesticated in other parts of the world. Among these are the subfamilies Ovinae (sheep) and Caprinae (goats and their allies), and the genera *Bos* (cattle), *Sus* (boar), and *Gallus* (fowl). Certain members of these subfamilies and genera are much more frequently mentioned by the explorers as being kept by the Negroes in the domesticated state than any other animal except perhaps the dog. The latter belongs to a genus (*Canis*) that is represented in the indigenous fauna of the Ethiopian zoogeographical region.

In his paper on the domestic animals of the Bantu (that is to say, on the Kafrids and *Pan 1*), Kroll[615] did not take sufficient account of the fundamental distinction between the part of Africa that is north of the Sahara and belongs to the Palaearctic zoogeographical region, and the Ethiopian region to the south. He describes each domesticated species as either 'African' or foreign (*fremd*), according to whether or not the wild species occurred in *any* part of Africa. He thus failed to make the necessary clear distinction between purely Palaearctic species that were tamed by Europids (in northern Africa or elsewhere) and subsequently introduced as domesticated animals into the Negrid part of the continent, and those that were tamed and domesticated by Negrids (if in fact there were any species that could properly be assigned to the latter category; see pp. 373–7). This treatment of the subject is liable to give an entirely incorrect impression of the capacity of Negrids to tame and domesticate wild animals, if the reader of his paper does not happen to be acquainted with the elementary principles of zoogeography and ethnography.

Long-horned wild cattle were formerly widely distributed in the Palaearctic zoogeographical region. They occurred, as the fossil record shows, in Europe, Africa north of the Sahara, and Asia, and also in the western part of North America. Some authorities recognize three species, but the distinctions do not appear to be clear-cut and it is probably best to refer all these forms to a single species, *Bos primigenius*.

Mesopotamian sculptures thought to date from about 3000 B.C. show *B. primigenius* being milked, and also in stalls with calves. Cattle were also used to draw funeral carts at this period.[514] It is generally supposed that domesticated members of the Asiatic race (*nomadicus*) were introduced into North Africa, where they may have interbred with the indigenous wild cattle (*opisthonomus*).[321] The Egyptians are known to have kept domestic cattle with both long and short horns during the period of the Nagada culture (about 3500–2600 B.C.).[117]

The only other ancestral cattle with which we are concerned here are commonly assigned to the species *B. indicus* or zebu, which, like *B. primigenius*, no longer survives in the wild state. The ancestor of the zebu is not known with certainty, but it is thought to have lived on the borders of the great deserts of Iran and Afghanistan and to have spread thence into the Indus Valley and thus to peninsular India and elsewhere. Zebu are short-horned cattle characterized chiefly by a large hump on the back, over the first to ninth thoracic vertebrae (Fig. 63A, p. 358). The hump consists of voluntary muscle fibres interspersed

63　*Zebu and sanga, the two chief types of cattle kept by Negrids*

A, zebu bull; B, sanga ox of the Nguni breed.　　　*Photographs by Mr. J. P. Maule.*

with adipose tissue, and must be regarded provisionally as a reservoir of nutriment that evolved in adaptation to semi-desert conditions.[747]

Tethered bull zebu are represented on vessels found in Baluchistan, supposed to date from 3000 B.C.[514] A domesticated zebu of a particular breed, with a hump situated rather far forward, appears in Egyptian tomb-paintings of the 18th dynasty (about 1557–1330 B.C.),[321, 514] but the typical zebu is not represented in ancient Egyptian monuments. It is thought to have been first brought from Arabia and the Persian Gulf to Africa at the 'Horn' in the seventh century A.D.[321]

These two kinds of cattle, *Bos primigenius* and *B. indicus*, were the ancestors of all the many breeds that existed in the secluded part of Africa when the explorers entered the interior of the continent; but whereas the zebu had retained its characteristic form, a typical representative of *B. primigenius* was not present. The long-horned cattle of the area belonged to the group of breeds termed *sanga* (Fig. 63B), which are characterized by a small, muscular hump, situated further forward than that of the zebu. There is adipose tissue between the muscles of the hump, but this tissue is not interspersed between the individual contractile fibres, and the muscle is thought to play a part in the movement of the forelimb.[747] The horns are usually long.

It seems almost certain that the sanga originated in Ethiopia. The name is Ethiopian in origin, and was applied to the giant-horned Galla cattle of past times, though sanga are no longer to be found in this country except in the territory of the Danakil tribe (Aethiopids).[711] Two hundred years ago James Bruce was present when Guangoul, chief of the Eastern Galla, came to pay his respects to the King of Ethiopia. He was mounted on a cow, 'not of the largest sort, but which had monstrous horns'.[155] This may well have been a sanga. It is significant that the cattle of the Bahima and Watusi are sanga, for these are Aethiopid people who have wandered into Negrid territory in the region between Lakes Albert and Tanganyika and in many places live as pastoralists in close association with Negrid tillers of the soil.

Three possibilities exist as to the mode of origin of sanga cattle. Frechkop[356] derives the '*race des Watusi*', as he calls them, from the zebu, but the resemblance to *primigenius* is closer. Sanga may have originated directly from *primigenius*, by selection, but a hybrid origin from the two species, *primigenius* predominating, is more probable. The horns of some breeds of sanga are even longer than those of the long-horned ancestor ever were, and this can only be due to long-continued selection.

The two types of cattle, sanga and zebu, with some intermediates, cover the whole of the secluded area, apart from desert and non-pastoral regions. The zebu is particularly characteristic of the east coast and the sanga of the central and western parts (though the Zulu of the south-east kept sanga cattle).

Although the Negrids originally received domesticated cattle as novelties introduced from the outside world, yet many of the tribes adapted themselves to a pastoral life in response to their new acquisition, and some of them developed more than a purely practical interest in their herds. Stringent rules evolved —varying in the different tribes—about the duties of the two sexes in relation to herding and milking, and about the propriety of consuming milk in the fresh or curdled state; in some tribes the slaughter of cattle was forbidden, and beef was replaced by blood taken from living animals. A fictitious value was placed on the animal, depending largely—in the case of the sanga—on the length of the horns. Cattle were used in place of money, especially in the purchase of wives.

So intense was the interest of some of the pastoral tribes in their herds that they despised and neglected the cultivation of crops and sometimes suffered starvation as a result. Baker writes of the 'Kytch', a Nilotid tribe, 'The misery of these unfortunate blacks is beyond description; they will not kill their cattle, neither do they taste meat unless an animal dies of sickness; they will not work, thus they frequently starve.'

Schweinfurth's remarks on cattle-worship among the Nilotid tribes are particularly interesting.

> Every idea and thought of the Dinka is how to acquire and maintain cattle: a kind of reverence would seem to be paid to them. . . . Only those that die naturally or by accident are used for food. . . . Indescribable is the grief when either death or rapine has robbed a Dinka of his cattle. He is prepared to redeem their loss by the heaviest sacrifices, for they are dearer to him than wife or child. . . . Not unfrequently in their sorrow the Dinka remain for days silent and abstracted, as though their trouble were too heavy for them to bear.

The Dinka castrated about one-third of their bulls. These castrated animals were useless, since, like other cattle, they were not slaughtered for eating nor used for riding or transport. 'Ask the Dinka what good they get from their possessions of oxen,' wrote Schweinfurth, 'and they have ever the answer ready that it is quite enough if they get fat and look nice.' One is reminded of the Melanesians of the northern New Hebrides, who put an extraordinary value upon the intersexual pigs that abound in certain islands, though these are useless from the practical point of view, since they cannot reproduce and are never eaten.[45, 46]

The origin of the domestic sheep, *Ovis aries*, is not known with certainty. Apart from some bones in Pleistocene caves,[1039] there do not appear to be any fossils that can be attributed to this species. The ancestry is sought in the moufflon, urial, and argali.

The moufflon, *O. musimon*, was formerly distributed over the whole of southern Europe from Spain to Greece, but is now restricted to Corsica and Sardinia; the urial, *O. vignei*, extends from Persia through Baluchistan to the Punjab, Kashmir, and Tibet; the huge argali, *O. ammon*, is a more northern form, ranging from Uzbek and Kirghiz to Tibet and the Gobi Desert. Both the moufflon and the urial are fertile in captivity with the domestic sheep;[330, 1039] the urial is fertile with the argali. [330] One strange fact is that the tails of all three supposed ancestors are short, while many domestic sheep have long tails.

There can be no doubt that Africa received its domestic sheep from Europe or Asia or both. They are known to have been kept in Egypt in Nagada times, and must have spread southwards from there and from other parts of North Africa. The breeds kept by the Negrids of the secluded part of the continent were all hairy, like the three wild species mentioned above, not woolly, like most of the domestic breeds of Europe. Galton was evidently surprised by the lack of wool on the sheep kept by the Ovaherero in South West Africa: 'the hair of their hides is like that of a calf,' he remarks. The sheep kept by the Negrids of the present day in eastern and southern Africa are of two main kinds, one thin and usually short-tailed, with small horns restricted to the male sex or else lacking horns in both sexes, the other fat-tailed, sometimes with coiled horns in the male.[711] The fat-tailed kind is especially characteristic of Ethiopia, and it was presumably from here that it spread southwards, mainly down the eastern side of the continent, while the thin-tailed sheep is found chiefly from the southern Sudan across Zaïre to Angola; but the areas occupied by the two kinds are not at all sharply separated.

Sheep were of considerable practical importance to some of the pastoral peoples, but they never affected culture and traditions to the same extent as cattle.

The Caprinae, like the Ovinae, are principally Palaearctic. It has already been mentioned that no member of the subfamily occurs naturally in the Ethiopian region. One species, *Capra nubiana*, lives in North Africa, but this is not regarded as the ancestor of domestic races. Many tame goats are almost indistinguishable from the wild *C. hircus*, especially the subspecies *aegagrus*, which extends from the Caucasus Mountains, Asia Minor, and certain Mediterranean islands to Persia, Afghanistan, and Baluchistan. It is uncertain, however, whether this is the sole ancestor, for *aegagrus* is fertile with the markhor, *C. falconeri*, where their ranges overlap in Baluchistan.[330]

Domestic goats were already kept in Egypt in Neolithic times, earlier than 3500 B.C. A lop-eared variety, recognized in Nagada sites, had become common by the third century B.C.[117] Schweinfurth mentions that the goats of the Dinka scarcely differed from the Ethiopian form. It seems probable that tame goats spread southwards from Egypt and other parts of North Africa, though some may have come much later from the east, when trade had been established across the Indian Ocean. Goats no doubt commended themselves to the Negrids by their hardiness and adaptability. The explorers mention them here and there, generally without giving much information about breeds. They provide no evidence that the goat became important in the social institutions of the Negrids. At the present day there are two main breeds in eastern and southern Africa, a larger, lop-eared kind and a smaller one with erect ears.[711]

The genus *Sus* is Palaearctic and Oriental, with some extension into the islands of the Australian zoogeographical region. The most likely ancestors of the domestic pigs of Europe and Asia are *Sus scrofa* and *S. cristatus*. The first-named is the European wild boar, which extends eastwards to Persia and southwards to Morocco and Algeria. Crossed with the domestic pig of Europe, it produces fertile progeny.[1039] The Indian wild boar, *S. cristatus*, is thought to be the ancestor of the domestic breeds of that country and of China. Importations have occurred from the latter country into Europe. Other species or subspecies of the genus have probably been domesticated elsewhere.

It is uncertain whether the domestic pigs of Egypt originated there from the North African *S. scrofa* or were imported in a domesticated state. It cannot be decided whether bones from the Egyptian Neolithic belonged to wild or tame specimens. The presence of domestic pigs in Egypt is not known with certainty till the third dynasty (about 2600–2550 B.C.), and from then onwards they continued to play a very subordinate role.[117]

Kroll[615] says that wild pigs were domesticated in Africa, but he must be referring to the part of the continent north of the Sahara, for no member of the genus *Sus* is native to southern Africa.[308] He allows that the domesticated pigs of the 'Bantu' were introduced from outside Africa.

The revulsion felt for the pig by Arabs and certain castes of Hindus may account for the very late introduction of the animal into the part of Africa under consideration here. It would be surprising if the early Portuguese colonists did not import pigs, but so far as is known the introduction only started about the beginning of the nineteenth century. The specimen produced at the court of the Chaka in 1824 caused considerable surprise. It was displayed in the seraglio for the amusement of the king's women, but unfortunately alarmed them so much that it was put to death forthwith. It would appear that pigs were not reported among the Basuto until 1874 nor among the Ovaherero till 1883.[711] It has not been possible to determine the origin of the pigs of the various tribes. No significant change in the cultural life of the people has anywhere resulted from their introduction.

It is generally agreed that dogs were among the first domestic animals. The Indian wolf, *Canis pallipes*, is commonly supposed to be the ancestor, though it is allowed that from early days onwards there may have been interbreeding with the European wolf, *C. lupus*. Certain authorities, however, consider that different species of the genus *Canis* were independently domesticated in different parts of the world. Keller goes to the extreme in this respect, for he names no fewer than seven ancestors.[577] For example, he derives the collie from *C. pallipes*, terriers from *C. aureus* (the jackal of south-west Asia), the Egyptian pariah-dog from *C. anthus* (North African jackal), and greyhounds from *C. simensis* (Abyssinian 'wolf'). At the other extreme it has been claimed that all modern domestic dogs derive from *C. lupus*.[118]

It seems that dogs were already domesticated in northern Europe by the pre-Neolithic (Mesolithic) Maglemosian people.[215] The skeletons of these animals suggest that the North African jackal was involved in their ancestry. In the period of the Nagada civilization in Egypt there were pariah-dogs and intermediate forms leading to greyhounds. Boessneck considers that the pariah-dogs of ancient Egypt represent the most primitive form of domestic dog, unaffected by deliberate selection.[117] He does not decide whether this dog was first domesticated in Egypt, nor does he name the wild ancestor. He regards the Egyptian pariah-dogs of the present day as somewhat different, since various domesticated breeds may have participated in their ancestry.

Short-legged, rather stout dogs with fairly large pricked ears, pointed muzzles, and tightly curled tails came into fashion in the Middle Kingdom (about 2133–1675 B.C.). They seem to have descended, like greyhounds, from the primitive pariah.

Typical hounds of the foxhound type are first seen in the New Kingdom (about 1557–1080 B.C.). These may have been imported.[117]

Keller considered that the hunting dog of the Hausa tribe descended from the ancient Egyptian greyhound.[577]

Kroll[615] lists the dog as one of the domestic animals of the 'Bantu' that were not of foreign origin; but the only wild species of the genus *Canis* endemic to southern Africa are the black-backed and side-striped jackals (*C. mesomelas* and *C. adustus*),[308] and neither of these is regarded as a possible ancestor of any kind of domestic dog.

Schweinfurth makes the interesting observation that the dogs of the Shillouk and Dinka tribes (both *Ni*) resembled the pariah-dogs of the Egyptians and Bedouins in lacking the dew-claw (hallux-claw) of the hind foot, which always exists (unless removed) in European dogs. He mentions that the Azande (*Pan 3*), a cannibal tribe occupying territory to the north-west of Lake Albert, main- tained a special breed of fat, short-haired dogs with large erect ears, pointed muzzles, and a short tail curled like that of a young pig. This breed, which was used partly for food, also lacked the dew-claw of the hind foot. Schweinfurth's drawing of this dog shows a remarkable resemblance to the breed fashionable in the Middle Kingdom of ancient Egypt, and provides strong evidence that the Azande obtained their dogs from the north.

It is probable that dogs spread through the continent from North Africa in an already domesticated state. Most of the explorers say little or nothing about distinct breeds, and it would appear that the same dogs were used indiscrimi- nately by many tribes for hunting and for warning of the approach of strangers.

Dogs do not seem to have inspired the origin of any special cults among the Negrids.

It is thought that the domestic fowl is a descendant of *Gallus bankiva*, the Indian jungle-fowl, which still survives in the wild state. The game-cock resembles the latter rather closely. Forms very similar to *G. bankiva*, perhaps to be regarded as subspecies of this, existed in the Pleistocene of Europe;[1039] but there is evidence that tame fowls were kept in Asia about 3000 B.C.[116] and this is very much earlier than any European record of a domestic specimen. Introduction to Africa appears to have followed after long delay. The earliest evidence is a realistic figure of a jungle-cock on an earthenware fragment attributed to the 19th Egyptian dynasty (1330–1200 B.C.) or thereabouts. This is supposed to represent part of a tribute-gift from an eastern country subjected at that time to Egypt. Actual domestication in North Africa appears to have started at a somewhat later date.

One cannot be sure that the fowls of the Negrids were derived chiefly from Egypt and other parts of North Africa, for they may have come directly from India when trade was established across the Indian Ocean. There is no question of the Negrids' having tamed the fowl, since the genus *Gallus* does not occur naturally in any part of Africa. The explorers found the domestic bird in various parts of the continent, but say little about particular breeds. Galton, however, mentions that bantams of a previously unknown kind were kept by the Ovambo of South West Africa.

The Monbuttu used fowls in augury, by administering poison or ducking them repeatedly in water. Survival was regarded as an omen of success in a projected war.

It follows from what has been said that all the principal domestic animals of the Negrids with whom we are concerned were introduced to them in an already domesticated state. The question whether the Negrids themselves tamed any wild animals at all will be considered in the next chapter (pp. 373–7).

Up to this point the present chapter has been devoted to the techniques, manufactured articles, and living organisms that reached the secluded part of Africa from the rest of the world. It cannot be brought to a close without mention of a sombre subject, concerned with the cargo taken away in some of the foreigners' ships.

'Nowhere in the world', says Schweinfurth, 'has slavery been so thoroughly engrafted and so widely disseminated as in Africa; the earliest mariners who circumnavigated its coasts found a system of kidnapping everywhere established on a firm basis, and extending in its business relations far into the interior of the continent.' Du Chaillu remarks of slavery in Gabon:

> In the first place I ought to state here that its existence has no connection at all with the foreign slave-trade. There were slaves here long before a barra-coon slave-depot was built on the coast. . . . Slavery has an independent existence, and is ruled by laws of its own. . . . from the seashore to the farthest point in the interior which I was able to reach, the commercial unit of value is a slave.

A Negrid king complained to him of the English, who were the cause of the stagnation of the slave-trade. Samuel Baker, who subsequently led an expedition to suppress the slave-trade in the Sudan and the region of the great lakes,[52] wrote on this subject:

> . . . the institution of slavery . . . is indigenous to the soil of Africa, and has *not been taught to the African by the white man*, as is currently reported, but . . . has ever been the peculiarity of African tribes. . . . It was in vain that I attempted to reason with them against the principles of slavery; they thought it wrong when they were themselves the sufferers, but were always ready to indulge in it when the preponderance of power lay upon their side.[51]

Livingstone describes how the king of the Balunda would organize an expedition to pounce on an unsuspecting village in his own territory, kill the headman, and sell every other inhabitant to a Negro slave-trader; or, if some of the people were too old to be useful as slaves, they were murdered, lest they should become troublesome afterwards by resorting to magic to avenge the attack on their village.

Slavery thus stands at the junction of this chapter with the next. It was undoubtedly indigenous, but foreign traders greatly increased its extent. Negrids who had been accustomed to sell slaves to others of their race were just as willing to sell them to foreigners. Indeed, as Baker remarks, 'All the best slave-hunters, and the boldest and most energetic scoundrels, were the negroes who had at one time themselves been kidnapped.'[51] A commerce existed; new buyers had arrived. When the explorers first entered the interior of Africa, they found that the foreign slave-traders had already established posts at considerable distances inland (pp. 336–9). Schweinfurth gives an impression of the vast extent of the trade. Year after year one of the principal 'kings' of the Azande, Mofio by name, yielded up 'thousands upon thousands' of slaves to foreign traders. He did this by raiding tribes in the surrounding territory, and also by simply handing over members of weaker tribes that had already been subjected to his rule. Comparable accounts are given by some of the other explorers.

The people chiefly influenced in their way of life by foreign intervention—the slaves themselves—were taken away to distant parts of the world and were therefore not able to affect the customs of those who were left behind. The latter, if not murdered, were left to mourn their loss, but not to adopt new modes of life.

A remarkable feature of slavery was its acceptance, in certain cases by those who were subjected to it. Du Chaillu records that some of the Ovaherero (Damara) 'court slavery. You engage one of them as a servant, and you find that he considers himself your property. . . . They have no independence about them. . . . They seem to be made for slavery, and naturally fall into its ways.' There is strong contrast here with certain other ethnic taxa of man, such as the Sanids, whom it has been found almost impossible to enslave.

# 20 The Negrids
## III. Indigenous culture

THE PREVIOUS chapter will have conveyed some impression of the ability of the Negrids, over a huge part of their territory, to make use of certain techniques, manufactured objects, and domesticated plants and animals that had had their origin among peoples belonging to races other than their own. What has been said makes it possible to disentangle the indigenous from the foreign in their culture, at least to some extent. In the present chapter we are concerned with the indigenous part, so far as it was observed and recorded by the seven explorers. The reasons for regarding the seven as unprejudiced and reliable witnesses have been given on pages 343–50. For references to their books see p. 343.

On entering Unyoro at the Karuma Falls, Baker was immediately struck by the clothing of the inhabitants (*Ka*). The men were wearing robes of bark-cloth arranged like the Roman toga. The women also were neatly dressed. Many exposed their breasts, but others wore a piece of bark-cloth across the chest and shoulders. The people of Unyoro 'considered the indecency of nakedness precisely in the same light as many Europeans'. Speke found particularly careful attention to attire among the Waganda at Mutesa's court. They wore 'neat bark cloaks resembling the best yellow corduroy cloth, crimp and well set, as if stiffened with starch, and over that, as upper cloaks, a patchwork of small antelope skins ... sewn together as well as any English glovers could have pieced them'. Speke's trousers were regarded as indecent. Curiously enough, however, the king's valets were stark naked women. The making of 'cloth' from the bark of *Ficus natalensis* was an elaborate process, described in some detail in *The indigenous trees of the Uganda Protectorate* by Eggeling and Dale.[301]

The ruling families of Unyoro and Buganda were partly of Aethiopid descent, and the fashions in dress, especially at court, may have been due to an imported culture. Throughout the rest of the secluded area a close approach to nakedness was much more usual. The Nilotids reached the extreme in this respect, for it is reported of the Shillouk, Nuer, and Dinka, and of the inhabitants of Ellyria (between the White Nile and the Latuko country), that males were absolutely naked, apart from armlets and other ornaments; and Baker's pictures show this to have been true also of the Kytch (except their chief) and Bari. All these were Nilotid tribes, and so perhaps were the men of a tribe adjacent to the Acholi, who made for themselves an elaborate headdress of human hair and of whom Baker remarks that 'a well-blacked barrister in full wig and nothing else would thoroughly impersonate a native of Lira'. Absolute nakedness of adult males was reported of only one tribe apart from the Nilotids, namely the Batonga (*Pan 1*), but the men of a large number of other tribes were described as nearly naked. Among the Zulu a small cap was worn on the penis, and so long as this was in position and the buttocks partly covered, a man was regarded as decently dressed; but it would have been considered extremely indecent to omit the penis-cap. A little apron of leather or grass was used by certain tribes to cover the male external genitalia. Several *Pan 3* tribes, the Azande among them, covered the loins with skins. Clothing was more extensive in districts where bark-cloth was used; for instance, in the Monbuttu country.

It was customary in many tribes for girls to wear no clothing while still unmarried, but the explorers do not anywhere state specifically that married women were actually naked, though in some tribes there was a close approximation to this, apart from ornaments (e.g. Ovambo (*Ka*), Abanga (*Pan 3*), and people near the source of the River Kasai (*Pan 1*)). The Monbuttu women, in contrast to the well-clothed men of their tribe, wore only a piece of bark-cloth about the size of a hand. Among most tribes it was customary for the married women to wear an apron of skin, a fringe of leather shreds, or a bunch of leaves or grass, hanging from the front of a girdle, and often a similar covering behind.

The Negrids of the secluded area did not anywhere use true tanning agents for skins, though these were available, at least in certain localities (for instance in Bongo territory). Skins were treated with ashes in certain places, and fat or oil was sometimes applied.[951, 373]

It was customary among the Nilotid tribes to extract or break off all four lower incisor teeth. The males of several *Pan 3* tribes, including the Azande and Fang, filed the incisor teeth to points, thus giving a ferocious expression to the face. Ears were commonly pierced to admit large ornaments. The women of various Palaenegrid tribes (and in one case the men also) pierced the upper lip and gradually extended the orifice until a shell (Batonga, *Pan 1*) or a circle of quartz, ivory, or horn (Mittu, *Pan 3*) could be inserted in it (Fig. 64, p. 368). The Azande were exceptional in practising no mutilation, apart from the filing of the incisor teeth. Several tribes, among them the Abanga (*Pan 3*) and Monbuttu, practised circumcision, and members of the latter tribe regarded Schweinfurth's Bongo and Mittu carriers as savages, because uncircumcised. It is uncertain whether circumcision can be regarded as indigenous among Negrid tribes. If not, it must have spread in the distant past from Arab or Turkish sources; but the Monbuttu circumcised at puberty, which is not the Muslim practice. It is a curious fact that none of the authors mentions clitoridectomy.

Attention to personal cleanliness varied extremely among different tribes. Fynn found the Zulu (*Ka*) exceptionally attentive to this matter. They were accustomed to wash daily in rivers. Schweinfurth considered cleanliness as one of the clearest signs of superior intellect, and regarded the Dinka (*Ni*) as preeminent among all Negrids in this respect. Speke remarked that 'the neat and cleanly nature of the Waganda [*Ka*] [was] a pattern to all other negro tribes'. Moist cloths, made from freshly drawn plantain-fibres, were used at Mutesa's court to wash the hands and face before and during meals. The inland people of Gabon stood at the opposite extreme in this respect. Du Chaillu remarks that they 'hardly know what it is to wash'. Galton described the Ovaherero (Damara) as 'the dirtiest and most vermin-covered of savages'.

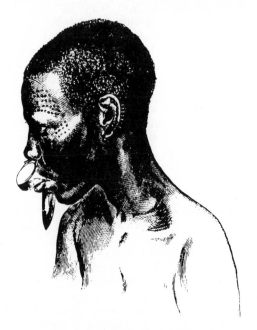

64    *Head of a Mittu woman, to show the mutilation of the lips practised by members of this tribe*

From Schweinfurth. [1951]

The sanitary laws of Buganda required every man to build for himself something corresponding to a lavatory, but no details of its construction are available. Schweinfurth says that the Negrids were generally more observant of 'decorum' (by which he presumably means privacy) in respect of defaecation 'than any Mohammedan'; but he never saw anything of the nature of a lavatory, with this single exception, that the king of the Monbuttu had a little conical hut, provided with sanitary arrangements identical with those usual in Turkish dwelling-houses. It is impossible to guess the circumstances in which some unknown person introduced this unique foreign appliance into such an extremely remote part of Africa.

The dwelling-houses of the Negrids, over the whole area traversed by the explorers, were without exception of one storey. The sight of a storeyed house caused amazement. In Ovamboland Galton met some runaway slaves who had seen the multi-storeyed houses of the Portuguese in Benguela. They spoke of them with 'great wonder'. When Livingstone reached the west coast at Loanda, his carriers from central Africa viewed the large stone houses with awe. He had never been able to convey to them how a house could be built of several storeys. Huts were built by sinking poles into the earth, and 'they never could comprehend how the poles of one hut could be founded upon the roof of another'. Some of the Makololo had seen Livingstone's little home at Kolobeng. In trying to describe it to their friends in their own country they remarked, 'It is not a hut; it is a mountain with several caves in it.'

The native huts were of two types: circular with conical roof, and rectangular. All were built of plant products, chiefly wood of *Acacia* and other trees, bamboo, leaf-stalks of palms, reeds, straw, and tough grasses; in some places there was strengthening by dried clay. The following are examples of tribes that lived in circular huts: *Nilotids*, Dinka, Dyoor, Shillouk; *Pan 3*, Azande, Bongo, Kredy, Mittu; *Kafrids*, Banyoro, Makololo, Ovambo, Wasagara, Zulu. Schweinfurth's drawing of a Bongo village (Fig. 65) gives a good general impression of the architecture of the circular huts. These tended to be uniform within each tribe, but there was considerable variety in the details of construction in different parts of the area under consideration, especially in the height of the wall and pitch of the roof. They varied in diameter from as little as $5\frac{1}{2}'$ (Ovambo) to a maximum of 40' (Dinka). The entrances to the huts of some tribes (Bongo, Makololo, Ovambo) were so low that it was necessary

65    *A Bongo village*

*From Schweinfurth.* [951]

to go on all fours to pass in or out. For a door the Bongo used 'a hurdle swung upon two posts so as to be pushed backwards and forwards at pleasure'. The Zulu fixed a vertical post on each side of the entrance, about two inches from it, and slipped wickerwork slats in between. The Ovambo used a mat for a door. No account is given of a door provided with a vertical hinge.

By far the most primitive dwellings were those of the Bergdama (*Pan 4*), who trained growing trees to provide themselves with shelter. A clump was selected and most of the lower branches removed; the tops of the trees were then bent downwards towards the ground and interlaced with one another to serve as roof and walls. Some of the branches were left to serve as internal walls, dividing the hut into two or three chambers. There was no door, but the entrance was a helical passage facing to leeward of the prevailing wind.

Rectangular huts were built by many Palaenegrid tribes (for instance, the Mpongwe (*Pan 1*), Apingi (*Pan 1*), Fang (*Pan 3*), and Monbuttu (*Pan 3*)). Those of the Fang were very small, 8'–10' long, 5' or 6' wide, and only 4' or 5' high. The Monbuttu built much larger houses, up to 30' long and 20' wide, divided into rooms. The huts of all these tribes had pitched roofs with longitudinal ridges.

Schweinfurth states that the houses of the Monbuttu had horizontal roofs, but this is contradicted by the only picture he gives of one of their villages. He is also wrong when he says that the Apingi (*Pan 1*) and Fang (*Pan 3*) built flat-topped huts. He was never much closer than a thousand miles to the territories of these tribes, and the only possible explanation is that he made a slip when writing notes on Du Chaillu's book.

Rectangular huts were also built by certain Kafrid tribes (Wagogo and Wanyamwezi). Much clay was used in their construction and Speke calls them 'mud huts'.

The Azande chiefs contented themselves with huts similar to those of their subjects, but some of the great kings, especially Munza of the Monbuttu (*Pan 3*) and Mutesa of the Waganda (*Ka*), had very special buildings for their accommodation. Munza is thought to have been ruler over a million subjects and to have been comparable in majesty to the famous Mwata Yamvo, king of the Balunda. His most sumptuous building was a hall for the reception of important visitors. It was at least 100' long and 50' broad. The roof, 40' high, rose with perfectly even vault from low walls on opposite sides; it was supported on straight tree-stems, placed in neat rows. The countless spars and rafters and other parts of the hall were made of petioles and midribs of the indigenous wine-palm (*Raphia vinifera*). The floor was of clay, as hard and smooth as asphalt. Schweinfurth's drawing of the interior shows an edifice of admirably precise and delicate construction, yet capable of withstanding tropical storms and hurricanes. It had replaced an even larger reception hall, at that time in decay.

Circular huts were generally grouped without system, so that there was nothing in a village that could be called a street. Among the Azande and usually among the Dinka the groups of huts were scarcely large enough to justify the name of village. The kraals of the Zulu consisted of from ten to one hundred huts, situated between two concentric fences; their cattle were herded at night within the inner fence. The villages of the Ovambo were surrounded by strong palisades, 8' or 9' high.

Rectangular huts lent themselves to orderly arrangement. The *Pan 1* usually placed them in two long, straight lines, with a wide street between (Fig. 66). Du Chaillu records a Fang village in which the street was 800 yards long. In some cases there were side-streets. The rectangular huts built by certain Kafrid tribes were usually arranged to form a square, with central enclosure; the group was called a *tembe*. The possibility that this arrangement was adopted under Arab influence must be kept in mind.

66   *A* Pan 1 *village near Panga, Zaïre, to show rectangular houses, arranged in two rows to form a street*

*From Stanley.* |1003|

By far the largest group of houses recorded by any of the explorers was at Linyanti, in Makololo territory, where there were six or seven thousand inhabitants.

Nearly everywhere in the secluded area, villages were connected by narrow tracks, admitting passage only in single file; but southern Buganda provided a striking contrast in this respect, for here there were roads as wide as those of Europe, all leading straight over hill and dale.

Canoes provided transport on lakes and rivers. They were made by excavating large trees, for, as Schweinfurth remarks, '... no people of central Africa seems to have acquired the art of joining one piece of wood to another, so that the craft of the cabinet-maker may be said to be unknown'. Nevertheless, some of the vessels used on the larger waterways were of considerable size. The Monbuttu had boats up to 38' long and 5' wide, capable of transporting cattle. Baker's party was ferried across the River Kafu in Unyoro in canoes upward of 4' wide, large enough to carry fifty men. The larger of the two canoes used in his journey on the Albert Nyanza was 32' long.

Although they did not join wood, many of the Negrid tribes showed considerable skill in carving it. Schweinfurth says that the platters of the Monbuttu were of 'patterns quite worthy of our own factories at home'. The large wooden bowls of the Azande, with pedestals of various forms, were 'admirable works of art'. The Bongo made well-carved four-legged stools (necessarily from a single piece of wood), for the use of women only; but in Buganda and neighbouring parts of Kafrid territory, no one was allowed to sit on an artificial seat except a king. When Speke was seen sitting in his camp-chair in Karagwe, it was at once assumed that he was a king in his own country.

The explorers seldom mention the methods adopted for the production of fire, but Schweinfurth describes a technique that appears to have been in use over a wide area of Nilotid and *Pan 3* territory. Two sticks of the wild custard-apple tree (*Annona chrysophylla = senegalensis*) were held at right angles to one another and rubbed together until a spark was emitted; this was allowed to fall on the partially charred remnant of a previous fire, and the incipient flame was fanned with dry grass. In Zululand the point of a stick was rotated in a notch cut in another piece of wood. Pith placed on the latter took fire, and transmitted the flame to dry grass.

The skill of various tribes in earthenware technique is highly praised by the explorers. The Banyeti (*Pan 1*) are said to 'excel in pottery'. Some of the beer-tanks of the Zulu held no less than sixty gallons. These large vessels, like most—or perhaps all—of the pottery throughout the secluded area, were made by women. The Wanyoro took what Baker calls 'the first step towards manufacturing art, by the fact of copying from nature', by imitating the shapes of various kinds of gourds in jet-black earthenware of fine quality. The Azande made pottery 'of blameless symmetry'. The water-bottles of the Monbuttu 'may fairly be said to rival in symmetry the far-famed examples of Egyptian art, and to betray a considerable faculty of plastic genius', despite the fact that these people, like other Negrids, were unacquainted with the use of the wheel. The Bongo women, too, 'without the help of any turning-wheel succeed in producing the most artistic specimens', some of them not less than a yard in diameter, with the whole outer surface ornamented by triangles and zigzag lines, arranged in concentric and spiral patterns. The Dyoor (*Ni*) women made 'immense vessels which, even to a critical eye, have all the appearance of being made on a wheel'—though in fact they were not.

In most Negrid tribes corn was ground by grasping a smaller stone in both hands and moving it over part of the surface of a larger one, which was gradually worn away in the centre as a result. This method was also in universal use at Khartoum at the time,[951] and one can only guess whether it was independently invented by Negrids. The smaller stone was in some cases a ball, presumably made spherical by repeated rotation in all directions during use (see pp. 394–5). The explorers make no mention of having seen a true quern or rotary hand-mill anywhere in Negrid Africa.

The wheel appears to have been unknown throughout the secluded area. Not only is there no record of its use in pottery or the grinding of corn, but no pivoted circular object, made by Negrids, is anywhere mentioned in the works of the explorers. The people of Linyanti, for instance, had never seen a wheeled vehicle till Livingstone arrived there. On a previous visit his arrival and departure with a waggon had not been witnessed; now, the whole population, amounting, as we have seen (p. 371), to six or seven thousand persons, turned out to see his vehicles in motion and thus for the first time to observe the rotation of a wheel. The Mpongwe (*Pan 1*) were accustomed to use unpivoted rollers to move a large canoe from the place where a tree had been felled and excavated to its launching-site.

On land, goods were usually transported from place to place by human labour without help from domestic animals or any mechanical device, and Katchiba, the chief at Obbo, was carried about 'pick-a-back'. Du Chaillu was strongly impressed by the fact that nowhere, in any part of the country that he traversed in the whole course of his explorations, had the people 'yet attained that primitive step in the upward march of civilization, the possession of beasts of burden'.

There is some indication that certain metals may possibly have been mined by Negrids before knowledge of metallurgy had been brought by foreigners to the secluded area. A sentence of Livingstone's suggests that there were native copper-mines at Ambriz, on the coast of Angola, north of Loanda, and that these were taken from their rightful owners by the Portuguese. Copper was already well known to the Monbuttu before the Nubians entered their country or contact had been made with the Muslim world. Schweinfurth thought that it must have come all the way from the mines of Angola, but one cannot tell whether these were then worked by Portuguese or Palaenegrids. Almost all the ornaments of the Monbuttu continued to be made of copper after this metal had become available from other sources. It was also reported to Livingstone that there were formerly silver-mines at Chicova, seventy miles north-west of Tete; but he could find no evidence of it, and the native inhabitants of the district knew nothing of the subject, and could not distinguish silver from tin. It is perhaps significant that copper and silver occur naturally in certain places in the elementary state, so that smelting is not required.

The agriculture of the Negrids, and the place of foreign plants and animals in it, have already been discussed in Chapter 19 (pp. 354 and 356–64; see also Appendix 9, p. 553). Although many tribes obtained flesh by hunting and had presumably done so since remote times, there would appear to be very few, if any, reliable examples of the full domestication of any species of wild animal* by Negrids, as a part of their indigenous culture, anywhere in the secluded area. 'During nine years' experience of Central Africa', says Baker, 'I never saw a tamed creature of any kind, not even a bird, or a young antelope in possession of a child. . . . a native of Africa, if of the Negro type, will never

---

* Throughout this book, in accordance with the invariable practice of zoologists, all living organisms other than plants and viruses are described as animals.

tame an animal. . . .'[53] The latter statement, however, is not quite correct, as we shall see.

A few animals became associated with Negrids in much the same way as the robin with Europeans, as much by the initiative of the animal as by that of man. The bush-pig, *Potamochoerus porcus*, provides an example. It associated itself in a half-tame state with the Monbuttu, a tribe that kept no truly domestic animal except poultry and dogs of the Azande breed. There is no question of the Monbuttu having housed or bred it. Rather similarly, the Dinka permitted snakes to live in the straw roofs of their huts. They called them 'brethren' and regarded it as criminal to kill them. The inhabitants of a house were said to call each guest-snake by an individual name. The snakes in question were harmless.

Full domestication may be said to proceed by four stages. Members of a wild species of animal (1) are caught and maintained in captivity; (2) are tamed and trained; (3) are bred, generation after generation; and finally (4) one or more varieties, differing from the wild type, are produced by selection (whether 'unconscious' or 'conscious', to use Darwin's terms).[257]

Livingstone witnessed an example of the first stage of domestication in central Africa, in a Balunda (*Pan 1*) village, near the source of the Zambesi. The people here kept 'canaries' in very neatly made cages, for the sake of their song. The cages were provided with traps on top, to entice wild birds into captivity. There were also tame pigeons in this village. The chief of the Barotse (*Pan 1*) also kept tame doves and birds described by Livingstone as 'canaries with reddish heads'. (The true canary, *Serinus canaria canaria*, is not indigenous to Africa.)

The Bongo (*Pan 3*) were accustomed to catch young wild cats (presumably *Felis libyca*) and reconcile them to life about their huts and enclosures, where they served a useful purpose by destroying rats. Members of this tribe also made long, cylindrical beehives of basket-work, with an opening in the middle about 6" square. The bees, said by Schweinfurth to have been of the European species, were 'wild or half-wild'. He does not say whether steps were taken to capture the swarms from these hives, nor is it certain that the species of bee in the hives was indigenous to tropical Africa. It is justifiable to claim, however, that the Bongo achieved the second stage of domestication, at any rate with the cats.

Schweinfurth mentions a remark of Livingstone's, unconfirmed by the latter's personal observation, that the natives of the Kalahari Desert were said to have trained the African hunting dog (*Lycaon pictus*) for use in the chase. With this possible exception there is no evidence in the books of the explorers that any of the Negrid tribes of the secluded area domesticated this animal, despite the fact that it was very abundant in some places (especially in Bongo territory). It has an enormous range from beyond Negrid territory in Somaliland, through Sudan and the eastern half of Africa to the south coast, and westward to Botswana and Angola (and incidentally to Ghana, but that is far outside the secluded area).[308] It is significant that Schweinfurth saw a tamed specimen in an Arab trader's camp in Bongo territory that showed all the docility of a domestic dog.

The wealth of animal life in Negrid Africa would have provided great opportunities for domestication, if this had been undertaken before 'ready-made' domestic animals had been introduced in abundance from abroad. Several animals, common in the wild state in the secluded area, are known to be easily tamed. A few examples are given here.

The guinea-fowl, *Numida meleagris*, is palatable, and very easily maintained in captivity, but the explorers nowhere mention its being kept as a domestic animal by Negrids. This is all the more remarkable in view of its great abundance. Schweinfurth estimates that he shot about a thousand of these birds in the course of his travels, 'generally two at a time', and in another part of his book he refers to 'the inevitable guinea-fowl'. He remarks that 'the traveller in Africa would be quite at a loss without them, as, with rare exceptions, they form the main commodity of his daily cuisine'. In Shillouk territory there were 'whole coveys' of them in the neighbourhood of dwellings. Guinea-fowl occur not only in the part of Africa explored by Schweinfurth, but in southern Africa as well; but Kroll,[615] in his detailed study of the domestic animals of the 'Bantu' (that is, of the Kafrids and *Pan 1*), makes no mention of this bird, and thus reinforces the negative evidence of the explorers.

The guinea-fowl occurs wild in Ethiopia, and was probably domesticated in that country and introduced thence into Egypt in ancient times. It would not appear, however, that there is any early record of tame guinea-fowl in Ethiopia. James Bruce did not use this bird as one of the species selected for special description in the fifth volume of his *Travels*,[155] and the earliest actual record of tame guinea-fowl in Ethiopia appears to be that of Hildebrandt in 1874. It was kept there at that time as an ornamental rather than a culinary bird.[490]

Guinea-fowl were probably first introduced into Europe from Egypt.[456] The Roman author Varro appears to have been the first to mention the presence of this bird north of the Mediterranean. In his *Rerum rusticarum libri tres*, produced in 37 B.C. when he was nearly 80 years old, he remarks that 'The African fowls, which the Greeks call Meleagrides, are large, speckled, and hump-backed. These newest fowls have passed from the kitchen to the couch of the diners as a result of the false refinement (*fastidium*) of men. They sell for a high price owing to their scarcity.'[1086] It follows that when Varro wrote, guinea-fowl were already domesticated in Greece, but still novelties in Rome. In his remarkably ill-arranged and scrappy book on the characteristics of animals, the Greek author Aelian mentions guinea-fowl twice. He remarks on the loud voice with which it was supposed to make a sound resembling the name 'Meleager', and he also says that it was regarded as sacred, so that it was never killed for food by religious people. In the island of Leros (one of the Dodecanese) even the birds of prey—so he says—would not injure it.[10] Aelian wrote this work late in the second or early in the third century A.D. The Greek term for the guinea-fowl is preserved in its modern specific name.

It is to be noted that nineteen centuries after it had become a domestic animal in Europe, the guinea-fowl had still not been tamed in the secluded* area.

---

* There are records of the keeping of domestic guinea-fowl by Negrids in what subsequently became northern Nigeria, and also in Togo, during the nineteenth century;[456] but these countries are far beyond the limits of the secluded area, and foreign influence must be suspected.

Among the species of antelopes, many of them extremely abundant in the wild state, there must have been a considerable number that could have been tamed for riding, transport of goods, and provision of meat and milk. The eland, *Taurotragus oryx*, is an example. It has an enormous range in Africa, covering almost the whole of the secluded area as far south as Mozambique, Rhodesia, Botswana, and South West Africa.[308] The eland is noted for its docility. 'Its gentle nature and capacity for domestication', says Gordon-Brown, 'should protect it from the sportsman unless food is a matter of dire necessity.'[423] Zeuner shows a photograph of Mr. Raymond Hook feeding one of these large animals out of a basin on the latter's farm in Kenya.[1169] Experiments on the domestication of the eland have been carried out by Europeans on quite a large scale in Africa. It can breed at any time of year, and the reproductive rate is higher than that of the zebu, since the period between one calving and the next is shorter. It presents the further advantage that it can feed on a wider range of plants than cattle can, and it thrives in hot, semi-arid districts. The meat is of excellent quality.[975] The eland has been used successfully as a draught animal in Rhodesia.[690] Four bulls and four cows were brought to the Askaniya-Nova Zoological Gardens in Ukraine in 1892 and from these no fewer than 408 descendants have been reared. Since 1963 experiments have been made on this stock to determine the suitability of the eland for practical use.[1066] The milk, though scanty, has been found to contain twice as much protein and fat as that produced by common domestic cattle. It must be remembered that all the studies have been made on unimproved stock, whereas the cattle with which they have been compared have been selected over periods of many centuries. Selection has now started at Askaniya-Nova.

One of the potentially most useful animals was the African elephant, *Loxodonta africana*, though on account of the very protracted periods of pregnancy and adolescence it does not lend itself well to the third or fourth stages of domestication. Livingstone and Schweinfurth knew that members of this species could be tamed for practical use, from the evidence of Roman medals. A small subspecies, *L. africana cyclotis*, occurred in the wild state in north-west Africa and in Libya in Roman times, and a small kind of elephant still exists in Sierra Leone; similar forms occur also in various parts of the secluded area (Cameroon, Gabon, Angola, Zaïre, and elsewhere).[1169, 308]

In its most typical form, *cyclotis* differs from *L. africana africana* in several respects apart from size. The ear is rounded rather than triangular (whence the subspecific name), and possesses no well-defined 'lobe'; the condyles of the lower jaw are ovoid (with the long axis transverse), not spherical as in the larger form; and there are several inconstant differences in the skull.[770] Specimens have been described that appear to be hybrids between the two races. There can be little doubt that *cyclotis* exists as a race, but whether all the small kinds of African elephant belong to it seems uncertain.

Members of the smaller race or races of *L. africana* have been tamed and used in war and industry from the third century B.C. onwards. General accounts of the domestication of elephants have been given by Zeuner[1169] and de Beer.[73] The Indian elephant had already been tamed in the fourth century B.C., and the early Ptolemies imported specimens of this species into Egypt. Indian trainers and drivers came with them. Experience with this animal no doubt made it easier to bring *cyclotis* into the service of man. The Egyptians were probably the first to tame it, for the Carthaginians are thought to have received tame specimens from Egypt before they themselves undertook the task of domestication. The animal was first used in the Carthaginian army in 262 B.C. Hannibal crossed the Pyrenees with thirty-seven elephants, mostly African, in 218 B.C. In the following year Ptolemy IV used seventy-three elephants, apparently all *cyclotis*, in battle against Antiochus III.

While still in possession of the Congo (now Zaïre) the Belgians tamed African elephants and by 1937 had distributed thirty-six trained animals for use in agriculture in the colony.[423]

So much for the indigenous element in the clothing (or lack of it), homes, technology, and domestic animals in the life of the Negrids. It remains to consider the interrelations of men and women in social life, their beliefs, fears, and amusements, and the regulation of their affairs by authority.

Throughout the secluded area, men obtained their wives by payment to the girls' fathers. In many tribes cattle were used as purchase-money; from five to fifty were needed in Zululand for a bride. The Bongo, not being herdsmen, used iron plates (presumably *loggoh kullutty* (p. 353)) and lance-heads instead of cattle. It will be noted that in both cases the payment involved an article that was ultimately of foreign origin, but one must suppose that the custom of paying for brides was indigenous. Nowhere was there any moral or legal barrier to polygamy. Bongo custom or law restricted the number of wives to three, but the Azande and Monbuttu set no limit. Some Zulu chiefs had fifty wives. Fynn says that polygamy was universal in this tribe, but no human ethnic taxon exists in which the sex-ratio is so unequal as to make this possible. The more polygamy, the more bachelors; the consequence is inescapable.

Zulu women preferred their husbands to be polygamous, because they valued the society of the other wives. Their husbands were not their companions. They seldom took notice of their wives in public, and were not accustomed to greet them, even on return from long journeys. In this respect there was a very marked difference from the Azande. Schweinfurth says:

> It is one of the fine traits of this people that they exhibit a deep and consistent affection for their wives. .... It was touching, through the moaning of the wind, to catch the lamentations of the Niam-Niam [Azande] men bewailing the loss of their captured [enslaved] wives; cannibals though they were, they were evidently capable of true conjugal affection.

Hardly any ransom was accounted too large by the Azande for the recovery of their wives taken prisoner in war. These facts should be more widely known, for it is often supposed that marital love, as Europeans understand it, does not exist in less advanced cultures.

Adultery was almost unknown among the Zulu, as a result of the severe penalty imposed (p. 389).

Unmarried Zulu were not forbidden by custom or law to indulge in a form of sexual intercourse with one another, but they were not permitted to have children. This was avoided by a practice called *ukuhlobonga*, described by

Fynn as 'the act of cohabitation on the outward parts of the girl between the limbs'.

Concubinage was permitted in certain tribes. Chaka had at least five thousand concubines. They lived in several separate seraglios, where decorum was observed, Fynn tells us, as exactly as in any European palace. Concubines were not permitted to bear children. Pregnancy was avoided by *ukuhlobonga*.

Music and dancing played large parts in the social life of the Negrids almost everywhere in the secluded area.

For the purpose of this book, music must be regarded from four separate points of view. One must ask oneself what capacities the Negrids exhibited first as inventors, and secondly as makers, of musical instruments; thirdly as composers, and fourthly as executant musicians. Only Schweinfurth enters into any detail on these subjects, but all the explorers contributed some relevant information, and one can at least gain a general impression bearing on this aspect of the ethnic problem.

The parts played by independent invention on one hand and diffusion on the other, in the origin and perfection of musical instruments, cannot be defined with confidence. Some of the simpler ones, such as the wooden drum, may perhaps have originated before the main ethnic taxa had evolved; if so, they neither originated independently in more than one population nor diffused from one to another, but passed by 'inheritance' (in the non-biological sense of the word), generation by generation, from a remote ancestral stock to groups that subsequently became morphologically distinct. Still, there are indications that certain instruments were invented by Negrids, and others about which there can be no certainty as to whether they spread to or from the people of this race.

The ground-bow (classified by Wachsmann[1111] as a single-stringed harp, though the string was not plucked) may well have been invented by Negrids. The Bongo practice was to stick one end of a bamboo rod vertically in the ground and attach a string to the top of it. The other end of the string was then pulled tightly and fixed firmly in the bottom of a cavity dug in the ground. The rod was thus bent in the shape of a bow. A piece of bark with a hole in it was placed over the cavity so as to complete the resonator. Sound was produced by beating the string with a splinter or twig of bamboo. Schweinfurth does not explain clearly how the pitch of the note was varied, but ground-bows were usually controlled by stopping the string with the hand not used to beat it. The player is said to have obtained additional resonance by holding his mouth over the upper end of the rod. Buzzing and humming airs were produced by the Bongo with this instrument, which has its counterparts among the tribes of southern Africa, including the Zulu.

The place of origin of the resonated xylophone or *marimba* is not known with certainty. It is difficult to believe that so complex an instrument as this could have been independently invented twice. It is used in Malaya, and the claim has been made that the Malayans invented it;[583] but this does not seem to have been proved, and it is possible that it originated in Negrid Africa.[44] The Zulu have a tradition that it was invented by a woman named Marimba, a chieftainess known as 'the Mother of Music'. She is said to have invented many musical instruments and given the Bantu-speaking people some of their oldest and most beautiful songs.[784] Livingstone gives a good drawing of the instrument, as used by the Balunda (*Pan 1*). There were fifteen or more slats in this instrument, each with a gourd of properly graduated size below it to act as resonator. The *handja* of the Fang (*Pan 3*) was similar, but with only six or seven slats and gourds. Fynn gives a careful description of a xylophone with fourteen slats and gourds, used by the Zulu. Livingstone implies (without actually saying so) that the Portuguese of Angola derived their marimba from the native xylophone. It was under this name that it crossed the Atlantic to Central America with Negro slaves.

The instrument known as the *sansa* may also have been invented by Negrids. It consists of a set of long, thin strips of iron or bamboo, clamped parallel to one another on a sounding board in such a way that their free ends project to different lengths. These ends are depressed by the thumbs and fingers, and suddenly released in such a way that they vibrate to give out musical tones. In the typical form of the instrument each key is provided with an adjustment for accurate tuning, but this is not evident in the illustration given by Du Chaillu of the type called *ibeka*, used by the Bakalai (*Pan 1*).

Considerable skill was shown by the Negrids in the construction of many of their musical instruments. This appears clearly enough in the illustrations provided by several of the explorers. Du Chaillu understates the case when he says that the *handja* of the Fang was 'not altogether unworthy of more civilized people'. Inventive capacity was shown in the application of local products to serve particular purposes. For instance, the Azande sometimes took wiry hairs from the tail of the giraffe to serve as strings for their arched harp (p. 351), and the Mittu used a half-shell (single valve) of a freshwater bivalve mollusc as a bridge for the *rababa* (p. 351).

The explorers express little appreciation of the ability of Negrids as composers of music, though some exceptions to this are to be found in their writings. Schweinfurth considered that among the many tribes he visited, only the Mittu (*Pan 3*) had any real talent for the composition of melodies. He gives in European notation a pleasant little air of theirs, sung in chorus by a hundred men, women, and children; 'they kept admirable time, succeeding in gradual cadence to procure some very effective variations' on this 'well-sustained air'. Baker mentions 'a most plaintive and remarkably wild, but pleasing air' sung by the chief of the Obbo people to the latter's accompaniment on the *rababa*, 'producing the best music that I ever heard among savages'. Du Chaillu, too, says that the airs of the Bakalai, played on their eight-stringed harp, were 'really pretty, though sad and monotonous'; and Galton mentions the 'manly choruses' of the Ovambo (*Ka*), the effect of which was 'charming'. Speke, on the contrary, remarks that Negroes are 'mentally incapacitated for musical composition, though as timists they are not to be surpassed'. This exaggerated statement contains an element of truth. The fact is that the explorers, being Europeans, looked for melody and harmony, and were usually disappointed; but they lacked the experience that would enable them to appreciate to the full the complexity of Negrid rhythms, which are perhaps unequalled in the music of any other race of mankind. Similarly, a Negrid might think poorly of

European music, on account of the relative simplicity of rhythm in most of it.

The explorers did appreciate the virtuosity of Negrids as executant musicians. It was revealed by their precision in timing and accuracy of pitch (whether of voice or tuning of instruments). A musician at the court of King Munza performed on an ivory horn so huge that he could scarcely hold it horizontally, yet on this instrument he 'executed rapid passages and shakes with as much neatness and decision as though he were performing on a flute'.[951] The capacity to sing in tune and in time seems to have been almost universal among the tribes visited by the explorers. The only striking exception to this generalization was provided by the Bongo (*Pan 3*), whose singing 'at one time suggests the yelping of a dog and at another the lowing of a cow ... everyone, without distinction of age or sex ... yelling, screeching, and bellowing with all their strength'. Music seems everywhere to have played a large part in the lives of the people, and in some cases it utterly absorbed their attentions for long periods. Schweinfurth, from his own experience, was half-inclined to believe Piaggia's statement that a member of the 'Niam-Niam' (Azande) tribe would go on playing an instrument all day and all night without thinking to leave off to eat or drink.

Most of the native dances witnessed by the explorers were of a voluptuous type. One must make allowance for the fact that there was reserve about sexual matters in Europe during a part of the nineteenth century, and Livingstone, as a missionary, could not be expected to approve; but Speke, Du Chaillu, and Fynn were what are called 'men of the world', and they too regarded these dances as grossly obscene. Speke, for instance, saw a dance of the Madi (?*Pan 3*) at a place east of the Nile, some thirty miles beyond its outflow from the Albert Nyanza. 'A more indecent or savage spectacle I never witnessed,' he remarks. The men and women 'made the most grotesque and obscene motions to one another'. Schweinfurth says of a Bongo dance, 'The license [*sic*] of their revelry is of so gross a character that the representation [drawing] of one of my interpreters must be suppressed. It made a common market-woman drop her eyes and called up a blush even to a poor sapper's cheek.' Du Chaillu 'abominated' what he saw at a dance of the Commi (*Pan 1*) tribe. The people lost all control at the sound of the tom-tom; 'the louder and more energetically the horrid drum is beaten, the wilder are the jumps of the male African, and the more disgustingly indecent the contortions of the women.' On another occasion women of the same tribe performed 'such dances as are not seen elsewhere. ... every woman was furiously tipsy, and thought it a point of honour to be more indecent than her neighbour.' At a dance of a group of women of the Oroungou (*Pan 1*) tribe, 'To attain the greatest possible indecency of attitude seemed to be the ambition of all six.' 'If the scene were witnessed in a lunatic asylum,' writes Livingstone of a Makololo (*Ka*) dance, 'it would be nothing out of the way, and quite appropriate even.' Fynn tells us that the Zulu dancers 'make the most indecent gestures; the songs, too, which accompany the dancing are of the most indecent kind'.

The ceremonial and martial dances, however, were of an entirely different character, and elicited nothing but praise from the explorers. Baker describes a grand performance by the people of Obbo (*Ni*). 'The dancing was most vigorous,' he says, '. . . the figures varying continually, and ending with a "grand gallop" in double circles, at a tremendous pace, the inner ring revolving in a contrary direction to the outer; the effect of this was excellent'—indeed, 'far superior' to anything he had seen during his extensive travels in Arab territory. Fynn and his companions were greatly impressed by a ceremonial dance performed by an immense number of Zulu. Without having actually witnessed it, they 'could not have imagined that a nation termed "savages" could be so disciplined and kept in order'. When Dingane replaced Chaka as king, the people performed such dances with even greater 'sedateness and formal regularity' than before.

It is an unfortunate fact that the explorers do not give sufficiently detailed information about the pictorial and plastic art of the Negrids to warrant an attempt at a general account in this chapter. It must suffice here to say that no example of a naturalistic picture or sculpture is recorded by any of them. There would perhaps have been general assent among them to a comment of Schweinfurth's relating to the Bongo, as applicable in a very general way to the artistic productions of most of the tribes they visited. Referring to some wooden carvings intended to represent deceased members of the tribe, he remarks:

> However rude these attempts must be pronounced, they nevertheless reveal a kind of artistic power certainly far from contemptible; at any rate, the very labour bestowed upon them indicates the appreciation which the artist entertained for his work. The Bongo, for their own part, regard their wooden images as incomparably superb, and persuade themselves that the likenesses of those who are represented are perfect.

Although Schweinfurth was a competent artist and Baker made many vigorous and useful paintings representative of Negrid life and culture, none of the explorers would have presumed to pose as an art critic.

It is not easy to provide a satisfactory general account of the religious beliefs and practices of the Negrids in the secluded area, on the evidence of the explorers' observations. Schweinfurth makes a candid comment that explains one cause of the difficulty. He remarks that his two years' residence among the Bongo 'only gave me after all a very superficial insight into the mysteries of their inner life'. There is yet another reason for the special difficulty of this subject. Each tribe had its own traditions in these matters, and one cannot easily distil the essence of what was common to many.

Nevertheless, there was one particularly widespread belief, involving one imaginary and two real categories of persons. Evil spirits, often regarded as the souls of the dead, were supposed to mingle in some mysterious way with the affairs of the living, for the purpose of harming them and depriving them of all earthly pleasures. Terror of these spirits was widespread. Referring to the people of all the many tribes among whom he travelled, Du Chaillu remarks that '. . . their whole lives are saddened and embittered by the fears of evil spirits, witchcraft, and other kindred superstitions under which they labour'. 'Their religion, if such it may be called,' says Livingstone, 'is one of dread.' He is here referring to a Palaenegrid tribe, though the fear of disembodied spirits was by no means confined to this subrace. 'Quite amazing', Schweinfurth remarks, 'is the fear which exists among the Bongo about ghosts.'

It was universally supposed that certain persons, often but by no means always old women, were capable of communing with the evil spirits, and did so in order to harm other people. They were naturally an added source of dread, and superstitions grew up about them. The Bongo thought that they wandered through the forest-glades at night to collect certain roots that somehow gave them access to the evil spirits. They believed that this nocturnal wandering might actually be taking place at the very time when the supposed witches gave every appearance of lying at repose in their huts.

A natural outcome of belief in witches was the existence of another group of persons, to whom the magical power of detecting witches was attributed. These people, always men, were called *izinyanga* (singular *inyanga*) by the Zulu, and by various names in other tribes. The usual rendering into English is the rather unfortunate one of witch-'doctor'. Fantastically dressed and decorated with strange objects such as the inflated gall-bladders of cattle, the *izinyanga* and their counterparts in other tribes obtained enormous and baneful influence over the people among whom they lived. They were supposed to be able to confer supernatural powers on objects of the most varied kinds—on sticks, stones, or even lumps of earth.[996]

Du Chaillu gives a detailed description of a Commi (*Pan 1*) witch-doctor.

I never saw a more ghastly object. He had on a high head-dress of black feathers. His eyelids were painted red, and a red stripe, from the nose upward, divided his forehead in two parts. Another red stripe passed round his head. The face was painted white, and on each side of the mouth were two round red spots. About his neck hung a necklace of grass and also a cord, which held a box against his breast. . . . A number of strips of leopard and other skins crossed his breast, and were exposed about his person; and all these were charmed, and had charms attached to them. From each shoulder down to his hands was a white stripe, and one hand was painted quite white. To complete this horrible array, he wore a string of little bells around his body.

Nearly all Negrids, according to Livingstone, had unbounded faith in the efficacy of fetishes, or, as he called them, 'charms'. It may be remembered that belief in fetishes, more than anything else, had caused Kant to regard Negrids as intellectually inferior (p. 19). Their nature and importance varied, however, among the different tribes. Teeth of crocodiles or leopards and skins of snakes were among the objects worn about the neck or waist for the sake of their supposed magical powers. As a general rule the fetishes of the Kafrids were portable. The *Pan 1* also carried small charms about with them, but they specialized in large idols of various kinds, which they kept in a special house in each village. Livingstone had lived for years among Kafrid tribes that were less addicted than most of the others to the use of fetishes, and he had never seen housed idols until he penetrated into Balunda (*Pan 1*) territory. 'As we go north,' he remarks with unusual asperity, 'the people become more bloodily superstitious.' One of the first such idols he encountered was an object resembling a crocodile, though regarded by the local people as a lion. It was made of grass plastered with clay; the eyes were cowrie-shells, and bristles from an elephant's tail were stuck in the neck to represent a mane. It stood in a shed, and the villagers were accustomed to pray and beat drums before it all night long when there was illness among them. Du Chaillu says that certain idols kept in special houses by the Palaenegrids of Gabon were believed to speak, nod the head, walk about, eat, and drink.

Of the multitude of superstitions recorded by the explorers, only a few examples will be related here.

The Azande (*Pan 3*) were firmly convinced that the possession of certain roots, charmed by a magician, gave success in hunting. Those who killed an exceptionally great number of antelopes or buffaloes were not credited, as a general rule, with any special skill in the use of their weapons: their achievement was attributed to the possession of the appropriate fetishes.

To determine which of his three sons should succeed Dagara, king of Karagwe, a minute drum was placed before them by the officers of state (*Ka*). In reality it was very light, but special fetishes had been inserted in it to render it extremely heavy to persons not entitled to the throne. Two of the claimants could not raise it from the ground; the third, Rumanika, picked it up with his little finger and thus became king. This was recorded by Speke, who spent more than six weeks in camp beside the palace, and became very friendly with Rumanika.

In Buganda (*Ka*), a chief who wanted to know when to make war against an adversary would call in a magician to tell him whether the time was propitious. The latter would then place a large earthenware vessel, half full of water, over a fire, and lay on it a grating of sticks. On the latter he would place a baby and a fowl, side by side, and cover them with a second large earthenware vessel. He would then steam them for a period of time determined by himself. Their survival or death would result in a decision to make war at once, or defer it. This was actually done by a magician named K'yenko on the order of Mutesa, king of Buganda, to determine whether it was safe to send an army through Unyoro to escort Speke to the north on his homeward journey. Speke remarks that extreme measures such as this were only used on the most important occasions.

Zulu (*Ka*) who required to be purified, because a relative had died or for some other sufficient reason, were required to slit open the side of a living calf, drain the gall-bladder, and distribute the bile over themselves, or in a particular place. The calves that had been treated in this way were allowed to die in agony, and were not eaten.

Among the Ovambo (*Ka*) there was fear of death by magic through partaking of a meal with a stranger. To avoid the supposed danger the stranger was required to sit, close his eyes, and raise his face. The person supposed to be endangered took water in his mouth, gargled with it, stood over the seated visitor, and squirted the water straight in his face. The king refused to eat with Galton because the latter would not submit to this ritual.

When Samuel Baker and Florence were seriously ill with a bilious fever at Obbo (*Ni*), the magician (who in this case was also the chief of his tribe) brought a small branch of a tree, filled his mouth with water, and squirted it over the leaves; he then waved the branch round the patients' heads and stuck it in the thatch above the doorway of their hut. This magician was also the rain-maker of his tribe. He imposed on his subjects by pretending to withhold rain, or send too much, unless provided with goats and corn.

The various tribes entertained very different ideas as to the existence of a God. Schweinfurth tells us that the Bongo certainly had no idea of a creator, or any kind of ruling power 'above'. Livingstone records the opinion of a Por-tuguese official at Tete that the Banyai (*Ka*), Barotse (*Pan 1*), and Balunda (*Pan 1*) 'have a clear idea of a Supreme Being, the maker and governor of all things'. He does not say that he confirmed this statement by his own obser-vations, but he does remark that the Bakonga (*Pan 1*) 'require no explanation of the existence of the Deity', and that the Bakuena (*Ka*) 'scouted the idea of any of them ever having been without a tolerably clear conception' of the existence of God.

The Bongo had no idea of immortality, but the works of the explorers con-tain several references to the survival of souls of the dead, at least for a time. Some of the Shillouk, for instance, thought that the dead 'are lingering among the living'. Du Chaillu mentions the placing of furniture, dress, and food at the graves of the recently dead, among the Gabon tribes (mostly *Pan 1*); but ap-parently this was done to appease the spirits, who were feared (cf. p. 381).

In many tribes there were public gatherings that might be called either religious ceremonies or invocations of fetishes, in connection with illness (cf. p. 383), death, famine, or drought; but in some, notably the Bakuena, noth-ing of the sort ever took place. Schweinfurth did not witness any form of public religious observance during five weeks' residence among the Monbuttu (*Pan 3*).

It is customary in more advanced societies to think of religions as combining a certain number of beliefs, not capable of proof by objective tests or reasoning, with rather detailed and explicit ethical codes. This combination was unusual or perhaps non-existent among the Negrids of the secluded area. Du Chaillu writes, 'Among the tribes with which I am familiar, there is no native generic term equivalent to our word *religion*.' Similarly Schweinfurth tells us that '. . . none of the natives of the Gazelle district [and this includes nearly all the tribes with which he came in contact] may be credited with the faintest con-ception of true religion', and 'All religion, in our sense of the word religion, is quite unknown to the Bongo.' These remarks must be taken to mean that there was nothing corresponding to a church where moral precepts could be taught publicly, and no clear correlation in their minds between such precepts and their unproven beliefs. There is not necessarily any implication, however, that there was no private inculcation of such precepts within the family. Intelligent men among the Bakuena told Livingstone that nothing regarded as sinful by the missionaries had ever in the past appeared to themselves as anything other than this, with the single exception of polygamy.

Although apparently there was nowhere any formulated ethical system, transmitted to congregations by persons corresponding to clergymen, bound together as ministers of a church, yet moral ideas must somehow have been in-culcated in most of the tribes. It is difficult to accept Galton's conclusion that the Ovaherero 'seem to have no perceptible notion of right and wrong'; and certainly the explorers witnessed several remarkable instances of selfless benevolence to total strangers, by people wholly uninfluenced by any foreign religion. Several examples have already been mentioned on pp. 346–7. Most, but not all, of the 'good Samaritan' acts recorded by the explorers were performed by women. A striking instance of a man's benevolence is related by Schweinfurth. A Bongo (*Pan 3*) told him that he had been severely wounded when helping Nubians to steal Dinka (*Ni*) cattle. He lay down just outside a Dinka house. The owner protected him, kept him till he was well, and then provided him with an escort to his home. The same author describes another remarkable act of mercy by a male Dinka. A man of this tribe had been one of Schweinfurth's bearers, but he was afflicted by guinea-worm (*Dracunculus medinensis*) when far from his own village, among people of another tribe. It was with difficulty that he could walk a single step, and he was reduced to living on scraps of food in a period of great scarcity. In his plight his father appeared unexpectedly to succour him. This remarkable man carried his son fifteen or sixteen leagues on his back to restore him to his home. 'This incident', says Schweinfurth, 'was regarded by the other natives as a mere matter of course.'

After long acquaintance with the Makololo (*Ka*), Livingstone came to the conclusion that in general they were less helpful to the unfortunate than more advanced peoples were, and '. . . a poor person who has no relatives, will seldom be supplied even with water in illness. It would be easy to enumerate instances of inhumanity which I have witnessed.' Among the Bakalai (*Pan 1*), too, there was no sympathy for those who were sick or aged and lacked friends to support them. They were driven out of their villages to die in loneliness in the forest. Du Chaillu twice saw old men driven out in this way. The emaciated corpse of one of them was found subsequently. Galton reports that among the Ovaherero 'A sick person meets with no compassion; he is pushed out of his hut by his relations away from the fire into the cold; they do all they can to expedite his death, and when he appears to be dying, they heap ox-hides over him until he is suffocated.' The possibility must be kept in mind that the explorer witnessed crude attempts to shorten the misery of lingering death.

In the explorers' records there is one instance of the expression of regret by Negrids for the suffering of an animal. During Du Chaillu's journey up the Rembo valley in Gabon, a female chimpanzee was shot and its baby wailed in misery. 'The whole camp was touched at his sorrows,' he writes, 'and the women were especially moved.'

Most of the explorers were not long enough in any one place to make a careful study of law and its administration. Du Chaillu writes of 'the total absence of any law but that of the strongest—the almost total ignoring of the right of property' among the tribes of Gabon; but even if this were true of the country through which he travelled, it certainly was not representative of the whole of the secluded area. In certain matters, especially in relation to hunting, quite complicated rules existed and were enforced. Some of these are related in detail by Livingstone. For instance, at a place between Zumbo and Tete (probably Banyai tribe (*Ka*)), when an elephant was wounded on one chief's land but died on another's, the lower half of the carcase (presumably that which lay next the soil) belonged to the landowner; and until the latter's representative arrived, the hunter could not legally start to cut up his prey. If he started too soon, he lost all right to tusk and flesh. On most branches of civil law, however, the explorers provide little information; for instance, we are given no details about land tenure or bequests. Among the Bechuana, minor complaints of one man against another were tried justly before a chief, the defendant being given full opportunity to present his case. Peremptory measures were usually adopted, however, when serious crimes had been committed and suspicion had fallen on particular persons.

The ideas entertained by Negrids in pre-colonial days on such subjects as the sanctity of human life and the imposition of the death penalty have been represented in recent years by certain authors and lecturers in terms for which one cannot find support in the writings of those who actually visited the interior of Africa while the native inhabitants were still in command of their own affairs. For instance, it has been stated that 'in most of Bantu Africa, long before the arrival of so-called western civilization, only a person who was a persistent murderer was put to death'.[645] 'Bantu Africa' can only mean those parts of the continent where the inhabitants spoke Bantu languages; that is to say, the territory of the Kafrids and *Pan 1*. Reference to Fig. 58 (p. 328) will show the area concerned. It will be noticed that it represents about one-half of the total area occupied by the entire Negrid population of Africa. It was visited by all the explorers except Schweinfurth, and four of them—Fynn, Livingstone, Galton, and Du Chaillu—never went outside it in the course of the journeys considered in this and the preceding chapters.

In this section of the present chapter, page-references are given to the reports of the explorers, so that the reader may check what is said as easily as possible, and form his own judgement on the reliability of the witnesses by reading their own words. The page-references to executions, given below within brackets, refer to pages in the explorers' books.[51, 200, 373, 378, 676, 951, 996]

Examples of summary executions in the course of warfare (of prisoners, women accompanying hostile armies, and persons suspected of spying, cowardice, or failure to follow up a success) are excluded from the account given below, which is entirely concerned with civil life.

It is convenient to start with Du Chaillu's[200] observations on the *Pan 1*; that is to say, with the 'Western Bantu' of Seligman.[957]

Slaves were treated by members of this group of Negrids in Gabon as though their lives were unworthy of consideration, for by native customs the right was accorded to all slave-owners to kill them at will (p. 21). In Oroungou territory Du Chaillu saw some of the skeletons of slaves, to the number of one hundred, who were killed to accompany a chief to the next world (p. 183). A large number of slaves were also tortured and killed at the funeral of a Mpongwe chief, in accordance with instructions left by him (p. 21). It must be recorded, however, that another chief of this tribe expressly forbade the killing of slaves at his funeral (p. 21).

Wives, like slaves, were in some cases subject to execution without public trial. Du Chaillu describes a terrible torture inflicted by a chief of the Shekiani on one of his wives, with the intention that it should end with her death. The explorer was in this case able to save her life (p. 157).

In most of the Gabon tribes it was usual, though not invariable, for one member of a pair of twins to be killed at birth. This happened at an Apingi village in which Du Chaillu was staying at the time.

It was believed that death was never a natural event, and fatal illness was always ascribed to sorcery (p. 338). Du Chaillu describes a method of execution commonly adopted by the Bakalai for those suspected of witchcraft. The suspect was led into the forest and tied to a tree. The whole surface of the body was lacerated and red pepper rubbed into the wounds, and the victim left to die. The recently dead corpse of a young woman who had been treated in this way was seen by Du Chaillu (p. 122). The latter also tells of a boy, aged ten years, who had been accused of sorcery and made some sort of confession. 'Hereupon the whole town seemed to be seized of the devil. They took spears and knives, and actually cut the poor little fellow to pieces. I had been walking out, and returned just as the dreadful scene was over.' The participants (Bakalai) 'were still frantic with rage, and were not quiet for some hours after' (p. 281).

In many parts of *Pan 1* territory it was customary for anyone charged with sorcery to be forced to drink an infusion of the root of a plant called *mboundou* (thought to be a species of *Strychnos* (p. 257)). It was supposed that only a guilty person would die. Du Chaillu makes repeated mention of trial by *mboundou* (pp. 272, 385, 395–8, 404–5). A single example must suffice. An aged friend of his, of the Camma tribe (*Pan 1*), was sick beyond the possibility of recovery. The explorer gives a terrible account of the execution of three women by *mboundou*, when a witch-doctor announced that they had killed the old man by sorcery (pp. 395–8).

The *Pan 1* territory through which Livingstone passed was far to the south-east of Gabon, but his experiences were in many respects similar to those of Du Chaillu. He describes ordeal by poison derived from a plant called *goho*, inflicted on women suspected of sorcery. Those who vomited were regarded as innocent, but those who defaecated were put to death by burning. The women eagerly desired the test, because they believed implicitly in its reliability and were certain that it would reveal their innocence (p. 621). In Angola a poisonous infusion of a certain tree was used. The accuser would repeat his charge if the woman vomited, and she would be forced to repeat the dose until she died. Every year hundreds of women came to a particular place near Cassange to undergo this ordeal, and perished as a result (p. 434). The people believed that death was in all cases due to one of two causes: either witchcraft, or failure to appease disembodied spirits by use of the appropriate charms (p. 440).

Livingstone states clearly that throughout all the country traversed by him from 20°S. northwards (that is to say, *Pan 1* territory), people were slaughtered to accompany the departed souls of chiefs.

Like Du Chaillu, Livingstone mentions the custom among certain tribes of putting to death one member of a pair of twins, and he also says that in one tribe a child that showed even a minor deformity (for instance, an unusual sequence in cutting of the teeth) was not allowed to live (p. 577).

We turn now from the *Pan 1* to the Kafrids.

Baker reports that Kamurasi, king of Unyoro, and his brother as deputy, were complete despots in the matter of life and death (vol. ii, p. 254). If they wished anyone to be executed, they had only to touch the person with the point of a lance or with a stick. By a curiously inverted custom, touching with a lance indicated that the man was to be clubbed to death; with the stick, to be killed by spearing. The sentence was executed instantly (vol. ii, pp. 199–200). When slaves were captured by Kamurasi, the old women among them were all killed by being beaten on the back of the neck with clubs, because they could not keep up with the rest of the party on the march (vol. ii, p. 202).

Mutesa, king of Buganda, was even more regardless of the sanctity of human life than Kamurasi. Speke had ample opportunity to make observations on this subject during his long sojourn at the court. The slightest infringement of the rules of conduct resulted in death. The Wakungu or officers of the court were required to be present during a certain number of months every year, however far distant their homes might be; if they failed in this obligation (pp. 323–4), or even if they saluted informally (p. 258), they were executed. Those persons at the palace who tied their bark clothing incorrectly, or exposed a small surface of naked leg when squatting, might be executed (pp. 255, 258). To touch the king's throne or clothes, even by accident, or even to look at his women, meant certain death (p. 256). If a page walked instead of running to deliver a message, it might cost him his life. Everyone in Buganda, apart from the royal family, found in possession of any article of foreign manufacture, other than beads or brass wire, was subject to execution (pp. 345, 490). Nearly every day, while Speke was residing within the precincts of the court, from one to three of the palace women were led out to execution (p. 358).

Some specific instances of summary executions under Mutesa's rule may be noted. A young woman had run away from her husband and taken shelter for a few days with a decrepit old man. The woman and old man, brought before Mutesa for trial, were not allowed to speak. They were ordered to be fed to preserve life as long as possible, and meanwhile gradually dismembered, and the parts cut off fed to vultures, until they died. Speke was present at the trial (p. 375). One day Mutesa was apportioning women to his officers, according to their merit. One man, to whom only one woman had been given, asked for more. He was sentenced to immediate execution, which was carried out on the spot by a blow behind the head with a heavy club (p. 377). This was witnessed by Speke's headman, Bombay, a trustworthy person who had served him on a previous expedition. Speke presented Mutesa with some carbines. The king loaded one of them and gave it to a page in Speke's presence, with instructions to shoot a man with it, to prove its effectiveness; this was immediately done (p. 298). Going for a walk with his officers in front and his women following behind, Mutesa noticed a woman tied by the hands to be punished for some offence. The king had with him a rifle presented to him by Speke, with which he shot her dead on the spot (p. 389).

It was the rule in Buganda that all the brothers of a new king, except two, were executed by burning at each accession to the throne; the two were allowed to survive in case accident should befall the ruler (pp. 254, 260, 281, 526–7).

In the Kafrid area traversed by Livingstone and Galton there was much clearer recognition of the sanctity of human life than in Unyoro, Buganda, and the huge *Pan 1* territory. Power was indeed entrusted to a few persons, but it was exercised more leniently. It is evident from Livingstone's account that among the Bakuena and Makololo, although the chief had power of life and death in his hands, there was no despotic cruelty comparable with that of Kamurasi and Mutesa; those who disagreed with a chief's judgement acquiesced in his decision—but were free to grumble (p. 184) (no small freedom, and not without ultimate effect).

To the south-east of the region just considered, conditions were very different. Chaka—or Shaka, as Fynn calls him—had displaced Dingiswayo before Fynn's arrival. The latter's observations were made over a period of nine consecutive years, mostly during Chaka's reign, but extending into a part of Dingane's.

Under Chaka's rule, as witnessed by Fynn, a movement of a royal finger, just perceptible to his attendants, sufficed to indicate that a man was to be taken away and executed. On the first day of Fynn's arrival at court, ten men were carried off to death, and he soon learnt that executions occurred daily (pp. 28, 75, 78). On one occasion Fynn witnessed the dispatch of sixty boys under the age of twelve years before Chaka had breakfasted (p. 28). The ordinary method of execution in Zululand was a sudden twisting of the neck, but in one case a man accused of witchcraft was suspended from a tree by his feet and burnt to death by a fire lit below him (p. 29). Sometimes people were killed by driving a stick into the body through the anus and leaving them to die (p. 140). On one occasion between four and five hundred women were massacred because they were believed to have knowledge of witchcraft (p. 156). In some cases very trivial offences resulted in death. One of Chaka's concubines was executed for taking a pinch of snuff from his snuff-box (p. 151). A group of cowherd boys was put to death for having sucked the nipples of cattle (p. 152).

It was the rule in Zululand that no one might eat from any crop until the king had partaken of the first-fruits of the year at a special ceremony. If anyone transgressed, every member of his kraal was executed (p. 304). At the ceremony the king was accustomed to have many people executed for no other reason than to show his power and cause him to be feared (p. 305).

Many besides the king could order executions. Nandi, his mother, had no compunction about having men and women put to death in her presence, sometimes by torture (p. 140). Every village chief was permitted to kill any of his people (p. 286). Any person accused by one of the *izinyanga* was immediately executed; their decisions were final (pp. 277, 318). Fynn witnessed this on several occasions (p. 70). Adultery was punished by death for both parties, and even the suspicion of adultery would authorize a husband to kill his wife (pp. 294–5).

The most terrible event of Chaka's reign that was actually witnessed by Fynn followed the illness and death of Nandi. Universal mourning was immediately ordered. The chiefs and people began to assemble in a crowd estimated at eight thousand. To eat or drink was forbidden; weeping was compulsory. Lamentations followed all night.

Those who could not force tears from their eyes—those who were found near the river panting for water—were beaten to death by others who were mad with excitement. Toward the afternoon I calculated that not fewer than 7,000 people had fallen in this frightful indiscriminate massacre. . . . Whilst masses were thus employing themselves, Shaka and his chiefs, the latter surrounding him, were tumbling and throwing themselves about, each trying to excel in their demonstrations of grief by alternate fits of howling (p. 133).

Fynn felt 'as if the whole universe were at that moment coming to an end' (p. 135). On his first appearance after the massacre Chaka ordered the execution of one of his aunts, who had been unfriendly to Nandi, and of all her attendants (some twelve or fourteen girls) (p. 133). Parties were sent out to execute those who had not come to express sorrow. During a period of one year after Nandi's death, all women found to be pregnant were executed with their husbands (pp. 136–7).

A very similar massacre had occurred previously, when an attempt had been made on Chaka's life (pp. 84–5).

Though milder at first, Dingane soon began to follow Chaka's example. Fynn says that he 'massacred numbers with the same unsparing hand as his predecessor' (p. 174). He secretly prejudged all cases that came before his council of chiefs (p. 163). Whenever a chief (*induna*) was suspected of witchcraft, poisoning, stealing royal cattle, or disobeying the king's orders, not only the man concerned but all related to or connected with him were executed, including children, except sometimes the young girls (p. 289). When a certain *induna* was accused of having had an amour with one of Dingane's wives, the man himself and every member of his village were inhumanely put to death (p. 241). In conformity with a practice general among many Negrid tribes, Dingane killed those of his brothers who were not able to escape (pp. 214, 241).

The foregoing account of executions has been restricted to some of those reported by the explorers in Bantu-speaking Africa, but it could easily have been extended to the rest of the secluded area if it had been considered justifiable to devote more space to this subject.

Over a very large part of the secluded area there is no evidence that human flesh was ever eaten, and no first-hand account of it is recorded by Fynn, Livingstone, Galton, Speke, or Baker. In several places the native inhabitants knew that cannibalism existed elsewhere; Speke and Baker give examples of this. Fynn mentions a tribe living in the vicinity of the Zulu that was stated to have taken to eating human flesh when their cattle were stolen; but this was not confirmed by direct observation, and the vast majority of Kafrid tribes were never cannibals, so far as is known. No suggestion is made anywhere that any Nilotid was ever a cannibal. Schweinfurth remarks of the Dinka (*Ni*), 'It is scarcely necessary to say that the accounts of the cannibalism of the Niam-Niam excite as much horror amongst them as amongst ourselves.'

Du Chaillu made his acquaintance with cannibalism in Fang (*Pan 3*) territory. He had been inclined to disbelieve in its reality, but the evidence was plain when he first entered a village of this tribe. 'I perceived some bloody remains which looked to me human,' he remarks; 'but I passed on, still incredulous. Presently we passed a woman who solved all doubt. She bore with her a piece of the thigh of a human body, just as we should go to market and carry thence a roast or steak.' The evidence accumulated inexorably as he travelled through Fang territory. The people showed no reserve in discussing the customary procedures with him, such as the division of a corpse, and the right of the king to a particular part of it. Human bones were thrown outside the houses of villagers, mixed with other offal. 'In fact, symptoms of cannibalism stare me in the face wherever I go, and I can no longer doubt.' It appeared to be the custom that when a villager was killed or died, his corpse was sent to another Fang village, for sale as food. 'This seems the proper and usual end of the Fangs.' Du Chaillu records the cutting up of the body of a man who had clearly died of disease. The villagers confirmed 'without embarrassment' that it was customary to eat such corpses. 'In fact, the Fangs seem regular ghouls, only they practise their horrid custom unblushingly, and in open day, and have no shame about it.' Unlike other tribes, the Fang had few slaves, partly because they were accustomed to eat prisoners taken in war; but they bought the bodies of slaves from other tribes for eating, paying ivory for them.

It was only among the Fang that Du Chaillu encountered positive evidence of cannibalism; but when he received a formal visit from the king of the Apingi (*Pan 1*), the latter immediately handed over to him a bound slave, with the remark, 'Kill him for your evening meal; he is tender and fat, and you must be hungry.' This incident must not be taken as proving that cannibalism existed among the Apingi. The coastal natives saw many slaves receiving food in depots ('barracoons') while awaiting shipment; and reports of this, filtering through to remote districts, had given rise to the belief that Negrids were fattened before being exported to serve as food for Europeans. Fear of this fate was, indeed, one of the miseries suffered by the slaves in the depots.

Reports of a tribe of cannibals called Niam-Niam, living in the region of the Bahr-el-Ghazal tributaries, began to trickle through to Khartoum about 1845.[556] This tribe, properly called the Azande, was much feared by its neighbours on account of its ferocity in war and addiction to the eating of human flesh. The name Niam-Niam, variously spelled, was used by all the early explorers. It had been bestowed on them by the Dinka, to convey (with understatement) the idea of 'great eaters'. The first person to penetrate into their territory was the British ivory-trader and H.M. consular agent in central Africa, John Petherick, who in 1858 spent a little more than a fortnight at a village called by its chief's name, Mundo, situated at the northern boundary of their tribe. In the course of his travels Petherick received information about cannibalism, but he did not witness it during his brief stay in the Azande village.[840]

In his valuable history of Nile exploration, Sir Henry Johnston makes the mistake of saying that in the course of Petherick's second expedition to the region of the Bahr-el-Ghazal tributaries, he revisited Niam-Niam territory. On this occasion he was accompanied by his wife, and the book describing their experiences consists of alternating sections, contributed by each of them in turn. [839] The book makes it perfectly clear that during this expedition (1862–3) they did not penetrate into any territory occupied by the Azande, though they approached it and received envoys from the tribe. It is worth remarking that their map is misleading in one respect. A red line is supposed to mark their route. So it does, in most places; but three long tracks leading off to the villages of Dari, Bofi, and Wanja are also marked in red, yet the account given in the Pethericks' book shows that neither of them travelled to these places. It is possible that members of their party did so.

Carlo Piaggia, an Italian who attached himself to traders in the Bahr-el-Ghazal region as a leader of their caravans, stayed in or near the country of the so-called Niam-Niam for about a year in 1863–4, mostly at the village of a chief named Tombo. Towards the end of 1863 he made a journey lasting twenty days into what was unquestionably Azande territory. [842] He only witnessed a single instance of cannibalism during his long stay in this part of Africa, when a foe slaughtered in warfare was eaten. Johnston uncharitably calls him 'the unlearned Piaggia' and in two places stigmatizes his explorations as 'unscientific'; but Schweinfurth remarks that with certain exceptions, not connected with cannibalism, 'Piaggia's observations seem acute enough.'

Schweinfurth was the first European to obtain full information about cannibalism among the Azande. He was passing southwards from the country of the Bongo and related tribes, and reached the territory of the man-eaters at its south-eastern extremity, in the region of the Nile-Congo watershed. He noticed piles of refuse with fragments of human bones strewn among them; all around were shrivelled human feet and hands, hanging on the branches of trees. The Azande made no secret of their use of human flesh as nutriment. They spoke freely on the subject, telling the explorer that no corpses were rejected as unfit for food, unless the person had died of some loathsome skin-disease. Skulls from which flesh and brains had been obtained were exhibited on stakes beside their huts. Any person who died without relatives to protect his body was sure to be devoured in the very district in which he had lived; and in times of war, any member of a conquered tribe was regarded as suitable for eating. Of the various oily and fatty substances employed in cooking, the one in most frequent use was human fat.

Schweinfurth came across a baby, about a day old, the offspring of a woman just taken away by slave-traders. It was left, gasping feebly in the full glare of the noon-day sun. The Azande awaited its death and the meal that was to follow.

It is noteworthy that among the Azande there were some who not only refused to eat human flesh, but would not take any food from the same dish as a cannibal. This shows that conformity is not always so rigidly enforced in less advanced societies as is sometimes supposed.

Schweinfurth remarks on the many similarities between the Fang, as described by other authors, and the Azande. There were resemblances not only in physical characters, but in dress and customs. In both tribes the incisor teeth were filed to sharp points; bodies were stained with a red dye derived from the wood of a tree; there was similar elaboration in the dressing of the hair; the chiefs wore leopard skins; both were hunting tribes. These resemblances are certainly remarkable, in view of the huge distance separating the territories of the two tribes. Traditionally the Fang had migrated from the north-east, and a common origin is not impossible.

Passing south again to the furthest point of his exploration, near the source of the River Uele ('Welle'), a tributary of the Congo, Schweinfurth entered the territory of the Monbuttu. He states that the members of this tribe were even more addicted to the consumption of human flesh than the Azande, and that they were in fact the most cannibalistic of all the then known tribes of Africa. The corpses of the enemy killed in war were distributed on the battlefield and dried for transport to the victors' homes. Prisoners were driven before them 'without remorse, as butchers would drive sheep to the shambles ... to fall victims on a later day to their horrible and sickening greediness'. Munza, king of the Monbuttu, told Schweinfurth of his order that cannibalism should be practised in secret during the latter's visit, since he knew that Europeans held the practice in aversion; nevertheless the explorer witnessed the preparation of parts of the human body for eating, and the great majority of the skulls brought to him by members of this tribe to add to his anthropological collection had been smashed to obtain the brains (and thus rendered useless). Some were still moist, and had the odour of recent cooking.

There is nothing in the works of the seven explorers that would explain satisfactorily the significance of cannibalism in Negrid Africa. Certainly there is no indication that the custom originated there from a desire to incorporate the power or influence of the person eaten. The reported adoption of cannibalism by a tribe deprived of its cattle (p. 390) might suggest that lack of sufficient protein food was the primary cause; but it has already been mentioned that the Fang and Azande were hunters. The Monbuttu, too, supplied themselves with all the meat they needed by hunting, and in addition brought back very large numbers of goats from their marauding excursions against their southern neighbours. Schweinfurth remarks that 'it is altogether a fallacy to pretend to represent that the Monbuttoo are driven to cannibalism through the lack of ordinary meat'.

An attempt will be made here to convey the general impressions of the explorers about the intellectual capacities of the Negrids in the secluded area. Some of the languages, for instance that of the Bechuana (*Ka*), were very rich in words, and the vocabulary of the Dinka was more copious than that of any European tongue in everything that related to cattle. Nevertheless Schweinfurth stresses the poverty of Negrid languages, in particular those of the Bongo and Azande, in words denoting abstract ideas. He mentions also a number of examples of single words, used by the Bongo to express similar but not identical ideas. For instance, there was no means of distinguishing verbally between *shadow* and *cloud*, or between *bitter* and *annoying*. Nevertheless, precision or grammatical accuracy in speech is recorded of more than one tribe. Livingstone says of the Basuto that 'both rich and poor speak correctly; there is no vulgar style'. Fynn makes a similar remark about the Zulu. Both Livingstone and Schweinfurth feared that native languages would be corrupted through the introduction of foreign words by missionaries.

There was no written language in any part of the secluded area, and indeed it was found difficult to convey to the native inhabitants the idea of what was meant by it. The Ovambo frankly disbelieved that Galton could express words by writing on paper, and he had to prove that this was possible by jotting down the names of a number of people and then reading them out. Livingstone says of the Makololo that 'It seems to them supernatural that we see in a book things taking place, or having occurred at a distance.' It is worth mentioning that thirteen years earlier, when lecturing on 'The hero as man of letters', Thomas Carlyle had expressed almost exactly the same opinion as the Makololo.

With the art of Writing, of which Printing is a simple, and inevitable and comparatively insignificant corollary, the true reign of miracles for mankind commenced. It related, with a wondrous new contiguity and perpetual closeness, the Past and Distant with the Present in time and place.[191]

Some of the Negrid peoples knew nothing of their history. Among the Rek, a section of the Dinka (*Ni*), '. . . all the lives and deeds of men have been long forgotten'. The people were 'without traditions, without history'. Speke writes of the Wanyamwezi (*Ka*) that 'There are no historical traditions known to the people.' The Ovaherero kept no count of years. Baker generalizes on this subject by saying that the natives of central Africa '. . . are not only ignorant of writing, but they are without traditions—their thoughts are as entirely engrossed by their daily wants as those of animals; thus there is no clue to the distant past; history has no existence'. Livingstone, however, did find here and there some clues to former times. A curious tradition was related to him as he ascended the Zambesi on his way to the west coast. A man was said to have left his own people, the Barotse, come downstream to a waterfall in Banyeti territory, and there excavated for himself an irrigation-canal to supply his garden. Livingstone does not say that he saw the canal, which presumably led from a pool above the fall, but the site of the garden was pointed out to him, in which 'an inferior kind of potato' still survived. 'Such minds must have arisen from time to time in these regions, as well as in our own country,' says Livingstone, wistfully; 'but, ignorant of the use of letters, they have left no memorial behind them.' On a rock situated about 170 miles inland from Loanda he saw a representation of a footprint, carved long ago as a memorial to the visit of a famous queen. 'In looking at these rude attempts at commemoration,' he remarks, 'one feels the value of letters.'

The same explorer provides some interesting examples of the way in which past events may be accidentally recorded for posterity—vaguely, it is true—in places where illiteracy and lack of interest in the past have blotted out nearly all records of former times. Two instances occurred while he was passing through Batonga territory to the east coast, towards the end of his transcontinental journey. He came upon the ruins of a very large town, and found among them a faint indication of its history. Lower millstones of hard rock were still lying about, and these had been worn down to the extent of $2\frac{1}{2}''$ where the upper stone had been rubbed against them. He inferred that the town had been inhabited for a long period. As he travelled onwards he passed through ruins of other towns, and in these he once again found lower millstones, accompanied here by great numbers of the quartz spheres that had acted as the upper components of the primitive mills. From the fact that these balls had been left in the ruins he drew the conclusion that the depopulation had been a sudden consequence of war.

Some knowledge of history did exist here and there, at any rate at the palaces of kings. Kamurasi, for instance, told Baker that his grandfather had been king not only (like himself) of Unyoro, but also of Buganda, Utumbi, and Chopi; but he denied all knowledge of ancient history, and could not comment on the belief, entertained by Baker, that there was a Galla (Aethiopid) element in his ancestry. In Buganda this royal history could be traced much further back, and many generations of the kings of Karagwe were still known by name. It was among the Zulu, however, that knowledge of the past was most complete. The annual 'first fruits' ceremony formed the basis for a history by years, going back to about 1750. It was possible, from the information supplied verbally by the people, to draw up quite a complicated genealogical table of the kings and their relatives, and to trace many details of the gradual fusion of the tribes.

There can be no doubt that many Negrids had considerable knowledge of geography. Writing of the people of Karagwe, Speke says he was surprised at 'the correctness of their vast and varied knowledge [of geography], as I afterwards tested it by observation and the statements of others'. One of them laid a long stick on the ground, pointing due north and south, and attached shorter ones directed towards the centre of each adjoining country. Schweinfurth, too, found Negrids in general very accurate in indicating the locations of distant places, by pointing with the finger (and incidentally also *time*, by pointing to where the sun would be, when some event was to occur). In Kafrid territory, people would readily draw maps on the ground for Livingstone, but he could not persuade the *Pan 1* of the Upper Zambesi to attempt this. Galton found that the Ovaherero had no map of a country in their minds, but only an infinity of local details; they had no name for a river as a whole, but a different one for nearly every reach of it.

Knowledge of mathematics was everywhere rudimentary, though there were differences between the tribes in this respect. The Ovaherero seem to have occupied an extreme position in the scale. Galton claimed that though they might possess words for higher numbers, they did not actually make use of any numeral higher than three. When they wished to express four, they used their fingers instead of an appropriate word. The Madi, according to Schweinfurth, only counted up to ten; greater numbers were generally indicated by gestures. To convey how many bearers were required, reeds were tied together in bundles of ten; these were handed to a chief to express the total number he was asked to supply. Similarly, a chief impersonating Kamurasi sent twenty-four small pieces of straw to denote the number of presents given to the latter by Speke, and ten to indicate the insufficiency of the number given by Baker. It seems possible, however, that in these cases words denoting number would have been used instead of symbols, if information had only to be transmitted from one native speaker to another, without any need to be certain that a foreigner understood it. The use of fingers to convey number was, however, widespread. The Zulu had numerals to express large numbers, but used their fingers nevertheless. Chaka asked Fynn to count a huge drove of oxen. He counted 5,654 and announced the result. The crowd of people who had watched this performance burst out laughing, since he had not once counted up to ten with his fingers; it was impossible to shake their incredulity. The Ovambo, on the contrary, counted Galton's oxen (a very much smaller number) as quickly as he could have done it himself. It is unfortunate that there is so little information in the explorers' books about the Negrids' ability to calculate. Galton says that it would 'sorely puzzle' the Ovaherero to realize that if one sheep cost two sticks of tobacco, two sheep would cost four. He regarded this tribe as 'intensely stupid', and intellectually very much inferior to the Ovambo. Schweinfurth tells of a game (probably not of Negrid origin) called *mungala*, played by most of the tribes in the Bahr-el-Ghazal country; this required considerable facility in ready reckoning.

It would not appear from the works of the explorers that the Negrids appreciated the independent or primary human value of knowledge about the natural world; or in other words, science (as opposed to technology) may be said to have been almost but not quite non-existent. Livingstone writes of the Bechuana, for instance, 'No science has been developed, and few questions are ever discussed except those which have an intimate connection with the wants of the stomach.' Generalizing more widely he remarks, 'All that the Africans have thought of has been present gratification.' Fynn, too, tells us that he seldom found any Zulu gifted with the inquisitiveness that makes people interested in knowledge, apart from the possibility of its immediate application to the practical affairs of their lives. These comments are too sweeping, however, for application to all the tribes of the secluded area. The Azande were keen helpers on Schweinfurth's botanical excursions, and he tells us that they could provide native names for all the plants; the Bongo, too, distinguished between two closely related species of antelopes, which he had at first been inclined to confuse.

A remarkable example of the pursuit of science was provided by Dagara, king of Karagwe, who wanted to know what was below the surface of the earth. To resolve this problem, a subterranean passage several yards long was dug at his command, and below this a cavern connected with the passage by a very small aperture. King Dagara was disappointed by the lack of new knowledge resulting from his geological investigation, and decided not to carry it further. Instead, he abandoned science for mysticism. It was stated with confidence that he was accustomed to resort to the cavern and stay there for many days at a time, without eating or drinking. In these periods of seclusion he was supposed to transform himself sometimes into a young man, at others into an old one, according to his whim at the time. Dagara's excavations were shown to Speke by Rumanika.

Livingstone found that the Barotse (*Pan 1*) had retentive memories on which he could rely for information about events that they themselves had actually witnessed long ago; but he found little evidence anywhere of *foresight* or thought about the distant future. It seemed to the local people a futile act on his part when he planted date-seeds near the head-waters of the Zambesi, in full knowledge that he would never see the fruit. He mentions it as a remarkable fact that the Batonga (*Pan 1*) even plant trees—'a practice seen nowhere else among natives'. Du Chaillu writes of the 'utter improvidence' of the Gabon tribes. Speke expresses the same idea when he says that the Negro 'thinks only for the moment'.

Speke's remark on the capacity of Negrid boys to absorb instruction has already been quoted (p. 348), and Baker was of opinion that children of this race were 'in advance, in intellectual quickness, of the white child of a similar age'; he adds, however, that 'the mind does not expand—it promises fruit, but does not ripen'.

The explorers appear to have encountered very few Negrids of markedly low intelligence. Speke did meet one lunatic, 'precisely a black specimen of the English parish idiot', but both Fynn and Livingstone remark on the rarity of actual insanity (apart from temporary aberrations).

Particular intelligence is attributed by the explorers to members of certain tribes. Those regarded as especially noteworthy in this respect were the Ovambo (*Ka*), Bunyoro (*Ka*), and Monbuttu (*Pan 3*). The latter are vividly described by Schweinfurth as 'men to whom one may put a reasonable question, and who will return a reasonable answer'. It is perhaps not irrelevant that there is evidence from physical anthropology of a Europid element in the ancestry of this tribe; indeed, Schweinfurth considered that they were related to the Fulbe. Fynn might have emphasized the relative intelligence of the Zulu (also hybrids, see p. 333), if his travels had made him acquainted with some of the *Pan 1* tribes. Livingstone remarks with surprising asperity of the Bashinje and neighbouring Angolan tribes (*Pan 1*) that they were 'by no means equal to the Cape Caffres [*Ka*] in any respect whatever'. Galton's low estimate of the intellectual calibre of the Ovaherero has already been mentioned.

Various opinions have been put forward to account for the fact that at the time when central Africa was first explored by foreigners, the culture of the Negrids was less advanced than that of certain other races of man. It has been suggested that the climate and soil were so unfavourable as to make mere survival in great numbers a considerable achievement, and that the effort to secure this left little opportunity or time for intellectual or spiritual advancement. Livingstone remarks of the Bakalahari, inhabitants of semi-desert territory, that '. . . no one [in Europe] can realize the degradation to which their minds have been sunk by centuries of barbarism and hard struggling for the necessaries of life'. It is true that in the interior of Africa, as in other parts of the world, there were places where life was hard. Starvation was witnessed by Baker in the Kytch tribe (*Ni*, see p. 360), and it was reported to Speke among the Wanyamwezi (*Ka*), though he himself did not see it; but over much the greater part of the secluded area the climate and soil were not unfavourable. Indeed, a very large number of references to the extraordinary fertility of the land are made by the explorers. A few of these will be recorded here. Their actual words must be used to give a true idea of the impression made upon them.

Schweinfurth remarks of the countryside at the border of Dinka (*Ni*), Dyoor (*Ni*), and Bongo (*Pan 3*) territory, 'The extreme productiveness of the luxuriant tropics is well exemplified in these fields, which for thirteen years have undergone continual tillage without once lying fallow and with no other manuring but what is afforded by the uprooted weeds.' The land of the Mittu

(*Pan 3*) '... is very productive. ... On account of its fertility the land requires little labour in its culture.' 'The Monbuttoo [*Pan 3*] land greets us as an Eden upon earth.' In some districts of the Azande '... the exuberance is unsurpassed. ... the cultivation of the soil is supremely easy. The entire land is preeminently rich in many spontaneous products, animal and vegetable alike, that conduce to the direct maintenance of human life.' Baker says of the country in what is now the borderland between Sudan and Uganda, '... we were in a beautiful open country, naturally drained by its undulating character, and abounding in most beautiful low pasturage'. He describes Shooa (Ladwong) in Acholi (*Ni*) territory, as '... "flowing with milk and honey"; fowls, butter, goats, were in abundance and ridiculously cheap'.

Schweinfurth's and Baker's comments on the fertility of certain Nilotid and *Pan 3* territories, given in the preceding paragraph, can easily be matched by what Livingstone says about the lands of the *Pan 1*. Of the catchment area of the River Kasai, a southern tributary of the Congo, he writes, 'To one who has observed the hard toil of the poor in old civilized countries, the state in which the inhabitants here live is one of glorious ease. ... Food abounds, and very little labour is required for its cultivation; the soil is so rich that no manure is required.' Further west, the valley of the Kwango '... is all fertile in the extreme. ... no manure is ever needed. ... the more the ground is tilled, the better it yields.' On his return from the west coast, Livingstone passed again through the Kasai valley, where he felt 'assured that there was still ample territory left for an indefinite increase of the world's population'. A similar thought occurred to him towards the end of his long journey, as he was passing through Batonga territory on his way to the east coast of the continent. 'There is certainly abundance of room at present in the country for thousands and thousands more of population.'

Further on towards the coast, now among the Banyai (*Ka*), Livingstone found the country 'extremely fertile, and the people cultivate amazing quantities of corn, maize, millet, ground-nuts, pumpkins, and cucumbers'. The same story could be told over and over again by examples from other Kafrid tribes. Speke tells us of the Wasagara, for instance, that 'the general state of prosperity was such, that the people could afford, even at this late season of the year, to turn their corn into malt to brew beer for sale; and goats and fowls were plentiful in the market'. West of the Victoria Nyanza 'It was a perfect paradise for negroes: as fast as they sowed they were sure of a crop without much trouble.' Galton writes of Kafrid territory on the western side of the continent, '... the charming corn-country of the Ovampo lay yellow and broad as a sea before us. ... The general appearance was that of most abundant fertility. ... As we journeyed on the next day, our surprise at the agricultural opulence of the country was in no way decreased.'

The examples that have been given, and many others that could be quoted, all point to the success of the Negrids (or perhaps one should say, of Negrid women) in agriculture; but they also show that further progress towards civilization was not rendered impossible by the harshness of the natural environment; nor is it possible to maintain that such progress was impeded by the necessity for perpetual labour to provide the purely material needs of man.

Labour was not perpetual, at any rate for the male sex. The explorers make this abundantly clear in their books. A few examples will be quoted. A remark of Schweinfurth's about the Monbuttu is representative of many written by the others.

Whilst the women attend to the tillage of the soil and the gathering of the harvest, the men, except they are absent either for war or hunting, spend the entire day in idleness. In the early hours of the morning they may be found under the shade of the oil-palms, lounging at full length upon their carved benches and smoking tobacco. During the middle of the day they gossip with their friends in the cool halls.

Baker makes this similar comment: '. . . it was the custom in Unyoro [*Ka*] for the men to enjoy themselves in laziness, while the women performed all the labour of the fields. Thus they were fatigued, and glad to rest, while the men passed the night in uproarious merriment.' Generalizing about Negrids he says, 'There are a lack of industry, a want of intensity of character, a love of ease and luxury.' Those who might have been expected to show enterprise in occupying themselves more intelligently seem to have been as deficient as the rest in this respect. At Mutesa's palace in Bunyoro (*Ka*), the Wakungu or court officers usually spent their time 'lounging about on the ground, smoking, chatting, and drinking pombé'. Remarks of a similar nature to these are frequent in the books of the explorers, and mere repetition of the same theme would be tedious. It must suffice to say that the failure to advance as quickly towards civilization as certain other races cannot be attributed to day-long devotion to the task of supplying the immediate needs of life.

The heavy incidence of ill health is sometimes suggested as a cause. It is unquestionable that the Negrids were afflicted by a number of illnesses against which they possessed no effective remedies. For instance, the explorers mention the occurrence of dysentery among the Zulu at a certain time of year, infestation of members of the same tribe with tapeworms, ophthalmia among the Makololo, seasonal sickness in Barotse country as the waters dried up, and smallpox at Obbo and elsewhere. Du Chaillu reports fevers, leprosy, a venereal disease, and virulent ulcers among the Bakalai. It is questionable, however, whether the inhabitants of the secluded area were in a worse situation, in respect of illness, than those of comparable tropical and subtropical countries elsewhere, in some of which, especially India, great advances in intellectual life had been made from remote times onwards. There seems also to be a tendency to overlook the fact that there were already centres of civilization in temperate countries in early times, when the inhabitants were still harassed by illnesses of various sorts, including epidemics fully comparable in virulence with those that beset the peoples of warmer climates. Some Europeans have in the past tended to overestimate the unhealthiness of Negrid Africa, partly on account of their own lack of immunity to certain diseases of that country, but mainly because the unhealthy coastal districts were for a long time the only parts of the continent that were known to them.

The explorers certainly do not present a picture of universal sickness among the inhabitants of the inland parts of Africa. Du Chaillu says of the Ashira (*Pan 1*), 'The natives are generally tolerably healthy. I have seen cases of what

I judge to be leprosy, but they have little fever among them, or other dangerous diseases.' Never in his travels did he come across a blind man, and deafness was very rare. Galton says of Ovamboland that 'There are no diseases in these parts except slight fever, frequent ophthalmia, and stomach complaints.' This country and that of the Ovaherero 'leave nothing to be desired' on the score of health. Schweinfurth makes more than one reference to the healthiness of the Azande territory. Referring to the hilly districts in which he had encountered this tribe and the Monbuttu, he remarks that 'My health was by no means impaired, but, on the contrary, I gained fresh vigour in the pure air of the southern highlands.' Baker, too, noted that when at Shooa (Ladwong), among the Acholi, '... the more elevated land was remarkably dry and healthy'. Livingstone was the only one among the seven explorers who was medically qualified, and his opinion therefore carries special weight (though the others were not ignorant in matters of health and sickness). In crossing what is now called the Batoka Plateau (in Zambia, between Livingstone and Lusaka), he remarked that the hilly ridges of this region 'may even be recommended as a sanatorium for those whose enterprise leads them on to Africa. . . . they afford a prospect to Europeans, of situations superior in point of salubrity to any of those on the coast'. He says also that '. . . they resemble that most healthy of all healthy climates, the interior of South Africa, near and adjacent to the [Kalahari] Desert'. It would not appear, therefore, on Livingstone's evidence, that even in former days, before European medicine had brought its benefits to central Africa, such tribes as the Batonga (Batoka), Bamangwato, Bakuena, and Bechuana lived in such an unhealthy climate that intellectual advancement was impossible.

It is sometimes suggested that the Negrids were subject to special disabilities as a result of the prevalence of hookworm disease and schistosomiasis in their country. It is true that these diseases are debilitating and that Negrids suffered from them, but hookworms (*Ancylostoma* and related genera) and species of the genus *Schistosoma* are not confined to their continent, but spread their ravages in other lands. Within Africa, too, they are far from restricting their parasitism to members of a particular race. From ancient times onwards they have been a source of affliction to one of the earliest of the great civilizations of the world. Egyptian papyri of about 1500 B.C. describe a form of anaemia almost certainly resulting from infestation of the alimentary canal with *Ancylostoma*, while eggs of *Schistosoma* have been found in mummified corpses of the Pharaohs.[442] It has long been known that the most advanced forms of schistosomiasis are seldom found in southern Africa,[381] and it is now realized that the main causative agent in that part of the continent is a separate species,[659] which seldom causes urinary obstruction through fibrosis of the neck of the bladder. Advanced stages of the disease are much commoner in Egypt, where the more virulent species, *S. haematobium*, is the prevalent parasite.[700]

*S. haematobium* has a wide distribution in Africa and the Near East. *S. mansoni* is another mainly African species, while *S. japonicum* represents the genus in Japan, China, and elsewhere.[700] All are human parasites, with freshwater gastropods as secondary hosts.

# 21 The Negrids
## IV. Miscellaneous observations

STUDY OF the works of other explorers than the chosen seven convinces me that the account of Negrid culture presented in the two preceding chapters, though necessarily incomplete and unsophisticated, is essentially a reliable one. Nevertheless the question must arise, whether there were particular parts of the secluded area that would have caused the explorers to present Negrid culture in a different light, if their routes had chanced to traverse them. Further, the reader would be justified in asking whether Negrid Africa outside the secluded area might hold evidence bearing so directly and powerfully on the ethnic problem that it would be wrong to exclude it entirely from consideration. These are subjects on which much could be written; but of the various aspects of the problem that might have been considered, three have been chosen as more important than all the rest. They form the subject of the present chapter.

Livingstone chanced to meet in Makololo territory some Negrids who had come all the way from their home in Manica, in what is now Mozambique, near the Rhodesian border. They gave him some very interesting and, on the whole, remarkably accurate information, telling him that in the vicinity of their native land there were 'walls of hewn stone, which they believe to have been made by their ancestors. . . . Two rivers, Motirikwe and Sabia or Sabe, run through their country into the sea.' The letters *l* and *r* are often confused, and *o* sometimes stands for an indefinite sound between consonants. It is therefore legitimate to rewrite the first-named river as Mtilikwe; the other is obviously the Sabi. Manica does in fact lie on the fringe of a huge district in which buildings of hewn stone are found, the very centre of which lies in the catchment area of the Sabi; and the most famous stone ruin of all, Zimbabwe, stands close to its tributary, the Mtilikwe. Livingstone's mention of this subject, published in 1857,[676] seems to have been strangely overlooked by historians of this now world-famous part of Africa. He himself never saw any of the stone buildings; but when he discovered the Victoria Falls, in November 1855, he was only forty-three miles from one of them. It was not until 1868 that a Europid at last re-entered Zimbabwe. This was Adam Renders, an American hunter. He himself did not publish an account of what he saw, but it was not long before others followed and made Zimbabwe known to the civilized world.

Ruins of hewn rock are scattered over an enormous area in Rhodesia, and they extend narrowly over the borders into Mozambique and northern Transvaal. From the extreme eastern limit of the Inyanga Terraces to the most westerly of all the ruins is a distance of no less than 475 miles, and it is 407 from Mapungubwe, just south of the Limpopo, to the most northerly of all, between Salisbury and the Zambesi. More than two hundred ruins have been located, but many of them are rather insignificant. Others, however, especially Khami, Dhlo-Dhlo, Naletale, Zimbabwe, and the Terraces, are imposing structures, which have been studied and reported on in detail.[559, 910, 911, 1026, 1027]

Problems spring instantly to the mind of anyone who sees the ruined stone buildings of Rhodesia. It is true that there are others in central and southern Angola, generally attributed to earlier generations of the Jaga (*Pan 1*) tribe; but these are on a comparatively minor scale, and with these exceptions, Negrids have always been accustomed, in all other parts of the secluded area, to build with plant material, supplemented in certain districts with suitable earth that hardens on drying. In most other countries of the world the existence of stone ruins would not cause much surprise, because building in this material has been usual since remote times. But did Negrids build the stone walls of Rhodesia? The problem does not concern only the identity of the builders, and the reason why they built here in stone: the *function* of some of the buildings remains obscure. A mystery presents itself, and it is this, rather than any special architectural excellence, that strikes chiefly on the mind— though one can, indeed, scarcely fail to be impressed in certain places by the grandeur of the scale. It has been calculated, for instance, that the external wall (Fig. 67) of the Great Enclosure at Zimbabwe contains some fifteen thousand tons of stone.[1026]

It is necessary at the outset to understand that the buildings in question are in no sense houses; the great majority of them are simply *walls* of two types: retaining walls, to support the extremities of terraces, and free-standing ones, to form enclosures or passages. At Khami, for instance, nearly all the stone structures are retaining walls (Fig. 68, p. 404); at Zimbabwe, most are of the other type. The inhabitants of both places evidently lived in circular huts, not made of stone. At Khami the terraces on which these were to be placed were hardened on the surface by ramming down a reddish building-earth (*daga*). Circular foundations laid on these show that the actual habitations of the people were huts of the usual Negrid type.

A partial exception to what was said at the beginning of the preceding paragraph may perhaps be glimpsed in the little 'Philips' ruin at Zimbabwe. Here there are indications that certain stone-built enclosures may possibly have been roofed. Where these were placed a little apart from one another, it looks as though wooden huts may have stood between them on the intervening ground, at a higher level. If so, this is the only approach—admittedly a very distant one—to a two-storey building in any part of the secluded area.

Near the frontier of Rhodesia with Mozambique, and reaching just beyond it into the latter country, there are very extensive retaining walls that evidently served another purpose than the support of a flat surface on which to build huts. It is clear that the Inyanga Terraces of this district formed the basis of some large-scale agricultural scheme. It is likely that these walls were built independently of the ones that cluster together in the catchment area of the Sabi, and perhaps by members of a different tribe.

The free-standing walls are the ones that present the great problem of func-

67  *Part of the external wall of the Great Enclosure at Zimbabwe, viewed from the outer side*

The wall is here about 30 feet high. *Photograph by the author, 1962.*

### 68　*The Hill Ruin at Khami*

A, photographed from the base of the Cross Ruin, to show the retaining walls. B, a 'chequer pattern' wall supporting the lowest ('A') platform. The white card is 15 cm (6″) high. *Photographs by the author, 1962.*

tion. Summers, one of the principal authorities on the subject, considers that the Great Enclosure at Zimbabwe was a church;[1026] Gayre argues that it was a fort;[396] Desmond Clark regards it as a 'palace', and compares it with the village of a Barotse (*Pan 1*) chief, built in stone instead of wood.[207] The other main building at Zimbabwe, nicknamed the 'Acropolis', is equally difficult to explain. Anyone standing to the south or south-west of it and looking up at the hill on which it stands would be likely to say that it was a fort, for the ascent to it is abrupt, indeed precipitous in places, and the great walls join the crags to one another in such a way as to present an appearance sufficient to deter anyone who had thoughts of aggression from that side; but climb to the top and look over the other side, and you will find no precipice there, but only an easy ascent. Anyone whose purpose was to defend the summit would have put his main walls on the side that nature had left defenceless; but there they are relatively puny. There is strong contrast in this respect between the 'Acropolis' and (for instance) Maiden 'Castle' (pp. 258–60), which was built more than a millennium before one stone was placed on another at Zimbabwe; for the whole structure of Maiden 'Castle' was obviously designed down to the last detail by people who had the clear purpose of transforming a hill into a defensive position.

Radio-carbon dating has made it possible to say that building in stone began at Zimbabwe at some time between the first half of the tenth and the first half of the thirteenth century; one may postulate A.D. 1100 or thereabouts as the most probable date.[1026] Gayre considers that the early builders were probably a mixed lot: Hottentots, Arabs based on Sofala, Negrid slaves brought in by the Arabs, and hybrids between these groups.[396] His paper deserves careful study, but the weight of evidence does not seem to give strong support to this view. Those who have made the most thorough investigation of the site incline to the opinion that local people of the Shona tribe (*Ka*) may have been responsible for the early work.[1026] The oldest masonry was of a primitive character (Fig. 69A, p. 406). There were no excavated foundations; the slabs of stone were only roughly trimmed, and the courses did not run in regular horizontal rows; joints between one stone and the next frequently lay immediately above another such joint. No free-standing wall was built in a straight line or in a regular curve of any shape whatever; mortar was never used.

During the fifteenth century there was a sharp change in the style of building. Foundations were dug; courses were laid horizontally in regular rows of trimmed blocks of accurate thickness; false jointing became much rarer. A fine example from a much later time, at Khami, is shown in Fig. 69B. In certain respects, however, there was continuity in structure and design. All building was still done in drystone, and walls were not erected in straight lines or determinate curves. Controversy persists about the identity of the builders, but the most commonly accepted view is that they were members of a group called Rozwi that detached itself from the Barotse (*Pan 1*) tribe and came south-eastwards into Kafrid territory. Here they remained, subject for a long time to a dynasty of kings called 'Mambo', until at last, during the thirties of the nineteenth century, they were overrun and almost exterminated by invaders belonging to the Ngoni tribe (*Ka*), who had themselves been driven out of Zulu territory by Chaka. A remnant of the Rozwi remained in the vicinity till about 1860, and some of their descendants are said still to exist elsewhere, incorporated in other tribes.[1026]

Many of the buildings, especially at Zimbabwe, obviously required the organization of a very large labour force. The number of actual builders, though considerable, must have been small in proportion to the total number required. The granite that was used in most of the buildings had to be quarried, brought to the site, and then transformed into blocks of suitable size. This involved the felling and transport of wood to make the fires that would heat the stone, so that it could be split by cooling with water; and masons were needed when carefully trimmed blocks were to be used.

69    *Early and late building styles in Rhodesia*

A, part of the south wall of the Western Enclosure of the 'Acropolis' at Zimbabwe, viewed from the inner side. The early or 'P' style of building is seen. B, part of the wall supporting the middle ('B') platform of the Hill Ruin at Khami, to show a late building style. The white card seen in the photographs is 15 cm (6″) high.
*Photographs by the author, 1962.*

One asks oneself why building in stone, on a scale that must have involved large labour forces, should have been confined almost entirely to a particular part of a vast territory. The answer must surely lie in the presence, in early days, of gold lying exposed in nuggets on the surface of the soil. The Negrids themselves were always much more interested in iron than in gold, for their own use; but the precious metal, or knowledge of it, spread eventually to the coast. Arab and Indian traders had established themselves at Kilwa, south of Zanzibar, by about A.D. 700, and by A.D. 900, before building in stone had begun at Zimbabwe, they were already at Sofala. When the Negrids discovered the insatiable desire of Europids for gold, trade inevitably began. Foreign beads and other trade-goods passed into the interior to pay labourers; gold passed out. The chiefs became rich beyond the desires of avarice; and just as today, in civilized countries, art-dealers tempt millionaires to display their wealth by paying immense fortunes for celebrated pictures, so the traders on the coast encouraged the owners of the land of gold to value the precious goods of the outside world. Ruin No. 1, to the N.N.W. of the Great Enclosure, has rendered up Chinese porcelain attributed to the thirteenth and fourteenth centuries, and from then onwards, century after century, treasures flowed into Zimbabwe, Khami, and the other great centres—Islamic painted glass and Persian faience of the thirteenth and fourteenth centuries, porcelain of the Sung and Ming dynasties with the so-called 'Céladon' glaze; the list could be extended to cover all the innumerable objects now exhibited in the National Museum at Bulawayo, the Queen Victoria Museum at Victoria, and the Museum at Zimbabwe itself. It is with a sense of bathos that one must descend from these glories of former days to mention an object that has helped to date the lower occupation-level at Dhlo-Dhlo—a square-sided gin-bottle, made in Holland about 1700 (lying incongruously beside a blue-and-white bowl of the Ming dynasty).

To supply the never-failing demand for gold, it became necessary to delve into the earth. One cannot tell whether the advice of foreigners was sought when the first shafts were sunk, some of which descended obliquely thirty feet and more below the surface. The actual labour of mining was presumably performed by the native inhabitants, and this involved the organization of a special labour force, in addition to that which had existed before.

It is clear that much the greater part of the building in hewn stone took place after contact had been made with foreign traders (Arab, Indian, Persian, and Indonesian) on the coast. The route followed in the export–import business is uncertain. It is usually supposed that the exports (ivory and slaves as well as gold) were taken first to the junction of the River Lundi with the Sabi and thence conveyed in canoes to the coast, some sixty miles south of Sofala; but arguments have been put forward for a much shorter direct route to the latter port, entirely by land.[1175] It is scarcely possible to believe that during all the centuries of active trade, foreigners did not frequently visit the ultimate sources of their income. The Portuguese arrived on the coast in 1505, and for a time dominated the trade with the northern goldfields. They established many inland settlements, and when these were eventually overrun about 1700, they left many prisoners in native hands, who may have influenced building techniques. Still, although building in stone would not have developed far without the immense stimulus of the gold-trade, it is impossible to attribute the overall design of the buildings to outsiders. The irregularity of the plans is not suggestive of foreign control. One cannot suppose that a literate person, in drawing the plan on paper, would have designed the Great Enclosure at Zimbabwe as it actually exists. Retaining walls, which form the major part of the ruins at Khami and elsewhere, cannot be attributed to Arabs, who were not accustomed to build them.

Nevertheless, the idea for all the buildings probably came from what was seen at Sofala by those whose function it was to transport the goods to and from the coast. The buildings at the town must have appeared magnificent to those who had never seen any part of the civilized world. The inland chiefs desired magnificence, and those of their subjects who had seen Sofala no doubt described it. It seems probable that Zimbabwe represents essentially a Negrid reflection of what had been seen of foreign architecture on the coast. If Arabs and other Europids had lived in any numbers at Zimbabwe and the other sites, one would expect to find many indications of their presence among the innumerable foreign objects that have been collected there; but these are almost exclusively trade-objects (especially beads) and prestige gifts for the chiefs (as well as ornaments, pottery, and other artifacts, obviously of Negrid origin). There are, however, some suggestions of foreign influence in minor details of architecture. It has been claimed that the chevron decoration at the top of the wall that encircles the Great Enclosure at Zimbabwe (Fig. 67), and other comparable decorations elsewhere, resemble Arabian designs.[54, 1175] The four little turrets on the western wall of the Western Enclosure of the 'Acropolis' may well represent someone's recollection of a minaret seen (but obviously not understood) at Sofala (cf. Gayre[396]). The high quality of the masonry at such places as Dhlo-Dhlo and Khami (Figs. 68 and 69B) may owe something, too, to Portuguese influence. A number of ecclesiastical objects found at Dhlo-Dhlo suggest that Catholic missionaries may have been there in the eighteenth century, when most of the building was probably done; and the stones arranged (now cemented) in the form of a cross on the flat surface of a boulder at the 'Cross' Ruin in Khami suggest (without proving) that Portuguese also resided at the latter site (cf. Robinson[910, 911]). It would be rash, however, to ascribe the actual lay-out or basic scheme of the stonework of the whole area to foreigners. Some of the decoration of the retaining walls at Dhlo-Dhlo and Khami, in particular the very effective 'chequer' pattern made by omitting alternate stones (Fig. 68A and B), is thought to be of Negrid origin.

In trying to form some general idea of the significance of the hewn-stone buildings, it is important to keep in mind some relevant facts about dates. The evidence that a few were erected some eight or nine hundred years ago may give a wrong impression of the antiquity of the buildings as a whole. Many of them were made much later. The most accurate and decorative masonry, presumably built to give added prestige to local rulers at Dhlo-Dhlo and Khami, is attributed to the eighteenth century; Naletale seems to have been constructed at about the same time;[207] and so was much of Zimbabwe, including the outer wall of the Great Enclosure.[1027] Antiquity is not the primary interest of the ruins: rather one must reflect on the administrative powers of those who organized and controlled the labour forces.

Zimbabwe has been included as one of the subjects of a fine book entitled *Vanished civilizations*.[821] It may be queried whether the term 'civilization' is fully applicable here. Decision must rest on the definition of the term (see pp. 506–8). There is much to admire in the sheer magnitude of Zimbabwe, and the decorative walling of Dhlo-Dhlo and Khami; but to what stage of culture had the rulers and labourers really advanced? There is no evidence that a wheeled vehicle was ever used during the period of occupation. Clark seems to convey an accurate impression when he speaks of the 'barbaric splendour' and 'barbaric ostentation' of Zimbabwe and the rest; and it is to be remembered that the splendour and ostentation were made possible by what was poured into the country from foreign lands. One must acknowledge the administrative capacity of the rulers, but may question the utility of the ends to which much of it was put. As Clark remarks, 'The many amulets, fetish figures, and other ritual objects unearthed in the diggings bear witness to a flourishing belief in and practice of witchcraft and magic.'[207] We see no sign of anything that might have been a school, far less a university; the people were illiterate, and no native record of anything exists, apart from the stones themselves, the objects found beneath and among them, and vague, almost incomprehensible traditions handed down to the descendants of those who survived the Ngoni onslaught. One must hope that old Arabic manuscripts somewhere exist, awaiting discovery by a scholar who will one day enable us to form a truer judgement about much that is today necessarily hypothetical.

The second topic of this chapter takes us well outside the secluded area into the territory of the Vai or Vei tribe (*Su*), in the vicinity of what subsequently became the frontier between Sierra Leone and Liberia. In *The races of man*, Deniker says of the Vai that '. . . alone among Negroes, they appear to possess a special mode of writing'.[268] Since the existence of literacy is commonly regarded as one of the criteria of civilization, it is necessary to review the facts that may substantiate or contradict Deniker's statement.

The curious history of this subject centres round a single member of the Vai tribe named Duwalu Bukele (spelled Doalu Bukara in the earlier literature, but there is no *r* in the Vai language). His home was at a village named Dshondu. Here he had been for many years under the influence of Islam, but a Christian missionary from Europe had given him instruction in reading over a period of three months. He was subsequently employed by traders to carry messages to distant places. Having reason to believe that some of the letters he carried back to his employers contained adverse comments on his own behaviour, he arrived at the conclusion that it would be advantageous to Negroes to have a method of their own for communicating secretly between widely separated places.

According to his own story, the idea of a script for the native language occurred to him in a dream. On awaking, he started to invent the necessary characters, but he soon brought in five other men, all, like himself, between the ages of 20 and 30. Together they constructed a set of two hundred and fifteen characters, each representing a syllable, not a letter. A few of these are reproduced in Fig. 70, p. 410. Some of the symbols showed the direct influence of the Latin alphabet; for instance, B stood for the sound of *gba*, and a mark resembling a handwritten M for *ma*. Others were evidently remembered from the past, but quite new sounds were assigned to them;[1078, 721] for instance, a mark like N for *po*. A few were hieroglyphs: for instance, a horizontal line thrown into ripples stood for the monosyllable *dshi*, meaning 'water'. It has been remarked that the same hieroglyph was used for this word by the ancient Egyptians,[1078] but derivation of the Vai script from this source may be discounted.[601] Many of the symbols were obviously invented by Bukele and his associates, and arbitrarily assigned to particular sounds. The Vai script is said to differentiate clearly between the two *b*'s of the language, the two *d*'s, the various labiovelars, and the nasalized forms of vowels.[598]

There is a suggestion that a very rudely developed system of picture-writing had existed from former times among the Vai people, and the idea has been put forward that Bukele's script may have been based partly on symbols derived from this system;[598] but the evidence for this is weak, and it has not been generally accepted. The Vai people of 1927 had no knowledge of the supposed picture-writing of their remote ancestors;[598] and in any case the great majority of the signs appear to be non-pictorial inventions of Bukele's group.

| symbol | sound | symbol | sound |
|--------|-------|--------|-------|
| | *ba* | | *pa* |
| | *da* | | *pe* |
| B | *gba* | | *pi* |
| | *ma* | N | *po* |
| | *ha*, also *ndo* | | *po* |
| | *mo* | | *ya* |

70    *Symbols from the Vai script*

*Copied from Koelle.* [601]

Since the script was phonetic, a person who had learnt the pronunciation of the syllables could read the language and be understood by Vai speakers, even if he himself did not know the exact meaning of what he was saying.

It was thus that there arose a phonetic, syllabic, mainly non-pictorial script. It was written with pens made of reeds, in ink derived from certain leaves obtained in the forest. The Negro ruler of the region established a school in Dshondu, where men, women, and children learnt to read and write their own language. The school and its books were burnt in a native war, but some of the scholars—Bukele among them—gathered together about five years later in a new town (written 'Bandakoro' in the only available record on the subject), situated some miles from where Dshondu had stood. Here they started once more to give instruction in reading and writing.

The first European to report the existence of the script was a naval officer, Lieutenant Forbes, who came across a specimen of it near Cape Mount, close to the western extremity of Liberia. He went to Fourah Bay in Sierra Leone in 1849, to enquire whether the missionaries there knew of its existence. The Revd. S. W. Koelle, a German missionary, was sent at once to investigate. After considerable difficulties caused by another native war he succeeded in reaching Bandakoro, where he chanced to meet Bukele, now about 40 years old, at the instant of his arrival. Koelle had spent about a week there, learning the script, when he was struck down by very severe fever; and as soon as he was well enough to face the journey, he made his way to the coast. His discovery was quickly published by the missionaries in a booklet written in English, in which the characters of the script were reproduced.[601] At the time of his visit, all the adult males of Bandakoro could read the script, at least to some extent, and there were literate persons in all the towns of Vai territory. It was still in use in most parts of the country in the middle of the present century, though known to few persons.

Koelle was struck by Bukele's intelligence and by his capacity to concentrate his mind on one subject over a long period.

New symbols were eventually added to the original ones by native exponents of the script. These were used to indicate modifications of the sounds and thus to represent some that occur in English but not in the Vai language. It has been claimed that the script thereby became a phonetically better system for representing certain words of our own speech than that provided by the English system of spelling.[598] Although this may well be true, it must be admitted that a syllabic system would have to be enormously enlarged if it were to be applicable to all the common words of the English language, and there is no evidence of the existence at any time of a large number of characters in the Vai script.

Strangely enough, another native script came to light in the Southern Province of Sierra Leone in 1932.[1028] It was invented by one Kisimi Kamala, a member of the Mende tribe (a subdivision, like the Vai, of the Mandingo group of tribes). The script consisted of 190 symbols. Like that of the Vai people, it was written from left to right, and it is considered to have been syllabic; but there are indications of what might be regarded as single letters. Thus the signs for *ma*, *mi*, and *mu* all have a single character in common, which can be taken as standing for the letter *m*; certain dots near this character indicate the different vowel sounds. This writing was occasionally scratched on the walls of buildings, but only a few hundred persons could read and write it, and it appears to have attracted little attention among the native population. It cannot be positively affirmed that Kamala was aware of the existence of the Vai script; but since there is no evidence that a set of written symbols has originated in any other part of Negrid Africa, it is very unlikely that the idea of inventing a script should have had two entirely independent origins in the narrow strip of borderland between Liberia and Sierra Leone. Kamala was a Muslim and must necessarily have been aware of the existence of the Koran. The idea of representing speech by symbols cannot be attributed to him.

We take an eastward leap of nearly 1,100 miles from the Sudanid-*Pan 2* borderland and find ourselves, for the first time in three chapters, in the middle of *Pan 2* territory. We are now among people of the Yoruba tribe, and are about to examine certain ancient pieces of sculpture unearthed in and near the town of Ife in Nigeria, 113 miles north-west of Benin and about the same distance north-east of Lagos. But first we must take a brief glance at Negrid sculpture in general.

Living organisms are seldom represented in lifelike form in Negrid sculpture. Some rough approximation to a naturalistic style may be found here and there. The sculptors of the Nok culture in northern Nigeria, for instance, produced tolerable likenesses of certain animals in terracotta; but their representations of the human head are not lifelike. It has been said that the Negrid sculptor produces his results by 'deliberately disregarding anatomical veracity'.[673] Segy, who has studied the sculpture of the Sudanids, *Pan 1*, *Pan 2*, and *Pan 3*, writes of its 'astonishing unity' in this respect throughout nearly every part of the vast territory occupied by these peoples.[955] Almost anyone who looks at pre-colonial Negrid art in a museum will allow that if the sculptures intended to represent men could come to life, no one would regard them as human. The uniformity stressed by Segy makes it possible to give at least some general impression of Negrid style in plastic art by the single photograph reproduced here in Fig. 71A. This is the head of a horseman, carved in wood by a Yoruba artist. The specimen may be seen in the Museum of Mankind (British Museum), among many of a similar nature. Segy remarks that in Negrid art there is no visual reality or imitation of nature. The reality is 'conceptual'; that is to say, the artist reveals ideas that are present in the mind.[955]

In view of these facts, it was natural enough that the discovery in Negrid Africa of strikingly realistic sculptures of the human head should have caused widespread astonishment. A German expedition (*Deutsche innerafrikanische Forschungsexpedition*) arrived in Nigeria in 1910, and in the same year its leader, Leo Frobenius, began to unearth at Ife a number of terracotta heads, unlike anything previously known from Negrid territory.[368, 369] No one could doubt that these heads, vitalized and restored to human bodies, would be universally recognized as human.

Frobenius carried out part of his work at Ebolokun, a grove (perhaps an ancient cemetery) situated about a mile north of the town. Before long he had obtained a fine head, similar in general style to some of the terracottas, but cast in bronze by the *cire perdue* method. It would appear that this head had been dug up by the Yoruba about the middle of the nineteenth century and given the name of Olokun, a divinity of the sea. It was buried again, and seems to have been brought to the surface annually thereafter for worship by members of the tribe. Frobenius had the good fortune to be allowed to photograph it.

From time to time in later years more heads were dug up at Ife, when foundations were being prepared for new houses. No fewer than thirteen bronze heads were found in 1938 in excavation for the foundations of a single house in the town.[60] In 1949 some more terracotta heads of the same type were excavated at Abiri, about ten miles from Ife. Altogether twenty bronze heads have been obtained, of which sixteen are of life size.[1141] One of them is a very fine mask, to which the name of Obalufon II has been assigned. The tradition is that this mask was not dug up, but has been kept continuously at the palace of the Oni (ruler) of Ife ever since it was cast.[1141]

Most of the Ife bronzes are in the Oni's palace, but a fine one is publicly exhibited in the Museum of Mankind (British Museum) in London, and two were brought by Bascom to Northwestern University, Evanston, Illinois.[60] The one shown in Fig. 71B was formerly in the British Museum, but has been returned to Nigeria. Many museums (including the British) possess good casts of some of the bronzes and terracottas. Casts of thirteen of the bronze heads belonging to the Oni were exhibited in 1962 at the National Gallery of the Federation at Salisbury, Rhodesia, as part of the First International Congress of African Culture.

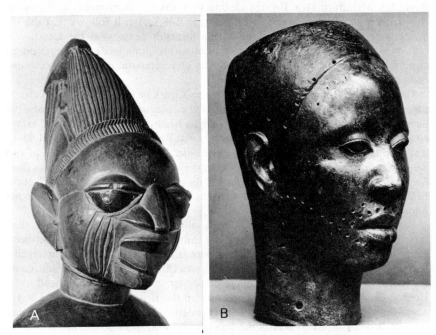

71   *A contrasting pair of sculptures from Nigeria*

A, a typical Negrid sculpture in wood: the head of a horseman (Yoruba tribe). B, bronze head found in the Wunmonije Compound at Ife.
*Both sculptures were formerly in the British Museum, but B has now been returned to Nigeria.*

There is universal agreement on the high technical quality of the Ife heads. Braunholtz says of one of the bronzes, 'In its vitality and the sensitive modelling of the features it challenges comparison with the finest sculpture of other times and countries.'[134] H. and V. Meyerowitz consider that 'The Ife heads are masterpieces and could not technically be improved upon.' They stress the 'amazingly sensitive surface treatment'.[739] Meinhard says that the Ife heads 'are technically and artistically on the highest level'.[731] Duckworth describes them as 'outstanding works of art of the highest quality',[291] and Sir William Rothenstein says that they are 'superb works of art, worthy to be set beside the best examples of sculpture of any period'.[916]

It has not been found possible to date the Ife heads with any accuracy. The extreme antiquity suggested by Frobenius is not accepted nowadays. E. L. R. Meyerowitz thinks that the numerous vertical lines incised on many of the faces suggest that the heads represent people who inhabited Ife before it was occupied by the Yoruba about the beginning of the twelfth century,[738] but the general opinion seems to be that they were probably made in the thirteenth[25] or fourteenth century, and it is supposed that in one or other of these centuries the naturalistic style and bronze-casting technique of Ife were carried thence to Benin (cf. Meinhard[731]). Bronze-casting was already in progress in the latter city when it was first visited by Europeans in 1485.[1141] It follows that the Ife heads were presumably sculptured in the fifteenth century at the latest.

It must be mentioned that realism did not survive long in Benin. The bronze-casters of this city soon reverted to forms characteristic of Negrid sculpture elsewhere.

The many excellent photographs in Pitt-Rivers's work on Benin art show this clearly enough.[846] One can indeed see that a few of the specimens represent Europids, but there is nothing approaching the realism of the Ife heads, and with a few partial exceptions (for instance, the Negrid heads shown in Pitt-Rivers's Figures 88–9 and 98–9) the sculptures represented are entirely unrealistic. Frobenius gives pictures of two naturalistic ears from Ife heads, and for comparison thirty-two unrealistic ones from Benin. He refers to the decadence (*Verfall*) of the pattern. [369] The technical skill of the Benin bronze-casters, which reached its climax in the sixteenth century, [134] is not disputed.

Although the metallic Ife heads are usually called bronzes, it appears that their composition is not in every case the same, and it might perhaps be more accurate to call some of them brasses. There is, however, no sharp, universally recognized distinction between the two classes of copper alloys. The source of the metal is unknown. The percentage of copper in the only bronze head from Ife that exists today in Europe (and is now in the British Museum) is 73·9. H. Maclear Bate, to whom we are ultimately indebted for this specimen (for it was he who brought it north across the Sahara in 1938), points out that copper is not known to occur naturally anywhere in Negrid Africa nearer to Ife than the Congo (now Zaïre).[62] Various suggestions as to the source of the metal have been put forward. It seems probable that it came from the north, by one of the caravan-routes across the desert.

One of the most difficult problems connected with the Ife heads is their assignment to correct positions in taxonomy. The names of important people in the history of the Yoruba tribe have been arbitrarily attached to several of them. Some scholars think that each may in fact be a portrait of a particular person; indeed, Frobenius[368] and Braunholtz[134] claim that there can be no doubt about this. The heads represent a wide range of ethnic taxa. The first fact that strikes one is that few of them represent typical Negrids of any subrace. One of the exceptions is a terracotta of a rather typical Sudanid shown in Plate 145 of Frobenius's *Das unbekannte Afrika*;[369] another Negrid, somewhat damaged and not referable to a particular subrace, is shown in Plate 146 of the same book. One of the casts exhibited in the Museum of Mankind (British Museum) (taken from a terracotta collected by Frobenius in 1910) appears to represent a *Pan 2* Negrid.

A few of the heads, especially the one shown in the lower right-hand corner of p. 594 of Bascom's article,[60] are suggestive of the Armenids, and another (shown in the middle photograph on the left side of the same page) is also clearly a Europid, though one could not assign it to a particular subrace without examining the actual specimen from various points of view.

Apart from the Negrid, Armenid, and certain other distinctive heads, there are some that appear to form a natural group. They are distinguished by possession in common of certain morphological features, and they give evidence of particular care on the part of the sculptor (and of the metal-caster, in the case of the bronzes) to produce heads of the highest possible technical excellence. Many of them show the vertical incised lines, to which reference has already been made; others (for instance, the bronze shown here in Fig. 71B) do not. I have examined carefully all the Ife heads exhibited in the British Museum and at the First International Congress of African Culture (p. 413), and also many photographs reproduced in books and papers, and can give the following general impression of those which fall into this special category. It must be remarked, however, that there is not complete uniformity within the group. In general the heads are high, with the vertex far back; the occiput does not project strongly. Most of them are scarcely or not at all prognathous, but the lips are rather thick and somewhat everted. The auricle (pinna) of the ear is rather large and lies against the head; it has a well-developed lower lobe, also lying against the head, and perhaps intended to represent an adherent lobe. The nose is somewhat wider than is usual in Europids, but it has quite a high bridge, projects moderately, and in some cases is slightly convex (Fig. 71B). In the male heads there are holes above and below the mouth and on the cheeks, evidently intended for the attachment of hair. The expression of these heads is one of serenity and self-confidence. It is convenient to have a collective name for the heads in this category, and, for want of a better word, it is perhaps legitimate to suggest that they may be said to belong to a 'ruler' group.

It is a very curious and indeed inexplicable fact that in most of the Ife heads, though not in those that represent Negrids, the upper eyelid is carried downwards on the nasal side in such a way as to cover the extremity of the lower lid. It is often said that these heads show the 'Mongoloid fold', but this is not correct.

The upper eyelids of man may be folded in two different places. Every upper eyelid is folded back on itself at its edge or margo, which bears the eyelashes. Some upper eyelids show a second fold, originating on their surfaces above the margo. The fold, properly called the *Mongolenfalte*, or plica naso-palpebralis superior of Aichel, [12] is the second fold, which sweeps down at the inner (nasal) extremity of the eye in such a way as to cover the margo (pp. 208–9 and 312 and Fig. 25B and C); and it often covers the inner extremity of the lower eyelid as well. On the outer or lateral side of the eye the second fold often extends *upwards* in the Mongolids, and thus gives an appearance of obliquity to the eye (Fig. 25C). Two folds of the upper eyelid, one partly covering the other, are *not* represented in the Ife heads.

It is stated by Bascom[60] that the 'Mongoloid fold' is 'found with fairly high frequency among Africans'. It is necessary to deny this. The *Mongolenfalte* is *rare* among Negrids.[12] A very short fold involving only a small part of the inner (nasal) end of the upper eyelid, but not hiding the corner of the eye or any part of the lower eyelid and not extending beyond the lower eyelid towards the nose, is indeed quite common in Negrids; but this type of lid, the *mediale Negerfalte* or plica tarsalis medialis,[12] is not represented in any of the Ife heads.

There is only one type of upper eyelid among all the ethnic taxa of man that seems to resemble closely the lid represented by the Ife sculptors in their 'ruler' heads (and certain others). This is the *Indianerfalte* or plica naso-marginalis of Aichel,[12] who gave it the former name because he first saw it among the Indianids (American Indians) in certain parts of Chile and Bolivia. In this type there is no second fold of the upper eyelid, but the true eyelash-bearing margo is continued obliquely downwards on its inner (nasal) side so as to overlap and hide the inner corner of the eye and part of the caruncle, and passes on towards the nose. This type of upper eyelid occurs sporadically in other races of man, including the Europid. Aichel gives a photograph of a head showing this fold (Fig. 35 on Plate XXI of his paper[12]), and the resemblance to the eyelids seen in the Ife heads is striking. He describes the possessor of this head as a Negro, without qualification, but the photograph appears to represent a member of one of the unclassified, hybrid (Europid-Negrid) tribes, that occupy a broad band of territory north of the *Pan 3* (Fig. 58, p. 328). Unfortunately he gives a wrong reference to the source of the photograph, and the original cannot be traced.

The Ife heads of the 'ruler' group cannot be assigned with confidence to any ethnic taxon that exists at the present day. Most of their morphological features suggest that they represent a racial hybrid, predominantly Europid in ancestry, possibly with some Negrid admixture indicated by the everted lips and slightly widened nose. It has been suggested that the people portrayed were Fulbe rulers of the Yoruba, but the morphological features do not confirm this. The Fulbe of the present day are markedly dolichocephalic, and somewhat prognathous below the nose; the lips are thin; and there is very little facial hair.[1084] In all these respects there is strong contrast with the heads in the 'ruler' group. It is unlikely that anyone intending to represent the Fulbe would put holes in their statues for the attachment of facial hair.

The identity of the sculptors has not been established. Frobenius himself considered that his discoveries 'disclosed nothing affording a clue for thinking that this great skill in art had been developed autogenetically, i.e. spontaneously in the country itself'.[368] He thought that if there had been local forerunners of the art, he would have come across evidence of their work in the course of his excavations, but he found nothing of the sort. He regarded the art-form as Mediterranean in origin, but could not attribute it confidently to any one locality. The heads have been examined by specialists in the sculpture of Africa (including Egypt), Persia, India, and Europe, but they have failed to find evidence that would definitely establish cultural affinities with any particular country.[739] Segy remarks on the 'enigma' that 'we witness the summit of a most accomplished artistic form and technique which suddenly came to an end, showing no survival or further development'. He considers that 'such an eruption of a new style as that of Ife must have been the effect of a foreign influence'.[955] In his opinion this style could only have been achieved by artists for whom it was already an established tradition. Like Frobenius, he inclines to the probability that the art was derived from the Mediterranean region, and he remarks that the heads 'have a classical Greco-Roman cast'. He thinks that all the bronze heads might be the products of a single 'master caster', or perhaps of two or three, and suggests that such a person or small group of persons might have accompanied one of the caravans that came south across the Sahara. One may rule out the possibility of Islamic influence, on account of the prohibition imposed by the Koran, but it is known that Greek sculptors wandered widely and implanted their style in distant lands.|955|

# PART FOUR

# Criteria of Superiority and Inferiority

# 22 Introduction to Part 4

ANYONE WHO accepts it as a self-evident truth, in accordance with the American Declaration of Independence, that all men are created equal, may properly be asked whether the meaning of the word 'equal' is self-evident. A definition is particularly necessary in discussions on the equality or inequality of human taxa. Is one concerned simply with the question whether the taxa are *similar* or *different*? If so, there can be no doubt as to the answer. Who could conceivably fail to distinguish between a Sanid and a Europid, or between an Eskimid and a Negritid, or between a Bambutid and an Australid? Clearly the members of these pairs of taxa are different and therefore unequal, in the sense that any two objects are unequal unless similar. The immediately obvious criteria of distinction between these taxa are, however, physical. Is one taxon *superior* to another? The great majority of adult Europids are obviously superior to the great majority of adult Sanids in stature, but in discussions of this subject it is desirable to avoid the use of the word 'superior' in this sense, and to employ some such alternative as 'larger' (and 'smaller' as its opposite) wherever this meaning is intended. The words 'superior' and 'inferior' are not generally used unless value-judgements are concerned.

Mere size of body or its parts makes it easier for members of certain human taxa to excel in particular sports, but it would scarcely be justifiable to speak of superiority or inferiority in this respect. It is worth while to notice briefly a few examples of crudely physical features that are advantageous or detrimental to members of certain taxa in sporting activities, without affecting the way in which these taxa should be regarded from the point of view of the ethnic problem.

There are certain games in which tallness is of obvious advantage. It would be absurd to suppose that Bambutids, Negritids, or Sanids could compete effectively with Sudanids, Nilotids, or Dinarids at basket-ball, and equally unreasonable to suggest that the three former taxa should be regarded as inferior on that account. It is much better to say simply that their stature is very much less. The relationship between a physical feature and success in sport is particularly obvious in this case, though it goes without saying that other factors as well are concerned in success at this game.

Long legs are unquestionably helpful towards speed in running, especially over short distances, and successful sprinters are usually tall. The Japanese population is mainly Palaemongolid, and members of this taxon are predominantly of short stature. The outcome can be seen readily enough in the results of the modern Olympic Games. In the whole period since these contests

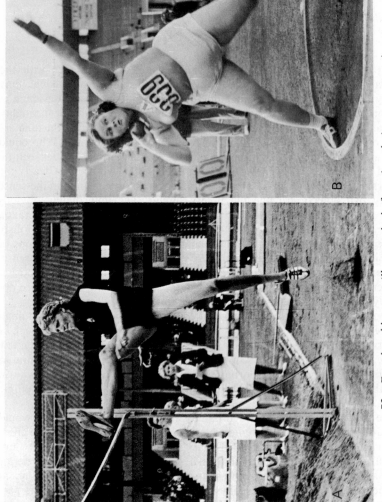

72   *Female athletes, to illustrate body-form in relation to success in sport*

A, Miss Iolande Balas, Romanian winner of the women's high jump at the Olympic Games in 1960 and 1964. B, Miss Tamara Tyshkyevich, shot-put champion of the Soviet Union and winner of the shot-put at the Olympic Games in 1956. A, *photograph by Mr. Gerry Cranham*; B, *Associated Press.*

were initiated in 1896 up till 1968 (inclusive), the Japanese never won a gold, silver, or bronze medal in any running race, single or relay, for men or women, at any distance whatever, with the exception of the Marathon. This is a race of more than twenty-six miles, in which speed is much less significant than endurance. In the 1936 Olympics Japanese competitors came in first and third in this race, winning gold and bronze medals respectively. Both these runners were examined by a competent physical anthropologist and judged to be predominantly Tungid, not Palaemongolid. Members of the Tungid subrace are generally rather short, but they are said to be 'particularly well suited, both psychically and physically, for this almost superhuman exertion'.[594] A Japanese runner won a bronze medal in the Marathon in 1964 and another a silver in 1968, but their morphological characters were not studied by physical anthropologists.

The Japanese are by no means unsuccessful at sports in which tallness is not important. On the contrary, an analysis of all the recorded results[726, 858] shows that they have won 52 gold medals, 43 silver, and 38 or 39 bronze.*

Long legs are at least as helpful in high jumping as in running. No Japanese man or woman has ever won any medal for this sport at the Olympic Games. The outstanding champion in the women's high jump has been Iolande Balas of Romania (Fig. 72A), whose record of 6' 2¾" in 1964[726] had never previously been closely approached at these Games. The population of Romania is predominantly Dinarid, and the facial features and tall stature, with especially long legs, characteristic of this subrace, are well shown in the photograph. To find someone who might compete successfully against Miss Balas, the British coaches looked specifically for a long-legged girl. The coach who found the most likely candidate for the task remarked of her, 'It was not so much the ease of her jumping which impressed me as the length of leg that was taking her over the heights.' He recognized the importance of skill and mental attitude, but put the main emphasis on a purely physical feature. Measured from the instep, the length of her leg on the inner side was 35½"; Miss Balas's, 36".[760]

The photograph shows that Miss Balas is a blonde. It is a recognized fact that Dinarids are quite frequently fair-haired. In his book on *Die Ötztaler*, Sauser gives a photograph of the head of a typical blond Dinarid, a male with features showing resemblances to Miss Balas's.[932] A special adjective, *'norisch'*, has been suggested for the blond type of Dinarid.[646] These blonds do not differ from the more usual dark-haired type in any morphological character. The flattened occiput, particularly characteristic of the Dinarids, is well shown in a photograph of Miss Balas published in the *Daily Mail*.[760]

In 1969 an appeal was made on British television, on behalf of the Amateur Athletic Association, for large women to come forward for training in the shot-put, javelin-throw, and discus-throw, with a view to possible participation in the Europa Cup competition.[1180] British women were said to have been unsuccessful in these sports. It is to be noted that on this occasion the entire emphasis was placed on bulk of body (though of course other qualities in addi-

---

* According to the rules of the Olympic Games, bronze medals should be awarded to both the unsuccessful semi-finalists in boxing events. It seems uncertain whether this was done in 1968. For details see Preston.[858]

tion would be necessary for success). The significance of corpulence in the shot-put is suggested by the photograph reproduced in Fig. 72B, which shows Miss Tamara Tyshkyevich, women's shot-put champion of the Soviet Union and winner of this event at the Olympic Games in 1956. She weighed 17 stone 4 lb. (242 lb., or about 109·8 kg).

In military training, obstacle races are sometimes arranged in the course of which the competitors are required to crawl through large drain-pipes. The diameter of the pipes being an arbitrary matter, there is no reason why narrow ones should not be selected, and advantage thereby given to Bambutids, Negritids, and Sanids. Indeed, one could easily make it as impossible for a normal Sudanid or Nordid to win (or even to complete the course), as it is for one of the pygmy taxa to win the shot-put. The arbitrary nature of the tests is obvious.

On the occasion of the Olympic Games held in Berlin in 1936, an attempt was made by a German physical anthropologist, W. Klenke, to estimate the proportion of competitors belonging to different ethnic taxa in the Japanese contingent.[594] He recognized that hybridity had occurred in the ancestry of most of them, but in the great majority the characters of one taxon predominated. If taxonomic position had been irrelevant in the selection of Olympic competitors, the majority of the contingent would have been Palaemongolid, since members of this taxon form the greater part of the population of Japan; but this was far from being so. Klenke assigned 44% of the Japanese contingent to the Sinid subrace, only 29% to the Palaemongolid, and 15% to the Tungid. 5% were Europids of the Ainuid subrace, 1% Polynesids, and the rest of a peculiar type called 'Jakonid' (probably Europid-Mongolid hybrids of indeterminate ancestry, but possibly Sinids influenced by unusual hormonal balance). The great numerical predominance of Sinids existed not only in the contingent as a whole (or in the representative sample studied in detail by Klenke), but also in each lesser group consisting of the persons competing in a particular sport. Klenke attributes this to the fact that Sinids are powerfully built, tall people, while the Palaemongolids (and incidentally the Tungids and Ainuids as well) are short. He notes that among boxers, Sinids were particularly predominant in numbers among the heavyweight categories (which was, indeed, predictable). It may be remarked that none of these heavy Sinids won a medal for boxing, nor did any Sinid win a medal for running or high jumping. This was presumably because there were too few Sinids in the whole population of Japan to make it probable that there would be a world champion among them.

Very nearly as many of the gymnasts were Palaemongolids as Sinids in the Japanese contingent (respectively 44% and 46%). Klenke attributes this to the fact that there are advantages in light weight in this branch of sport.

Certain taxa possess physical characters that are advantageous in boxing. Henry Cooper, the heavyweight boxer, has said that projecting cheek-bones are disadvantageous, because they are apt to cause splitting of the skin, and blood tends to get into the eye.[1178] This would mean that Nordids have an advantage, because it is characteristic of this subrace that the zygomatic arches slope away backwards, while their strongly projecting counterparts in Tungids would reduce the chances of this subrace in the ring. A thick skull would favour a boxer, because its inertia would lessen the shaking of the brain caused by a heavy blow. Broca remarked long ago of the Negro, 'In him, the bones of the cranium are conspicuously thicker than ours, and have at the same time much greater density; they scarcely contain any diploë, and their resistance is such that they can sustain truly extraordinary blows without breaking.'[138] The extreme thickness of the skull and the replacement of diploë by compact bone in Australids has already been mentioned (p. 279). *Pithecanthropus*, too, was guarded against heavy blows to the head by the thickness of his cranial walls, and he would have been well fitted to stand up to battering in the boxing ring.

Some remarks on the effect of grading competitors into groups by body-weight on the success of certain ethnic taxa in sports will be found in Appendix 10 (p. 554).

It has been usual since remote times for people of various ethnic taxa to regard themselves as outstripping others not so much through the possession of greater physical powers of the kind we have been discussing, as by superiority in the moral or intellectual sense. Several examples have already been mentioned in this book, especially in Part 1. Contemptuous words have often been used to designate particular taxa or tribes, and these have in some cases become so widely used that they have tended to supplant the names that the despised people apply to themselves. The *Pan 3* tribe that called itself the Lwoh was named 'Dyoor' by the Dinka (*Ni*). This scornful word, meaning 'wild men',[951] became the name by which the tribe in question was generally known, and one finds it inscribed on maps. Similarly, the Monbuttu applied the word 'Momvoo' to their neighbours on the southern side, and this word too, implying the extremity of degradation, has been used as though it were the correct name of the tribe.[951]

Perhaps no taxon or tribe has been more universally disdained than the people called by missionaries 'Bergdama' and provisionally designated *Pan 4* in this book. Its members live in isolated groups in the hilly regions of South West Africa. Many of them were mercilessly massacred by the Hottentots, who enslaved most of those who survived. The *Pan 4* adopted the language of their masters and forgot their own. They did not even remember the name of their tribe, but sometimes called themselves 'Nu Khoin', or black people, for distinction from the 'Awa Khoin', the 'red people' or Hottentots. The latter used the word 'Dama' or 'Daman' as an inclusive term for the Ovaherero (*Ka*) and Bergdama, distinguishing the latter as 'Chou-daman' ('*chou*' meaning filthy) or *Xoudama* ('*xou*' = human excrement).[1089, 1090]* The Ovaherero called them 'Ovazorotua' (inferior blacks), and like the Hottentots they killed and enslaved them. Certain anthropologists have vied with the oppressors of the *Pan 4* in denigrating these unfortunate people. Deniker[268] says that they are 'miserable savages who live by hunting and plunder', Haddon[450] that they are 'practically a pariah people and may be a degraded offshoot of the OvaMpo' (an un-

* The Hottentots sometimes called the *Pan 4* 'Haukhoin'. Seligman [957] says that the name means 'dung people', but this is incorrect. It means foreign men, which is itself a misnomer, since these people were the original inhabitants of the country. See Vedder. [1089]

likely hypothesis). A standing joke against them among their neighbours (not so funny in view of modern knowledge of human evolution in general) was that they descended from monkeys—a belief apparently accepted at one time by themselves.[378] It is to be remarked that Galton[378] and Vedder,[1090] who knew the *Pan 4* personally, did not concur in the opinions expressed by their detractors, and the former relates a very remarkable instance of the honesty of one of them.

Galton calls the *Pan 4* 'Ghou Damup', probably a misheard version of ' ⧻ Nu Dama' (the symbol ⧻ representing a Hottentot sound not represented in any European language). Missionaries usually call them 'Bergdama' or 'Hill Damara', but they do not appear to belong to the same subrace (*Ka*) as the Damara (=Ovaherero). They are not very uniform in physique, and further study will be necessary before they can be fitted with confidence into any taxonomic scheme (cf. Vedder [1089]).

The foregoing remarks relate to only a few extreme examples of a widespread tendency for members of certain ethnic taxa to regard others as inferior. The question arises whether any reality at all may underlie opinions of this sort. Is it possible to obtain objective evidence that would help to solve the ethnic problem? It may be profitable, at the outset, to consider certain arguments of a very general nature, admittedly only tentative and exploratory, but nevertheless helpful, in my opinion, in orientating the mind towards thought on this difficult problem.

It is not to be supposed that genes conferring genuine 'superiority' of any sort, if such exist, would be easily susceptible to genetic analysis. One would anticipate the cumulative effect of many genes, each having a small effect (pp. 158–9 and 190–91). In these circumstances there would be no sharp segregation of characters in the F2 generation, when members of two different ethnic taxa had mated together and produced hybrid offspring who had married similar hybrids. For the solution of the ethnic problem, however, one is not immediately concerned with the question whether the analysis of human polygenes is possible, or likely to become so. The relevant question is altogether different. One wants to know whether it is conceivable that members of two taxa may differ in large numbers of groups of genes affecting many parts of the body, but not at all in those that affect the nervous and sensory systems and therefore play a part in determining mental qualities. In addressing oneself to this problem it is helpful to consider any two taxa of mammals, other than man, that differ from one another in morphological characters about as much as a Sanid does from a Europid, or an Eskimid from a Negritid, or a Bambutid from an Australid, and then note whether two such taxa of animals are ever identical in their habits, and therefore in their mental qualities. The conclusion will almost necessarily be reached that identity in habits is unusual even in pairs of taxa that are morphologically much more similar to one another than are members of the pairs of human taxa that have just been mentioned. The subspecies of gorilla, for instance, are not nearly so different from one another morphologically as Sanids are from Europids, but they differ markedly in their modes of life (pp. 114–15).

In this connection it is relevant to mention that even a trained anatomist would take some time to sort out correctly a mixed collection of the skulls of

Asiatic jackals (*Canis aureus*) and European red foxes (*Vulpes vulpes*), unless he had made a special study of the osteology of the Canidae; whereas even a little child, without any instruction whatever, could instantly separate the skulls of Eskimids from those of Lappids (pp. 195–7). In reflecting on this fact the reader should hold in mind that the jackal and fox, though so similar in their skulls, belong not only to different species, but to different *genera*. Their habits are different. The jackal often hunts in packs, while the fox is solitary; both kill small animals for food, but the jackal relies more than the fox on carrion and vegetable matter; it utters a very distinctive howl at night, while the fox is quieter, and yelps rather like a small dog.[330, 691, 841, 861, 1011]

For comparison, ten adult skulls of the Asiatic jackal (*Canis aureus indicus*) and ten of the European red fox (*Vulpes vulpes vulpes*) were selected at random from specimens in the British Museum (Natural History).[49] There is overlap in size, but most jackal skulls are slightly larger than those of the fox, and the facial region of the former tends to be slightly wider. The temporal ridges, which converge as they run backwards on the dorsal side of the skull to unite posteriorly in the sagittal crest, generally remain separate further back in the fox than in the jackal, but three of the ten jackal skulls resembled those of the fox in this respect. The supra-orbital process is somewhat hollowed out above in the fox, but scarcely or not at all in the jackal. The constriction behind the supra-orbital process, marking the boundary between the interorbital and temporal regions of the skull, is generally deeper in the fox, but one of the jackal skulls showed as deep a constriction as one of the foxes'. By taking note of these distinguishing features, it should be possible to separate skulls of the two animals, but the differences are small. For further remarks on these differences, see Appendix 11 (p. 555).

Keeping in mind the close similarity of the skulls of jackal and fox, and the differences in their habits, one may find it difficult to suppose that two human taxa differing so profoundly in cranial characters as (for instance) the Eskimid and Lappid can be identical in all the genes that control their nervous and sensory systems; and if this seems unlikely, one must ask oneself whether it is conceivable that the mental qualities of each human taxon, though differing, must somehow add themselves together in such a way that all taxa are necessarily to be regarded as 'equal' mentally, in the special sense that no taxon is superior to any other. What known cause of evolution could have produced this result? Is it not more probable that natural selection has adapted taxa to different environments, and that as a result some of them have a greater tendency than others to produce persons possessing special agility and versatility of mind? And if one introduces a value-judgement by predicating that agility and versatility of mind are superior to mental sloth, is it not at least *likely* that superiority and inferiority are realities (even though, as was pointed out at the beginning of the book (p. 6), all taxa include mentally inferior persons)?

Natural selection may have produced the mental diversity of human taxa in response to different environments (physical and biological) in much the same way as artificial selection has produced mental diversity in the various breeds of dogs and other domestic animals, which also differ, breed from breed, in their mental qualities. As Darwin remarks of dogs, 'The degree to which the various breeds differ in the perfection of their senses, dispositions, and inherited habits is notorious to everyone.'[257] It is found easiest to train dogs of different breeds for different purposes, such as guiding blind persons, carrying messages in war, indicating the position of game, and performing on the stage.[789] Darwin found comparable differences in the mental equipment of different breeds (or 'races' as he called them) of pigeons.

The manner of flight, and certain inherited movements, such as clapping the wings, tumbling in the air or on the ground, and the manner of courting the female, present the most singular differences. In disposition the several races differ. Some races are very silent; others coo in a highly peculiar manner.[257]

Darwin provides very strong evidence that all the breeds to which he refers in these remarks derive from a single species, *Columba livia*, and that they were produced by artificial selection (both 'methodical' and 'unconscious'), which he describes as the 'foundation-stone in the formation of new races' (i.e. breeds).[257]

The retreat of the ice after the last glacial epoch opened up vast areas of the northern hemisphere and offered great opportunities to people who could adapt themselves to a new mode of life and develop the foresight needed for the maintenance of large populations under strongly seasonal climatic conditions, very different from those in many parts of the world, where a more equable environment made it less necessary to look far into the future. Certain potentially favourable environments are more demanding than others, and thus favour the natural selection of an enterprising type of mind.

It does not follow from what has just been said that extremely adverse environmental conditions would lead to the natural selection of the most enterprising and far-seeing persons. On the contrary, it seems that some of the less progressive ethnic taxa of man have been forced out of the most favourable habitats and have learnt to obtain a specialized livelihood in regions that did not offer much opportunity for large-scale enterprise and the resulting increase of population that would be necessary for the development of civilization.

It must be kept in mind that certain taxa have remained primitive or become paedomorphous in their general morphological characters, and none of these has succeeded in developing a civilization. It is among these taxa in particular that one finds some direct indication of a possible cause of mental inferiority in the small size of the brain (see p. 292). The relation between brain-size and intelligence is not, however, direct. This follows obviously enough from the fact that a large part of the brain is concerned with non-intellectual processes, especially the mere transmission (as opposed to origination) of nervous impulses, and with the co-ordination of muscular contractions throughout the body. The proportion of the brain that is concerned with thought-processes varies greatly in the different taxa of mammals, so that direct comparison of total brain-size cannot throw light on the subject under consideration unless it is instituted between closely related forms, in which the proportional sizes of the various parts are nearly the same. For this reason, and because there is a correlation between the size of the body and that of the brain, the fact that elephants and dolphins have large brains is not immediately relevant.

When man alone is considered, certain facts bearing on the relation between brain-size and intelligence do stand out. In particular, the fossil evidence shows clearly enough that the organ has increased progressively in volume in the course of human evolution, and that those ethnic taxa (the Australid, for instance) that are primitive morphologically in other respects have retained to some extent the smaller cranial capacity of man's ancestors. Further, no person recognized as eminent in mathematics, science, philosophy, or any other purely intellectual subject has ever been a member of a taxon in which the average cranial capacity is low. If it could be shown that a positive relationship existed between brain-size and intellectual capacity, one would have an objective method for assessing the latter in the various ethnic taxa.

During the nineteenth century the brains of a number of distinguished Europeans were studied, and data were collected about those who had died in earlier times. Interest centred chiefly on the total brain-weight and on the degree of convolution of the cerebral cortex.[529, 1115] Unfortunately, the weights were often given in a rather unsatisfactory way. In many cases precise particulars were omitted as to whether the organ was weighed fresh or after preservation, and if preserved, in what fluid. The amount of blood remaining in the vessels, and of cerebro-spinal fluid in the ventricles, must also have affected the recorded figures. The data are nevertheless not without value. Cranial capacity (the volume of the cavity of the brain-case) provides a good indication of the volume of the organ, and obviously determines its upper limit. Skulls are many, freshly removed brains few, and as a result much more information is available about cranial capacity than about the weight of the contained organ. What seem to be reliable data relating human brain-weight to cranial capacity are available. A table of these is given by Welcker.[1135]

The facts given in Welcker's table may be expressed almost exactly by the equation

$$1 \cdot 065v - 195 = w,$$

where $v$ is the cranial capacity in millilitres and $w$ the weight of the brain in grams. [49]

For comparison with those of distinguished persons, the brain-weights of unselected European males aged 21 and over are represented diagrammatically in Fig. 73, p. 430. The weights, obtained directly by use of the balance, are taken from the table given by Wagner.[1115] For the present purpose they have been arranged in groups (900–999 g, 1,000–1,099 g, etc.), and the number falling in each group counted and expressed by the height of the column. The mode or largest group is seen to be 1,300–1,399 g, but the frequency-polygon is not symmetrical, and the arithmetic mean of European males may be taken as about 1,410 g,[1062] or 1,424 g at the age (30 or thereabouts) at which the organ is said to be slightly heavier than at earlier or later ages.[529]

Some of the early records supposed to represent the brain-weights of celebrities are extremely high. Oliver Cromwell was credited with a gigantic brain, weighing no less than $6\frac{1}{4}$ lb.[529] This figure was presumably obtained with Troy weights. If so, it would be equivalent to 2,332 g; if avoirdupois, still more. In either case, the record is incredible.

The history of Cromwell's skull and brain after death is not without interest. He died on 3 September 1658 and his body was buried in Westminster Abbey. John Evelyn tells us in his diary how on 30 January 1661 his 'carcass' and

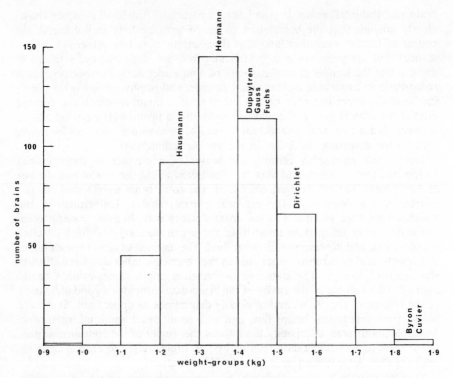

73  *Brain-weights of European males aged 21 and over, shown in a frequency-*
*polygon*

The names of certain eminent and distinguished men are referred to the weight-ranges to which their brains
belonged.                    *Diagram drawn from the tabulated data of R. Wagner.* [1115]

those of two of his associates were 'dragg'd out of their superb tombs in Westminster among the Kings to Tyburne, and hang'd on the gallows there from
nine in the morning till six at night, and then buried under that fatal and ig-
nominious monument in a deepe pit'.[318] His head, however, was not buried.
On the contrary, it was cut off and exposed on the top of Westminster
Hall.[1126] How long it remained there, and when or where or by whom the
brain was removed and weighed, does not appear to be known; but eventually
the skull came to Oxford, and Huschke[529] gave careful instructions for
discovering 'whether the above-mentioned statement [about the weight] may be
a historical falsehood'. He suggested that the skull (presumably repaired after
removal of the brain) should be filled with water maintained at 4·1°C, and that
the contained water should then be weighed so as to provide an approximation
to the weight of the organ it had originally contained (due allowance being
made for the specific gravity of brain-matter). There does not appear to be any
record that the Oxford anatomists followed this well-meant advice, but the
delay of at least three years between death and weighing, and the huge figure
given for the weight, leave no doubt that Huschke was right in suspecting error.

If the weight had really been 2,332 g, and if it is permissible to apply the equation given above to extrapolate from Welcker's data, Cromwell would have had a cranial capacity of 2,373 ml, which is not credible.

Cuvier was another celebrity to whom a huge brain (weighing more than five *livres*) was formerly ascribed. Wagner, having carefully reviewed the evidence, allows him the large weight of 1,861 g. It has been suggested that the great zoologist suffered slightly from hydrocephaly, at least in youth, but there was little fluid in the ventricles of his brain at death.[1115]

Byron's brain was said to have weighed six 'medicinal pounds', but his corpse was brought from Greece to England, and unfortunately no one knows where it was when the brain was removed and weighed. In England at that time (1824) avoirdupois would have been used, in which case six pounds would have meant 2,239 g, again an incredible weight. Wagner thinks that the brain was weighed in mainland Greece, or perhaps on the island of Zante, and that Venetian weights were used. He mentions that at that time there was a close connection between Venice and Greece. If his surmise is correct, the weight would represent 1,807 g. This is a very large but credible figure, which may perhaps be accepted. The organ was hyperaemic. [1115]

The weight-groups to which the brains of these and certain other notable men belonged are shown in Fig. 73.

The brain of P. G. L. Dirichlet (German mathematician, expositor of Gauss's discoveries) weighed 1,520 g. Several men of high intellect are known to have possessed brains above the mean weight for European males: for instance, C. H. Fuchs (German pathologist), 1,499 g; Gauss, 1,492 g.[1115] The cranial capacity of Immanuel Kant was 1,715 ml.[620] The equation given on p. 429 suggests that his brain weighed 1,631 g.

The mental specialist who opened Schumann's skull, after his death in an asylum, reported that the composer's brain weighed 1,475 g. This is a surprisingly high figure, in view of the fact that his cranial capacity is stated to have been 1,510 ml.[933] The latter figure would suggest a brain of about 1,413 g, almost exactly the mean weight for male Europeans. Several distinguished persons are known to have possessed brains of moderate or small size. There is no evidence, however, that any illustrious person ever had a brain that was very small in comparison with those of normal Europeans, and it would appear that sufferers from microcephaly are invariably idiots.

The brain of the French surgeon G. Depuytren weighed 1,437 g; of the philologist C. F. Hermann, 1,358 g; of the German mineralogist Hausmann, only 1,226 g. [1115] The cranial capacity of Raphael is given variously as 1,400–1,420 and 1,450–1,500 ml,[933] and it therefore seems certain that his brain was not a large one. Wagner quotes the brain of a woman aged 25 years that weighed only 720 g, and he describes and illustrates that of another person of unstated sex, aged 26 years, that registered only 300 g on the balance. In such organs there is no reversion to the structure seen in pongids, except in the simplicity of the convolutions in the frontal lobes. [1115] These are pathologically defective, not primitive brains.

Since there tends to be less convolution of the cerebral cortex in members of ethnic taxa regarded on other grounds as primitive (p. 292) or paedomorphous (pp. 319 and 322), and far less again in pongids, it has naturally occurred to anatomists to enquire whether intellectually eminent persons show peculiarities in this respect. The subject was considered in some detail long ago by Wagner, who obtained permission from Gauss's son to open the preserved head of the mathematician, mainly for the purpose of studying the degree of convolution of the cortex.[1115] Wagner also examined the brain of Dirichlet, and in the cases of both these mathematicians he found the gyri particularly complicated and the intervening sulci unusually deep. His figures amply illustrate what he says; but he drew no firm conclusion from what he saw in these two brains, because he did not find similar complexity in the cerebral cortices of Hermann or Hausmann. The prominent anatomist who examined Beethoven's brain found only the usual complexity of convolution, and the sulci were not particularly deep.[933]

It was suggested that the total surface-area of the cerebral hemispheres (including the part that dips down into the sulci) might be greater in eminent than in undistinguished persons, but though very elaborate measurements were made in an attempt to test this hypothesis,[1113] the work was done on too few persons to carry much weight.

There is no actual proof that all the pongid and paedomorphous characters in the brains of Australids and Sanids respectively are directly concerned in determining the intellectual faculties, but they add themselves to the other morphological features that suggest a less advanced or more childlike condition. The most important differences between bright and dull minds in normal members of any one species or *Formenkreis* probably depend to a large extent on factors more subtle than those that can be seen by the naked eye or registered by the balance.

Some exceptionally interesting experiments bearing on this problem have been carried out on animals. R. C. Tryon of the University of California started work with a stock of laboratory-bred rats (presumably *Rattus rattus*). He proceeded to derive from these animals two inbred stocks, by selection on the basis of their tendencies to run through a particular maze with the smallest or greatest number of wrong turnings.[1069] Each rat ran through the maze nineteen times, and the total number of errors made was recorded. The brightest rats (those that made fewest errors) in the brightest litters were kept for breeding together, and so were the dullest in the dullest litters. After seven generations had been subjected to this selective process, two distinct stocks had been produced. The members of the dull stock commonly made about six times as many errors as the bright, and very little overlapping in the performances of the two stocks remained. Further selection over many generations had negligible effects. The two stocks were inbred continuously, and about twenty years later they were tested on three mazes, all different from the one used in the original selection experiment. In each of the tests the members of the bright stock made significantly fewer errors than the dullards.[921] The very surprising fact, and the one immediately relevant to the subject under discussion, is that the weight of the cerebral cortex was found to be *greater* in the dull than in the bright stock.[75] Something beyond mere size of the cortex is obviously concerned with the type of intelligence needed for easy learning of mazes.

Despite what was said in the preceding paragraph, it remains a fact that if rats are kept in groups provided with 'toys' and set to find their way through mazes, their cortices do become heavier than those of members of the same stock caged singly in a quiet room with nothing to stimulate their mental activity.[75] This applies to rats of both bright and dull stocks. It must be supposed that in the wild remote ancestors of the laboratory rat, large cerebral cortices were normal, since no wild rat could survive if it behaved like the isolated specimens in the experiments. In other words, the enlargement of the cerebral cortex was the normal response to stimuli roughly equivalent to those occurring naturally in the environment of wild life, and the capacity to respond to this environment evolved, like other characters, through the operation of natural selection.

These facts have relevance for human affairs. One might perhaps suppose that the small size of the brain in Australids and certain other ethnic taxa was due to an environmental cause operating in individual development, namely, the lack of appropriate mental stimulation. This opinion cannot be sustained. If it were true, one would have to suppose that the remote ancestors of the Australids lived in mentally stimulating environments and evolved the capacity to grow large brains. The facts do not support this hypothesis. On the contrary, they suggest that the brains of Australids are small because they *retain* the size characteristic of a particular stage in human evolution beyond which most other ethnic taxa have evolved. There is no evidence or likelihood that the ancestors of the Australids were at any time civilized, and it is unthinkable that natural selection could have caused the brains of the ancestral Australids to evolve the potentiality to increase in size, during the course of individual development, in response to a stimulating environment that did not exist at the time. The Australid is not comparable to the isolated rat, which had the inborn potentiality to grow a brain of the same size as that of its remote ancestors, if allowed to develop in a suitable environment.

Among normal individuals of large-brained taxa, the exact size of the brain is not the fact that sets a limit to mental activity. The physical basis of intelligence presumably depends, in such persons, on the arrangement and complexity of the processes by which the nerve cells (neurones) of the cerebral cortex communicate with one another. On cursory examination under the microscope these cells in any one species of animal generally look very similar to the corresponding ones in members of related species, and indeed in members of related genera and even families, despite the great differences in behaviour. These differences must depend ultimately on the branching outgrowths that have originated from the neurones in the course of embryonic development, and have put one cell in communication with another.

The junctions between neurones are called *synapses*. They commonly occur where the end of a long process (axon) from one neurone branches repeatedly and interlaces with several much shorter ramifications (dendrites) of another neurone. The latter may pass on the impulse through its own axon to yet another neurone, and so on, repeatedly in some cases, until it reaches an effector organ (muscle or gland). One of the methods employed to reveal the branched processes of neurones is called the Golgi-Cox technique, after the names of the histologists who originated and perfected it.[230] It involves impregnation of the tissue with mercuric chloride; the mercuric compound is slowly reduced and the cell darkens. Thin slices (sections) of brain material made by this method are shown in Fig. 74. It is a curious feature of the Golgi-Cox technique that although it generally darkens only about 3% of all the neurones in a piece of brain, those that it does reveal are darkened throughout, to the tips of their processes. It follows that when the dendrites of a particular cell are clearly seen under the microscope in a preparation made by this method, the terminal branches of the axon that brings nerve-impulses to them from another neurone are usually not visible, because the darkening reaction did not occur in the cell of which the axon was a process. It is for this reason that the dendrites show clearly in Fig. 74, but the interlacing of branching axon-processes with them is not seen.

Although an enormous number of minute projections ('spikes') can be seen projecting from the long, vertically ascending processes in Fig. 74B, there are probably very many more that are too small to be seen with the optical microscope. The electron microscope has revealed numbers of diminutive ones, only about 23 nm in diameter, in the brain of the cat.[817] Such minute objects as these could not possibly be resolved by the optical microscope, and it is very doubtful whether they could be visualized at all. The structure of the brain may eventually be found to be considerably more complicated than has been supposed. The significance of the very small dendrites, revealed by electron microscopy, does not appear to be known with certainty. It is probable that they are not concerned with the formation of synapses.

The ultimate branches of each axon are expanded at their tips into little swellings called 'end-feet', which are implanted on the dendrites or in some cases directly on the cell-body of the neurone to which the axon transmits the nervous impulse. The latter is transmitted across the excessively minute intervening space (only about 20 nanometres wide) by the passage of a chemical messenger. A large number of end-feet is usually implanted on a single neurone; often they originate from the axons of several other neurones. It is easiest to estimate the number of end-feet, or actually to count them, when they are implanted not on dendrites, but on the cell-body itself. There are in some cases hundreds of them on a single neurone. A clear picture of such a case is shown in Fig. 75, p. 436. The object illustrated is a model of a neurone in the spinal cord of the cat. One can see the thin threads (minute terminal branches of an axon or axons) that bring impulses to it, and their termination in end-feet. The cell illustrated had 434 end-feet implanted on it.

The model was made as follows.[455] A piece of the spinal cord of the cat was treated by the method 4ª of Ramon Cajal; that is to say, after fixation by formaldehyde it was impregnated with silver nitrate solution, and the silver ion was subsequently reduced by pyrogallol.[872] The material treated in this way was sectioned at 4 $\mu$m. A particular cell could be followed through many consecutive sections. A model, magnified 2,000 times in linear dimensions, was made of the part of the cell that was included in each section, and all the models were stuck together in correct sequence and orientation to produce the composite model depicted in Fig. 75.

It would have been an almost superhuman task to find the origins of all the 434 threads ending on the feet applied to the cell shown in Fig. 75, and this would have been only the start of an investigation planned to reveal all the paths of nervous impulses passing to and from this particular cell. Yet this was a neurone from the spinal cord of an animal, not from the brain of man; and it is estimated that the cortex of the human cerebral hemispheres contains some fourteen thousand million neurones,[967] interrelated in an extremely complicated way.

Fig. 74 gives a glimpse of the increase in complexity of the human brain during the development of man. It shows a few of the neurones in a minute part of the cortical region of the superior frontal gyrus of the frontal lobe; that is to say, in a part of the brain believed to be concerned in the intellectual and emotional processes of the mind. It will be remembered that this is a Golgi-Cox

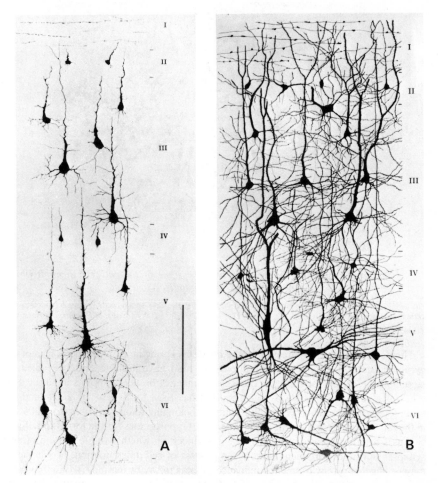

74    *Neurones (nerve-cells) in the cerebral cortex of a child at birth* (A) *and of another at the age of six years* (B)

Vertical sections through the superior frontal gyrus show the outgrowth and increasing ramification of the dendrites. The cell-bodies (perikarya) and dendrites have been darkened by the Golgi-Cox method.
*From Conel.*[221] *The scale placed between the two drawings, added by the author, represents 120 μm.*

preparation, and that therefore only a small proportion of the cells that were present in the thin section is seen; and the axon-processes that make contact with the dendrites have not been revealed. In A one sees the cells in the brain of a new-born infant; in B, the corresponding cells at the age of six years. The great increase in the complexity of the dendrites is clearly shown. The precise age at which they achieve their ultimate degree of ramification in man appears not to be known, but it is probably much later in life. Opportunity is given here for the influence of paedomorphosis, in the evolution of certain ethnic taxa.

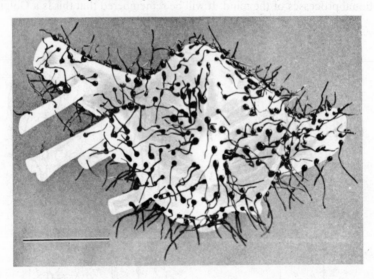

75    *A model of a neurone (nerve-cell), to show some of the end-feet through which other neurones send impulses to it*

The cell is a motor neurone of the lumbo-sacral enlargement in the cat's spinal cord. The scale (added by the author) represents 30 μm.                                                                *From Haggar and Barr.*|455|

The outgrowth and ramification of the dendrites springing from the perikarya of the pyramidal cells in the middle frontal gyrus of man have been accurately studied. In layer 3 of the cortex, for instance, the mean number of branching-points in all the dendrites of a single cell is only 3·1 at birth, but has risen to 40·8 in the adult; and the mean total estimated length of all the dendrites belonging to one cell rises from 203 μm in the former case to 6,836 μm in the latter. |934| Opportunities for the formation of new synapses are thus greatly increased. It is still uncertain whether the formation of new synapses during development is wholly a process of self-differentiation, or whether it may be affected by environmental influences, that is to say by learning. |1142, 1032, 1000|

In whatever way the number of synapses may be increased during development, it seems clear that their proliferation must somehow be related, in the case of the frontal lobes of the brain, to the increase in the capacity for thought. As the neurologist Kappers has remarked, 'The selective character of the interneuronal connections is the most important feature of the nervous system. It is only from this selectivity that the efficiency of the nervous system results.'[571] The pathways in the brain show some analogy with the electrical wiring in telephone exchanges. If there were two such exchanges, comparable in size and complication, and if in one of them some of the necessary wires were missing or wrongly connected, one might find it very difficult, by morphological inspection alone, to be sure that the exchange in question would work less effectively than the other. Indeed, this might well be impossible unless one had a wiring-diagram provided by the engineer who designed the exchange. The difficulties are immensely greater with the brain; for not only is the morphological problem very much harder to solve on account of the extreme complication, minute size, and inaccessibility of the parts, but it is very difficult indeed to perform experiments corresponding to the rather simple ones that the electrical engineer employs when he seeks to locate a fault.

Ideally it would be possible to reveal the morphological basis of complex thought-processes by study with the optical or electron microscope. If this could be achieved, one would have objective visual evidence bearing on the similarity or differences in nervous mechanisms among the various ethnic taxa of man. In the arrangement and degree of complexity of the interneuronal connections in the frontal lobes of the brain one might find evidence of primitiveness in the Australids, for instance, and of paedomorphosis in Sanids. This is a problem for the future, when biological microtechnique has advanced sufficiently for it to be tackled without the immense expenditure of time and energy that would be required today. Even the gross structure of the brain in these taxa is still very imperfectly known at the present time (see pp. 292–5, 319, and 322). In the existing circumstances, reliance must be placed on easier, though still very difficult, observations—not on the source of mental activities in the cerebral hemispheres, but on their results as manifested in the activities of man. We turn now to the intellectual faculty—that which in its highest form has given rise to philosophy, mathematics, science, technology, history, literature, law, and religion; in a word, to civilization.

# 23 The assessment of cognitive ability

## INTRODUCTION

THE ATTEMPT to define the word 'intelligence', in its ordinary sense, is deferred to later pages in this book (pp. 495–7), but it is necessary to remark at the outset that it is composed of separate parts, which can be defined. Unfortunately only one of these, the cognitive (p. 496), is capable of being systematically tested. It may be roughly defined as the general ability to perceive, comprehend, and reason, without regard to the other essential components of true intelligence: namely, judgement in choosing appropriate subjects for study, eagerness to acquire, transmit, and (if possible) add to knowledge and understanding, and capacity for sustained effort. The cognitive element may perhaps be regarded as basic, despite its uselessness if the others be absent; and an enormous amount of study has been devoted to methods for its assessment. The so-called 'intelligence tests' are intended to measure cognitive ability, and they are undoubtedly to a large extent successful. In this book they are called cognition tests.

No one who has not taken the trouble to study these tests in sufficient detail to recognize their possibilities and limitations is qualified to express an opinion on the ethnic problem. There is, perhaps, no aspect of this problem more deserving of serious study by anthropologists than the systematic testing of cognitive ability. The following account is addressed specifically to those who interest themselves in the differences between the ethnic taxa of man.

It is appropriate to begin with Alfred Binet. Like all great innovators, he had his 'forerunners'. In the later editions of *The origin of species*, Charles Darwin dutifully mentions a number of persons who were ahead of him in publication of some of his ideas.[256] It is one thing, however, to have an idea and publish it incidentally and briefly in a work on a different subject, but quite another to develop it independently in such massive and persuasive form that it gains general acceptance and initiates an important new line of investigation; and this is what Binet achieved in the domain of cognition testing.

Binet was born in 1857. He spent most of his adult life at the Sorbonne, as Directeur-adjoint and subsequently Directeur of the Laboratory of Physiological Psychology. At first his interests ranged widely over the fields of biology and psychology, and he published a number of books and papers not directly connected with cognitive ability. He wrote, for instance, on the behaviour of Protozoa and of the germ-cells of plants and animals,[90] and on the ventral nerve-cord of Crustacea and insects.[91] In these early works he shows already the clear, unpretentious style and marked capacity to write interestingly that never deserted him throughout life. His book *The psychology of reasoning* contains a fascinating account of some of his experiences in this field, especially in the parts concerned with his experiments in hypnosis.[92]

About the turn of the century he began to interest himself in the intellectual powers of two very cooperative girls in their early teens, named Marguerite and Armande. His study of their mental powers foreshadows his main life-work, which was crowded into the few years that remained to him before his early death in 1911. Readers of his book on Marguerite and Armande[93] will note the originality of the tests they so willingly underwent, and also the striking differences from ordinary school examinations intended to reveal what has been learnt in formal lessons.

Shortly after the publication of this book, the French Minister of Public Instruction began to interest himself in the teaching of mentally abnormal children, and he appointed a Commission to study this subject. The Commission reported that children suspected of being intellectually retarded should not be removed from ordinary schools unless they had been submitted to an examination that proved them to be incapable of profiting from the ordinary curriculum.[95] It was this decision that set Binet and his collaborator, T. Simon, on the path to their *'echelle métrique de l'intelligence'*. Thus their initial purpose was simply to determine whether a child was so subnormal mentally as to require education in a special school. 'Our aim,' they said, 'when a child shall be placed in our presence, is to take the measure of his intellectual capacities, in order to know whether he is a normal or a retarded person.'[96] This was the clear statement of what they had in mind; and they proceeded to give a preliminary, theoretical account of the procedure to be followed.

Binet and Simon adopted an unsophisticated, matter-of-fact attitude in defining the subject of their enquiry.

It seems to us that there exists in intelligence a fundamental element, the lack or alteration of which has the greatest significance for practical life. It is discernment [*jugement*], or in other words common sense, practical sense, initiative, the faculty of adapting oneself. To discern well, to understand well, to reason well, these are the essential springs [*ressorts*] of intelligence.

Their test was intended to display the presence or absence of this fundamental element. From the beginning it was always their rule that each child should be tested separately by spoken questions, most of them requiring spoken answers.

The two collaborators followed up these ideas by applying them practically to normal children, and also to mentally abnormal ones, some of whom still remained at primary schools, while others had been sent to hospitals. The object of their study was to establish what could be expected of normal children at the ages of three, five, seven, nine, and eleven years, in response to questions intended to trace the development of the fundamental element defined in their earlier paper. The questions were devised in such a way that the results of the test would depend as little as possible on knowledge acquired in formal education.

Their long paper on their first test, published in 1905,[97] need not be considered in any detail, because it was followed three years later by another, which has provided a basis for the construction of individual verbal cognition tests ever since.[98] They had set themselves to study *'l'intelligence sans culture'* and to devise methods for its measurement. Their choice of the words *'l'intelligence sans culture'* is important, because it seems to imply that they themselves recognized that this was not the whole of intelligence, but unfortunately they lost sight of this later on; for towards the end of their paper they distinguish sharply between *'l'intelligence'* (which was assessed by their test) on one hand, and *'la faculté scolaire'* on the other. The latter they define as 'the faculty of learning at school, the faculty of assimilating the education given at school, by the methods used at school'. It was highly desirable that techniques should be devised for measuring the part of intelligence that is not taught at school, and Binet and Simon's contribution to this end was outstanding; but it was very unfortunate that they lent the weight of their authority to the use of the word 'intelligence' in a severely limited sense. It has given rise to the widespread idea that the results of so-called 'intelligence tests' may be taken as reliable assessments of intelligence in the wide sense. It is necessary to stress that these tests (or rather the best of them) are invaluable *not* because they test the whole of intelligence (for they do not), but because they provide a measure of *one essential constituent* of it. This subject is further discussed in Chapter 26.

It is perhaps understandable that Binet and Simon used the word 'intelligence' as they did. Their main object throughout was to be able to distinguish children who were genuinely subnormal mentally from those who seemed stupid only because they were uneducated. They knew that some of the children who were regarded as subnormal had received scarcely any formal education, and that their potentiality for intellectual work might have been seriously underestimated. It was for this reason that Binet and Simon studiously avoided the results of education in their tests, and included only such subjects as were matters of almost universal knowledge among the children to whom the tests were applied. They did not say that the capacity to absorb instruction was an unimportant constituent part of intelligence in the ordinary sense of the word.

Binet and Simon's test consisted of questions arranged in groups; all or nearly all the questions in a group were supposed to be answerable by average children of a particular age. There was a group of questions for each age in yearly steps from three to thirteen. The whole test was thus a *graduated series* or *scale* of such groups of questions, and they called it an *'echelle'*. Unfortunately the word 'scale' is often used loosely for cognition tests that do not consist of graduated groups of questions.

The following examples will give a general impression of the test at various levels in the scale. The children were asked to repeat a series of unit numbers (two to seven of them, according to age) or a phrase of several (six to twenty-six) syllables; to count numbers in reverse; to think of as many different words as possible in a minute; to define abstract words (e.g. *'charité'*); to distinguish between words, such as *'plaisir'* and *'bonheur'*, having similar but different meanings; to recognize absurdities in statements; to say what is supposed to be happening in a picture, or in a human situation briefly described in words; to complete drawings of people from which certain parts (e.g. the nose) were missing; to draw a square or other simple geometrical form; and—much the most difficult of all—to solve the problem called *'découpage'*. To set this problem the person conducting the test folded a piece of paper twice in view of the child, and then cut out a part of it through all the folds at once; the child was required to say what the paper would look like if unfolded.

The authors admit that their tests include some questions (especially those relating to vocabulary) in which scholastic training might be helpful to the child under test; but they claim that, despite this, their method does in fact reveal *'la belle intelligence native'* of uneducated children.

Each child was placed provisionally at the *'niveau'* of the most advanced group of questions that he could answer correctly, or with only one mistake. This, however, was not necessarily his final level; for he was granted an advance of one year if he could answer at least five questions in tasks intended for older children than those of his provisional level, and an advance of two years if he could answer at least ten such questions.

The authors give instructions for using their test to classify stupid children into grades advancing from the lowest, *'idiot'*, through *'imbécile'* to *'débile'*. 'To establish the category of a young abnormal,' they explain, 'we are obliged to take account of two different factors: his age and his intellectual level.' They express the child's mental capacity by relating these two factors; that is to say, by stating the number of years of retardation or advancement.

The final version of the test was published by Binet as sole author in the year of his death.[94] The changes were not very large.

He found a few of the questions too scholastic, or too dependent on information derived from parents. The tests for ages eleven and twelve had been found too difficult and were made easier; that for age thirteen was omitted, and others for age fifteen and for adults added. As before, the *niveau intellectuel* could be raised by a sufficient number of correct answers to questions intended for older persons.

## DEFINITIONS

In the literature of cognition testing, several important words are used in different senses by different authors, often without definitions. It is necessary to state here the exact meanings that will be attached to certain terms that will be used repeatedly in the rest of this chapter and in the next. The reader who prefers to skip the definitions given below is asked to turn back to these pages if in any doubt as to the sense in which any of them is used.

*'Test'* will mean a particular set of tasks proposed by an author or group of authors. A single example of a test cannot be used indefinitely, because it would become widely known and the correct answers learnt by rote. All examples of a test prepared by the same person or persons and based on exactly the same principles will be regarded as belonging to the same test, not as separate tests. The word *'form'* will be used for the various examples of a particular test (for example, forms 'L' and 'M' of the 1937 Stanford–Binet; see p. 444). A few forms of a test are commonly made public, the rest

restricted in distribution. When a test is reissued with distinctly modified features, it will be called a *'version'* of the earlier test; though if the change is considerable, it is legitimate to regard it as a new test and to give it a new name. The separate tasks that together constitute a test will be called *'items'*; these will be distinguished as *'questions'* if they are interrogative and as *'problems'* if they are not (e.g., if the testee has to find the way out of a printed maze, or to perform an act). It would seem appropriate to call a person subjected to a test a 'subject', but this results in confusion with the same word used to mean the topic or theme of a test or item. 'Candidate' is too suggestive of scholastic examinations. The rather unattractive word *'testee'*, which occurs frequently in the literature of mental testing, will be used instead. It has at least the merit that its meaning is obvious. For the person who conducts the test, the word *'tester'* seems preferable to 'examiner'.

Tests such as those of Binet and Simon, in which the tester interviews the testees one by one, will be called *'individual tests'*. *'Group-tests'* will mean those that are intended to be set to several or many testees simultáneously.

The term *'verbal'* will be applied to tests or items that require the testee to speak, write, or underline or otherwise mark words or sentences. The term will not imply that the test or item is intended to investigate the testee's fluency or his ability to express himself grammatically. Questions intended to test his understanding of the meanings of words in his own language will be called *'vocabulary'* items.

The term *'non-verbal'* will be applied to all tests or items in which the testee is not required to speak, write, or make marks to indicate words. The term will not imply that the tester will not use speech to explain what the testee is required to do. In the great majority of cases he will in fact speak for this purpose, necessarily in the testee's language, but there are some tests that can be explained by action without any use of words. The action is called *'pantomime'* in the literature of cognition tests, and this term will be used here. Non-verbal items are often included in verbal tests, but a test will not be called 'non-verbal' if it includes verbal items. Pencils or other writing instruments may be used in certain items of non-verbal tests (for instance, to indicate the way out of a printed maze).

The term *'performance test'* has unfortunately been used in different senses. Some authors use it to mean a test of manipulative skill, but this has no necessary connection with cognitive ability. A 'performance' item or test will be used here to mean a non-verbal problem or set of problems in which the testee is required to make his response by a simple act, not requiring manipulative skill, and not involving the use of a writing instrument.

*'Mental age'* is always used in the literature of mental testing to replace Binet and Simon's *'niveau intellectuel'*. It is usual to express mental age as a percentage of *chronological* (actual) age. The cognitive ability of the average child will thus be represented by the figure 100, unless a test has been inaccurately adjusted to the ability of average children. The 'average children' referred to here are average *Europid* children, since all the early work on the assessment of cognitive ability was done (in western Europe and the U.S.A.) on Europids, mostly Alpinids, Nordids, and Mediterranids, and hybrids between these. The percentage is commonly called the *'intelligence quotient'*, although 'cognitive percentage' would express the meaning more exactly. The abbreviated form *'IQ'* is universally used, and it would be impossible to replace it. The letter *I*

may be regarded as standing for a particular part of intelligence, and $Q$ for a quotient transformed into a percentage.

The reader will find it convenient to bear in mind that it has been customary to regard persons having IQs below 70 as 'mentally defective', and from 140 upwards as 'gifted'. The figures quoted are not, however, universally agreed. Some would substitute 75 for 70, and children with IQs down to 132 have in certain cases been admitted to the 'gifted' group.

The expression 'retarded' is sometimes used as more or less synonymous with 'mentally defective', but it follows from the definition of 'IQ' that any figure less than 100, if reliable, indicates some degree of retardation in relation to the average Europid child of western Europe and the U.S.A.

'Mental age' and especially 'IQ' are expressions of such importance in the assessment of cognitive ability that it is worth while to mention their introduction into the literature of psychology. It does not appear that the history of this subject has been treated with the care it deserves.

We have seen (p. 441) that up to his death in 1911, Binet continued to use the word *'niveau'* to mean what subsequently became known as 'mental age'. The German psychologist Bobertag, writing in that year on the application of Binet and Simon's test to children in the schools of Breslau, several times uses *'Niveau'* as though it were a neuter German noun (*'das intellectuelle Niveau eines Kindes'*).[1115] William Stern, Bobertag's colleague at Breslau University, used *'Intelligenzalter'* with the same meaning in his book *Die differentielle Psychologie*, also published in 1911.[1009] In June of the same year Dr. H. H. Goddard used the expressions 'Mental Age' and also 'chronological age' in describing his administration of Binet and Simon's test to American children.[417] In his paper he lays no claim to the invention of these terms, but it seems unlikely that anyone (except possibly himself) had ever previously used them in print. Another American psychologist, F. Kuhlmann, appears to have been the next to use these two terms, in a paper published in March 1912.[616] He refers to Goddard's paper and seems to imply (without definitely saying so) that he took 'mental age' from it. In the same year an author using the initials J.C.B., in the course of a general review of literature on the Binet tests, uses the term 'mental age' in discussing Goddard's paper.[40] The widespread adoption of the term may have resulted from this review. It does not occur, however, in any of the four papers published by Terman and Childs in 1912.[1037] These authors use 'test age' instead. They do, however, use 'chronological age'.[1037]

The term *'Intelligenzquotient'* and its abbreviation 'IQ.' were introduced by Stern in 1912. He remarks that the simple difference between LA., *Lebenzalter* [chronological age], and IA., *Intelligenzalter* [mental age], has not the same significance at different ages. He mentions that another author (Kramer) had already pointed out that a given retardation (say three years) would indicate more serious defect if it applied to a child aged eight than it would to one aged twelve. Stern says that one can only be satisfied with LA. — IA. when comparing the intelligences of children of about the same age, and he proceeds forthwith to recommend the use in all other cases of the *Intelligenzquotient*.

It specifies not the difference, but the relation of IA. to LA., and is therefore independent, over a certain range, of the absolute value of LA. The formula runs $IQ. = \dfrac{IA.}{LA.}$ The value in children that stand exactly at the normal *Niveau* = 1; in children with advanced intelligence, more than 1; in children with retarded intelligence, a proper fraction.

He gives as an example, 'An eight-year-old child with IA.6 thus has an IQ. $= \frac{6}{8} = 0.75$; the same IQ. applies to a twelve-year-old child with IA.9.'[1010]

It has been stated here and there in the literature of cognition testing that in 1912 Kuhlmann, as well as Stern, made the suggestion that the quotient should be used instead of the difference between chronological and mental ages, to indicate advance or retardation. This may perhaps be correct, but I have not been able to confirm it. I have not seen a reference to anything written by Kuhlmann that would support the claim. There is nothing of the sort in his papers published in March, June, and September 1912, all of which deal with mental testing.[616, 617, 618]

## SUCCESSORS TO THE BINET–SIMON TEST

The verbal individual test introduced by Binet and Simon has been reissued in many versions. The most important of all have been those of Terman, who unquestionably improved them greatly, and adjusted them more accurately to chronological age-standards by trials on a far larger number of persons. His tests have been used on an enormous scale. As Professor of Psychology at the Leland Stanford Junior University he called his first test 'The Stanford Revision and Extension of the Binet–Simon Intelligence Scale'. He published a full explanation of it and guide to its use in 1916.[1035] It is sufficiently distinct to receive a separate name, and may conveniently be referred to as the 1916 Stanford–Binet. It is not necessary to say much about it, because it was supplanted by another in 1937, devised by Terman in collaboration with Maude A. Merrill.[1038] Two forms of the new version, distinguished as 'L' and 'M', were printed in full in their book. No one who studies this work can fail to be impressed by the amount of thought that was lavished upon it. It is based on the study of over three thousand normal, American-born Europids, aged $1\frac{1}{2}$–18 years, and also a number of older persons. It summarizes the results of what was probably the most elaborate attempt ever made to establish the average growth-rate of cognitive ability in Europid children, and thus provides a trustworthy guide for the establishment of mental ages. Despite the improvement of the test since the time of Binet and Simon, one can still detect clearly enough the influence of the originators. Various versions of the 1937 Stanford–Binet have been produced, adapted to the needs of British testees unfamiliar with certain words in common use in the U.S.A.

Many readers of the present book have probably been subjected to one of the versions of the 1937 Stanford–Binet, and are familiar with its general character. As in Binet's final version[94] of the Binet–Simon Test, there are questions designed for adults but available also to upgrade the mental age of any children who can answer them. The tests for adults are intended to be answered respectively by those who are 'Average', 'Superior I', 'Superior II', and 'Superior III'.

Among the items regarded by the authors as the most reliable indicators of what they call 'intelligence' are vocabulary, detection of absurdities, comprehension, naming of opposites, completion of drawings and statements, rote memory for digits, and conceptual memory (capacity to retain ideas and express them by paraphrase). Binet and Simon's *'découpage'* problem, admitted by themselves to be very difficult for children of thirteen years (though set for them), is used in its original form under the name of 'paper cutting', but regarded as suitable for adults of the highest grade (SA III). It seems to me to be one of the best problems in the whole test, and least susceptible to environmental influences.

The item in the 1937 Stanford–Binet that gives the closest correlation with the results of the test as a whole is that which is concerned with the candidate's *vocabulary*; that is to say, with his understanding of the meanings of words. It is presented in exactly the same form to all children from the age of six upwards, and also to adults. It begins with familiar words, such as 'orange', 'envelope', 'straw', and 'puddle', and ends with others ('casuistry', 'homunculus', 'sudorific', 'retroactive', and 'parterre') that would not be in common use among all sections of society. Most of the questions and problems in the 1937 test are far less affected by differences in the testee's home environment than the vocabulary item is, and it is surprising that the results of the latter give such close correlation (0·81; see p. 453) with those of the test as a whole.

The Stanford–Binet Test was once more revised in 1960.[358] A single form, designated 'L-M', was presented. The new version was based on studies of very nearly five thousand testees, aged $2\frac{1}{2}$–18 years. Further experience had made it necessary to eliminate certain questions and to allocate others to persons of different ages, but the modifications were not fundamental. One interesting change was that the IQ tables were extended to include the chronological ages seventeen and eighteen, because it was found that the mental abilities measured by the Stanford–Binet method do develop at least to the latter age.

It has long been recognized that beyond the age of fourteen or thereabouts it becomes increasingly difficult to assess IQ by the usual methods, and it was formerly supposed that the capacity to score high marks in cognition tests does not increase after the age of fifteen or sixteen. Professor G. H. Thomson pointed out, however, that the tests in common use were supposed to be based on knowledge that was the common property of everyone, and that after a certain age (about fourteen) it became increasingly difficult to invent questions that were confined to such knowledge and yet hard enough to extend the brighter children. He suggested that if suitable questions could be devised, it would be found that the capacity to score high marks would go on developing into adult life.[1047] The extension of IQ tables in the 1960 Stanford–Binet, mentioned above, seems to support this opinion.

Whether Thomson's conclusions be accepted or not, it remains a fact that the IQs of persons older than 18 cannot in any case be measured directly in the usual way. Nevertheless, figures roughly equivalent to IQs can be obtained. In his 1916 book, Terman assumed adults to be sixteen years old, and was thus able to make an assessment of their IQs, if their mental ages were sixteen or less.[1035] It is more satisfactory to proceed by first obtaining an adult's 'percentile rank'; that is to say, finding out where he stands, in serial order, among a representative sample of all the adults in a population. His 'rank' is the number of persons, expressed as a percentage, who obtain lower scores in a test than he does. Percentile ranks do not lend themselves very well to statistical treatment, but they have the advantage that there is a convenient method for converting them to the equivalents of IQ.[599] Briefly, an adult is given the same IQ as a child who stands at the same percentile rank as himself. What are called 'standard scores' are less readily comprehensible than percentile ranks, though better from the statistical point of view; and they, too, can be converted to IQ equivalents.[1038] Whether these conversions are really very helpful appears, however, to be questionable. On the whole, IQs are probably most reliable when obtained by tests on children less than fifteen years old.

Several tests based on the 1908 Binet–Simon or on Binet's 1911 version of it have been devised apart from Terman's. F. Kuhlmann of the Minnesota School for Feeble-Minded and Colony for Epileptics made an extended study of the 1908 Binet–Simon and produced an American revision of it in 1912,[616, 617, 618] and he continued long afterwards to make important contributions to the techniques of cognition testing. Other verbal individual tests of the same general type, but not based so directly on the Binet–Simon, have been invented and have played their parts in the assessment of cognitive ability.

If one examines the Binet–Simon tests and their various versions and derivatives, one gains certain impressions about the thoughts that must have been present in the minds of those who designed them. Clearly, they took it for granted that the testees would be children accustomed to the everyday life of Europe, North America, or countries having similar cultures; but with this reservation, they tried to think of items that would be as fair as they could make them for those whose socio-economic statuses, and environments in general, were different. It seems certain that they did not consider the possibility of their tests being applied to persons living under entirely different cultural systems. There are many parts of the world where not only 'casuistry' and 'retroactive' but perhaps also *'charité'* would be untranslatable, and where it would be impossible to ask a child to distinguish in native words between *'plaisir'* and *'bonheur'*. But translation was perhaps the least of the difficulties that would have to be surmounted, if the tests were to be presented to children living in uncivilized communities who had never seen or even heard of many of the objects mentioned or used in the tests. One might be inclined to think that tests of the Binet–Simon type would be irrelevant in such circumstances. Actually this is not so. Such tests play their part indirectly. It is possible to devise tests, very different from the Binet–Simon, that are to a large extent 'culture-fair' for people living in circumstances quite unlike those of Europe and North America, and some might even be classified as nearly 'culture-free'. Tests of these types, which will be considered in the next section of this chapter, can then be administered to children whose IQs have been established by use of the Stanford–Binet or some other reliable test. If the results show a high correlation (p. 453), the 'culture-fair' or 'culture-free' test can be used with some confidence in comparing the cognitive abilities of people living in very different cultural environments, in remote parts of the world. Such tests as the 1937 or 1960 Stanford–Binets, based as they are on very accurately assembled data, provide *standards of reference* for the calibration of other tests, more suitable for general use.

The great disadvantage of individual verbal tests is that they occupy so much of the tester's time. To administer the 1937 Stanford–Binet to one young child usually takes from thirty to forty minutes; to an older one, about an hour. The simultaneous administration of a test to a group of persons is much more convenient for the tester (though some authorities regard it as less desirable, if time is available). Many verbal group-tests, some of them showing influence from the Stanford–Binet, others quite different, have been devised. They are only applicable to literate testees. Such tests have been administered on a vast scale to schoolchildren (pp. 471–3, 484–6, and 490–94), and to adults too (pp. 474–80).

It is usual to set time-limits for the completion of group-tests, and in some cases for that of each item in them. The desirability of demanding speed in the testing of cognitive ability is, however, debatable. It is commonly claimed that people of high mental ability think quickly, and time-limits are therefore regarded as helpful.[1095, 599] Experiments with recruits to the American Army during the First World War[1164] showed that doubling the time allowed for the 'alpha' group-test did not result in any significant increase in the scores for the test as a whole, though there was a tendency for the testees to do better in one of the eight items. (The item in question was 'arithmetical reasoning', which does not fall within the scope of most tests of cognitive ability.) If, however, those who excel when time-limits are imposed also reveal their superiority when they are not, it may be argued that the value of the limit (apart from mere convenience to tester and quick-minded testees) is not obvious. In any case it is undesirable to follow the example of Bonser,[126] who stopped all testees from writing answers to each item of his test as soon as one of them announced that he had finished. A person of low cognitive ability might finish quickly and thus prevent others from revealing the full extent of their superiority. Davis and Eells make some useful comments on the subject of speed in mental testing.[262] They point out that quickness in solving problems is strongly influenced by cultural attitudes. Competitiveness, conscientiousness, compulsiveness, and anxiety all play their parts in producing speed or slowness, as the case may be. None of these attributes is necessarily linked with cognitive ability. It is worth remembering that in the year of publication of his work *On the origin of species*, Charles Darwin wrote in a letter to Sir Charles Lyell, the geologist, 'I suppose I am a very slow thinker.'[259] His son Francis remarks that Charles Darwin 'used to say of himself that he was not quick enough to hold an argument with anyone, and I think this was true'.[259]

NON-VERBAL TESTS

It has already been pointed out (p. 446) that the tests of the Binet–Simon type, invaluable though they undoubtedly are when used in appropriate circumstances, cannot possibly be of universal application. Can any type of test be 'culture-free',* or even 'culture-fair'* except in a very limited sense?

It is appropriate to insert here a few words on the general subject of fairness

---

* It is to be hoped that substitutes will be introduced for these clumsy terms, in which a noun is used to qualify adjectives.

in cognition testing. Some students of the subject have doubted the possibility of making any tests genuinely fair. Professor Otto Klineberg of Columbia University points out that the score obtained by a testee may be affected not only by the language in which a test is administered, but also by his previous experience in general, his education, his familiarity with the subject-matter of the test, the strength of his wish to succeed, his attitude towards the tester, and his emotional state while under test.[597] All this is true, but one must not overlook the fact that the designers of cognition tests, from Binet and Simon onwards, have striven to avoid the pitfalls. For instance, the necessity to have regard for the emotional states of persons undergoing tests was clearly recognized by Binet and Simon themselves, and has been held in mind by their successors ever since. Terman and Childs, describing in 1912 the application of their revised version of the Binet–Simon test to American testees, mentioned that 'Extreme care was taken to win the confidence of the child and to rid him of any embarrassment before beginning the tests.'[1037] Kuhlmann, in the same year, introducing independently another revision of the same test, gave careful instructions for arousing the testee's interest, encouraging him, and making the test 'appeal to him as a game'.[618] Forty-one years later, in the same spirit, the inventors of an ingenious test suggested that it should be called 'the Davis–Eells Games', and the name has stuck.[262]

When a particular test is such that environmental differences are likely to affect the scores obtained, care is taken to define the group of persons for whom it is designed. The Davis–Eells Games, for instance, are specifically intended for children living in American towns and cities. It is claimed that within that particular environment, they are suitable for administration to children of all social classes; but the authors themselves mention that the Games may give misleading results if used in rural districts of the same country.[262] They are only 'culture-fair' when used in towns or cities.

Some of the non-verbal tests inevitably approximate more closely than the verbal ones to the 'culture-free' ideal, and these are of particular interest and promise to students of the ethnic problem who want to investigate the cognitive abilities of people living far beyond the range of civilization. Non-verbal tests have been regarded by some authorities[386] as supplementing rather than replacing verbal ones; but in fact the best of them are extremely ingenious and much more independent than the others of the cultural environment of the testee. Ideally, the designer of a culture-free test would take for granted in the testee only such knowledge (as opposed to cognitive ability) as was common to everyone in the world who was not actually feeble-minded, idiotic, or severely handicapped by physical debility. As in all other fields of endeavour, the ideal cannot actually be reached; but that is certainly no reason why the attempt should not be made to get as close as possible to it, and some of the best non-verbal tests do not fall far short.

The difficulty of making any approach to a culture-free or even a culture-fair test appears to have been overstressed by some psychologists, who argue that the environmental handicaps suffered by children in particular homes, even in a single community, may affect the results given by tests intended to be fair to all subjected to them. To resolve this problem, the attempt has been made to assess home environments on a numerical scale, ascending from worst to best, and to use the resulting data to find whether a mathematical correlation (p. 453) could be established between two sets of numbers: (a) the figures representing home environments, and (b) the marks scored by the children who lived in the assessed homes. Cases have been reported in which a positive correlation was found to exist, even when culture-fair or culture-free tests had been used; and this has been taken to show that the supposed 'fairness' or 'freedom' of the tests was unreal.[1097] It must be borne in mind, however, that this conclusion is not necessarily well founded. Parents of very low cognitive ability would be likely not only to provide poorer home environments than others, but also to transmit their low cognitive ability to their offspring (see Chapter 24). It is not justifiable to assume without further evidence that the results of the tests were wholly—or even partly—ascribable to environmental circumstances.

It must be mentioned that many good non-verbal tests are not intended to be culture-free, and some of those that are culture-fair for most people living in civilized communities would be quite unsuitable for use in remote parts of the world. For instance, the Pintner–Cunningham requires an understanding that a lock and key are somehow associated with one another, and those who attempt the American Army 'beta' test should be acquainted with the mechanism of an adjustable spanner. These objects would be as meaningless to the inhabitants of many isolated regions as the implements used by unsophisticated peoples for making fire without matches would be to most of those who live in the great cities of the civilized world. Fairness and unfairness in cognition testing will be further considered in the chapter devoted to racial differences in cognitive ability (see especially pp. 468–70).

A few examples of non-verbal tests are briefly described below. They have been selected partly because of the special ingenuity that has been displayed in the design of some of them, and partly because all of them, except perhaps the first, appear to be well suited for administration to people living at very different cultural levels. The underlying principles of each test are explained, and references given to books and papers in which actual examples of the tests have been published. It is to be hoped that anthropologists about to work in remote parts of the world would consider the possibility of using cognition tests on a much larger scale than heretofore. It might be possible to reach some agreement as to which test or tests are the most suitable for the purpose, and thus make reliable comparisons possible. Raven's 'Progressive Matrices' (p. 450) would have a high claim for selection.

Spearman's 'Figure Classification' is a particularly good example of a non-verbal test designed to assess the most essential components of cognitive ability. Many verbal tests are obviously the product of strongly developed common sense, but such non-verbal ones as Spearman's and Raven's give evidence of marked originality and special intellectual powers in their originators.

Figure Classification requires no more elaborate apparatus than a pencil and a sheet of paper bearing printed geometrical figures. It can be used as a group-test or individually. The items are all similar in principle but graded in difficulty. Each consists of two *groups of shapes*, which may include such figures as, for instance, lines, rectangles, and triangles, variously orientated. One group is labelled 'I', the other 'II', but other symbols could be used, if necessary, with illiterate testees. It is the testee's task to discern in what respect all the shapes in group I differ from all those in group II. He is also presented with separate groups of shapes, called 'test symbols', which are all different from those in groups I and II; but some of them agree with those in group I in the features by which the latter differ from those in group II. He is required to put a tick against the test symbol that belongs logically to group I. He can only succeed if he can form an idea of the common features that distinguish the shapes in group I from those in group II and can realize that the underlying plan is capable of extension so as to include one particular set of test symbols, but not the others. Some of the Figure Classification problems require a lot of thought. Useful examples are given in Thurstone's *Primary mental abilities.*|1055|

It is questionable whether anyone, however fluent in the native tongue, could interest uncivilized people sufficiently in Spearman's test to make them take the trouble to understand what was required of them. This does not apply, however, to another equally ingenious non-verbal test, Raven's 'Progressive Matrices'. Although it would be preferable to have the help of a fluent speaker, it would actually be possible for someone totally ignorant of the testee's language to administer the latter test by pantomime. It is a performance test, not requiring the use of a pencil. Each 'matrix', in Raven's sense, is a series of designs, printed on hard, flat surfaces.|876, 877, 878| The problem is to detect a uniform feature running through and expanding regularly in the series of designs. At the end of the series there is a blank space in the form of a slot or recessed area. The testee is provided with a number of flat pieces, each of which will fit into the slot. These all bear designs, but on only one of them is there a design that carries forward the idea that is implicit in the series. All the rest are 'wrong', for they do not carry forward the idea. The testee is required to do nothing except select the correct piece and place it in the slot. The separate problems are progressive in the sense that the first is so obvious that anyone, even a little child, could at once select the correct piece, while the others are arranged in a particular order, such that they become more and more difficult. No one, I think, could instantly select the right piece in the most difficult problems. The same set of matrices may be administered to anyone from the age of six or seven years upwards. He may go on trying until he can get no further, for no time-limit need be set. Physical abnormalities, other than severe defects of vision, are no bar to success, provided that the testee can somehow indicate which piece should be placed in the slot.

A novel pattern-completion test, named 'PATCO', has been designed by Hector|483, 484| to help in judging the suitability of Negrids for employment in industry. It has been used in the aptitude-test centre of a South African mine.

The testee is provided with a rectangular frame, on which three elongated rectangular pieces of cardboard, all exactly similar, have been placed in special positions by the tester. The testee is given another exactly similar rectangle and required to put it in such a position that the four, taken together, produce a bilaterally symmetrical figure; or, to look at it in a different way, one half of the figure is now a 'mirror' or 'folding' image of the other. Many different problems of graded difficulty can be set in succession. In another set of items the testee must put his rectangle in such a position in relation to the other three that if two of the rectangles could be rotated on the frame, without losing their relative positions, they would exactly coincide with the other two. In my experience this 'rotation' problem is much harder, in general, than the 'folding' one, though rather easy problems can be set. The necessary apparatus is easy to make and light to transport, but it is essential that someone fluent in the native tongue should explain carefully what the testee is required to do. It is not nearly so easy to explain as the Progressive Matrices.

Cattell's 'Culture-Free' is a non-verbal test, specifically intended (as its name implies) to be so far as possible unaffected by the particular environment to which the testee has been accustomed. One of the items is a tapping-sequence problem. Four wooden cubes are placed before the testee, and the tester taps them in a particular sequence. The testee is required to tap them in the same sequence. The tester repeats the process over and over again, making the sequence progressively longer and more complicated. This is particularly suitable as a general introduction to the test as a whole (and indeed to other tests), because anyone could quickly understand what was required of him. One could easily gather a group of people of any culture round one, to watch the 'game' in progress, and this would encourage participation in the other items (perhaps several days later, when the idea of such a thing as a test had become familiar and created interest).

In another item of the same test, the testee has to look at a row of simple drawings that can be seen to form a series (for instance, pictures of similar leaves, regularly orientated in sequence in relation to one another), and to select, from six other pictures, the one that completes the series. A picture illustrating this item and others in Cattell's test is given by Freeman.[357] The least satisfactory item, for students of the ethnic problem, is the one called 'pool reflections'. The testee is shown a picture of a simple object (for instance, a cup with a handle), and required to mark which of six drawings is the one that would represent it if reflected in a pool of water. There must be many people in various parts of the world to whom reflections in still water are familiar, while others, living in desert regions, have less frequently had opportunities to see them. The remaining items are pattern-completion problems, based on the same general principles as Raven's.

Cattell's test has the advantage for the traveller that only a few wooden cubes and some pencils and sheets of paper need be carried, not the heavier equipment that is required for certain performance tests that might be suitable in other respects. There is no question of the testee being required to write, but if necessary he must be given practice in making a mark with a pencil before attempting the test.

Piaget's tests are very different in scope from any of those mentioned above. Some of them require a few words of response by the testee and therefore cannot be classified as non-verbal, and one of them requires the understanding of written numbers. The tests are intended for young children. Those that are concerned with conservation and visualization are non-verbal, and appear to be suitable for use in a wide range of cultural environments. The term 'conservation' implies that the testee, having perceived certain facts about length, area, or volume by examination of objects exhibited to him, must hold in mind the ideas derived from his perceptions and use them in solving simple problems. For instance, the testee is shown a dish and a bottle half filled with coloured liquid, and required to indicate how far the liquid would rise in the dish if the fluid from the bottle were poured into it. 'Visualization' means the perception of form and realization of how the appearance would change as a result of change in orientation. The same bottle containing coloured fluid may be used in this test. It is exhibited to the testee in an upright position and then placed behind a screen and tilted through 45°, with only the top of it visible to him. He is required to indicate, on an outline drawing of the bottle, how the level of the water would now appear if he could see it. The problems in conservation and visualization are very diverse. Full particulars of some of them are given by Vernon.[1097] Piaget's tests require explanation by someone fluent in the testee's language.

Brief general accounts of many cognition tests are given in textbooks of mental testing (for instance, those by Garrett and Schneck,[386] Thurstone,[1055] Mursell,[783] Freeman,[357, 358] and Thorndike and Hagen[1051]). The last-named is especially useful, because it contains a chapter on the method one should adopt to obtain more detailed information about particular tests.

## THE ANALYSIS OF COGNITIVE ABILITY

One naturally asks oneself whether cognitive ability is demonstrably composite, and if so, what the component elements or 'factors' may be. This has particular significance for the ethnic problem. One would in any case wish to know whether there were any general differences in cognitive ability among the various ethnic taxa, expressible, for instance, in IQs, and this has to some extent been achieved, as we shall see in Chapter 25 (though much remains to be done). It would, however, be of special interest to discover whether the taxa differ from one another in respect of particular factors. This is a subject on which little is known, and the present section is written in the hope that it may play some small part in encouraging further study. It might perhaps be found that certain taxa, known to give low median IQs in response to general tests, possess high ability in some particular cognitive factor or factors.

To tackle this subject at its root, it is necessary to go back to 1904, the year before Binet and Simon published the first version of their test.[97] It was then that there appeared in an American psychological journal a long article by the British psychologist and mathematician Charles Edward Spearman (1863–1945) entitled '"General intelligence", objectively determined and measured'.[993] This very interesting paper is concerned with correlations between the attainments of schoolchildren in different subjects. Spearman elaborated on the same theme in papers and books published during the subsequent quarter of a century.

Spearman's procedure can perhaps best be illustrated by an actual example taken from his general paper on the mathematics of correlation, published in

1922.[994] He makes use here of data collected by an American psychologist, F. G. Bonser, in a study of the reasoning ability of children.[126] The testees were the boys and girls of the upper fourth, fifth, and sixth grades of a single school. Bonser arranged the students in order of ability as shown by their responses to tests in four separate subjects, which he called 'mathematical judgement' (actually simple arithmetic), 'controlled association' (supply of missing words in sentences, and naming of opposites to given words), 'selective judgement' (selection of sensible reasons for familiar facts), and 'literary interpretation' (explanation in the testees' own words of the meanings of poems). It will be observed that the questions were different from the great majority of those that have already been considered in this chapter, because instruction given in school would affect the capacity to answer.

Spearman set himself the task of finding the correlations between the placings of the children in serial order in the four different items of the test. The reader who does not happen to be conversant with the mathematics of correlation must hold in mind that if two variable quantities of any sort are completely linked to one another, so that if one increases or decreases, the other varies in the same direction and to exactly the same extent, the two are said to be completely correlated, and the degree of correlation is expressed by the figure 1·00. If the two sets of figures vary entirely independently of one another, the correlation is 0·00. Intermediate degrees of correlation are indicated by intermediate figures. The number that expresses the degree is properly called the *correlation coefficient*, though the second of these two words is often omitted, because understood without mention. It is represented in mathematical expressions by the symbol *r*. Thus, if all children who stood first in 'mathematical judgement' stood first also in 'literary association', and so also with the second, third, and fourth children, up to the last, the correlation between them in the two subjects would be 1·00. If, on the contrary, there were no correspondence whatever between the orders in which the children stood in the two items, the correlation would be 0·00. Some degree of correlation would be expressed by an intermediate figure, capable of being worked out with mathematical precision.

The mathematical treatment of correlation, with worked-out examples, is simply explained in Anastasi's *Psychological testing*,[18] pp. 72–5, and in Chapter 16 of Moroney's *Facts from figures*[768] (see especially pp. 289–91). It may be remarked that when one variable decreases as the other increases, there is *negative* correlation; but this is rarely encountered in mental testing. An example may be found, however, on p. 494 of the present book, and another, presumably insignificant, can just be detected at the bottom left-hand corner of Fig. 76, p. 465.

One may work out correlations between *placings* in different subjects (first, second, third, etc.) or between the actual *marks* (scores) awarded. Bonser and Spearman used placings.

The children's placings varied in the different subjects, but Spearman's mathematical analysis revealed a considerable degree of correlation between them. For instance, the correlation coefficient (*r*) between their placings in 'mathematical judgements' and 'controlled associations' was 0·485; that between their placings in 'literary interpretations' and 'selective judgements' was less close, namely 0·335. If, now, these two numbers are multiplied together, the result (to three significant figures) is 0·162. The same process may be repeated, with the children's placings in the different items considered in different pairs. Thus the correlation between their placings in 'mathematical judgements' and 'selective judgements' may be multiplied by that between their placings in 'controlled associations' and 'literary interpretations'. The resulting figure is 0·158. The reader will notice that the two products, 0·162 and 0·158, are close to one another.

The facts are best stated in general terms by a mathematical expression. Let the placings in the four different items be represented by the letters A, P, B, and Q, and the correlation between A and P by $r_{ap}$, that between B and Q by $r_{bq}$, between A and Q by $r_{aq}$, and between P and B by $r_{pb}$. The facts found by experiment may then be expressed very nearly by the equation:

$$r_{ap} \times r_{bq} - r_{aq} \times r_{pb} = 0.$$

This equation, commonly called the tetrad equation, was published by Spearman in his book *The abilities of man*.[995] He stated that it was the mathematical expression of his findings that he himself preferred. In his earlier papers they were certainly expressed in less convenient forms.[993, 994, 475]

Spearman's great achievement, so far as mental ability is concerned, was his proof, by application of his general mathematical analysis of correlations, that wherever the observed facts agreed with the equation, *two* factors affecting mental ability were concerned. One of these is that which he at first called variously 'General intelligence', the *'common and essential element in the intelligence'*, the 'common fundamental Function', the 'central Function', and the 'central factor';[993] but later he preferred to call it the 'General Factor',[475] and at last he used simply '*g*'.[995] The other is the 'specific factor' or '*s*', which varies from one ability to another. If two abilities are really essentially the same (as, for instance—to use his own example—the ability to cross out with accuracy the letter *e* wherever it occurs in a page of print, and to cross out the letter *g*), the equation does not hold, and this fact in itself shows that the abilities are not to be regarded as distinct.[995] 'Every performance depends, not only on this General Factor, but also in varying degree on a factor specific to itself and all very similar performances.'[475] *g* remains unchanged for any one person for all the correlated abilities; *s*, on the contrary, varies not only (like *g*) from one individual person to another, but from one ability of each individual person to another of his abilities.

In his first paper on the subject Spearman remarked that the correlations between different branches of intellectual activity were due to their being 'variously saturated with some common fundamental Function (or group of functions)'. He devised methods for calculating the greater or less relative influence of *g* in some of the abilities tested. In the talent for classics *g* was to *s* as 15 : 1; in that for music 1 : 4.[993] The idea of 'saturation' with *g* has been much used in the literature of mental testing.

Strangely enough, Spearman found that the capacity to discriminate 'pitch' in the acoustic sense was highly saturated with *g*.[993] Not much attention appears to have been devoted to this finding in subsequent discussions of mental testing.

Spearman's approach to mental testing was so radically different from that of other psychologists that controversy necessarily arose, and it has continued intermittently since then. It has revolved principally round two questions: whether the specific factors are as numerous as Spearman supposed, and whether there is in fact any general factor or $g$ at all. L. L. Thurstone, Professor of Psychology in Chicago University, and G. H. Thomson, Professor of Education at Edinburgh, were prominent in opposition to Spearman's views.[1048, 1054, 1055, 1056, 1058]

It seems impossible to deny that if a particular mental ability consists of two elements, one general (that is to say, shared by many or all cognitive abilities) and the other actually specific to a particular task, the facts are necessarily in conformity with the tetrad equation. This truth, however, does not exclude the possibility that there may be other cognitive abilities, neither general nor wholly specific to particular tasks. Strong evidence has been obtained that there is a limited number of what may be called semi-specific factors of cognitive ability, each available for use in a whole *group* of different though related situations. One may hold this view while retaining belief in the existence of a central factor, though there are some authorities who regard the semi-specific factors as *primary*, in the sense that the supposedly single central factor is actually composite.

It must be mentioned in passing that the use of the word 'factor' by psychologists is liable to give rise to misunderstanding. It is used by them to mean a constituent part of cognitive ability. Unfortunately it is still sometimes used as a synonym for gene. For instance, Burt and Howard[172] call the polygene theory of mental inheritance the 'multifactorial' theory, while Thurstone[1054, 1056] uses the term 'multi-factor analysis' to mean the analysis of factors in the psychological, not the genetical sense. It must be understood that the 'primary factors' and 'group factors' discussed by psychologists have nothing to do with the idea of 'factor' as the word is sometimes used in genetics, as a synonym for gene. It is out of the question that a 'factor' in the psychological sense could be determined by a single gene.

Among those who allow the existence of semi-specific primary factors or group factors, general agreement has not been reached as to the number of them that should be recognized; but eight occur commonly in the literature. These are the factors that give capacity for comprehension of words, verbal fluency, induction, deduction, numerical calculation, rote memory, recognition of spatial relations, and quickness in perceiving relevant detail embedded in irrelevant material (cf. Thurstone;[1055] Thurstone and Thurstone;[1058] Wolfle;[1149] Vernon[1096]). The 'numerical calculation' referred to in this list is of the simple arithmetical kind, not involved to any great extent in higher mathematics. The Thurstones reported some degree of obscurity about the separate existence or exact nature of the capacities for deduction and perceptual quickness.[1058] They preferred to call induction simply 'reasoning', and thus, apparently, to let deduction merge with it. Vernon recommended that a battery of tests should measure in particular the capacities for comprehension of words, induction, numerical calculation, and recognition of spatial relations.[1096]

Perhaps the least hypothetical way of regarding the factors of cognitive ability is to consider them not abstractly, as though one possessed all-embracing knowledge of mental activity, but empirically, in relation to the results of a particular battery of tests. An ability that was involved in only one test among a battery of several would be regarded as a *specific* factor, so far as that battery was concerned; another, involved in two or more of the tests, would be a *common* factor; if it manifested itself in all the tests it would be the *general* factor, *so far as that particular battery of tests was concerned* (cf. Thurstone[1056]). In relation to that battery, and to the specific and general factors involved in it, the tetrad equation would presumably hold true.

The probability must be kept in mind that some of the factors of cognitive ability are not in fact quite separate; they may, so to speak, 'overlap' with one another (cf. Thomson[1048]). There may be an area of cognitive ability in which several factors all overlap with one another—and this may be the real significance of *g*. Each factor concerned in the overlapping would consist of a shared and an unshared part; but the latter could not exist alone.

Ideally, on the assumption that more or less separate factors of cognitive ability do in fact exist, one would have a special test for each of them. Although this has not been fully achieved, certain tests seem to be much more highly 'loaded' for one factor than for others; that is to say, they are so designed that they assess it particularly well. Such tests are highly specialized, whereas it is both the virtue (from one point of view) and the defect (from another) of such tests as the Binet–Simon that they are diverse in content and non-analytical (though their separate items may be more precise).

Probably the easiest ability to assess separately is rote memory (the parrot-like retention of information in the mind, without understanding of it). This seems genuinely to stand somewhat apart from other cognitive abilities. Conceptual (so-called 'logical') memory develops much later in life than the other, and is regarded by Jensen as a part of *g*.[551] Binet and Simon must have had rote memory in mind when they wrote of '*la mémoire*':

> One may have common sense and lack memory. The opposite also frequently occurs. We are at this very moment observing a retarded girl who displays before our astonished eyes a much greater memory than our own. We have measured this memory, and we are not the dupes of any illusion. Nevertheless this poor girl presents the finest classical type of imbecility.[96]

Jensen remarks that some children with very low IQs find it easy to memorize personal names or meaningless series of digits.[551] Very intelligent people are often forgetful of names. It is to be noted that no test loaded for rote memory is included in the battery of tests recommended by Vernon (pp. 455–6), and Knight omits what he calls 'retentiveness' from his definition of 'intelligence'.[599]

As its name implies, the Minnesota Spatial Relations test is highly loaded for one particular factor, and the results it gives show very low correlation ($r = 0.18$) with those given by a reliable 'general' test (the Otis).[386] One might suppose that Piaget's problems in 'conservation' and 'visualization' (pp. 451–2) would also assess primarily the ability to recognize spatial relations, but Vernon finds them heavily loaded for $g$.[1097]

Such tests as Spearman's Figure Classification and Raven's Progressive Matrices are obviously highly loaded for inductive capacity, since they require the discovery of a rule or principle. The deduction as to which 'test-symbol' to indicate by a tick, or which flat piece to place in the slot, is generally rather obvious once the induction has been made. It must be allowed, however, that even a person highly endowed with inductive capacity would fail in these tests if it were possible for such a person to be very deficient in the ability to recognize spatial relations, for he could not readily grasp the conformities and differences presented by the various shapes placed before him.

Raven's test correlates rather closely with the Stanford–Binet and other tests of the same type, which are regarded as giving good assessment of cognitive ability in general.[876, 358] This may seem surprising, since most of the generally recognized factors of cognitive ability would not appear to be directly tested by it. It seems, however, that the Matrices do measure something that is fundamental in cognition. Spearman himself regarded his Figure Classification—a very similar test, in principle—as one of the best tests for $g$.[1055] One may express this in another way by saying that a large part of inductive capacity 'overlaps' all the other factors. If so, the capacity to induce seems to be a particularly significant, indeed basic part of cognitive ability. This would be an important conclusion for those interested in the ethnic problem, since tests highly loaded for inductive capacity do not necessarily require that either tester or testee should understand any particular language; pantomime may suffice (see p. 450).

Hector suggests that his new Pattern-Completion Test (pp. 450–51) assesses the same abilities as Raven's Progressive Matrices. It seems likely, however, that the loading of the former for recognition of spatial relations is higher, and for inductive capacity much lower.

Extremely important though the abilities for deduction and numerical calculation are in certain intellectual fields, it would not appear that they overlap very largely with the other factors of cognitive ability (or, to express a similar idea from another point of view, they do not seem to overlap to any particularly large extent with $g$). So far as mere numerical ability is concerned, extreme examples of it are sometimes found in persons who are feeble-minded or even half-idiots in other respects. Hankin gives some remarkable examples of this, among those curiously talented people usually called 'calculating geniuses'.[467] It appears that their capacity to calculate at astonishing speeds may be due to freedom from deflection of thought through association of numbers with real objects or events; and it is said that some of these 'geniuses' work subconsciously. People who have no marked ability in this respect may have noticed that they have occasionally solved a simple mathematical problem quickly, and only afterwards realized that the thought-processes had been subconscious.

It is unusual for great mathematicians to be calculating geniuses, but such persons have existed. Srinivasa Ramanujan was one. An anecdote about this remarkable man is perhaps worth mentioning. While ill in hospital he was visited by a fellow mathematician, who chanced to have noticed that his taxicab bore the figure 1729 as its registration mark. He mentioned to the patient that this seemed rather a dull number. 'No,' replied the Indian, 'it is a very interesting number; it is the smallest number expressible as a sum of two cubes in two different ways.'[469]($1^3 + 12^3 = 9^3 + 10^3 = 1729$.)

It would appear that mathematicians ordinarily combine exceptional capacity for deduction with some numerical ability. In an article on Comte's philosophy in the *Fortnightly Review* published in 1869, T. H. Huxley described mathematics as that subject 'which knows nothing of observation, nothing of experiment, nothing of induction, nothing of causation'.[537] Sylvester hurried to oppose this opinion, in an address to the Mathematical and Physical Section of the British Association;[1031] nevertheless it surely contains a considerable element of truth.

From what has been said it follows that no test or battery of tests is complete unless it includes items highly loaded for inductive ability, and this is obviously important for the student of the ethnic problem. But induction is also relevant to this problem in an entirely different way. This is a matter that fits in here as well as anywhere else in the book, though it constitutes a digression from the main theme of the chapter. In brief, an insufficient capacity for induction may result in failure to comprehend fully certain branches of biology that are inextricably bound up with the ethnic problem. Mathematicians who have interested themselves in biology have made very important contributions to certain branches of this science, particularly genetics; but some of them appear not to possess very high capacities for the recognition of spatial relations or for induction—two of the most essential requirements for work in taxonomy. As a result they may tend to overlook or minimize the importance of morphological anthropology; and they sometimes overstress the significance that should be attached to one or two differences in gene-frequencies between ethnic taxa. This may lead them to separate widely certain taxa that are shown, by a mass of evidence based on conformity in the anatomy of many parts of the body, to be in fact closely related. The high esteem in which geneticists are rightly held may lead astray some of those who have not made a careful study of the anatomical basis of human taxonomy. If ever the polygene problem (pp. 190–91 and 203) is solved, anatomists and geneticists are likely to find themselves no longer in disagreement.

# 24 The inheritance of cognitive ability

DURING THE development of every organism there is interplay between genetic and environmental influences in determining the structure and function of the various parts of the body. No one can doubt, for instance, that if two human beings were genetically identical, but one was well fed throughout life while the other was kept on a diet approaching the starvation level, they would differ in the size and form of their bodies. Examples of such differences between monozygotic ('identical') twins have been carefully recorded.[963] Yet there is obviously a genetic element in stature, for it is not lack of nourishment that causes the members of certain ethnic taxa to be pygmies. It must be recognized that the environment plays a particularly important part in the development of certain characters that distinguish different individuals, while genetic causes predominate in others (such as blood-groups). There are certain ethnic taxa of man in which the skin only darkens slightly when exposed to bright sunlight, others in which it darkens strongly in the same circumstances, and others again in which it is dark whether exposed to bright light or not (see p. 158).

It is scarcely necessary to insist that the environment plays a part in the development of cognitive ability. Theoretically it would be possible to rear a child without ever allowing him to see anything, or to move about and thereby gain ideas of space, or handle separate objects and thus conceive of numbers, or hear any external sound, or even be aware of the existence of any other human being. It is unthinkable that such a child could evince any but the most rudimentary cognitive ability. His genes might be such that if he had experienced the ordinary upbringing of the great majority of children in the world, he would have displayed an IQ of 140 or more; in the circumstances his mental potentiality would remain hidden. What we have before us in any organism, including man, is the result of interaction between inheritance and environment.

It is of the utmost importance for the ethnic problem to find out what part the genetic element plays in the development of cognitive ability. Two main types of observations can be used to throw light on this subject.[170] In one type (here called type A) one studies persons who have been exposed to *similar* environments but may reasonably be suspected of being *genetically different* in cognitive ability. For observations of the other type (B) one requires those who have been exposed to *different* environments but are likely to be *genetically identical or similar*. In both cases the persons concerned must be subjected to one or more cognition tests of the types described in the previous chapter.

An investigation reported in 1931 is a good example of type A.[643] The testees were children in a 'home' for illegitimate boys and girls in England. None of them had ever lived with their fathers, who had in every case deserted their mothers. On the average the children had lived with their mothers during the first six months of their lives. From then onwards the environment of all was the same, that of the 'home'.

Wherever possible, the social classes of the fathers and mothers of the children were recorded. Five such classes were recognized. These ranged from A, the professional class, to E, which included street pedlars and paupers. Only those children were tested whose fathers and mothers were classifiable by social class. The cognitive abilities of the children were tested by a version of the 1916 Stanford–Binet, adapted to the needs of English testees, and also by a group-test (the 'Simplex') that gave rather good correlation with the Stanford–Binet. The group of children as a whole showed an almost exactly normal distribution of cognitive ability by both tests. The report on this investigation contains no fewer than eighteen tables recording the IQs of the children. These are arranged according to the sexes of the children and the social classes of their parents (either of the fathers or of the mothers, or about midway between the two). One of the tables is reproduced here as an example, with IQs given to the first place of decimals. It shows the result of applying the modified Stanford–Binet to boys. It is to be noted that the tabulation is here in accordance with the social class of the *fathers*, without consideration of that of the mothers.

| Fathers' social classes | Mean IQs of boys | Number of boys tested |
|---|---|---|
| A | 102·0 | 20 |
| B | 106·0 | 43 |
| C | 99·9 | 72 |
| D | 98·2 | 23 |
| E | 92·0 | 2 |

In every one of the eighteen tables there was some degree of positive correlation between the classes of the parents and the mean IQs of their offspring.

Observations by the late Sir Cyril Burt on the IQs of illegitimate children accorded well with those of Lawrence just described. He had noticed that even among children whose mothers belonged to the poorest class of the community, there was a small proportion having IQs well over 100. In such cases he commonly found later on that these particular children were the offspring of fathers belonging to a superior social class.[169]

Although observations of this type have their value, the evidence becomes much stronger when the cognitive abilities of the parents, instead of their social classes, can be assessed; and Burt carried out an investigation of this sort over a period of fifteen years.[169] The children involved in his study had been received during early infancy into residential schools and orphanages, where the environment was more or less similar for all. In some cases information could be obtained bearing on the cognitive abilities of the parents. Burt concentrated his attention on the children of mothers with IQs assessed at the low grade of 70–85. For the purpose of analysis he considered in one group those of their children whose fathers were of very low to medium ability (assessed at IQ 65–100); another group consisted of the children whose fathers were of high cognitive ability (assessed at IQ 120–145), but whose mothers belonged to the group of low-grade IQ. There were 105 children in the first group, 67 in the second. The children were subjected to a test of the Binet type. Those in the first group showed a mean IQ of 88·6; in the second, 103·2. The difference in IQ was thus 14·6 (standard error 2·1).

Investigations on the cognitive ability of hybrids between races should perhaps be regarded as belonging to type A, but it seems on the whole more appropriate to treat them as distinct, and they will be considered in the chapter on racial differences in cognitive ability (see pp. 471–3 and 493–4).

The facts just related have a strong bearing on the inheritance of cognitive ability, but observations of type B are still more impressive. The best method of all for studying the problem in question is to assess the cognitive abilities of persons related in different degrees, who have been exposed to different environments. The special importance of identical twins in investigations of this kind was recognized by Francis Galton nearly a century ago.[380] He remarks that he sought 'for some new method by which it would be possible to weigh in just scales the effects of Nature and Nurture, and to ascertain their respective shares in framing the disposition and intellectual ability of men. The life-history of twins supplies what I wanted.' He did indeed make a start in this promising line of enquiry; but it seems that none of the twin-pairs he investigated had been reared separately, and at that time no suitable tests were available by which cognitive ability could be accurately assessed. He does, however, mention cases in which 'closely similar' twins maintained their resemblance to one another in mental features into old age, despite very different environmental circumstances in adult life.

A digression is necessary at this point. The evidence suggests that cognitive ability, in so far as it is inherited, resembles most measurable physical characters of man in that it is controlled by the cumulative action of a considerable number of genes, each having such small effect that its passage from generation to generation cannot be traced separately. It is agreed by those who have studied the subject that the genetic control of such characters as, for instance, stature (body-height), span (greatest distance between middle finger-tips when the arms are held horizontally), and length of forearm (middle finger-tip to bent elbow) is of this nature. In early studies of the genetics of these 'quantitative compound characters', as they were called, it was assumed that dominance and recessivity would occur. It was the British mathematician G. U. Yule, in 1906, who first clarified the whole subject by making the assumption that each pair of allelomorphic genes, when present together, would have an intermediate effect. He concluded that 'in the case of perfect blending', and in the absence of modification by different environments, the coefficient of correlation between the characters of an individual and those of his parent, grandparent, and great-grandparent would be respectively $\frac{1}{2}$, $\frac{1}{4}$, and $\frac{1}{8}$.[1168] This conclusion is nowadays accepted. If a character is under the control of polygenes and dominance does not occur, and if, further, there is no tendency towards 'assortative mating' (for instance, for tall persons to choose tall partners in marriage, and short to choose short), one would expect the following correlations (on the average of a large number of examples), provided that there was no systematic or regular interference from environmental effects:

*coefficient of correlation (r)*

| | |
|---|---|
| between father and son, or mother and daughter . . | 0·50 |
| between grandparents and grandchildren . . . . | 0·25 |
| between brothers or sisters . . . . . | 0·50 |
| between uncle (or aunt) and nephew (or niece) . . | 0·25 |

Measurements of adult stature, made on several thousand pairs of persons, show a rather close correspondence with these figures, namely, 0·507, 0·322, 0·543, and 0·287 respectively.[172] It will be noticed that the correlations are all somewhat higher than one would expect; that is to say, the members of each pair are, on average, rather more nearly of the same height than the simple theory would suggest. This is attributed in the main to the tendency towards assortative mating, the reality of which had already been recognized by Karl Pearson and Miss Lee in their paper published in 1903.[831]

Fisher[336] considered how the simple expectations listed above (correlations of 0·50, 0·25, 0·50, and 0·25 respectively) would be affected by assortative mating and also by the partial dominance of genes. Applying Fisher's corrections to the simple expectations, Burt and Howard obtained remarkably close approximations to the observed figures.[172] In fact, the average discrepancy in the four correlations was only about 0·01.

Having found the 'multifactorial theory' (polygene hypothesis) fully upheld by these considerations, Burt and Howard applied it forthwith to the results of cognition tests, with allowance for partial dominance and assortative mating in this case also (for there is evidence of some tendency for people of high cognitive ability to intermarry, and similarly with those at the other end of the scale). They concluded that 12% of the correlation was due to unreliability of the tests and environmental influences, and the rest to genetic constitution.[172]

Although there is thus evidence that assortative mating and partial dominance do affect to some extent the correlations obtained in genetical studies of cognitive ability, it will suffice for the present purpose to keep in mind the simple expectations, based on the assumption of full genetic control without complications, and to note what departures from the figures are obtained in practice. In addition to the four correlations listed above, the following should be memorized:

*coefficient of correlation (r)*

| | |
|---|---|
| between monozygotic ('identical') twins . . . . | 1·00 |
| between first cousins . . . . . . . | 0·25 |
| between second cousins . . . . . . . | 0·06 |

An actual example will make the matter more concrete.

One of the earlier writers on this subject was Dr. A. H. Wingfield of Toronto University, whose book *Twins and orphans*, published more than forty years ago, is still well worth study today.[1143] He used two recognized tests (Multimental Scale and National Intelligence Test) to assess the 'general intelligence' (cognitive ability) of his testees, and thus obtain figures for IQ. Some of the correlations he obtained were as follows:

|  | coefficient of correlation ($r$) |
|---|---|
| between 'physically identical' twins | 0·90 |
| between siblings (brothers and sisters, not twins) | 0·50 |
| between parent and child | 0·31 |
| between 'cousins' (presumably first cousins) | 0·27 |
| between grandparent and grandchild | 0·15 |
| between unrelated children | 0·00 |

To determine the coefficient of correlation in the case of identical twins, Wingfield took the $x$ variable as referring in each case to the twin with the higher IQ, and the $y$ variable as referring to the one with the lower IQ. $x$ is the deviation of a measurement from the mean of the first series (brighter twin of each pair), and $y$ is the deviation from the mean of the second series (less bright twin of each pair). This appears to be the usual procedure in such studies, but it is not always stated in published reports.

Bearing in mind the degree of genetic relationship existing between the individuals comprising the above groups one is forced, literally forced, to draw the conclusion that *the closer the genetic relationship between individuals, the closer is the degree with which they will resemble each other in intelligence.*[1143]

This conclusion is justified, and Wingfield has deservedly earned recognition for his important contribution to our knowledge of the inherited element in cognitive ability.

For the sake of accuracy in the history of this subject, it is nevertheless desirable to point out certain defects in Wingfield's contribution that appear to have been overlooked by those (e.g. Sandiford [926]) who have reproduced his table of correlations. Wingfield did not explain that his correlations for parent–child, cousin–cousin, and grandparent–grandchild were not based on the same tests of what he calls 'general intelligence' as those used in his own study of twins and siblings. For the parent–child figure he relied on Schuster and Elderton's data, which were based on evidence of fathers' and sons' *academic* achievements. [948] He says he also got his data for cousins from Schuster and Elderton, but these authors did not consider cousins. His figure is actually from a paper by Elderton alone, [306] but he states it wrongly. She gave a correlation of 0·34 for first cousins, based on subjective impressions of the mental ability of the persons concerned. Wingfield quotes the figure of 0·27, but this is Elderton's mean figure for health, temper, mental ability, and general success in life, taken together. Wingfield does not state where he obtained his figure (a remarkably low one) for the grandparent–grandchild correlation.

Many similar investigations have been undertaken. Perhaps the most extensive have been those of Erlenmeyer-Kimling and Jarvik in the United States[312] and Burt in Great Britain.[171] One of the most interesting of the findings of the American authors is that the IQs of monozygotic twins reared apart were much more closely correlated than those of unrelated persons reared together. Jensen provides a full review of the information available on this whole subject, and summarizes it in Table 2 on p. 49 of his paper.[551] From the data in this table I have selected those items that are most significant and reproduced them in graphical form in Fig. 76. They are more significant than the others because they relate to persons who either (a) are known on positive evidence to have been reared separately, or else (b) are likely to have been reared separately in most cases, in view of the distance of the relationship. The data represented in Fig. 76 refer to persons in both these categories. The monozygotic twins, siblings, and unrelated children belong to category a; those related as uncle (or aunt) to nephew (or niece), and as cousins, to category b. The reader is asked to pay particular attention to this figure, because the information it conveys is of first-rate importance for the subject of this book. The figure is fully explained in the accompanying legend. It will be understood that the *black* spots represent the actual facts, that is to say the average (median) correlations between the IQs of the groups in pairs. The *hollow* (white) spots, joined by vertical lines to the black ones, represent what the correlations would have been, if nothing had influenced IQs except genes inherited from ancestors. For three reasons one would not expect exact superposition of the black and white spots. First, the differences of environment must have had some effect. Secondly, the positions of the hollow spots indicate the 'raw' expectations, not corrected for assortative mating or partial dominance. Thirdly, it is impossible to make cognition tests perfectly reliable in every case. Despite the inexactitude of superposition, the general congruity between the positions of the black and hollow spots is striking, and the obvious conclusion about the correlation between IQ and genetic relationship must be drawn.

It is a curious fact that the black spots in Fig. 76 representing pairs of persons actually known to have been reared apart lie *below* the attached hollow spots, while those that represent pairs of persons not positively known to have been reared separately lie *above* the hollow spots. One seems to see here, graphically represented, the effects of *different* environments in reducing to some extent the phenotypic expression of genes affecting cognitive ability, and of *somewhat similar* environments in increasing this expression.

The suggestion has been made that monozygotic twins reared apart might resemble one another in IQ because their environments, though different, would tend to be similar; but Sir Cyril Burt denies this.[171] 'Selective placement' did not occur in the cases he studied. One of the twins was usually brought up in his or her parents' home, the other in the environment of a different social class. He points out that childless couples in well-to-do circumstances often adopt children from less wealthy classes.

A study of monozygotic twins by Shields[963] deserves detailed consideration, because it has become a subject of an important controversy as to the role of heredity and environment in the development of cognitive ability.

The testees in Shields's investigation were 38 pairs of separated monozygotic twins, 36 pairs of unseparated ones, and eight pairs of dizygotics.* Nearly all were adults or

* For the sake of accuracy it is just worth mentioning that a few pairs of twins participated in one test but not in the other.

adolescents; only four were less than fifteen years old. Two very different tests were used. One was a pattern-completion test called 'Dominoes', which gives high correlation in results ($r = 0.74$) with Raven's Progressive Matrices (p. 450), and has even higher $g$-saturation than the latter. The other was essentially a vocabulary test (the 'Synonyms' section of Raven's Mill Hill Vocabulary Scale). This was a less satisfactory test for the purpose, because separated twins may chance to be exposed in everyday

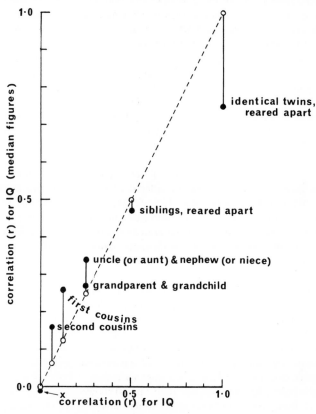

76     *The correlations in IQ between members of pairs of persons related in different degrees*

The graph is constructed as follows. Both ordinate and abscissa represent correlation coefficients ($r$) between the IQs of pairs of related persons (e.g. monozygotic twins). The *black spots* represent the coefficients (expressed as medians) obtained from data actually recorded by various investigators. They are to be read off on the ordinate scale. Each black spot is connected by a vertical line with a *hollow spot*, representing what the correlations would have been if genetic factors had operated without influence from the environment (on the assumption that there was neither selective mating nor partial dominance). The hollow spots are to be read off on either ordinate or abscissa. (The oblique broken line passing through the hollow spots reminds the reader that they are related equally to ordinate and abscissa.) $x$ = unrelated children, reared apart. *Graphical representation drawn from the tabulated data of Jensen.* |551|

life to very different vocabularies (though when huge numbers of children who attend similar schools are tested, a suitable vocabulary item may give good correlation with a reliable general test; see p. 445).

The tests were scored in marks ('points'). Shields and Gottesman converted all marks in both tests into 'IQ equivalents'.

The manuscript in which they explain their method of conversion does not appear to have been published; but in the pattern-completion test 28 marks were regarded as equivalent to an IQ of 100, and the corresponding figure for the vocabulary test was 19 marks. For certain purposes the marks given for the vocabulary test were doubled (on account of their smaller spread) and then added to the marks given for the pattern-completion test; the resulting figure was regarded as the 'total intelligence score'. It would seem possible that the doubling may have somewhat overemphasized the results of the vocabulary test in relation to the other.

The mean intra-pair difference in 'total intelligence score' was 7·38 marks for the unseparated and 9·46 for the separated monozygotics; 13·43 for the dizygotics. The corresponding intra-class correlation coefficients were 0·76, 0·77, and 0·51. The figures 0·77 and 0·51 agree closely with those represented graphically in Fig. 76 (in which unseparated twins are not included).

In the pattern-completion test, 30% of the separated monozygotic pairs scored exactly the same number of marks or differed by only one or two marks. The corresponding figure for dizygotics was 13%. Of the separated pairs of monozygotics, 24% differed by 9 marks or more; the corresponding figure for dizygotics was 50%.

In the vocabulary test, 24% of the separated monozygotic pairs differed not at all in marks, or only by one mark; of the dizygotic pairs, 14%. However, 24% of the separated monozygotic pairs differed by 6 marks or more in this test; 29% of the dizygotics did likewise.

Shields remarks that if both early environment and heredity had effects on a trait, the percentage of pairs that resembled one another closely would decrease from unseparated monozygotics to separated monozygotics to dizygotics, and the proportion of pairs showing a large difference would increase from unseparated monozygotic to separated monozygotic to dizygotic. This is exactly what his results show. They are well represented graphically in the figure at the bottom of p. 142 of his paper.

Both Gottesman[424] and Kagan[561] emphasize that at least 25% of the separated monozygotic pairs (that is to say, about nine pairs) showed differences exceeding 16 IQ points in at least one of the two tests. Some difference was to be expected in the vocabulary test, for the reason stated above; and it is significant that two of the separated pairs had been subjected to particularly dissimilar environments. Of the rest, four pairs were very unequal physically, since *one only* of a pair was an epileptic in one case, *one only* had disseminated sclerosis in another, *one only* had had birth injury in a third case, and in a fourth *one only* of the pair had high blood-pressure. Shields himself regarded these as relevant social and physical causes of intellectual differences between members of the six separated monozygotic pairs. Among the unseparated monozygotics there was only one example of any comparable social or physical cause (one member of one pair had had concussion). These facts have been overlooked in the controversy that the investigation has aroused.

Despite the social and physical differences between some of the separated monozygotics, the extreme difference among them amounted to only 10 IQ points in the pattern-completion test. The corresponding figure for the unseparated monozygotics was almost exactly the same (9 units). If the conversion to IQs was reliable, it follows that the members of pairs of separated monozygotics were remarkably similar to one another in cognitive ability as revealed by the test, despite the social and physical differences between members of some of the pairs, as related in the previous paragraph.

It follows that this investigation does not contradict but on the contrary supports the abundant evidence from other sources.

# 25 Racial differences in cognitive ability

## INTRODUCTION

ONE PARTICULAR argument is commonly levelled against all attempts to compare different ethnic taxa by the application of cognition tests. It is remarked, truly enough, that the inventors of these tests were civilized Europids, and so also, in the early days of psychometry, were the testers and testees; and from this premise it has been argued that psychologists have been influenced, in the importance they attach to various factors of mental ability, by the practical needs of a particular culture. If this were true, the values set upon those factors would be arbitrary and lack all claim to universal application. It would follow that non-Europid races would necessarily appear inferior when subjected to the tests. The only fair procedure would be to make a special set of tests for each ethnic taxon—and thus, incidentally, render it impossible to compare the taxa in respect of mental ability. An extreme form of this doctrine may be quoted, as follows: 'Had the first IQ tests been devised in a hunting culture, "general intelligence" might well have turned out to involve visual acuity and running speed, rather than vocabulary and symbol manipulation.'[294]

There are reasons, however, why arguments of this sort cannot be accepted. It is scarcely credible that members of any human taxon would be incapable of distinguishing between physical and intellectual qualities, or would regard someone as stupid simply because he could not see very clearly or run rapidly. No one acquainted with primitive peoples is likely to believe such a thing possible. One might suppose, from the pleas of those who seek to discredit the value of mental testing in studies of the ethnic problem, that Binet and his successors were only anxious to spot the children most likely to turn out as 'successes' in highly competitive and acquisitive societies. It has been made clear in the historical introduction to Chapter 23 that the exact opposite was the case. The *primary* purpose of Binet and Simon was to provide methods for the early detection of those children who could never be anything but mentally defective, and who should therefore be educated, so far as that was possible, in special institutions. Terman and Childs, writing in 1912, made a statement to the same effect, in reference to the tests available in their time, including their own version of Binet and Simon's. Their opinion was that 'the tests in general are significant not so much for displaying the child's intelligence in its entirety, as for detecting that type of mind which is not capable of profiting from its social environment'.[1037] Persons possessing that type of mind, when adult, would be recognized as defective in every human society, however primitive. Subsequently, when the scope of methods for mental testing was extended, no attention was paid to the opinions of persons engaged in industry, commerce, or any mundane department of civilized life in the twentieth century. On the contrary, psychologists turned back to the philosophers who had considered deeply the problems of mind over a period of centuries, and in the writings of those scholarly men they found a mass of closely reasoned thought about the nature of mental activity in general, which has not been found inadequate even at the present day. In every human society the capacities for comprehension, deduction, induction, and the other factors of cognitive ability are relevant, and it is proper to use methods for their assessment.

Despite this, it must be admitted that there are difficulties in assessing cognitive ability in parts of the world where not only languages but also cultures and physical environments are very different from those that exist in the countries where psychometry was invented and evolved. This subject has been carefully considered by many psychologists. Dr. S. Biesheuvel's position as Director of the National Institute of Personnel Research at Johannesburg has brought him into intimate contact with it, and he has expressed opinions widely shared by others. Much of what he says about the difficulty of obtaining clear evidence of genetic differences in 'intelligence' (cognitive ability) between the various ethnic taxa of South Africa is relevant elsewhere. Dr. Biesheuvel considers that there are objections to all tests involving the study of pictures or diagrams, or the use of pencil and paper. He mentions several tests that are generally supposed to be 'culture-free', but in his opinion are not. He argues that the low scoring of Negrids in items involving the ability to recognize spatial relations may be due to environmental circumstances. The superiority of Europids in these items may result from the playing of children's games with blocks, the arrangement of furniture, the placing of pictures on walls, the laying of tables for meals, familiarity with the lay-out of reading matter on the page, and so on. He has found it necessary to abandon tests in which the rectangular form, or appreciation of vertical and horizontal planes, play too prominent a part. He suggests also that 'intelligence' may be affected by vitamin deficiencies in pre-natal and early post-natal life. Even the urban Negrids of South Africa have not fully acquired the dietary habits of Europeans. He remarks that thoroughly detribalized Negrids, living social lives similar to those of Europids, should be used as testees in attempts to compare the mental abilities of the two races; but, as he points out, one would then have no certainty that the Negrids used in such tests were not a selected group, unrepresentative of their race as a whole.[83, 84]

The reader may care to be reminded that the subject of fairness in cognition tests has already been considered in a general way in Chapter 23 (pp. 447–9). Biesheuvel's publications deserve serious consideration by those who plan to work among peoples of different ethnic taxa in various parts of the world, but one may hope that no one will be dissuaded from a projected task in mental testing simply because difficulties are likely to be encountered. The possibility must be borne in mind that they may have been exaggerated. For instance, it is not to be assumed that pencil and paper are always to be avoided where they are not familiar objects of everyday life. Professor S. D. Porteus used his well-known Mazes successfully with wild aborigines in the central desert of Australia, who had never even seen pencil or paper before (and could not speak a word of English).[851] The testees were very much interested and quickly understood what they were required to do with the pencil. Incidentally, one of them gave a lesson to those psychologists who lay exaggerated emphasis on the necessity for ensuring the complete relaxation of the testee. The aborigine in question was a murderer who had speared several men. He was chained by the leg to his principal accuser when he worked at the Mazes, and a policeman sat beside him with a loaded pistol; yet he became so absorbed in the test that Porteus thought the man could safely have been left free and unguarded until he had finished it.

It is unfortunate that there has been so little conformity in the tests administered to peoples living in remote parts of the world. An investigator in one place may use only one test, another working elsewhere a different one; and perhaps neither test has been calibrated (or is even capable of calibration) against one of established validity. Reports on the results of such tests may have considerable intrinsic interest, but general conclusions cannot be drawn. It would be possible to review here in turn, and analyse in detail, a large selection of the many tests that have been carried out in this way; but not much light would be thrown on the ethnic problem. A definite intention to try to solve this problem is the first requirement; beyond that, one needs careful selection of tests as culture-free as they can be made, and some uniformity in their application—and reliable evidence, too, as to the taxa (not the nations) to which the testees belong. A difficulty that must be faced in some places is uncertainty as to the chronological ages of children, which must be known, at least approximately, if IQs are to be determined. It would be helpful to have more information about dental succession in various ethnic taxa, to overcome this difficulty. If the ages of children cannot be determined, adult testees must be used, and comparisons made with adults of other races.

Fortunately there is a great expanse of the world's surface from which an immense store of relevant information is available. North America is unique in the advantages it presents to the student of racial differences in cognitive ability. Four races are well represented in the resident population: Europid, Negrid, Mongolid, and Indianid (American 'Indian'). The two first-named share a common mother-tongue. Literacy is general (though not universal), and verbal group-tests can therefore in many cases be used. Almost everywhere the ages of children are known with precision. In no other country in the world has cognition testing been so actively pursued; and although the American investigators have administered a very large number of different tests, several of the most reliable ones have been used so widely that valid comparisons are possible.

The rest of this chapter will be devoted to the study of cognition testing among the resident races of North America.

## NORTH AMERICAN NEGROES: EARLY STUDIES

By a curious convention, anyone in North America who shows clear evidence of Negrid ancestry is regarded as a Negro, even if it is obvious that the person in question is predominantly Europid (see pp. 228–31). In conformity with this convention, the term will be used in this chapter to include all grades of the Europid–Negrid hybrids resident in North America, as well as the non-hybrid Negrids of that country. The Negrid element in the North American population derives predominantly from Sudanid and Palaenegrid 1 and 2 ancestors, not from those Negrid subraces (Kafrid and Nilotid) that received a certain amount of Europid admixture in their native land.

The Europids of North America, with whom the Negrids will be compared, are derived mainly from Nordid, Mediterranid, Alpinid, and Ashkenazim (hybrid Armenid) stock. The three first-named subraces are much hybridized with one another.

The Europids and Negroes of North America live in a society that is at least to some extent integrated, or at any rate neither of the two peoples lives out its life in geographically delimited areas or 'reserves', nor is there a social convention that separates them so exclusively as that which keeps (or used to keep) some of the castes of India as strangers from one another. Thus the difficulties that have faced students of the ethnic problem in many parts of the world have not been nearly so severe in the U.S.A. and Canada. Not only has the sharing of a common mother-tongue made it easy to use verbal tests and vocabulary items; beyond that, pencil and paper and the everyday objects of civilized life are familiar to all, and education at schools in many parts of the country is nowadays roughly comparable or actually the same. A general discussion of the influence of their environment on the IQs of Negroes will be found on pp. 488–90.

Three investigations of special significance for the ethnic problem were made during the second decade of the present century. Their interest is by no means only historical: on the contrary, they provide a valuable introduction to modern thought on the subject. The three have been chosen because each illuminates a different aspect of the problem, and each aspect is important.

The earliest of the three investigations was carried out by the American psychologist G. O. Ferguson in 1914.[327] It concerns the scores obtained in cognition tests by Negroes of various grades of hybridity. Those North Americans who show any clear evidence of Negrid ancestry tend to adopt freely the convention mentioned above, whereby they are all regarded as falling into the category of Negroes, even if there is obviously a large Europid element in their genetic make-up; and a fellow-feeling seems to unite them all. If, as is claimed, the mere fact of being a Negro (in this sense) is an 'environmental disadvantage', affecting the ability to succeed in cognition tests (p. 489), it must act equally on all; and if the races differ in genetic constitution affecting cognitive ability, one would expect some correlation between grades of hybridity and marks obtained in tests.

Ferguson administered cognition tests to 269 Europid and 319 Negro children of both sexes in the schools of Richmond, Virginia. His main analysis of the results, illustrated by an elaborate series of diagrams, was restricted to those aged twelve to seventeen. His data for younger and older pupils than these were incomplete, and he omitted them from his main analysis. The Negro and Europid children attended separate schools.

He also tested a smaller number of schoolchildren in two other towns in the same state, but did not consider the results sufficiently complete for incorporation in his main analysis.

An important feature of Ferguson's study is that at the time when it was made, the Negro population was not so much mingled by intermarriage as it is today, and it was possible for anyone who had studied the physical characters of hybrids of different grades to recognize them with some degree of accuracy. Ferguson made his classification on the basis of skin-colour, form of face and skull, and texture of hair. He admits that certainty was not possible, but he claims that any errors would balance one another; that is to say, there would be no systematic error inclining in one direction or the other. From a study of their physical characters he assigned each Negro child to one of four categories:

'pure negroes' (here designated $\frac{4}{4}$)

'three-fourths pure negroes' ($\frac{3}{4}$)

'mulattoes proper' ($\frac{2}{4}$)

'quadroons' (offspring of mulatto with Europid) ($\frac{1}{4}$).

In the notation used here, the numerator of the fraction may be regarded as the estimated number of unhybridized Negrids among the child's grandparents, the rest being Europids. In the main part of the investigation Ferguson combined the $\frac{1}{4}$ and $\frac{2}{4}$ Negroes into a group that will here be called $\frac{1}{4} + \frac{2}{4}$, and the others into a group here called $\frac{3}{4} + \frac{4}{4}$. The former group consisted mainly of 'mulattoes proper', on account of the small number of quadroons among the schoolchildren.

Three cognition tests were administered, two of them of the type called 'mixed relations', and the other a 'completion' test. All three were group-tests.

The mixed-relations questions, though widely varied in content and difficulty, were all of the same general type as this: 'As cat is to fur, so bird is to what?' The other test required the completion of sentences from which words had been omitted. Here again the difficulty varied over a considerable range.

Since six age-groups (12–17) of each sex attempted each of three tests, thirty-six comparisons of the three groups of testees (Europids, $\frac{1}{4} + \frac{2}{4}$ Negroes, and $\frac{3}{4} + \frac{4}{4}$ Negroes) were available for analysis. The results obtained by the three groups are perhaps most clearly set forth in the following form (though this way of summarizing his results was not adopted by Ferguson himself).

*Number of cases in which each group*
*obtained the highest mean marks*

|  | Europids | $\frac{1}{4} + \frac{2}{4}$ Negroes | $\frac{3}{4} + \frac{4}{4}$ Negroes |
|---|---|---|---|
| Boys | 14 | 4 | 0 |
| Girls | 16 | 2 | 0 |
|  | 30 | 6 | 0 |

Some readers who study these figures may be inclined to minimize their significance by laying emphasis on the fact that the Europids did not attend the same schools as the Negroes. Since all the Negroes attended the same schools, it is particularly interesting to disregard the Europids and consider the Negroes alone. The following figures emerge.

*Number of cases in which each group*
*gained the higher mean marks*

| | $\frac{1}{4} + \frac{2}{4}$ Negroes | $\frac{3}{4} + \frac{4}{4}$ Negroes |
|---|---|---|
| *Boys* | 14 | 4 |
| *Girls* | 12 | 6 |
| | 26 | 10 |

It is important to mention that the means used in establishing the data recorded above are derived from individual scores that range rather widely. There is no question of a universal or almost universal superiority of the Europids. No less than 22·7% of the $\frac{3}{4} + \frac{4}{4}$ children scored marks that exceeded the mean marks scored by the Europids. It is significant for the ethnic problem, however, that many more of the $\frac{1}{4} + \frac{2}{4}$ children (34·7%) than of the $\frac{3}{4} + \frac{4}{4}$ exceeded the Europid mean.

The figures given below represent the mean marks obtained by all the Negro boys and girls aged twelve to seventeen, of each group separately, expressed as percentages of the mean marks of the Europids.

| | |
|---|---|
| $\frac{4}{4}$ . . . . . | 73·7 |
| $\frac{3}{4}$ . . . . . | 77·8 |
| $\frac{2}{4}$ . . . . . | 81·3 |
| $\frac{1}{4}$ . . . . | 94·0 |

If the Negroes of North America suffer any disadvantage in cognition tests from their cultural environment in general, or as a result of their separate education, or merely through 'being black' (p. 489), the handicap is shared by all. The comparison of hybrid Negroes of various grades with one another and with non-hybrid Negrids is thus potentially of particular value in studies of the ethnic problem. Although Ferguson's work was done so long ago, it seems to have been one of the best planned, most detailed, and most fully reported of all the investigations of its kind that have ever been carried out. In some (though not all) of the more recent studies, the degree of hybridity has been judged by reliance on skin-colour alone, which is an unsafe criterion. Someone adequately trained in physical anthropology should participate in studies of this kind, if the actual ancestry of each testee is not known with certainty. In general, it has been found in most cases that the obvious hybrids have done better in cognition tests than non-hybrid Negrids and those showing little evidence of Europid ancestry; but this has not invariably been so. The subject of Negro hybridity in relation to cognitive ability has been reviewed by Tyler[1077] and Shuey.[966] An experiment of particular interest carried out on Indianid (American 'Indian') hybrids is described on pp. 493–4.

The second investigation carried out in the second decade of the century and chosen for special mention here is of importance for the ethnic problem partly on account of its vast scale, and partly because of the vigorous controversy it aroused, which has smouldered on into recent times. No one interested in the ethnic problem can afford to overlook it, whatever opinion he may hold when he has fully considered its implications.

After the entry of the United States into the First World War, it was suggested by American psychologists that they could help the war effort by grading the 'intelligence' of recruits. The suggestion was accepted by the Army, and between September 1917 and the end of January 1919 no fewer than 1,726,966 men were subjected to tests. A book on this great experiment appeared in 1920,[1167] and in the following year an official report was published, amounting to 890 large pages. This was a corporate work, edited by Lieut.-Col. R. M. Yerkes.[1164] Negroes and Europids were considered separately in it. In accordance with the usual custom the former name was taken to include all who showed any physical evidence of Negrid ancestry. All the Negroes had been born in the U.S.A., and English was their mother-tongue.

A test called 'alpha' was administered to the great majority of the testees. This is a verbal group-test, designed for literate persons. It consists of eight items, of which six were quite well adapted for the assessment of cognitive ability, by the standards of the time, though two were less so (p. 475). Many of the testees, however, were illiterate, and for them a special test called 'beta' was designed. This was calibrated to alpha by the administration of both tests to a large number of literate testees. Many recruits were also subjected to individual tests (either the Stanford–Binet or the Yerkes–Bridges Point Scale), and a special non-verbal test, consisting mainly of performance items, was provided for use in appropriate cases. Full consideration of all the available evidence resulted in the assignment of every recruit to one of eight grades, called 'letter ratings', as follows: **E,** too inferior for ordinary employment in the Army; **D–,** very inferior; **D,** inferior; **C–,** low average; **C,** average; **C+,** high average; **B,** superior; **A,** very superior. Those recruits relegated to rating **E** were not further considered in the main analysis of the investigation.

The general result, so far as comparison between Europids and Negroes is concerned, is set out in a table (unnumbered) on p. 707 of Yerkes's report.[1164] The reader is referred to pp. 555–9 and 707 of the report for an exact explanation of the basis on which the figures were compiled. The facts are represented in the present book by a diagram (Fig. 77, p. 476), which shows the percentage of Europids and Negroes falling into each of the letter ratings from **D–** to **A.**

The investigators noticed a marked difference between the letter ratings of Negroes from northern and southern states. To analyse the matter further they made a special study of Illinois, Indiana, New Jersey, New York, and Pennsylvania, as representing the northern states, for comparison with Alabama, Georgia, Louisiana, and Mississippi for the southern. The numbers of Negro testees from the two groups of states were respectively 4,705 and 6,846. The data, set out in table 268 of the report, are here represented graphically in Fig. 78, p. 477. The very great difference between the two regions is at once obvious, and comparison with Fig. 77 shows that although the northern Negroes did not attain such high ratings, on the whole, as the Europids, they did approximate very much more closely to the Europid pattern than did the southern Negroes, or the Negro draft as a whole.

How are these facts to be explained? One will at once consider the possibility that differences in education between north and south might be the cause. It can scarcely be doubted that facilities for school education (for Europids as well as Negroes) would have been better in the more urban, northern states than in the largely rural districts of the south. If the tests had been culture-free, this should not have made much difference; but in fact the tests had not the degree of freedom from cultural influences that characterizes, for instance, Raven's Progressive Matrices (p. 450), which were introduced at a much later date. In particular, the capacity to succeed in the Arithmetic and General Information items of the alpha test was necessarily affected by education in school. A few examples will make this clear.

The following is a question set in the Arithmetic item. 'A certain division contains 3,000 artillery, 15,000 infantry, and 1,000 cavalry. If each branch is expanded proportionately until there are in all 20,900 men, how many will be added to the artillery?' As regards the General Information item, it is important to recognize that a test of purely cognitive ability is supposed to involve only such knowledge as is likely to be the common property of all or as nearly as possible all the persons whom it is desired to compare. For instance, all would be familiar with the words 'cat', 'fur', 'bird', and 'feather', and one may therefore properly *use* these words in a test designed to assess reasoning ability (p. 472). It is an entirely different matter to ask questions designed to find out how much a testee *already knows*. Thus, in a perfect cognition test one would not ask such questions as these (the correct answers to be underlined): 'Rosa Bonheur is famous as a poet painter composer sculptor'; 'The author of "The Raven" is Stevenson Kipling Hawthorne Poe'. One can imagine two persons of equal cognitive ability, of whom one could answer these questions, while the other could not. Yet these are examples of questions set in the General Information item of the alpha test. It is important to note that 30·1% of all Negroes in Group IV (intended to represent the Negro draft as a whole) and 58·2% of Group V (representing the Negroes of the northern states) took the alpha test.

Fig. 78 gives a good general impression of the difference between the northern and southern states in the matter under discussion. Very misleading impressions are given if states are specially selected for consideration simply because they point towards particular conclusions. One could easily choose a state in which the Europids did exceptionally well and another in which the Negroes did exceptionally badly, and thus emphasize the results in order to support a particular hypothesis of Europid superiority. The error of selectivity may be amusingly illustrated by taking the state of New Mexico as an example. Here, the result of the test appears staggering at first sight. No fewer than 55·5% of the Negro recruits from this state were assigned to letter rating **A**. There was no part of the whole country in which anything remotely similar to this achievement was attained by the Europid recruits. Only 4·1% of 93,973 Europids attained this distinction. One's admiration is suddenly deflated, however, when one discovers that the percentage was 55·5% of *nine* recruits! The strange chance by which five out of nine New Mexican Negroes recruited to the American Army were rated **A** is not commented on in the official report, and it would be rash to draw any conclusion from it. In reflecting on the New Mexican data, it is well to hold in mind the less flattering ones from Georgia.

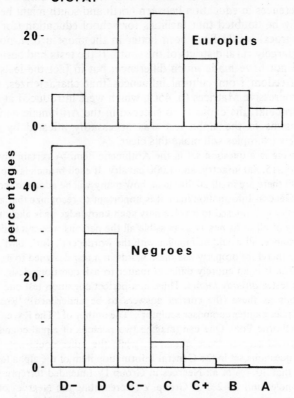

**Europids**

percentages

**Negroes**

D−   D   C−   C   C+   B   A

77   *The relative cognitive abilities of Europid and Negro recruits to the American Army during the First World War, as assessed by the 'alpha' test*

The capital letters denote 'letter ratings' (D−, lowest; A, highest). The heights of the columns indicate the percentage of recruits assigned to each letter rating. For fuller particulars see text.
*Diagram drawn from the data of Yerkes.* [1164]

More Negroes were recruited from this state than from any other (2,187 in all). The percentage of them that achieved the **A** rating was 0·1 (two individuals).

Professor Otto Klineberg and certain other psychologists have analysed the results of the Army tests in a selective manner, by choosing for comparison the four [596, 597, 14] or three[74] northern states in which the Negroes did particularly well for comparison with the four or three southern states in which the Europids did particularly badly. Klineberg was able to show by this selective process that the Negro recruits of certain northern states, especially Ohio, achieved higher median scores in the alpha test than did the Europid recruits of certain southern ones, especially Mississippi. He quotes 49·50 as the median score for Negroes of Ohio in the alpha test, and 41·25 for Europids of Mississippi.

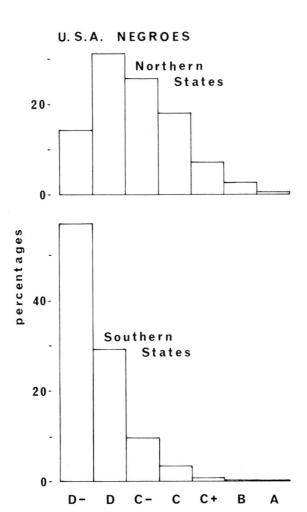

**U. S. A.   NEGROES**

Northern
States

Southern
States

percentages

D−   D   C−   C   C+   B   A

78   *The relative cognitive abilities of Negro recruits to the American Army* from northern and southern states *during the First World War, as assessed by the 'alpha' test. For further particulars see text, and legend to Fig. 77*

*Diagram drawn from the data of Yerkes.* [1164]

Since, as we have seen, there can be no doubt that formal education must affect the scores obtained in the alpha test, and since it was easier to provide good education in the largely urbanized northern states than in the more rural south, it might naturally suggest itself to an investigator that the best plan would be to compare Europid with Negro in a northern state and Europid with Negro in a southern state. I have followed Klineberg in choosing Ohio and Mississippi for the purpose of this comparison. The scores obtained in the alpha test are given by Yerkes in tables 200 and 248 of his report. The exact medians cannot be quoted, since the marks obtained by each recruit are not printed separately, but a close approximation can be given. It will be helpful to the reader to mention that rating **C** (supposed to represent average 'intelligence') extends from 45 to 74 marks. The comparison given here deserves study.

| State | Testees | Median marks fell within these ranges |
|---|---|---|
| Ohio | Europids | 65–69 |
| " | Negroes | 45–49 |
| Mississippi | Europids | 40–44 |
| " | Negroes | 10–14 |

The letter ratings for recruits from Ohio and Mississippi are shown diagrammatically in Figs. 79 and 80. In studying the marks and letter ratings it is important to bear in mind that I have used these two states in the table and figures simply because Klineberg chose them to show Negroes at their best and Europids at their worst, in northern and southern states respectively.

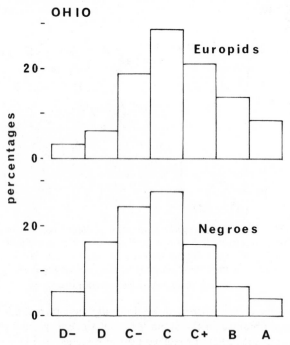

**OHIO**

79    *The relative cognitive abilities of Europid and Negro recruits to the American Army* from Ohio *during the First World War, as assessed by the 'alpha' test. For further particulars see text, and legend to Fig. 77*

Diagram drawn from the data of Yerkes. [1164]

Against all expectation, the superiority of the Europids became *more* evident when beta marks were taken into consideration. The statisticians employed by the Army worked out a method for integrating the results of the alpha and beta tests into a combined mark. When this method was applied to the four northern states chosen by Klineberg as those in which the Negroes did best and the four

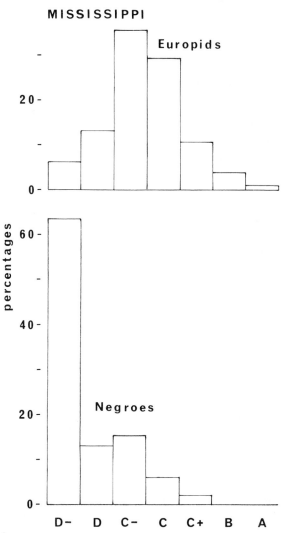

80    *The relative cognitive abilities of Europid and Negro recruits to the American Army* from Mississippi *during the First World War, as assessed by the 'alpha' test. For further particulars see text, and legend to Fig. 77*

*Diagram drawn from the data of Yerkes.* [1164]

chosen by him as the southern ones in which the Europids did worst, the following results were obtained:[14]

|  | *Mean marks on 'combined scale'* *(alpha and beta combined)* |
|---|---|
| Southern Negroes | 9·9 |
| Northern Negroes | 12·0 |
| Southern Europids | 12·7 |
| Northern Europids | 14·1 |

It thus transpired, when the fullest information was brought to bear, that the Europids of the four states in which they did *worst* surpassed the Negroes of the four states in which the latter did *best*. Alper and Boring[14] attribute this result to the 'educational disadvantages' of the Negroes, but almost everyone who examines the details of the alpha and beta tests is likely to pronounce the latter as *less* dependent on what is taught at schools than the alpha.

In the controversy over the Army tests, the suggestion was made that the Negroes who migrated northwards from their main centre in the southern states might tend to be those who were more active mentally than the ones who stayed behind. The migrants to the north, or their descendants who inherited their mental qualities, would then tend to do better in the tests set by the Army's psychologists. This hypothesis of 'selective migration' is certainly plausible, but it was attacked in various publications, and Professor Klineberg devoted a whole book to the subject.[595] He produced evidence that those Negro children who had arrived recently in the north were not mentally superior to those of the same age and sex who had remained in the south. The most striking piece of evidence in his book comes from a study of twelve-year-old girls in northern schools, subjected to the National Intelligence Test. When their marks were plotted against their length of residence in the north, the graph (on p. 30 of his book) showed a remarkably consistent rise with the passage of years in the more favourable environment. It must be remarked, however, that the marks scored by twelve-year-old boys in a similar experiment were much less consistent. One does not know how it happened that the group of boys who had been only one or two years in the north scored nearly as many marks, on average, as those who had been born in the north. Still, most of the evidence quoted in his book supports his opinion that selective migration does not account for the facts. It is noteworthy, however, that results obtained from non-verbal tests, which tend to be much more culture-free than the ones on which he relies, do not support his views nearly so effectively. 'It should be added', as he remarks in another book, 'that with the performance tests this result is not so clear, and that the environmental effect appears largely to be restricted, as far as these studies go, to tests with a definite linguistic component.'[596]

Professor Klineberg's arguments against the hypothesis of selective migration have been disputed by Professor Henry E. Garrett,[384] who has examined the original data on which the former's account is based. He points out certain significant omissions by Klineberg, and draws attention also to a slip, by which too high a figure for average IQ was attributed to a group of Negro children resident in Los Angeles. It has also been pointed out, by an informant present in Los Angeles at the time of the test, that the children in question were the offspring of highly selected Negro parents.[837] Klineberg's writings on this subject should nevertheless be seriously considered by anyone who wishes to reach a balanced opinion on the possibility that some of the results of the Army's test may have been due to selective migration.

The whole subject has been reviewed in considerable detail by Professor Audrey M. Shuey.[966] The evidence indicates that in more modern times northern and southern Negro children have differed less in cognitive ability than did recruits from the two regions in the First World War. From the results of many different tests she puts the average difference between them at seven IQ points, in favour of the northern. It happens, however, that a considerable number of southern-born Negro children live in the north and attend the same schools as their northern-born counterparts. When these two lots of children are subjected to cognition tests, it is found that the northern-born testees surpass the southern-born by only three or four IQ points, instead of seven. Shuey draws the conclusion that roughly one-half of the difference in IQ between northern and southern Negro children is to be attributed to environmental differences, and the rest to selective migration by their parents.

In discussions on the differences between the performance of Negroes in northern and southern states, one relevant circumstance seems to have been overlooked. On four occasions on which censuses were made in the U.S.A. during the second half of the nineteenth century, the mulattoes* were counted separately. It was found that where the proportion of Negroes to Europids was lowest, the proportion of mulattoes to 'total Negroes' was highest. In 1890, mulattoes constituted only 14% of the Negro population of Kentucky, Tennessee, Alabama, Louisiana, Arkansas, Oklahoma, and Texas, while in the New England states they amounted to 32·7%.[1015] One cannot be sure whether similar figures would have been obtained if a similar enumeration had been carried out at the time of the test made by the American Army; but it seems probable that differences in the amount of hybridity may have affected the results. (See Chapter 13, pp. 229–30.)

What are the main conclusions, then, that must be drawn from the Yerkes report and the resulting controversy? The most important appear to be these. Foremost of all, every effort should be made to avoid the selection of data that will tend towards a particular conclusion. When, in a huge and diverse country, it is desired to compare two groups of persons (Europids and Negroes in this case) by means of tests that make no claim to be culture-free, it is only fair to institute comparisons in regions where the environment, in the widest sense, is roughly the same (mainly rural, for instance, or largely urban). In many parts of the U.S.A., at the time of the Army's investigation, the education of Negroes was probably less good than that of Europids. This may indeed have affected the responses to those particular questions, in a few of the items, that were related to scholastic studies; but it seems difficult to suppose that this can account for the general tendency everywhere for the Europids, on average, to sur-

---

* It would appear that in these censuses the word 'mulattoes' was used loosely to mean Negroes whose appearance gave clear indication of a Europid element in their ancestry.

pass the Negroes (though it must never be forgotten that there was considerable overlap in the results). Finally, the Negro recruits from the four northern states, selected as being those from which the Negro recruits did best in the tests, did *not* surpass the Europid recruits from the four southern states, selected as being those from which the Europid recruits did worst; the reverse was shown to be the case, when the results of both alpha and beta tests were taken into consideration.

The last of the three investigations dating from the second decade of the century is chosen because it illustrates particularly well a trap into which students of the ethnic problem have fallen from time to time, from those early days of cognition testing onwards. In several respects Sunne's experiment[1030] was admirably designed. She took precautions to ensure that the Europid and Negro testees were as comparable as possible. All of them were English-speaking children who lived in New Orleans, and all of them were subjected to several tests (Binet, Yerkes Point Scale, and others). All the Europid children attended a school situated in one of the very poorest districts in the city, and the schools for Negroes were in the same district. This was arranged in order that the environmental conditions at home and at school should be as nearly as possible the same. *All* the Europid children in grades II to V were used as testees; there was no selection among them. So far, so good. But here error stepped in. The Negro children were deliberately selected as being those boys and girls who were '*of as nearly the same age and grade as possible*' (her italics) as the Europid children. In other words, the intention was to have a set of Negro children who were as similar to the Europids in school advancement, age for age, as possible. Now advancement in schools is obviously dependent to a considerable extent on cognitive ability. The proper selection would have been by age alone; grade should not have been considered. It would only have been one step further than Sunne went if a group of Europid boys and girls had been matched as exactly as possible with a group of Negro boys and girls of the same chronological *and mental* ages. In that case the IQs of Europids and Negrids would have been found to be the same—not surprisingly! The real differences between the races could not be disclosed in full by Sunne's method. Actually, on the average of Sunne's tests, the Negro children were somewhat retarded in relation to the Europid; but the method of comparison concealed the extent of the real difference between the races.

A seemingly inexplicable fact about Sunne's experiment is that all the 122 Europid boys and girls were in grades II to V, while among the 126 Negro children there were ten from grades VI and VII.

## LATER STUDIES OF NORTH AMERICAN NEGROES

The cognitive ability of North American Negroes has been considered in many reviews published from the early days of psychometry onwards. Ferguson himself, in the introductory part of his long paper, mentions the earliest use of Binet's test in an attempt to compare Negroes with Europids in respect of this ability.[327] R. S. Woodworth of Columbia University published a brief survey of the subject shortly after Ferguson's paper appeared, and reported on the latter's investigation in the course of it.[1155] In some of the reviews all aspects of mental differences between races are considered in a very general way, without special emphasis on cognitive ability. This applies, for instance, to Garth's review in 1931,[389] Tyler's (2nd edition) in 1956,[1077] and Dreger and Miller's in 1960.[278] These three authors agree that North American Negroes show less cognitive ability, on average, than the Europids of the same country, and they attribute this, with varying emphasis, to environmental differences.

Garth presents his case rather dogmatically. 'It is useless', he remarks, 'to speak of the worthlessness of so-called "inferior peoples" when their worth has never been established by a fair test;'[389] but he does not tell us who speaks of worthlessness, nor does he bring evidence that would prove all tests unfair. Dreger and Miller also blame the tests for the results. According to them, Negro children behave in the circumstances of everyday life in the way expected of Europid children whose IQs are 10 points higher; and these authors thus seem to imply that subjective impressions are more reliable than the results of mental tests. Indeed, they even seem to deny that it is worth while to try to improve the methods of testing. 'The search for a culture-free test', they announce, 'is illusory.'[278] Tyler presents her case with moderation and carefully reasoned argument.[1077] She mentions the remarkable fact, contrary though it is to the main tenor of her opinion, that in Kent County, Ontario, where the socio-economic status of Negro and Europid was more nearly comparable than anywhere else in the country and racial discrimination was at a minimum, the Europids were found to surpass the Negroes by an average of 15 to 19 IQ points on all tests, verbal and non-verbal. Everyone can profit from a study of this fair-minded presentation of a difficult problem, written by an author who inclines to the environmentalist interpretation.

In 1958 there appeared a work by Professor Audrey M. Shuey of Randolph-Macon Woman's College which differed from other reviews of the subject in being almost entirely confined to the results of cognition tests (in the wide sense of the term; some tests falling into this category include one or two items that are not strictly cognitive in scope). Shuey's book, entitled *The testing of Negro intelligence*,[965] was more comprehensive and systematic than any that had appeared previously on this subject. Dreger and Miller[278] found it 'polemic'; but it seems that these authors employ the adjective in an unusual sense, for the book is not aggressively controversial, nor is there any offensive personal attack on those who hold opinions differing from those of the author. The results of a very large number of tests are set out in a standardized tabular form and critically discussed.

Eight years later, in 1966, Shuey published a new and greatly enlarged edition of her book.[966] This monumental work cannot be overlooked by anyone interested in the subject. She deals separately with the various types of persons that constitute North American society: young children, schoolchildren, high school and college students, the armed forces in both World Wars, veterans and other adult civilians, gifted and retarded persons, delinquents, and criminals. In each category Negroes are compared with Europids. To consider the data she presents and the conclusions she draws about each of these categories would occupy too large a space for accommodation in the present book, which attempts to cover all aspects of the ethnic problem (except practical applications). It seems best to concentrate attention mainly upon the part of her book that deals with schoolchildren, and on results that can be presented in terms of IQ. The idea of IQ loses part of its significance when the attempt is made to apply it to adults, despite the ingenuity that has been devoted to this end; and it is questionable whether it conveys very much useful information about children below school age. Schoolchildren seem to be the ideal testees, not only because 'mental age' (and therefore IQ) has more direct meaning when applied to them than it has at later stages of life, but also because these children are readily available in large numbers for tests.

Verbal group-tests will be considered first, because they are easier to administer than tests of other types and consequently have been used on a much larger number of testees. Shuey reports on the results of applying these tests to more than sixty thousand Negro schoolchildren, and also to a large number of comparable Europids. Eighteen different tests were used by various investigators. They included such well-known ones as the Kuhlmann–Anderson and National Intelligence Tests. Not all of them gave results that could be expressed in terms of IQ, and it is recognized that the IQs given by different tests do not always exactly coincide; but it was found possible to calculate a 'combined mean IQ' to represent the results of studies by verbal group-tests administered to about fifty thousand of the Negro schoolchildren. The mean figure was 84·0. It will be remembered that IQs are expressed on a scale in which 100 represents as accurately as possible the mean cognitive ability of a random sample of the Europid children of the U.S.A. The mean IQ of Negro schoolchildren in the southern states was 80·6; of those in the intermediate ('Border') and northern states, respectively 89·8 and 89·7. Europid children were tested as well as Negroes in fifty-eight of the studies on which Shuey reports. In fifty-seven of these they obtained higher average marks. Some of the investigators reported the percentage of Negro children that overlapped the average score of the Europids. The mean of all the overlaps was 10%.

It does not seem to be possible, from the available data, to distinguish the overlaps beyond the medians from those beyond the means; but IQs tend to follow closely the normal curve of frequency distribution, and it is unlikely that the means and medians were far apart.

Shuey reports on non-verbal group-tests administered by different investigators to nearly fifteen thousand Negro schoolchildren, and many Europids as well. The tests were very diverse in character. They included Raven's Progressive Matrices, the Army 'beta', Davis–Eells Games, Pintner–Cunningham, Dearborn A, and a dozen others. Over nine thousand of the Negro testees were subjected to tests that gave results in IQ. The combined mean IQ, as calculated by Shuey, was 85, but the figures varied considerably in different parts of the country, from 77 in the *northern* rural districts to 91 in the intermediate urban. The Europids scored higher average marks than the Negroes in eighteen of the nineteen investigations in which children of the same localities were compared. The Progressive Matrices were tried with Negro and

Europid children aged seven to nine in a population of low socio-economic grade in a north-eastern city. The mean Negro IQ resulting from this test was 80·5, the Europid 90·8. It may be remembered that this very ingenious culture-free test involves inductive reasoning and is supposed to be highly loaded for *g* (see pp. 450 and 457).

Data are available for nearly ten thousand Negro schoolchildren subjected to individual tests, including the Stanford–Binets of 1916, 1937, and 1960, and others almost equally well-known. Fourteen different individual tests are included in Shuey's survey. Over seven thousand Negro schoolchildren took tests that gave results presentable as IQs, and the combined mean IQ of this group was between 84 and 85. Those in the intermediate urban areas once again did best, with a combined mean IQ of 90. The southern rural areas did least well in individual tests, with a combined mean IQ of only 77. The range of combined mean IQs, which thus extended from 77 to 90, was almost exactly the same as that which resulted from the non-verbal group-tests. Europid children were included in twenty-three of the investigations by individual tests. They were superior to the Negroes, on average, in twenty-one of these. In the other two there was equality. In one of these, many of the Europid children came from homes where English was not spoken, and the testees must therefore have been at some disadvantage in viva voce tests, even though the language spoken at school was English.

The fact that verbal group-tests, non-verbal group-tests, and individual tests all gave the Negro schoolchildren combined mean IQs of 84–85 is one of the most striking in the whole of Shuey's elaborate analysis.

It would be possible to pass in review all the groups of Negroes mentioned on p. 483, but there is no need to do so here. The reader who requires all the detailed information that Professor Shuey provides should refer to her book, where it is readily available. It must suffice to say that the results given by tests on schoolchildren are confirmed by those administered to the other groups; for there is a general tendency for the Europids to surpass the Negroes in cognition tests, usually by about the same margin.

In 1966, the year in which Professor Shuey's book was published, there also appeared a report of a huge investigation of the mental abilities of American schoolchildren, carried out in the previous year under the auspices of the U.S.A. Department of Health, Education, and Welfare.[216] The book will here be referred to, for short, as the Coleman Report, though in fact Coleman was only the first-named in a list of seven authors. Some impression of the magnitude of this study will be conveyed by the fact that nearly twenty thousand school-teachers were needed to administer the tests in the classrooms of the nation. The tests (all of them group-tests) were of five kinds, intended to assess verbal ability, non-verbal ability, reading comprehension, mathematics achievement, and general information. Coleman and his colleagues considered that they were testing *achievement*, and they remarked that the tests 'are not in any sense "culturally fair"'. The two called mathematics achievement and general information, and probably also the one called verbal comprehension, are indeed classifiable as tests of achievement, or (better) of *attainment*; but the examples they give of the tests in verbal and non-verbal ability show that these clearly fall into the general category of cognition tests. The ability to absorb and reproduce scholastic learning is not assessable by the items of which they consist. They seem to have been fair for all who had had the opportunity to profit from the general experience of school life in the U.S.A. (such as the ability to read and write), with the reservation that those whose mother-tongue was not English, or who were bilingual in everyday life, must have been at some disadvantage in the verbal tests (cf. p. 490).

In all the schools the tests were administered to children in grades 1, 3, 6, 9, and 12. It is to be regretted that the testees were classified by school grade, without consideration of their ages. Two different non-verbal tests were administered to those in grade 3; with this exception there was one verbal and one non-verbal test for each grade. In the report, the results are conveniently set out in the form of diagrams, showing the outcome of each test by the percentile method. The median point (50th percentile) is marked in each diagram. All the children in each classroom took the tests together; but separate diagrams are used in the report to represent the scores of testees classified into the following groups: 'Whites' (Europids not hybridized with other races), 'Negroes', 'Oriental Americans' (Mongolids), 'Mexican Americans', and 'Puerto Ricans'. The two latter groups, consisting of mixed and hybridized peoples, are not further considered in the present chapter. For the marks gained by the Mongolids and Indianids in these tests, see pp. 492 and 493 respectively.

The two largest groups—Europids and Negroes—were each divided into eight subgroups on a regional basis, as follows: *Metropolitan* (north-east, midwest, west, south, and south-west), and *Non-metropolitan* (north and west, south, and south-west).

In the tests of both verbal and non-verbal ability, in each of the five school grades (including both non-verbal tests set to grade 3), the Europids of every one of the eight regions (including in each case that region in which they did worst) surpassed in median marks the Negroes of every one of the eight regions (including that in which they did best). In most cases the median of the Europids was at about the same figure as the 75th percentile of the Negroes. In other words, those Negroes who attained the median mark of the Europids surpassed about 75% of the Negro group as a whole.

It must not be forgotten that in nearly every relevant investigation a certain percentage of Negroes goes beyond or 'overlaps' the median of the Europids; that is to say, they gain a higher mark or higher IQ than do 50% of the Europids with whom they are compared. Shuey brings together in her book the available facts bearing on this subject. She reaches the conclusion that the overlap percentage amounts, on average, to 11%. The extent of the average overlap appears to have been considerably exaggerated by some authors, as a result of the repeated citation in the literature of a high figure that was not based on a sufficient number of investigations.

Figures for overlap, taken by themselves, necessarily give incomplete information, since most of the overlappers might be bunched near the median. The variability curve might be markedly 'skew' in this respect, or it might be of normal shape, but indicate a narrow range (cf. Garrett[385]). One wants to know how far the range of cognitive ability extends towards high levels. Several authors have looked for Negro children of exceptionally high IQ, and the existence of others has come to light in the course of investigations not primarily directed towards this end.

The earliest large-scale investigation that threw light on this subject was initiated by Terman, who published his results in 1926.[1036] His purpose was to discover the children with the highest IQs in certain Californian cities. His search covered practically the whole of Los Angeles, San Francisco, and Oakland, most of Berkeley, and part of Alameda. By sending circular letters to school-teachers he obtained the names of a large number of children regarded by them as particularly bright, and from these he gradually filtered off the brightest of all by the administration of a succession of cognition tests. The final test was the complete Stanford–Binet. All children who achieved IQs of 140 and above by this test were regarded as 'gifted'; to this highly select group a few others with IQs from 132 upwards were also admitted. The total number in the gifted group was 643, of whom about 99% were Europids; they had been chosen from a total of about 168,000. (The Chinese children at their own schools were not included in the search.) More than two-thirds of the gifted were in the IQ ranges 140–144, 145–149, and 150–154; a single individual reached the 200–204 rating.

Since the gifted children represented about 0·38% of the total number from whom the selection had been made, this may be taken as representing roughly the figure for the Europid children of the five cities as a whole. In these cities, Negroes amounted to about 2% of the population, and the number of Negro children among the total group from whom the selection was made must have been roughly 2% of 168,000. Of these, only two reached the gifted group, almost exactly 0·06%. Thus the percentage of the gifted among the Europid children was about six times higher than among the Negroes. Both of the Negro children in the gifted group are described by Terman as 'part white'. Their positions in the IQ scale are not recorded.

Since Terman made his investigation, many studies of the same subject have been carried out in various parts of North America. They have involved altogether a much larger number of Negro children (though fewer Europids). Shuey's analysis of the results reveals a higher proportion of gifted children in both groups.[966] The figures suggest that the percentage of gifted individuals is about eight times higher among the Europids than among the Negroes.

A certain number of Negro schoolchildren attain very high IQs. The most celebrated case is that of a girl,* aged nine years and four months, reported on in 1935 by Witty and Jenkins, of Northwestern University in Illinois.[1144] This remarkable child, referred to as 'B' and described by the authors as 'one of the most precocious and promising children in America', attained the astonishing IQs of 200 by Stanford–Binet, 180 by Otis S.A. (Intermediate, Form A), 185 by Army alpha (1925 revision), and 170 by McCall Multimental. Her achievement on performance tests was good but not outstanding. 'B' was stated by her

---

* In his recent book, *Race, intelligence and education*, Professor H. J. Eysenck lays stress on the fact that Negro girls and women are more successful, on average, in both cognition and attainment tests than Negro boys and men. [319]

mother to be 'of pure Negro stock'. Her mother was a school-teacher, her father a graduate of a College of Applied Science. Witty and Jenkins attribute her ability 'to a fortunate biological inheritance plus a fairly good opportunity for development'.

Jenkins followed up the study of gifted Negroes in later years by searching for all published accounts of Negroes with IQs of 130 and above. In the course of this study, published in 1948, he found records of eighteen Negro children who surpassed IQ 160 on the Stanford–Binet test; seven of the eighteen went beyond 170, four beyond 180, and one (presumably 'B', though this is not stated) attained 200.[549] Two of these talented children had completed their high-school studies and been enrolled as university students at the age of thirteen. Unfortunately Jenkins makes no mention in this paper of the degrees of hybridity, if any, among the highly gifted Negroes.

Cases such as these must necessarily influence our outlook on the ethnic problem, but, as Jenkins says, their incidence is 'much lower' among Negroes than among Europids. Without committing himself to a definite opinion, he suggests that the lower proportion of highly gifted Negroes may be due to differences of environment.

It does not appear that any very precise information is yet available that would make it possible to list with confidence those special factors of cognitive ability in which Negroes are strongest and weakest. The lack of exact knowledge on this subject is probably due to the fact that many investigators prefer to use tests, such as the Stanford–Binet, that are not selective for any particular factor, but give reliable assessments of cognitive ability as a whole. The individual items of such tests are more selective, but separate reports on the reponses to each are not usually published. One has little more to guide one than the general impressions of those who have mentioned the subject in their writings. In general, Negroes do not shine in tests that are culture-fair or claim to be culture-free, and they do better in verbal than in non-verbal ones. Indeed, there seems to be rather general agreement that they show considerable verbal facility, and their capacity for rote memory is high; but they seem to be weak in reasoning and abstract thought in general, in numerical calculation, and in conceptual memory (cf. Jensen,[551] Peterson,[838] Pintner,[844] Shuey,[966] Tyler,[1077] and Yerkes[1164]).

The influence of the environment on the results of cognition tests has already been discussed in a general way (see pp. 447–9, 459, 469–70, and 483), but a few words must be added here about the special case of the North American Negroes, since so much has been written about it. It scarcely needs to be said that the environmental differences between Negro and Europid in North America are very small in comparison with those that separate peoples living at primitive cultural levels in remote regions of the world from the inhabitants of highly civilized countries. Nevertheless, some students of the subject do emphasize strongly the differences that actually exist in North America; and when faced with evidence that efforts are made in cognition testing to avoid error arising from these differences, they sometimes fall back on arguments that seem rather to evade the issue than to attack it by the suggestion of new techniques. Professor J. F. Crow of Wisconsin University, for instance, allows that efforts to eliminate environmental effects are in fact made, and that the average IQs of Negroes nevertheless remain lower than those of Europids; but he considers it arguable 'that being black or white in our [American] society changes one or more aspects of the environment so importantly as to account for the difference'.[233]

Dr. F. C. McGurk has made a special study of what he calls 'the culture hypothesis'. In his general review of it[724] he claims that despite the marked improvement in the cultural environment and social status of American Negroes since the time of the First World War, their 'overlap' figures have remained more or less constant. It would be interesting to see all the available facts relating to this matter re-analysed in terms of median IQs.

McGurk carried out a rather elaborate experiment to find out how the cultural environment of the home affects responses to a cognition test.[723, 724] The testees were High School students, 213 of them Negroes and the same number Europids. Each Negro was 'matched' as exactly as possible with a Europid by consideration of his age and of a wide variety of social and economic factors, including the school he attended and the curriculum he followed. The intention was that the members of each of the 213 pairs should resemble one another as closely as possible in the environment to which they had been subjected. The test included a wide variety of questions. A group of 78 psychologists was employed to study all the questions in the test and to pick out from among them those that were 'cultural' (i.e. dependent on cultural experience) and those that were 'noncultural'. The Europids surpassed the Negroes easily on the non-cultural questions, but by a *smaller* margin on the cultural ones.

Closer analysis of the results revealed a still more striking fact. A group of almost exactly one-quarter of all the Negroes, consisting of those who were judged 'lowest' in socio-economic status, and their matched Europid counterparts, were considered separately. It was found that in this selected group the Europids again did better than the Negroes on the non-cultural questions, by a significant margin; but on the cultural ones the Negroes *surpassed* the Europids (though the difference was not statistically significant).

Several independent investigators, including McGurk,[723, 724] have studied the differences in IQ attained by Negro children belonging to different socio-economic classes. Shuey has reviewed the evidence on this subject.[966] She finds that those in the 'high' class have tended, in general, to attain an IQ rating much lower than that of Europids of the same class; lower, in fact, by no less than 20·3 IQ points, on average. This difference is considerably greater than that which distinguishes the average Negro schoolchild from his or her counterpart in the Europid population of the U.S.A.(about 15 or 16 IQ points). The Negro children of the 'high' socio-economic class have shown a mean IQ 2·6 points *below* that of the Europids of the 'lower' and 'lowest' socio-economic classes. Yet the latter must almost inevitably have experienced a less favourable environment, from the general cultural point of view, than the Negro children of the 'high' class. The reader is referred to Shuey's book for suggestions as to the causes that may have resulted in the low IQs attained by Negro children of the 'high' class.

All such experiments suggest that the cultural environment of the home is not so important in determining success in cognition tests as some writers on the subject have supposed. This, however, should not surprise us unduly. From the time of Binet onwards, and increasingly so in more modern times, designers of the best tests have tried to avoid, so far as possible, the setting of items involving knowledge that is not widely available to the testees who would be likely to attempt them. The intention has been to assess cognitive ability, not special knowledge.

## MONGOLIDS

Most of the Chinese and Japanese immigrants to North America have presumably been Sinids, Palaemongolids, and hybrids between these. The physical characters of some of the Mongolid subraces are briefly described in Appendix 1 (pp. 537–9).

The Mongolids who have been tested in North America have mostly been bilingual children, speaking their immigrant parents' language at home and English at school. Bilingual persons are thought to be at a disadvantage in verbal cognition tests. Indeed, this is held to account for the low IQs often assigned to the offspring of Portuguese and Italian immigrants to North America.

Kwoh Tsuen Yeung appears to have been the first person to administer a reliable cognition test, giving results in terms of IQ, to Mongolid children resident in North America. He reported his findings in 1921.[1166] The testees were 109 Chinese of both sexes, aged five to fourteen, all born in America and living in San Francisco or its vicinity. Their parents had come principally from the region of Canton. This is in the part of China inhabited principally by Palaemongolids (or Chukiangids, as Liu calls them[675]). Most of the children's fathers were laundry-workers or ranchers. The children attended public schools and received the same education (in English) as the Europids, but at home they spoke their mother-tongue and retained all the ancestral customs of their people. They were tested by the Stanford–Binet, with omission of the vocabulary item. The median IQ of the whole group was 97, and the mode fell in the range 96–105; one child attained an unspecified IQ in the range 136–145.

Although Yeung's experiment was made at such an early date and on such a small scale, the result it gave is representative of nearly all that have succeeded it. The fact is that the IQs of Mongolid children in North America are generally found to be about the same as those of Europids, though in some cases their bilingual habit depresses their marks in those items in which verbal proficiency is particularly important. In non-verbal tests they often surpass the Europids. A few more examples will be given, to confirm this statement. The general tendency towards a single conclusion makes it unnecessary to quote a large number. The contrast with the Negroes is striking.

T. Fukuda, of Northwestern University, carried out a small study of Japanese children in Denver, Colorado.[371] They comprised all the forty-three Japanese children aged three to twelve, of both sexes, who were available in the city; thus they were an unselected group. Their parents were all immigrants and belonged to various socio-economic classes. The children spoke Japanese at home but English at school. Like Yeung, Fukuda used the Stanford–Binet test. He omitted the vocabulary item and one other that required fluency in English, but provided suitable alternatives for these. The median IQ of the whole group was found to be 95; of those of the children who attended public schools, 97. One girl aged ten years and two months, who had been born in Japan, attained an IQ of 143.

The two studies that have been briefly recorded above were made on small numbers of children. A much larger investigation, planned by Professor P. Sandiford of Toronto University, was carried out by Miss Ruby Kerr on an unselected group of 276 Japanese and 224 Chinese boys and girls attending public elementary schools in Vancouver. The Pintner–Paterson Performance Test was used, and the home-language difficulty thus avoided. The median IQ of the Japanese (sexes not treated separately) was 114·2; of the Chinese 107·4. No fewer than 80% of the total Japanese group and more than 71% of the Chinese equalled or exceeded the median score of the Europid children of the vicinity, with whom they were compared. Sandiford concluded that the Japanese were 'the most intelligent racial group resident in British Columbia with the Chinese a more doubtful second'. He obviously uses the word 'intelligent' in the sense usual in the literature of psychometry, to mean superior in cognitive ability. He attributes the superiority of the Japanese to differential migration ('selection'), but does not support this surmise by factual evidence.[928, 927]

Four different methods of scoring the Pintner–Paterson Performance Test are recognized, and the results they give differ to some extent. Miss Kerr used the 'year scale' method, and her figures for mental age (and thus IQ) were derived from this. In reporting the results obtained, Sandiford states that the year-scale method gives 'substantially accurate' results, 'a trifle higher than the true values'. There cannot be much discrepancy, since this has been shown to give a correlation coefficient of 0·81 with 'Binet' (? Stanford–Binet).[928]

An extensive investigation of Japanese children was made by a group under the direction of Terman, and reported in great detail by M. L. Darsie.[249] The testees covered by the main part of the report were 570 unselected children aged ten to fifteen, attending schools in the cities and towns of California. They were fluent in English, but their parents almost without exception spoke Japanese in their homes. The tests used were the complete Stanford–Binet and the Army beta. By good fortune the original standardization of both these tests had been carried out on urban Europid children of the same state. The median IQ of the Europid children, by Stanford–Binet, was 99·5; of the whole Japanese group aged ten to fifteen, 89·5. Many of the older Japanese children had left their schools, and it was felt that the older ones who remained behind were somewhat unrepresentative. The median IQ of the ones aged ten to thirteen was approximately 91. One of the most significant parts of Darsie's report is his analysis of the way in which the Japanese and Europid testees responded to the separate items in the Stanford–Binet test. The Japanese were found to be inferior in the definitely linguistic items. The following table will serve as an example of the difference between the two sets of testees when faced with an item of this type.

| Vocabulary item at level intended for children aged | Percentage of 12-year-old testees who passed in this item | |
|---|---|---|
| | Japanese | Europid |
| 10 years | 37 | 100 |
| 12 years | 9 | 65 |
| 14 years | 2 | 20 |

In those items, however, in which the verbal element was small or absent, the Japanese equalled or surpassed the Europids. For instance, they did better than the Europids in the induction item, which depends far less on environmental circumstances than does knowledge of words.

The non-verbal Army beta test was regarded as suitable only for the younger children. The Japanese testees aged ten and eleven got almost exactly the same mean scores as their Europid counterparts; at age twelve the Japanese were markedly superior.

The reader is referred to pp. 485–6 for a description of the investigation of the mental abilities of American schoolchildren of all races carried out in 1965 under the auspices of the U.S.A. Department of Health, Education, and Welfare.[216] In verbal ability, in which the Mongolids were necessarily at a disadvantage, the median score of the Europids was greater than that of the Mongolids in all five grades. In non-verbal ability the median scores of the Mongolids were superior to those of the Europids in three grades (including both tests set to grade 3), and equal in two; the median scores of the Europids surpassed those of the Mongolids in two grades.

'Equal' in the preceding paragraph means that the median marks of the Mongolids fell at approximately the middle range of the seven Europid medians. In grade 12 not every Europid regional subgroup surpassed the Mongolids in verbal ability (on median marks); nor, in the same grade, did the latter surpass every Europid regional subgroup in non-verbal ability.

In both verbal and non-verbal tests (including both the non-verbal tests set to the children of grade 3), and in all the five grades, the median marks of the Mongolids exceeded those of the Negroes, in all the latter's eight regions, by wide margins in every case. The median score of the Mongolids also exceeded that of the Indianids in every case.

## INDIANIDS

Apart from the Eskimids, there are four rather distinct Indianid subraces in North America. It is not possible to treat them separately in respect of cognitive ability, because many of the tests have been administered at schools that have drawn their pupils of this race from all parts of the United States, and have thus included members of all four subraces.

The most extensive investigation of the cognitive ability of Indianids has been that carried out under the auspices of the U.S.A. Department of Health, Education, and Welfare in 1965 (see pp. 485–6).[216] In this study, as in all other comparable ones that include verbal items, the Indianid schoolchildren were at a disadvantage in relation to Negroes, since many of them did not speak English as their mother-tongue, or at any rate not as their only everyday language; and further, it is thought that their cultural environment was less well adapted to succcess in the tests than that of the Negroes. Nevertheless, the median marks of the Indianids exceeded those of the Negroes in all five school grades (1, 3, 6, 9, 12), in both verbal and non-verbal tests, including both the non-verbal tests set to children in grade 3.

It must be mentioned that in the verbal ability test set to grades 3 and 12 and in the non-verbal test set to grade 1, the median Indianid marks exceeded the medians attained by *most but not all* of the eight regional subgroups of Negroes.

In none of the five school grades, either in verbal or in non-verbal tests, did the Indianid median mark reach that of the Mongolids.

In each one of the five grades, in tests of both verbal and non-verbal ability, the Europids of every one of the eight regions (including that in which they did worst) surpassed the Indianids in median marks.

In tests of non-verbal ability set to grades 3 (both tests), 9, and 12, the median marks of the Indianids approached that of the regional group of Europids that did worst (that is to say, the Non-metropolitan south region in each case).

Although one may make full allowance for the linguistic disadvantage suffered by the Indianids in verbal tests, one can scarcely fail to be surprised by the low IQs and marks that have been reported in certain cases, even when competent testers have used reliable tests. Garth, for instance, administered two different verbal group-tests to three large groups of Indianids of several different tribes attending United States Indian Schools, and reported median IQs in the lower 70s and even down to the upper 60s. [389] As one would expect, they generally do much better in non-verbal tests, but even here there are exceptions. A pupil of Garth's administered the Pintner Non-Language Test to a group of 667 Indianid children, and recorded a median IQ of only 71·6. [389]

Such a low figure as this with a non-verbal test is not characteristic of Indianids. Jamieson, himself an Indianid, administered the Pintner–Paterson Performance Test to Iroquois schoolchildren in southern Ontario, and obtained a median IQ of 92·5. With the Pintner Non-Language (the same test as that by which Garth's pupil had recorded such a very low IQ with a different set of testees), he found a median IQ of no less than 96·9.[548] It is perhaps significant that all Jamieson's testees in southern Ontario had some element of Europid ancestry, though few of them had so much as a Europid parent or grandparent.

There is one particular study of Indianids that merits special consideration, because it provides one of the best examples of the use of hybridity in attempts to estimate the effect of race on cognitive ability. The investigation in question was carried out by Hunter and Sommermeir, of the University of Kansas, at an Indian Institute in that state.[528] The testees were 711 schoolchildren of both sexes, aged fourteen and over. They had come to the Institute from all over the U.S.A., and no fewer than sixty-five tribes and fourteen different tribal mixtures were represented. Nearly two-thirds of them, however, were Europid–Indianid hybrids. There was in no case any evidence of Negro forbears. By good fortune the ancestry of every child has been inscribed in the school records, and it was thus possible to classify them all in one of the following groups:

$\frac{4}{4}$ = non-hybrid Indianids

$\frac{3}{4}$ = all degrees of hybridity below $\frac{4}{4}$ down to $\frac{3}{4}$ (the latter fraction indicating three Indianid and one Europid grandparent)

$\frac{1}{2}$ = two Indianid and two Europid grandparents

$\frac{1}{4}$ = all degrees of hybridity with Europids less than $\frac{1}{2}$ (but the great majority of the $\frac{1}{4}$s had one Indianid and three Europid grandparents)

The symbols and their meanings are taken from Hunter and Sommermeir's paper. A closely (but not exactly) similar notation has been used in the present book (p. 472) in describing Ferguson's work on hybridity in Negroes.

The children were subjected to the Otis Group Intelligence Test. The median marks of the Indianids and hybrids, to the nearest unit, were as follows: $\frac{4}{4}$, 67; $\frac{3}{4}$, 78; $\frac{1}{2}$, 91; $\frac{1}{4}$, 109. For comparison it must be mentioned that the median mark of American Europids aged 15 is 122·6. A positive correlation was found to exist between the marks scored and the number of months that the testees had spent at the school, and also between their marks and ages. It was possible, in the statistical analysis of the results, to make accurate allowance for these two factors, in working out the correlation between degree of hybridity and marks. It was found that there was a correlation of $-0.41$ between the proportion of Indianid ancestry and the marks obtained.

The authors say, '... we get a correlation of $+0.41$ for degree of Indian blood and total score with the factors of age and months of schooling constant.' It is unquestionable that '$+0.41$' should be '$-0.41$'. In their own words, 'There is a significant positive [sic] relation between degree of Indian blood and score, the score falling as degree of white blood falls.'

The fact that the Otis Test is partly verbal may have played some part in the result; but of the three items that the testees found most difficult, only one was verbal. It is noteworthy that the $\frac{3}{4}$ testees scored considerably higher mean marks than the $\frac{4}{4}$. It is rather difficult to believe that one Europid grandparent, probably living in a remote part of the U.S.A. or perhaps dead, could have had much influence of an environmental kind on success in verbal items. The experiment supports the evidence for a genetic difference in cognitive ability between the Europid and Indianid races.

The evidence suggests that the Indianids tend, on average, to be superior in cognitive ability to the Negroes of North America, but inferior to the Mongolids and Europids of that country.

# 26 Racial differences in achievement
## I. Introduction

PSYCHOLOGISTS OFTEN use the word 'intelligence' as a technical term meaning cognitive ability. Professor E. G. Boring is quoted as saying (perhaps in jest) that intelligence, by definition, is what intelligence tests measure.[127] It must once again be regretted that the unquestionable value of cognition tests should be lessened by the attachment of a wrong label to them. The label has misled the general public as to what it is that they assess. Achievement in the intellectual field does indeed require cognitive ability, but it requires a great deal else besides. Intelligence is what is needed, in the wide sense in which that word is used in ordinary speech.

It may be useful to quote a few definitions of intelligence, to give an impression of their diversity. Several authors, especially those who wrote in the early days of cognition testing, adopted an eminently practical attitude. They were thinking of intelligence as operating in the world of everyday experience, without much regard for the use of the mind in highly intellectual studies. In his last paper Binet lists and discards five definitions, and then tells us 'his favourite theory' about the meaning of the word. 'Intelligence', he tells us, 'reveals itself by the best possible adaptation of the individual to his environment.'[94] One can find in the literature a number of definitions that follow this line; for instance, 'conscious adaptation to new situations', 'the ability to utilize previous experience in meeting new situations', and 'the ability to act effectively under given conditions'. William Stern, one of the most prominent German workers in the field of cognition testing in the second decade of the century, defined intelligence as 'the general ability of an individual to engage his thought consciously on new requirements; it is general mental ability to adapt to new tasks and conditions of life'.[1010] Other authors stress the practical use of what has been *learnt*. A nomenclature committee of the American Psychological Society, reporting in the 1920s, suggested alternative definitions: 'ability to learn and to utilize in new situations knowledge or skill acquired by learning', and 'selective adaptation through acquired knowledge'.[1118] Others, however, have looked on the word in quite a different light, regarding it as 'the power of attention', 'the ability to reason well and to form sound judgements', and 'the ability to think in abstract terms'. Some psychologists have adopted an almost despairing attitude towards the attempt to define it. Raven tentatively suggested 'an individual's innate disposition to modify his conduct in such a way that he continues to preserve his individuality in a changing environment'; but he doubted whether the word can be said 'to be anything more than a person's ability to do what an examiner thinks is "intelligent"'.[879] Spearman went further still. 'In the last act,' he concluded, 'the truth stands revealed, that the name really has no definite meaning at all; it shows itself to be nothing more than a hypostatized word, applied indiscriminately to all sorts of things.'[995] One may perhaps wonder what Spearman meant by the word 'hypostatized' in this connection.

It seems gradually to have dawned on those who invented what they called 'intelligence tests' that it might be worth while to have a look at what the great philosophers of the past had written about the activities of the human mind; and certain terms that Descartes, Leibnitz, Kant, and others had used began to appear during the 1920s in the writings of psychometrists.

The influence of Kant eventually became particularly important. In his *Critik der Urtheilskraft* he divides the faculties of the mind, taken as a whole, into three parts, namely, (1) *Erkenntnisvermögen* (cognitive faculty), (2) *Gefühl der Lust und Unlust* (feeling of pleasure and displeasure), and (3) *Begehrungsvermögen* (faculty of desire).[566] This classification, though well known on the Continent, appears to have been largely overlooked in Great Britain until introduced by William Hamilton, the Scottish philosopher of the so-called 'common sense' school, who used it in his lectures on metaphysics to the undergraduates of Edinburgh University from 1836–7 onwards.

It was Hamilton who brought the word 'cognitive' into common use in philosophy. The meaning of the term 'Cognitive Faculties' is explained in some detail in the posthumous edition of his lectures.[464] It will suffice here to say that he included under this term self-consciousness, the mental processes by which external objects are perceived, and the sensations derived from them, referred to external causes; retention of the information so received and its passage into the unconscious mind, with capacity for its recall; and what he called 'the Elaborative Faculty'; that is to say, essentially the ability to synthesize, analyse, and generalize the information received by the mind, and thus to reason by deduction and induction. These are the principal mental processes that are assessed by the best-known 'intelligence tests', and it is for this reason that I have substituted the term 'cognition tests' (p. 438).

Such tests, however, give no indication of the testee's mental faculties that belong to Kant's second category, which Hamilton called 'The phænomena of our Feelings, or the phænomena of Pleasure and Pain'; and it follows that a person may have high cognitive ability, but little or no feeling for value-judgements. But even if he has genuine interests in intellectual subjects, he will achieve nothing if he has not the ability to exert himself. As Binet and Simon remarked long ago, *'Un intelligent* [in their restricted sense of the word] *peut être très paresseux.'* For success in scholastic studies, as they admitted, 'there is need for qualities that depend above all on attention, will, character (for instance, a certain docility), a regularity of habits, and especially on continuity of effort'.[98] Yet, as Knight remarks in his book *Intelligence and intelligence testing*, 'a high degree of intelligence [cognitive ability is meant] is often accompanied by a temperamental aversion from continuous work, by a lack of persistence and perseverance'.[599]

Spearman himself, inventor of one of the most ingenious cognition tests (pp. 449–50) and discoverer of *g*, recognized the limitations of mental testing as usually applied. 'Obviously', he wrote, '. . . *g* alone would never make a big man of any sort. For it measures the cognitive aspect of mental activity.'[995]

It is arguable, however, that in this remark Spearman undervalues his own discovery of *g*. It would have been better if he had written, 'Obviously . . . cognitive ability alone would never make a big man of any sort;' for it would appear that *g* may indicate something in addition to cognitive ability. I have not seen nor heard any discussion of this subject, which appears to warrant study by psychologists and statisticians. Spearman did not originally derive his idea of 'general intelligence' or *g* from the results of cognition tests, but from data of scholastic attainment in classics, French, English, and mathematics; and indeed he took sensory functions into consideration.[993] Scholastic attainment involves the second and third as well as the first of Kant's three faculties of the mind.

Most of the methods available for the assessment of the non-cognitive factors involved in intellectual studies—the 'Feelings' and 'Conative powers', as Hamilton called them—are not nearly so objective as cognition tests. In psychological literature they are usually referred to as tests of personality or temperament (though some authors regard the former as a wider term that includes the latter[278]). Short descriptions of some of these are given in the textbooks of psychological testing (see especially Anastasi's[18]). They are useful for throwing light on people's suitability for various occupations. There is generally no question, however, of grading the testees in order of excellence. Indeed, in the brief instructions given to those about to answer Thurstone and Thurstone's *Personality schedule*,[1057] it is stated candidly that this is 'not a test in any sense because there are no right or wrong answers to any of the questions'. Persons filling up 'self-report inventories' may even in some cases have the deliberate intention to deceive.[18]

It seems possible, however, to gain some information about the conative faculty by objective means. The Pauli test, for instance, does measure the capacity for sustained mental effort of a particular kind.[899] It is applicable to anyone who has even the most rudimentary knowledge of mathematics. The testee is required to add together as many pairs of single-digit numbers as he can, during the period of one hour. He must work, from beginning to end of the test, at his maximum capacity for speed and accuracy. The test no doubt gives important information for certain purposes, but it may be doubted whether the results would be closely correlated with the ability to concentrate the mind mainly on one particular intellectual subject over a period of many months or years. Charles Darwin 'would say that he had the power of keeping a subject or question more or less before him for a great many years';[259] and this no doubt played a large part in his achievement.

What has been said on p. 496 may now be rewritten in the form of a short definition of intelligence, in the straightforward, everyday sense of that word. It is the ability to perceive, comprehend, and reason, combined with the capacity to choose worth-while subjects for study, eagerness to acquire, use, transmit, and (if possible) add to knowledge and understanding, and the faculty for sustained effort towards these ends (cf. p. 438). One might say briefly that a person is intelligent in so far as his cognitive ability and personality tend towards productiveness through mental activity.

One of the most obvious effects of intelligence is the ability to succeed in ordinary examinations at school or university, or in the similar ones that psychologists call 'achievement tests' but for which the term 'attainment tests' is preferred here. If all the testees subjected to such tests had experienced the same environments throughout life, the results would give some indication of their relative intelligences. In practice, the environments of all the testees have never been exactly the same; but relevant information bearing on the ethnic problem may nevertheless be obtained. The reader of Chapter 25 will remember that an enormous investigation of American schoolchildren was undertaken by the U.S.A. Department of Health, Education, and Welfare in 1965.[216] Two of the subjects of the tests (verbal and non-verbal ability) have already been considered, because they were essentially cognition tests; but there were also tests of 'reading comprehension', 'mathematics achievement', and 'general information', all three of which, with the possible exception of the first, were attainment tests. The second of these three subjects is the most significant for study here, because it is the least liable to be affected by home environment. The great majority of children acquire their knowledge of mathematics mainly at school, whereas general information depends to a large extent on parents' conversation and the availability of newspapers at home; and reading comprehension is affected by the mother-tongue of testees and by facilities provided at home for reading.

It will be remembered that in the investigation mentioned in the previous paragraph, the testees were examined together by group-tests in their classrooms, but that in the presentation of the results the Europids, Negroes, Mongolids, and Indianids were treated separately. For statistical purposes (calculation of median marks, etc.) the United States were divided into eight regions, and the Europids and Negroes were treated separately in each of these. The Mongolids and Indianids were not sufficiently numerous for this subdivision by territory to be considered necessary. The reader who requires fuller information about the general plan of the investigation should turn back to pp. 485–6 to refresh his memory.

The results of the 'mathematics achievement' test deserve study in some detail. The tests were set in this subject to all children in grades 3, 6, 9, and 12. It is convenient to begin by considering the relative attainments of Negroes and Indianids in this subject. In all four grades the median marks of the Indianids exceeded those of the Negroes of all the eight regions (though the Negroes of two of the eight regions came close in grade 6, and so did those of three of the regions in grade 9).

The median score of the Mongolids exceeded that of the Indianids in all four grades, generally by wide margins. In fact, in grades 6, 9, and 12 the median mark of the Mongolids almost exactly equalled or surpassed the 75th percentile of the Indianids; that is to say, those Indianids who attained the median mark of the Mongolids equalled or surpassed about 75% of the Indianid group as a whole.

Thus the Indianids surpassed the Negroes, and the Mongolids easily surpassed the Indianids. The Mongolids and Europids were much more nearly even. In grades 3 and 6 the median marks of the Europids of all eight regions did exceed the median marks of the Mongolids, but only by small margins. In grade 9 and also in grade 12 the median marks of the Mongolids exceeded those of the Europids of three of the eight regions; the median marks of the Europids of the remaining five regions exceeded the median marks of the Mongolids. It would be rash to draw any conclusion about the relative attainment-potential of Mongolids and Europids from the marks obtained by members of the two races in this investigation.

It is not necessary to institute comparisons between pairs of the four races in all their six possible permutations, as regards their attainments in the mathematical test, but one more may be mentioned. The Europids of that region in which they did worst in the test not only scored a higher median mark than did the Negroes of the region in which the latter did best; they did so much better than the Negroes that their median mark in the region in which they did *worst* exceeded the 75th percentile mark of the Negroes of the region in which the latter did *best*. All this applies to the tests in school grades 6, 9, and 12, and also in grade 3, with this exception. In this lowest of the four grades the Negroes of the two regions in which they did best scored a mark at the 75th percentile that *just* surpassed the median mark of the Europids of the region in which the latter did worst.

In view of the widespread belief that Negroes are at particular disadvantage in the southern schools of the U.S.A., it is worth remarking that the two regions in which the Negroes did their best in mathematics at grade 3 were the south Metropolitan and south-west Non-metropolitan.

The unreliability of cognition tests, taken by themselves, as indicators of potential intellectual attainment, has been revealed from time to time by investigations carried out on 'gifted' Europid children. It is appropriate at this point to mention the results of attainment tests administered to Negroes who had been shown to be gifted in cognitive ability by tests carried out previously.

Witty and Jenkins, the psychologists who had reported on the remarkable Negro girl 'B' (see pp. 487–8), subsequently made independent studies of Negroes who had registered high IQs several years earlier. Among eight thousand Negro children in grades 3–8 in the elementary schools of Chicago, Jenkins had detected 103 having IQs of 120 and above. Six years later, Witty and Theman traced 84 of these young people and administered to them attainment tests in English, social studies, mathematics, science, and understanding of contemporary affairs. [1145] In general, they found their attainment 'by no means' so outstanding as that reported in investigations of other groups of gifted children; but since some of the latter investigations were carried out on children with IQs of 140 and above, they finally concentrated their attention on the 24 Negroes who fell into this category. In general, the Negroes do not appear to have entirely lived up to the early promise suggested by their high cognitive ability revealed at the earlier test; but they seem to have surpassed the average attainment of the Europid population. It must be admitted, however, that the exact standards of comparison do not appear to be clearly indicated in every part of the report. Jenkins, in his paper 'The upper limit of ability among American Negroes', reached similar conclusions. He shows that although the highly gifted Negro child usually goes on to fulfil her or his early promise, failure is also frequent. [549]

Unfortunately 'B' does not appear to be mentioned in any follow-up report, but Witty and Theman do record a remarkable accomplishment by one of the children recorded in their study. This Negro boy graduated from grade 8 at the age of ten years and six months, and from the University of Chicago at sixteen; he went on to receive the degree of Doctor of Philosophy at nineteen.[1145] The authors do not say whether he revealed any evidence of hybrid ancestry.

The results of the mathematical attainment test briefly summarized above (pp. 498–9) are impressive, and it is possible to feel confident that the whole of the message they convey is attributable to environmental causes. In particular it seems unlikely that the environment of Indianids in the U.S.A. is better adapted to attainment in mathematics than that of Negrids. Nevertheless it remains 'true that some error might arise from environmental differences, even with tests in a subject so little affected (in most cases) by parental influence as mathematics; for the surroundings necessarily have more influence on the outcome of attainment tests of the usual type, even in this subject, than on those that assess cognitive ability.

One of the principal achievements of man has been the invention and development of language. The level of achievement in this respect varies widely among the different ethnic taxa. One of the most primitive languages that have been carefully studied is that of the Arunta, an Australid tribe sparsely scattered over a wide area in central Australia, chiefly southwards from the Macdonnell Range to the vicinity of Lake Eyre. When their speech was first recorded in the nineteenth century, there were some two thousand of them, but their numbers have greatly diminished since then. Those who recorded it were explorers and missionaries, untrained in the niceties of linguistics; and they fitted the words into the grammatical scheme of their own European tongues. A Norwegian linguist, Professor Alf Sommerfelt, who had never visited Australia, made a detailed study of everything that had been written about this language and came to certain remarkable conclusions.[990] The primary words are all of a single syllable, or have an *a* prefixed, and all are affirmations expressing actions or states. It follows that they are essentially verbs; but there is no part of the conjugation of a verb to which they can properly be assigned. They have been compared to gerunds,[310] but this would imply that they resemble nouns, and as Sommerfelt says, 'The Arunta language only expresses ... action and state; the notion of the object does not exist.' Nor is there any word classifiable as an adjective, for notions of quality are not directly expressed.

The words here described as primary are the *éléments formatifs* of the rest of the language, for they are agglutinated together to produce all the remaining words. All the *éléments formatifs* are words, and are therefore not to be regarded as prefixes or suffixes.

Only what is concrete is conveyed by the words of the Arunta language; abstract ideas do not appear to be represented. Even the words that designate time denote actions. Sommerfelt remarks that 'The absence of abstract ideas manifests itself especially in numeration;' for the words regarded by travellers and missionaries as numerals (there are, in fact, only two of fundamental character, translated by them as 'one' and 'two') are not properly to be so regarded, in Sommerfelt's opinion. The Arunta, he says, '... possesses nothing that he must necessarily count', and the words translated as numerals 'differ profoundly' from this category of words. The Arunta '... has no system of names for number'.

Sommerfelt freely admits the perplexity that a European must experience in trying to grasp the nature of the Arunta language.

> It is very difficult for us to understand a system that does not know our fundamental categories of noun, verb, adjective, and pronoun. ... ideas are much less differentiated than in modern languages. ... We must therefore emancipate ourselves from the conventions of the European grammarian and try to grasp the true character of the system. ... gestures play a large role. ... the words are practically incomprehensible if one does not know the situation in which they have been said.[990]

In the eighteenth century, long before there was any knowledge of so primitive a language as that of the Arunta, a great thinker had already suggested that the earliest words to be invented were probably verbs. Adam Smith added to the later editions of his *Theory of moral sentiments* some 'Considerations concerning the first formation of languages'.[978] In this article he suggests that the earliest words may have been impersonal verbs of the same type as the Latin *pluit*, *ningit*, and *tonat*, which unfortunately cannot be translated into English without introducing the abstract idea of 'it': '(it) rains', '(it) snows', '(it) thunders'. From such words as these, in Smith's opinion, there might arise a general concept of '(it) menaces', associated by usage with a word corresponding to the Latin *venit* ('(it) comes'). Only later in the evolution of language would a particular object come to be associated with this formerly impersonal verb, and thus the noun would originate ('the lion comes'). So far as I know, Adam Smith's anticipation of the type of language spoken by the Arunta and certain other Australid tribes has not been noticed.

If one were asked unexpectedly to name the greatest intellectual achievement of man and given no time for reflection, one's thoughts might turn first of all towards the work of some great philosopher or mathematician or scientist, or one might be inclined to suggest some marvellous modern advance in technology, such as the placing of a man on the moon; but on less hasty consideration one might perhaps be as likely to argue that the invention of parts of speech, and especially of the sentence, would qualify for this distinction. This invention appears to have been made independently in different ethnic taxa, and there is reason to believe that it must have been a product not of any society as a whole, but of its most intelligent members only; for when a language comes to be dominated by mass media of communication, even in highly civilized societies, the parts of speech tend to be blurred, the sentence to be corrupted, and ideas to be vaguely conveyed by the mere apposition of words without logical connections. Languages are often studied and learnt without any thought about differences in their potentiality for the precise transfer of information and ideas from one person to others; and it is relevant to the purpose of this book to consider which ethnic taxa have evolved the clearest and which the least clear methods of communication by words. The matter is complicated by the spread of language from one taxon to another, often with forgetfulness of its original tongue by a dominated people.

A language may reveal its superiority or inferiority, and that of those members of the taxon who were responsible for its origin and development, not only by its grammatical precision but also by the scope of meaning attached to its words; for this gives clear indication of the inductive capacity of its inventors. Take, for instance, the Akan languages, spoken by a compact group of Sudanid tribes on the Guinea Coast of West Africa. A student of this language, P. P. Brown, remarks that it is very rich in words denoting particular objects, but very poor in those that embrace related ones under a single term.[147] Thus, there are five unrelated words for baskets of different kinds, but there is no word for basket; the idea of classification seems scarcely to exist. There is a word that can be attached to *eat* or *sleep* to make *eat-time* or *sleep-time*, and another that converts them into *eat-place* and *sleep-place*; but these two conversion words are never used for the abstract ideas of *time* and *place*. The language is thus deficient in words involved in reasoning and abstract thought, but suffices for persons principally interested in objects that can be immediately perceived by the senses.

In the Akan language the same word is used to mean 'May I go?' 'Can I go?' 'Shall I go?' 'Must I go?' These ideas, respectively of permission, capability, futurity, and necessity, are not logically comprehensible under a single, wider idea. It must unfortunately be admitted, however, that in the deterioration of the English language through the media of mass communication, 'can' and 'could' are nowadays more and more frequently used to mean 'may' and 'might', and the superiority of English over Akan has thus begun to dwindle in the few decades since Brown published his article.

As Brown remarks, 'The basis of thought is the seeing of relationships,' and in this connection he notes the deficiency of Akan in prepositions.[147] Adam Smith had written on the significance of the preposition in relation to intellect long before. 'A preposition denotes a relation, and nothing but a relation,' he insists. 'But before men could institute a word, which signified a relation, and nothing but a relation, they must have been able, in some measure, to consider this relation abstractedly from the related objects .... The invention of such a word, therefore, must have required a considerable degree of abstraction.'[978] It is indeed true that the full and correct use of this part of speech is a good indication of intelligence in speakers of the Romance and English languages, and its invention in any language was a notable achievement.

The inadequacy of reasoning power evidenced by the absence of group-names for genuinely comparable objects (e.g. different kinds of baskets, in Akan) presents itself also to the zoologist when his studies take him into the society of primitive peoples. In the northern New Hebrides, for instance, I came across particular individuals who possessed considerable knowledge of the local fauna, and could name a large number of different species; but I was unable to obtain group-names for such familiar and obvious taxa as butterflies and beetles.

This is a matter, however, on which the English-speaking world should not pride itself unduly. One repeatedly hears the expression 'animals and birds'. What, then, are animals supposed to be? So far as one can make out, the word is used in common speech in reference to an entirely heterogeneous sample of animal life (mammals, particular reptiles, Amphibia, and a random assortment of several invertebrate taxa).

One must ask oneself whether the deficiency of a language is a cause or an effect. Brown does not commit himself as to whether Akan is deficient because its speakers' thought has been inadequate, or their thought is deficient because of the inadequacy of their language. Biesheuvel finds himself faced with the same problem in his study of Negrids (presumably mainly Kafrids) in South Africa. 'Racial groups have frequently been stigmatized as of inferior mentality', he says, 'because their language habits prevented them from thinking in the same way ... as Western man.'[85] May it not be that in this passage he puts the cart before the horse? Languages required to be invented (by gradual improvement over long periods), and those taxa that included a sufficient proportion of people possessing high capacity for logical and abstract thought invented languages suited to their intellectual needs.

It would be absurd to claim any superiority of all Europids over all Negrids, on the evidence of achievement in the intellectual field; yet it must be allowed that the contributions of Negrids to the world of learning have, on the whole, been disappointing, despite all the improvements in facilities for their education. American Negroes are better known for their mass appeal in public affairs and popular entertainment than for great achievements in such subjects as philosophy, mathematics, science, or technology.

Just as in the case of cognition tests, so also in this of intellectual achievement, the infrequency of notable success by Negroes is often attributed to environmental causes. It is necessary to hold constantly in mind that the characters of organisms, including man, are the result of interplay between genetic and environmental causes, and that in some cases (e.g. eye-colour and cognitive ability) the former prevails in a wide variety of circumstances.

It will be remembered, too, that evidence bearing on the differences between races in cognitive ability can be obtained by studies of hybrids (pp. 471–3 and 493–4). We are concerned here not with cognitive ability alone, but with all three factors of the mind involved in achievement in the intellectual field; and here again evidence is available from the same source.

From the nineteenth century onwards there have been numerous reports from Africa that the ruling families are distinguishable from their subjects by physical characters, and that these suggest a Europid (Aethiopid) element in their ancestry. To take only one example, Speke remarks that King Rumanika of Karagwe (west of the Victoria Nyanza) and also his sons 'had fine oval faces, large eyes, and high noses, denoting the best blood of Abyssinia'.[996] This was in a region where the bulk of the population was of the ordinary Kafrid type. Evidence from this source, however, is not of great value in the absence of conclusive proof that superior intelligence derived from Aethiopid ancestors had played a part in enabling the founders of such kingdoms to gain control of native populations. The evidence from hybrids living in the United States is much more valuable. It certainly appears that hybrids having a particularly large Europid element in their ancestry have played a dominant role in the struggle for the advancement of Negroes in American society. This is so, whether one looks at the first or the seventh and early part of the eighth decades of the present century.

Several authors were already calling attention to this matter in the first decade. H. S. Dickerman summarized the matter shortly and clearly enough in these words: 'There are full-blooded negroes of ability, but a very large proportion of those one sees in places of responsibility and honor among negroes are of mixed race. It is so with teachers, ministers, and physicians.'[273] G. S. Hall, writing in an educational journal in 1905, mentioned eight of the most prominent Negroes of his time and called attention to the fact that neither they, nor a score of other comparable persons, were typical members of their race.[460] He mentions that not only quadroons and octoroons, but also those with only one sixteenth or one thirty-second part of Negro ancestry, or even less, were regarded as Negroes, without qualification. A. H. Stone, writing a few years later, made exactly the same point: 'Practically all the so-called Negroes of distinction are not real Negroes at all,' he claimed; and in another part of the same book, 'There can no longer be a question as to the superior intelligence of the mulatto over the Negro—of his higher potential capacity.... the Negro masses [are] almost invariably led by the mulatto.'[1015] In the same year R. S. Baker made the same point in a book written to support the Negro cause. 'This much', he remarked, 'I know from my own observation: most of the leading men of the race to-day in every line of activity are mulattoes.'[50] Like Hall, he made a list of them. Several occur in both lists (Dr. W. E. B. Du Bois, sociologist, leader of the radical intellectual group working for the Negro cause; C. W. Chesnutt,* the novelist; H. O. Tanner, a celebrated artist; Booker T. Washington, educationist). Baker's contribution to the subject is, however, much more important than Dickerman's, Hall's, or Stone's, for he provides clear photographs of some of the 'Negroes' he mentions. So far as morphological characters are concerned, Du Bois shows no indication of Negrid ancestry, apart from a slightly swollen lower lip; Chesnutt, Tanner, and Mary Church Terrell (educationist) show no trace whatever. In these persons there may have been slight darkening of the skin, though the photographs do not reveal it. Baker says that he met men and women who asserted that they were Negroes, but whom he could only regard as such 'in defiance of the evidence of my own senses'.[50]

Booker Taliaferro Washington seems by his own account in *Up from slavery*[1120, 1121] to have been the son of a Europid father. R. S. Baker describes him as a mulatto.[50] Photographs show that his lips were not very thick,† and his ear was large, with large, free lobe.[50, 557, 1120] At the age of twenty-three or thereabouts he had a 'flowing' moustache.[507] Sir Harry Johnston, who met him at Tuskegee in 1908, describes him as having 'an odd look of an Italian about him' and a complexion resembling pale *cafe-au-lait*.[558] The evidence suggests that his father was a man named Tagliaferro, either born in Italy or of Italian descent, who was an overseer in the slave plantation where Booker Washington was born.[558] His mother was certainly a Negress. His most obviously Negrid morphological features were the somewhat prognathous jaw and 'funnel-shaped' nose (cf. p. 331 and Fig. 60C).

* The spelling of Chesnutt's name varies in different texts.

† Sir Harry Johnston says in one of his books [558] that Washington's lips were 'Negroid', but photographs, including one in another book by Johnston himself,[557] contradict this statement.

The case of George Carver is not so clear-cut. It seems to be generally assumed that he was of purely Negrid stock; and Sir Harry Johnston, who had had very extensive experience of Negrids in various parts of Africa before he met him at Tuskegee, describes him in one book as 'an absolute Negro'[557] and in another as 'a full-blooded Negro'.[55] Nevertheless, a photograph[507] and drawing[863] show that he had a strongly projecting nose, large ears with large, free lobes, and a thick moustache. Indeed, one of his biographers describes him at the age of thirty-six as having 'handlebar moustaches' and 'the beak of a nose, rather Semitic, jutting from between deep-set eyes'.[507]

It has already been indicated that the bearing of hybridity on achievement in the intellectual field could have been presented equally well by examples taken from the 1960s and early 1970s instead of from the early years of the century. I have made a small collection of photographs of some of the most distinguished American Negroes of modern times, which bears this out. Copies of these could be made available for study by physical anthropologists interested in the problem.

# 27 Racial differences in achievement
## II. Civilization

IT IS arguable that the clearest evidence of the superiority of a race might be derived from the ability of its members, or some of them, to create a civilization. The difficulty in applying this argument lies in the definition of the crucial word. There are some, indeed, who claim that civilization cannot be defined, and others who define it in such a way as to defend narrowly conceived political ideas. Others, Sommerfelt[991] and Radin[871] among them, evade the issue by calling the cultures of even the most primitive societies their 'civilizations'. No one, surely, should be at a loss who has actually lived in an advanced and also in a primitive society. It is scarcely credible that such a person could not observe differences and express them in words. An attempt at a definition will be made here. The word 'civilization' will refer throughout to a particular state of society, not to the process of its creation.

An attempt at a realistic definition of civilization was made nearly a century ago by the American anthropologist Lewis H. Morgan, who had had wide practical experience of human societies at different levels of culture.[766] He recognized three grades or 'statuses', to which he gave the names of 'Savagery', 'Barbarism', and 'Civilization'. The first two names are admittedly unfortunate, for some of the people at the lowest grade (essentially the food-gatherers, who do not cultivate their sources of nutriment) have not been savage in the ordinary sense of the word, except when provoked by intolerable persecution inflicted by persons nominally of higher grades; and 'barbarians' is a needlessly offensive word for people of the intermediate status. Nevertheless the classification, apart from the terms used, has its merits.

Morgan assigns people to the intermediate grade if they have started to make pottery; and they still remain in this grade when they begin to domesticate animals or to use irrigation in the cultivation of plants. At the most advanced level of the intermediate status they invent the smelting of iron from its ores. The crucial separation of civilization from the intermediate status is placed by Morgan at the invention of the phonetic alphabet and 'the use of writing in literary composition'. He allows that hieroglyphic writing on stone may be admitted as an equivalent.

Morgan may have been right in supposing that the use of a script, as opposed to a series of pictures representing a succession of events, is the most salient distinguishing feature of a civilized society. It is open to anyone to choose a single feature that seems to him to separate civilized from uncivilized societies, but it is unlikely that any particular criterion would command wide acceptance. It seems best to avoid all sophistication in this matter and simply make a list of the most obvious features by which societies, commonly regarded as civilized in the everyday sense of the word, are distinguished from others to which this term is not ordinarily applied. No two persons would make exactly the same list; but I think it probable that most people would regard a society as civilized if a considerable majority of the requirements listed below were satisfied. No society exists or ever has existed in which all the requirements were satisfactorily fulfilled. In the case of certain extinct cultures, many of the items on the list cannot help one in reaching a decision, because there is not enough reliable information. There may be no decipherable script that gives sufficient information about the daily life and customs of the people. In such cases one can only be guided by the special excellence or inferiority of the artifacts that have resisted decay, or by the writings of explorers who visited the country in question before the culture was changed through external influence.

It may be suggested, then, that in societies ordinarily regarded as civilized, the majority of the people comply with most of the following requirements.

1. In the ordinary circumstances of life in public places, they cover the external genital organs and the greater part of the trunk with clothes. (This is mentioned first, because the fact of a person's being naked or clothed is usually his or her most immediately obvious feature.)

2. They keep the body clean and take care to dispose of its waste products.

3. They do not practise severe mutilation or deformation of the body, except for medical reasons.

4. They have knowledge of building in brick or stone, if the necessary materials are available in their territory.

5. Many of them live in towns or cities, which are linked by roads.

6. They cultivate food-plants.

7. They domesticate animals and use some of the larger ones for transport (or have in the past so used them), if suitable species are available.

8. They have a knowledge of the use of metals, if these are available.

9. They use wheels.

10. They exchange property by the use of money.

11. They order their society by a system of laws, which are enforced in such a way that they ordinarily go about their various concerns in times of peace without danger of attack or arbitrary arrest.

12. They permit accused persons to defend themselves and to bring witnesses for their defence.

13. They do not use torture to extract information or for punishment.

14. They do not practise cannibalism.

15. Their religious systems include ethical elements and are not purely or grossly superstitious.

16. They use a script (not simply a succession of pictures) to communicate ideas.

17. There is some facility in the abstract use of numbers, without consideration of actual objects (or in other words, at least a start has been made in mathematics).

18. A calendar is in use, accurate to within a few days in the year.

19. Arrangements are made for the instruction of the young in intellectual subjects.

20. There is some appreciation of the fine arts.

21. Knowledge and understanding are valued as ends in themselves.

A few words must be added about items 20 and 21. These are overlooked or underrated in societies in which art is vulgarized and nothing valued unless it serves crudely sensual or materialistic ends. Gobineau's comment on this subject is worth quoting: '. . . material well-being has never been anything but an external appendage of civilization.'[409] Toynbee has suggested that as an 'identification-mark' (but not as a definition), civilization might be equated with '. . . a state of society in which there is a minority of the population, however small, that is free from the task, not merely of producing food, but of engaging in any other of the economic activities—e.g. industry and trade'.[1063] This freedom of a minority is indeed relevant to items 20 and 21, but much must depend on the way in which it is used. There have been societies, properly regarded as uncivilized, in which about one-half of the adult population possesses the freedom in question (see p. 399).

Item 21 overlaps item 15, in so far as knowledge and understanding prevail against superstition.

A few of the requirements (nos. 2, 13, 20) have been met by certain peoples still at the stage of food-gatherers, and several others by those at Morgan's intermediate status ('Barbarism', as he called it). In seeking to arrive at a judgement, one would bear in mind that some of the items (such as nos. 11–14) are more important than others; and particular excellence in those of them in which much variation is possible (e.g. nos. 16–18) should be offset against deficiencies in others. The extremes of variation are to be found in such subjects as mathematics (no. 17). In recent times there have been subraces and even perhaps whole races in which mathematics may be said to have been non-existent, while already in the remote past members of certain Europid subraces had made considerable advances in several major branches of this subject. For instance, an algebraic equation and its solution are given in an Egyptian papyrus of about 1550 B.C.,[179] and this document is said to have been founded on a much earlier work.[793]

In this chapter we are concerned primarily with the ability of members of various races to *originate* civilization. There seems to be little doubt that this status arose independently more than once in the course of history, and cultural interchange between one self-civilizing society and another seems to have been sporadic, and not important in the early stages. The cultures that appear (1) to qualify as civilized, (2) to have been built up at the start with little or no influence from any other contemporary civilization, and (3) subsequently to have given rise to great civilizations in other parts of the world, are the Sumerian (or Sumero-Akkadian), ancient Egyptian, Helladic-Minoan, Indus Valley, and Sinic. All other undoubted civilizations appear to have derived, directly or indirectly, from these, in some cases from more than one of them.

The development of civilization naturally stretched over a very long period in each of the societies in which it arose independently or nearly so, and it would be futile to name a date on which the process could be regarded as having been brought to completion. Nevertheless, the order in which the five civilizations just mentioned arose is more or less clear, and very rough dates may be suggested. Few would deny that the Sumerian is the earliest civilization of which we have concrete knowledge, and one would probably not be very far out if one suggested that it dated from the last half of the fourth millennium B.C. The Egyptian was a little later, about the turn of the millennium; the Helladic-Minoan somewhere in the first half of the third, the Indus halfway through it, and the Sinic considerably later than the others, halfway through the second millennium B.C. Different authorities would naturally give other dates, according to their differing criteria of civilization.

A question of fundamental importance for the ethnic problem now arises, to which everything that has so far been said in this chapter directly leads. To what races did the peoples belong who originated civilizations? Two chief sources of information are available for the solution of this problem: the representations of themselves left for posterity in their works of art, and the remains of the bodies that they interred in their cemeteries.

It is convenient to begin with the earliest of all civilizations, though the temporal order will not be maintained throughout, for reasons that will become apparent.

The Sumerian civilization is often called the Sumero-Akkadian, but the Akkadians learnt much from the Sumerians, and we are concerned here with origins. There is no intention to disparage the Akkadians, for at later stages they added much to the joint civilization properly termed Sumero-Akkadian.

The Sumerian artists left an abundant supply of images, mostly bas-reliefs in profile view, intended to represent the two kinds of people that formed the population of the southern parts of Mesopotamia in ancient times. The shaven heads and faces of the Sumerians stand in sharp contrast to the long-haired and heavily bearded Akkadians; but in the early period, before the incursion of Armenids into any part of the region, the physical features of the peoples, as opposed to their differences in coiffure and clothing, were not very marked. In their own representations of themselves the Sumerians generally appear with protruding occiput and extremely receding forehead. The pointed nose projects strongly forward; it is narrow, with small alae, and straight or slightly convex; the chin and mouth are small, the lips narrow, the eyes and ears large (Fig. 81, p. 510).[737, 580] The strong projection of the pointed nose, combined with the recession and insignificance of the chin, give a curiously birdlike appearance, which is emphasized when the nose is slightly convex. Almost any book on Sumerian civilization will provide numerous examples (e.g. Delaport,[266] Fig. 3; King,[580] Figs. 3–5). The figurines are mostly less reliable as images than the bas-reliefs, because in so many cases the pointed noses have been blunted accidentally.

There is no known human taxon, past or present, that presents precisely this form of head and face. The closest approach to it that I have been able to find anywhere is given by two photographs in which Kurds are seen in profile view. These are in papers by Chantre[204] (the top left figure in his Plate XIII) and von Luschan[685] (Fig. 2 in his Plate XXIV). If one somewhat exaggerates the features seen in these photographs, one has an approximation to those that the Sumerian artists were accustomed to provide; but rather a wide variety of types is found among the Kurdish population.

81    *A shell-inlay plaque, to show the Sumerian head as usually represented in the early period*

The site is unknown (possibly Uruk). *Ashmolean Museum, Oxford.*

A considerable proportion of the Kurdish people are fair, with blue eyes. The colouring of the Sumerians does not appear to be known. The Kurds are sometimes described as 'Proto-Nordic', but there does not appear to be any strong reason, based on morphological features, for not attaching them to the Mediterranid-Orientalid-Nordindid group of taxa. Chantre considered them as descendants of the Kushites, who seem to have been the main element in the population of the country round the Persian Gulf in ancient times.[203]

For more reliable information one naturally turns to the bones left behind in the cemeteries of ancient peoples of this part of the world.

During the last few millennia before Christ, in the periods of the Sumero-

Akkadian and Indus Valley civilizations, two types of human beings having different skull forms were very widely distributed in the countries we now call Iraq, Iran, and Pakistan. It will be convenient to include skulls from Iran in this discussion, although the civilizations with which we are primarily concerned are those of Mesopotamia and the Indus Valley. Every scrap of information about the ancient skulls of this whole region is worth using, for the material is pitifully scarce. It is a sad fact that in searching in the Near East for every little piece of pottery or other artifact of former times, archaeologists have sometimes actually thrown away the skeletal remains disclosed in the course of their excavations.[681]

The British anthropologists Dudley Buxton and Talbot Rice[177] found both types of skulls among human remains excavated at the Sumerian palace at Kish in Mesopotamia, and at a near-by mound. These remains were assigned to the eighth to fifth centuries B.C. The same or similar two types were found again by the French anthropologist H. V. Vallois among remains collected at Sialk, halfway between Tehran and Isfahan, some 415 miles east by north of Kish, in deposits extending in date from before the beginning of the age of metals up to the ninth century B.C.[1083] More than a thousand miles east-south-east from here is Mohenjo-Daro, one of the best-known sites of the Indus Valley civilization, and here again the same two types of skulls were found by Col. R. B. S. Sewell and Dr. B. S. Guha of the Zoological Survey of India.[961]

The civilization of the Indus Valley is often called 'Chalcolithic', because copper and bronze had not entirely replaced stone in making certain implements. As Mackay points out, the term used might suggest that the civilization was rather primitive, which is very far from being true. The stone implements are ribbon flakes of flint, serving as cheap knives.[694]

The physical anthropologists mentioned above give detailed descriptions of each skull. The following account is an attempt to give an impression of each of the two types by compressing the mass of available information into short statements. Actually there was a considerable amount of variation.

In one type the skull is dolichocranial, or just beyond the borderline to mesocranial; it is 'well-filled', but rather small. Superciliary ridges are slight, and the glabella scarcely projects; the forehead does not recede strongly (indeed, it is almost vertical in specimens regarded as female); the vault is rather high. The pterion is spheno-parietal. Muscular impressions are not strongly marked. The face is rather long. The zygomatic arches recede (i.e., the face has no tendency to flatness). The orbits are moderately high. The nasion is not much depressed; the bony bridge of the nose is narrow and projects considerably. The nasal aperture falls into the category of mesorrhine; its lower border is usually (but not always) oxycraspedote. The palate is rather elongated, and there is a tendency to slight prognathism. The mandible is rather feebly built, but the chin is fairly prominent.

The few available long bones suggest that the stature was rather low.

The skulls of this type are obviously Europid. Buxton and Rice say that in many ways they resemble the Mediterranean; Sewell and Guha say more definitely, 'This type of skull we consider to represent the true Mediterranean race' (i.e. the Mediterranid subrace). Vallois assigns it to the *type proto-méditerranéen* on the grounds that the structure is coarser than in modern

Mediterranids, the ridges more marked, and the cranial index slightly lower. It is permissible to describe the skulls of this type as in a broad sense Mediterranid, with the reservation that Orientalids and Nordindids have very similar skulls, so that certainty on this point is not easily reached when no other part of the body is available for comparison.

Such differences as exist between these three subraces reside chiefly in the soft parts of the body,[302] and in frequencies of the genes for blood-group 'B' and of the set of Rhesus factors (cf. Schwidetzky [953]). Indeed, the Nordindids were formerly termed *die ostmediterrane Rasse*.[302] Vallois regards the Orientalids as a subdivision of the Mediterranids (or, to use his terminology, the *race sud-orientale* is a *sous-race* of the *race méditerranéenne*); and he says that the Nordindids (*race indo-afghane*) do not differ fundamentally from the Mediterranids. [1085]

The skulls of the second type found at Kish, Sialk, and Mohenjo-Daro are also described in detail by the authors mentioned above. Once again there is considerable variation, but it is possible to form an impression of the general type. An attempt is made in the following paragraph to condense the main facts into a short statement.

The skull is thick-walled and extremely dolichocranial (hyper- and even in one case ultradolichocranial), as a result of the exceptionally long extension of the occiput behind the external auditory meatus. It is 'ill-filled', for the sides rise almost vertically, and then, as they turn inwards towards the middle line, they are again somewhat flattened, and there is in some cases a keel-like ridge where they meet (i.e., the skull is scaphocranial); but the cranial capacity is remarkably high. The glabella and supraciliary ridges are prominent and the forehead recedes behind them; but the cranium rises to a high vault (i.e., it is hypsicranial). The muscular impressions are strongly indicated, and those of the temporal muscles are situated exceptionally close to the middle line. The zygomatic arches do not recede quite so much as those of the Mediterranid type.* The face is rather long, like that of the Mediterranids. The orbits are high. The nasion is markedly depressed. The bony bridge of the nose resembles that of the Mediterranids in being narrow, but it projects rather more strongly. The nasal aperture is mesorrhine or even platyrrhine; its lower border is usually oxycraspedote. There is marked subnasal and some general prognathy, and in correspondence with this the palate is very long. The mandible is robust, with powerful ramus, and the chin is powerfully developed. The bite is edge-to-edge, not overlapping.

The scanty remains of long bones again suggest rather low stature.

This brief description may be still further summarized by saying that the skull is in several ways rather primitive, but in strong contrast with this the cranial capacity is particularly high (higher than in Mediterranids).

A skull of remarkably similar form to this, with an almost complete skeleton, was discovered in 1909 in a deposit of early Aurignacian age at Combe-Capelle, near Montferrand in the Dordogne, central France. The discoverer was the enthusiastic archaeologist O. Hauser, who has left a graphic account of the circumstances in a paper containing excellent photographs and a detailed description of the skull and the rest of the skeleton by Professor H.

---

* It has been stated that the founders of the Indus Valley civilization were 'flat-faced'.[244] This cannot be substantiated. The term is not applicable to either of the peoples who formed almost the whole of the population of the Valley, so far as is known.

Klaatsch.[590] I take the opportunity to suggest the name Combe-Capellid, or Capellid for short (*aurignacensis* Hauser in Linnean nomenclature), for people of this type, who may be regarded as forming a subrace of the Europid race.

It is claimed that people of this type survive to this day in places scattered over western Europe and North Africa, and for that reason they have been called 'Eurafrican'. This, indeed, is the name applied by Buxton and Rice to the specimens of this type that were found at Kish, but unfortunately it is subject to strong objections. The name 'Eurafrican' had previously been used by Sergi [959] in an entirely different sense; and further, it is misleading, because it unintentionally suggests a Negrid element in the ancestry. Vallois' term '*type hyperdolichocéphale proto-iranien*' is too long for general use.

Sewell and Guha at first placed their Capellid skulls from Mohenjo-Daro in a 'Proto-Australoid race',[961] a surprising assignment in view of the very high cranial capacity (among other features); but later, when he had had the opportunity to examine Buxton's skulls at Oxford and Keith's at the Royal College of Surgeons, Guha became convinced that the hyperdolichocranial ones from Mohenjo-Daro were in fact 'Caucasic'[439] or 'Caucasian';[441] that is to say, Europid. It was Guha's opinion that Capellids entered what is now Pakistan during the Neolithic age, and have survived there and in India. 'Mixed with the long-headed Mediterranean race which constituted the major part of the Indus Valley people in Chalcolithic times,' he writes, 'it forms today the bulk of the population of the Peninsula and a considerable proportion of Northern India.'[439] He does not make it clear whether he uses the word 'mixed' to mean 'interspersed' or 'hybridized'. The latter seems the more probable, for it would probably be hard to find a typical Capellid among the population of India, Pakistan, or Bangladesh today.

A few brachycephalic skulls were found at Kish, and were regarded by Buxton and Rice as probably Armenoid.[177] Some were also found at Sialk, though none from the most ancient deposits. Vallois classified the older brachycephalic skulls as Armenoid, and provisionally assigned the more recent ones to the Alpine group.[1083] Sewell and Guha found two brachycephalic skulls at Mohenjo-Daro. They considered that one of these was Alpinid, while the other showed resemblances to certain Naga skulls.[961] It must be allowed, however, that Naga skulls do not by any means conform to a single type.

'No traces', say Buxton and Rice,[177] 'have as yet appeared of either Negroid or East Asiatic [Mongoloid] blood at Kish,' and with the exception of a single skull at Mohenjo-Daro, mentioned in the preceding paragraph, the same remark applies to the latter place and to Sialk.

At Kish and Mohenjo-Daro, then, the populations consisted mainly of Mediterranids (or some closely similar people) and Capellids. The majority of the skulls from Kish were Capellid,* of those from Mohenjo-Daro Mediterranid; but there were not enough from either place to justify the drawing of conclusions about the relative numbers in the populations. The numbers of Mediterranid and Capellid skulls found at Sialk were almost exact-

---

* Vallois [1083] makes a slip in saying that most of Buxton and Rice's skulls from Kish belonged to his *Groupe dolichocéphale II*, that is to say to the Mediterranid subrace. The British authors say clearly that most of their skulls were what they call 'Eurafrican'.

ly equal, but there were also quite a lot of brachycranials at this site, except in the earliest period.

Since the population of Kish consisted of Sumerians and Akkadians, one is tempted to pronounce one type of skull as Sumerian and the other as Akkadian, though puzzled to decide which is which. Buxton and Rice were themselves unable to decide whether the two types corresponded to the two elements in the population, whose dress, coiffure, and language are known from their monuments to have been so very different. The matter is complicated by the opinion of Sir Arthur Keith that there were not two types of skulls in ancient Mesopotamia, but only one variable type.[575]

Keith's skulls had been excavated by the joint British and American expedition led by Leonard Woolley.[461] Some of them had been obtained at Ur, others from the 'later cemetery' at the neighbouring site of Al-'Ubaid.[1157] There is no positive evidence of the presence of Akkadians at either of these two places, when the people represented by the skulls were living. Another ancient people, the prehistoric makers of painted pottery, had indeed occupied Al-'Ubaid in earlier times, but there is no indication that any of their remains were interred in the later cemetery. The archaeological evidence obtained by Woolley himself led him to conclude that the skulls from Al-'Ubaid studied by Keith were those of Sumerians belonging to the First to Third Dynasties. In one of them there was a clay vase, 'of a type that runs through virtually the whole period covered by the cemetery'; it bore an inscription in Sumerian characters. Woolley concluded that this evidence alone would suffice to show that the cemetery belonged to the fully developed Sumerian period. The skulls from Ur were from a very much later period. Woolley's estimate was between 1900 and 1700 B.C.

Keith regarded all the skulls from Al-'Ubaid and Ur as Sumerian and assigned them to a single taxon, which he identified as 'Arab' (presumably Orientalid). Having examined Buxton and Rice's specimens at Oxford, he maintained the same conclusion about these also. 'I have no doubt', he says, 'that the same race ['Arab'] now occupies the lower plains of the Tigris and Euphrates that occupied them in ancient times.'[575] He remarks that the diversity 'is not more than is met with in races [subraces] of mankind considered to be pure'; but it is difficult to accept this opinion.

It seems unlikely that one could find any modern Orientalid skull with such extreme Capellid characters as his No. II skull, shown in his Plates LXIII and LXIV. This skull has strongly marked glabella and supraciliary ridges, and the occiput projects enormously; the cranial wall is seven millimetres thick along the vault and ten at the parietal eminence. Keith admits his doubt when he makes this remark: 'It is possible that in no Arab community of today does there exist a group of individuals with such large heads, big brains, and massive jaws as those whose remains Mr. Woolley recovered at al-'Ubaid [i.e. the skulls from that site which he (Keith) studied and described].' Sewell and Guha place Keith's skulls Nos. I, II, III, IV, and VII (all from Al-'Ubaid) in the group here termed Capellid.[961]

A photograph in Keith's Plate LXVI shows that his skull No. VIII (from Al-'Ubaid) was orygmocraspedote.

There are skulls among those described by Keith that seem to fall into the

Mediterranid category (in the wide sense of that term), as well as Capellids and intermediates. It is not easy to draw a sharp dividing-line in his material, and the possibility of hybridization in southern Sumeria cannot be excluded. Vallois found no intermediates between the types here termed Mediterranid and Capellid in his material from Sialk.[1083]

Guha considered it probable that 'the Mediterranean group' were responsible for the origin of the Indus Valley civilization.[440] He appears to have based this opinion on the fact that skulls of this type were more numerous than Capellid ones in the available material.

What, then, is certain and what possible about the taxonomic position of the Sumerians and the founders of the Indus Valley civilization? Certainly there is no evidence of any Mongolid or Negrid element in these Europid people, nor were they Armenids (though members of the latter taxon played a large part in the later development of civilization in Babylonia). The people who originated civilization in Sumeria and the Indus Valley may have been Mediterranid (with the reservation mentioned on p. 512), or may have belonged to the somewhat similar Capellid taxon, or may indeed have belonged to both, and may have included hybrids between the two.

It may be remarked in passing that it would be useful to have a comprehensive name for the Mediterranids and the other peoples that cannot be clearly distinguished from them by cranial criteria. This might turn out to be a valid taxon.

The physical anthropologist finds himself confronted with new problems when he turns from Mesopotamia and the Indus Valley to the territories of the Helladic-Minoan civilization. He no longer has the support of detailed, skull-by-skull descriptions, conveniently arranged in large monographs. Instead he must rely mainly on short papers, many of them giving tantalizingly inadequate information on account of the fragility and incompleteness of the specimens. In some cases the investigator has actually feared to remove a skull from the deposit in which it lay lest he should damage it in the process, and has therefore taken such measurements as he could while it was still only partly exposed.[292] In many cases no information is available apart from the cranial index; indeed, from some accounts of the ancient peoples of Crete one might almost suppose that the task of the physical anthropologist was simply to determine this useful but very insufficient guide to taxonomic position. Another difficulty is that many of the descriptions are not accompanied by information about artifacts that would make possible the assignment of the human remains to a particular age.

There is not a great deal of trustworthy information about the physical characters of the 'pre-Greek' people of Greece who founded the Helladic civilization. These were presumably the 'Pelasgians' of classical Greek authors;[1022] but most of the ancient bones that have been found in Greece in the vicinity of the Helladic civilization cannot be referred with certainty to this or any other people mentioned in Greek literature.

As an example one may take Virchow's careful report on a considerable number of ancient skulls, which appear to have been a random lot from various localities.[1103] It seems scarcely possible to draw any general conclusions from what he says, except that the skulls he studied varied from ultradolichocranial to brachycranial, and that none of his descriptions fits the Capellid type.

Most of the early students of the subject, Sergi [958, 959] and Ripley [905] among them, considered that the country was originally inhabited by people of the 'Mediterranean race'. One branch of this taxon, called by Sergi the Pelasgi, were thought by him to have spread across the sea from a place near the present frontier between Libya and Egypt, some travelling to southern and eastern Italy, others to Pelasgia itself (Greece and the country surrounding the Black Sea), and others again to Crete. [958] Sergi coined the term *'Ellipsoides pelasgicus'* for a type of skull thought to be characteristic of this branch of the 'Mediterranean race'. Measurement of his photograph of a skull of this type, viewed from above, gives a cranial index of about 66·5 (ultradolichocranial).

Both Sergi and Ripley conclude that brachycephalic immigrants subsequently spread down from the north into Greece (mainly, it seems, from Albania, during the Christian era). It would not appear that later studies have disproved this opinion. Even in modern times the proportion of dolichocephalic people remains highest in the southern parts of Greece, in which the centres of Helladic civilization were situated.

In the earliest days there seems not to have been very much contact between Crete and the mainland, and the full influence of the island only began to be felt in Greece in the Late Helladic phase (from about 1550 B.C. onwards). [1022]

Our knowledge of the physical characters of the Cretan people in ancient times is moderately satisfactory, despite the fragility of the bones. Some of the earliest investigators, including Boyd Dawkins, [264] W. L. H. Duckworth, [292] and Felix von Luschan, [686] were first-rate anatomists, and they made good use of such material as they could obtain. Indeed, it is allowed at the present day that the information collected early in the century, from 1901 onwards, is still the best available. [531] It is not too much to say that Boyd Dawkins, with only a few skulls at his disposal, drew conclusions that have stood the test of time. He concluded that the early Cretan skulls he examined resembled those of the dolichocranial pre-Greek people of Attica (that is to say, of the region of the Helladic civilization); that this was the aboriginal taxon of the Mediterranean shores and islands; and that the invasion by round-headed peoples occurred subsequently. 'If this view be accepted,' he says, 'the skulls found by Mr. Hogarth in Crete belong to the small dark Mediterranean people, the oldest, if not the only, ethnical element in the Pelasgians of Crete.' [264] Duckworth studied ancient skulls and modern heads, and noted the change from a high percentage of dolichocranials (65% among males, 71% females) in ancient times to a preponderance of brachycephals in the population at the beginning of the present century. [292] Writing a couple of years later to add notes on a few more Early Minoan II and Late Minoan III skulls, Hawes found no reason to dispute Duckworth's conclusion, though he brought evidence that a few brachycephals were present in Crete from quite early times. [479] The general tendency for change from long-heads in the Middle Minoan to round-heads in the present century was confirmed by the comprehensive study published by von Luschan in 1913. [686]

The skulls that have been described in detail give no indication that there was ever any Capellid element in the ancient population of Crete.

A considerable number of long bones have been found in ancient Cretan cemeteries, and these give a uniform impression of the small stature of the old population. The estimated mean height of adult males in early Minoan I times was only about 163 cm (5' 4").[1067] This supports the evidence derived from skulls that the people were in fact Mediterranids.

As we have seen (pp. 509–10), the Sumerians' attempts at self-portraiture were rather crude and unrealistic, and therefore not of much assistance to the physical anthropologist; but the frescoes left to posterity at the Palace of Knossos do in fact provide strong confirmation of the evidence from skulls. There is nothing in these charming representations of themselves to contradict the belief that the Minoans were Mediterranids, and there is much to support it. The profile painting of a young woman, reproduced in monochrome by Arthur Evans in 1901[316] and subsequently nicknamed 'La Parisienne', would serve as well as any other single portrait to substantiate this statement; but Sir Arthur's massive set of volumes on the Palace, amply illustrated in colour as well as black-and-white, should be studied by anyone who wants to gain a general impression of how the Minoans saw themselves.[317] The most famous picture of all is that which shows the 'Cup-bearer' (opposite p. 707 in Vol. 2 (Part 2) of his book); but perhaps the most useful to the physical anthropologist are the numerous frescoes of groups of Minoan women reproduced in Volume 3.

One rather peculiar feature is worth mentioning. A considerable proportion (though only a minority) of these women show a slight projection forward of the tip of the nose. This feature is rather marked in 'La Parisienne'.

Evans himself considered that a particular portrait from the Middle Minoan II period might represent a priest-king belonging to an Anatolian (presumably Armenid) ruling caste.[317] This opinion does not carry conviction. Evans was influenced by what he regarded as an 'aquiline' nose, but the figure he reproduces (Fig. 2a in Vol. 1) does not resemble an Armenid, and anyhow the members of this subrace did not possess noses that could be accurately described as aquiline. Evans provides a few pictures of persons showing Negrid characters, and suggests that 'partly negroized elements' may have been brought to Crete as captives.

No one has ever suggested, on evidence either from skulls or pictures, that any non-Europid people participated in the origin or development of Cretan civilization.

Contrast between the scarcity of well-preserved ancient skulls from Hellas and Crete on one hand and their abundance from Egypt on the other is striking in the extreme. More study has been devoted to the craniology of ancient Egypt than to that of any other country in the world.[761] Our knowledge of the skulls is largely due to the studies of a British anthropologist, G. M. Morant, who analysed statistically not only the detailed measurements made by his collaborators on nearly one thousand skulls, but also the data included in every available publication on ancient Egyptian skulls that dealt with more than twenty specimens.[761] He thus had at his disposal a mass of detailed information derived from five thousand skulls in all, covering all major periods from predynastic to Roman times. In addition, whole skeletons and hair from mummies have been available to many investigators, and very numerous monuments depict the ancient Egyptians as their artists saw them.

From predynastic times onwards a principal part of the population of Egypt appears to have been composed of a section of the Aethiopid subrace (pp. 225–6), but with this stock there coexisted for a time an 'Aeneolithic' (Chalcolithic) people that disappeared before the beginning of the First Dynasty. The skulls of the latter people show that they were related to the main population, but distinct from it.[761] Whether they vanished by extinction or by incorporation is unknown, but since they founded no civilization, they are not immediately relevant to the subject under discussion here.

In their monuments the dynastic Egyptians represented themselves as having a long face, pointed chin with scanty beard, a straight or somewhat aquiline nose, black irises, and a reddish-brown complexion. On the evidence of their mummies it would appear that the head-hair was curly, wavy, or almost straight, and very dark brown or black. Facial and body-hair was scanty apart from the chin tuft of males. The skeletons show that stature was low, and the bones are slight and suggest a rather feeble frame. The skulls stand near the dividing-line between meso- and dolichocranial, with bulging occiput; viewed from on top they appear coffin-shaped or ovoid; supraciliary ridges are poorly developed or absent; the forehead is nearly vertical. The cheeks are narrow, the nose rather broad. The lower jaw is feeble, and the pointed chin confirms the reliability of their images. There is some tendency towards projection of the face and jaws (mesognathy) (cf. Smith[981]).

Sergi, the originator of the idea of a 'Mediterranean race' ('*stirpe mediterranea*'), regarded the Aethiopids in general as a part of its 'African branch';[958] and there is general agreement among those who have written on this subject that the Europid element in the Egyptians from predynastic times onwards has been primarily Mediterranid, though it is allowed that Orientalid immigrants from Arabia made a contribution to the stock.[981, 302] It is agreed, too, by the British anatomist Elliot Smith,[981] who worked for many years in Egypt, and by Morant,[761] that the Negrid contribution to the Egyptian stock was a small one. Morant showed that all the sets of ancient Egyptian skulls that he analysed statistically were distinguishable by each of six criteria from Negrid skulls (represented by a considerable number of specimens from each of eight different Kafrid, Palaenegrid, and 'Northern Negro' tribes); and he concluded that the whole of the Negrid contribution (if indeed there were any, for he would not decide definitely on this point) must have been made in predynastic times.

Morant's six criteria were all associated with the facial part of the skull. The nasal height $(NH_1R)$* of the Egyptians was significantly greater, the nasal breadth (NB) less, and the nasal index $(100\ NB/NH_1R)$ therefore much less; and the tendency of the Negrid face towards prognathy resulted in significant differences in the basilar angle $(B \prec)$, and especially in the profile and nasial angles $(P \prec$ and $N \prec)$.

Although the inhabitants of Egypt throughout the dynastic period were similar to one another in many respects, they were differentiated at first into

---

* The meanings of the symbols given in capital letters in this paragraph are familiar to students of craniology. They are given here for the sake of precision. For explanations of them see Morant's paper,[761] or better, that by Fawcett and Lee.[322]

two local forms, one of them occupying the Fayum and parts of the country in the vicinity of the lower Nile, and the other living far upstream, in the region called the Thebaid. In anthropological studies the former region is referred to as 'Lower Egypt', though it does not correspond exactly with the modern province of that name; the other is called 'Upper Egypt'. The Upper Egyptians had narrower skulls, and consequently somewhat lower cranial indices (commonly about 73·5, in comparison with 75·0 or rather more among the Lower Egyptians) and one may condense a very large body of statistical data into a few words by saying that in all the six criteria by which Egyptian skulls can be distinguished from Negrid ones, the Upper Egyptian skulls approximated at first a little more closely towards the Negrid condition than did those from Lower Egypt. This differentiation did not persist, however. Extremely gradually, as one dynasty succeeded another, over an immense period, the skulls of the Upper Egyptians changed, until at last they were scarcely distinguishable from those of the Lower Egyptians, even by the most refined statistical techniques.[761] Morant considers two possible causes of the change: either miscegenation in Upper Egypt on a very large scale, with eventual predominance of the Lower Egyptian element, or an independent evolutionary change in the Upper Egyptian population. He does not decide the question, but the former possibility seems much the more probable of the two. Eickstedt maintained a third opinion, that the Upper Egyptians were pushed out of the country towards the south by their relatives from downstream.[302] Whichever hypothesis is correct, the population of the whole country became almost homogeneous, with attenuation of the Negrid element. The Fellahin and Copts of modern Egypt are regarded as scarcely modified descendants of the Egyptians of late dynastic times.

In turning from the origin of the Egyptian to that of the Sinic civilization we leave behind us what might be regarded as an almost overwhelming mass of skeletal material to find ourselves faced with a disappointing lack of it. The Sinids are, however, on the whole, remarkably uniform in physical characters over huge areas, and there is no reason to think that markedly different ethnic taxa occupied any part of China from the beginnings of civilization to the present day.

The Shang Kingdom (about 1500–1100 B.C.) roughly coincided with the Shansi Province of modern China. An Yang and the other archaeological sites are situated in the vicinity of the Hwang (Yellow) River. There had been traditions of an ancient kingdom in this region since very early times, but until the present century there was no positive information about it. Inscribed bones and tortoise-shell had been found from time to time since the last year of the nineteenth century, and in 1928 the first expedition was sent by Academia Sinica to excavate in the vicinity of An Yang. The ancient traditions, which had been viewed with some scepticism by Chinese scholars, were now amply confirmed.[1165,340] Whether, from the available evidence, the Shang culture can be regarded as fulfilling the requirements of the items listed on pp. 507–8 must be regarded as uncertain; but there can be scarcely any doubt that the movement towards civilization in China started here. By L. H. Morgan's criterion there can be no doubt at all, for the Shang people unquestionably had an actual script, not mere picture-writing (item 16), and that script was a very archaic form of the Chinese characters as they have been known ever since. The Shang people made and cast bronze (item 8), and they domesticated several species of animals (item 7); glazed pottery has been discovered, almost certainly turned on the wheel (item 9). It is not known, however, that they built in stone or brick (item 4); and they appear to have been grossly superstitious (item 15). Inscriptions have been found on more than one hundred thousand fragments of bone and tortoise-shell, and these appear to be mostly questions put to dead ancestors, with replies in some cases.[1165]

The Chou Dynasty replaced the Shang about 1100 B.C., but the culture and apparently the people survived; indeed, Fitzgerald regards the Shang culture as 'the direct ancestor, or rather the childhood, of the later Chinese culture'; and he considers that a considerable proportion of the Chinese people of today are the posterity of Shang ancestors.[340] In the existing state of knowledge it must be regarded as probable that the Shang people belonged to the local forms of Sinids that inhabit the region of the Hwang River today and are called by Liu the Huanghoids.[675] Liu says that they are popularly known in China by a term meaning 'the Northerners', and he claims that they occupy the 'cradle' of the Chinese people and their culture. (For the physical characters of the Huanghoids, see Appendix 1, p. 538.)

The five civilizations that have been mentioned—the Sumerian, ancient Egyptian, Indus Valley, Helladic-Minoan, and Sinic—seem to have been the only ones that originated independently or nearly independently. One must say 'nearly', because it would appear that no civilization, except the first, originated in complete independence of any other, unless one regards the Andean and Middle American cultures as civilizations (pp. 521–5 and Appendix 13, 558–9). In his book *East-west passage,* Michael Edwardes claims that complete 'idea-systems' do not travel, but only fragments tend to be transmitted.[298] Fragments do seem to have reached the Sinic world from Europe in very early times. For instance, the bronze socketed celt appears to have spread from Europe across Siberia and reached China during the Chou period.[340]

It can scarcely be doubted, however, that 'idea-systems' do move about, for what Toynbee[1063] calls 'affiliated' and 'satellite' civilizations receive more than fragments from pre-existing sources. It seems doubtful whether these two types of civilizations can be sharply distinguished from one another, but it is unquestionable that certain civilizations owe some of their main characteristics to others that established themselves earlier, and in this sense they are dependent, directly or indirectly, on the independent or nearly independent ones. Thus, for instance, the Hittite was ultimately dependent on the Sumerian (through the Sumero-Akkadian), the Mycenaean and Hellenic on the Helladic-Minoan, the Hindu on the Indus Valley, the Japanese on the Sinic, and so on; but each developed characters of its own. Some civilizations have been dependent on two or more others. All the great independent and dependent civilizations developed among Europid and Mongolid peoples.

The only race other than the Europid and Mongolid in which any close approximation to civilization ever originated is the Indianid. Two subraces of this race achieved this distinction, the Andids in western South America and the Zentralids in Central America. The most obvious physical differences between these two subraces are briefly described in Appendix 12 (pp. 556–7). These Indianid cultures almost certainly originated independently of all the civilizations of the Old World, although several remarkable similarities do exist (for instance, certain weaving techniques and *cire perdue* metal-casting in the Andean culture[1063]). These two Indianid cultures seem also to have originated independently of one another, though 'fragments' do appear to have made their way to and fro between them from time to time, despite their wide geographical separation;[1082] and there appears to have been sporadic interchange between the Andean and Polynesian cultures.[64, 168]

In the Andean region and also in Middle America, the conquerors—respectively the Incas and Aztecs—might almost be said to have been absorbed by the peoples they subjected; for although, to a varying degree, the rulers imposed uniformity on the subject tribes, the latter had already created for themselves the basis on which the advance towards civilization took place.

L. H. Morgan placed both the Andean and the Middle American cultures in what he called the 'Middle Status of Barbarism'; that is to say, not even in the highest category of the intermediate range. He relegated them to this status on the grounds that they did not know how to smelt iron from its ores, had not invented a phonetic alphabet, and did not use writing in literary composition.[766] If, however, he had had the knowledge that is available today, it is doubtful whether he would have allowed deficiency in these elements of culture to weigh quite so heavily against others in the scale. If the matter be judged by the items listed on pp. 507–8, one may perhaps claim that in the period before the Spanish conquest in the 1530s, the Andeans were civilized in ten (nos. 1, 2, 4–8, 14, 19, and 20) and perhaps marginally so in five others (nos. 3, 13, 15, 17, and 18); (cf. Baudin;[64] Burland;[168] Hemming[486]). In items 11 and 12, both concerned with the legal system, and item 21, it seems impossible to reach a firm decision. In three important items (nos. 9, 10, and 16), however, they did not reach the level of civilization. They had no properly established monetary system, but relied mainly on barter; they had no knowledge of the use of the wheel for any purpose; and they had no script. Hemming, in his work on the Spanish conquest, emphasizes three inventions that they lacked, namely writing, the wheel, and the true arch, 'three discoveries that we would regard as fundamental' in deciding whether the usual standard of civilization is reached;[486] but the superb craftsmanship of their stonemasons in most respects surely outweighs one shortcoming. Too much emphasis, however, may perhaps have been laid by some authors on their *quipu,* a device consisting of knots and loops arranged on strings in such a way as to record numbers on a denary* system. The *quipu* was useful for sending exact

---

* 'Denary' is used here in preference to 'decimal', because the latter word is liable to cause misunderstanding. The statement that a particular tribe or nation uses 'decimal' numeration may give rise to the impression that fractions of unity are represented by decimal notation, when in fact the people concerned have no knowledge of this method.

numerical information from one place to another, as it was light and easily carried; but it could not be used in calculation.[179]

The people of Middle America originally comprised several nations that shared a basic culture, with local variations. Their achievement was unequal, but customs that had grown up in one nation tended to spread gradually to another. Some of them attained a high culture in certain respects. Whether they are entitled to be classified as civilized will be briefly considered in the light of evidence from several independent sources.[99, 174, 382, 695, 944, 1043, 1082]

The Maya, whose territory included what are now Guatemala, British Honduras, the western end of Honduras and of El Salvador, with neighbouring parts of Mexico, were the first nation to rise to a high cultural level and the nation that eventually rose highest. What has been called their 'meteor-like glory' was limited to six centuries starting about A.D. 300.[1043] Thereafter there was an unexplained dispersal towards Yucatan and elsewhere, and a marked decline resulting in an actual collapse of culture before the Spanish conquest in the second quarter of the sixteenth century. Meanwhile the Aztecs had arrived in the neighbourhood of what is now Mexico City, had adopted the culture of the local people, and to a certain extent had dominated those of a considerable part of what is now southern Mexico. The Aztecs were at the summit of their cultural advance when Cortés landed in Middle America in 1519.

In mathematics, astronomy, and the calendar (items 17 and 18), the Middle Americans, especially the Maya, were greatly superior to the Andeans, and indeed to the members of every ethnic taxon that has ever existed other than certain subraces of Europids and Mongolids. The Mayan system of numeration was vigesimal (i.e. based on the number 20), with the exception that *uinal*, 20 units, was followed by a set of only 18 numbers, and this stage is numeration was thus duodevigesimal instead of vigesimal. This irregular step was no doubt introduced because it was convenient in the construction of the calendar, since they counted their year as consisting of $(20 \times 18) + 5$ days (see Appendix 13, pp. 558–9). It is often said loosely that the great virtue of Mayan mathematics was that they introduced a symbol for zero. This, in itself, is a rather trivial matter. What is essential is that they invented a 'local value' (or 'place-notational') system of numeration that involved zero; that is to say, a system in which the value of each numerical symbol depended on its position in a series of such symbols, and the zero took its place (if required) in this series. The invention of a local-value system with zero was a great mathematical achievement, as Laplace remarked long ago. In writing on this subject he was unaware that the Maya had invented the idea and applied it to their vigesimal system before the Indian mathematicians had thought of it and used it in denary notation; but his remarks on the subject in the third edition of his *Exposition du système du monde*[634] are applicable here, with the necessary alteration of 'India' to 'Middle America' and 'ten' to 'twenty' in the first sentence.

It is from India that there comes to us the ingenious method of expressing all numbers by ten characters, by giving them at the same time an absolute value and a value of position; a shrewd and important idea that now appears to us so simple that we are scarcely aware of its merit. But this simplicity itself, and the extreme facility that results from it in all calculations, places our system of arithmetic in the first rank of useful inventions; and one will appreciate the difficulty of reaching it, if one considers that it evaded the genius of Archimedes and Apollonius, two of the greatest men by whom antiquity honours itself.[634]*

It is important to realize that this Mayan invention was undoubtedly independent of the Hindu, which is almost everywhere in use today. Not only was it vigesimal instead of denary, but the symbols were entirely different and their sequence was vertical, not horizontal.[179] The independent origin in different parts of the world of something so intellectually demanding as the idea of local value with zero provides a striking disproof of the diffusionist doctrine in its extreme form, according to which nothing has ever been independently invented more than once.

The Babylonians introduced a place-notational method for writing numbers into their sexagesimal system at some time between 2300 and 1600 B.C.;[179] that is to say, probably about two millennia before the beginning of the 'classic' period of Mayan culture. It is a strange fact that they did not use a symbol for zero until long afterwards, and their use of the method was therefore completely satisfactory only in those cases in which this symbol was not required. They at last introduced a symbol for zero about 200 B.C., but they are said not to have used it in calculations.[179]

The sexagesimal numeration of the Babylonians and the vigesimal-duodevigesimal system of the Maya must have made their multiplication tables very difficult to commit to memory. The denary system of Hindu-Arabic mathematics, now used almost universally throughout the world, is much superior.

Some of the Middle American peoples, especially the Maya, made remarkably accurate astronomical observations, though they were handicapped by their failure to invent instruments to help them in this work. Their measurement of the length of the year was good enough to provide a basis for reliable calendars. Middle American calendars, based on that of the Maya, merit study because they furnish a good example of talented people falling a little short of maximum achievement by the introduction of unnecessary complications. They are comparable in this respect, though on a very much higher plane, with the systems of 'kinship' notation used by certain primitive tribes. Many descriptions of these calendars are too short to provide the requisite information, while others are unnecessarily complicated ways of explaining unnecessarily complicated systems. The attempt is made in Appendix 13 (pp. 558–9) to provide a clear but not oversimplified account of the Aztec calendar, which is very similar to that of the Maya.

The Middle Americans attained high standards in architecture, even though they never approached nearer to the true arch than its corbelled counterpart. Their pyramidal temples were huge and magnificent. Great cities were built that astonished the Spanish invaders.[695] The Aztec capital is said to have accommodated a population of about three hundred thousand.[1082]

When all these great achievements are held in mind, one might be inclined to pronounce these people as civilized without further consideration. But further consideration is precisely what is necessary. It must be remembered that the

* In the second edition of his *Exposition*,[633] Laplace had hesitantly attributed the invention to Archimedes.

Middle Americans had nothing that could properly be called a narrative script. Their numerals were inscribed, sometimes on stone, sometimes on surfaces beaten out from the bark of a particular tree and folded in a special way to form what may be called a book; but nearly all of their inscriptions were concerned with numbers and the calendar. Their hieroglyphs were mainly ideographic, though some only indirectly, through use of the 'rebus' or pun principle. There was no way of writing verbs, and abstract ideas (apart from number) could not be inscribed.[382, 1082] It would not appear that the technique even of the Maya lent itself to a narrative form, except in a very limited sense. Most of the Middle Americans conveyed non-calendrical information only by speech or by the display of series of paintings.

On the basis of what has already been said, one might still be inclined to classify the Middle Americans, or at any rate the Maya, as civilized; but anyone who does not happen to have studied their culture will learn with a shock that they had no weights (unlike the Andeans), no metal-bladed hoes or spades, and no wheels (unless perhaps a few toys were actually provided with wheels and really formed part of the Mayan culture).[382, 1043] Throughout Middle America exchange was effected by barter; and money, in the accepted sense, can scarcely be said to have existed. Beyond all this, the Middle Americans were excessively superstitious. Their religions, which actually governed their lives, contained no other element than superstition. Their entire concentration was on trying to understand and propitiate the magical influences that were supposed to govern their lives. As Vaillant tersely remarks of the Aztecs, 'Religion . . . did not enter into the fields of ethics,'[1082] and this statement was equally applicable to the other nations.

There was one particular feature of Middle American culture that seems decisive, for it makes it almost impossible to regard these people, so talented in many respects, as civilized. It was their custom to make war with the sole purpose of obtaining prisoners, who were kept in cages until required and then killed at special ceremonies by a cruel method involving the slitting open of the living body and the tearing out of the still-pulsating heart. Special festivals were held during every twenty-day cycle of the year, and prisoners were slaughtered in this way at most of these. At one festival each year, babies were killed instead. Exact details of the procedure at each of the eighteen festivals each year, as practised by the Aztecs, are given by Bancroft in Volume 2, Chapter 9, of his book on *The native races of the Pacific states of North America*.[55] He gives a list of the references on which he bases his account. A summary of it is given by Vaillant.[1082] On special occasions huge numbers of prisoners were slaughtered. Twenty thousand are said to have suffered at the dedication of the enlarged Great Temple.[1082] Whether this figure is exaggerated one cannot tell; but it was confirmed by educated Aztecs, and certainly the Spanish conquistadors counted thousands of victims' skulls placed on a special rack at the capital city;[1082] and helplessly they saw the gruesome process enacted on their fellows who had been taken prisoner.[695] All this was no temporary aberration, due to the fanaticism of some particular dictator; on the contrary, it was the settled custom of the people from remote times, as ancient monuments show.

The slaughter was not all. During the long period of the Aztec domination, the custom of eating the flesh of sacrificed persons became almost universal.[55] It has been claimed from time to time that the Maya practised ritual slaughter and cannibalism less frequently than the people of the other nations of Middle America; but it was in fact an essential part of their way of life.[382] Incidentally, it is a curious fact that some of the few Mayan hieroglyphs that can be deciphered so as to give information in narrative form are descriptions of the preliminaries leading up to slaughter and the process of incision preparatory to the tearing out of the heart.[353]

The slaughter and eating of prisoners was intended to propitiate the gods, and for this reason the suggestion has been made that the eating 'was not cannibalism in the general meaning of the word'.[382] It is evident, however, that the motives of the eaters were mixed. For instance, the Maya reserved the hands and feet of the victims for the high priest and supreme lord, as 'the most delicate morsels'; and at one of the cyclical feasts, merchants were accustomed to invite friends to 'partake of the human flesh and other choice viands'.[55] As to the 'general meaning' of the word, cannibalism is defined in the Oxford *New English dictionary* as 'The practice of eating the flesh of one's fellow-creatures'[782] and in the American *Century dictionary* as 'The eating of human flesh by human beings'.[1139]

The mathematics, astronomy, and calendar of the Middle Americans suggest unqualified acceptance into the ranks of the civilized, but other features of their culture flatly forbid it. The Andeans must be regarded as coming closer to the mark, without reaching it. In attempting to assess the achievement of these two Indianid peoples it must be remembered that they were completely isolated from the civilized world and very nearly so from one another, whereas the civilizations of the Old World, even those regarded as 'independent', did have some influence on one another, with the exception of the Sumerians in their early phase.

There can be little doubt that civilization has always originated and developed through the presence in a population of a small proportion of very talented people. Although this thought must have been present in many minds, one does not often come across a direct statement of it in print. The French evolutionary biologist J. B. Lamarck stated it with characteristic vigour (and a good deal of exaggeration) in a discourse delivered in 1802 or thereabouts and subsequently printed.[627] E. L. Thorndike, Professor of Education at Columbia University, expressed the same idea in much more moderate words in a book published in 1910. His statement is as clear as can be. 'The origination of advances in civilization is a measure of ability,' he wrote, 'but the abilities that have originated them have probably been confined to a very few men.' He points out the factors that result in the presence of these few men in a population:

   ... the chance of men of great gifts being born is the result not only of the central tendency* of a race and its variability, but also of its size. Other

* Thorndike explains at the beginning of his book that he uses the term 'central tendency' to mean the median.

things being equal, there is a far greater chance of the birth of a man of great ability in a tribe of a million than in one of a thousand. Since one such man may add to the knowledge and improve the habits of the entire group regardless of its size, civilization will progress more rapidly in large than in small groups, in a condition of isolation.[1050]

Thorndike introduces the words 'in a condition of isolation' to indicate that civilization may exist in a population, small or large, as a result of its having been introduced from outside, even though the factors necessary for its origin and development were not present in the population itself. It must be remarked, however, that if civilization had never arisen independently in a particular race, that race would presumably be less likely to originate new advances than would the race that had created the civilization that was introduced. It is also true that there are ethnic taxa that have not yet proved their capacity to absorb civilization from outside (though this does not mean that such absorption is necessarily impossible).

Professor A. R. Jensen has referred briefly to this subject. 'It may well be true', he says, 'that the kind of ability we now call intelligence was needed in a certain percentage of the human population for our civilization to have arisen.'[551] This can, indeed, scarcely be doubted; but the other faculties of the mind besides cognitive ability (which is what Professor Jensen means by 'intelligence') must have been necessary as well.

If it be accepted that the independent origin and development of civilization result from the activities of a small but significant proportion of the members of a particular ethnic taxon, the existence of these exceptional individuals might be regarded as a secondary character of that taxon, just as (for instance) the existence of a small but significant proportion of the Australids having a fronto-temporal pterion is a secondary character of that taxon, which distinguishes it from those taxa in which this form of pterion very rarely occurs (see pp. 298–300).

The term 'group intelligence' is sometimes used in psychological literature. The idea behind the use of this term seems to be that wide dispersal of mental ability among the members of a population may be more important than the presence in it of a small proportion of people of very high intelligence (though the presence of the latter would in fact almost necessarily be associated with high median intelligence of the group as a whole). It has been suggested that the best indication of high 'group intelligence' is the ability of the group to survive, and that for this reason any test of mental ability that gives rather similar results with all surviving populations must be a good test. Lest anyone should doubt the seriousness of this suggestion, I quote the relevant passage.

The simple fact is that these primitive folk are our contemporaries. In other words, they are still here, and in many cases are maintaining themselves against pressure and competition from 'superior' peoples.

Hence, any test that relates the divisions of mankind closer together must be, generally speaking, the best measure.[852]

The author of these words quotes a particular test (the Porteus Maze Test) that is 'good' by this criterion. Two points must be noted. First, if one were to devise a very simple test, it would necessarily be 'good' by the criterion just stated. Yet one could devise such a simple maze (not on paper, but on the ground) that dogs and other intelligent animals could perform it as certainly as human beings. In just the same way, a little child may be as successful as a mathematical genius in multiplying two by two. Secondly, mere survival is not a reliable criterion of mental ability. Multitudes of species of animals, both vertebrate and invertebrate, are able to survive, some of them in huge numbers, yet no one would be likely to claim that all these animals are comparable in intelligence with any normal human being. It would be absurd to make survival a surer test of intelligence than the capacity to advance towards civilization. Survival is only one element in that advance—an element shared by every one of the millions of species of animals that exist today.

Explanations are frequently suggested for the failure of certain peoples to make this advance. Thus Professor A. Sommerfelt excuses the fact that the Arunta had no numerals (in the proper sense of the word) on the ground that 'The Arunta who lives far from all influence of whites has no need of a system of numerals comparable to ours. He possesses nothing that he must necessarily count, no domestic animals, no merchandise, no money.'[990] One is left to assume that if they had had something to count, the Arunta would have invented numerals. But *why* had they nothing to count? *Why* were they content with this situation? One is forcibly reminded of John Stuart Mill's remark that it is 'better to be Socrates dissatisfied than a fool satisfied'.[745] Members of all ethnic taxa of man must have experienced stages in their histories at which they possessed no domestic animals, no merchandise, and no money, but in many of these taxa there were people who were not satisfied.

The failure of Negroes and members of certain other taxa, living in civilized countries, to reach the same average scores in cognition and attainment tests as Mongolids and Europids has often been attributed to environmental causes (pp. 448–9, 469, 483, and 488–9). In just the same way, it has repeatedly been suggested that those ethnic taxa that have never attained to civilization by their own endeavours in their native lands have been held back by the unfavourable nature of their habitats. Some authors are dogmatic on this subject. Sommerfelt, for instance, says that the differences between 'peoples and tribes' are due to 'natural surroundings and history, not to innate characteristics of these peoples'.[991] This, however, is not by any means always the experience of those who have actually travelled among primitive peoples in their natural environments. Livingstone, for instance, was struck by the mental differences between members of different races living in the Kalahari Desert. The Bakalahari, a Kafrid tribe, had been forced into this environment in the remote past.

> Living ever since on the same plains with the Bushmen, subjected to the same influences of climate, enduring the same thirst, and subsisting on the same food for centuries, they seem to supply a standing proof that locality is not always sufficient of itself to account for differences in races.[676]

And how, on the environmental hypothesis, can one explain the fact that the Negrids inhabiting the tropical rain-forest of central Africa made not even a start in mathematics, while the Maya of the Guatemalan tropical rain-forest, equally cut off from all contacts with civilized people, made astounding progress in this subject, and at one time were actually ahead of the whole of the rest of the world in one important branch of it? (See pp. 522–3.)

It would be wrong to suppose that civilization developed wherever the environment was genial, and failed to do so where it was not. Indeed, it might be nearer the mark to claim the opposite. It has been pointed out by an authority on the Maya that their culture reached its climax in that particular part of their extensive territory in which the environment was least favourable, and in reporting this fact he mentions the belief that 'civilizations, like individuals, respond to challenge'.[1043] Similarly A. H. Brodrick, in his book *Man and his ancestry*, says that civilization came to Europe from the east, 'where the change of climate had driven men to exercise their ingenuity in new conditions'.[142] The Sumerians found no Garden of Eden awaiting them in Mesopotamia and the adjoining territory at the head of the Persian Gulf, but literally made their environment out of unpromising material by constructing an elaborate system of canals for the drainage and watering of their lands. A very large number of Aztecs and members of several other Middle American tribes lived and made their gardens on artificial islands that they themselves constructed with their hands. These are nothing more than particularly striking examples of the fact that the environment oi all but the most primitive human beings is to a large extent man-made; and it is made not by instinct, like that of certain animals, but by the use of reason. No specialist in the physical geography of America, ignorant of its human history, could guess that the Andes with the narrow coastal strip beside the mountain range constituted the environment of the highest culture that the Indianids ever attained in any part of the continent. It is true that less cultured tribes may be pushed aside into exceptionally unfavourable environments, but the idea that environment determines culture, whether at the pre-civilized or civilized state, is untenable.

It is sometimes argued that a few thousand years are a short time in relation to the whole period of man's existence, and that consequently one should not lay much stress on the time at which the civilized state has been attained. It will never be possible to find out with certainty whether any of the races in which civilization did not appear independently would ever have attained it independently if given sufficient time, because no considerable tract of inhabited country exists anywhere today to which some inkling of civilization has not yet penetrated from outside, or will not soon penetrate. Two facts, however, must be borne in mind in this connection. The first is the unreality of orthogenesis. The section of Chapter 8 concerned with this subject (pp. 138–46) was introduced specifically in relation to this question. There is no internal driving force within organisms, causing them automatically and necessarily to evolve. Evolution is not related to development in the embryological sense; the two processes have nothing to do with one another. Secondly, one must not underestimate the immense advance made by certain races of man in passing from the food-gathering to the intermediate status of culture. That passage has been well named 'the Neolithic revolution',[215] and genius was needed then, just as it was needed later on when further progress was made in the origin and improvement of civilization. It must not be forgotten that certain races of man not only never attained independently to the status of civilization, but never independently reached the intermediate phase.*

It must also be borne in mind that most of the Indianid subraces never made any close approach to civilization by their own unaided efforts, and some of the Mongolid and Europid subraces (the Ainuids, for instance, among the latter) have played no major part in the origin and advance of civilization (though other subraces of these two races, in which civilization did not appear independently, have played important parts in its subsequent history).

* It is probable that many ethnic taxa that have not yet made any important contributions to the advancement of man could progress rapidly by encouraging the intermarriage and fertility of their most intelligent members.

# CONCLUSION

# Conclusion

TO THE reader who has followed this account of a vast and very diverse subject throughout the long journey to the present page, it is perhaps unnecessary to point out the coherence of the available evidence bearing on the ethnic problem. One might conceivably have found that civilization originated among ethnic taxa regarded on morphological evidence as primitive (pp. 124–9) or particularly paedomorphous (pp. 137–8), or among those that were less successful than others in tests of cognitive ability or scholastic attainment. Nothing of the sort is revealed by scrutiny of the actual facts. The Australids, shown to be primitive by morphological criteria (Chapter 16), did not progress on their own initiative beyond the food-gathering status; nor did those classic prototypes of paedomorphosis, the Bushmen or Sanids (Chapter 17). A parallel conclusion is forced upon us if we look at the results of cognition and attainment tests carried out on members of various races living under conditions of civilized life (Chapter 25 and pp. 498–9). The Mongolids and Europids did best in both of these types of tests; they were followed (at some distance) by the Indianids, and the Negrids were still less successful. In conformity with these results, the races among which civilization originated and advanced were the Mongolids (pp. 519–20) and Europids (pp. 509–19); two Indianid subraces approached nearer to civilization than any other taxon (pp. 521–5), and indeed in certain respects (though certainly not in others) one of these subraces advanced to an impressively high level of culture (pp. 522–3); and here again the Negrids fell behind (Chapter 20). The reader will not have overlooked the fact that repeatedly, in each relevant context, the possibility of environmental causes has been reviewed in some detail and rejected as an insufficient explanation of the facts (pp. 397–400, 448–9, 469–73, 488–90, and 527–8).

Emphasis has been laid in this book on the morphological differences between typical members of different races. Any reader who may be inclined to minimize these differences might care to refresh his memory by turning once more to Fig. 56. Chapters 11, 12, 13, 16, and 17 are mainly occupied with this subject, to which insufficient attention has been paid in recent years. Most of our knowledge about the structural differences between the various taxa of man is derived from study of bones and external characters. Cranial capacity is, of course, directly relevant to the ethnic problem, since it sets a limit to the size of the brain in the different taxa; but all morphological differences are also relevant in an indirect way, since it is scarcely possible that any taxa could be exactly the same as one another in all the genes that control the development and function of the nervous and sensory systems, yet so different from one another in structural characters in other parts of the body as many taxa in fact are. Apart from this, considerable morphological differences in the brains of different taxa have in some cases been observed (pp. 292–5, 319, and 322).

The decrease in interest in major morphological differences between human taxa is due to the fact that no one has discovered how to investigate genetically the system of polygenes (pp. 158–9, 190–91, 203, and 458) that controls the development of the structures in question; and there is a disposition nowadays to ignore whatever cannot be traced to its causes. Yet facts are facts, and remain so whether or not at a particular stage in the progress of biology one can explain them. Attention is focused today on those 'secondary' differences (pp. 185–91) that are due to genes that can be studied singly and occur in most ethnic taxa, though in different proportions in different taxa. The study of these genes has been of great intrinsic interest, but it has necessarily led, from its very nature, to a tendency to minimize or even disregard the extent to which the ethnic taxa of man do actually differ from one another (pp. 188, 190–91, 203, and 458).

There is one point that I particularly want to take this opportunity of stressing. It is the absurdity (for no weaker term is applicable) of classifying various taxa together as 'coloured',* and even suggesting that no other character than the pigmentation of the skin distinguishes one human taxon from another. It is not necessary to repeat here what has already been said with sufficient emphasis on this subject (pp. 15–16, 159–60, 181–2, and 307); but it may be remarked that the error stands in relation to physical anthropology as illiteracy does to the study of literature, and no educated person should be guilty of it.

Here, on reaching the end of the book, I must repeat some words that I wrote years ago when drafting the Introduction (p. 6), for there is nothing in the whole work that would tend to contradict or weaken them.

Every ethnic taxon of man includes many persons capable of living responsible and useful lives in the communities to which they belong, while even in those taxa that are best known for their contributions to the world's store of intellectual wealth, there are many so mentally deficient that they would be inadequate members of any society. It follows that no one can claim superiority simply because he or she belongs to a particular ethnic taxon.

Nevertheless, the facts summarized in the first paragraph of this Conclusion must be borne in mind. One must deny, as Rousseau did long ago, the 'fine dictum of morality' that men are everywhere the same. We may reject many of his speculations about the nature of primitive man, yet grant his earnest wish, printed in the original French at the very beginning of this book, that we should 'learn to know men by their conformities and by their differences'.

---

* What is said in this paragraph does not refer to the word 'Coloured' when used as a technical term to distinguish a particular hybrid population in South Africa from the Negrids and Europids of the same country.

# APPENDICES
# AND BIBLIOGRAPHY

# 1 The physical characters of certain Mongolid subraces

THE TUNGIDS, Sinids, and Palaemongolids are chosen for description here, since these are the subraces most frequently mentioned in the book. The Mongolids are differently classified by different authors, some of whom give different names to the same subrace (e.g., Lundman[682] calls the Tungids '*die altaide Rasse*', and Liu[675] regards the Palaemongolids of southern China as the 'Chukiangid subtype' of the Sinids). The attempt is made here to give a short description of the most obvious physical features of each of the three subraces, as represented by their most typical members. Several of the physical characters that distinguish the Mongolids from other races of mankind are more strongly marked in the Tungids than in any other Mongolid subrace. Lundman describes the '*gobide*', one of the local forms of Tungids, as having '*sehr extreme Mongolenzüge*'.[682] For this reason the Tungids are described first, and the characters of the other two subraces then presented by comparison.

The *Tungids* ('Mongols') are the principal inhabitants of Inner Mongolia, Mongolia, and Central Siberia. The Tungus are one of the many tribes of Tungids.

The stature is medium to low. The trunk is broad, and long in relation to total height. The head is very brachycephalic. The zygomatic arches project strongly. The forehead is low and receding. The face is broad and particularly flat. The chin does not usually recede in males.

The mesorrhine nose is broad and flattened in the region between the eyes; the bridge is rather low, and straight or somewhat concave. The eyes are far apart. The space between upper and lower eyelids is horizontal and slit-like; the *Mongolenfalte* (pp. 208 and 415) is strongly developed. The lips are slightly thicker than those of Europids.

There is very little body-hair and little facial hair in males.

The skin is yellow to yellow-brown and the eyes dark brown.

(The skull of Tungids is mentioned in Chapter 13 (pp. 220–21).)

Most of the inhabitants of China (including Manchuria), except Tibet and the part bordering on the South China Sea, are *Sinids*. Members of this subrace differ from the Tungids in being rather tall and slender, with longish legs. The head is mesocephalic and very high (hypsicephalic). The forehead and chin recede slightly. The zygomatic arches are less prominent than those of the Tungids.

The mesorrhine nose is straight, and long from sellion to tip. The space between upper and lower eyelids is more widely open than that of the Tungids except at its lateral extremity, where in many cases it rises to give slight obliquity to the eye. The *Mongolenfalte* is not strongly developed.

The most familiar form of Sinid anatomy is shown by those who dwell in the drainage-basin of the River Yangtse-Kiang and are called by Liu[675] the Changkiangids; but the northern Chinese, who inhabit the valley of the River Hwangho and are also well represented in Manchuria and Korea, are regarded by some as approximating more closely to the archaic form from which the Changkiangids arose by hybridization. The northerners, called Huanghoids by Liu, differ from the Changkiangids principally by being taller and having longer heads and less flat faces; their eyes tend to be slitlike and provided with a *Mongolenfalte*; the nose is narrow and in some cases slightly aquiline.

The Manchu of north-western Manchuria used to constitute a distinct type, described in great detail by Baelz[41] under the name of '*der koreanisch-mandschurische Typus*'. It seems uncertain whether these people have maintained their identity since Baelz wrote, some seventy years ago. They were not confined to their homeland, but extended also to Korea and Japan, in which countries they seem at one time to have been especially numerous in aristocratic circles. The chief distinguishing features were extreme brachycephaly combined with a narrow face and somewhat aquiline nose; the alae were not sharply marked off from the rest of that organ. The eyes were slitlike and long, and rose upwards laterally; the *Mongolenfalte* was present. The mouth was small; the chin narrow and receding. Many portraits of Japanese women painted in the second half of the eighteenth century appear to be stylized representations of members of this taxon.[49] The women in question could not conceivably have been Palaemongolids. Baelz considered that the type was formerly emphasized in Japan by deliberate sexual selection of particular women.

There are a number of points of resemblance between the Korean-Manchurian and Huanghoid types, but they seem to have differed considerably in the length of the head, if the descriptions are correct.

The somewhat paedomorphous peoples grouped together by Eickstedt[302] as *Palaemongolids* have a very wide distribution from Japan (where they form the bulk of the population) through southern China, Tibet, and Indo-China to the Malayan Peninsula and Archipelago; but they have become considerably hybridized with other taxa in various parts of their range.

The stature is short, generally below that of the Tungids. The head is less markedly brachycephalic. The forehead, unlike that of Tungids (and most Sinids), rises steeply. The face is wider in its lower part and less flattened than that of the Tungids. The chin recedes, especially in women.

The nose is mesorrhine and short from sellion to its rounded tip; its bridge is low and the alae tend to spread rather widely. The eyes are oblique (highest laterally) and are held much more widely open than those of the Tungids and Sinids; the *Mongolenfalte* is weakly developed or absent. There is slight alveolar prognathy. The mouth is large and the lips somewhat swollen.

The brownish-black or black scalp-hair is finer than that of Tungids and less rigid.

The skin is pale brown or yellowish-brown.

# 2  A classification of the genera of Primates mentioned in the book

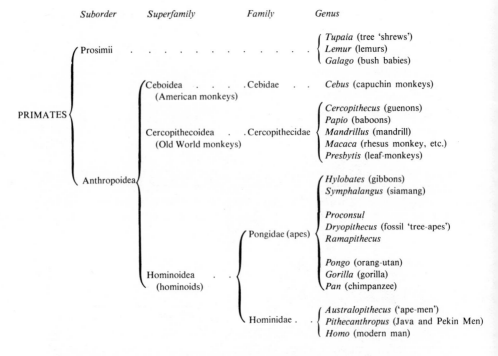

| Suborder | Superfamily | Family | Genus |
|---|---|---|---|
| Prosimii . . . . . . . . . . | | | *Tupaia* (tree 'shrews')<br>*Lemur* (lemurs)<br>*Galago* (bush babies) |
| | Ceboidea . . . .Cebidae . .<br>(American monkeys) | | *Cebus* (capuchin monkeys) |
| | Cercopithecoidea . .Cercopithecidae<br>(Old World monkeys) | | *Cercopithecus* (guenons)<br>*Papio* (baboons)<br>*Mandrillus* (mandrill)<br>*Macaca* (rhesus monkey, etc.)<br>*Presbytis* (leaf-monkeys) |
| Anthropoidea | | Pongidae (apes) | *Hylobates* (gibbons)<br>*Symphalangus* (siamang)<br><br>*Proconsul*<br>*Dryopithecus* (fossil 'tree-apes')<br>*Ramapithecus*<br><br>*Pongo* (orang-utan)<br>*Gorilla* (gorilla)<br>*Pan* (chimpanzee) |
| | Hominoidea . .<br>(hominoids) | Hominidae . . | *Australopithecus* ('ape-men')<br>*Pithecanthropus* (Java and Pekin Men)<br>*Homo* (modern man) |

PRIMATES

For more comprehensive and somewhat different classifications, see especially Simpson.[968, 972] Some modern authorities place Java and Pekin Men in the genus *Homo*, and the gorilla with the chimpanzee in *Pan*. The gorilla was first placed in the same genus as the chimpanzee by Richard Owen in 1853.[814]

# 3 The nomenclature of the Australasids

SOME READERS may require the following explanation of the choice of names for the subspecies (race) *australasicus* Bory, 1825, and for the subraces *australasicus* Bory, 1825, *melaninus* Bory, 1825, and *tasmanianus* Gregory, 1921.

The name *alfuri* was formally bestowed by von Eickstedt on a taxon comprising the Australids, Melanesians, and Papuans.[303] He adopted it 'ex Lesson 1827'. Lesson[661] applied the name *Alfourous* to two separate '*Rameaux*' of the *Race Noire*, namely the *Alfourous-Australien* (Australian aborigines) and the *Alfourous-Endamène* (who seem, so far as one can judge from his brief description, to have been some of the peoples, related to the Senoi of the Malay Peninsula, scattered in remote parts of various East Indian islands). There are two reasons for not accepting the name *alfuri*. (1) Bory's *australasicus* has priority of two years. (2) Lesson and von Eickstedt referred the names *Alfourous* and *alfuri* to what were clearly infrasubspecific taxa. It follows from the *International code of zoological nomenclature*[1014] that *alfuri* cannot be the correct name of the subspecies.

Bory de Saint Vincent made the Australian aborigines the eighth of the 15 '*espèces*' into which he divided mankind.[128] He gave it the name of '*Homo Australasicus*'. From this taxon he excluded the Melanesians and Papuans; but it appears to follow from clauses I.24(a) and X.45(d) of the *Code* that the taxonomist who subsequently brings them into the same taxon as Bory's *Australasicus* must include them under the same name. It must be remarked that Bory does not use the terms 'Léiotriques' and 'Oulotriques' as formal categories that could be regarded as taxa major to *Australasicus*; he divides *Homo* directly into '*espèces*'.

The Melanesians and Papuans present problems of both classification and nomenclature. Bory[128] separated sharply his '*espèce*' *Homo Melaninus* from the '*race Papoue*' of his '*espèce*' *Homo Neptunianus* (which also included the Malays and Polynesians). Von Eickstedt seems to have supposed that Bory was describing under these terms respectively the Melanesians and Papuans, and he therefore adopted the names '*melaninus* Bory' and '*papuensis* ex Bory' for the two peoples.[303] Actually Bory's *Melaninus* included the population of most of New Guinea, and the '*race Papoue*' was an ill-defined hybrid taxon (*Neptunianus* × *Melaninus*) occupying only one peninsula of New Guinea with a few little neighbouring islands.

It is questionable whether the Papuans as a whole can be regarded as subracially distinct from the Melanesians. Some Papuans have convex noses, with the tips turned down, and in certain cases the nasal bones are very narrow at their upper ends; some of the skulls are higher than those of most Melanesians. Still, the general resemblance is close, and it seems safer to make a single taxon. If so, *melaninus* is clearly the correct name. The common name 'Melanesid' is used in this book for the subrace *melaninus*, despite the fact that von Eickstedt used it (in the form '*die Melanesiden*') *both* for the inclusive taxon and also as one of his names for the Papuans only.[302]

It seems justifiable to include the Tasmanids in the race *australasicus*, for they showed many resemblances to the Melanesids and more distantly to the Australids. Most writers on the subject emphasize the difference in the form of the hair, which was 'woolly' rather than 'frizzy' or curly, and grew in spiral tufts. It appears to have been considerably shorter than that of the Melanesids, but there has been some misunderstanding about this. The Tasmanids paid great attention to their hair, which they cut short, tuft by tuft, using one stone as a knife and another as a chopping-block.[989] Although the skulls of Tasmanids are similar in many respects to those of the rest of the race, there are several statistically significant differences between theirs and those of 'type A' Australids.[763] The most obvious of these is the remarkable projection of the parietal eminences, which results in the maximum breadth of the skull being greater than that of the Australids, though the transverse diameter of the skull in every region except the parietal is less than in the latter subrace. The apertura pyriformis is even wider in proportion to its height than in the Australids, and the distance in a straight line from the nasion to the prosthion is remarkably short. The orbits are very low in proportion to their width.

The Tasmanids became extinct (apart from their hybrid progeny) in 1877,[989] but no one seems to have brought them into the Linnean system of nomenclature until 44 years later, when Gregory proposed the name *tasmanianus*.[433]

# 4 *List of Australid skulls that show certain features particularly clearly*

| Collection | Serial no. | Special feature |
|---|---|---|
| British Museum (Natural History) | 1911/11/14/5 | Very large and heavy skull |
| ,, ,, | 1897/10/10/2 | Very thick bones |
| ,, ,, | AUS.30.987 | Typical orygmocraspedote, and outer border of orbit widely rounded |
| ,, ,, | AUS.1016.B | Orygmocraspedote though not prognathous |
| ,, ,, | AUS.30.989 | Typical bothrocraspedote |
| ,, ,, | AUS.20.1 | Well-developed nasal spine, although orygmocraspedote and with strong alveolar prognathism |
| ,, .. | AUS.30.438 | Ditto |
| ,, ,, | AUS.80.5 | Extreme alveolar prognathism |
| ,, ,, | AUS.30.442 | Strongly developed posterior lacrimal crest |
| ,, ,, | AUS.30.984 | Very short ethmo-lacrimal sutures, especially on right side |
| ,, ,, | AUS.50.994 | Long lower canine tooth on left side |
| Department of Zoology, Oxford | 836*b* = 987 | Typical amblycraspedote |
| ,, ,, | 838*a* = 995 | Typical pseudo-oxycraspedote, and outer border of orbit widely rounded |

# 5 Types of aperturae pyriformes found in Australid skulls

THE TABLE below records the structure of the lower border of the apertura pyriformis in all those skulls and parts of skulls in the British Museum (Natural History) and the Departments of Zoology and Human Anatomy at Oxford in which this part could be observed. Intermediates have been assigned to the category to which they approximate most closely, except those that stand so exactly between two categories that this was not possible.

| *Type of craspedoty* | *No. of specimens* | |
|---|---|---|
| Epalxi- | 5 | |
| Intermediate between epalxi- and orygmo- | 1 | |
| Orygmo- | 46 | 80 |
| Intermediate between orygmo- and ambly- | 10 | |
| Ambly- | 18 | |
| Intermediate between ambly- and bothro- | 1 | |
| Bothro- | 12 | 16 |
| Pseudo-oxy- | 4 | |
| Intermediate between pseudo-oxy- and epalxi- | 1 | |

The table shows that 80 specimens lacked complete separation by a ridge (or ridges) between the nasal floor and the alveolar slope. In 17 a ridge or ridges separated the nasal floor from the alveolar slope. (One could not be assigned with confidence to either group.)

# 6  *The rock art of the Bushmen (Sanids)*

IN SOME of those ethnic taxa that never advanced on their own initiative beyond a very primitive mode of life, there have been certain individuals who have attained remarkable proficiency in particular domains of culture. The Bushmen provide an example; for their rock art, practised at a time when they were still living as food-gatherers, is justly celebrated. Some of the artists, chiefly living in the more central part of Sanid territory, engraved on rock surfaces; others, mostly in the peripheral districts, were painters. It will suffice to confine ourselves to the latter here.

In many parts of southern Africa the outcrops of granite have weathered in such a way as to leave roofs overhanging shallow recesses, providing partial protection from the elements. The process of weathering has given a smooth surface to the back walls of some of these shelters. On many of these convenient substitutes for canvas, spread out to the light of day and often covering an expanse of several yards, a magnificent set of coloured pictures greets the eye.

Some authorities, notably Frobenius,[370] have been inclined to attribute the origin of the art to the spread of culture from distant parts of the world; but there is no positive evidence that any foreigners did actually visit the territory of the Bushmen at the time, many centuries ago, when rock art was establishing itself and developing. There seems to be little doubt that Bushmen painted all the pictures that survive today, and no reason to suppose that members of any other taxon taught them how to do it.

Those who actually knew the Bushmen of the nineteenth century provide clear evidence that the paintings on the rock faces of southern Africa were the work of members of their taxon. Gustav Fritsch, one of the best authorities on native customs in that part of the world, attributes the paintings to them without the slightest hesitation.[367] George Stow, author of a classical work, *The native races of South Africa*,[1016] probably knew the Bushmen of old better than anyone else. He lived in southern Africa from 1843 onwards and was still there when he wrote the preface to his book in 1880.* He was intimately acquainted with many of the old Bushmen, who remembered well the events of earlier times. He obtained a considerable amount of evidence bearing on the identity of the artists and had no doubt that they were Bushmen. Theophilus Hahn worked among the Bushmen of south-western Africa in the sixties and seventies of the nineteenth century, studying five tribes that occupied part of the long mountain range that stretches northwards from the

* It was not published till 25 years later, after his death.

lower course of the Orange River. He found artists of all five tribes actively engaged in painting the rocks.[458]

Those who have been inclined to attribute the origin of the art to external influence, and have even doubted whether Bushmen were the artists, seem to have overlooked the significant anatomical features of the human form as represented stylistically in the paintings. The short, horizontal penes and emphasized buttocks of the men, and the pelvic posture (p. 322), steatopygia (pp. 317–18), steatomeria (p. 318), and often ludicrously exaggerated labia minora of the women (Fig. 55) are obvious Sanid features in a very large proportion of the pictures. For an extreme example of emphasis on the peculiarities of the female anatomy of Sanids the reader is referred to one of George Stow's copies of Bushman paintings, reproduced as Plate 7 in *Rock paintings in South Africa*, edited by Dorothea Bleek.[1017]

Negrids are seen in a small proportion of the Bushmen's paintings. The artists adopted a more lifelike style in representing members of taxa other than their own. Naturally enough they made the Negrids considerably larger than members of their own taxon, and frequently they showed clear appreciation of other distinguishing features, including even some rather inconspicuous ones, such as the projecting heel and the toe-region, which is much more widely splayed than in their own feet. These two minor features as well as the prognathous face are very clearly shown in the realistic picture of a Negrid in another collection of Stow's copies of Bushman paintings (Plate 11 in another book edited by Bleek[1018]). In the same picture there are two Bushmen, painted in the stylistic manner in which the artists represented members of their own taxon.

If, however, the Bushmen had left us nothing but paintings of human beings, we should have had no means of knowing that there were experts in naturalistic art among them. This was reserved for paintings of animals, many of which may be pronounced masterpieces in their genre for their delicate beauty, accuracy, and technical excellence. Hahn must be referring to the animals when he says that the forms 'are more accurately conceived and more correctly depicted than in many old Egyptian and Indian paintings'.[457] Anyone who has seen the rock paintings of southern Africa is likely to confirm Fritsch's comment, that 'Nature was instructress to the Bushman for the pictorial representation of the objects that surrounded him.'[367] Two very small details from rock paintings in Mashonaland, Rhodesia, are shown in Fig. 82, to provide a glimpse of the Bushmen's naturalistic art. Each of the original paintings covered about five feet by four. Careful copies of them by Mrs. E. Goodall, in colour, are included in the fine work *Prehistoric rock art of the Federation of Rhodesia and Nyasaland.*[1025]

One of the most interesting features of Bushman art is the custom of combining visually realistic and highly schematic forms in the same picture. A painting in a gorge in the Brandberg Mountains, north of Walvis Bay in South West Africa, provides an example of this. It is reproduced in colour in the book on Bushman art by Obermaier and Kühn.[809] Five antelopes, moving in single file, are seen. They are represented naturalistically, apart from the colours, but they are being chased by an utterly fantastic human being. As usual in represen-

**82** *Bushman art: small details from two rock paintings in Mashonaland, Rhodesia*

A, an antelope, with male and female Sanids. B, an antelope, with part of a hippopotamus below and an indeterminate object above.

*Copies made by Mrs. E. Goodall from the original rock paintings. Her copies of the complete paintings, in colour, are reproduced in Summers.*[1025]

tations of members of their own taxon, the hunter lacks facial features; but he more than makes up for this deficiency by the possession of two butterfly wings and four spidery limbs, each represented by a single line, bent at the joints. The arms are outstretched in front, as though to grasp the hindmost antelope. The contrast between naturalism and fantasy is striking and highly reminiscent of surrealism.

Actual animals and stylized Bushmen, with their accoutrements, are the principal subjects in most of the paintings; but in some of them there are also imaginary beasts and strange inanimate objects, not resembling anything present in the real world. Frobenius refers to the latter as 'absolutely inexplicable delineations, which are so peculiar in comparison with the other pictures that we can do nothing better than comprehend them under the general idea of *Formlinge*. Tuberous roots, rock boulders, and other motifs are here in such wonderful confusion, that a comparative study lasting many years would be necessary to solve the riddle of the whole subject.'[370] Frobenius does not explain why he chose the word *'Formlinge'* for these strange objects, but it has found its way into the literature of Sanid rock art. It is (or was) sometimes used in Germany for blocks of compressed coal-dust.

The recognized artists are known to have been males, and as a general rule only the exceptionally talented members of the communities were entitled to decorate the shelters and caves. The handiwork of particular painters can be recognized by experts, and it appears that certain individuals may have left their imprint on rocks situated more than a hundred miles apart.[207]

It was customary in many cases to paint one picture on top of another, and this has made it possible to trace the gradual evolution of the art from uniform colour-wash to bichrome and polychrome paintings, with concomitant improvement in the ability to represent animals as seen from different points of view. It is significant that composite pictures in which white Angora goats are represented belong exclusively to the polychrome period. These animals were first brought to southern Africa in 1689.[809] The artists relied on haematite, in its various forms, for their yellows, yellow-browns, and reds; charcoal for black; kaolin, chalk, and zinc 'oxide' (carbonate is more probable) for white.[458, 809]

The significance of the Bushmen's paintings has been much discussed. A magical or religious meaning has been attached to them by certain authors, especially Kühn.[809] It is true that some of them appear to represent religious ceremonies; but if so, the artist would have been acting simply as a recorder of events, like a press photographer, without any intention of trying to influence the course of affairs by the magic of his art. Stow, Hahn, and Sollas deny most positively that artists painted for any religious or magical purpose; they insist that the Bushmen practised their art because they valued it for the pleasure it gave.[1016, 457, 458, 989]

Whatever may have been the motive behind some of the more abstruse paintings, the genuine artistry of the Bushmen is recognized by nearly all who have studied their work. Even the best reproductions scarcely do justice to them. Summers allows this, in his foreword to the work, already quoted, on the rock art of Rhodesia and Nyasaland.[1025] As he says, the pictures in the book are as accurate as they can be made, but they lose a great deal of their vividness in reproduction. To appreciate these works of art at their full worth one needs to step from the open veldt to the entrance to a rock shelter, and see them thus suddenly displayed. In describing the painting of animals in the White Rhino shelter in the Matopo Hills, Rhodesia, Cooke says that it 'shows what complete mastery the artist had over both his subject and his materials'.[223] Verworn reproduces a painting of a rhinoceros and remarks that 'The extraordinarily naturalistic posture and movement in the reproduction is characteristic.'[1098] So, indeed, it is; but the Bushman's art had the merit of not restricting itself to naturalism. The artists maintained what was excellent in the work of their ancestors, while showing readiness to explore in new directions. Sollas sums up their achievements in these words, 'They haunt no more the sunlit veldt, their hunting is over, their nation is destroyed; but they leave behind an imperishable memory, they have immortalized themselves in their art.'[989]

Bushman art is important in several ways in studies of the ethnic problem. Above all, it shows how a taxon may be eminent in one of the factors of civilization, even if deficient in most of the rest. As Hahn remarked, in words for 'which there is unfortunately no English equivalent, '... der Sab [the Bushman] ist ein "verbummeltes Genie"'.[457] Verbummelt he may have been, but the artist of this subrace was a genius nevertheless; and the capacity to produce occasionally a person of this calibre was an important secondary character of the taxon—a character that should warn us to think hard before making any dogmatic statement about the superiority of one taxon over another. Only a small proportion of people in most races of mankind could even imitate successfully—far less initiate and perfect—the rock art of these simple people. It must be remembered, too, that although the artists were few, they flourished because other members of their communities were endowed with the faculty of appreciating their work.

# 7 Classified list of the chief Negrid tribes mentioned by the seven explorers

IN THIS list the names of all tribes are spelled exactly as the explorers spelled them. Readers who are familiar with the names of the Negrid tribes of Africa, as written in the accepted modern spelling, will be able to recognize most of them. In some cases the explorers used incorrect names, or did not name the people of a particular district; in other cases two authors used different names for the same tribe. In these cases, where possible, the correct modern name is given in italics.

Some of the tribes mentioned by the explorers are better regarded as sections of larger tribes, but it has seemed right to list the names of the smaller sections here, for the convenience of readers of the explorers' books.

Certain tribes occupying lands near the border between Kafrid and Palaenegrid 1 territory are intermediate in physical characters, and a few of those that I have classified as Palaenegrid 1 might almost as well be regarded as Kafrid (and perhaps *vice versa*).

Baker[51]
> PALAENEGRID 3.  Madi,* Makkarika (? = *Azande*)
> KAFRID.  *Banyoro*
> NILOTID.  *Acholi*, Bari, natives of Ellyria, Kytch, Nuēhr (=*Nuer*), natives of Obbo, Shir

Du Chaillu[200]
> PALAENEGRID 1.  Apingi, Ashira, Bakalai, Camma = Commi, Mpongwe, Oroungu, Shekiani
> PALAENEGRID 3.  Fang (=*Pangwe*)

Fynn[373]
> KAFRID.  Zulu (a combination of many tribes)

Galton[377]
> PALAENEGRID 4.  Ghou Damup (=*Bergdama* = *Haukhoin*)
> KAFRID.  Damara = Ovaherero, Ovampo

Livingstone[676]
> PALAENEGRID 1.  Balonda (=*Lunda*), Banyeti, Barotse (=*Lozi*), Bashinge, Basongo, Batoka, Chiboque (? = *Chokwe*)
> KAFRID.  Bakalahari, Bakuéna = Bakwain, Bamangwato, Banyai, Batonga, Bechuana, Makololo

---

* The Madi of Baker and Speke were not the same tribe as the Madi of Schweinfurth, nor the A-Madi of the latter author. These were three separate tribes. See Schweinfurth, 1951 Vol. 1, p. 523 (footnote).

Schweinfurth[951]

  PALAENEGRID 3.  A-Banga, A-Madi,* Babackur, Bongo, Kredy, Madi,* Mittoo, Monbuttoo (=*Mangbettu*), Niam-Niam = Zandey (=*Azande*)

  NILOTID.  Dinka, Dyoor, Nueir (=*Nuer*), Shillouk

Speke[996]

  PALAENEGRID 3.  Madi*

  KAFRID.  Waganda (=*Baganda*), Wanyambo, Wanyamwesi, Wanyoro (=*Banyoro*), Wasagara, Wazaromo, Wazinza

# 8  *Livingstone on evolution by sexual selection*

A NOTEWORTHY fact about Livingstone, which seems to have been overlooked by historians of biology, is that he made a very short but very significant remark on sexual selection in relation to evolution. This was published in 1857, the year before Charles Darwin's preliminary paper was read before the Linnean Society, and two years before it was published. Livingstone remarks on the small size of most kinds of domestic animals in tropical Africa, and goes on: 'It is not from the want of care in the breeding, for the natives always choose the larger and stronger males for stock, and the same arrangement prevails in nature, for it is only by overcoming their weaker rivals, that the wild males obtain possession of the herd. Invariably they show the scars received in battle.'|676| In his preliminary paper Darwin calls attention to 'the struggle of the males for the females. These struggles are generally decided by the law of battle. . . . The result of the struggle among the males may be compared in some respects to that produced by those agriculturists who pay less attention to the careful selection of all their young animals, and more to the occasional use of a choice male.'|253| Darwin introduced the term 'Sexual Selection' in 1859, in the first edition of his work *On the origin of species*.|254| He defines it as the form of selection that 'depends, not on a struggle for existence, but on a struggle between the males for possession of the females; the result is not death to the unsuccessful competitor, but few or no offspring. Generally, the most vigorous males, those which are best fitted for their places in nature, will leave most progeny.' In his book on *The descent of man, and selection in relation to sex*, published in 1871,|258| Darwin records Livingstone's remark about scars received in fights between males, but he makes no mention of the latter's idea of evolution through sexual selection, which is clearly implied in Livingstone's words recorded above.

# 9 List of all plants mentioned by the seven explorers (p. 343) as having been cultivated by Negrids, except those that cannot be identified with tolerable certainty from the information given

MANY OF the names in the list below are not those used by the explorers.

The plants most frequently mentioned by the explorers are named in heavy type; those very seldom mentioned are placed within parentheses.

| | | Place of origin |
|---|---|---|
| Moraceae | (*Ficus natalensis*, bark-cloth tree) | indigenous |
| Cannabinaceae | (*Cannabis sativa*, Indian hemp) | central Asia |
| Euphorbiaceae | **Manihot utilissima,** cassava | tropical America |
| Papilionaceae | **Arachis hypogaea,** ground-nut | South America |
| | (*Phaseolus vulgaris*, runner-bean) | |
| | (*P. mungo*, Urd bean) | ? indigenous |
| | *P. lunatus*, butter-bean | ? Asia |
| | (*Vigna sinensis*, Catiang bean) | India |
| | (*Canavalia ensiformis*, horse-bean) | West Indies |
| | *Voandzeia subterranea*, Bambarra ground-nut | ? indigenous |
| Convolvulaceae | **Ipomoea batatas,** sweet potato | |
| Pedaliaceae | *Sesamum indicum*, sesame | indigenous |
| Labiatae | (*Hyptis spicigera*, kendee) | ? America |
| Solanaceae | *Nicotiana rustica*, Mexican tobacco | Mexico, Texas |
| | **N. tabacum,** South American tobacco | South America |
| Cucurbitaceae | *Cucurbita maxima*, pumpkin | |
| | *Cucumis melo*, melon | |
| | (*C. sativus*, cucumber) | |
| | (*Citrullus vulgaris*, water-melon) | indigenous |
| Dioscoreaceae | **Dioscorea** sp., yam | |
| Bromeliaceae | (*Ananas sativus*, pineapple) | South America |
| Gramineae | *Pennisetum typhoideum*, bajra | |
| | **Sorgum durra,** dhurra | |
| | **Eleusine corocana,** telaboon | |
| | **Zea mays,** maize | South America |
| | (*Triticum vulgare*, wheat) | |
| | (*Oryza sativa*, red rice) | India |
| | *Panicum miliaceum*, millet | Egypt, Arabia |
| | **Saccharum officinarum,** sugar-cane | tropical Asia |
| Palmae | (*Borassus flabellifer*, Palmyra palm) | indigenous |
| | *Elaeis guineensis*, oil-palm | indigenous |
| | (*Cocos nucifera*, coconut) | |
| Araceae | (*Richardia (Calla) africana*), Arum lily | indigenous |
| | *Colocasia antiquorum*, taro | |
| Musaceae | (*Musa ensete*, ensete) | indigenous |
| | **M. sapientium,** plantain and banana | |

# 10 Remarks on the grading of competitors in sports by body-weight, and the advantage thus given to members of certain ethnic taxa

THE ADVANTAGES gained by members of certain taxa through their greater stature or bulk have been mentioned on pp. 421–5. It must be pointed out, however, that in those events in which competitors are graded into groups by body-weight, advantage may be gained by nations in which the population consists largely of people belonging to taxa in which small stature is one of the characteristic features. This results from the establishment of a number of categories for small persons of different weights. Thus in free-style wrestling there are separate competitions for flyweights, bantamweights, featherweights, and welterweights; and in the Olympic Games medals are awarded for success in each category. In a nation consisting mainly of Sudanids or Nordids, for instance, only a small proportion of the population would be eligible for any of these competitions. In a predominantly Palaemongolid nation, on the contrary, one could select from a large proportion of the population. Japanese, predominantly Palaemongolid, have won no fewer than six gold, three silver, and three bronze medals for free-style wrestling in the categories mentioned above. They have never won any medal for free-style wrestling in the middleweight, light-heavyweight, or heavyweight categories.*

* The Olympic records were analysed over the period 1896–1968.

# 11 *Notes on the differences between the skulls of dog and jackal*

T. H. HUXLEY distinguished what he called 'Thooid' (doglike) from 'Alopecoid' (foxlike) species of Canidae primarily on the basis of a careful comparison of a single Thooid skull (that of the South American wild dog, *Canis azarae*) with a single Alopecoid one (that of the common red fox, *Vulpes vulpes*).[539] The purpose of this note is to call attention to certain features that differed in these two particular specimens but do *not* serve to distinguish skulls of the jackal, *Canis aureus indicus*, from those of the common red fox, *Vulpes vulpes vulpes*, though these two species are respectively Thooid and Alopecoid.

The ascending processes of the premaxillae do *not* ordinarily reach the anterior processes of the frontal in the fox; indeed, they do not approach them more nearly than they do in the jackal. The last premolar and the two molar teeth of the upper jaw are set in a similar curve in jackal and fox; their arrangement does *not* approximate more nearly to a straight line in the jackal. In the external form of their skulls the Thooid (jackal) and Alopecoid (fox) are more alike than anyone would be likely to expect from reading Huxley's conclusions based on *single skulls only* of *C. azarae* and *V. vulpes*, though the separation of the two genera is fully justified on other grounds.

# 12  The physical characters of Andids and Zentralids

THE PURPOSE of this Appendix is to provide the evidence on which the two Indianid subraces that came closest to civilization are assigned to separate subraces. Naturally they both present certain features common to most Indianids, such as scantiness of facial hair in males, thickness and rigidity of the individual hairs of the scalp, dark brown iris, swollen thorax, wide shoulders and pelvis, and very high frequency of the gene for blood-group 'O'.

The following account of the most obvious physical features of the Andids is based mainly, but not entirely, on the careful observations made by the French zoologist Alcide d'Orbigny, who had the advantage of studying them before any extensive hybridization with immigrants had occurred.[811]

The stature of the Andids is low—medium, adult males averaging about 1·60 m. They are rather massively built and the trunk is very long in relation to total height. The scalp hairs are very long and very straight. The head is brachycephalic. The face is wide, but the zygomatic arches do not project excessively. The forehead is broad and low, and its lowness is exaggerated by the insertion of the scalp-hair far down on it; it retreats moderately, the vault being highest at the back. (One of the tribes, the Aymara, used to exaggerate this feature artificially to such an extent that at first glance one would not recognize the skull as human.) The nose is very characteristic. It is rather broad, long from sellion to tip, and markedly aquiline; the alae spread widely. The chin is short vertically, but rather massive and not retreating. The eye-slits are narrow and horizontal; the margin of the upper eyelid falls at the nasal side as an *Indianerfalte* (plica naso-marginalis).[12] The cornea is pale yellow. The ears are long, narrow, and very obliquely placed. The skin is moderately dark olive-brown.

Among secondary characters one may mention the presence of a Wormian bone, the epactal, between the parietals and the occipital. This occurs so frequently, in both normal and artificially deformed skulls,[268] that it receives the name of 'Inca bone'. Some members of the subrace have a distinctive odour, the same in both sexes.

Orbigny stresses strongly the peculiarities of the Andids (or '*Race Ando-Péruvienne*', as he calls this taxon). 'The Peruvians', he remarks, 'differ entirely from all other races in the world.' It is significant for the subject of the present book that he qualifies this rather exaggerated statement by adding, '. . . it is an altogether distinct type, that is similar only to the Mexican peoples' (i.e. presumably the Zentralids).

The following brief account of Zentralid anatomy is based principally on Eickstedt's account.[302]

The stature is about the same or perhaps a little less than that of the Andids, but the Zentralids are more slender. They are more brachycephalic than the former subrace. Except in skin-colour, the face resembles that of Europids more closely than does that of any other Indianid subrace. The zygomatic arches do not project so much as in the other subraces, and the forehead is steep, high, and narrow, which is exceptional in the Indianid race. (The Maya, however, like the Aymara among the Andids, used formerly to flatten the forehead artificially in some cases.) The nose is generally straight or slightly convex, but never actually aquiline. The tip is pointed, but the organ is rather broad, with fairly wide alae. The mouth tends to turn downwards at the sides, especially in females. The chin is broad and rather square, and retreats somewhat. The eyes are very different from those of the Andids in being held widely open, to show a somewhat almond-shaped space between the eyelids; there is no *Indianerfalte*. The skin is rather dark brown; darker, in fact, than that of any other Indianid subrace of Central or North America. There is a distinctive body odour.

# 13 *Middle American calendars*

THE SOLAR year was clearly recognized by the Aztecs. It was regarded as consisting of 365 days. It seems uncertain whether they realized that the year was in fact about 0·24 day longer than this, and if so what method, if any, was adopted by them to correct the resulting cumulative error.|1082|

There was no attempt to use a lunar month. In accordance with the vigesimal system of numeration, days were counted in groups of twenty. Each of the twenty days was given a name, and these were always used in the same order. These six will serve as an example: 'reed', 'jaguar', 'eagle', 'vulture', 'motion', and 'flint-knife' (in that sequence). It seems that when the calendar was instituted, the first New Year's Day was 'reed'. When eighteen cycles of twenty days each had been completed, there remained five days ('reed', 'jaguar', 'eagle', 'vulture', and 'motion') before the next New Year; thus the latter started on 'flint-knife'. The following New Year started five days later in the series again with 'house', and the next five days later again with 'rabbit'. After that 'reed' was once more, necessarily, the day on which the next New Year must start; and these four ('reed', 'flint-knife', 'house', and 'rabbit') were the only days on which a New Year could start.

A separate cycle, of thirteen days, operated continuously alongside the 20-day cycle. The days of this short cycle were distinguished by numbers instead of names. It seems that the very first New Year's Day started, for some unexplained reason, on day 2 (cf. Vaillant|1082|).

Thus each day was given a number in the 13-day cycle and also a name in the 20-day cycle. The first New Year's Day having been '2-reed', the very next day was '3-jaguar'; this was followed by '4-eagle' and '5-vulture' and so on until thirteen days had been completed, when the shorter cycle began again with '1-death's-head' (the latter being the name of the fourteenth day in the longer cycle). The result was that every day received a different combination of number and name from all other days until 260 (= 13 × 20) days had passed, when the turn for '2-reed' came round again, and the same sequence as before began to be repeated endlessly. The reader who cares to work it out for herself or himself will find that when 365 days had been completed, the next New Year's Day fell on '3-flint-knife', the sixth day after the eighteenth 20-day cycle had ended.

If, then, the first year started on '2-reed', the next began on '3-flint-knife', the next after that on '4-house', and the one following on '5-rabbit'; 'reed' appeared again on the next New Year's Day in the form of '6-reed'. When 52 (= 13 × 4) years had elapsed, '2-reed' at last occurred again *on New Year's Day* (though it had recurred repeatedly on other days). The recurrence on New Year's Day follows from the fact that the lowest common multiple of 365 and 260 days is 365 × 52 days, i.e. 52 years. This explains the immense emphasis placed by the Aztecs on the period of 52 years. It was supposed that when this cycle was completed, the world might come to an end; and tremendous rejoicing greeted the rising of the sun on the day on which it had been thought possible (genuinely, it seems) that another dawn might never come.

The Maya are regarded as the inventors of the Middle American calendars. The Aztecs' system was very similar to theirs, but differences existed. In particular, the Maya were able to extend their calendar back into the remote past, whereas the Aztecs had no method of distinguishing one 52-year cycle from another,[1082] and considerable difficulties are encountered by historians as a result. The names of the days in the 20-day cycle referred to the same objects in the two calendars, but each nation used its own language to designate them.

The Maya clearly recognized that the year was slightly longer than 365 days,[382] and they are said to have introduced a system of intercalary days almost as exact as our own.[99]

# Bibliography

EACH AUTHOR is listed under a single name only. Several authors have spelled their surnames differently in their various publications, or used different initials or names differing in other ways. In nearly every such case the name given in this bibliography is that used by the author himself in his earliest publication listed here.

The works of a single author are arranged in the order of their dates of publication, with the exception that the editions and translations of a single work are listed in direct sequence without regard to the dates of publication of other works by the same author. If the name of a book was changed in a new edition, however slightly, the new name is here written out in full.

Spelling and the use or omission of accents follow the original exactly.

Sources of information not contained in printed works are listed separately on p. 605.

1. **Abbie, A. A.,** 1965. 'Incidence of hairy pinna in Australian aborigines.' *Nature, 206,* 533–4.

2. —— 1966. 'The anthropological status of the Australian aborigines.' *Homo, 17,* 74–88.

3. —— **& Rao, P. D. P.,** 1965. 'Hairy pinna in Australian aborigines.' *Human Biol., 37,* 162–73.

4. **Adachi, B.,** 1903. 'Hautpigment beim Menschen und bei den Affen.' *Ztschr. Morph. Anthrop., 6,* 1–131.

5. —— 1937. 'Das Ohrenschmalz als Rassenmerkmal und der Rassengeruch ("Achselgeruch") nebst dem Rassenunterschied der Schweissdrüsen.' *Ztschr. f. Rassenk., 6,* 273–307.

6. —— **& Fujisawa, K.,** 1903. 'Mongolen-Kinderfleck bei Europäern.' *Ztschr. Morph. Anthrop., 6,* 132–3.

7. **Adanson, M.,** 1757. *Histoire naturelle du Sénégal: coquillages.* Paris (Bauche).

8. **Addison, T.,** 1849. 'Disease of the supra-renal capsules.' *London med. Gazette, 43,* 517–18.

9. —— 1855. *On the constitutional and local effects of disease of the supra-renal capsules.* London (Highley).

10. **Aelian [C.],** 1958. *On the characteristics of animals.* Greek text with English translation. 3 vols. London (Heinemann).

11. **Agassiz, L.,** 1850. 'De la classification des animaux dans ses rapports avec leur développement embryonnaire et avec leur histoire paléontologique.' *Biblioth. univ. Genève: Arch. des Sci. phys. et nat., 5,* 190–204.

12. **Aichel, O.,** 1933. 'Ergebnisse einer Forschungsreise nach Chile-Bolivien. 4. Epicanthus, Mongolenfalte, Negerfalte, Hottentottenfalte, Indianerfalte.' *Ztschr. Morph. Anthrop., 31,* 123–66.

13. **Allison, A. C., Blumberg, B. S., & Rees, — ap,** 1958. 'Haptoglobin types in British, Spanish Basque and Nigerian African populations.' *Nature, 181,* 824–5.

14. **Alper, T. G., & Boring, E. G.,** 1944. 'Intelligence-test scores of northern and southern white and Negro recruits in 1918.' *J. abnorm. soc. Psychol., 39,* 471–4.

15. **Ammon, O.** (edited by), 1899. *Zur Anthropologie der Badener. Bericht über die von der Anthropologischen Kommission des Karlsruher Altertumsvereins an Wehrpflichtigen und Mittelschülern vorgenommenen Untersuchungen.* Jena (Fischer).

16. —— 1900. 'Zur Theorie der reinen Rassentypen.' *Ztschr. Morph. Anthrop., 2,* 679–85.

17. **Amoore, J. E., Johnston, J. W., & Rubin, M.,** 1964. 'The stereochemical theory of odor.' *Sci. Amer., 210,* 42–9.

18. **Anastasi, A.,** 1968. *Psychological testing.* 3rd edit. London (Macmillan).

19. **Anati, E.,** 1963. *Palestine before the Hebrews.* London (Cape).

20. **Anderson, J. G. C.,** 1938. Comment added to Tacitus.[1034]

21. **Andree, R.,** 1881. *Zur Volkskunde der Juden.* Bielefeld (Velhagen & Klasing).

22. —— 1889. *Ethnographische Parallelen und Vergleiche.* Neue Folge. Leipzig (Veit).

23. **Anon.,** 1684*a*. 'Extrait du Journal d'Angleterre, contenant plusieurs choses remarquables.' *Journ. des Sçavans* (vol. not numbered), 39 (only).

24. —— 1684*b*. 'Nouvelle division de la terre, par les différentes espèces ou races d'hommes qui l'habitent.' *J. des Sçavans* (vol. not numbered), 85–89.

25. —— 1955. *A summary guide to the exhibition galleries of the British Museum.* London (Trustees of the British Museum).

26. —— 1960. *South Africa 1910–1960.* Pretoria (South African Information Office).

27. —— 1967*a*. 'One of America's leading Negro spokesmen.' *Daily Telegraph,* 25 April.

28. —— 1967*b*. 'Rusk's daughter marries Negro.' *Daily Telegraph,* 22 Sept.

29. —— 1968. 'Biological views of race.' *Lancet, 2,* 762–3.

30. **Anoutchine [D.],** 1878. 'Sur la conformation du ptérion chez diverses races humaines et les primates.' *Bull. Soc. d'Anthrop. Paris, 1,* 330–3.

31. —— 1882. 'Über einige Anomalien am menschlichen Schädel mit besonderer Berücksichtigung des Vorkommens der Anomalien bei verschiedenen Rassen.' (Abstract from original in Russian.) *Biol. Centralbl., 2,* 38–51.

32. **Anstruther, I.,** 1956. *I presume: Stanley's triumph and disaster.* London (Bles).

33. **Asher, M.,** 1970. 'Israel defines a Jew.' *Daily Telegraph,* 12th March.

34. **Ashley-Montagu, M. F.,** 1933. 'The anthropological significance of the pterion in the Primates.' *Amer. J. phys. Anthrop., 18,* 159–336.

35. —— 1940. Review of McCown & Keith.[720] *Amer. Anthrop., 42,* 518–22.

36. —— 1946. *Man's most dangerous myth: the fallacy of race.* New York (Columbia University Press).

37. **Ashmore, H. S.** (edited by), 1961. *Encyclopædia Britannica: a new survey of universal knowledge.* 24 vols. London (Encyclopædia Britannica, Ltd.).

38. **Audouin, I. B., & others,** 1825. *Dictionnaire classique d'histoire naturelle.* Vol. 8. Paris (Rey & Gravier).

39. **Augé, C. & P.** (edited by), 1947. *Nouveau petit Larousse illustré: dictionnaire encyclopédique.* Paris (Larousse).

40. **B., J. C.,** 1912. 'Recent literature on the Binet tests.' *J. educ. Psychol., 3,* 101–10.

41. **Baelz, E.,** 1901. 'Menschen-Rassen Ost-Asiens mit specieller Rücksicht auf Japan.' *Ztschr. f. Ethnol., 33* (*Verh. Berl. Ges. Anthrop. Ethnol. Urges.,* 166–90).

42. **Baer, K. E. v.,** 1828. *Über Entwickelungsgeschichte der Thiere. Beobachtung und Reflexion.* Erster Theil. Königsberg (Bornträger).

43. —— 1876. Article 'Ueber Darwins Lehre' in *Reden gehalten in wissenschaftlichen Versammlungen und kleinere Aussätze vermischten Inhalts.* Vol. 2. St. Petersburg (Schmitzdorff).

44. **Baines, A.** (edited by), 1969. *Musical instruments through the ages.* (Reprinted with revisions.) Harmondsworth (Penguin Books).

45. **Baker, J. R.,** 1928. 'Notes on New Hebridean customs, with special reference to the intersex pig.' *Man, 28,* 113–18.

46. —— 1929. *Man and animals in the New Hebrides.* London (Routledge).

47. —— 1968a. 'Cro-Magnon man, 1868–1968.' *Endeavour, 27,* 87–90.

48. —— 1968b. 'Observations on the cranium of Broken Hill Man, *Homo rhodesiensis* Woodward.' *Ztschr. Morph. Anthrop., 60,* 121–7.

49. —— 1973. Observations not previously published.

50. **Baker, R. S.,** 1908. *Following the colour line: an account of Negro citizenship in the American democracy.* London (Doubleday, Page).

51. **Baker, S. W.,** 1866. *The Albert N'Yanza, great basin of the Nile, and explorations of the Nile sources.* London (Macmillan).

52. —— 1874. *Ismailïa: a narrative of the expedition to central Africa for the suppression of the slave trade organized by Ismail, Khedive of Egypt.* 2 vols. London (Macmillan).

53. —— 1890. *Wild beasts and their ways. Reminiscences of Europe, Asia, Africa, and America.* 2 vols. London (Macmillan).

54. **Balsan, F.,** 1962. 'Les routes de l'or du Matabéléland.' *Acta geographica (Paris), 44,* 3–7.

55. **Bancroft, H. H.,** 1875–6. *The native races of the Pacific states of North America.* 5 vols. New York (Appleton).

56. **Bargmann, W.,** 1939. 'Blutgefäss- und Lymphgefässapparat innersekretorische Drüsen', constituting Vol. 6, Part 2, of Möllendorff & Bargmann.[751]

57. **Barker, E.,** 1914. *Nietzsche and Treitschke: the worship of power in modern Germany.* London (Oxford University Press).

58. **Barnicot, N. A., Garlick, J. P., Singer, R., & Weiner, J. S.,** 1959. 'Haptoglobin and transferrin variants in Bushmen and some other South African peoples.' *Nature, 184,* 2042 (only).

59. **Bartels, P.,** 1911. 'Histologisch-anthropologische Untersuchungen der Plica semilunaris bei Herero und Hottentotten, sowie bei einigen Anthropoiden.' *Arch. mikr. Anat., 78,* 529–64.

60. **Bascom, W. R.,** 1939. 'The legacy of an unknown Nigerian "Donatello": the simple beauty of the mysterious bronze heads recently discovered at Ife.' *Illustrated London News, 194,* 592–4.

61. **Bastian, A.,** 1874. *Die deutsche Expedition an der Loango-Küste, nebst älteren Nachrichten über die zu erforschenden Länder.* 2 vols. in 1. Jena (Costenoble).

62. **Bate, H. M.,** 1956. *South Africa without prejudice.* London (Werner Laurie).

63. **Bather, F. A.** (edited by), 1928. *Rhodesian man and associated remains.* London (British Museum (Natural History)).

64. **Baudin, L.,** 1961. *Daily life in Peru under the last Incas.* Transl. by W. Bradford. London (Allen & Unwin).

65. **Baur, E., Fischer, E., & Lenz, F.,** 1931. *Human heredity.* Translated, with corrections, from the 3rd German edition. London (Allen & Unwin).

66. **Becker, S. W., Fitzpatrick, T. B., & Montgomery, H.,** 1952. 'Human melanogenesis:

cytology and histology of pigment cells (melanodendrocytes).' *Arch. Dermatol. Syphilol.*, *65*, 511–23.

67. **Beda, —[Venerable Bede]**, 1473. *Bedae historia ecclesiastica gentis Anglorum.* (Place of publication and publisher not named.)

68. —— 1847. *The Venerable Bede's ecclesiastical history of England. Also the Anglo-Saxon chronicle.* Edited by J. A. Giles. London (Bohn).

69. **Beddoe, J.,** 1885. *The races of Britain: a contribution to the anthropology of western Europe.* Bristol (Arrowsmith).

70. **Bedoukian, P. Z.,** 1953. Article on 'Perfumes: synthetics and isolates' in Kirk & Othmer.[584] pp. 17–38.

71. **Beer, G. R. de,** 1951. *Embryos and ancestors.* Oxford (Clarendon Press).

72. —— 1965. *Genetics and prehistory.* Cambridge (University Press).

73. —— 1969. *Hannibal: the struggle for power in the Mediterranean.* London (Thames & Hudson).

74. **Benedict, R., & Weltfish, G.,** 1943. 'The races of mankind.' *Public affairs Pamphlet No. 85.* New York (Public affairs Committee).

75. **Bennett, E. L., Diamond, M. C., Krech, D., & Rosenzweig, R.,** 1964. 'Chemical and anatomical plasticity of brain.' *Science, 146,* 610–19.

76. **Bennett, J.,** n.d. *Giacomo Meyerbeer.* London (Novello, Ewer).

77. **Berchem, B. van,** 1789. 'Réflexions sur la maniere de distinguer les espèces, les races & les variétés dans les animaux quadrupèdes; d'après leurs caracteres extérieurs.' *Hist. et mém. Soc. Sci. phys. Lausanne, 2,* 45–64.

78. **Berg, L. S.,** 1926. *Nomogenesis or evolution determined by law.* Translated from the Russian. London (Constable).

79. **Bergman, H.,** 1954. *The autobiography of Solomon Maimon.* Transl. from the German. London (East & West Library).

80. **Bernatzik, H. A.,** 1929. *Zwischen weissem Nil und Belgisch-Kongo.* Wien (Seidel).

81. **Bertin, L. C.,** 1958. Article on 'Sexualité et fécondation' in Grassé.[427] Vol. 13, Fasc. 2, 1584–652.

82. —— **& Arambourg, C.,** 1958. Article on 'Super-ordre des Téléostéens (Teleostei)' in Grassé.[427] Vol. 13, Fasc. 3, 2204–500.

83. **Biesheuvel, S.,** 1949. 'The measurement of intelligence and aptitudes of African peoples.' *African Regional Scientific Conference, Johannesburg,* E(n)*4,* 1–5.

84. —— 1952*a.* 'The study of African ability. Part I. The intellectual potentialities of Africans. Some problems in the study of interracial mental differences.' *African Studies, 11* (2), 45–58.

85. —— 1952*b.* 'The study of African ability. Part II. A survey of some research problems.' *African Studies, 11* (3), 105–17.

86. **Bigelow, R. S.,** 1965. 'Hybrid zones and reproductive isolation.' *Evolution, 19,* 449–58.

87. **Billingham, R. E.,** 1948. 'Dendritic cells.' *J. Anat., 82,* 93–109.

88. —— 1949. 'Dendritic cells in pigmented human skin.' *J. Anat., 83,* 109–15.

89. —— **& Silvers, W. K.,** 1960. 'The melanocytes of mammals.' *Quart. Rev. Biol., 35,* 1–40.

90. **Binet, A.,** 1889. *The psychic life of micro-organisms. A study in experimental psychology.* Transl. from the French. London (Longmans, Green).

91. —— 1894. *Contribution à l'étude du système nerveux sous-intestinal des insectes.* Paris (Alcan).

92. **Binet, A.,** 1899. *The psychology of reasoning based on experimental researches in hypnotism.* Transl. from the 2nd French edition. London (Kegan Paul, Trench, Trübner).

93. —— 1903. *L'étude experimental de l'intelligence.* Paris (Schleicher).

94. —— 1911. 'Nouvelles recherches sur la mesure du niveau intellectuel chez les enfants d'école.' *Année psych., 17,* 145–201.

95. —— **& Simon, T.,** 1905*a.* 'Sur la nécessité d'établir un diagnostic scientifique des états inférieurs de l'intelligence.' *Année psych., 11,* 163–90.

96. —— —— 1905*b.* 'Méthodes nouvelles pour le diagnostic du niveau intellectuel des anormaux.' *Année psych., 11,* 191–244.

97. —— —— 1905*c.* 'Application des méthodes nouvelles au diagnostic du niveau intellectuel chez des enfants normaux et anormaux d'hospice et d'école primaire.' *Année psych., 11,* 245–336.

98. —— —— 1908. 'Le developpement de l'intelligence chez les enfants.' *Année psych., 14,* 1–94.

99. **Birket-Smith, K.,** 1965. *The paths of culture: a general ethnology.* Transl. from the Danish. Madison (University of Wisconsin Press).

100. **Blacker, C. P.,** 1952. *Eugenics: Galton and after.* London (Duckworth).

101. **Blair, P. H.,** 1960. *An introduction to Anglo-Saxon England.* Cambridge (University Press).

102. **Blakeslee, A. F.,** 1932. 'Genetics of sensory thresholds: taste for phenyl thio carbamide.' *Proc. Nat. Acad. Sci. U.S.A., 18,* 120–30.

103. **Blanchard, R.,** 1883. 'Etude sur la steatopygie et le tablier des femmes boschimanes.' *Bull. Soc. zool. France, 8,* 34–75.

104. **Bloch, A.,** 1896. 'Des rapports du système pileux avec la coloration de la peau. *Bull. Soc. d'Anthr. Paris, 7,* 524–8.

105. **Blum, H. F.,** 1959. *Carcinogenesis by ultraviolet light.* Princeton (University Press).

106. **Blumenbach, I. F.,** 1776. *De generis humani varietate nativa liber.* Goettingae (Vandenhoeck).

107. —— 1781. *De generis humani varietate nativa liber.* Editio altera (2nd edit.) Goettingen (Vandenhoek).

108. —— 1795. *De generis humani varietate nativa.* 3rd edit. Gottingae (Vandenhoek & Ruprecht).

109. —— 1790. *Beyträge zur Naturgeschichte.* Göttingen (Dieterich).

110. —— 1865. *The anthropological treatises of Johann Friedrich Blumenbach.* Transl. by T. Bendyshe. London (Longmans).

111. **Blunt, K., & Cowan, R.,** 1930. *Ultraviolet light and vitamin D in nutrition.* Chicago (University Press).

112. **Boas, F.,** 1911. *The mind of primitive man.* New York (Macmillan).

113. —— 1912. *Changes in bodily form of descendants of immigrants.* New York (Columbia University Press).

114. —— 1940. *Race, language and culture.* New York (Macmillan).

115. **Bobertag, O.,** 1911. 'Über Intelligenzprüfungen (nach der Methode von Binet und Simon).' *Ztschr. angew. Psych. u. psych. Sammelforsch., 5,* 105–203.

116. **Boddie, G. F.,** 1961. Article on 'Poultry' in Law.[642] Vol. 11, pp. 142–6.

117. **Boessneck, J.,** 1953. 'Die Haustiere in Altägypten.' *Veröff. zool. Staatssamm., München, 3,* 1–50.

118. **Bohlken, H.,** 1961. 'Haustiere und zoologische Systematik.' *Ztschr. Tierzücht. u. Züchtungsbiol., 76,* 107–13.

119. **Bolk, L.,** 1926*a*. 'Neue Ansichten über die Menschwerdung.' *Verh. Anat. Ges., 35* Versammlung; 76 (only).

120. —— 1926*b*. *Das Problem der Menschwerdung.* Jena (Fischer).

121. —— 1926*c*. 'Die Entstehung des Menschenkinnes: ein Beitrag zur Entwicklungsgeschichte des Unterkiefers.' *Verh. Kön. Akad. van Wetenschappen, Amsterdam,* Sect. 2, *23* (5), 1–95.

122. —— 1929. 'Origin of racial characteristics in man.' *Amer. J. phys. Anthrop., 13,* 1–28.

123. —— **Göppert, E., Kallius, E., & Lubosch, W.** (edited by). 1936. *Handbuch der vergleichenden Anatomie der Wirbeltiere.* Vol. 4. Berlin (Urban & Schwarzenberg).

124. **Bonin, G. von,** 1912. 'Zur Morphologie der Fossa praenasalis.' *Archiv f. Anthrop., 11,* 185–95.

125. —— 1963. *The evolution of the human brain.* London (University of Chicago Press).

126. **Bonser, F. G.,** 1910. *The reasoning ability of children of the fourth, fifth, and sixth school grades.* New York (Teachers College, Columbia University).

127. **Boring, E. G.,** n.d. Quoted without reference by Jensen.[551]

128. **Bory de Saint-Vincent, G.],** 1825. Article on 'Homme. *Homo*' in Audouin & others[38], Vol. 8, pp. 269–346.

129. **Boule, M.,** 1911. 'L'homme fossile de La Chapelle-aux-Saints.' *Ann. de Paléont, 6,* 109–72.

130. —— 1912–13. 'L'homme fossile de La Chapelle-aux-Saints.' *Ann. de Paléont., 7,* 21–56 & 85–192; *8,* 1–67.

131. —— **& Vallois, H. V.,** 1957. *Fossil men: a textbook of human palaeontology.* London (Thames & Hudson).

132. **Boulenger, E. G.,** 1915. *Reptiles and batrachians.* London (Dent).

133. **Bouvier, E.-L., & Fischer, H.,** 1898. 'Étude monographique des pleurotomaires actuels.' *Arch. Zool. exp., 6,* 115–80.

134. **Braunholtz, H. J.,** 1940. 'Bronze head from Ifé, Nigeria.' *Brit. Mus. Quart., 14,* 75–7.

135. **Bredius, A.,** 1936. *The paintings of Rembrandt.* London (Allen & Unwin).

136. **Brinkmann, A.,** 1909. 'Ueber das Vorkommen von Hautdrüsenorganen bei den anthropomorphen Affen.' *Anat. Anz., 34,* 513–20.

137. **Brinkmann, R.,** 1929. 'Statistisch-biostratigraphische Untersuchungen an Mitteljurassischen Ammoniten über Artbegriff und Stammesentwicklung.' *Abh. Ges. Wiss. Göttingen, Math.-Phys. Kl., 13* (3), 1–249.

138. **Broca, P.,** 1858. 'Mémoire sur l'hybridité en général, sur la distinction des espèces animales et sur les métis obtenus par le croisement du lièvre et du lapin.' *J. de la Physiol., 1,* 433–71 & 684–729.

139. —— 1859. Ditto. *J. de la Physiol., 2,* 218–58 & 345–96.

140. —— 1859–60. 'Des phénomènes d'hybridité dans le genre humain.' *J. de la Physiol., 2,* 601–25; *3,* 392–439.

141. —— 1873. 'Sur les Celtes.' *Bull. Soc. Anthropol. Paris, 8,* 247–52.

142. **Brodrick, A. H.,** 1960. *Man and his ancestry.* London (Hutchinson).

143. **Broom, R.,** 1947. 'Discovery of a new skull of the South African ape-man, *Plesianthropus.*' *Nature, 159,* 672 (only).

144. —— 1951. *Finding the missing link.* London (Watts).

145. —— **& Robinson, J. T.,** 1950. 'Further evidence of the structure of the Sterkfontein apeman Plesianthropus.' *Transvaal Mus. Mem., 4* (1), 7–83.

146. **Brosnahan, L. F.,** 1961. *The sounds of language: an inquiry into the role of genetic factors in the development of sound systems.* Cambridge (Heffer).

147. **Brown, P. P.,** 1949.·'Learning a European language.' *Year Book of Education* (vol. not numbered), 338–41.

148. **Brown, W. L., & Wilson, E. O.,** 1954. 'The case against the trinomen.' *System. Zool., 3,* 174–6.

149. **Browne, L.,** 1930. *The story of the Jews from the earliest times to the present day.* London (Cape).

150. **Browne, T.,** 1646. *Pseudodoxia epidemica: or, enquiries into very many received tenents, and commonly presumed truths.* London (Dod).

151. —— 1658a. *Hydriotaphia urne-burial. Or, A brief discourse of the sepulchrall urnes lately found in Norfolk;* bound with second edition of *Pseudodoxia epidemica: or enquiries into very many received tenents, and commonly preserved truths.* London (Dod).

152. —— 1658b. *Hydriotaphia, or urne-buriall, or, a discourse of the sepulchrall urnes lately found in Norfolk.* London (Brome).

153. —— 1669. *Hydriotaphia, urn burial; or, A discourse of the sepulchral urns lately found in Norfolk. Together with The garden of Cyrus; or, The quincuncial lozenge, or network plantations of the ancients, artificially, naturally, mystically considered: with sundry observations.* London (Brome).

154. —— 1965. *Religio medici and other writings.* London (Dent).

155. **Bruce, J.,** 1790a. *Travels to discover the source of the Nile, in the years 1768, 1769, 1770, 1771, 1772, and 1773.* 5 vols. London (Robinson).

156. —— 1790b. *An interesting narrative of the travels of James Bruce, Esq., into Abyssinia, to discover the source of the Nile.* Abridged by S. Shaw. London (Shaw).

157. **Buchanan, G.,** 1582. *Rerum Scoticarum historia.* Edinburgh (Arbuthnet).

158. **Budgett, J. S.,** 1903. 'On the breeding habits of some West-African fishes, with an account of the external features in development of *Protopterus annectens,* and a description of the larva of *Polypterus lapradii.*' *Trans. Zool. Soc. Lond., 16,* 115–36.

159. **Buffon, G. L. L. de,** 1749. *Histoire générale des animaux* and *Histoire naturelle de l'homme,* constituting Vol. 2 of Buffon, Daubenton, & La Cepède.[165]

160. —— 1766. *Histoire naturelle, générale et particulière, avec la description du cabinet du roi.* Vol. 4. Paris (Imprimerie royale).

161. —— (edited by), 1771–86. *Histoire naturelle des oiseaux.* 10 vols. Paris (Imprimerie Royale).

162. —— 1776. Supplément III to Buffon, Daubenton, & La Cepède.[165]

163. —— 1777. Article on 'Le serin des Canaries' in Buffon,[161] Vol. 4.

164. —— 1778. Article on 'Des mulets in Buffon, Daubenton, & La Cepède.[165] Suppl. 4.

165. —— **Daubenton, L., & La Cepède, E.,** 1749–1804. *Histoire naturelle, générale et particulière, avec la description du Cabinet du Roy.* 38 vols. & 7 Suppl. Paris (Imprimerie Royale).

166. **Burkitt, A. St. N., & Hunter, J. I.,** 1923. 'The description of a Neanderthaloid Australian skull, with remarks on the production of the facial characteristics of Australian skulls in general.' *J. Anat., 57,* 31–54.

167. —— **& Lightoller, G. H. S.,** 1923. 'Preliminary observations on the nose of the Australian aboriginal, with a table of aboriginal head measurements.' *J. Anat., 57,* 295–312.

168. **Burland, C. A.,** 1967. *Peru under the Incas.* London (Evans).

169. **Burt, C.,** 1943. 'Ability and income.' *Brit. J. educ. Psychol., 13,* 83–98.

170. —— 1946. 'Intelligence and fertility: the effect of the differential birthrate on inborn mental characteristics.' *Occ. Pap. Eugen.* |Eugenics Society|, *2*, 1–43.

171. —— 1966. 'The genetic determination of differences in intelligence: a study of monozygotic twins reared together and apart.' *Brit. J. Psychol., 57*, 137–53.

172. —— & Howard, M., 1956. 'The multifactorial theory of inheritance and its application to intelligence.' *Brit. J. statist. Psychol., 9*, 95–131.

173. **Burton, R. F., & M'Queen, J.,** 1864. *The Nile basin.* London (Tinsley).

174. **Bushnell, G. H. S.,** 1961. Article on 'America: archaeology' in Law.[642] Vol. 1, pp. 345–53.

175. **Buxton, L. H. D.,** 1936*a*. Article on 'The sea raiders' in Buxton.[176]

176. —— (edited by), 1936*b*. *Custom is king.* London (Hutchinson).

177. —— & Rice, D. T., 1931. 'Report on the human remains found at Kish.' *J. Roy. Anthrop. Inst., 61*, 57–119.

178. **Cain, A. J.,** 1963. *Animal species and their evolution.* London (Hutchinson).

179. **Cajori, F.,** 1928. *A history of mathematical notations.* Vol. 1. *Notations in elementary mathematics.* Chicago (Open Court).

180. **Callan, H. G.,** 1957. 'The lampbrush chromosomes of *Sepia officinalis* L., *Anilocra physodes* L. and *Scyllium catulus* Cuv. and their structural relationship to the lampbrush chromosomes of Amphibia.' *Pubbl. Staz. Zool. Napoli, 29*, 329–46.

181. —— 1963. 'The nature of lampbrush chromosomes.' *Internat. Rev. Cytol., 15*, 1–24.

182. —— & Lloyd, L., 1960. 'Lampbrush chromosomes of crested newts *Triturus cristatus* (Laurenti).' *Phil. Trans. Roy. Soc. B, 243*, 135–219.

183. —— & Spurway, H., 1951. 'A study of meiosis in interracial hybrids of the newt, *Triturus cristatus*.' *J. Genet., 50*, 235–49.

184. **Camper, P.,** 1782*a*. *Natuurkundige verhandelingen van Petrus Camper over den orang outang en eenige andere aap-soorten. Over den Rhinoceros met den dubbelen horen; en over het Rendier.* Amsterdam (Meijer & Warnars).

185. —— 1782*b*. *Kleinere Schriften die Arzneykunft und fürnehmlich die Naturgeschichte betreffend.* Vol. 1. Transl. from the Dutch by J. F. M. Herbell. Leipzig (Crusius).

186. —— 1791*a*. *Naturgeschichte des Orang-Utang und einiger andern Affenarten, des Africanischen Rashorns und des Rennthiers.* Transl. from the Dutch by J. F. M. Herbell. Düsseldorf (Dänzer).

187. —— 1791*b*. *Dissertation physique de Mr. Pierre Camper, sur les différences réelles que présentent les traits du visage chez les hommes de différents pays et de différents ages.* Transl. from the Dutch by D. B. Q. D'Isjonval. Utrecht (Wild & Altheer).

188. —— 1913. *De oculorum fabrica et morbis.* (Facsimile.) Amstelodami (van Rossen).

189. **Cappell, D. F.,** 1961. Article on 'Blood groups' in Law.[642] Vol. 2, pp. 372–7.

190. **Carlyle, T.** (anon.), 1833–4. 'Sartor resartus.' *Fraser's Mag. for Town & Country, 8*, 581, to *10*, 193 (not continuous).

191. —— 1967. *Sartor resartus* and *On heroes and hero worship.* London (Dent).

192. **Cat, — le,** 1740. *Traité des sens.* Rouen (publisher not named).

193. —— (anon.), 1751. *Refutation du discours du citoyen de Geneve, qui a remporté le prix a l'Academie de Dijon, en l'année 1750.* Londres (Kelmarneck).

194. —— 1765. *Traité de la couleur de la peau humaine en général, de celle des negres, en particulier, et de la métamorphose d'une de ces couleurs en l'autre, soit de naissance, soit accidentellement.* Amsterdam (publisher not named).

195. **Caylus, Comte de,** 1767. *Recueil d'antiquités Égyptiennes, Étrusques, Grecques, Romaines et Gauloises.* Vol. 7. Supplément. Paris (Tilliard).

196. **Chadwick, N. K.,** 1963. *Celtic Britain.* London (Thames & Hudson).

197. **Chai, C. K.,** 1967. *Taiwan aborigines: a genetic study of tribal variations.* Cambridge, Mass. (Harvard University Press).

198. **Chaillu, P. B. Du,** 1860a. [No title to paper.] *Proc. Boston Soc. Nat. Hist., 7,* 296–304.

199. —— 1860b. [No title to paper.] *Proc. Boston Soc. Nat. Hist., 7,* 358–67.

200. —— 1861. *Explorations & adventures in equatorial Africa; with accounts of the manners and customs of the people, and of the chace of the gorilla, crocodile, leopard, elephant, hippopotamus, and other animals.* London (Murray).

201. **Chamberlain, H. S.,** 1899. *Die Grundlagen des neunzehnten Jahrhunderts.* 2 vols. München (Bruckmann).

202. —— 1911. *The foundations of the nineteenth century.* Transl. by J. Lees. with an Introduction by Lord Redesdale. 2 vols. London (Lane).

203. **Chantre, E.,** 1885–7. *Recherches anthropologiques dans le Caucase.* Bâle (Georg).

204. —— 1895. 'Recherches anthropologiques dans l'Asie occidentale. Missions scientifiques en Transcaucasie. Asie mineure et Syrie. 1890–1894.' *Archives Mus. d'Hist. nat. Lyon, 6,* i–xvii & 1–250.

205. **Charles, A.,** 1959. 'An electron microscopic study of the human axillary apocrine gland.' *J. Anat., 93,* 226–32.

206. **Chouke, K. S.,** 1929. 'The epicanthus or Mongolian fold in Caucasian children.' *Amer. J. phys. Anthrop., 13,* 255–79.

207. **Clark, J. D.,** 1959. *The prehistory of southern Africa.* Harmondsworth (Penguin).

208. **Clark, J. G. D.,** 1961. Article on 'Kossinna' in Law.[642] Vol. 8. pp. 262–3.

209. **Clark, W. E. Le G.,** 1964. *The fossil evidence for human evolution.* London (University of Chicago Press).

210. —— 1967. *Man-apes or ape-men? The story of discoveries in Africa.* London (Holt, Rinehart, & Winston).

211. **Clarkson, T.,** 1788. *An essay on the slavery and commerce of the human species, particularly the African.* 2nd edit. London (Phillips).

212. **Cleaver, J. E.,** 1968. 'Defective repair replication of DNA in xeroderma pigmentosum.' *Nature, 218,* 652–6.

213. **Cleland, J. B., & Johnston, T. H.,** 1938. 'Blood-grouping of aborigines of the Northern Flinders Ranges in South Australia.' *J. Trop. Med. & Hyg., 41,* 26–7.

214. **Cobb, F. C.,** 1877. 'The Celt of Wales and the Celt of Ireland.' *Cornhill Mag., 36,* 661–78.

215. **Cole, S.,** 1959. *The Neolithic revolution.* London (British Museum).

216. **Coleman, J. S., & six others,** 1966. *Equality of educational opportunity.* Washington (U.S. Government Printing Office).

217. **Collignon, ——** [R.]. 1896. Discussion following paper by Matignon.[713]

218. —— **& Deniker, J.,** 1896. 'Les Maures du Sénégal.' *L'Anthropol., 7,* 257–69.

219. **Collins, H. B.,** 1925. 'The pterion in Primates.' *Amer. J. phys. Anthrop., 8,* 261–74.

220. —— 1926. 'The temporo-frontal articulation in man.' *Amer. J. phys. Anthrop., 9,* 343–8.

221. **Conel, J. LeR.,** 1939–67. *The postnatal development of the human cerebral cortex.* 8 vols. Cambridge, Mass. (Harvard University Press).

222. **Cook, J.,** 1773. 'An account of a voyage round the world in the years MDCCLXVIII, MDCCLXIX, MDCCLXX, and MDCCLXXI.' Contribution to Hawkesworth.[482]

223. **Cooke, C. K.,** 1959. Chapter on 'Rock art in Matabeleland' in Summers,[1025] pp. 112–62.

224. **Coolidge, H. J.,** 1929. 'A revision of the genus *Gorilla*.' *Mem. Mus. Comp. Zool. Harvard*, *50*, 291–381.

225. —— 1933. '*Pan paniscus*. Pigmy chimpanzee from south of the Congo River.' *Amer. J. phys. Anthrop.*, *18*, 1–59.

226. **Coon, C. S.,** 1939. *The races of Europe*. New York (Macmillan).

227. —— 1963. *The origin of races*. London (Cape).

228. —— **& Hunt, E. E.,** 1966. *The living races of man*. London (Cape).

229. **Coupland, R.,** 1923. *Wilberforce, a narrative*. Oxford (Clarendon Press).

230. **Cox, W. H.,** 1891. 'Imprägnation des centralen Nervensystems mit Quecksilbersalzen.' *Archiv f. mikr. Anat.*, *37*, 16–21.

231. **Crandall, L. S.,** 1964. *The management of wild animals in captivity*. London (University of Chicago Press).

232. **Crofts, D. R.,** 1929. *Haliotis*. Liverpool (University Press).

233. **Crow, J. F.,** 1969. 'Genetic theories and influences: comments on the value of diversity.' *Harvard educ. Rev.*, *39* (2), 301–9.

234. **Cummins, H.,** 1955. 'Dermatoglyphics of Bushmen (South Africa).' *Amer. J. phys. Anthrop.*, *13*, 699–709.

235. —— **& Setzler, F. M.,** 1951. 'Dermatoglyphics in Australian aborigines (Arnhem Land).' *Amer. J. phys. Anthrop.*, *9*, 455–60.

236. **Cumont, F.,** 1913. *Catalogue des sculptures et inscriptions antiques (monuments lapidaires) des Musées royaux de Cinquantenaire*. 2nd edit. Bruxelles (Vromant).

237. **Cunningham, D. J.,** 1886a. 'The lumbar curve in man and apes.' *Nature*, *33*, 378–9.

238. —— 1886b. 'The lumbar curve in man and the apes, with an account of the topographical anatomy of the chimpanzee, orang-utan, and gibbon.' *Cunningham Memoirs of the Royal Irish Academy*, *2*, 1–148.

239. **Cutbush, M., Mollison, P. L., & Parkin, D. M.,** 1950. 'A new human blood group.' *Nature*, *165*, 188–9.

240. **Cuvier, G.,** 1817. 'Extrait d'observations faites sur le cadavre d'une femme connue à Paris et à Londres sous le nom de Vénus Hottentotte.' *Mém. Mus. d'Hist. nat.*, *3*, 259–74.

241. —— 1824. Article on 'Femme de race Boschismanne' in Geoffroy & Cuvier.[400]

242. **Dall, W. H.,** 1889. 'Report on the Mollusca. Part II. Gastropoda and Scaphopoda' [obtained by the U.S. Coast Survey Steamer 'Blake']. *Bull. Mus. Comp. Zool. Harvard*, *18*, 1–492.

243. **Dally, ——,** 1873. 'Sur les Celtes'. *Bull. Soc. Anthropol. Paris*, *8*, 243 (only).

244. **Daniel, G. E.,** 1961. Article on 'Indus Valley civilization' in Law.[642] Vol. 7. pp. 435–7.

245. **Dankmeijer, J.,** 1938. 'Some anthropological data on finger prints.' *Amer. J. phys. Anthrop.*, *23*, 377–88.

246. **Dapper, O.,** 1668. *Kaffrarie of Lant der Kaffers*. See reprint and translation into English in Schapera.[937]

247. **Darlington, C. D.,** 1947. 'The genetic component of language.' *Heredity*, *1*, 269–86.

248. —— 1955. 'The genetic component of language.' *Nature*, *175*, 178 (only).

249. **Darsie, M. L.,** 1926. 'The mental capacity of American-born Japanese children.' *Comp. Psychol. Monog.*, *3* (15), 1–89.

250. **Dart, R. A.,** 1925. 'Australopithecus africanus: the man-ape of South Africa.' *Nature*, *115*, 195–9.

251. —— 1931. Quoted by Keith.[576]

252. **Dart, R. A.,** 1937. Chapter on 'Racial origins' in Schapera.[938] pp. 1–31.

253. **Darwin, C.,** 1859a. 'Extract from an unpublished work on species, by C. Darwin, Esq., consisting of a portion of a chapter entitled, "On the variation of organic beings in a state of nature; on the natural means of selection; on the comparison of domestic races and true species."' *J. Proc. Linn. Soc., Zool., 3*, 46–50.

254. —— 1859b. *On the origin of species by means of natural selection, or the preservation of favoured races in the struggle for life.* 1st edition. London (Murray).

255. —— 1866. *On the origin of species by means of natural selection, or the preservation of favoured races in the struggle for life.* 4th edition. London (Murray).

256. —— 1872. *The origin of species by means of natural selection, or the preservation of favoured races in the struggle for life.* 6th edition. London (Murray).

257. —— 1868. *The variation of animals and plants under domestication.* 2 vols. London (Murray).

258. —— 1871. *The descent of man, and selection in relation to sex.* 2 vols. London (Murray).

259. **Darwin, F.** (edited by), 1902. *Charles Darwin: his life told in an autobiographical chapter, and in a selected series of his published letters.* London (Murray).

260. **Daubenton, L.,** 1754. Article on 'Le mouflon et les autres brebis' in Buffon. Daubenton, & La Cepède,[165] Vol. 11.

261. **Davenport, C. B.,** 1925. 'Notes on physical anthropology of Australian aborigines and black-white hybrids'. *Amer. J. phys. Anthrop., 8*, 73–94.

262. **Davis, A., & Eells, K.,** 1953. *Davis–Eells test of general intelligence or problem-solving ability.* London (Harrap).

263. **Davis, J. B.,** 1867. *Thesaurus craniorum. Catalogue of the skulls of the various races of man.* London (printed for the subscribers).

264. **Dawkins, W. B.,** 1900–1. 'Skulls from cave burials at Zakro.' *Ann. Brit. Sch. Athens, 7*, 150–5.

265. **Dean, G.,** 1963. *The porphyrias: a story of inheritance and environment.* London (Pitman).

266. **Delaporte, L.,** 1925. *Mesopotamia: the Babylonian and Assyrian civilization.* Translated from the French. London (Kegan Paul, Trench, Trübner).

267. **Demours, A. P.,** 1818. *Traité des maladies des yeux.* Vol. 4. Paris (published by the author).

268. **Deniker, J.,** 1900. *The races of man: an outline of anthropology and ethnography.* London (Scott).

269. —— 1904. 'Les six races composant la population actuelle de l'Europe.' *J. Roy. Anthrop. Inst., 34*, 181–206.

270. **Desor, E.,** 1848. 'On the embryology of *Nemertes*, with an appendix on the embryonic development of *Polynöe*; and remarks upon the embryology of marine worms in general.' *Boston J. nat. Hist., 6* (1), 1–18.

271. **Deutsch, M., Katz, I., & Jensen, A. R.** (edited by), 1968. *Social class, race, and psychological development.* London (Holt, Rinehart, & Winston).

272. **Devaux, É.,** 1933. *Trois problèmes: l'espèce, l'instinct, l'homme.* Paris (Le François).

273. **Dickerman, H. S.,** n.d. Quoted by Hall, G. S.[460]

274. **Diodorus,** 1939. *The library of history of Diodorus of Sicily.* With translation by C. H. Oldfather. Vol. 3. London (Heinemann).

275. **Distant, W. L.,** 1902. 'Biological suggestions. Animal sense perceptions.' *Zoologist, 6*, 161–78.

276. **Dixon, A. F.**, 1904. 'On certain markings, due to nerves and blood-vessels, upon the cranial vault; their significance and the relative frequency of their occurrence in the different races of man.' *J. Anat. Physiol., 38*, 377–98.

277. **Dobzhansky, T.**, 1944. 'On species and races of living and fossil man.' *Amer. J. phys. Anthrop., 2*, 251–65.

278. **Dreger, R. M., & Miller, K. S.**, 1960. 'Comparative psychological studies of Negroes and whites in the United States.' *Psychol. Bull., 57*, 361–402.

279. **Drennan, M. R.**, 1931. 'Pedomorphism in the pre-Bushman skull.' *Amer. J. phys. Anthrop., 16*, 203–10.

280. —— 1932. 'L'ordre d'éruption des dents permanentes chez les Boschimans.' *L'Anthrop., 42*, 491–5.

281. —— 1937. *A short course on physical anthropology.* Cape Town (Mercantile-Atlas).

282. **Dresser, H. E.**, 1902–3. *A manual of palœarctic birds.* 2 vols. London (publ. by the author).

283. **Dreyer, T. F.**, 1936. 'The significance of the Bushman skull.' *Soöl. Navors. nas. Mus. Bloemfontein, 1*, 25–31.

284. **Driesch, H.**, 1908. *The science and philosophy of the organism.* 2 vols. London (Black).

285. **Drochmans, P.**, 1960. 'Electron microscope studies of epidermal melanocytes, and the fine structure of melanin granules.' *J. biophys. biochem. Cytol., 8*, 165–80.

286. —— 1961. 'Étude au microscope électronique du mécanisme de la pigmentation mélanique: la distribution des grains de mélanine aux cellules malpighiennes.' *Pathol. et Biol., 9*, 947–54.

287. **Dronamraju, K. R.**, 1960–61. 'Hypertrichosis of the pinna of the human ear. Y-linked pedigrees.' *J. Genet., 57*, 230–43.

288. **Drury, J., & Drennan, M. R.**, 1926. 'The pudendal parts of the South African Bush race.' *Med. J. South Africa*, November. (Pages not numbered in reprint.)

289. **Dubois, E.**, 1894. *Pithecanthropus erectus. Eine menschenaehnliche Uebergangsform aus Java.* Batavia (Landesdruckerei).

290. —— 1924. 'Figures of the calvarium and endocranial cast, a fragment of the mandible and three teeth of *Pithecanthropus erectus.' Proc. Kon. Akad. Wetens. Amsterdam, 27*, 459–64.

291. **Duckworth, E. H.**, 1939. Quoted by Meyerowitz, H. & V.[739]

292. **Duckworth, W. L. H.**, 1902–3. Excavations at Palaikastro. II (11). 'Human remains at Hagios Nikolaos.' *Ann. Brit. Sch. Athens, 9*, 344–55.

293. —— 1904. *Morphology and anthropology: a handbook for students.* Cambridge (University Press).

294. **Duncan, O. D.**, 1968. Quoted by Jensen.[551]

295. **Dürer, A.**, 1528. *Herinn sind begriffen vier Bücher von menschlicher Proportion.* (Place of publication and publisher not named.)

296. **DuShane, G. P.**, 1935. 'An experimental study of the origin of pigment cells in Amphibia.' *J. exp. Zoöl., 72*, 1–31.

297. **Ebert, J. D.**, 1965. *Interacting systems in development.* London (Holt, Rinehart & Winston).

298. **Edwardes, M.**, 1971. *East-west passage.* London (Cassell).

299. **Edwards, A. M.**, 1864. 'Recherches anatomiques, zoologiques et paléontologiques sur la famille des chevrotains.' *Ann. des Sci. nat., Zool., 2*, 49–167.

300. **Edwards, E. A., & Duntley, S. Q.**, 1939. 'The pigments and color of living human skin.' *Amer. J. Anat., 65*, 1–33.

301. **Eggeling, W. J., & Dale, I. R.,** [1951]. *The indigenous trees of the Uganda Protectorate.* Entebbe (Government Printer).

302. **Eickstedt, E. von,** 1934. *Rassenkunde und Rassengeschichte der Menschheit.* Stuttgart (Enke).

303. —— 1937. 'Geschichte der anthropologischen Namengebung und Klassifikation (unter Betonung der Erforschung von Südasien). II Teil. 2 Hälfte. B. Die jüngere Erforschungsgeschichte der Südasiaten.' *Ztschr. f. Rassenk., 6,* 151–210.

304. **Eimer, G. H. T.,** 1888–1901. *Die Entstehung der Arten auf Grund von Vererben erworbener Eigenschaften nach den Gesetzen organischen Wachsens. Ein Beitrag zur einheitlichen Auffassung der Lebewelt.* Vol. 1, Jena (Fischer). Vols. 2 & 3 (with collaboration of C. Fickert & M. von Linden), Leipzig (Engelmann).

305. —— 1890. *Organic evolution as the result of the inheritance of acquired characters according to the laws of organic growth.* Translation of Vol. 1 of Eimer.[304] London (Macmillan).

306. **Elderton, E.,** 1907. 'On the measure of the resemblance of first cousins.' *Eugenics Lab. Mem. (University of London), 4,* 1–53.

307. **Ellerman, J. R., & Morrison-Scott, T. C. S.,** 1951. *Checklist of Palaearctic and Indian mammals 1758–1946.* London (British Museum).

308. —— —— **& Hayman, R. W.,** 1953. *Southern African mammals 1758 to 1951: a reclassification.* London (British Museum).

309. **Ellis, H.,** 1905. *Studies in the psychology of sex: sexual selection in man.* Philadelphia (Davis).

310. **Entwistle, W. J.,** 1961. Article on 'Languages of the world' in Law.[642] Vol. 8, pp. 335–61.

311. **Erasmus, [D.],** 1516. *Novum instrumentū omne, diligenter ab Erasmo Roterodamo recognitum & emendatum.* Basiliae (publisher not named).

312. **Erlenmeyer-Kimling, L., & Jarvik, L. F.,** 1963. 'Genetics and intelligence: a review.' *Science, 142,* 1477–9.

313. **Erxleben, I. C. P.,** 1777. *Systema regni animalis per classes, ordines, genera, species, varietates cum synonymia et historia animalium.* Lipsiae (Weygandianis).

314. **Esher, Viscount,** 1921. *The tragedy of Lord Kitchener.* London (Murray).

315. **Estes, R. D.,** 1967. 'The comparative behaviour of Grant's and Thomson's gazelles.' *J. Mammal., 48,* 189–209.

316. **Evans, A. J.,** 1900–01. 'The palace of Knossos. Provisional report of the excavations for the year 1901.' *Ann. Brit. Sch. Athens, 7,* 1–120.

317. —— 1921–35. *The palace of Minos: a comparative account of the successive stages of the Cretan civilization as illustrated by the discoveries at Knossos.* 4 vols. London (Macmillan).

318. **Evelyn, J.,** n.d. *The diary, 1641 to 1706, of John Evelyn, Esq., F.R.S.* London (Thomson).

319. **Eysenck, H. J.,** 1971. *Race, intelligence and education.* London (Temple Smith).

320. **Falk, B.,** n.d. *Rachel the immortal: stage queen: grande amoureuse: street urchin: fine lady.* London (Hutchinson).

321. **Faulkner, D. E., & Epstein, H.,** 1957. *The indigenous cattle of the British Dependent Territories in Africa* (Colonial Advisory Council of Agriculture, Animal Health and Forestry; Publication No. 5). London (H.M. Stationery Office).

322. **Fawcett, C. D., & Lee, A.,** 1902. 'A second study of the variation and correlation of the human skull, with special reference to the Nagada crania.' *Biometrika, 1,* 408–67.

323. **Fayrer, J.,** 1885. Discussion following paper by Jacobs.[545]

324. **Fechner, G. T.,** 1849. 'Die mathematische Behandlung organischer Gestalten und Processe.' *Ber. Verh. kön. sächs. Ges. Wiss., math.-phys. Classe* (vol. not numbered), 50–64.

325. **Federbush, S.,** 1959. *World Jewry today.* London (Allen).

326. **Fenner, F. J.,** 1939. 'The Australian aboriginal skull: its non-metrical characters.' *Trans. Roy. Soc. South Australia, 63* (2), 248–306.

327. **Ferguson, G. O.,** 1916. 'The psychology of the Negro: an experimental study.' *Archives of Psychol., 5* (36), 1–138.

328. **Fiala, F.,** 1896–9. 'Die Ergebnisse der Untersuchung prähistorischer Grabhügel auf dem Glasinac im Jahre 1894; im Jahre 1895; im Jahre 1896.' *Wiss. Mitth. Bosn. Hercegov., 4,* 3–32; *5,* 3–28; *6,* 8–32.

329. **Finch, O.,** 1880. 'Ueber die Bewohner von Ponapé (östl. Carolinen). Nach eigenen Beobachtungen und Erkundigungen.' *Ztschr. f. Ethnol., 12,* 301–32.

330. **Finn, F.,** n.d. *The wild beasts of the world.* London (Jack).

331. **Fischer, E.,** 1931. Chapter on 'Description of the races of man (anthropography)' in Baur, Fischer, & Lenz.[65]

332. **Fischer, J. B.,** 1829. *Synopsis mammalium.* Stuttgardtiae (Cottae).

333. —— 1830. *Addenda, emendanda et index ad Synopsis mammalium.* Stuttgardtiae (Cottae).

334. **Fischer, P.,** 1887. *Manuel de conchyliologie et de paléontologie conchyliologique.* Paris (Savy).

335. **Fischer, ——, & Bernardi, ——,** 1856. 'Description d'un pleurotomaire vivant.' *Journ. de Conchyl., 5,* 160–66.

336. **Fisher, R. A.,** 1918. 'The correlation between relatives on the supposition of Mendelian inheritance.' *Trans. Roy. Soc. Edin., 52,* 399–433.

337. —— 1952. Contribution to UNESCO.[1080]

338. —— **& Ford, E. B.,** 1947. 'The spread of a gene in natural conditions in a colony of the moth *Panaxia dominula* L.' *Heredity, 1,* 143–74.

339. —— —— **& Huxley, J. S.,** 1939. 'Taste-testing the anthropoid apes.' *Nature, 144,* 750 (only).

340. **Fitzgerald, C. P.,** 1961. *China: a short cultural history.* London (Cresset).

341. **Fitzpatrick, T. B., Brunet, P., & Kukita, A.,** 1958. Article on 'The nature of hair pigment' in Montagna & Ellis,[755] pp. 255–303.

342. **Flemming, W.,** 1882. *Zellsubstanz, Kern und Zelltheilung.* Leipzig (Vogel).

343. **Fleure, H. J.,** 1922. 'Some aspects of race study.' *Eugenics Rev., 14,* 93–102.

344. —— **& James, T. C.,** 1916. 'Geographical distribution of anthropological types in Wales.' *J. Roy. Anthrop. Inst., 46,* 35–153.

345. **Flourens, ——,** 1849. 'Éloge historique de Jean-Frédéric Blumenbach, un des huit Associés étrangers de l'Académie.' *Mém. Acad. roy. des Sciences de l'Instit. de France, 21,* i–xxiv.

346. —— 1865. 'Memoir on Blumenbach' in Blumenbach.[110]

347. **Flower, W. H.,** 1870. *An introduction to the osteology of the Mammalia.* London (Macmillan).

348. —— 1875. 'On the structure and affinities of the musk-deer (Moschus moschiferus, Linn.).' *Proc. zool. Soc. London* (vol. not numbered), 159–89.

349. —— **& Murie, J.,** 1867. 'Account of the dissection of a Bushwoman.' *J. Anat. Physiol., 1,* 189–208.

574    BIBLIOGRAPHY

350. **Footman, D.,** 1946. *The primrose path: a life of Ferdinand Lassalle.* London (Cresset).

351. **Ford, E. B.,** 1945. *Butterflies.* London (Collins).

352. —— 1955. *Moths.* London (Collins).

353. **Förstemann, E.,** 1906. 'Commentary on the Maya manuscript in the Royal Public Library of Dresden.' *Archaeol. & Ethnol. Papers Peabody Mus., 4* (2), 49–267.

354. **Fort, R. L. de,** 1890. *La topographie cranio-cérébrale: applications chirurgicales.* Paris (Alcan).

355. **Fox, A. L.,** 1932. 'The relationship between chemical constitution and taste.' *Proc. Nat. Acad. Sci. U.S.A., 18,* 115–20.

356. **Frechkop, S.,** 1955. Article on 'Super-ordre des Ongulés (Ungulata Linné 1766)' in Grassé.[427] Vol. 17 (1), pp. 484–693.

357. **Freeman, F. S.,** 1950. *The theory and practice of psychological testing.* London (Pitman).

358. —— 1962. *Theory and practice of psychological testing.* 3rd edit. New York (Holt, Rinehart, & Winston).

359. **Friedenthal, H.,** 1910. *Beiträge zur Naturgeschichte des Menschen. Lief. 5. Sonderformen der menschlichen Leibesbildung.* Jena (Fischer).

360. **Frigerio, L.,** 1888. 'L'oreille externe: étude d'anthropologie criminelle.' *Archives d'Anthrop. crim., 3,* 438–81.

361. **Frisch, J. L.,** 1763–1817. *Vorstellung der Vögel Deutschlandes und beyläufig auch einiger Fremden; nach ihren Eigenschaften beschrieben.* Berlin (Birnstiel).

362. —— n.d. Quoted by Blumenbach.[108]

363. **Frisch, K. von,** 1962. 'Dialects in the language of the bees.' *Sci. Amer., 207* (2), 78–87.

364. —— 1965. *Tanzsprache und Orientierung der Bienen.* Berlin (Springer).

365. —— 1966. *The dancing bees: an account of the life and senses of the honey bee.* (Translated.) London (Methuen).

366. **Fritsch, G.,** 1872. *Die Eingeborenen Süd-Africa's, ethnographisch und anatomisch.* Breslau (Hirt).

367. —— 1880. 'Die afrikanischen Buschmänner als Urrasse.' *Ztschr. f. Ethnol., 12,* 289–300.

368. **Frobenius, L.,** 1913. *The voice of Africa being an account of the travels of the German Inner African Exploration Expedition in the years 1910–1912.* 2 vols. London (Hutchinson).

369. —— 1923. *Das unbekannte Afrika: Aufhellung der Schicksale eines Erdteils.* München (Becksche Verlagsbuchhandlung).

370. —— 1933. *Kulturgeschichte Afrikas. Prolegomena zu einer historischen Gestaltlehre.* Zürich (Phaidon).

371. **Fukuda, T.,** 1923. 'Some data on the intelligence of Japanese children.' *Amer. J. Psychol., 34,* 599–602.

372. **Furneaux, W.,** 1896. *Life in ponds and streams.* London (Longmans, Green).

373. **Fynn, H. F.,** 1950. *The diary of Henry Francis Fynn.* Edited by J. Stuart. Pietermaritzburg (Shooter & Shooter).

374. **Gall, J. G.,** 1952. 'The lampbrush chromosomes of Triturus viridescens.' *Exp. Cell. Res.,* Suppl. *2,* 95–102.

375. —— 1954. 'Lampbrush chromosomes from oocyte nuclei of the newt.' *J. Morph., 94,* 283–351.

376. —— 1958. Article on 'Chromosomal differentiation', in McElroy & Glass.[722] pp. 103–35.

377. **Galton, F.,** 1853. *The narrative of an explorer in tropical South Africa.* London (Murray).

378. —— 1890. *Narrative of an explorer in tropical South Africa being an account of a visit to Damaraland in 1851*. 3rd edit. London (Ward, Lock).

379. —— 1869. *Hereditary genius: an inquiry into its laws and consequences*. London (Macmillan).

380. —— 1883. *Inquiries into human faculty and its development*. London (Macmillan).

381. **Gamble, F. W.**, 1910. Article on 'Platyhelminthes and Mesozoa' in Harmer & Shipley.[471] Vol. 2, pp. 1–96.

382. **Gann, T., & Thompson, J. E.**, 1931. *The history of the Maya from the earliest time to the present day*. London (Charles Scribner's Sons).

383. **Garn, S. M.**, 1961. *Human races*. Springfield, Ill. (Thomas).

384. **Garrett, H. E.**, 1960. 'Klineberg's chapter on race and psychology: a review.' *Mankind Quart., 1* (1), 15–22.

385. —— 1963. 'Misuses of overlap in racial comparisons.' *Mankind Quart., 3* (4), 254–6.

386. —— **& Schneck, M. R.**, 1933. *Psychological tests, methods, and results*. New York (Harper).

387. **Garrison, F. H.**, 1929. *An introduction to the history of medicine*. London (Saunders).

388. **Garstang, W.**, 1922. 'The theory of recapitulation: a critical re-statement of the biogenetic law.' *J. Linn. Soc., 35*, 81–101.

389. **Garth, T. R.**, 1931. *Race psychology: a study of racial mental differences*. New York (McGraw-Hill).

390. **Gates, R. R.**, 1946. *Human genetics*. 2 vols. New York (Macmillan).

391. —— 1961a. 'The histology of skin pigmentation.' *J. Roy. micr. Soc., 80*, 121–30.

392. —— 1961b. 'Todas and Kotas of the Nilgiri Hills.' *Mankind Quart., 2*, 35–47 & 92–9.

393. —— (n.d.). *Race crossing*. Roma (Instituto 'Gregorio Mendel').

394. **Gay, A.**, 1871. 'Die Circumanaldrüsen des Menschen.' *Sitz. Kais. Akad. Wiss. Wien, 63* (II Abt.), 329–32.

395. **Gayre of Gayre, R.**, 1963. 'Early Hebrew and Palestinian ethnology.' *Mankind Quart., 3*, 238–53.

396. —— 1965. 'Zimbabwe.' *Mankind Quart., 5*, 212–43.

397. **Gedda, L.**, 1967. Chapter on 'A study of racial and subracial crossing' in Kuttner.[622]

398. **Geoffroy, —— de [É. Geoffroy-Saint-Hilaire]**, 1798. 'Sur un prétendu orang-outang des Indes, publié dans les actes de la Société de Batavia.' *J. de Physique, de Chimie, d'Histoire naturelle et des Arts, 3*, 342–6.

399. —— 1829. *Cours de l'histoire naturelle des mammifères*. Paris (Pichon & Didier).

400. —— **& Cuvier, F.**, 1824–42. *Histoire naturelle des mammifères, avec des figures originales, coloriées, dessinées d'après des animaux vivans*. 4 vols. Paris (Belin).

**Geoffroy-Saint-Hilaire, É.**, see **Geoffroy, de.**

401. **Gerasimov, M.**, 1971. *The face finder*. Transl. from the German by A. H. Brodrick. London (Hutchinson).

402. **Gérault, H.**, 1860. 'Mémoire sur les caractères différentiels de la conformation cranienne chez les Lapons et les Esquimaux.' *Mém. Soc. d'Anthrop. Paris, 1*, 177–86.

403. **Gerber, A., & Greef, A.**, 1878–1903. *Lexicon Taciteum*. Lipsiae (Teubner).

404. **Ghirshman, R.**, 1938–9. *Fouilles de Sialk près de Kashan, 1933, 1934, 1937*. 2 vols. Paris (Guethner).

405. **Giacomini, C.**, 1882. 'Annotazioni sopra l'anatomia del negro. 2a Memoria.' *Giorn. Accad. med. Torino, 30*, 729–40.

406. **Giacomini, C.,** 1897. 'La "plica semilunaris" et le larynx chez les singes anthropomorphes.' *Arch. ital. de Biol., 28,* 98–119.

407. **Glass, B., & Li, C. C.,** 1953. 'The dynamics of racial intermixture—an analysis based on the American Negro.' *Amer. J. human Genet., 5,* 1–20.

408. **Gmelin, J. F.,** 1788. See Linnaeus.[671]

409. **Gobineau, A. de,** 1853–5. *Essai sur l'inégalité des races humaines.* 4 vols. (comprising 6 *Livres*). Paris (Didot).

410. —— 1856. *The moral and intellectual diversity of races, with particular reference to their respective influence in the civil and political history of mankind.* Translation |of *Livre premier*| with an analytical introduction and copious historical notes, by H. Hotz. Philadelphia (Lippincott).

411. —— 1915. *The inequality of human races.* Transl. by A. Collins. London (Heinemann).

412. —— 1958. *Lecture des textes cunéiformes.* Paris (Didot).

413. —— 1874. *Les Pléiades.* Paris (Plon).

414. —— 1966. *Sons of kings (Les Pléiades).* Transl. by D. Parmée. London (Oxford University Press).

415. —— 1924. *The golden flower.* Transl. and with an introduction by B. R. Redman. London (Putnam).

416. —— 1970. *Gobineau: selected political writings.* Introduced and edited by M. D. Biddiss. London (Cape).

417. **Goddard, H. H.,** 1911. 'Two thousand normal children measured by the Binet measuring scale of intelligence.' *Pedagog. Sem., 18,* 232–59.

418. **Golling, J.,** 1915. 'Anthropologische Untersuchungen über das Nasenskelett des Menschen.' *Ztschr. Morph. Anthrop., 17,* 1–82.

419. **Gontcharoff, M.,** 1961. Article on 'Embranchement des Némertiens' in Grassé.[427] Vol. 4 (1), pp. 783–886.

420. **Goodsir, J.,** 1868. *The anatomical memoirs of John Goodsir F.R.S., late Professor of Anatomy in the University of Edinburgh.* 2 vols. Edited by W. Turner. Edinburgh (Black).

421. **Gordon, M.** (edited by), 1959. *Pigment cell biology.* New York (Academic Press).

422. **Gordon, R. M.,** 1961. Article on 'Worm infestations in man' in Law.[642] Vol. 14, pp. 740–3.

423. **Gordon-Brown, A.,** 1956. *The year book and guide to East Africa.* London (Hale).

424. **Gottesman, I. I.,** 1968. Chapter on 'Biogenetics of race and class' in Deutsch, Katz, & Jensen,[271] pp. 11–51.

'425. **Grant, M.,** 1917. *The passing of the great race, or the racial basis of European history.* London (Bell).

426. —— 1920. Introduction to Stoddard.[1013]

427. **Grassé, P.-P.** (edited by), 1952–72. *Traité de zoologie: anatomie, systématique, biologie.* 17 vols. Paris (Masson).

428. —— 1955. Article on 'Ordre des Fissipèdes (Fissipeda, Blumenbach, 1791): caractères anatomiques' in Grassé.[427] Vol. 17 (1), pp. 194–291.

429. —— **& Dekeyser, P. L.,** 1955*b*. Article on 'Ordre de rongeurs' in Grassé.[427] Vol. 17 (2), pp. 1321–573.

430. **Gratiolet, P.,** n.d. |1854|. *Mémoire sur les plis cérébraux de l'homme et des Primatès.* Paris (Bertrand).

431. —— **& Alix, P.-H.-E.,** 1866. 'Recherches sur l'anatomie du *Troglodytes aubryi.*' *Nouv. Arch. Mus. d'Hist. Nat. Paris, 2,* 1–264.

432. **Gregory, W. K.,** 1920. 'Studies in comparative myology and osteology, No. 5.—On the anatomy of the preorbital fossæ of Equidae and other ungulates.' *Bull. Amer. Mus. Nat. Hist., 42,* 265–84.

433. —— 1921. 'The origin and evolution of the human dentition: a palæontological review. Part 5. Later stages in the evolution of the human dentition; with a final summary and a bibliography.' *J. dent. Res., 3,* 87–228.

434. —— 1925. 'The biogenetic law and the skull form of primitive man.' *Amer. J. phys. Anthrop., 8,* 373–8.

435. —— 1947. 'The monotremes and the palimpsest theory.' *Bull. Amer. Mus. Nat. Hist., 88,* 1–52.

436. —— **& Hellman, M.,** 1927. 'The dentition of *Dryopithecus* and the origin of man.' *Anthrop. Papers, Amer. Mus. Nat. Hist., 28,* 1–123.

437. **Greenwood, P. H.,** 1958. 'Reproduction in the east African lung-fish *Protopterus æthiopicus* Haeckel.' *Proc. Zool. Soc. Lond., 130,* 547–67.

438. **Griggs, E. L.,** 1936. *Thomas Clarkson, the friend of slaves.* London (Allen & Unwin).

**Guérault, H.,** see **Gérault.**

439. **Guha, B. S.,** 1935. Article on 'Racial affinities of the peoples of India' in Hutton.[532] Vol. 1, Part III, pp. i–lxxi.

440. —— 1944. 'Racial elements in the population' [of India]. *Oxford Pamphlets on Indian Affairs, 22,* 1–31.

441. —— **& Mitra, A. H.,** 1962. 'Progress in anthropology in India since 1938. Part II.' *Mankind Quart., 2* (3), 200–10.

442. **Gulick, J. T.,** 1873. 'On diversity under one set of external conditions.' *J. Linn. Soc. Zool., 11,* 496–505.

443. —— 1887. 'Divergent evolution through cumulative segregation.' *J. Linn. Soc., 20,* 189–274.

444. **Günther, A.,** 1884. 'Note on some East-African antelopes supposed to be new.' *Ann. Mag. Nat. Hist., 14,* 425–9.

445. **Gusinde, M.,** 1952. 'Bericht über meine sudafrikanische Forschungsreise 1950/51.' *Anthropos, 47,* 388–404.

446. **Haacke, W.,** 1893. *Gestaltung und Vererbung. Eine Entwickelungsmechanik der Organismen.* Leipzig (Weigel Nachfolger).

447. **Hackett, L. W.,** 1937*a. Malaria in Europe, an ecological study.* Oxford (University Press).

448. —— 1937*b*. 'Recent additions to our knowledge of "*Anopheles maculipennis*" races.' *League of Nations Bull. Health Org., 6,* 1–16.

449. —— **& Missiroli, A.,** 1935. 'The varieties of *Anopheles maculipennis* and their relation to the distribution of malaria in Europe.' *Rivista di Malariologia, 14,* 45–109.

450. **Haddon, A. C.,** 1924. *The races of man and their distribution.* Cambridge (University Press).

451. **Haeckel, E.,** 1866. *Generelle Morphologie der Organismen.* 2 vols. Berlin (Reimer).

452. —— 1874. *Anthropogenie oder Entwickelungsgeschichte des Menschen. Gemeinverständliche wissenschaftliche Vorträge über die Grundzüge der menschlichen Keimes- und Stammes- Geschichte.* Leipzig (Engelmann).

453. —— 1898. *Natürliche Schöpfungs-Geschichte.* 9th edit. 2 vols. Berlin (Reimer).

454. —— 1902. *Le monisme, lien entre la religion et la science: profession de foi d'un naturaliste.* Paris (Schleicher).

455. **Haggar, R. A., & Barr, M. L.,** 1950. 'Quantitative data on the size of synaptic end-bulbs in the cat's spinal cord.' *J. comp. Neurol., 93,* 17–35.

456. **Hahn, E.,** 1896. *Die Hausthiere und ihre Beziehungen zur Wirtschaft des Menschen. Ein geographische Studie.* Leipzig (Duncker & Humblot).

457. **Hahn, T.,** 1870. 'Die Buschmänner. Ein Beitrag zur südafrikanischen Völkerkunde.' *Globus, Illustrirte Zeitschrift für Länder- und Völkerkunde, 18,* 65–155 (not continuous).

458. —— 1879. 'Felszeichnungen der Buschmänner.' *Ztschr. f. Ethnol., 11 (Verh. Berl. Ges. Anthrop. Ethnol. Urges.,* 307–8).

459. **Haldane, J. B. S.,** 1932. *The causes of evolution.* London (Longmans, Green).

460. **Hall, G. S.,** 1905. 'The Negro in Africa and America.' *Pedag. Semin., 12,* 350–68.

461. **Hall, H. R., & Woolley, C. L.,** 1927. *Ur excavations. Vol. 1. Al-'Ubaid. A report on the work carried out at Al-'Ubaid for the British Museum in 1919 and for the joint expedition in 1922–3.* London (Oxford University Press).

462. **Halloy, d'O. d',** 1873. Quoted by Lagneau.[626]

463. **Hamilton, G.,** 1955. *In the wake of Da Gama. The story of Portuguese pioneers in East Africa.* London (Skeffington).

464. **Hamilton, W.,** 1859–60. *Lectures on metaphysics.* 4 vols. Edited by H. L. Mansel & J. Veitch. Edinburgh (Blackwood).

465. **Hamy, E.-T.,** 1869. 'De l'épine nasale antérieure dans l'ordre des primates.' *Bull. Soc. d'Anthrop. Paris, 4,* 13–28.

466. —— 1907. 'La figure humaine dans les monuments chaldéens, babyloniens et assyriens.' *Bull. Mém. Soc. Anthrop. Paris, 8,* 116–32.

467. **Hankin, H.,** 1926. *Common sense and its cultivation.* London (Kegan Paul, Trench, Trubner).

468. **Hardy, A. C.,** 1954. Article on 'Escape from specialization' in Huxley, Hardy, & Ford.[534]

469. **H[ardy], G. H.,** 1921. 'Srinivasa Ramanujan, 1887–1920.' (Obituary notice.) *Proc. Roy. Soc. A,* 99, xiii–xxix.

470. **Hare, A. W.,** 1884. 'On a method of determining the position of the fissure of Rolando and some other cerebral fissures in the living subject.' *J. Anat. Physiol., 18,* 174–81.

471. **Harmer, S. F., & Shipley, A. E.,** 1910. *The Cambridge natural history.* 15 vols. London (Macmillan).

472. **Harris, E.,** 1961. Article on 'Painting' in Law,[642] Vol. 10, pp. 326–30.

473. **Harris, H.,** 1959. *Human biochemical genetics.* Cambridge (University Press).

474. **Harrison, G. A.,** 1957. 'The measurement and inheritance of skin colour in man.' *Eugenics Rev., 49,* 73–6.

475. **Hart, B., & Spearman, C.,** 1912. 'General ability, its existence and nature.' *Brit. J. Psychol., 5,* 51–84.

476. **Hartmann, R.,** 1872. 'Beiträge zur zoologischen und zootomischen Kenntniss der sogenannten *anthropomorphen* Affen.' Part 1. *Arch. Anat. Physiol. wiss. Med.* (vol. not numbered), 107–52.

477. **Hauschild, M. W.,** 1921. 'Die kleinasiatischen Völker und ihre Beziehungen zu den Juden.' *Ztschr. f. Ethnol., 53,* 518–28.

478. **Hausrath, A.,** 1914. *Treitschke, his life and work.* Transl. anonymously. London (Allen & Unwin).

479. **Hawes, C. H.,** 1904–5. 'Excavations at Palaikastro. IV (7). Larnax burials at Sarandári.' *Ann. Brit. Sch. Athens, 11,* 293–7.

480. **Hawkes, C. F. C.,** 1961. Article on 'Pre-Roman iron age' in Law,[642] Vol. 5, pp. 461–6.

481. **Hawkes, J. & C.,** 1949. *Prehistoric Britain.* London (Chatto & Windus).

482. **Hawkesworth, J.** (edited by), 1773. *An account of the voyages undertaken by the order of his present Majesty for making discoveries in the Southern Hemisphere.* Vols. 2 & 3. London (Strahan & Cadell).

483. **Hector, H.,** 1958. 'A new pattern completion test.' *J. Nat. Inst. Personnel Res., 7,* 132–4.

484. —— 1959. 'A coloured version of the pattern completion test.' *J. Nat. Inst. Personnel Res., 7,* 204–5.

485. **Helmholtz, H.,** 1853. 'Ueber Goethe's naturwissenschaftliche Arbeiten.' *Allg. Wiss. u. Lit.* (vol. not numbered), 383–98.

486. **Hemming, J.,** 1970. *The conquest of the Incas.* London (Macmillan).

487. **Herder, J. G. von,** 1828. *Ideen zur Philosophie der Geschichte der Menschheit.* Third edit. Leipzig (Hartknoch).

488. **Hickmann, H.,** 1949. *Catalogue général des antiquités égyptiennes du Musée du Caire. Instruments de musique.* Le Caire (Imprimerie de l'Institut français d'Archéologie orientale).

489. **Hiernaux, J.,** 1968. *La diversité humaine en Afrique subsaharienne: recherches biologiques: études ethnologiques.* Bruxelles (Institut de Sociologie, Université libre de Bruxelles).

490. **Hildebrandt, J. M.,** 1874. 'Gesammelte Notizen über Landwirthschaft und Viehzucht in Abyssinien und den östlich angrenzenden Ländern.' *Ztschr. f. Ethnol., 6,* 318–40.

491. **Hill-Tout, C.,** 1921. 'The phylogeny of man from a new angle.' *Trans. Roy. Soc. Canada,* Sect. II, *15,* 47–82.

492. —— 1924. 'New trends in anthropology.' *Rep. Brit. Ass. Adv. Sci., 92,* 417 (only).

493. **Hirsch, N. D. M.,** 1927. 'Cephalic index of American-born children of three foreign groups.' *Amer. J. phys. Anthrop., 10,* 79–90.

494. **Hitler, A.,** 1925–7. *Mein Kampf.* 2 vols. München (Eher Nachfolder).

495. —— 1942. *Mein Kampf.* Transl. by J. Murphy. London (Hurst & Blackett).

496. **Hodgkin, R. H.,** 1952. *A history of the Anglo-Saxons.* 2 vols. 3rd edit. Oxford (University Press).

497. **Hoernes, M.,** 1889. 'Hallstatt en Autriche, sa nécropole et sa civilisation.' *Rev. d'Anthropol., 4,* 328–36.

498. —— 1892. *Die Urgeschichte des Menschen nach dem heutigen Stande der Wissenschaft.* Wien (Hartleben).

499. —— 1905. 'Die Hallstattperiode.' *Arch. f. Anthrop., 3,* 233–81.

500. —— 1912. *Kultur der Urzeit.* 3 vols. Leipzig (Göschen).

501. **Hoffmann, E.** (edited by), 1890. *C. Iulii commentarii cum supplementis A. Hirtii et aliorum.* Vindobonae (Gerold).

502. **Höfler, M.,** 1913. 'Zur Somatologie der Gallokelten.' *Archiv f. Anthrop., 12,* 54–74.

503. **Holl, M.,** 1882. 'Ueber die fossae prænasales der menschlichen Schädel.' *Wiener med. Woch., 24,* 721–2, & *25,* 754–6.

504. **Holmes, T. R.,** 1908. *Caesar's commentaries on the Gallic war translated into English.* London (Macmillan).

505. —— 1931. *Caesar's conquest of Gaul.* Oxford (University Press).

506. —— 1936. *Ancient Britain and the invasions of Julius Caesar.* Oxford (University Press).

507. **Holt, R.,** 1947. *George Washington Carver.* London (Phoenix House).

508. **Home, H.,** 1774. *Sketches of the history of man.* Edinburgh (Creech).

509. **Homma, F. C.,** 1926. 'On apocrine sweatglands in white and negro men and women.' *Bull. Johns Hopkins Hosp., 38,* 365–71.

510. **Hooke, B. G. E., & Morant, G. M.,** 1926. 'The present state of our knowledge of British craniology in late prehistoric and historic times.' *Biometrika, 18,* 99–104.

511. **Hooton, E. A.,** 1918. 'Some early drawings of Hottentot women.' *Harvard Afr. Studies, 2,* 83–99.

512. —— 1959. *Up from the ape.* Revised edit. New York (Macmillan).

513. **Horstmann, E.,** 1957. Article on 'Haut und Sinnesorgane' in Möllendorff & Bargmann.[751] Vol. 3, Part 3.

514. **Howard, M. M.,** 1962. 'The early domestication of cattle and the determination of their remains.' *Ztschr. Tierzücht. u. Züchtungsbiol., 76,* 252–64.

515. **Howells, W. W.,** 1937a. 'Anthropometry of the natives of Arnhem Land and the Australian race problem.' *Pap. Peabody Mus., 16* (1), 1–97.

516. —— 1937b. 'The Iron Age population of Great Britain.' *Amer. J. phys. Anthrop., 23,* 19–29.

517. —— 1966. 'Homo erectus.' *Sci. Amer., 215* (5), 46–53.

518. **Hrdlička, A.,** 1928. 'Catalogue of the human crania in the United States National Museum collections.' *Proc. U.S. Nat. Mus., 71* (24), 1–140.

519. —— 1937. 'The gluteal ridge and gluteal tuberosities (3rd trochanters).' *Amer. J. phys. Anthrop., 23,* 127–98.

520. **Huc, É. V.,** 1854. *L'empire chinois.* Paris (Imprimerie Impériale).

521. **Hughes, H. S.,** 1952. *Oswald Spengler: a critical estimate.* London (Scribner).

522. **Hülle, W.,** 1936. 'Vorbemerkung' to Kossinna.[607]

523. **Hume, D.,** 1747. *Essays, moral and political.* 3rd edit. London (Millar).

524. **Hunter, J.** (physician), 1775. *Disputatio inauguralis, quædam de hominum varietatibus, et harum causis, exponens.* Edinburgi (Balfour & Smellie).

525. —— 1865. 'Inaugural dissertation' [on the varieties of mankind and their causes]. English translation of the Latin edition of 1775, published as an Appendix to Blumenbach.[110] pp. 357–94.

526. **Hunter, J.** (surgeon and anatomist), 1787. 'Observations tending to shew that the wolf, jackal, and dog, are all of the same species.' *Phil. Trans. Roy. Soc., 77,* 253–66.

527. —— 1789. 'A supplementary letter on the identity of the species of the dog, wolf, and jackal.' *Phil. Trans. Roy. Soc., 79,* 160–61.

528. **Hunter, W. S., & Sommermeir, E.,** 1922. 'The relation of degree of Indian blood to score on the Otis Intelligence Test.' *J. comp. Psychol., 2,* 257–77.

529. **Huschke, E.,** 1854. *Schædel, Gehirn und Seele des Menschen und der Thiere nach Alter, Geschlecht und Raçe. Dargestellt nach neuen Methoden und Untersuchungen.* Jena (Mauke).

530. **Hutchinson, H. N., Gregory, J. W., & Lydekker, R.,** n.d. *The living races of mankind.* 2 vols. London (Hutchinson).

531. **Hutchinson, R. W.,** 1968. *Prehistoric Crete.* Harmondsworth (Penguin).

532. **Hutton, J. H.** (edited by), 1935. *Census of India, 1931.* Vol. 1, Part III. Simla (Government of India Press).

533. **Huxley, J. S.,** 1938. 'Clines: an auxiliary taxonomic principle.' *Nature, 142,* 219–20.

534. —— **Hardy, A. C., & Ford, E. B.** (edited by), 1954. *Evolution as a process.* London (Allen & Unwin).

535. **Huxley, T. H.,** 1863. *Evidence as to man's place in nature.* London (Williams & Norgate).

536. —— 1865. 'On the methods and results of ethnology.' *Fortnightly Rev., 1,* 257–77.

537. —— 1869. 'The scientific aspects of positivism.' *Fortnightly Rev., 5,* 653–70.

538. —— 1871. *A manual of the anatomy of vertebrated animals.* London (Churchill).

539. —— 1880. 'On the cranial and dental characters of the Canidae.' *Proc. Zool. Soc. Lond.* (vol. not numbered), 238–88.

540. —— 1913. *Huxley's lectures and lay sermons.* London (Dent).

541. **Hyatt, A.,** 1889. 'Genesis of the Arietidae.' *Mem. Mus. Comp. Zoöl. Harvard, 16* (3), 1–238.

542. —— 1897. 'Cycle in the life of the individual (ontogeny) and in the evolution of its own group (phylogeny).' *Proc. Amer. Acad. Arts and Sci., 32,* 209–24.

543. **Illig, K. G.,** 1902. 'Duftorgane der männlichen Schmetterlinge.' *Zoologica, 38,* 1–34.

544. **Isaacs, N.,** 1936–7. *Travels and adventures in eastern Africa.* 2 vols. Edited by L. Herrman. Cape Town (van Riebeeck Society).

545. **Jacobs, J.,** 1885a. 'On the racial characteristics of modern Jews.' *J. anthr. Inst., 15,* 23–62.

546. —— 1885b. 'The comparative distribution of Jewish ability.' *J. anthr. Inst., 15,* 351–79.

547. **Jäger, G.,** 1876. 'Ueber die Bedeutung der Geschmacks- und Geruchsstoffes.' *Ztschr. f. wiss. Zool., 27,* 319–31.

548. **Jamieson, E., & Sandiford, P.,** 1928. 'The mental capacity of southern Ontario Indians.' *J. educ. Psychol., 19,* 313–28.

549. **Jenkins, M. D.,** 1948. 'The upper limit of ability among American Negroes.' *Sci. Monthly, 66,* 399–401.

550. **Jenkins, T., & Steinberg, A. G.,** 1966. 'Some serum protein polymorphisms in Kalahari Bushmen and Bantu: gamma globulins, haptoglobins and transferrins.' *Amer. J. human Genet., 18,* 399–407.

551. **Jensen, A. R.,** 1969. 'How much can we boost IQ and scholastic achievement?' *Harvard educ. Rev., 39* (1), 1–123.

552. **Jepsen, G. L.,** 1949. 'Selection, "orthogenesis", and the fossil record.' *Proc. Amer. Phil. Soc., 93,* 479–500.

553. **Jerie, H. G.,** 1970. 'From photogrammetry to photogrammetric system engineering.' *Jena Rev., 15* (3), 159–67 and coloured supplement.

554. **Joest, W.,** 1893. 'Ethnographisches und Verwandtes aus Guayana.' *Internat. Arch. f. Ethnogr., 5* (Suppl.), 1–102.

555. **Johnston, H. H.,** 1897. *British Central Africa: an attempt to give some account of a portion of the territories under British influence north of the Zambesi.* London (Methuen).

556. —— 1903. *The Nile quest: a record of the exploration of the Nile and its basin.* London (Lawrence & Bullen).

557. —— 1910. *The Negro in the New World.* London (Methuen).

558. —— 1923. *The story of my life.* London (Chatto & Windus).

559. **Jones, N.,** 1960. *Guide to the Zimbabwe ruins.* Bulawayo (Commission for the Preservation of Natural and Historical Monuments and Relics).

560. **Jung, K. E.,** 1882. *Der Weltteil Australien.* Vol. 1. *Der Australkontinent und seine Bewohner.* Leipzig (Freytag).

561. **Kagan, J. S.,** 1969. 'Inadequate evidence and illogical conclusions.' *Harvard educ. Rev., 39* (2), 274–7.

562. **Kaiser, E.,** 1926. *Die Diamantenwüste Südafrikas.* Vol. 2. Berlin (Reimer).

563. **Kames, Lord** (anon.), 1774. *Sketches of the history of man.* 2 vols. Edinburgh (Creech).

564. **Kant, I.,** 1775. *Von den verschiedenen Racen der Menschen,* reprinted in Kant.[569] Vol. 2. pp. 427–43.

565. —— 1785. *Bestimmung des Begriffs einer Menschenrace.* Reprinted in Kant. [569] Vol. 8. pp. 89–106.

566. —— 1790. *Critik der Urtheilskraft.* Berlin (Lagarde & Friederich).

567. —— 1952. *The critique of judgement.* Transl. by J. C. Meredith. Oxford (Clarendon Press).

568. —— 1798. *Anthropologie in pragmatischer Hinsicht.* Königsberg (Nicolavius).

569. —— 1910–37. *Kant's gesammelte Schriften.* 22 vols. Berlin (Reimer).

570. **Kappers, C. U. A.,** 1929. 'The fissures on the frontal lobes of *Pithecanthropus erectus* Dubois compared with those of Neanderthal Men, *Homo recens* and chimpanzee.' *Proc. Kon. Akad. Wetens. Amsterdam, 32,* 182–95.

571. —— 1932. Chapter on 'Principles of development of the nervous system (neurobiotaxis)' in Penfield.[834] Vol. 1, pp. 45–89.

572. **Kawaguti, S., & Baba, K.,** 1959. 'A preliminary note on a two-valved saccoglossan gas-tropod, *Tamanovalva limax,* n. gen., n. sp., from Tamano, Japan.' *Biol. J. Okayama Univ., 5,* 177–84.

573. **Keane, A. H., Quiggin, A. H., & Haddon, A. C.,** 1920. *Man, past and present.* Revised edit. Cambridge (University Press).

574. **Keith, A.,** 1925. *The antiquity of man.* 2nd edit. 2 vols. London (Williams & Norgate).

575. —— 1927. Chapter entitled 'Report on the human remains' in Hall & Woolley.[461] pp. 214–40.

576. —— 1931. *New discoveries relating to the antiquity of man.* London (Williams & Norgate).

577. **Keller, C.,** 1902. *Die Abstammung der ältesten Haustiere.* Zurich (Amberger).

578. **Kerr, J. G.,** 1900. 'The external features in the development of *Lepidosiren paradoxa* Fitz.' *Trans. Roy. Soc. B, 92,* 299–330.

579. **Kersten, O.** (edited by), 1871. *Baron Carl Claus von der Decken's Reisen in Ost-Afrika in den Jahren 1862 bis 1865.* Vol. 2. Leipzig (Winter).

580. **King, L. W.,** 1910. *A history of Sumer and Akkad. An account of the early races of Babylonia from prehistoric times to the foundation of the Babylonian monarchy.* London (Chatto & Windus).

581. **King, W. R.,** 1870. 'The aboriginal tribes of the Nilgiri Hills.' *J. Anthrop., 1,* 18–51.

582. **Kingsnorth, G. W.,** 1962. *Africa south of the Sahara.* Cambridge (University Press).

583. **Kirby, P. R.,** 1937. Chapter on 'The musical practices of the native races of South Africa' in Schapera,[938] pp. 271–89.

584. **Kirk, R. E., & Othmer, D. F.,** 1947–60. *Encyclopedia of chemical technology.* 15 vols. & 2 supplements. New York (Interscience Encyclopedia).

585. **Kirk, R. L.,** 1965. 'The distribution of genetic markers in Australian aborigines.' *Austr. Inst. Aborig. Stud., Occ. Papers, 4,* 1–67.

586. **Klaatsch, H.,** 1908a. 'Das Gesichtsskelett der Neandertalrasse und der Australier.' *Verh. Anat. Ges., 22,* 223–73.

587. —— 1908b. 'The skull of the Australian aboriginal.' *Rep. Path. Lab. Lunacy Dept. N.S.W., 1* (3), 43–167.

588. ——— 1920. *Der Werdegang der Menschheit und die Entstehung der Kultur*. Berlin (Bong).

589. ——— 1923. *The evolution and progress of mankind*. (Edited translation of Klaatsch[588]). London (Fischer Unwin).

590. ——— & Hauser, O., 1909. 'Homo Aurignacensis Hauseri, ein paläolithischer Skelettfund aus dem unteren Aurignacien der Station Combe-Capelle bei Montferrand (Périgord).' *Praehist. Ztschr.*, *1*, 273–338.

591. **Kleinschmidt, O.,** 1897. (No title to paper.) *J. f. Ornith.*, *45*, 518–19.

592. ——— 1926. *Die Formenkreislehre und das Weltwerden des Lebens*. Halle-S. (Gebauer-Schwetschke).

593. ——— 1930. *The Formenkreis theory and the progress of the organic world*. London (Witherby).

594. **Klenke, W.,** 1938. 'Zur Anthropologie japonischer Weltkämpfer.' *Ztschr. f. Rassenk.*, *8*, 151–61 & 264–93.

595. **Klineberg, O.,** 1935a. *Negro intelligence and selective migration*. New York (Columbia University Press).

596. ——— 1935b. *Race differences*. London (Harper).

597. ——— 1951. *Race and psychology*. Paris (UNESCO).

598. **Klingenheben, A.,** 1933. 'The Vai script.' *Sierra Leone Studies*, *19*, 137–49.

599. **Knight, R.,** 1959. *Intelligence and intelligence tests*. London (Methuen).

600. **Knowles, M. D.** (edited by), 1952. *The heritage of early Britain*. London (Bell).

601. **Koelle, S. W.,** 1849. *Narrative of an expedition into the Vy country of West Africa, and the discovery of a system of syllabic writing recently invented by the natives of the Vy tribe*. London (Seeleys).

602. **Koenigswald, G. H. R. von,** 1956. *Meeting prehistoric man*. London (Thames & Hudson).

603. **Kölliker, A.,** 1867. *Handbuch der Gewebelehre des Menschen, für Aerzte und Studirende*. Leipzig (Engelmann).

604. **Kollmann, J.,** 1885. 'Das Ueberwintern von europäischen Frosch- und Tritonlarven und die Umwandlung des mexikanischen Axolotl.' *Verh. naturf. Ges. Basel*, *7*, 387–98.

605. **Kossinna, G.,** 1912. *Die deutsche Vorgeschichte, eine hervorragend nationale Wissenschaft*. 1st edit. Würzburg (Kabitzsch).

606. ——— 1921. *Die Indogermanen: ein Abriss*. Leipzig (Kabitzsch).

607. ——— 1936. *Die deutsche Vorgeschichte: eine hervorragend nationale Wissenschaft*. 7th edit. Leipzig (Kabitzsch).

608. **Kramer, S. N.,** 1961. *History begins at Sumer*. 2nd edit. London (Thames & Hudson).

609. **Kraus, B. S.,** 1951. 'Carabelli's anomaly of the maxillary molar teeth. Observations on Mexicans and Papago Indians and an interpretation of the inheritance.' *Amer. J. human Genet.*, *3*, 348–55.

610. **Krause, W.,** 1844. Article on 'Haut' in Wagner.[1114]

611. ——— 1876. *Handbuch der menschlichen Anatomie*, Vol. 1. 3rd edit. Hannover (Hahn).

612. **Krogman, W. M.,** 1930. 'Studies in growth changes in the skull and face of anthropoids.' *Amer. J. Anat.*, *46*, 303–13.

613. ——— 1932. 'The morphological characters of the Australian skull.' *J. Anat.*, *66*, 399–413.

614. ——— 1967. 'The role of genetic factors in the human face, jaws and teeth: a review.' *Eugenics Rev.*, *59*, 165–92.

615. **Kroll, H.,** 1928. 'Die Haustiere der Bantu.' *Ztschr. f. Ethnol.*, *60*, 177–290.

616. **Kuhlmann, F.,** 1912*a*. 'The present status of the Binet and Simon tests of the intelligence of children.' *J. Psycho-Asthenics, 16,* 113–39.

617. —— 1912*b*. 'The Binet and Simon tests of intelligence in grading feeble-minded children.' *J. Psycho-Asthenics, 16,* 174–91.

618. —— 1912*c*. 'A revision of the Binet–Simon system for measuring the intelligence of children.' *J. Psycho-Asthenics, Monog. Suppl., 1* (1), 1–41.

619. **Kukita, A., & Fitzpatrick, T. B.,** 1955. 'Demonstration of tyrosinase in melanocytes of the human hair matrix by autoradiography.' *Science, 121,* 893–4.

620. **Kuppfer, C., & Hagen, F. B.,** 1881. 'Der Schädel Immanuel Kant's.' *Archiv. f. Anthrop., 13,* 359–410.

621. **Kuttner, R. E.,** 1967*a*. Article on 'Biochemical anthropology' in Kuttner.[622] pp. 197–221.

622. —— (edited by), 1967*b*. *Race and modern science. A collection of essays by biologists, anthropologists, sociologists and psychologists.* New York (Social Science Press).

623. **Labouret, H.,** 1959. *L'Afrique précoloniale.* Paris (Presses universitaires).

624. **Lacépède\*, [E. de], & Cuvier, [G.],** 1801. *La ménagerie du Muséum national d'Histoire naturelle, ou les animaux vivants.* Paris (Miger & Patris).

625. **Lafargue, P.,** 1927. Article on 'Personal recollections of Karl Marx' in Ryazanoff.[924]

626. **Lagneau, G.,** 1873. 'Sur les Celtes.' *Bull. Soc. Anthropol. Paris, 8,* 236–41.

627. **Lamarck, J. B.,** n.d. *Recherches sur l'organization des corps vivans.* (Based on a discourse delivered in year X of the French Republic.) Paris (Maillard).

628. **Langer, C.,** 1884. *Anatomie der äusseren Formen des menschlichen Körpers.* Wien (Toeplitz & Deuticke).

629. **Langerhans, P.,** 1868. 'Ueber die Nerven der menschlichen Haut.' *Arch. f. path. Anat., Physiol., klin. Med. (Virchow), 44,* 325–37.

630. —— 1869. Dissertation, quoted by Bargmann.[56]

631. **Lankester, E. R.,** 1891. *Zoological articles contributed to the Encyclopaedia Britannica.* London (Black).

632. **Lantz, L. A., & Callan, H. G.,** 1954. 'Phenotypes and spermatogenesis of interspecific hybrids between *Triturus cristatus* and *T. marmoratus.*' *J. Genet., 52,* 165–85.

633. **Laplace, P. S.,** An VII (probably 1799). *Exposition du système du monde.* 2nd edit. Paris (Duprat).

634. —— 1808. *Exposition du système du monde.* 3rd edit. Paris (Courcier).

635. **Lapouge, G. V. de,** 1887. 'La dépopulation de la France.' *Rev. d'Anthrop., 16,* 69–80.

636. —— 1899. *L'Aryen: son role social.* Paris (Fontemoing).

637. —— 1902. Introduction to Haeckel.[454]

638. **Lartet, É.,** 1856. 'Note sur un grand singe fossile qui se rattache au groupe des singes supérieurs.' *C. de hebd. Séanc. Acad. Sci. Paris, 43,* 219–23.

639. **Lartet, L.,** 1868. 'Une sépulture des troglodytes du Périgord (crânes des Eyzies).' *Bull. Soc. d'Anthrop. Paris, 3,* 335–49.

640. **Latham, R. G.,** 1851. *Man and his migrations.* London (Van Voorst).

641. **Lavrin, J.,** 1948. *Nietzsche: an approach.* London (Methuen).

642. **Law, M. D.** (edited by), 1961. *Chambers's Encyclopædia.* New edition. 15 vols. London (Newnes).

643. **Lawrence, E.,** 1931. 'An investigation into the relation between intelligence and inheritance.' *Brit. J. Psychol., Monog. Suppl., 16,* 1–80.

\* Formerly La Cepède.

644. **Laycock, T.,** 1840. *A treatise on the nervous diseases of women.* London (Longmans).

645. **Leakey, L. S. B.,** 1961. *The progress and evolution of man in Africa.* London (Oxford University Press).

646. **Lebzelter, V.,** 1929. 'Anthropologische Untersuchungen an tiroler Kaiserjägern.' *Mitt. anthrop. Ges. Wien, 59,* 209–28.

647. **Leers, J. v.,** 1934. *Spenglers weltpolitisches System und der Nationalsozialismus.* Berlin (Junker & Dünnhaupt).

648. **Leguat, F.,** 1708. *Voyage et avantures de Francois Leguat, & de ses compagnons, en deux isles desertes des Indes orientales.* Vol. 2. London (Mortier).

649. **Lehmann, H., & Cutbush, M.,** 1952a. 'Sickle-cell trait in southern India.' *Brit. med. J., 1,* 404–5.

650. —— —— 1952b. 'Sub-division of some southern Indian communities according to the incidence of sickle-cell trait and blood-groups.' *Trans. Roy. Soc. Trop. Med. & Hyg., 46,* 380–83.

651. **Lemche, H.,** 1957. 'A new living deep-sea mollusc of the Cambro-Devonian class Monoplacophora.' *Nature, 179,* 413–16.

652. **Lenin, N.,** 1927. Article on 'Marxism' in Ryazanoff.[924]

653. **Lennier, G.,** 1883. 'Note sur l'expédition française des terres australes pendant les années 1802 à 1804.' *Bull. Soc. zool. France, 8,* 1–8.

654. **Lermontov, M. Y.,** 1940. *A hero of our own times.* Transl. from the Russian. London (Oxford University Press).

655. —— 1962. *A hero of our time* (in Russian). Moscow (Library for Non-Russian Schools).

656. **Lerner, A. B.,** 1961. 'Hormones and skin colour.' *Sci. Amer., 205,* 98–108.

657. —— & **Fitzpatrick, T. B.,** 1950. 'Biochemistry of melanin production.' *Physiol. Rev., 30,* 91–126.

658. —— & **McGuire, J. S.,** 1961. 'Effect of alpha- and beta-melanocyte stimulating hormones on the skin colour of man.' *Nature, 189,* 176–9.

659. **LeRoux, P. L.,** 1958. 'The validity of *Schistosoma capense* (Harley, 1864) amended as a species.' *Trans. Roy. Soc. Trop. Med. & Hyg., 52,* 12–14.

660. **Leschi, J.,** 1950. 'Empreintes digitales et races: essai de synthese.' *L'Anthrop., 54,* 35–66.

661. **Lesson, R.-P.,** 1827. *Manuel de mammalogie, ou histoire naturelle des mammifères.* Paris (Roret).

662. **Letourneau, C.,** 1873. Review of Giglioli's book. *Studii craniologicae. Rev. d'Anthrop., 2,* 126–32.

663. **Lewis, C. T., & Short, C.,** 1879. *A Latin dictionary founded on Andrews' edition of Freund's Latin dictionary.* Oxford (Clarendon Press).

664. **Leydig, F.,** 1857. *Lehrbuch der Histologie des Menschen und der Thiere.* Hamm (Grote).

665. **Liddell, H. G., & Scott, R.,** 1883. *A Greek–English lexicon.* 7th edit. Oxford (Clarendon Press).

666. **Liley, N. R.,** 1966. 'Ethological isolating mechanisms in four sympatric species of poecilid fishes.' *Behaviour,* Suppl. *13,* i–vi & 1–197.

667. **Lindholm, W.,** 1927. 'Kritische Studien zur Molluskenfauna des Baikalsees.' *Trav. Comm. Étude Lac Bajkal, 2,* 139–86.

668. **Linnaeus, C.,** 1746. *Fauna Svecica sistens animalia Sveciæ regni.* Lugduni Batavorum (Wishoff & Wishoff).

669. —— 1758. *Systema naturæ per regna tria naturæ.* 10th edit. Vol. 1. Holmiæ (Salvius).

670. —— 1766. Ditto, 12th edit. Vol. 1, Part 1. Holmiæ (Salvii).

671. **Linnaeus, C.,** 1788. *Systema naturae per regna tria naturae, secundum classes, ordines, genera, species.* 13th edit. Vol. 1, Part 1. Edited by J. F. Gmelin. Lipsiae (Beer).

672. —— 1894. *Systema naturae. Regnum animale.* 10th edit., republished. Lipsiæ (Engelmann).

673. **Little, K. L.,** 1961. Article on 'Negro' in Law,[642] Vol. 9, pp. 745–8.

674. **Little, W., Fowler, H. W., & Coulson, J.,** 1955. *The shorter Oxford English dictionary.* Oxford (Clarendon Press).

675. **Liu, C. H.,** 1937. 'A tentative classification of the races of China.' *Ztschr. f. Rassenk., 6,* 129–50.

676. **Livingstone, D.,** 1857. *Missionary travels and researches in South Africa; including a sketch of sixteen years' residence in the interior of Africa, and a journey from the Cape of Good Hope to Loanda on the west coast; thence across the continent, down the river Zambesi, to the eastern ocean.* London (Murray).

677. **Locy, W. A.,** 1915. *Biology and its makers.* New York (Holt).

678. **Long, E.,** 1774. *The history of Jamaica. Or, general survey of the antient and modern state of that island: with reflections on its situation, settlements, inhabitants, climate, products, commerce, laws, and government.* 3 vols. London (Lowndes).

679. **Ludolfus, I.,** 1691. *Ad suam historiam aethiopicam antehac editam commentarius.* Francofurti (Zunneri).

680. **Lundman, B.,** 1962. 'Serologische Beiträge zur Regionalanthropologie von Grossbrittanien (und Irland).' *Homo, 13,* 70–72.

681. —— 1963. 'The racial history of the Near East.' *Mankind Quart., 3,* 179–88.

682. —— 1967. *Geographische Anthropologie: Rassen und Völker der Erde.* Stuttgart (Fischer).

683. **Lundström, A.,** 1955. 'The significance of genetic and non-genetic factors in the profile of the facial skeleton.' *Amer. J. Orthodont., 41,* 910–16.

684. **Luschan, F. v.,** 1906. 'Bericht über eine Reise in Südafrika.' *Ztschr. f. Ethnol., 38,* 863–95.

685. —— 1911. 'The early inhabitants of western Asia.' *J. Anthrop. Inst., 41,* 221–44.

686. —— 1913. 'Beiträge zur Anthropologie von Kreta.' *Ztschr. f. Ethnol., 45,* 307–93.

687. **Luschka, H. v., Koch, J. A., Götte, A., & Görtz, C.,** 1868. 'Anatomische Untersuchung eines Buschweibes.' (Review of 4 papers.) *Archiv f. Anthrop., 3,* 306–8.

688. **Luther, M.** (anon.), [1522]. *Das newe Testament Deutzsch.* Wittemberg (publisher not named).

689. **Lydekker, R.,** 1898. *The deer of all lands.* London (Ward).

690. —— 1926. *The game animals of Africa.* London (Rowland Ward).

691. —— n.d. *Wild life of the world: a descriptive survey of the geographical distribution of animals.* 3 vols. London (Warne).

692. **Macalister, A.,** 1893. (Presidential address, no title.) *Rep. Br. Ass. Advmt. Sci.,* 62nd Meeting (1892), 886–95.

693. —— 1898. 'The apertura pyriformis.' *J. Anat. Physiol., 32,* 223–30.

694. **Mackay, E.,** 1935. *The Indus civilization.* London (Lovat Dickson & Thompson).

695. **Madariaga, S. de,** 1942. *Hernán Cortés conqueror of Mexico.* London (Hodder & Stoughton).

696. **Magnen, J. Le,** 1948. 'Un cas de sensibilité olfactive se présentant comme un caractère sexuel secondaire féminin.' *C. r. hebd. Séanc. Acad. Sci. Paris, 226,* 694–5.

697. —— 1949. 'Variations spécifiques des seuils olfactifs chez l'homme sous actions androgène et œstrogène.' *C. r. hebd. Séanc. Acad. Sci. Paris, 228,* 947–8.

698. **Malpighi, M.,** 1665. *De externo tactus organo anatomica observatio.* Neapoli (Ægidium Longũ).

699. —— 1686. Article entitled 'Exercitatio epistolica de lingua' (originally published in 1665), reprinted in *Marcelli Malpighii opera omnia.* London (Scott).

700. **Manson-Bahr, P. H.,** 1966. *Manson's tropical diseases: a manual of the diseases of warm climates.* 16th edit. London (Baillière, Tindall, & Cox).

701. **Marshall, J.** (anatomist), 1864. 'On the brain of a Bushwoman; and on the brains of two idiots of European descent.' *Phil. Trans. Roy. Soc., 154,* 501–58.

702. **Marshall, J.** (archaeologist), 1931. *Mohenjo-Daro and the Indus civilization, being an official account of archæological excavations at Mohenjo-Daro carried out by the Government of India between the years 1922 and 1927.* 3 vols. London (Probsthain).

703. **Marshall, W. E.,** 1873. *A phrenologist amongst the Todas.* London (Longmans, Green).

704. —— n.d. Quoted by Topinard.[1062]

705. **Martial,** 1950. *Epigrams.* 2 vols. London (Heinemann).

706. **Martin, R.,** 1926. Chapter 'Zur Anthropologie der Buschmänner' in Kaiser.[562] pp. 436–90.

707. —— 1928. *Lehrbuch der Anthropologie.* 2nd edit. *Vol. 2. Kraniologie, Osteologie.* Jena (Fischer).

708. —— **& Saller, K.,** 1956–62. *Lehrbuch der Anthropologie in systematischer Darstellung, mit besonderer Berücksichtigung der anthropologischen Methoden.* 3 vols. Stuttgart (Fischer).

709. **Marx, K. F. H.,** 1865. 'Life of Blumenbach' in Blumenbach.[110]

710. **Mason, H. S.,** 1959. Article on 'Structure of melanins' in Gordon.[421]

711. **Mason, I. L., & Maule, J. P.,** 1960. *The indigenous livestock of eastern and southern Africa.* Farnham Royal (Commonwealth Agricultural Bureaux).

712. **Mather, K., & Harrison, B. J.,** 1949. 'The manifold effect of selection.' *Heredity, 3,* 1–52 & 131–62.

713. **Matignon, J. J.,** 1896. 'Stigmates congénitaux et transitoires chez les Chinois.' *Bull. Soc. d'Anthrop. Paris, 7,* 524–8.

714. **Matthew, W. D.,** 1926. 'The evolution of the horse; a record and its interpretation.' *Quart. Rev. Biol., 1,* 139–85.

715. **Maupertuis [P.-L. M. de],** 1768. Article on 'Vénus physique' 'first published 1745), in *Œuvres de Maupertuis.* Nouvelle édition. 4 vols. Lyon (Bruyset).

716. **Mayaud, N.,** 1940. 'Considérations sur les affinités et la systématique de *Larus fuscus* et *Larus argentatus.' Alauda, 12,* 80–98.

717. **Mayr, E.,** 1959. 'Trends in avian systematics.' *Ibis, 101,* 293–302.

718. —— 1963a. *Animal species and evolution.* Cambridge, Mass. (Harvard University Press).

719. —— 1963b. Chapter on 'The taxonomic evaluation of fossil hominids' in Washburn,[1119] pp. 332–45.

720. **McCown, T. D., & Keith, A.,** 1939. *The stone age of Mount Carmel: the fossil remains from the Levalloiso-Mousterian.* Vol. 2. Oxford (Clarendon Press).

721. **McCulloch, M.,** 1950. *The peoples of Sierra Leone Protectorate.* London (International African Institute).

722. **McElroy, M. D., & Glass, B.** (edited by), 1958. *A symposium on the chemical basis of development.* Baltimore (Johns Hopkins Press).

723. **McGurk, F. C. J.,** 1953. 'On white and Negro test performance and socioeconomic factors.' *J. abnorm. soc. Psychol., 48,* 448–50.

724. **McGurk, F. C. J.,** 1961. 'Psychological test score differences and the "culture hypothesis".' *Mankind Quart., 1* (3), 165–75.

725. **McLachlan, D.,** 1967. Article entitled 'Dean Rusk's daughter weds a Negro' in *Daily Mail,* 22 Sept.

726. **McWhirter, N. D. & A. R.,** 1967. *Guinness book of Olympic records.* London (Transworld).

727. **Meckel, J. F.,** 1811. *Beyträge zur vergleichenden Anatomie.* Vol. 2. Leipzig (Carl Heinrich Reclam).

728. **Meiners, C. ('M'),** 1790a. 'Ueber die Natur der afrikanischen Neger und die abhangende Befreyung, oder Einschränkung der Schwarzen.' *Götting. Hist. Mag., 6,* 385–456.

729. —— 1790b. 'Von den Varietäten und Abarten der Neger.' *Götting. Hist. Mag., 6,* 625–45.

730. —— 1811. *Untersuchungen über die Verschiedenheiten der Menschennaturen (die verschiedenen Menschenarten) in Asien und den Südländern, in den Ostindischen und Südseeinseln, nebst einer historischen Vergleichung der vormahligen und gegenwärtigen Bewohner dieser Continente und Eylande.* Vol. 1. Tübingen (Cotta).

731. **Meinhard, H.,** 1961. Article on 'Bronzework: West Africa' in Law,[642] Vol. 2, pp. 609–10.

732. **Meise, W.,** 1928. 'Die Verbreitung der Aaskrähe (Formenkreis *Corvus corone* L.).' *J. f. Ornith., 76,* 1–203.

733. **Meisenheimer, J.,** 1921. *Geschlecht und Geschlechter im Tierreich.* Vol. 1. *Die natürlichen Beziehungen.* Jena (Fischer).

734. **Meredith, H. V., & Hixon, E. H.,** 1954. 'Frequency, size, and bilateralism of Carabelli's tubercle.' *J. dent. Res., 33,* 435–40.

735. **Mertens, R., & Müller, L.,** 1940. 'Die Amphibien und Reptilien Europas. (Zweite Liste, nach dem Stand vom 1 Januar 1940.)' *Abh. Senckenb. naturf. Ges., 451,* 1–56.

736. **Merton, B. B.,** 1958. 'Taste sensitivity to P.T.C. in 60 Norwegian families with 176 children. Confirmation of the hypothesis of single gene inheritance.' *Acta genet. stat. med., 8,* 114–28.

737. **Meyer, E.,** 1909. *Geschichte des Altertums.* 2nd edit. Vol. 1. Stuttgart (Cotta).

738. **Meyerowitz, E. L. R.,** 1940. 'Four pre-Portuguese bronze castings from Benin.' *Man, 40,* 129–32.

739. **Meyerowitz, H. & V.,** 1939. 'Bronzes and terra-cottas from Ile-Ife.' *Burlington Mag., 75,* 151–5.

740. **Michael, R. P., & Keverne, E. B.,** 1968. 'Phenomones in the communication of sexual status in Primates.' *Nature, 218,* 746–9.

741. **Miklucho-Maclay, N. von,** 1881. 'Haarlose Australier.' *Ztschr. f. Ethnol., 13 (Verh. Berl. Ges. Anthrop. Ethnol. Urges.,* 143–9).

742. —— 1884a. 'Remarks on a skull of an Australian aboriginal from the Lachlan district.' *Proc. Linn. Soc. N.S.W., 8,* 395–6.

743. —— 1884b. 'On a very dolichocephalic skull of an Australian aboriginal.' *Proc. Linn. Soc. N.S.W., 8,* 401–3.

744. —— 1885. 'On a complete debouchement of the sulcus Rolando in some brains of Australian aborigines.' *Proc. Linn. Soc. N.S.W., 9,* 578–80.

745. **Mill, J. S.,** 1861. 'Utilitarianism.' *Fraser's Mag., 64,* 391–673 (not consecutively).

746. **Millot, J., & Anthony, J.,** 1958. Article on 'Crossoptérygiens actuels' in Grassé,[427] Vol. 13, (3), 2553–97.

747. **Milne, A. H.,** 1955. 'The humps of east African cattle.' *Empire J. exp. Agric., 23,* 234–9.

748. **Minkowski, A.,** 1967. *Regional development of the brain in early life.* Oxford (Blackwell).

749. **Mitsukuri, K.,** 1897. 'A living specimen of *Pleurotomaria beyrichii.' Annot. zool. Jap., 1,* 67–8.

750. **Moll, J. A.,** 1857. 'Bemerkungen über den Bau der Augenlider des Menschen.' *Arch. f. Ophthalmol., 3,* Abt. 2, 258–68.

751. **Möllendorff, W. v., & Bargmann, W.** (edited by), 1929–66. *Handbuch der mikroskopischen Anatomie des Menschen.* 7 vols. Berlin (Springer).

752. **Monboddo, Lord** (anon.), 1773–92. *On the origin and progress of language.* Edinburgh (Kincaid & Creech).

753. **Montagna, W.,** 1962. *The structure and function of skin.* New York (Academic Press).

754. —— **Chase, H. B., & Lobitz, W. C.,** 1953. 'Histology and cytochemistry of human skin. V. Axillary apocrine sweat glands.' *Amer. J. Anat., 92,* 451–70.

755. —— **& Ellis, R. A.,** 1958. *The biology of hair growth.* New York (Academic Press).

**Montagu, M. F. A.,** see **Ashley-Montagu.**

756. **Montaigne, M. de,** 1587. *Essais de Messire Michel, Seignevr de Montaigne.* Revised & augmented edit. 2 books in one. Paris (Richer).

757. **Montandon, G.,** 1937. 'Homo palaeniger et Homo niloticus.' *Ztschr. f. Rassenk., 6,* 107–9.

758. **Montelius, O.,** 1901. 'La chronologie préhistorique en France et en autres pays celtiques.' *L'Anthrop., 12,* 609–23.

759. **Montesquieu [C. de S.]** (anon.) [1748]. *De l'esprit des lois.* Geneve (Barrillot).

760. **Moor, R.,** 1966. 'Find a girl with long legs.' *Daily Mail,* 9 July.

761. **Morant, G. M.,** 1925. 'A study of Egyptian craniology from prehistoric to Roman times.' *Biometrika, 18,* 56–98.

762. —— 1926. 'A first study of the craniology of England and Scotland from Neolithic to early historic times, with special reference to the Anglo-Saxon skulls in London museums.' *Biometrika, 18,* 56–98.

763. —— 1927*a.* 'A study of the Australian and Tasmanian skulls, based on previously published measurements.' *Biometrika, 19,* 417–40.

764. —— 1927*b.* 'Studies of Palaeolithic Man. II. A biometric study of Neanderthaloid skulls and of their relationships to modern racial types.' *Ann. Eugen., 2,* 318–81.

765. —— 1930–31. 'Studies of Palaeolithic man. IV. A biometric study of the Upper Palaeolithic skulls of Europe and of their relationships to earlier and later types.' *Ann. Eugen., 4,* 109–214.

766. **Morgan, L. H.,** 1877. *Ancient society or researches in the lines of human progress from savagery, through barbarism to civilization.* London (Macmillan).

767. **Morgan, T. J.,** 1959. Article on 'Breton language' in Law,[642] Vol. 2, p. 531 (only).

768. **Moroney, M. J.,** 1965. *Facts from figures.* 3rd. edit. Harmondsworth (Penguin).

769. **Morris, F. O.,** 1871. *A natural history of British moths.* 4 vols. London (Knox).

770. **Morrison-Scott, T. C. S.,** 1947. 'A revision of our knowledge of African elephants' teeth, with notes on forest and "pygmy" elephants.' *Proc. Zool. Soc. Lond., 117,* 505–27.

771. **Morton, F.,** 1955. *Hallstatt und die Hallstattzeit: viertausend Jahre Salzkultur.'* Hallstatt (Musealverein).

772. —— 1956. *Salzkammergut: die Vorgeschichte einer berühmten Landschaft.* Hallstatt (Musealverein).

773. **Mourant, A. E.,** 1954. *The distribution of the human blood groups.* Oxford (Blackwell).

774. —— **Kopeć, A. C., & Domaniewska-Sobczac, K.,** 1958. *The ABO blood groups: comprehensive tables and maps of world distribution.* Oxford (Blackwell).

775. **Müller, F.,** 1864. *Für Darwin.* Leipzig (Engelmann).

776. —— 1869. *Facts and arguments for Darwin.* London (Murray).

777. **Müller, H.,** 1860*a*. 'Epithel der Bindhaut der Ratte.' *Verh. physical.-med. Ges. Würzburg, 10,* p. xxiii (only).

778. —— 1860*b*. 'Bewegungs-Erscheinungen an ramificirten Pigment-Zellen in der Epidermis.' *Würzb. naturwiss. Ztschr., 1,* 164–6.

779. **Müller, H. J.,** 1952. Contribution to UNESCO.[1080]

780. **Müller, J.,** 1852. *Über Synapta digitata und über die Erzeugung von Schnecken in Holothurien.* Berlin (Reimer).

781. **Munro, R.,** 1890 (*sic,* actually 1900). *Rambles and studies in Bosnia-Herzegovina and Dalmatia.* 2nd edit. Edinburgh (Blackwood).

782. **Murray, J. A. H., Bradley, H., Craigie, W. A., & Onions, C. T.** (edited by). 1888–1926. *A new English dictionary on historical principles; founded mainly on the materials collected by the Philological Society.* 10 vols. Oxford (Clarendon Press).

783. **Mursell, J. L.,** 1950. *Psychological testing.* New York (Longmans, Green).

784. **Mutwa, C. V'M.,** 1971. *My people: writings of a Zulu witch-doctor.* Harmondsworth (Penguin).

785. **Nägeli, C. W. v.,** 1884. *Mechanisch-physiologische Theorie der Abstammungslehre.* München (Oldenbourg).

786. **Napier, J. R. & P. H.,** 1967. *A handbook of living primates.* London (Academic Press).

787. **Nasr, A. N.,** 1967. 'Histochemically demonstrable lipids in human eccrine and apocrine sweat glands.' *J. roy. micr. Soc., 86,* 427–32.

788. **Navarro, J. M. de,** 1952. Article on 'The Celts in Britain and their art' in Knowles.[600]

789. **Naylor, L. E.,** 1961. Article on 'Dog' in Law.[642] Vol. 4, pp. 578–80.

790. **Nersessian, S. D.,** 1965. Chapter on 'Between east and west: Armenia and its divided history' in Rice.[902] pp. 63–82.

791. **Nestle, E.** (edited by), 1926. H ΚΑΙΝΗ ΔΙΑΘΗΚΗ. London (British & Foreign Bible Society).

792. **Neubauer, A.,** 1885. 'Notes on the race-types of the Jews.' *J. anthr. Inst., 15,* 17–23.

793. **Neugebauer, O. E.,** 1961. Article on 'History of mathematics, ancient and medieval' in Ashmore.[37] pp. 84–6.

794. **Neumayr, M.,** 1889. *Die Stämme des Thierreiches.* Vol. 1. Wien (Tempsky).

795. —— **& Paul, C. M.,** 1875. 'Die Congerien- und Paludinenschichten Slavoniens und deren Faunen. Ein Beitrag zur Descendenz-Theorie.' *Abh. der K. K. Geol. Reichsanst. Wien, 7* (3), 1–106.

796. **Neustätter, O.,** 1895. 'Ueber die Lippensaum beim Menschen, seinen Bau, seine Entwickelung und seine Bedeutung.' *Jenaische Ztschr. f. Naturwiss., 29,* 345–90.

797. **Neuville, H.,** 1933. 'L'espèce, la race et le métissage en anthropologie: introduction à l'étude de l'anthropologie générale.' *Arch. Inst. Paléont. humaine, Mém., 11,* 1–515.

798. **Newman, H. H., Freeman, F. N., & Holzinger, K. J.,** 1937. *Twins: a study of heredity.* Chicago (University Press).

799. **Nichols, E. M.,** 1968. 'Microspectrophotometry in the study of red hair.' *Ann. Human Genet., 32,* 15–26.

800. **Nicoli, R. M., Ranque, J., & Martel, J. L.,** 1968. 'Étude séro-anthropologique. XXIV. Recherches sur les Arméniens en Provence.' *L'Anthrop., 72,* 89–96.

801. **Niekerk, I. J. M. van,** 1965. 'The anatomy of the duct system of the Bantu pancreas.' *Mankind Quart., 6,* 37–53.

802. **Niethammer, G.** (edited by), 1937. *Handbuch der deutschen Vogelkunde.* Vol. 1. Leipzig (Akademische Verlagsgesellschaft).

803. **Nietzsche, F.,** 1881. *Morgenröthe. Gedanken über die moralischen Vorurtheile.* Chemnitz (Schmeitzner).

804. —— 1903. *The dawn of day.* Transl. by J. Volz. London (Unwin).

805. —— 1883–91. *Also sprach Zarathustra. Ein Buch für Alle und Keinen.* Parts 1–3, Chemnitz (Schmeitzner); Part 4, Leipzig (Naumann).

806. —— 1960. *Thus spake Zarathustra.* Transl. by A. Tille & M. M. Bozman, with an Introduction by R. Pascal. London (Dent).

807. **Nordenskiöld, E.,** 1946. *The history of biology: a survey.* New York (Tudor).

808. **Nott, J. C.,** 1856. Appendix to Gobineau.[410]

809. **Obermaier, H., & Kühn, H.,** 1930. *Bushman art: rock paintings of South-West Africa.* London (Oxford University Press).

810. **Oken, L.,** 1816. *Lehrbuch der Naturgeschichte.* Vol. 3, Part 2. Jena (Schmid).

811. **Orbigny, A. d',** 1839. *L'homme américain (de l'Amérique méridionale) considerée sous ses rapports physiologiques et moraux.* 2 vols. & Atlas. Paris (Pitois-Levrault).

812. **Osborn, H. F.,** 1934. 'Aristogenesis, the creative principle in the origin of species.' *Amer. Nat., 68,* 193–235.

813. **Osborne, R. H., & George, F. V. De G.,** 1959. *Genetic basis of morphological variation: an evaluation and application of the twin study method.* Cambridge, Mass. (Harvard University Press).

814. **Owen, R.,** 1853. (Paper has no title.) *C. r. hebd. Séanc. Acad. Sci. Paris, 37,* 385–9.

815. —— 1862. 'Osteological contributions to the natural history of the chimpanzees (*Troglodytes*) and orangs (*Pithecus*). No. V. Comparison of the lower jaw and vertebral column of the Troglodytes Gorilla, Troglodytes niger, Pithecus Satyrus, and different varieties of the human race.' *Trans. Zool. Soc. Lond., 4,* 89–113.

816. **Pandit, S. R.,** 1934. 'Blood-group distribution in the Todas.' *Indian J. Med., 21,* 613–15.

817. **Pappas, G. D., & Purpura, D. P.,** 1961. 'Fine structure of dendrites in the superficial neocortical neuropil.' *Exp. Neurol., 4,* 507–30.

818. **Park, M.,** 1816–17. *Travels in the interior districts of Africa: performed in the years 1795, 1796, and 1797. With an account of a subsequent mission to that country in 1805. To which is added an account of the life of Mr. Park.* New edit. 2 vols. London (Murray).

819. —— 1969. *Mungo Park's travels in Africa.* London (Dent).

820. **Parker, T. J., & Haswell, W. A.,** 1910. *A text-book of zoology.* 2 vols. London (Macmillan).

821. **Parrish, M.** (edited by), 1963. *Vanished civilizations: forgotten peoples of the ancient world.* London (Thames & Hudson).

822. **Parry, E. J.,** 1947. Article on 'Musk' in Whiteley.[1138]

823. **Pascal, R.,** 1960. Introduction to Nietzsche.[805]

824. **Pasteels, J.,** 1958. Article on 'Développement des Dipneustes ou Choanichthyiens' in Grassé,[427] pp. 1743–54.

825. **Paterson, A. M.,** 1893. 'The human sacrum.' *Sci. Trans. Roy. Dublin Soc., 5,* 123–238.

826. **Patrick, D.** (edited by), 1908. *The illustrated Chamber Encyclopædia: a dictionary of universal knowledge.* New edition. 10 vols. London (Chambers).

827. **Paul-Boncour, G.,** 1912. *Anthropologie anatomique: crâne, face, tête sur le vivant.* Paris (Doin).

828. **Pavlow, A. P.,** 1901. 'Le Cretacé inferieur de la Russie et de sa faune. Seconde partie. Céphalopodes du Néocomien supérieur du type de Simbirsk.' *Nouv. Mém. Soc. imp. Nat. Moscou, 16* (3), 51–87.

829. **Peake, H., & Hooton, E. A.,** 1915. 'Saxon graveyard at East Shefford, Berks.' *J. Roy. Anthrop. Inst., 45,* 92–130.

830. **Pearson, K.,** 1905. *National life from the standpoint of science.* Second edit. London (Black).

831. —— **& Lee, A.,** 1903. 'On the laws of inheritance in man. 1. Inheritance of physical characters.' *Biometrika, 2,* 357–462.

832. **Pedersen, P. O.,** 1949. Quoted by Krogman.[614]

833. **Pelseneer, P.,** 1888. 'Report on the Pteropoda collected by H.M.S. Challenger during the years 1873–76.' *Report on the scientific results of the voyage of H.M.S.Challenger during the years 1873–76, 23,* 1–93.

834. **Penfield, W.** (edited by), 1932. *Cytology & cellular pathology of the nervous system.* 3 vols. New York (Hoeber).

835. **Péron, F., & Lesueur, C. A.,** 1883. 'Observations sur le tablier des femmes hottentotes.' *Bull. Soc. zool. France, 8,* 15–33.

836. **Peters, H. B.,** 1937. 'Die wissenschaftlichen Namen der menschlichen Körperformgruppen. Eine Zusammenstellung nach den internationalen Nomenklaturregeln.' *Ztschr. f. Rassenk., 6,* 211–41.

837. **Petersen, J., & Lanier, L. H.,** 1929. 'Studies in the comparative abilities of whites and Negroes.' *Mental Measurements Monographs, 5,* 1–156.

838. —— 1923. 'The comparative abilities of white and Negro children.' *Comp. Psychol. Monog., 1* (5). 1–141.

839. **Petherick [B. H. & J.],** 1869. *Travels in Central Africa and explorations of the Western Nile tributaries.* 2 vols. London (Tinsley).

840. **Petherick, J.,** 1861. *Egypt, the Sudan and central Africa, with explorations from Khartoum on the White Nile to the regions of the equator.* Edinburgh (Blackwood).

841. **Phillips, W. W. A.,** 1935. *Manual of the mammals of Ceylon.* Colombo (Colombo Museum).

842. **Piaggia, C.,** 1877. *Dell' arrivo fra i Niam-Niam e del soggiorno sul Lago Tzana in Abissinia.* Lucca (Giusti).

843. **Pillsbury, D. M., Shelley, W. B., & Kligman, A. M.,** 1956. *Dermatology.* London (Saunders).

844. **Pintner, R.,** 1924. *Intelligence testing: methods and results.* London (University of London Press).

845. **Pirie-Gordon, H.,** 1961. 'Hybrid nomenclature.' *Mankind Quart., 1,* 208–10.

846. **Pitt-Rivers [A.],** 1900. *Antique works of art from Benin.* (Privately printed).

847. **Plate, L.,** 1908. *Selectionsprinzip und Probleme der Artbildung: ein Handbuch des Darwinismus.* Leipzig (Engelmann).

848. **Pliny,** 1963. *Natural history, with an English translation in ten volumes.* Vol. VIII. Transl. by W. H. S. Jones. London (Heinemann).

849. **Pöch, R.,** 1911. 'Die Stellung der Buschmannrasse unter den übrigen Menschenrassen.' *Korr.-Bl. deutsch. Ges. Anthr. Ethn. Urges., 42,* 7–78.

850. **Poli, I. X.,** 1826. *Testacea utriusque Siciliae eorumque historia et anatome.* Vol. 3. Parmae (ex Regio Typographeio).

851. **Porteus, S. D.,** 1933. *The maze test and mental differences.* Vineland, N.J. (Smith).

852. —— 1967. Chapter on 'Ethnic groups and the maze test' in Kuttner,[622] pp. 409–27.

853. **Pouchet, G.,** 1858.- *De la pluralité des races humaines: essai anthropologique.* Paris (Baillière).

854. —— 1864a. *De la pluralité des races humaines: essai anthropologique.* 2nd edit. Paris (Masson).

855. —— 1864b. *The plurality of the human race.* Transl. from the 2nd edit. by H. J. C. Beavan. London (Longman).

856. —— 1895. 'Liste des ouvrages et mémoires publiés de 1855 à 1894 par Charles-Henri-Georges Pouchet.' *Nouv. Arch. du Mus. d'Hist. nat. Paris, 7,* after p. 284.

857. **Powell, T. G. E.,** 1958. *The Celts.* London (Thames & Hudson).

858. **Preston, F.** (edited by), 1969. *The Chambers's Encyclopaedia yearbook 1969; a record of the events, developments and personalities of 1968.* London (International Learning Systems Corporation).

859. **Prince, J.,** 1963. 'Rickets among immigrants.' *Daily Telegraph,* 21 Sept.

860. **Procter, E. E. S.,** 1961. Article on 'Spanish history' in Law,[642] Vol. 13, pp. 27–33.

861. **Protheroe, E.,** n.d. *New illustrated natural history of the world.* London (Routledge).

862. **Pruner-Bey, —,** 1865. 'De la chevelure comme caractéristique des races humaines d'après des recherches microscopiques.' *Mém. Soc. d'Anthrop. Paris, 2,* 1–35.

863. **Pullen, A. M.,** 1946. *Despite the colour bar: the story of George Carver—scientist.* London (S.C.M. Press).

864. **Purpura, D. P., & Schadé, J. P.** (edited by), 1964. *Growth and maturation of the brain.* London (Elsevier).

865. **Pycraft, W.,** 1925. 'On the calvaria found at Boskop, Transvaal, in 1913, and its relationship to Cromagnard and Negroid skulls.' *J. roy. Anthrop. Inst., 55,* 179–98.

866. —— 1928. Article on 'Rhodesian Man: description of the skull and other human remains from Broken Hill' in Bather.[63]

867. **Quatrefages, A. de, & Hamy, E. T.,** 1882. *Crania ethnica: les crânes des races humaines.* Paris (Baillière).

868. **Quetelet, A.,** 1846. *Lettres à S.A.R. le Duc Régnant de Saxe-Cobourg et Gotha, sur la théorie des probabilités, appliquée aux sciences morales et politiques.* Bruxelles (Hayez).

869. —— 1849. *Letters to H.R.H. the Grand Duke of Saxe Coburg and Gotha, on the theory of probabilities, as applied to the moral and political sciences.* Transl. by O. G. Downes. London (Layton).

870. **Race, R. R., & Sanger, R.,** 1950. *Blood groups in man.* Oxford (Blackwell).

871. **Radin, P.,** 1953. *The world of primitive man.* London (Abelard-Schuman).

872. **Ramón Cajal, S.,** 1910. 'Las fórmulas del proceder del nitrato de plata reducido y sus effectos sobre los factores integrantes de las neuronas.' *Trab. Lab. Invest. biol., 8,* 1–26.

873. **Ranke, J.,** 1898. 'Der Stirnfortsatz der Schläfenschuppe bei den Primaten.' *Sber. bayer. Akad. Wiss. (math.-physik. Classe), 28,* 227–70.

874. **Rao, P. D. P.,** 1963-4. 'Finger-prints of aborigines at Kalumburu Mission in Western Australia.' *Oceania, 34,* 225–33.

875. —— 1964–5. 'Finger and palm prints of the aboriginal children at Yuendumu Settlement in Central Australia.' *Oceania, 35,* 305–12.

876. **Raven, J. C.,** 1941. 'Standardization of progressive matrices, 1938.' *Brit. J. med. Psychol., 19,* 137–50.

877. —— 1947. *Progressive matrices, set 1.* London (Lewis).

## 594    BIBLIOGRAPHY

878. **Raven, J. C.,** 1956. *Coloured progressive matrices, sets $A_1$, $A_B$, B.* London (Lewis).

879. —— 1966. *Psychological principles appropriate to social and clinical problems.* London (Lewis).

880. **Rawles, M. E.,** 1947. 'Origin of pigment cells from the neural crest in the mouse embryo.' *Physiol. Zoöl., 20,* 248–66.

881. **Ray, J.,** 1686. *Historia plantarum species hactenus editas aliasque insuper multas noviter inventas & descriptas complectens.* Vol. 1. London (Faithorne & Kersey).

882. —— 1691. *The wisdom of God manifested in the works of the creation.* London (Smith).

883. **Réaumur, — de [R. A. F. de],** 1749. *Art de faire éclorre et d'élever en toute saison des oiseaux domestiques de toutes especes.* Paris (Imprimerie Royale).

884. **Redesdale, Lord,** 1911. Introduction to Chamberlain.[202]

885. **Redman, B. R.,** 1924. Introduction to Gobineau.[415]

886. **Reed, T. E.,** 1969. 'Caucasian genes in American Negroes.' *Science, 165,* 762–8.

887. **Reeve, L.,** 1844. Article entitled 'Monograph of the genus *Triton*', subsequently bound in Reeve,[888] Vol. 24.

888. —— 1850–81. *Conchologia iconica: or illustrations of the shells of molluscous animals.* (Place of publication & name of publisher not mentioned.)

889. **Reicher, M.,** 1913. 'Untersuchungen über die Schädelform der abendländischen und mongolischen Brachycephalen. 1. Zur Characteristic einiger brachycephaler Schädel-formen.' *Ztschr. Morph. Anthrop., 15,* 421–526.

890. —— 1914. Ditto, '2. Vergleich der alpenländischen brachycephalen Schädel mit den mongoloiden.' *Ztschr. Morph. Anthrop., 16,* 1–64.

891. **Rensch, B.,** 1928. 'Grenzfälle von Rasse und Art.' *J. f. Ornith., 76,* 222–31.

892. —— 1933. 'Zoologische Systematik und Artbildungsproblem.' *Verh. Deut. Zool. Ges., 35,* 19–83.

893. —— 1957. 'Die stammesgeschichtliche Sonderstellung des Menschen.' *Arbeitsgem. Forsch. Landes Nordrhein-Westfalen, 64,* 1–45.

894. —— 1959. *Evolution above the species level.* London (Methuen).

895. **Retzius, A.,** 1845. 'Ueber die Schädelformen der Nordbewohner.' Transl. from the Swedish. *Arch. Anat. Physiol. wiss. Med. (Müller)* (vol. not numbered), 84–129.

896. —— 1846. 'Mémoire sur les formes du crâne des habitants du nord.' Transl. from the Swedish. *Ann. des Sci. nat. Zool., 6,* 133–72.

897. —— 1864. *Ethnologische Schriften von Anders Retzius nach dem Tode des Verfassers gesammelt.* Stockholm (Norstedt).

898. **Retzius, G.,** 1896. *Das Menschenhirn: Studien in der makroskopischen Morphologie.* Stockholm (Königliche Buchdruckerei).

899. **Reuning, H.,** 1957. 'The Pauli test: new findings from vector analysis.' *J. Nat. Inst. Personnel Res., 7,* 3–27.

900. **Rhyne, V. C. W. ten,** 1686. *Schediasma de Promontorio Bonæ Spei; ejusve tractus incolis Hottentottis.* Schafusii (Meister).

901. —— n.d. *An account of the Cape of Good Hope and the Hottentotes, the natives of that country.* Transl. from the Latin. Schaffhausen (publisher not named).

902. **Rice, D. T.** (edited by), 1965. *The dark ages: the making of European civilization.* London (Thames & Hudson).

903. **Richardson, J.,** 1956. *Rachel.* London (Reinhardt).

904. **Richter, R.,** 1938. 'Beobachtungen an einer gemischten Kolonie von Silbermöwe (*Larus argentatus* Pont.) und Heringsmöwe (*Larus fuscus graellsii* Brehm).' *J. f. Ornith., 86,* 366–73.

905. **Ripley, W. Z.,** 1900. *The races of Europe: a sociological study.* London (Kegan Paul, Trench, Trübner).

906. **Rivers, W. H. R.,** 1906. *The Todas.* London (Macmillan).

907. **Roberts, D. F., & Hiorns, R. W.,** 1962. 'The dynamics of racial intermixture.' *Amer. J. hum. Genet., 14,* 261–77.

908. **Robin, C.,** 1845. 'Sur un espèce particulière de glandes de la peau de l'homme.' *Ann. des Sci. nat., Zool., 4,* 380–81.

909. **Robinson, A.** (edited by), 1913. *Cunningham's text-book of anatomy.* 4th edit. Edinburgh (Frowde and Hodder & Stoughton).

910. **Robinson, K. R.,** 1959. *Khami ruins.* Cambridge (University Press).

911. —— n.d. *A guide to the Khami ruins.* Place of publication not stated (Commission for the Preservation of Natural and Hi...rical Monuments and Relics).

912. **Rode, P.,** 1937. 'Les Primates de l'Afrique.' *Publ. Com. d'Étud. hist. sci. Afrique occ. franç., B 2,* 1–223.

913. —— 1941. 'Étude d'un chimpanzé pygmée adolescent (*Pan satyrus paniscus*).' *Mammalia, 5,* 50–68.

914. **Rolleston, H. D.,** 1888. 'Description of the cerebral hemispheres of an adult Australian male.' *J. Anthrop. Inst., 17,* 32–42.

915. **Roth, C.,** 1961. Article on 'Jewish History' in Patrick,[826] Vol. 8, pp. 92–100.

916. **Rothenstein, W.,** 1939. Quoted by Meyerowitz, H. & V.[739]

917. **Rothman, S., Krysa, H. F., & Smiljanic, A. M.,** 1946. 'Inhibitory action of human epidermis on melanin formation.' *Proc. Soc. exp. Biol. N. Y., 62,* 208–9.

918. **Rousseau, J. J.,** 1755. *Discours sur l'origine et les fondemens de l'inegalité parmi les hommes.* Amsterdam (Rey).

919. —— 1782. *Discours sur l'origine et les fondemens de l'inegalité parmi les hommes.* London (publisher not named).

920. —— 1946. *The social contract and discourses.* Transl. by G. D. H. Cole. London (Dent).

921. **Rozenzweig, M. R., Krech, D., & Bennett, E. L.,** 1960. 'A search for relations between brain chemistry and behaviour.' *Psychol. Bull., 57,* 476–92.

922. **Rückert, J.,** 1892. 'Zur Entwicklungsgeschichte des Ovarialeies bei Selachiern'. *Anat. Anz., 7,* 107–58.

923. **Ruzicka, L., & Stoll, M.,** 1934. 'Über die Herstellung von 2-methyl und 7-methyl-cyclopentadecanon-(1). Beiträge zur Synthese des *d,l*-Muscons.' *Helv. chim. Acta, 17,* 1308–18.

924. **Ryazanoff, D.** (edited by), 1927. *Karl Marx: man, thinker, and revolutionist.* London (Lawrence).

**Saint-Hilaire, É. Geoffroy de,** see **Geoffroy, de.**

925. **Salaman, R. N.,** 1911. 'Heredity and the Jew.' *J. Genet., 1,* 273–92.

926. **Sandiford, P.,** 1928. *Educational psychology: an objective study.* London (Longmans, Green).

927. —— 1938. *Foundations of educational psychology.* London (Longmans, Green).

928. —— **& Kerr, R.,** 1926. 'Intelligence of Chinese and Japanese children.' *J. educ. Psychol., 17,* 361–7.

929. **Santiana, A.,** 1953. 'Los Indios del Ecuador y sus caracteristicas serológicas.' *Ztschr. f. Ethnol., 78,* 262–71.

930. **Sarasin, F.,** 1922. Volume 'C' on *Anthropologie der Neu-Caledonier und Loyalty-Insulaner* in Sarasin & Roux.[931]

931. —— **& Roux, J.,** 1916–22. *Nova Caledonia: Forschungen in Neu-Caledonien und auf den Loyalty-Inseln.* 6 vols. & Atlas. Wiesbaden (Kreidel).

932. **Sauser, G.,** 1938. *Die Ötztaler: Anthropologie und Anatomie einer Tiroler Talschaft.* Innsbruck (Naturwissenschaftlich-medizinischer Verein).

933. **Schaaffhausen, H.,** 1885. 'Einige Reliquien Berühmter Männer.' *Corresp.-Blatt deut. Ges. Anthrop. Ethnol. Urges., 16,* 147–9.

934. **Schadé, J. P., Backer, H. van, & Colon, E.,** 1964. Chapter on 'Quantitative analysis of neural parameters in the maturing cerebral cortex' in Purpura & Schadé,[864] pp. 150–75.

935. **Schaffer, J.,** 1924. 'Über Anal- und Circumanaldrüsen. I Mitteilung Geschichtlicher Überblick.' *Zeitschr. f. wiss. Zool., 122,* 79–96.

936. **Schapera, I.,** 1930. *The Khoisan peoples of South Africa: Bushmen and Hottentots.* London (Routledge).

937. —— (edited by), 1933. *The early Cape Hottentots.* Cape Town (Van Riebeeck Society).

938. —— 1937. *The Bantu-speaking tribes of South Africa.* London (Routledge).

939. **Schepers, G. W. H.,** 1950. 'The brain casts of recently discovered *Plesianthropus* skulls.' *Transvaal Mus. Mem., 4,* 85–117.

940. **Schiefferdecker, P.,** 1917. 'Die Hautdrusen des Menschen und der Säugetiere, ihre biologische und rassenanatomische Bedeutung sowie die Muscularis sexualis.' *Biol. Zentralbl., 37,* 534–62.

941. —— 1922. 'Die Hautdrüsen des Menschen und der Säugetiere, ihre biologische und rassenanatomische Bedeutung, sowie die Muscularis sexualis.' *Zoologica, 72,* 1–154.

942. **Schindewolf, O. H.** (edited by), 1938. *Handbuch der Paläozoologie.* Vol. 1. Berlin (Borntraeger).

943. **Schmidt, G. A.,** 1934. 'Ein zweiter Entwicklungstypus von *Lineus gesserensis ruber* O. F. Müll. (Nemertini).' *Zool. Jahrb., Abt. Anat. u. Ont., 58,* 607–60.

944. **Schmidt, M.,** 1926. *The primitive races of mankind: a study in ethnology.* London (Harrap).

945. **Schneider, K. C.,** 1908. *Histologisches Praktikum der Tiere für Studenten und Forscher.* Jena (Fischer).

946. **Schotte, J. P.,** 1782. *A treatise on the Synochus atrabiliosa, a contagious fever.* London (Murray).

947. **Schouteden, H.,** 1931. 'La chimpanzé de la rive gauche du Congo.' *Bull. Cercle Zool. Congol., 7,* 114–19.

948. **Schuster, E., & Elderton, E. M.,** 1907. 'The inheritance of ability, being a statistical study of the Oxford class lists and of the school lists of Harrow and Charterhouse.' *Eugenics Lab. Mem. (University of London), 1,* 1–42.

949. **Schwarz, E.,** 1929. 'Das Vorkommen des Schimpansen auf den linken Kongo-Ufer.' *Rev. Zool. Bot. Afr., 16,* 425–6.

950. —— 1934. 'On the local races of the chimpanzee.' *Ann. Mag. Nat. Hist., 13,* 576–83.

951. **Schweinfurth, G.,** 1873. *The heart of Africa. Three years' travels and adventures in the unexplored regions of central Africa. From 1868 to 1871.* 2 vols. London (Sampson Low, Marston, Low, & Searle).

952. **Schweppenburg, H. G. von,** 1938. 'Zur Systematik der *fuscus-argentatus* Möwen.' *J. f. Ornith., 86,* 345–65.

953. **Schwidetzky, I.** (edited by), 1962. *Die neue Rassenkunde.* Stuttgart (Fischer).

954. **Sclater, P. L., & Thomas, O.,** 1894–1900. *The book of antelopes.* London (Porter).

955. **Segy, L.,** 1961. *African sculpture speaks.* New York (Hill & Wang).

956. **Seiner, F., & Staudinger, R.,** 1912. 'Beobachtungen und Messungen an Buschleuten.' *Ztschr. f. Ethnol., 44,* 275–88.

957. **Seligman, C. G.,** 1961. *Races of Africa.* London (Oxford University Press).

958. **Sergi, G.,** 1895. *Origine e diffusione della stirpe mediterranea: indusioni antropologiche.* Roma (Società editrice Dante Alighieri).

959. —— 1901. *The Mediterranean race: a study of the origin of European peoples.* London (Scott).

960. —— 1908. 'Di una classificazione razionale dei gruppi umani.' *Atti Soc. ital. Prog. Sci., 1,* 232–42.

961. **Sewell, R. B. S., & Guha, B. S.,** 1931. Chapter on 'Human remains' in Marshall, J.,[702] Vol. 2, pp. 599–648.

962. **Shelley, W. B., & Hurley, H. J.,** 1953. 'The physiology of the human axillary apocrine sweat gland.' *J. Invest. Dermatol., 20,* 285–97.

963. **Shields, J.,** 1962. *Monozygotic twins brought up apart and brought up together.* London (Oxford University Press).

964. **Shrubsall, F.,** 1897. 'Crania of African Bush races.' *J. Anthrop. Inst., 27,* 263–92.

965. **Shuey, A. M.,** 1958. *The testing of Negro intelligence.* Lynchburg, Virginia (Bell).

966. —— 1966. *The testing of Negro intelligence.* 2nd edit. New York (Social Science Press).

967. **Sicard, H.,** 1970. 'Le pas de la réflexion.' *Soc. d'Étud. préhist. Les Eyzies, 19,* 46–68.

968. **Simpson, G. G.,** 1945. 'The principles of classification and a classification of mammals.' *Bull. Amer. Mus. Nat. Hist., 85,* v–xvi & 1–350.

969. —— 1951a. 'The species concept.' *Evolution, 5,* 285–98.

970. —— 1951b. *Horses: the story of the horse family in the modern world and through sixty million years of history.* New York (Oxford University Press).

971. —— 1953. *The major features of evolution.* New York (Columbia University Press).

972. —— 1963. Chapter on 'The meaning of taxonomic statements' in Washburn,[1119] pp. 1–31.

973. **Singer, R.,** 1953. 'The sickle cell trait in Africa.' *Amer. Anthrop., 55,* 634–48.

974. **Sisson, S., & Grossman, J. D.,** 1953. *The anatomy of the domestic animals.* London (Saunders).

975. **Skinner, J. D.,** 1967. 'An appraisal of the eland as a farm animal in Africa.' *Anim. Breed. Abstr., 35,* 177–86.

976. **Slatis, H. M., & Apelbaum, A.,** 1963. 'Hairy pinna of the ear in Israeli populations.' *Amer. J. hum. Genet., 15,* 74–85.

977. **Smit, H. P.** (edited by), 1928. *The native tribes of South West Africa.* Cape Town (Cape Times).

978. **Smith, A.,** 1797. *The theory of moral sentiments; or, an essay towards an analysis of the principles by which men naturally judge concerning the conduct and character, first of their neighbours, and afterwards of themselves. To which is added, A dissertation on the origin of languages.* 8th edit. 2 vols. London (Strahan).

979. **Smith, G. E.,** 1904*a*. 'The so-called "Affenspalte" in the human (Egyptian) brain.' *Anat. Anz., 24,* 74–83.

980. —— 1904*b*. 'The morphology of the occipital region of the cerebral hemisphere in man and the apes.' *Anat. Anz., 24,* 436–51.

981. —— 1923. *The ancient Egyptians and the origin of civilization.* London (Harper).

982. **Smith, M.,** 1954. *The British amphibians and reptiles.* Revised edit. London (Collins).

983. **Smith, R. A.,** 1905. *A guide to the antiquities of the early Iron Age of central and western Europe.* London (British Museum).

984. **Smith, S. S.,** 1788. *An essay on the causes of the variety of complexion and figure in the human species.* Edinburgh (Elliot).

985. **Sneath, P. H. A.,** 1967. 'Trend-surface analysis of transformation grids.' *J. Zool. Lond., 151,* 65–122.

986. **Snyder, L. H.,** 1932. 'Studies in human inheritance. IX. The inheritance of taste deficiency in man.' *Ohio J. Sci., 32,* 436–40.

987. **Soemmerring, S. T.,** 1784. *Über körperliche Verschiedenheit des Mohren vom Europäer.* Mainz (publisher not named).

988. —— 1785. *Ueber die körperliche Verschiedenheit des Negers vom Europäer.* Frankfurt (Barrentrapp & Wenner).

989. **Sollas, W. J.,** 1911. *Ancient hunters and their modern representatives.* London (Macmillan).

990. **Sommerfelt, A.,** 1938. *La langue et la société: charactères sociaux d'une langue de type archaïque.'* Oslo (Ascheoug).

991. —— 1944. 'Is there a fundamental mental difference between primitive man and the civilized European?' *Earl Grey Memorial Lectures (King's College, Newcastle upon Tyne), 26,* 1–8.

992. **Sorokin, P.,** 1928. *Contemporary sociological theories.* New York (Harper).

993. **Spearman, C.,** 1904. '"General intelligence", objectively determined and measured.' *Amer. J. Psychol., 15,* 201–93.

994. —— 1922. 'Correlation between arrays in a table of correlations.' *Proc. Roy. Soc. A, 101,* 94–100.

995. —— 1927. *The abilities of man: their nature and measurement.* London (Macmillan).

996. **Speke, J. H.,** 1863. *Journal of the discovery of the source of the Nile.* Edinburgh (Blackwood).

997. **Spengler, O.,** 1923. *Der Untergang des Abendlandes: Umrisse einer Morphologie der Weltgeschichte.* 2 vols. München (Beck).

998. —— 1959. *The decline of the west.* Transl. by C. F. Atkinson. London (Allen & Unwin).

999. —— 1934. *Preussentum und Sozialismus.* München (Beck).

1000. **Sperry, R. W., & Hibbard, E.,** 1968. Chapter on 'Regulative factors in the orderly growth of retino-tectal connexions' in Wolstenholme & O'Connor,[1150] pp. 41–52.

1001. **Spurway, H.,** 1953. 'Genetics of specific and subspecific differences in European newts.' *Symp. Soc. exp. Biol., 7,* 200–37.

1002. **Stadtmüller, F.,** 1936. Chapter on 'Kranium und Visceralskelett der Säugetiere' in Bolk, Göppert, Kallius, & Lubosch.[123]

1003. **Stanley, H. M.,** 1890. *In darkest Africa or the quest rescue and retreat of Emin Governor of Equatoria.* London (Sampson Low, Marston, Searle, & Rivington).

1004. **Stegman, B.,** 1930–31. 'Die Vögel des dauro-mandschurischen Übergangsgebietes.' Parts 1 & 2. *J. f. Ornith., 78,* 389–471, & *79,* 137–236.

1005. —— 1934. 'Ueber die Formen der grossen Möwen (subgenus *Larus*) und ihre gegenseitigen Beziehungen.' *J. f. Ornith., 82,* 340–80.

1006. **Steller, G. W.,** 1774. *Beschreibung von dem Lande Kamtschatka, dessen Einwohnern, deren Sitten, Nahmen, Lebensart und verschiedenen Gewohnheiten.* Frankfurt (Fleischer).

1007. **Stern, C.,** 1953. 'Model estimates of the frequency of white and near-white segregants in the American negro.' *Acta genet. stat. med., 4,* 281–98.

1008. —— 1960. *Principles of human genetics.* 2nd edit. London (Freeman).

1009. **Stern, W.,** 1911. *Die differentielle Psychologie in ihren methodischen Grundlagen.* Leipzig (Barth).

1010. —— 1912. 'Die psychologischen Methoden der Intelligenzprüfung.' *Ber. Kong. exp. Psychol., 5,* 1–109.

1011. **Sterndale, R. A.,** 1884. *Natural history of the Mammalia of India and Ceylon.* Calcutta (Thacker, Spink).

1012. **Stock, St. G.** (edited by), 1898. *Caesar de bello gallico,* books I–VII according to the text of E. Hoffmann. Oxford (Clarendon Press).

1013. **Stoddard, L.,** 1920. *The rising tide of colour against white world-supremacy.* London (Chapman & Hall).

1014. **Stoll, N. R.** (edited by), 1961. *International code of zoological nomenclature adopted by the XV International Congress of Zoology.* London (International Trust for Zoological Nomenclature).

1015. **Stone, A. H.,** 1908. *Studies in the American race problem.* London (Doubleday, Page).

1016. **Stow, G. W.,** 1910. *The native races of South Africa: a history of the intrusion of the Hottentots and Bantu into the hunting grounds of the Bushmen, the aborigines of the country.* Edited by G. McC. Theal. First edition (1905), reprinted. London (Swan Sonnenschein).

1017. —— **& Bleek, D. F.,** 1930. *Rock paintings in South Africa from parts of the Eastern Province and Orange Free State.* London (Methuen).

1018. —— —— n.d. *Photographs of Stow's copies of Bushman paintings not included in 'Rock paintings in South Africa'.* Typescript descriptions by D. F. Bleek. (In the Library of Rhodes House, Oxford.)

1019. **Stratz den Haag, C. H.,** 1903. 'Das Problem der Rasseneinteilung der Menschheit.' *Archiv f. Anthrop., 1,* 189–200.

1020. **Stresemann, E., & Timofeeff-Ressovsky, N. W.,** 1947. 'Artenstehung in geographischen Formenkreisen. 1. Der Formenkreis Larus argentatus-cachinnans-fuscus.' *Biol. Zentralbl., 66,* 57–76.

1021. **Stuart, J.,** 1950. Introduction to Fynn.[373]

1022. **Stubbings, F. H.,** 1961. Article on 'Greece: Archaeology' in Law.[642] Vol. 6, pp. 532–6.

1023. **Studer, ——,** 1911. 'Eine neue Equidenform aus dem Obermiocän von Samos.' *Verh. Deut. Zool. Ges.* (vol. not numbered), 192–200.

1024. **Stuhlmann, F.,** 1894. *Mit Emin Pascha ins Herz von Afrika. Ein Reisebericht mit Beiträgen von Dr. Emin Pascha, in seinem Auftrage geschildert.* Berlin (Reimer).

1025. **Summers, R.** (edited by), 1959. *Prehistoric rock art of the Federation of Rhodesia and Nyasaland.* Salisbury, Rhodesia (National Publications Trust).

1026. —— 1963. Chapter on 'City of black gold: the riddle of Zimbabwe' in Parrish.[821]

1027. —— **Robinson, K. R., & Whitty, A.,** 1961. 'Zimbabwe excavations.' *Occ. Pap. Nat. Mus. S. Rhodesia, 3,* 157–332.

1028. **Sumner, A. T.,** 1932. 'Mendi writing.' *Sierra Leone Studies, 17,* 29–33.

1029. **Sunderland, E.,** 1956. 'Hair-colour variation in the United Kingdom.' *Ann. human Genet., 20,* 312–30.

1030. **Sunne, D.,** 1917. 'A comparative study of white and Negro children.' *J. appl. Psychol., 1,* 71–83.

1031. **Sylvester, J. J.,** 1870. Address to the Mathematical and Physical Section of the British Association. *Rep. Brit. Assoc. Adv. Sci. (Exeter 1869), 39,* Notices & Abstracts. 1–9.

1032. **Szentágothai, J.,** 1968. Chapter on 'Growth of the nervous system: an introductory survey' in Wolstenholme & O'Connor,[1150] pp. 3–12.

1033. **Tacitus, C.,** 1935. *The Germania of Tacitus: a critical edition.* Edited by R. P. Robinson. Middletown, Conn. (American Philological Association).

1034. —— 1938. *Cornelii Taciti de origine et situ Germanorum.* Edited by J. G. C. Anderson. Oxford (Clarendon Press).

1035. **Terman, L. M.,** 1916. *The measurement of intelligence: an explanation of and a complete guide for the use of the Stanford revision and extension of the Binet–Simon Intelligence Scale.* Boston (Houghton Mifflin).

1036. —— 1926. *Genetic studies of genius.* Vol. 1. *Mental and physical traits of a thousand gifted children.* Stanford (University Press).

1037. —— **& Childs, H. G.,** 1912. 'A tentative revision and extension of the Binet–Simon measuring scale of intelligence.' Parts I–III. *J. educ. Psychol., 3,* 61–82. 133–43, 198–208, 277–89.

1038. —— **& Merrill, M. A.,** 1937. *Measuring intelligence: a guide to the administration of the new revised Stanford–Binet tests of intelligence.* London (Harrap).

1039. **Thévenin, R.,** 1947. *Origine des animaux domestiques.* Paris (Presses universitaires).

1040. **Thierry, A.,** 1828. *Histoire des Gaulois depuis les temps les plus reculés jusqu'à l'entière soumission de la Gaule à la domination romaine.* 3 vols. Paris (Sautelet).

1041. **Thompson, D'A. W.,** 1916. 'Morphology and mathematics.' *Trans. Roy. Soc. Edin., 50,* 857–95.

1042. —— 1917. *On growth and form.* Cambridge (University Press).

1043. **Thompson, J. E. S.,** 1963. Chapter on 'The gods that failed: the glory and decay of Mayan culture' in Parrish,[821] pp. 139–68.

1044. **Thompson, R. H. S., & King, E. J.,** 1964. *Biochemical disorders in human disease.* London (Churchill).

1045. **Thomson, A., & Buxton, D.,** 1923. 'Man's nasal index in relation to certain climatic conditions.' *J. Roy. Anthrop. Inst., 53,* 92–122.

1046. —— **& Randall-Maciver, D.,** 1905. *The ancient races of the Thebaid.* Oxford (Clarendon Press).

1047. **Thomson, G. H.,** 1924. *Instinct, intelligence and character: an educational psychology.* London (Allen & Unwin).

1048. —— 1939. *The factorial analysis of human ability.* London (University of London Press).

1049. **Thomson, M. L.,** 1955. 'Relative efficiency of pigment and horny layer thickness in protecting the skin of Europeans and Africans against solar ultraviolet radiation.' *J. Physiol., 127,* 236–46.

1050. **Thorndike, E. L.,** 1910. *Educational psychology.* 2nd edit. New York (Columbia University).

1051. **Thorndike, R. L., & Hagen, E.,** 1955. *Measurement and evaluation in psychology and education.* London (Chapman & Hall).

1052. **Thurston, E.,** 1896. 'Anthropology of the Todas and Kotas of the Nilgiri Hills, and of the Bráhmans, Kammálans, Pallis, and Pariahs of Madras City.' *Bull. Madras Govt. Mus., 4,* 141–236.

1053. —— n.d. Quoted by Gates (1961a).[391]

1054. **Thurstone, L. L.,** 1935. *The vectors of the mind: multiple-factor analysis for the isolation of primary traits.* Chicago (University Press).

1055. —— 1938. *Primary mental abilities.* Chicago (University Press).

1056. —— 1947. *Multiple-factor analysis: a development and expansion of* The vectors of the mind. Chicago (University Press).

1057. —— **& T. G.,** 1929. *Personality schedule, 1929 edition.* Chicago (University Press).

1058. —— —— 1941. *Factorial studies of intelligence.* Chicago (University Press).

1059. **Tiedemann, F.,** 1836. 'On the brain of the negro, compared with that of the European and the orang-outang.' *Phil. Trans. Roy. Soc., 126,* 497–527.

1060. **Tobias, P. V.,** 1955–6. 'Les Bochimans Auen et Naron de Ghanzi. Contribution à l'étude des "Anciens Jaunes" sud-africains.' *L'Anthrop., 59,* 235–52, 429–61; *60,* 22–52, 268–89.

1061. **Topinard, P.,** 1885. *Éléments d'anthropologie générale.* Paris (Delahaye & Lecrosnier).

1062. —— 1894. *Anthropology.* Transl. from the French. London (Chapman & Hall).

1063. **Toynbee, A. J.,** 1961. *A study of history.* Vol. 12. *Reconsiderations.* London (Oxford University Press).

1064. **Toynbee, J. M. C.,** 1964. *Art in Great Britain under the Romans.* Oxford (Clarendon Press).

1065. **Tratman, E. K.,** 1950. 'A comparison of the teeth of people: Indo-European racial stock with the Mongoloid racial stock.' *Dental Rec., 70,* 31–53 & 63–88.

1066. **Treus, V., & Kravchenko, D.,** 1968. 'Methods of rearing and economic utilization of eland in the Askaniya-Nova Zoological Park.' *Symp. Zool. Soc. Lond., 21,* 395–411.

1067. **Trevor, J. C.,** 1968. Unpublished; quoted by Hutchinson.[531]

1068. **Trotter, M., Duggins, O. H., & Setzler, F. M.,** 1956. 'Hair of Australian aborigines (Arnhem Land).' *Amer. J. phys. Anthrop., 14,* 649–59.

1069. **Tryon, R. C.,** 1940. 'Genetic differences in maze-learning ability in rats.' *Yearbook Nat. Soc. Stud. Educ., 39* (1), 111–19.

1070. **Turgenev, I. S.,** 1959. *A nest of gentlefolk and other stories.* Transl. from the Russian. London (Oxford University Press).

1071. —— 1963. *A nest of gentry* (in Russian). Moscow (State Publishers of Artistic Literature).

1072. **Turner, W.,** 1884. 'Report on the human crania and other bones of the skeletons collected during the voyage of H.M.S. Challenger, in the years 1873–76.' Part 1. 'The crania.' *Report of the scientific results of the voyage of H.M.S. Challenger during the years 1873–76. Zoology,* Vol. 10, 1–130. London (Longmans).

1073. —— 1886a. Ditto, Part 2. 'The bones of the skeleton.' *Report of the scientific results of the voyage of H.M.S. Challenger during the years 1873–76. Zoology,* Vol. 16, 1–136. London (Longmans).

1074. —— 1886b. 'The sacral index in various races of mankind.' *J. Anat. Physiol., 20,* 317–23.

1075. —— 1886c. 'The lumbar curve of the spinal column in several races of men.' *J. Anat. Physiol., 20,* 536–43.

1076. **Turner, W.,** 1891. 'The relations of the dentary arcades in the crania of Australian aborigines.' *J. Anat. Physiol., 25,* 461–474.

1077. **Tyler, L. E.,** 1956. *The psychology of human differences.* 2nd edit. New York (Appleton-Century-Crofts).

1078. **Tylor, E. B.,** 1865. *Researches into the early history of mankind and the development of civilization.* London (Murray).

1079. **Tyson, E.,** 1699. *Orang-outang, sive Homo sylvestris: or, the anatomy of a pygmie compared with that of a monkey, an ape, and a man.* London (Bennet).

1080. **UNESCO** (Anon.), 1952. *The race concept: results of an enquiry.* Paris (UNESCO).

1081. **Urbain, A., & Rode, P.,** 1940. 'Un chimpanzé pygmée (*Pan satyrus paniscus* Schwarz) au Parc Zoologique du Bois de Vincennes.' *Mammalia, 4,* 12–14.

1082. **Vaillant, G. C.,** 1961. *The Aztecs of Mexico: origin, rise and fall of the Aztec nation.* Harmondsworth (Penguin).

1083. **Vallois, H. V.,** 1939. Article on 'Les ossements humains de Sialk. Contributions à l'étude d'histoire raciale de l'Iran ancient' in Ghirshman,[404] Vol. 2, pp. 113–92.

1084. ———— 1941. 'Recherches anthropologiques sur les Peuls et divers noirs de l'Afrique occidentale d'après les mensurations de M. Leca (Mission Labouret 1932).' *Bull. Mém. Soc. d'Anthrop. Paris, 2,* 20–74.

1085. ———— 1960. *Les races humaines.* 5th edit. Paris (Presses universitaires).

1086. **Varro, M. T.,** 1912. *Rerum rusticarum libri tres.* Edited by G. Goetz. Lipsiae (Teubner).

1087. **Vaugondy, R. de,** 1778. *Nouvel atlas portatif destiné principalement pour l'instruction de la jeunesse, d'après la géographie moderne de feu l'Abbé Delacroix.* Paris (Fortin).

1088. **Vaurie, C.,** 1951. 'Adaptive differences between two sympatric species of nuthatches (*Sitta*).' *Proc. X Internat. Ornith. Congr.* (1950), 163–6.

1089. **Vedder, H.,** 1923. *Die Bergdama.* 2 vols. Hamburg (Friederichsen).

1090. ———— 1928. Chapter on 'The Berg Damara' in Smit,[977] pp. 37–78.

1091. **Verne, J.,** 1930. *Couleurs et pigments des êtres vivans.* Paris (Colin).

1092. **Verneau, R.,** 1886. 'La race de Cro-Magnon: ses migrations, ses descendants.' *Rev. d'Anthrop., 1,* 10–24.

1093. ———— 1891. *Cinq années de séjour aux Îles Canaries.* Paris (Hennuyer).

1094. ———— 1906. *Les grottes de Grimaldi (Baoussé-Roussé: Anthropologie).* Monaco (Imprimerie de Monaco).

1095. **Vernon, P. E.,** 1940. *The measurement of abilities.* London (University of London Press).

1096. ———— 1961. *The structure of human abilities.* 2nd edit. London (Methuen).

1097. ———— 1965. 'Environmental handicaps and intellectual development.' Parts I & II. *Brit. J. educ. Psychol., 35,* 9–20 & 117–26.

1098. **Verworn, M.,** 1917. *Zur Psychologie der primitiven Kunst.* Jena (Fischer).

1099. **Villiers, H. de,** 1961. 'The tablier and steatopygia in Kalahari Bushwomen.' *South Afr. J. Sci., 57,* 223–7.

1100. **Vincent, L.,** 1872. 'Contributions à l'ethnologie de la côte occidentale d'Afrique: les Boschimans.' *Rev. d.Anthrop., 1,* 452–6.

1101. **Virchow, R.,** 1886. 'Buschmänner.' *Ztschr. f. Ethnol., 18* (*Verh. Berl. Ges. Anthrop. Ethnol. Urges.,* 221–39).

1102. ———— 1887. 'Physische Anthropologie von Buschmännern, Hottentotten und Omundonga.' *Ztschr. f. Ethnol., 19* (*Verh. Berl. Ges. Anthrop. Ethnol. Urges.,* 656–66).

1103. —— 1893. 'Über griechische Schädel aus alter und neuer Zeit und über einen Schädel von Menidi, die für den des Sophokles gehalten ist.' *Sitzungsber. Kön. preuss. Akad. Wiss. Berlin* (vol. not numbered), 677–700.

1104. —— 1896. 'Die Beschreibung eines Schädels aus der alteren Hallstatt-Zeit vom Mühlhart.' *Ztschr. f. Ethnol.*, 28 (*Verh. Berlin Ges. Anthropol. Ethnol. Urges.*, 243–6).

1105. **Vogt, C.,** 1863. *Vorlesungen über den Menschen, seine stellung in der Schöpfung und in der Geschichte der Erde.* 2 vols. Giessen (Nicker).

1106. —— 1864. *Lectures on man: his place in creation, and in the history of the earth.* Transl. from the German. London (Longman, Green, Longman, Roberts).

1107. **Voltaire, F. M. A.** (anon.), 1756. *Essay sur l'histoire génèrale, et sur les moeurs et l'esprit des nations, depuis Charlemagne jusqu'a nos jours.* Place of publication not named (Cramer).

1108. —— ('Bazin'), 1765. *La philosophie de l'histoire.* (Place of publication and publisher not named.)

1109. —— ('M. de V.'), 1777. *Questions sur l'encyclopédie.* Geneve (publisher not named).

1110. —— 1879. *Les lettres d'Amabed,* reprinted in *Œuvres complètes de Voltaire,* Vol. 21. Paris (Garnier).

1111. **Wachsmann, K. P.,** 1969. Chapter on 'The primitive musical instruments' in Baines.[44]

1112. **Wade, G. W.,** 1934. *The documents of the New Testament translated & historically arranged with critical introductions.* London (Murby).

1113. **Wagner, H.,** 1864. *Maassbestimmungen der Oberfläche des grossen Gehirns.* Cassel (Wigand).

1114. **Wagner, R.,** 1844. *Handwörterbuch der Physiologie mit Rücksicht auf physiologische Pathologie.* Vol. 2. Braunschweig (Vieweg).

1115. —— 1860. *Vorstudien zu einer wissenschaftlichen Morphologie und Physiologie des menschlichen Gehirns als Seelenorgan.* 2 vols bound together. Göttingen (Dieterischen Buchhandlung).

1116. **Wallace, A. R.,** 1876. *The geographical distribution of animals, with a study of the relations of living and extinct faunas as elucidating the past changes of the earth's surface.* 2 vols. London (Macmillan).

1117. —— 1912. *Darwinism: an exposition of the theory of natural selection with some of its applications.* London (Macmillan).

1118. **Warren, H. C., & others,** 1925. 'Definitions and delimitations of psychological terms. III.' *Psychol. Bull.*, 22, 370–74.

1119. **Washburn, S. L.** (edited by), 1963. *Classification and human evolution.* New York (Wenner-Gren Foundation).

1120. **Washington, B. T.,** 1901. *Up from slavery: an autobiography.* London (Doubleday, Page).

1121. —— 1961. *Up from slavery: an autobiography.* London (Oxford University Press).

1122. **Weber, M.,** 1927–8. *Die Säugetiere: Einführung in die Anatomie und Systematik der recenten und fossilen Mammalia.* 2 vols. Jena (Fischer).

1123. **Webster, W.,** 1908. Article on 'Moors' in Patrick.[826]

1124. **Wecker, S. C.,** 1963. 'The role of early experience in habitat selection by the prairie deer mouse, *Peromyscus maniculatus.*' *Ecol. Monog.*, 33, 307–25.

1125. —— 1964. 'Habitat selection.' *Sci. Amer.*, 211 (4), 109–16.

1126. **Wedgwood, C. V.,** 1964. *The trial of Charles I.* London (Collins).

1127. **Weidenreich, F.,** 1936. 'The mandibles of *Sinanthropus pekinensis:* a comparative study.' *Palaeont. Sinica*, D, 7 (3), 1–163.

1128. **Weidenreich, F.,** 1943. 'The skull of Sinanthropus pekinensis: a comparative study on a primitive hominid skull.' *Palaeont. Sinica,* D. *10,* i–xxi & 1–485.

1129. —— 1947. *Apes, giants and man.* Chicago (University Press).

1130. **Weiner, J. S.,** 1954. 'Nose shape and climate.' *Amer. J. phys. 'Anthrop., 12,* 615–18.

1131. —— **& Zoutendyk, A.,** 1959. 'Blood-group investigation on central Kalahari Bushmen.' *Nature, 183,* 843–4.

1132. **Weisbach, A.,** 1897. 'Prähistorische Schädel vom Glasinac (Bosnien).' *Wiss. Mitth. Bosn. Hercegov., 5,* 562–76.

1133. **Weismann, A.,** 1892. *Das Keimplasma. Eine Theorie der Vererbung.* Jena (Fischer).

1134. —— 1893. *The germ-plasm: a theory of heredity.* Translated from the German. London (Scott).

1135. **Welcker, H.,** 1886. 'Die Capacität und die drei Hauptdurchmesser der Schädelkapsel bei den verschiedenen Nationen.' *Archiv f. Anthrop., 16,* 1–159.

1136. **Wells, L. H.,** 1955. 'The place of the Broken Hill skull among human types.' *Proc. Third Pan-African Congress on Prehistory,* 172–4.

1137. **Wenz, W.,** 1938. Article on 'Gastropoda' in Schindewolf.[942]

1138. **Whiteley, M. A.** (edited by). 1947. *Thorpe's dictionary of applied chemistry.* Vol. 8. London (Longmans. Green).

1139. **Whitney, W. D.,** 1889. *The Century dictionary: an encyclopedic lexicon of the English language.* Vol. 1. New York (Century Co.).

1140. **Wiener, A. S.,** 1962. *Blood groups and transfusion.* London (Hafner).

1141. **Willett, F.,** 1967. *Ife in the history of West African sculpture.* London (Thames & Hudson).

1142. **Windle, W. F.,** 1967. Chapter on 'Maturation of the brain related to variables in the environment' in Minkowski,[748] pp. 395–409.

1143. **Wingfield, A. H.,** 1928. *Twins and orphans: the inheritance of intelligence.* London (Dent).

1144. **Witty, P. A., & Jenkins, M. D.,** 1935. 'The case of "B"—a gifted Negro girl.' *J. soc. Psychol., 6,* 117–24.

1145. —— **& Theman, V.,** 1943. 'A follow-up study of educational attainment of gifted Negroes.' *J. educ. Psychol., 34,* 35–47.

1146. **Wolf, L.,** 1886. 'Volkstämme Central-Afrika's.' *Ztschr. f. Ethnol., 18 (Verh. Berl. Ges. Anthrop. Ethnol. Urges.,* 725–52).

1147. **Wolfenden, J.,** 1961. 'Race relations.' *Official Year-Book of the National Assembly of the Church of England,* 78th year, 11–15.

1148. **Wolff, W.,** 1886. 'Einige Beobachtungen an den Negern und Buschmännern Afrika's.' *Arch. mikr. Anat., 28,* 421–4.

1149. **Wolfle, D.,** 1940. *Factor analysis to 1940.* Chicago (University Press).

1150. **Wolstenholme, G. E. W., & O'Connor, M.,** 1968. *Growth of the nervous system.* London (Churchill).

1151. **Wolterstorff, W.,** 1922. 'Übersicht der Unterarten und Formen des *Triton cristatus* Laur.' *Blätter f. Aquar.- u. Terrarienk., 34,* 120–21.

1152. **Wood-Jones, F.,** 1929. 'The Australian skull.' *J. Anat., 63,* 352–5.

1153. —— 1931. 'The non-metrical morphological characters of the skull as criteria for racial diagnosis. Part 1. General discussion of the morphological characters employed in racial diagnosis.' *J. Anat., 65,* 179–95.

1154. **Woodward, M. F.,** 1901. 'The anatomy of *Pleurotomaria beyrichii.' Quart. J. micr. Sci.,* *44,* 215–68.

1155. **Woodworth, R. S.,** 1916. 'Comparative psychology of races.' *Psychol. Bull., 13,* 388–97.

1156. **Woollard, H. H.,** 1930. 'The cutaneous glands of man.' *J. Anat., 64,* 415–21.

1157. **Woolley, C. L.,** 1927. Chapter on 'The later cemetery' in Hall & Woolley.[461] pp. 172–213.

1158. ——— 1929. *The Sumerians.* Oxford (Clarendon Press).

1159. **Wright, S.,** 1931. 'Evolution in Mendelian populations.' *Genetics, 16,* 97–159.

1160. ——— 1932. 'The roles of mutation, inbreeding, crossbreeding and selection in evolution. *Proc. 6th Internat. Congr. Genet., 1,* 356–66.

1161. ——— 1948. 'On the roles of directed and random changes in gene frequency in the genetics of populations.' *Evolution, 2,* 279–94.

1162. ——— 1951. 'Fisher and Ford on "The Sewall Wright effect."' *Amer. Sci., 39,* 452–8.

1163. **Yamashina, Y.,** 1948. 'Notes on the Marianas mallard.' *Pacific Sci., 11,* 121–4.

1164. **Yerkes, R. M.** (edited by), 1921. 'Psychological examining in the United States Army.' *Mem. Nat. Acad. Sci., 15,* 1–890.

1165. **Yetts, W. P.,** 1933. 'The Shang-Yin Dynasty and the An Yang finds.' *J. Roy. Asiatic Soc.* (vol. not numbered), 657–85.

1166. **Yeung, K. T.,** 1921. 'The intelligence of Chinese children in San Francisco and vicinity.' *J. appl. Psychol., 5,* 267–74.

1167. **Yoakum, C. S., & Yerkes, R. M.,** 1920. *Mental tests in the American Army.* London (Sidgwick & Jackson).

1168. **Yule, G. U.,** 1906. 'On the theory of inheritance of quantitative compound characters on the basis of Mendel's laws—a preliminary note.' *Rep. 3rd Internat. Congr. Genet.,*140–42.

1169. **Zeuner, F. E.,** 1963. *A history of domesticated animals.* London (Hutchinson).

1170. **Zimmermann, A. A.,** 1950. 'The development of epidermal pigmentation in the negro fetus.' *Zoologica, 35,* 10–12.

1171. **Zittel, K. A.,** 1885. *Handbuch der Palæontologie.* 1 Abt., II Band. München (Oldenbourg).

1172. **Zuckerkandl, E.,** 1875. *Reise der österreichischen Fregatte Novara um die Erde in den Jahren 1857, 1858, 1859. Anthropologischer Theil.* 1 Abt. *Cranien der Novara-Sammlung.* Wien (Staatsdruckerei).

*Sources of information not contained in printed works*

1173. **Anon.,** 1962. Exhibit of trade-goods at the Uganda Museum, Kampala (Speke Centenary Celebrations).

1174. **Asher, M.,** 1970. Personal communication.

1175. **Balsan, F.,** 1962. Personal communication.

1176. **Blacker, C. E. D.,** 1966. Personal communication.

1177. **Carrington, D.,** 1966. Personal communication.

1178. **Cooper, H.,** 1969. Interview on television by the British Broadcasting Corporation (B.B.C.1) on 11 October.

1179. **Donnellan, P., & Lytton, D.,** 1966. 'The Abbey of the English.' Television film (B.B.C.1). 22 December.

1180. **Hartman, M.,** 1969. Appeal on behalf of the Amateur Athletic Association on television (B.B.C.1), 16 October.

1181. **McManus, J. F. A.,** n.d. Personal communication.

# Index

Page-numbers printed in **bold type** refer to subjects of greater importance than others listed under the same heading; those printed in *italics* refer to illustrations; those enclosed within parentheses are less likely than the rest to refer to information required by readers.

The Index does not cover the preliminary pages (pp. i–xviii), to which the reader should refer for the tabulated matter given in them (chapter-headings, etc.). It is concerned chiefly with facts, theories, events, peoples, investigators, and authors of books and papers. Few geographical names are listed, apart from those (such as Ife, La Tène, Mohenjo-Daro, and Zimbabwe) that are intimately bound up with the main theme of the book. For a list of the chief Negrid tribes mentioned in the book, see pp. 550–51. For a classified list of the chief human races and subraces mentioned in the book, turn to the end of it (pp. 624–5).

# Table of races and subraces

THE TABLE includes most of the modern and recently extinct races and subraces of *Homo sapiens* L. that are mentioned at all frequently in this book. The Bambutids (African pygmies) and Negritids (Negritos) are omitted, because their affinities with other ethnic taxa are still obscure. The names of the taxa as printed on this page are intended to accord with the *International code of zoological nomenclature*,[1014] but the code does not lay down strict rules for taxa minor to subspecies. The classification is the author's.

| Subspecies (races) | | Subraces | |
|---|---|---|---|
| *Names* | *Authorities for names* | *Names* | *Authorities for names* |
| australasicus | Bory, 1825[128] | australasicus | Bory,† 1825[128] |
| | | melaninus | Bory, 1825[128] |
| | | tasmanianus | Gregory, 1921[433] |
| albus* | Gmelin, 1788[408] | curilanus | Fischer, 1830[333] |
| | | europaeus | Linnaeus, 1758[669] |
| | | pelagius | Fischer, 1829[332] |
| | | indoafghanus | Gregory, 1921[433] |
| | | arabicus | Bory, 1825[128] |
| | | syriacus | Chamberlain, 1899[201] |
| | | dinaricus | Lapouge, 1899[636] |
| | | alpinus | Lapouge, 1899[636] |
| | | slavonicus | Fischer, 1829[332] |
| | | eurasicus | Sergi, 1908[960] |
| | | africanus | Sergi, 1908[960] |
| afer | Linnaeus, 1758[669] | palaeniger | Montandon, 1937[757] |
| | | aethiopicus | Bory, 1825[128] |
| | | niloticus | Montandon, 1937[757] |
| | | cafer | Bory, 1825[128] |
| hottentotus | Bory, 1825[128] | hottentotus | Bory, 1825[128] |
| | | huzuana | Fischer, 1830[333] |
| asiaticus | Linnaeus, 1758[669] | tatarus | Erxleben, 1777[313] |
| | | sinicus | Bory, 1825[128] |
| | | palaemongolicus | Eickstedt, 1937[303] |
| americanus | Linnaeus, 1758[669] | centralis | Eickstedt, 1937[303] |
| | | andinus | Eickstedt, 1937[303] |
| | | brazilianus | Eickstedt, 1937[303] |

* The correct name for this subspecies is disputed (possibly *europaeus* Linnaeus, 1758, or *sapiens* Linnaeus, 1758).
† For convenience in printing this table, Bory de Saint Vincent's name is contracted throughout to Bory.

The classification on this page agrees exactly, line for line, with that on the opposite page, but the names of the taxa (except Australasid and Melanesid) are those introduced by Eickstedt[303] and Peters[836] as standardized 'Trivialnamen'. These authors have done more than anyone else to clarify the nomenclature of the ethnic taxa of man.

| Races | Subraces | | |
|---|---|---|---|
| Names used in this book | Names used in this book | Alternative names roughly or exactly corresponding | Examples of places where typical specimens can be or have been found |
| Australasid | Australid | Australian aborigine | Australia |
| | Melanesid | Melanesian | New Hebrides |
| | Tasmanid | Tasmanian | Tasmania |
| Europid | Ainuid | Ainu | Kurile Islands |
| | Nordid | Nordic | Norway |
| | Mediterranid | Mediterranean | Southern Italy |
| | Nordindid | Indo-Afghan | Pakistan |
| | Orientalid | 'Arab' | Arabia |
| | Armenid | Assyroid | Armenian S.S.R. |
| | Dinarid | Illyrian | Yugoslavia |
| | Alpinid | Alpine | Switzerland |
| | Osteuropid | Est-baltique | Northern Russia |
| | Turanid | Turki | Kazakh S.S.R. |
| | Aethiopid | Eastern Hamite | Ethiopia |
| Negrid | Palaenegrid | Congolese | Zaïre |
| | Sudanid | Western Sudanese | Senegal |
| | Nilotid | Eastern Sudanese | Southern Sudan |
| | Kafrid | Zambesian | Rhodesia |
| Khoisanid | Khoid | Hottentot | South West Africa |
| | Sanid | Bushman | Kalahari Desert |
| Mongolid | Tungid | Mongol | Mongolia |
| | Sinid | Chinese | Central China |
| | Palaemongolid | Southern Mongol | Vietnam |
| Indianid | Zentralid | (No equivalent name) | Mexico |
| | Andid | Ando-Péruvienne* | Peru |
| | Brasilid | Brasilio-Guarienne* | Brasil |

* Orbigny.[811]